The Hidden Ground of Love

THE HIDDEN GROUND OF LOVE

The Letters of
THOMAS MERTON
on Religious Experience
and Social Concerns
selected and edited by
William H. Shannon

Farrar · Straus · Giroux

NEW YORK

Library of Congress Cataloging in Publication Data
Merton, Thomas, 1915–1968. / The hidden ground of love.
1. Merton, Thomas, 1915–1968. 2. Trappists—United States—Correspondence.
I. Shannon, William Henry. II. Title.
BX4705.M542A275 1985   271'.125'024   84-26045

Preface

Letters are valuable and entertaining in proportion to the wit and ability, and above all the imprudence, of those who write them. Honest letters are more informative, more amusing, more pathetic, more vital than any considered autobiography. Of all documents, these are the most essentially human.

C. E. VULLIAMY

When Thomas Merton made the decision to enter the Abbey of Gethsemani on December 10, 1941, to test whether or not he had a monastic vocation, he brought with him into the monastery all the instincts of a writer. He knew he was bringing them, as he revealed in *The Seven Storey Mountain*. He had in fact already produced a not inconsiderable amount of writing, though most of it was unpublished. Yet he was prepared—at least so he thought in his initial enthusiasm for Trappist life—to sacrifice his writing talents to the higher calling of being a contemplative. It came as a surprise to him (and perhaps a secret relief that he might not have admitted to himself) when his Superiors asked him to make no such sacrifice. On the contrary, they insisted that he keep on writing.

Though entrance into the monastery did not "cost" him his gift of writing, it did modify the direction his writing would take. Being a monk ruled out one kind of writing—fiction—he had long been drawn to. It can scarcely be said, however, that by becoming a monk he had given up a promising career as a novelist. Four of his novels had been rejected by Robert Giroux, then a young editor at Harcourt, Brace and Company, to whom Merton's literary agent, Naomi Burton, had sent them. Giroux, who had known and published Merton as an undergraduate at Columbia College, concluded that the "novels" were too obviously versions of the author's unresolved struggles to find meaning in his own life. This rejection of his novels because they were masked autobiography had something of the prophetic about it. For it was a book of undisguised autobiography, *The Seven Storey Mountain*, that established once and for all his reputation as a writer. Its success may well have released Merton from his attraction to fiction and turned him toward a form of writing more congenial to his talent.

The Seven Storey Mountain was not only a memorable success: it was an augury of what was to come. In writing it, Merton found himself as an author, and the best writings he produced thereafter are those which, in one way or another, are autobiography. He was at his best in sharing his experiences with others. He recognized this. When he received the first copy of *Seeds of Contemplation*, he recorded in *The Sign of Jonas*: "Every book I write is a mirror of my own character and conscience."

When the "fan" mail began to pile up as he became well known, and the circle of friends with whom he corresponded grew wider and wider, Thomas Merton became very adept in a literary form that is essentially autobiography in miniature—letter writing. Early in his writing career, Merton had been advised by Evelyn Waugh, who edited the British edition of his autobiography under the title *Elected Silence*, "to put books aside and write serious letters and to make an art of it." Understandably, Merton's Superiors did not take kindly to this suggestion. Trappists wrote few letters; letter writing was not a part of their tradition. Yet, tradition notwithstanding, Merton's correspondence during his years in the monastery, and especially during the 1960s, became so extensive that by itself it would establish him as a writer of distinction.

He wrote hundreds of letters. In sheer quantity they almost rival his published works. At the Thomas Merton Studies Center at Bellarmine College in Louisville, Kentucky, there are some 3,500 letters addressed to well over a thousand correspondents. Nor does this tell the whole story, since more and more letters continue to turn up from the people to whom Merton wrote, or from their estates.

The scope and variety of his correspondents are staggering. He wrote to poets and heads of states; to popes, bishops, priests, religious and lay people; to monks, rabbis, and Zen masters; to Catholics, Protestants, Anglicans, Orthodox Christians, and Jews; to Buddhists, Hindus, and Sufis; to literary agents and publishers; to theologians and social activists; to old friends and young ones, too.

The range and contents of his letters are almost as diverse as the number of his correspondents. He wrote about Allah, Anglicanism, Asia, the Bible, the Blessed Virgin, Buddhism, China, Christ, Christendom, Church, conscience, contemplation, and the cold war; about Eckhart, ecumenism, God, happiness, his hermitage, and his hospital interludes; about illusions, Islam, John of the Cross, Julian of Norwich, Martin Luther King, Jr., the Koran, Latin America, liturgy, the love of God, poetry, political tyranny, precursors of Christ, prophets, psalms, silence, solitude, and *sobornost*; about technology, Trinity, unity, the will of God, his own writings. The subjects of his letters parallel, and often shed light on, the wide variety of topics in his published articles and books.

But there is quality, too. Many of the letters are skillfully, if almost always hurriedly, crafted. One has the feeling that letter writing was not for him the chore that it often is for others. He seems to have enjoyed it as a serious literary endeavor. A considerable number of the letters could stand alone as brief and insightful essays on the topics they deal with. The care he took, at least during the 1960s, and especially from 1963 on, to preserve his letters (both his own and those written to him) suggests that he had a premonition of their importance.

Their importance can scarcely be overestimated. They reveal an aspect of his character and thought that does not appear, at least with the same clarity and personal touch, in his published works. This is true not only because the very nature of letter writing tends to make it more personal but also because he wrote with much greater freedom in his letters than in his published works. Almost to the last, the things he wrote for publication were carefully scrutinized by the censors of his Order and of the Church. Their chief concern (especially that of the Cistercian censors) was that Merton's writings conform to the image of what a Trappist monk was expected to be. The problem of course was that, by the 1960s at least, Merton had ceased to be a "typical" Trappist monk (if indeed he had ever been). On May 5, 1967, with his characteristic flair for paradox, he wrote to Rosemary Radford Ruether: "I am now convinced that the first way to be a decent monk is to be a non-monk and an anti-monk, so far as the image goes." Yet he was convinced that he could do this only by remaining a monk. For in this same letter he goes on to reject Ruether's suggestion that the logic of his stance on social issues called for him to leave the monastery and the hermitage and come out into the "real" world to do battle with the "principalities and powers." "I am certainly quite definite," he wrote, "about wanting to stay in the bushes, provided I can make some sort of noises that will reach my offbeat friends." It was these "noises" and the "offbeat friends" that upset and riled the censors. That is why he could make the "noises" and reach the "offbeat friends" more readily through his letters than through his published works.

Yet it would be a mistake to think that Merton delighted in being different and saying what was startling and "offbeat" (though it must be said that at times he was not above this). He was essentially a man of tradition, striving to recover authentic Christian and monastic values in a time of change and upheaval, during which he often read the signs of the times better and more clearly than others. He never claimed to have the answers to all questions. He did feel certain that he had some of the right questions; and he probed them relentlessly, with a greater sense of freedom in his letters than elsewhere. He wrote at a time when the very foundations of Christian life and culture were being shaken. One of the reasons he was sometimes misunderstood was that he was doing a bit of the shaking himself.

His style was admirably suited to the art of letter writing: it was personal and intimate; almost always lively and almost never heavy; at times deadly serious and deeply perceptive; at other times carefree, jovial, and even hilariously funny; never solemn, often light, and even breezy. He once compared himself to Newman: "I have absolutely nothing in common with Cardinal Newman, except for the fact that we are both converts and both wrote autobiographies. He writes beautiful prose, I write slang." Merton is of course exaggerating, for he, too, was capable of writing excellent prose, yet without doubt the slang is there, too, and slang is the language of intimacy and an accepted part of the vocabulary of letter writing.

I have been invited by the Thomas Merton Legacy Trust to act as the general editor of the Merton Letters, a task I accept with genuine pleasure. Because the letters are so numerous as to make the editing of them by a single person an almost insuperable task, I have, with the approval of the Trustees, invited the collaboration of three well-known Merton scholars: Dr. Robert E. Daggy, curator of the Thomas Merton Studies Center in Louisville, who gives so generously of his time to those who come to work at the Center; Professor Michael Mott of Bowling Green University in Ohio, author of the authorized Merton biography; and Brother Patrick Hart, who so often and so unselfishly has placed his own extensive Merton scholarship at the service of other scholars.

Four volumes are planned. The present volume contains the letters on religious experience and social concerns. Subsequent volumes will present letters to relatives and special friends, letters to contemporary writers, letters on spiritual direction and monastic renewal. They will include only Merton's letters, not those of his correspondents. Indeed, the necessity of keeping them within a reasonable length has required a prudent "cutting" of some of the letters. This has been done with care, and often with reluctance, but always with the intention of preserving their essence, and with the hope of serving the reader better.

WILLIAM H. SHANNON
General editor of the Merton Letters

Introduction

This first volume contains the Merton letters dealing with religious experience and social concerns. These two topics are put together in one volume because they are intimately linked in Merton's letters and also in his life—two facets, the inside and the outside, of a single life. His religious experience gave Merton the motivation for his ever deepening commitment to peace, justice, and human equality. For in the religious experience he met God and discovered his own true self in God; but more than that: he also confronted, in God, his fellow men and women— not as a faceless mass, but as persons, each infinitely precious and all linked to one another in a network of relationships, grounded in God, that made them one. This is to say that Merton discovered God as the ground of his own being and in that same ground he found the rest of reality, especially his brothers and sisters, in a unity that was beyond all separateness.

This perception that God and the world, though distinct, are yet not separate (how could a being be separate from its ground?) is central to Merton's thought. It appears not infrequently in the letters, as well as in other writings. For example, on April 13, 1967, addressing Amiya Chakravarty and the students at Smith College in Northampton, Massachusetts, on the occasion of their celebrating a "Merton Day," he writes of "the happiness of being one with everything in that *hidden ground of love* for which there can be no explanation." These words which see God not as a being among other beings but as the ground of all beings, and even more precisely the ground of love in which all beings find their identity and uniqueness, provide a most appropriate title for this volume.

It will be helpful to clarify for the reader the meaning I intend to convey by the words "religious experience." Initially I had intended to use the term "ecumenical letters," which after some reflection I rejected on at least two counts. First, the historical meaning "ecumenical" has acquired tends to restrict it to interreligious dialogue among different Christian traditions. Such an understanding would exclude the many letters Merton wrote to people who belonged to religious traditions that are not Christian. Second, even if the word "ecumenical" is used in a broader sense to include interreligious dialogue with non-Christian traditions, it does not capture the perspective that was most important to Merton's vision of reality. Ecumenical dialogue is generally concerned with refining doctrinal formulations to identify points of agreement and disagreement—with the hope, at least among Christians, of working toward eventual reunion of the churches.

Merton's principal interest lay elsewhere. He let the "professional" ecumenists seek to recover a unity that had been lost because of human frailties and infidelities to the truth. His own search he directed toward a unity that has never been lost, because it is beyond the reach of human weakness. This unity is discoverable only at the level of the religious experience—something that can never be adequately expressed in doctrinal formulations. In the notes he prepared for a talk he was to deliver in Calcutta in October 1968, he had written:

True communication on the deepest level is more than a simple sharing of ideas, conceptual knowledge, or formulated truth. The kind of communication that is necessary at this level must also be "communion": beyond the level of words, a communion in authentic experience which is shared not only on a "preverbal" level but also on a "postverbal" level.

In the talk he actually gave at Calcutta, he expressed the conviction that communication at this deepest level is indeed possible:

And the deepest level of communication is not communication, but communion. It is wordless. it is beyond words, and it is beyond speech, and it is beyond concept. Not that we discover a new unity. We discover an older unity. My dear brothers [and sisters], we are already one. But we imagine that we are not. And what we have to recover is our original unity. What we have to be is what we are.

"We are already one. But we imagine that we are not." It is at the level of doctrinal formulations that we recognize our differences; it is at the level of the religious experience that we can come to realize our oneness. Merton's concern is consistently at this second level rather than the first. In a revealing letter to Dona Luisa Coomaraswamy, written on January 13, 1961, he speaks of a vision of peace that can only be achieved by men and women who, without belonging to any movement, "are able to unite in themselves and *experience* in their own lives all that is best and most true in the various great spiritual traditions."

It was the phenomenon of the religious experience that Merton felt called to explore. It was at this level, he believed, that various religious traditions could be especially enriched, not through synthesis or syncretism, but through the sharing of such experience. The words "religious experience" are therefore more appropriate than "ecumenical" to describe the letters that deal with various religious traditions.

The other letters in this volume relate Merton to the social concerns of his day. In a letter written on August 3, 1965, to Shinzo Hamai, the Mayor of Hiroshima, Merton says: "I never cease to face the truth symbolized by Hiroshima." The danger of nuclear war and the threat of it in a bloody and indefensible war in Vietnam are topics he writes about frequently to his correspondents. The cold war, racial injustices, the oppression of black people in the United States, and of Third World people in so many places of the world are other social concerns discussed, often with strong passion, in the letters.

A word needs to be said about the order of the letters in this volume. They are arranged in sets according to correspondents, and within each set the letters are presented chronologically; thus, for example, the letters to Dorothy Day are all together and in chronological order.

The sets of letters are arranged alphabetically by correspondents— with one exception. An alphabetical rather than a topical arrangement was chosen because in scarcely any of the letters does Merton confine himself to a single topic. He moves readily from prayer and contemplation to reflections on his reading, to discussions of various religious traditions, to issues of war and peace and justice. This continual interrelating and overlapping of subject matter would make a topical arrangement confusing and even unfaithful to the contents of the letters. There is, however, one departure from this alphabetical arrangement. The set of letters to Catherine Doherty has been placed first, because it is the only set that includes very early letters, written before Merton had decided to enter the monastery. This unique feature would seem to justify a special place for these letters.

I am well aware that the arrangement of these letters by sets rather than by years is a departure from what is the more usual practice in editing letters. Such a departure is, I believe, appropriate and even necessary here. First of all, the large majority of the letters were written over a relatively brief period of time—which would tend to make a purely chronological arrangement awkward and confusing. Second and more important, the arrangement by sets to individual persons allows the reader to experience the sequence, progress, and development of so many friendships that were important to Thomas Merton. And we need to realize that letter writing was for him a way of making friendships and of enabling them to grow. Most of us have other ways of building friendships: visiting with our friends, spending time with them. Merton's life-style, to a large degree, denied him the types of friendship-building contacts which we so easily take for granted. Because he prized friendship so highly, he had no other choice: he *had* to write letters.

Every effort has been made to help the reader enter into and experience these friendships. This accounts for the short biographical note given at the head of each correspondence. This is also the reason for the brief connecting links that are occasionally placed between letters to preserve the continuity of the dialogue between Merton and his friend.

Each set of Merton letters—this is primarily true of the longer sets— is a partial biography of Thomas Merton, and all the sets taken together are a kind of latter-day *Seven Storey Mountain*. They tell in his own words the thoughts, the concerns, the dreams, and the activities of a Merton who had gone far beyond the stiffness and narrowness of his early autobiography. The letters tell the story of the maturing of a contemplative.

The first person to select and edit Merton letters was of course Merton himself. In 1962, after he had been forbidden to write about war and peace, he put together a selection of letters he had written mostly in 1961 and 1962. Called the *Cold War Letters*, they were circulated among his friends in mimeographed form. An expanded version, which ran to 180 pages and included 110 letters (numbered consecutively, except that there are two letters #24 and no letter #30), was issued early in 1963. The thirty-seven *Cold War Letters* included in this volume have been duly indicated.

W.H.S.

Acknowledgments

I wish to express my gratitude to the Merton Legacy Trust for having appointed me as the general editor of the Merton Letters and for giving me access to all the Merton letters that are stored at the Thomas Merton Studies Center at Bellarmine College, Louisville, Kentucky. I am grateful, too, to the many correspondents of Merton (or the directors of their estates or archives) who so graciously cooperated with me in the task of locating letters that were missing from the collection. Some of the correspondents whom I have met and who supplied me with letters and/or valuable background information are: Canon A. M. Allchin, Sr. M. Emmanuel, O.S.B., Wilbur H. Ferry, James H. Forest, Hildegard Goss-Mayr, Etta Gullick, Marco Pallis, Linda Sabbath, Zalman Schachter, John Yungblut. Correspondents with whom I have been in touch by mail or phone, without having met them personally, include: A. Reza Arasteh, Abdul Aziz, Jeanne Burdick, Richard Chi, James Douglass, John Tracy Ellis, Bernard Haring, C.S.S.R., John Harris, John Heidbrink, William Johnston, S.J., Martin Lings, Raymond H. Prince, Rosemary Ruether, Bruno Schlesinger, Carleton Smith, R. J. Werblowsky, Gordon Zahn. I want especially to express my gratitude to Ch. Abdul Aziz of Karachi, Pakistan, who, at considerable inconvenience to himself, was able to locate a number of important letters that Merton had sent to him. I am grateful to Mrs. Abraham J. Heschel, who discovered a valuable letter from Merton to her late husband; to Mrs. Edward Deming Andrews, who sent me three letters that completed the correspondence between Merton and her late husband; to Mrs. Chakravarty, who furnished letters of Merton to her husband, Dr. Amiya Chakravarty, who was too ill to respond to me himself. From Madonna House in Combermere, Canada, I received a number of the early letters that Merton wrote to Catherine Doherty; and from the Erich Fromm Archive (in Tubingen, West Germany), under the capable direction of Dr. Ranier Funk, I have received additional

Merton and Fromm letters and valuable background information. Dr. Funk has been a very helpful colleague and scholar. Phillip M. Runkel, assistant archivist at Marquette University, and Daniel Mauk, of the Catholic Worker, have been helpful in supplying letters of Merton to Dorothy Day. John C. H. Wu, Jr., sent me, from Formosa, some sixteen letters of Merton to his father. Information about Sr. Penelope has come to me from Sr. Joan, C.S.M.V., librarian at St. Mary's Covent, Wantage, England. Mrs. Magdelen Goffin of Tunbridge Wells, Kent, England, has generously furnished me with biographical material about her father, E. I. Watkin, as well as several letters of Merton to him. I am grateful to Ms. Barbara L. Morris, Vice President for Academic Planning at St. John's University, Jamaica, New York, for a copy of the complete correspondence between Merton and the late Dr. Paul Sih, and to Dr. William Marshall, of the Special Collections' Division of the University of Kentucky Libraries, for the Merton–Suzuki correspondence. Just in time to get them into this volume, I have received letters that Merton wrote to Charles S. Thompson. They came to me through the courtesy of Ms. Valerie Flessati of the London Pax Christi.

It will surprise no one who has any contact with Merton studies when I name Brother Patrick Hart of the Abbey of Gethsemani and Dr. Robert E. Daggy of the Thomas Merton Center in Louisville as two persons whose generous help and sound advice were indispensable to the preparation of this volume. And it would not have reached its happy conclusion without the interest, involvement, and assistance of my editor, Mr. Robert Giroux.

It is appropriate, too, that I express my gratitude to Ms. Elizabeth Fake, Associate Professor Emeritus of Nazareth College, Sr. Margaret Teresa Kelley, S.S.J., Professor Emeritus of Nazareth College, and Sr. Therese Hanss, S.S.J., for their kind help in proofreading the entire volume; and to Ms. Diane Burruto for her very capable typing of it.

W.H.S.

The Hidden Ground of Love

To Catherine de Hueck Doherty

Catherine de Hueck Doherty, born into a wealthy Russian family in 1900, was married at the age of fifteen to Baron Boris de Hueck. When she was twenty she and her husband were forced to flee Soviet Russia, and they arrived penniless in Canada. Her business astuteness, combined with hard work, enabled her to recoup their fortunes, and by 1930 she had become wealthy again. Wealth did not satisfy her, however, since for a long time she had been haunted by Jesus' words: "Sell all you have, give to the poor and come follow me."

In 1930 she made the decision to live among the poor, first in the slums of Toronto (where she established the first Friendship House), and then in New York City in Harlem. It was there that she met Eddie Doherty, the well-known journalist, whom she married in 1943. They founded Madonna House in Combermere, Ontario, Canada, a rural community that has become a place for the sharing of life and prayer, and a center of training for the lay apostolate.

In 1941, Thomas Merton at twenty-six was teaching English at St. Bonaventure College, Olean, New York, where Catherine had come to speak. After hearing her, Merton volunteered to help out at Friendship House in Harlem, and thus their friendship started. The letters written to her during these crucial months in his life reveal why and how he decided that his vocation was to be a Trappist monk. He arrived at Our Lady of Gethsemani monastery in Kentucky on December 10, 1941, and was received as a postulant on December 13, 1941. The first three letters here are the only ones in this book Merton wrote before becoming a monk.

St. Bonaventure College
October 6, 1941

First, thanks very much for letting me stand around Friendship House for a couple of weeks of evenings: I hope I can do that more often.

I liked most of all the clothing room, but wasn't there much. I think the "cubs" are certainly very smart fine kids, and think about them a lot . . .

You will be interested in this one: I have a nun in a freshman English class (one from the kitchen here—the only nun I've got in regular classes for this year), and she wrote an essay about St. Bonaventure in which she listed all the things that had impressed her since she had first come here. Baroness de Hueck was outstanding on this list: the sister was very impressed with what you said, and although she didn't go into details, evidently agrees with you. Well, I nearly gave her an A on the strength of this, but I didn't. Charity is one thing: art another. In heaven they are identical, on earth too often distinct. A for charity, B-plus for technique was what I gave the sister, only the first grade remained unspoken, and that was just as well too, because today she gave me a big argument about some obscure point of grammar.

For a couple of minutes I talked to a Quaker woman who was passing through here. She had spent the summer in Kansas working among Negro sharecroppers, not without some guarded hostility on the part of the local authorities. She had with her a lot of students from Allegheny College, Meadville. I talked of you and Friendship House and got a smarter and more enthusiastic reaction than you get from the average Catholic . . .

Right now besides my work I am doing a lot of reading and studying and meditation, and a little writing but nothing systematic, just notes on what I am thinking about, when I am thinking about anything that doesn't look disgusting as soon as it gets on paper.

Mostly it has something to do, in general, with the question of lay vocations, both in an academic sense and in a personal one too. The academic sense is maybe more interesting. There is one problem about lay vocations that interests me a lot, and it is obviously very important to Friendship House too: except that you probably have it all doped out to your satisfaction. I haven't yet. The problem is this: where does Catholic Action stop and politics begin?

First of all, it seems to me that you yourself illustrate the proper balance between them. That is: Catholic Action, which is another word for Charity, that is Love, means, for one thing, feeding the poor, clothing the needy, and after that, saving souls. A person who is really interested in that must also necessarily be interested in certain political movements which tend to help feed the poor, clothe the needy, etc. Also, a person who is charitable, and really loves the poor, realizes just how little pure political action, without any charity behind it, really means.

If you make laws to provide the nation with old age pensions and the nation is populated by people who beat up their grandmothers, your old age pension law doesn't mean much.

If you make a law (and this time nobody is being funny) providing the unemployed with unemployment insurance, and then refuse to employ certain classes, or types, or races of people in any decent job, your law is never going to eliminate unemployment . . .

When you get down to it, Catholic Action means not voting for anybody but going out and being a saint, not writing editorials in magazines, even, but first of all being a saint.

I said it was a problem. In any place where people are engaged in doing things, as you are at Friendship House, for the love of the poor and, through them, God, there isn't much of a problem. Where it comes in with me is trying to explain guys like Franco, or some of the Medieval Popes, in whom Catholic Action (or what they imagined to be that) got totally submerged in a completely materialistic and political struggle between certain social and political groups. The problem I am getting at is, is it possible for there to be a completely Catholic government? Is there any point in these Catholic political parties, like the ones that used to exist in Germany and Italy? and so on.

If a Catholic gets into a position of power in a country where the political atmosphere is made up of struggles between a lot of irreligious and frankly selfish minorities, how can he ever do anything at all except by compromising with religious principles, or, worse than that, fooling himself that he is leading a crusade, and then turning the country upside down in the name of religion, the way Franco did, or the way the Third and Fourth Crusades did to Europe. I think the Reformation was a divine punishment for the Fourth Crusade, in which the businessmen of Venice inveigled the whole army of Crusaders (recruited with promises of plenary indulgences if they died in battle) to conquer, for Venetian business, the Christian empire at Constantinople!

On the other hand, I believe there is only one free and just state in the world, and that is the Vatican City: but that is less a state than a glorified monastery. Now assuming all the people in a given country were good Catholics, it might be possible for that country to be ruled the way the Vatican City is ruled: that is, politics would be, all down the line, subordinated to salvation, and ordered to the salvation of souls as its ultimate end. Then you would have real freedom, real justice, and everything else.

Which brings us back to the same conclusion: the first thing to do is to feed the poor and save the souls of men, and in this sense, feeding the poor means feeding them not by law (which doesn't do a damn bit of good), but first of all at the cost of our own appetites, and with our own hands, and for the love of God. In that case, feeding the poor and saving them are all part of the same thing, the love of our neighbor . . .

And when it comes to saving souls, once again writing and talking and teaching come *after* works of love and sanctity and charity, not before. And the first thing of all is our own sanctification, which was the lesson

I got out of my retreat at the Trappists,* and keep finding out over and over again every day . . .

If I can only make myself little enough to gain graces to work out my sanctification, enough to keep out of hell and make up for everything unpleasant, in time, the lay vocation, as far as I'm concerned, presents no further problems, because I trust God will put in my way ten million occasions for doing acts of charity and if I am smart maybe I can catch seventeen of them, in a lifetime, before they get past my big dumb face.

At this point I realize that this letter is disordered and obscure and badly written and probably extremely uninteresting to everybody. But even if it doesn't make sense, the very fact that I used up so many words talking about lay vocations and writing means that I think I am finding out something about writing and about the lay vocation for me: which is that my vocation is probably to go on finding out this same thing about writing over and over as long as I live: when you are writing about God, or talking about Him, you are doing something you were created to do, even if you don't feel like a prince every minute you are doing it, in the end it turns out to be right: but when you are writing or talking about some matter or pride or envy to advance your own self, you feel lousy while you are doing it and worse afterwards and ten times worse when you read the stuff over a week later . . .

Meanwhile, I hope you will come up here again† and make some more speeches. The seminarians could do with some ideas about Harlem. I understand the clerics (who have now long ago returned to Washington) are still in a ferment. I'm going to write to one of them and find out, anyway. By the time I get to writing to him, I will probably have thought up another dull and complicated treatise instead of a letter!

But I think a lot of Harlem, and I'll tell you the one reason why: because Harlem is the one place where I have ever been within three feet of anyone who is authentically said to have seen visions—what was the old lady's name? I have forgotten. But believe me when the angels and saints appear among us they don't appear in rich men's houses, and the place I want to be is somewhere where the angels are not only present but even sometimes visible: that is slums, or Trappist monasteries, or where there are children, or where there is one guy starving himself in a desert for sorrow and shame at the sins and injustice of the world. In comparison with all these, St. Bonaventure occasionally takes on the aspects of a respectable golf club, but then again I won't say that either, because the place is, in spite of everything, holy, and when you live under the same roof as the Blessed Sacrament there is no need to go outside looking for anything . . .

* Merton made a retreat at Gethsemani monastery during Holy Week, 1941, as recorded in The Seven Storey Mountain.
† The story of her earlier visit to St. Bonaventure College is also told in SSM.

This letter is being written not according to plan, but according to the clock, and now it is time for me to wind up and turn in. Maybe you are lucky. But anyway, God bless everybody in Friendship House and in Harlem and hear all your prayers, and please pray sometimes for us here . . .

November 10, 1941

. . . I feel rather astonished, to begin with, at the subtle way you interpreted the big fanfare of speculation that came along with each one of those two letters I sent to Canada, because, when I wrote them, I was deliberately steering clear of anything that might be interpreted as having anything to do with vocation . . . So when you started out, in the car, while we were riding back from Buffalo, by saying that any person who asked all those questions probably wanted to be a priest, you (1) surprised me, (2) woke me up to the fact that maybe I am very bad at being abstract about anything, (3) you scared me. The priest business is something I am supposed to be all through and done with. I nearly entered the Franciscans. There was a very good reason why I didn't, and now I am convinced that Order is not for me and never was. So that settles that vocation.

Meanwhile, about being at St. Bonaventure: that's easy. I cannot even give myself half an argument that this is the place for me to stay. From the moment I first came here, I have always believed nothing about the place except that, for me, it was strictly temporary. It is not enough. There is something lacking, for me. I have plenty of time to write, and that has been nice, I am sure. The teaching is like a sort of harmless hobby: about on the plane of stamp collecting. In any visible results it may have, as regards the Kingdom of God, it is just about as valuable as stamp collecting, too. But of course this is only my second year. And besides, visible results aren't much, and it is a kind of weakness to strain your eyes looking for the results that men are capable of seeing on earth . . .

I don't know what it is that will help me to serve God better: but whatever it is, it doesn't seem to be here. Something is missing. Whenever I read about the young rich man in the Gospels, who asked the Lord what he should do, beyond keeping the Commandments, and turned away, sad, "because he had great possessions," I feel terrible. I haven't got great possessions, but I have a job, and this ease here, this safety, and some money in the bank and a pile of books and some small stocks my grandfather left me, nothing that the average housemaid or A & P clerk doesn't have, in good times. But I don't feel comfortable at all when I think of that sentence in the Bible. I can't read that and sit still. It makes me very unquiet.

And then when I am filled with that unquietness, I have learned at last that the only thing that will take it away again is to go down into the church and try to tell God that everything I have, I give up to Him, and beg Him to show me how He wants me to give it to Him, in what way, through whom?

Just before you came down here, and I wasn't really thinking of Friendship House at all, I had been saying that prayer and finally started a novena to find out how to give God what He was asking of me: thinking all the time of possessions: maybe some poor person would be brought to my knowledge and I could give him something of what I have received through God's goodness.

So then you turned up. If you are surprised that I gave you one feeble argument and then shut up, that is why. Not that I wouldn't, in ordinary circumstances, be so full of arguments I couldn't even see straight. But in this case it was altogether too clear for argument, nor have I been able to work up even the slightest interest in any argument against leaving here since you have left . . .

However, at least by God's grace I know what to pray for harder and harder every day. Nothing but the strength of His Love, to make me love to deny my fears every time they come up. A nice high ideal. The very thought of how I have always been, under difficulties, makes me so ashamed there is nothing more to do but shut up.

Also, there is this.

I don't know if you are concerned about the past of people who come to work for you. I am bringing this up because it might possibly be important. I got in some trouble once, which I don't particularly want to tell anybody about. If you absolutely want to know, I will tell you, but otherwise I can say in good conscience that I don't believe, myself, that it would disqualify me from working in Friendship House, or bring any scandal to be connected with FH in any way, or reflect on you or anybody else, nor is it anything that makes me in any way different from anybody else, but once I did get in some trouble, enough for it to be an impediment to my becoming a *priest*. I repeat, to the best of my knowledge it does not in any way affect my fitness to work at Friendship House. On the other hand, it is something that definitely demands a whole life of penance and absolute self-sacrifice: so that if I thought the Trappists would take me, I think I would want to go to them. But I have to do penance, and if Harlem won't have me, then where may I turn?

If I had never mentioned this, I am sure that it never would have come up in any other way, and I am sure it could not possibly be dragged up out of the past, because it remains only something between me and God and the other persons involved, with whom I have unfortunately lost all contact: or so it seems. Maybe it would have been better to have ignored the whole thing.

However, it came up and spoiled my last "vocation" [see *SSM*, pp. 296–98], and I don't want to leave anything in the background to spoil this one. I assure you that it is something which, if the president of this college knew, I don't think he would fire me for. I just got a sudden attack of scruples, maybe, when I brought it up.

But if you have any doubts at all, say so, and I will tell you the whole story, in which I am no white-haired hero, no model of self-sacrifice or of holiness either.

The general burden of this letter is to let you know that, in me, you are getting no bargain, and I feel I should especially tell you this, because you have done me an inestimably great honor, far above my own worthlessness, in asking me to come to FH, even before I got around to asking it myself. I believe that, since with God all things are possible, with His help I can some day be a Saint, if I pray without ceasing and give myself totally to Him. In all this, I depend on a miracle: but His grace is always a miracle. Apart from that miracle, however, there is the present fact that I am not only not a Saint but just a weak, proud, self-centered little guy, interested in writing, who wants to belong to God, and who, incidentally, was once in a scandal* that can be called public, since it involved lawyers. So that's the dirt. Never forget me in your prayers!

December 6, 1941

Many thanks for your fine letter from Chicago. I feel very guilty for bringing up all that business while you had so many other things to worry about, especially since certain things have occurred since then that make it seem pretty definitely that I am not to have the privilege of trying a year or two at FH.

But the problem I felt I had to put before you had been bothering me so much: and the fact I brought it up shows that; and also, it finally led me to do something I ought to have done long ago.

You see, I have always wanted to be a priest—that is, ever since my conversion. When someone told me that there was an impediment against my ever being ordained, I was very unhappy, and really, since then, I had been really quite lost, in a way. I knew I wanted to belong to God entirely, but there didn't seem to be any way particularly suited to fill up everything in me that I had hoped would be filled by the priesthood. I tried to get as close to it as possible by coming to Bona's and living just like the priests here, under the same roof as the Blessed Sacrament: but the work itself didn't seem to mean an awful lot, and everything seemed to be a little dead. I simply stayed here, praying and waiting to be shown what I was to do.

When you came along, everything you said made perfect good sense, and I was glad to think that perhaps this was what I had been praying

* It is now generally known that the "scandal" referred to was the fact that, while at Cambridge University, Merton fathered a child. Merton's guardian, Tom Bennett, made arrangements to care for the mother and child.

for. I saw FH, and liked it: what actually inspired me was the idea of complete poverty, *real* poverty, without security: and also the fact that Harlem is where Christ is, where the Blessed Mother is more likely to appear than anywhere—except, perhaps, a Trappist monastery! As to the actual routine of work, I can't say it meant any more to me than St. Bonaventure and teaching. I like teaching . . . But always it would seem to me like marking time, like waiting for something else, filling in an interval.

Meanwhile I had made a couple of Trappist retreats, and was practically driven silly by the conflict between my desire to share that kind of life and my belief that it was absolutely impossible. Of course, the obvious thing to do was to ask somebody else about this impediment: whether it was really as serious as I had been told.

There were two reasons why I hesitated. First, I had been told it was a total, complete, irrevocable impediment in such strong terms that it seemed fantastic even to question them. Second, the devil made use of this to try and kid me that all this thinking about a religious vocation was just a silly, dramatic self-indulgence, and that I would never really be able to stand up under the life, in actuality, and that I had best forget all about it. Well, I could not forget about it, but I stalled around, having argued myself into such a state that it was almost impossible to do anything: and all along I had been *arguing* with myself instead of praying, which of course didn't help matters, but definitely guaranteed that I would end up in what you refer to as a "pretzel": and what a pretzel! A regular Gordian knot of a pretzel I was in!

Well, when I had agreed to go to Harlem, it seemed as though the question was answered, for the time being. I could try Harlem, and if the question came up again, well, then I could see about it then.

Then I made Father Furfey's retreat. His retreat was all about Harlem and nothing about Trappists, except that it dealt with the one infinite source of life that nourishes both Friendship House and the Trappists, the Mystical Body of Christ: but all from the point of view of the former. It was a terrific retreat, and I came back here all on fire with it.

And what happened? I started thinking about the Trappists again. This time, I was in such a pretzel that it was evident there was no use fooling any more, the question had to be settled. This time I didn't argue, I prayed, and the most apparent thing after that was the desire to question this impediment, and question it with every question I knew how. In short, I went to one of the priests here, who ought to know, and he told me at once that in his opinion there *was no* impediment and never had been. He was so definite, in his turn, that it knocked me flat. I rushed out of the room saying all I could remember of the *Te Deum* and went and fell on my face in the chapel and began to pray and beg and implore Almighty God to let me be admitted to the Trappists as a choir religious.

So then I wrote to the Trappists, simply saying I was coming for a retreat, and, this was in line with the priest's directions: I intended to ask for admission then, nothing about it in the letter. Of course, it *might* possibly happen that the retreat would change my mind (which just seems absurd) and then I would return to the idea of Harlem. What is much more likely, it might happen that the Trappists would not have me anyway. Then, again, I would know I should try Harlem for a while. But anyway, I was now getting to some definite answer to all my problems.

A few days later, another thing happened, that now rules out Harlem for good.

All this time I had been assuming that the classification 1B I got from the Draft Board last spring was going to be definite for a while. However, they now want to reclassify me; and if they make me 1A I am liable to be sent off at once. What is going to happen about *that* is still unknown. It is all in God's hands. I have asked for three months, to find out whether or not the Trappists will take me. I still don't know whether the Draft Board will give me that time, or merely drag me into the army without any more speech. All I can do is pray, and wait patiently to do God's will, meanwhile begging Him with every breath that He may forgive me for resisting my vocation so long, and may now, in His infinite bounty, let me be accepted into the cloister, not by reason of any merit in me, but only because of His goodness.

That is what has been happening. So you see, it is apparently not God's will that I should serve Him in Harlem now. Needless to say, all this has felt like being ground between two millstones, but one thing is more and more clear each time the stones go round: I don't desire *anything* in the world, not writing, not teaching, not any kind of consolation or outward activity: I simply long with my whole existence to be completely consecrated to God in every gesture, every breath and every movement of my body and mind, to the exclusion of absolutely everything except Him: and the way I desire this, by His grace, is the way it is among the Trappists. FH made sense to me, but I was not eaten up with this kind of longing for the lay apostolate that I seem to have for a contemplative community and a life of prayer and penance. Only these things and the thought of them makes me live, interiorly, now. Everything else actually seems not only dry, but painful: but the thought, and fact of prayer and fasting are totally sweet and peaceful. Never forget me in your prayers, B., especially now. I am unshakably rooted in faith in this vocation: but there is the army [that] may try to kill it in me. So pray for me! My love to everybody. Bob Lax wants to be a staff worker: he is a very good guy.

P.S. Remember me especially between the 14th and 20th when I expect to be down at Gethsemani, Kentucky, trying to be admitted!

Abbey of Gethsemani, Trappist, Kentucky
December 13, 1941

I entered the community as a postulant this afternoon. After that it will no doubt be hard, but at least I will know there is nothing keeping me from God any more—I can belong entirely to Him by simply consenting to each trial as it presents itself, and that is enough! It is everything. I only want to belong entirely to Him. I will never forget FH in my prayers! And pray for me! And write, sometime! Merry Christmas.

In 1948 The Seven Storey Mountain *was published. It became a national bestseller and brought fame to its monk-author.*

February 14, 1949

After all these years I have an excuse to say hello and ask your prayers. The excuse is this. A lady in California thought, for some reason, that she ought to give away seventy copies of *The Seven Storey Mountain*, a book I wrote, for people to read. My job was to get them distributed. Friendship House in New York distributed twenty, and forty more went to prisons, and I thought you would be able to handle six. I am also sending one to you personally in case you have not read it. Not that it is so wonderful.

But I would be very grateful if you could handle this for us. As you know, out here we are not in touch with spots where these things would do the most good.

In the last seven years I have found out somewhat of what God wants to do with people, and what His love means. When I say this life is wonderful it doesn't mean that every other vocation isn't wonderful too: but to be in the sort of place where God wants one: that is certainly a marvelous thing. As soon as you get set in your groove, boy do things happen!

People still accuse me of being enthusiastic, but I guess I am a little saner than I used to be? Anyway it is good to be quiet enough to let God work and not get too much in His way with one's own pep, because when my own steam obscures everything things don't move nearly as fast.

It seems funny to talk about things moving in a place where nothing ever happens. But more has happened here in seven years than I would have imagined could happen anywhere else in seven centuries. And yet, on the surface, nothing has happened. Somewhere in it all there have been a lot of prayers for you and for Friendship House and I know I have been getting a lot in return. In fact now that I have written a book, I am being prayed for much more than I have prayed for others and this reversal of the usual situation for a Trappist is disconcerting. But it is also very nice, because I sure feel the benefit of those prayers. Maybe I can store some up for the future . . . But if I can't I'll take it out in trust.

This is my first chance to say how happy I was to hear of your marriage [to Eddie Doherty in 1943] and to send you congratulations and best wishes and blessings. I can see where being married can bring those whose vocation it is much closer to God. Also it is good to hear, once in a while, that Friendship House is branching out here and there.

We read your book on FH in the refectory and it made a big impression, and I read *Dear Bishop* and thought it packed a great big punch. I hope it has done some good. But I can guess what kind of letters you got. I got one or two myself. Including one priest who flattered me by saying he didn't like me any more than he liked you. So we are sitting in the same boat. Let us pray that it may speed us to heaven with a million or two Americans for our companions and crown, something to give to Our Lord. His Providence certainly designed a rough age for us to be saints in.

So let us pray that we will get there: or you, who are on the way, pray for me who have been seven years starting and not getting very far. But I like it anyway.

August 22, 1956

. . . I am so glad we are getting around to the publication of that ancient, prehistoric *Journal* [first called *The Cuban Journal*, finally published in 1959 as *The Secular Journal*]. But I am especially glad that it keeps me in your growing spiritual family. I am a member of the Domus Domini,* at least by virtue of a manuscript which works for you in my place. I hope you will let me know the details of what is growing into a firmly established institute . . .

Now, as always, God's real work remains obscure and humble in the eyes of the world. Now more than ever, we have to be suspicious of results that are achieved by the efficient, over-efficient technological means of which the world is so proud. Christ works always humbly and almost in the dark, but never more than now . . .

Nothing is more important than prayer and union with God, no matter where we may be. Christ is the source and the only source of charity and spiritual life. We can do nothing without Him and His Spirit, and I know you are now, as always, seeking no other Mover than the Spirit of Christ. That is why the Cross will cast its shadow, still, over your life. But then, in that shadow, you will see the Light of Christ, the Light of the Resurrection. He lives in us, and through our poverty He must reign. And I need not tell you how poor He makes us in order to reign in us. If we knew how poor and desolate we would have to be when we began to follow Him, perhaps we would have fallen back.

* Domus Domini *means a diocesan pious union (*Domus Domini *for men,* Domus Dominae *for women). Such pious unions were approved by Pius XII in 1947. Madonna House was officially erected as a diocesan pious union in 1960 by the Bishop of Pembroke, Ontario.*

Thus we are left as children, as the saved remnant which is forgotten, we are like the animals in Noah's ark, which floats off on the waves of the deluge of materialism without anyone but God knowing where we will end up.

We have got to be people of hope, and to be so we have to see clearly how true it is that the hopes of a materialistic culture are the worst form of despair. We have to build a new world, and yet resist the world while representing Christ in the midst of it. I have been taken to task for yelling so loud that this is a perverse generation and no doubt I have put a lot of my own frustration into the cries: the people of the generation are good, so good, so helpless, some of them: the culture, the generation, is perverse and I see little hope for it. Why? Because by its very essence it is against Christ. I hope that I am wrong.

In the end, no theory that neglects real people can be of any value. It is in those that He sends to you that you see Him and love Him, and there you have a reality which cannot be taken away, a treasure like the one for which St. Lawrence died on the gridiron. You have Christ . . .

December 28, 1957

We have all been waiting a long time for the final judgment of the censors of the Order as to the publication of the *Cuban Journal.* Naomi Burton may have told you that it finally got to a fourth censor and the score, at the close of the thirteenth-inning, was three against publication and one in favor. There are apparently to be no more innings after that. In other words the Order is officially and definitely against. So much so that the Abbot General has written me a very long letter to this effect, instructing me as to the attitude which I myself am to take in the matter. He tells me that he feels it is my duty, in the circumstances, to ask you if you would consider forgoing your right to publish the book. In other words, while you do in fact retain the right to publish the book if you want to, he asks you in charity to take into consideration the feelings of the Order in the matter. He is concerned above all with passages which he feels would shock certain readers coming from a priest, a member of this Order, and the effect of the shock would make itself felt in a harmful way, he believes.

My position is such that in practice I have no choice but to conform to these wishes of my Highest Superior (below the Pope), and hence I have to communicate these wishes to you as my own. I am very sorry to have to do so. But, knowing that you, as well as I, will be disposed to see the whole business in the light of faith, and to accept the judgment of those higher up in the Church as God's will for us—always remembering of course that *you* haven't made any vow of obedience to my Superior, and you remain free to do what you want. I think we can certainly differ, privately and speculatively, with this opinion of censors who may not be blessed with a superabundance of judgment in such matters. Yet at the same time, they have reasons of a different order, and I think it would be rash for us to ignore these altogether. Incidentally there was no question of anything definitely against faith or morals, just the general tone of carping criticism of "nice" people which they think is undesirable in one of my present status. Maybe so. It certainly is somewhat adolescent, and I thought the preface took sufficient account of this fact. They did not agree.

If you are still very anxious to publish the book, the only hope I can offer is the vague possibility that they *might* consent after abundant cuttings—but perhaps the cutting would be so abundant that the bulk of the book would be gone. My own opinion is that we ought to just drop the idea for the moment, and if God wills, we will have another chance some time later on.

So you see, the Cistercians of the Strict Observance are very much opposed to any voice with even a slightly radical sound being raised in their midst. I do not know whether or not I feel this is something for which we ought to be proud. However, every Order has its own spirit, and our General has been clamping down on all expressions of anything, on the rather reasonable theory that the monks came to the monastery in the first place to shut up. I cannot deny the validity of the argument. Father Abbot tells me that there was a $500 advance on the ms. and that we will take care of that, so that at least you will have got something out of the transaction.

I was happy to have a few words with Eddie [Doherty] when he was down here . . .

February 11, 1958

Today we are celebrating the hundredth anniversary of Lourdes, and part of the celebration, for me, is to send you a piece of good news. It shows that Our Lady is with us, and that there is still a very solid hope that the *Secular Journal (Cuban Journal)* will be published after all.

Yesterday afternoon I heard from the Abbot General again. I had written him a letter after receiving your humble acceptance of his demands about the book. I explained to him simply that I still wondered if we were entitled to deprive your cause of such an important source of support. Previously he had shown himself opposed to the publication of the book *even if* I made the changes suggested by the censors. Now however I repeated the plea that at least I might be allowed to make those changes and submit the book once more.

Father General agreed to this, and expressed himself very content with the way both you and I had acted, and promised to reconsider the whole thing after the corrections had been made. The book will start off again to the two censors (or two out of that group of four) after I have made the corrections . . . I am sorry to have to mutilate it a bit, but perhaps it is just as well. My plan at present is simply to cut, not to change or rewrite if I can help it. However, it may turn out that some passages could be kept with a little rewriting, and if that seems to be so, I will try my hand at it.

There is one consolation in all this: I don't feel that the book is of such a nature that it has to be preserved intact the way it was written. I mean, it is not the same kind of document as the *Autobiography* of the Little Flower and nothing much depends on the fact that it may have been changed here and there, since in this case the changes may well be for the better. I wasn't a saint when I wrote the book, and I am probably still less a saint now, not that anyone knows anything about who is or who isn't a saint. Because all, even the saints, are sinners—except, as today reminds us, Our Lady.

The emendation of the *Secular Journal* might well be a matter of suppressing material that is sinful, offensive against charity perhaps. If that is true, then the job will be a welcome one. Pray in any case that I do it the way the Holy Spirit wants it to be done.

I am happy to have this chance to wish you joy on Our Lady's feast.

Now, most important of all. I will have to write a new preface, and this will give me an opportunity to talk about Madonna Villa and all that it stands for and all you are trying to do. Please send me all the material possible, so that I can get a good clear idea of what is going on. I didn't even know until recently that you and Friendship House had parted company. Tell me all about the Institute (?), how you stand, what are your rules, etc. What is the official title again??? (Do you think it is smart to have an official name in Latin?) (Or don't you have an equivalent in English?) . . .

September 18, 1958

Your deeply moving letter came the other day, just before I received from New York proofs of the *Secular Journal* . . . I wish you would look over the proofs of the preface and straighten out any errors. You are forbidden, under obedience, to delete any compliments addressed to your person . . .

The great paradox of Superiorship is that no one can be a Superior unless he is fully worthy, and yet no one is fully worthy. There is only one solution: that Christ Himself, in us, must be the Superior, for He alone is worthy. And we must be content to struggle to keep out of His way. Above all, as you say so wisely, we must be glad if those under us *see* our defects, and are even aware of our sins in some way. Because that means that they will not expect too much from us, and will place their hopes in Christ. The crux of the whole "problem" of being a Superior is right there, in the shame we feel at letting everyone down, the shame at not being up to our task, the fear that everything will be known, that our nothingness will be seen and realized. So many Superiors, thrown into a panic by this fear, become harsh and demanding or suspicious and resentful. And that is not to "govern" but to "dominate." The same thing works the other way, of course, a hundred times over. Because there are subjects also who want to dominate, and who do not want the Superior to know their shame, and who try to get in the first blow . . . May God spare you from such.

In the end, though, the solution is Love—you have said it. And love, it seems to me, implies the realization that perhaps already those subject to us know our failings very well, and accept them with love, and would not dream of holding them against us, because they know these things do not matter. That is the great consolation: in the joy of being known and forgiven, we find it so much easier to forgive everything, even before it happens.

Pray for me, Catherine, in my own sins and struggles. After so boldly advertising to the world that I was out to become a saint, I find I am doing a pretty bum job of it. It is really funny, and I am not surprised or distressed to see what a damn fool I have been: maybe I have a call to that peculiarly Russian form of sanctity—*yurodivetsvo*—to be a fool for Christ and to really enjoy it, in a quiet and inconspicuous way, because in a way He enjoys it . . .

But it certainly is a wonderful thing to wake up suddenly in the solitude of the woods and look up at the sky and see the utter nonsense of *everything*, including all the solemn stuff given out by professional asses about the spiritual life: and simply to burst out laughing, and laugh and laugh, with the sky and the trees because God is not in words, and not in systems, and not in liturgical movements, and not in "contemplation" with a big C, or in asceticism or in anything like that, not even in the apostolate. Certainly not in books. I can go on writing them, for all that, but one might as well make paper airplanes out of the whole lot.

I must stop now and devote myself to the folly of getting up a conference for the novices. But it is not so bad: I prepare conferences and then tell them something entirely different. If I gave them what I had prepared, then that would really be folly.

Catherine, one of my mad ideas—which is really mad and I don't pay attention to it—is to break off and start a new kind of small monastery in Ecuador, a sort of an ashram for local intellectuals and men of good will and Indians, part of the time devoted to discussions and spiritual works of mercy (and some corporal, like a clinic) and part of the time devoted to sitting in a hermitage and getting the straws out of my hair. The whole thing from a certain aspect looks more like Madonna House than O.C.S.O. [Order of Cistercians of the Strict Observance]. Anyway, there is no indication that it would possibly be the will of God, or at least not in the extreme form, and so I put it away as a temptation . . .

July 22, 1961

Your letter was written on May 26 (anniversary of my ordination) and here we are already at the Feast of St. Mary Magdalen. I am sorry for all the delay, but I did want to acknowledge your letter with at least a brief note of some sort. Your two poems were very welcome and they will be posted on the novices' board for their enlightenment. They can use some. I keep trying to remind them that they are not alone in the world, and that they have brethren suffering and struggling very often with much greater problems than we have here, and much greater difficulties. We remain pretty bound up in our relatively small concerns.

However, no one is exempt from anguish. I share the agony of spirits you speak of, and for the same reasons. There is no doubt that we are all involved in a social structure that is rotting from within. The fact that so many good people are able to identify this futile and transient structure with Christian civilization or even, worse still, the body of Christ, is enough to cause anyone agony. I think this agony is simply the inevitable form our suffering takes at such a time. We feel useless, bound, helpless . . . We are stopped, blocked, tongue-tied. When we open our mouths we run into so much contradiction that we wonder whether or not we can believe our own convictions. As Christians we are not really "with" any of the big social movements in one direction or another, left or right. We no longer have the support of a really Christian society. When we lean on the society that is built on what used to be Christian, it gives way and we fall with it . . . yet we cannot commit ourselves to the even more transient secularism that claims to possess the key to the future. It is a very salutary solitude, and one in which I for one think more and more that I will have to stop preaching or to preach only by silence, because no matter what you say, you seem to be saying yes to something you cannot in conscience approve of.

I send you a poem in return for yours. Not exactly a nice little spiritual nosegay. Pray that I may be allowed to print it somewhere. That is not yet by any means certain. I will send along one on the "bomb" which, by some miracle, is getting printed ["Original Child Bomb"] . . .

[*Cold War Letter* 79]

June 4, 1962

Your long, wonderful letter has gone for nearly three months without an answer. But you can guess all the reasons. And now perhaps if I answer it is because the voice which was shouting, momentarily, about peace, has been told to shut up. And I have a little time to return to other things such as writing letters.

I knew I didn't have much time to get said what I felt ought to be said. So I got it all out as best I could, in a jumble of words and articles, and even finished a book. The book is on stencils, and when the last stencil was typed the order came in not to print or publish anything more on topics "not befitting a contemplative monk." Apparently the most crucial problems, and the struggle with the demon, these are out of range of a contemplative monk. I was told it would be all right if I prayed over these matters, however.

You ask me if I am weary? Sure. Perhaps not as weary as you are, but weary in the same way, weary of the same things. It is complicated by the fact that one is tempted to feel he has no right to be weary of the actions and pronouncements of a lot of very good, sincere people who are themselves weary of something or other. We are like a bunch of drunken men at the last end of a long stupid party falling over the furniture in the twilight of dawn. I hope it is dawn. Probably not, though. But the thing that eats one up is the anguish over the Church. This of course leaves me inarticulate because I know that anyone can show where and how and why I am not a good Catholic, a good Christian, a faithful member of Christ. And yet there is this conviction that the Church is full of a terrible spiritual sickness, even though there is always that inexpressible life . . .

It is at such a time as this that one has to have faith in the Church, and the fact that we suffer from the things that make us suffer, the fact that we cannot find any way out of the suffering, is perhaps a sign of hope. I do not pretend to understand the situation or to analyze anything. Your answer is correct. What is wanted is love. But love has been buried under words, noise, plans, projects, systems, and apostolic gimmicks. And when we open our mouths to do something about it we add more words, noise, plans, etc. We are afflicted with the disease of constant talking with almost nothing to say. From that point of view I suppose it is just as well that I am saying nothing more about the war business. Saying things does not help. Yet what is there to do? You're right again, that what one must do is meet the needs that He brings before us, when and as He does so. We will not see anything clear, but we must do His will. We have to be heroic in our obedience to God. And that may mean cutting through a whole forest of empty talk and clichés and nonsense just to begin to find some glimmer of His will. To obey always and not know for sure if we are really obeying. That is not fun at all, and people like to get around the responsibility by entering into a routine of trivialities in which everything seems clear and noble and defined: but when you look at it honestly it falls apart, for it is riddled with absurdity from top to bottom . . .

November 12, 1962

. . . I was deeply moved by the Poustinia [i.e., hermitage] project. That is ideal. It is just right. It will be a wonderful contribution. It is the kind of thing that is most needed. And though it is certain that we must speak if and when we can, silence is always more important. The crises of the age are so enormous and the mystery of evil so unfathomable: the action of well-meaning men is so absurd and tends so much to contribute to the very evils it tries to overcome: all these things should show us that the real way is prayer, and penance, and closeness to God in poverty and solitude. Yet there is no question that sometimes this too is also preached as an invasion of responsibility. It is a terrible situation, and each case must be judged on its merits, with fear and trembling, by the gift of Counsel. Indeed it is very hard now to simply lay down a line of action and say this is it. I will not deviate from this. The next moment you may be forced to change your direction.

So it is usually when I have just resolved firmly to be perfectly silent that I find I have to speak: and when I have resolved to speak out boldly, that I am reduced to silence. At the moment I am pretty well reduced to silence on the war question, and that is all right. It is what I expected, and what I accept. And yet behind it is an evasion, a failure to measure up to the test of the times, for the Church has been too slow to speak and to take a definite position, and this has been weakness and betrayal on the part of those whose responsibility it was: they have been too deeply identified with secular interests.

. . . On the other hand I have the greatest sympathy for the rough and tumble peace movement with its all kinds of wacky people. They are certainly not saints, and some of them think themselves atheists. They are not all leading what we would call good lives. Yet perhaps the peace movement, begun imperfectly and followed with all kinds of errors and misjudgments, may be their way to find the real meaning of love. I know many such people who have despaired of finding love in our cold institutional gatherings and our official pronouncements. God alone knows what He means to do through these people. And He knows too that they are not easy to handle or to live with, for Dorothy Day has had her share of difficulty with them. And yet they are there, and I suppose it is my job to be at least remotely the Church's arm around them, as nobody else much (in the clergy) seems interested.

. . . I think what I need to learn is an almost infinite tolerance and compassion. At least this is I think my great need, because negative thought gets nowhere. I am beginning to think that in our time we will correct almost nothing, and get almost nowhere: but if we can just prepare a compassionate and receptive soil for the future, we will have done a great work. I feel at least that this is the turn my own life ought to take.

. . . This must end here, though there would be much more to say. I am editing and correcting a manuscript of a Russian Orthodox scholar called Bolshakoff, who is at Oxford but doesn't write very good

English. It is about the Russian mystics and full of very interesting material . . .

November 21, 1964

. . . I have known for a long time that in the contemplative Orders of this country the accepted framework has not been adequate to take care of the vocations. The monasteries both of common life and of hermits (if one can call a hermit group a monastery) are organized in a rigid and stereotyped way for one kind of life only, which is not bad in its own way, and which seems to persist because it is relatively easy to keep in order. It is a matter of rules and observances which keep the monk busy and enable him to live a life of comparative recollection and prayer, protecting him against some of the distractions of life, keeping him in trim by a certain amount of austerity.

Unfortunately this regimented form of existence, which is sound enough when based on the best traditions, tends to be rather empty and frustrating, to many vocations, and indeed there is a very general feeling that the life easily becomes a dead end. It retains its meaning for those who have some kind of responsibility in the community or who work in a way that contributes to the community, while for others, well, they tend to vegetate. There are few real contemplatives who can continue simply to live the monastic life as it is organized and really *grow* as they go on. The older generation still manage it. The younger ones, after my age group, tend to be more and more dissatisfied and disoriented.

There is no question that the hermit life is a legitimate and traditional development of the monastic vocation. Simply to block this off and forbid it has kept the question from being raised in the past. It can no longer be kept out of sight. I think in fact that in the monastic Orders we are going to frankly face the need of allowing temporary or permanent hermitages for some of our members. And in fact I already have a dacha or something, which I suppose is somewhat like yours, though perhaps bigger because it was originally built to house groups of ministers coming for dialogue. They go there to converse with us, not to live there. It is a three-room cottage, very simple.

There is also a very keen sense of need for a simpler, more "open" type of monastic life, in which the work will be more "real" and there will be more sense that one is living as ordinary poor people live, not as institutionalized and dressed-up "poor monks" with personal poverty in a rich community. This is one of the great trends in the Order today. It is shaking the Order up quite a bit, especially in Europe. There we have Dutch monks who want to go out and work in factories. Their aspiration is good but the way of fulfilling it seems to me to be off the track. At least for monks.

You say they come to you with all sorts of complicated questions.

Yes, that is true. They have been reading and hearing all sorts of things, and in many cases they may be, though smart, spiritually confused. The basic trouble is perhaps that they are still very immature in the spiritual life, because they are very centered on a "self" for which they want to attain the best of ends: they want to possess "contemplation" and "God." But to think contemplation is something that one can "attain" and "possess" is just to get off on the wrong road from the very beginning. What they really need is solid and simple direction, and more than that, what they need is the kind of really basic sort of training that the Desert Fathers and the early monasteries gave: to shut up and stop all their speculation and get down to living a simple laborious life in which they forget themselves. I am sure that around Madonna House you can help them find a more authentic and realistic simplicity than they may have had in monasteries.

As for the "hermit," well, the danger is that there is no precedent among us and no one to lead the way. It would be a great shame if what I think to be a genuine movement proceeding from God would in fact be discredited by a lot of false and immature hermits trying it out and making a mess of it. I would say that very probably at Madonna House you could really be of service to two or three mature and trained monks with a capacity to be hermits . . .

My advice in the concrete would be to have a couple of hermitages, or three near Madonna House, and allow well-tested men to try out there temporarily, say for Lent, or for three months in summer, etc., and see what develops . . .

I must close now. I am involved in this myself, and have definite hopes of living in a hermitage here in the woods sometime in the not too distant future. In fact I do spend much time there already, and sleep there, etc. I am sure it can all be worked out very simply and quietly, but unfortunately people have a mania for organization and complication, trying to draw up detailed programs for everything all the time, and they forget to just live. I hope they will just let me get out there and live with God and work things out in a simple practical way as time goes on, instead of making up a rigid and legalistic set of rules. However, I will take whatever my Superiors see fit to impose . . .

January 12, 1966

I have been wanting to answer your Christmas letter and your Advent anguish. It is probably gone now, unless the Lord has been keeping you in it as He sometimes does. Living in the hermitage permanently now I am learning the ways of anguish better and the ways of tears too, but also I am taking myself in hand about it, because I am coming to realize that there is a subtle way in which the world grips us and will not set us free: for we must realize that the tyranny of worldly power today holds people precisely by continual anguish and torments them with insecurity, in order every day to get a little better grip. That is the demonic thing about this cold war and hot war and the ceaseless news . . . One must weep for the world, like Staretz Silouane, whom I love as you do. One must even, as he did, keep our souls in "hell" without despairing. But also we must gradually get so that the world and its rule of terror does not reach in to try to dominate our inner soul.

That is why with the business of Dan Berrigan, for example, it is not so great a reason for anguish as one might at first sight think and Dorothy [Day] in the *Catholic Worker* I think is quite right when she says it was perhaps a good thing for him to be shipped out. As far as I know, the authentic story is this: it is not as simple as those protesting against it have made it out to be. Rather his Provincial is a fairly good sort, is trying to be broad-minded and open, and is generally loosening things up, but there were fears in the province that because of Dan the General might descend on the Provincial and spoil everything. Thus (and I don't doubt the Chancery had a hand in it) it was thought wise to smuggle Dan out for a while (I know him very well). Actually, the uproar was justified in the sense that, taking Dan as an occasion, people simply expressed their disgust once for all with the "old way" of doing things, a way which has in any case been deplored by the Council itself. Hence, on this occasion, people simply began to vent their wrath on this particular Superior indeed, but aiming at *all* Superiors who have habitually and flagrantly abused their power for years, consistently tricking and circumventing subjects, never frank with them, always trusting them in a way that is an implicit insult to the dignity of the Christian person, and so on. The lid had to come off at last and it did. I am sure there will be more of the same, and there is no indication that there can be any really widespread change without it. The old ways are established and I suppose that most people just seem to think they are the right ways and there can be no other. Well, the Church will never wake up unless there is a change in this also, as in the Holy Office (I bet it will take time for that one to change too). Thank heaven there are plenty of good Superiors too, who are open-minded and ask for nothing better than to give their subjects some initiative especially in things like race relations. I am sure there is no question of impeding Dan Berrigan in this regard: it is the "pacifism" that is the trouble, in Cardinal Spellman's bailiwick.

I thought it might be useful to say these things, as we are going to have more and more of these same alarms. Let us pray for one another to grow in hope and freedom and do so precisely in and by that anguish which is really a great good though we would certainly prefer any other at the time it is with us . . . I was very anguished myself over Roger La Porte's burning himself alive and had a six weeks' struggle with the peace people I am associated with, Dorothy included, but we came out all right, and I think we have all profited by it. Some tried to make out that Roger was a martyr, but in fact I think he was a kind of sign of judgment, in his well-intentioned confusion, something to teach the Catholic peace movement that there is something far more important than just getting coverage in the press and on TV.

Well, we won't really get out of the wilderness until everything is pressed out and there is nothing left but the pure wine to be offered to the Lord, transubstantiated into His Blood. Let us look forward to that day when we will be entirely in Him and He in us and the Father in and over all. Then there will be true peace which the world cannot give . . .

To A. M. Allchin

The Reverend Arthur MacDonald Allchin is a Canon Residentiary at Canterbury Cathedral, England, living within the cathedral precincts. On October 4, 1983, I interviewed him about his correspondence with Thomas Merton, and about the three visits he made to the Abbey of Gethsemani in the 1960s. We sat in his garden, the huge central tower of the cathedral rising above us against a bright blue sky. When he first wrote to Merton, Fr. Allchin was at Oxford, serving as librarian at Pusey House and as chaplain for students. His lifelong concern for Christian unity has made him a leading figure in interreligious dialogue, especially between the Christian East and West. He chairs the Council of St. Alban and St. Sergius, and has served as editor of their journal, Sobornost. *He is also warden of the community of the Sisters of the Love of God (sometimes called the Fairacre Sisters, from their street in Oxford), a cloistered community of Anglican nuns who follow a modern rule though shaped by the Carmelite tradition.*

Canon Allchin's writings express his keen interest in monasticism, his research into the works and influence of various religious figures (especially the seventeenth-century divines), as well as his enthusiasm for Welsh literature, culture, and spirituality. His interest in Wales sparked Merton's fascination with his own Welsh heritage, his last note being a request that together they "do Wales" in the spring of 1969. Merton wrote this from Delhi, on the Asian journey from which he never returned.

Fr. Allchin came to North America for the first time in the summer of 1963 to participate in a Faith and Order meeting at Montreal. Later that summer he visited Dr. Dale Moody, professor at the Baptist Seminary in Louisville, with whom he had become good friends at Oxford. Dr. Moody, who had visited Merton nearby with students from his seminary, arranged for Canon Allchin to meet Merton. His first letter to Merton received this reply.

July 4, 1963

It was a pleasure to receive your letter. Certainly you will be very welcome at the Abbey, and if you wish to stay a couple of days, it would be fine. If you come some time in the afternoon of the 6th of August, and stay over a couple of days, I will get permission to see you on the seventh or eighth.

Meanwhile I will inform the people in the guesthouse to expect you. I look forward to seeing you and Dr. Moody, whom I have not seen for some time now. He is close, but I am cloistered, so we do not see much of each other, though one of our monks was at the Baptist Seminary recently.

I hope you will forgive my abominable typing. My handwriting is far worse still.

Fr. Allchin asked Merton if he would be willing to write an introduction to a book of translations of the sermons of Isaac of Stella being done by Sr. Penelope, C.S.M.V., of Wantage.

October 21, 1963

Thanks for your letter. I find the proposal to do an introduction on Isaac for Sister Penelope irresistible, though I am making firm resolutions to stop all prefaces. But no, not this one. I certainly want to do it, if I can; and the fact that there is no hurry is a big help. How much space do I have? And I would like to see some of the translations. Glad they will be for the layman!

Thanks too for sundry books and offering to send more. I have a thing called a "cervical disk" and have been lying in traction, where for some reason I have taken to reading George Herbert. I told Etta Gullick I found him a little trite, but really I don't always. He is sometimes most moving. Vaughan I have—one of my favorites. I once thought of bringing out an edition of his translation of Eucherius's *De Contemptu Mundi*— but that would be complicated. How are the Cambridge Platonists? Law I would like to have.

I have been reading Dame Gertrude More. Will send you a thing about her and also some other mimeographed booklets. Please overlook innumerable mistakes!

December 1, 1963

Thank you so much for the [Thomas] Traherne. It will be very valuable if and when I come to carry out my intention to write about Anglican mystics. I have read some of the chapters, and of course it is somewhat less inspired than his other books, but I like it. Etta Gullick has sent William Law, and I know I will like him very much too.

I have still never heard anything from Fairacres, but the Rev. Mother need not be afraid to write if she has something to ask, though I do not pretend to be the world's best correspondent. I hope the copies of *Monastic Studies* reached everyone.

Everyone is still a bit numb from the awful events of ten days ago [the assassination of President John F. Kennedy]. They have been to some extent a revelation of the good and the bad in the country, and if the bad has seemed bad, perhaps worse than we thought, perhaps also the good has appeared as a little better than we thought. I don't know how much one can say about it.

April 25, 1964

Have I yet thanked you for the remarkable little book of essays on the Blessed Virgin [*The Blessed Virgin Mary: Essays by Anglicans*, edited by E. L. Mascall and H. S. Box]? I particularly liked your essay on the seventeenth-century divines and am interested in all the other quotes from Anglican sources throughout the book. I liked the whole tone of the book very much, and was especially interested in the balanced and sensible approach of H. S. Box on the Assumption and Immaculate Conception.

Meanwhile I have been getting on with other Anglican reading. Thornton on *English Spirituality* was of course attractive for its thesis that emphasized Benedictine, Cistercian and Victorine bases for Anglican spirituality. I did not agree with some of his rather oversimplified judgments but liked the book as a whole. I am reading Stranks on *Anglican Devotion*, which is informative. Also McAdoo on the *Moral Theologians*.

It seems to me that the best of Anglicanism is unexcelled, but that there are few who have the refinement of spirit to see and embrace the best, and so many who fall off into the dreariest rationalism. For my part I will try to cling to the best and be as English a Catholic as one in my position can be. I do think it is terribly important for Roman Catholics now plunging into the vernacular to have some sense of the Anglican tradition. This, however, is only a faint hope in my own mind, because on one hand so many of the highest Anglicans are outrageously Latin, and on the other the beauty of the *Book of Common Prayer*, etc., is out of reach of the majority in this country now, and is perhaps no longer relevant. But the spirit and lingo of modern Roman Catholicism in English-speaking countries has been in so many ways a disaster!

Now how about Sister Penelope? I don't mean that I am in a great lather to begin something as I still have some irons in the fire that I want to get out (sorry for the scrambled metaphors). But I would be interested to know when to expect something, and what . . .

Etta Gullick often says she has been next to you in a church.

May 22, 1965

Please believe that I am covered with the most utter confusion. I knew I owed you a letter, and finally today impelled by some angel I found your letter and looked into it again, finding to my horror that you had asked me to send you something for *Sobornost*. There is nothing I would rather do, and I am ashamed that I completely forgot the request. But I know you will understand, as I am being asked for things all the time, all kinds of things, and my memory has no place for them all. But it should have a place for *Sobornost*. I think the explanation is that your letter came during the annual retreat when the mail is piled up and then lands on one in a deluge after it is all over.

If I get a chance I will try to write something monastic . . . I have written some rather fiery treatments of modern problems of Western monks, but surely *Sobornost* is not interested in that particularly. There is an article called "Contemplation and Ecumenism" which is coming out in a very small Dominican magazine in California, so that leaves it out in the open for you people. But perhaps you would want me to reshape it, since I did not have the Orthodox in mind . . .

The meditation on the Poorer Means is for the nuns at Hayward's Heath [Anglican sisters of the community of the Holy Cross, Sussex]. I think my passage on Anglicans is perhaps a bit silly, in fact I know it is. Now if you would want that and could perhaps get it out before they do (which surely would not be hard) and can arrange it with them, all right. It would also require some changes, and I would gladly make them. The long thing on hermits is more for your interest than anything else. The "Notes on Sacred Art" have never appeared anywhere except in little bits. Perhaps you too could take little bits . . .

It seems that I am going to be living permanently in the hermitage, in fact practically am now. This is a great cause for rejoicing but it does mean that I will not be seeing people, except perhaps rarely and exceptionally. I do not know if I can see Etta Gullick in September if she comes, for instance. Perhaps not. But it means of course that I am most unlikely to be ordered anywhere, even to Norway, where we are probably making a foundation. I would love to be ordered somewhere via Oxford, and might even consent to go to Rome if I thought I could go via Oxford, but hardly otherwise. [Fr. Allchin had asked in his letter: "Can you be ordered to Rome via Oxford?"] It is the last place in the world I would go to otherwise than bodily dragged (to the stake).

I . . . have been using *Andrewes Preces* [*Privatae*] at night in the hermitage.

July 22, 1966

. . . I can count on permission to see you when you are in this country next year, as I will still be meeting some who come here, so to speak, in an ecumenical way. So by all means plan on coming down if you can.

The preface I wrote for Sister Penelope is being typed, but the typists are very slow and unreliable now . . . Why doesn't she try Burns Oates?

In January 1967 Fr. Allchin came to New York City to teach for a semester at General Seminary.

January 14, 1967

I hope this will meet you in New York and find you well and ready for action. Certainly I look forward to seeing you here after Easter. Any time after Easter would be all right for me. The weather is not yet perfect at the end of March, but it is usually all right. Spring does not really begin until the middle of April. But suit yourself, Kentucky weather is unpredictable and it could be foul in May.

Yes, I am sending off some notes to the monks at Crawley Down [a small Anglican community of men, the Congregation of the Servants of the Will of God]. As to the Shakers, I have not done anything more but there is a vast amount of material in various centers where furniture, manuscripts and so on have been collected. There are one or two places quite near New York. The people at the seminary can probably tell you about them. There is a place down here [Shakertown, Pleasant Hill] that has some of the old buildings, but not much else.

You are right that things are in a state of general turmoil here perhaps even more than in England, but here we are used to turmoil and no one much minds. But I do rather think that the RCs are getting themselves into the same sort of confusion as the Protestants, with anyone and everyone rushing about in all directions. Doubtless the old monolithic business was too rigid, but still one feels that a certain agreement on basic truths might be desirable. The monks are busy with their own problems and not really getting anywhere . . .

Fr. Allchin visited Gethsemani for a second time in early April 1967.

June 16, 1967

So many things to thank you for. It seems a long time since your visit, when the weather was fine, and when it was good to walk and talk in the woods. Now it is stifling. Come again when the weather is fine again. Did you say you were to be here in the fall, or next spring?

Then the books: R. S. Thomas is for me a marvelous discovery. A poet like Muir, perhaps better than Muir, with such a powerful spirit and experience, so well conveyed. I must try to write something on him: is there anything about his life, or who he is? Thanks also for the book on Muir, which I am saving for a quiet afternoon, or a series of quiet afternoons.

Yes, the people at *Frontier* sent Stevie Smith's address, but I have not written to her yet. After all, a declaration of love is no mean thing . . . Etta Gullick was here as you know and we had a delightful picnic.

That was in the fine weather too. Now the valley is steaming and one can barely see the hills on the other side.

Hoping to see you again one of these days. Thanks again.

September 15, 1967

I have two letters of yours to answer, and the first one is the second. There is no problem at all about your coming here before Easter. Come whenever you can. Just let us know.

The other one—I think your idea [of spending a sabbatical year living the monastic life at Crawley Down] is very good. For my own part I am all in favor of people going to monasteries for a year or two. In fact I am more and more persuaded that, as we go on, that is going to be one of the main functions of a monastery. I think our monasteries should be quite small and simple places, not great triumphal and solemn castles of prayer, and these simple places should be manned by a small group of permanent members, some of them more active, others so to speak con-templatives and megaloschemoi. And then there would always be another group, perhaps half of those in residence at any time, simply there for a year or two. Zen monasteries are like that: places where one goes for a short time to learn—and perhaps to return on and off later. I think that the idea of getting everyone tied up with solemn vows for life is simply no longer workable for a great number of people who nevertheless have monastic vocations of a modified kind.

I have meant to write a note some time to Fr. Gregory, in answer to his nice note . . . Thanks for *Sobornost*, a good issue. Would it be possible for me to have half a dozen copies, please? . . .

This afternoon I am going to take off into the woods. I have a rather fascinating book about a Crow Indian who made fasting retreats on moun-taintops in order to get suitable visions and "medicine" in order to triumph in battle. It is quite fascinating—a study of a mystical military life! And of an establishment with which he got in trouble because he seems to have forced the visions a bit. A really interesting book. Also I am working on Melanesian Cargo cults. If you turn up anything new and interesting on them, I hope you will let me know.

I haven't read the *Sobornost* piece on Ann Griffiths yet, because I am entirely swept away by my discovery of David Jones. He is a real revelation, I like his work immensely. When I have learned from his kind and convenient notes to pronounce a few Welsh words, I'll turn to Ann . . .

From the Desk of Father Louis O.C.S.O.

February 1, 1968

Pardon the pretentious note paper. Someone thought it would be a good gift, and it is useful.

Though I am not too sure of dates in March I think April 3rd or 4th sounds all right, and so let's plan on it.

I might really write on David Jones, and would write to him. Do you have his address? I am even running a small temporary magazine and would love to have something of his in it. I wonder if much of R. S. Thomas has been published over here? I could definitely use some of his.

We have a good new Abbot: one of the other hermits.

March 24, 1968

The hermitage looks like this even today [a picture of the hermitage in winter]—though we are supposed to be in "spring." However, I hope things will be better when you come early in April.

I will look for you Wednesday 3rd. When? I am provisionally reserving two rooms from Tuesday night on in case you arrive late. I will be down Wednesday morning about nine and look for you then. As for the idea of going to Shakertown, that is splendid. Glad there is a car. Wonderful. We can take the whole day Thursday. Oh, looking back at your letter I see you'll be arriving afternoon of 3rd. That's all right. I'll either be down in the monastery or expect you at hermitage on your own time—you can find it? If you're driving from Dayton, you'll get here about two I'd imagine.

Thanks for Ann Griffiths' poems—wonderful material very Greek sounding. I think before publication in the *Pond* I'd have to make them more "poetic"—or you or Hodges. But I really do hope to do something with at least some of them.

I will offer Mass for Madeleine Lossky—and Vladimir too. Must go back to his Eckhart book again.

Yes, I think I have a short thing for the *Fairacres Bulletin*. We can talk of that.

I haven't written to D. Jones or even to Stevie Smith—in spite of best of intentions. The Sysiphean, or better Sisyphean (Sisyphic?) labor of letters makes it impossible to do many things I'd like in the way of opening new contacts.

Fr. Allchin arrived on April 3. The next day they visited Shakertown at Pleasant Hill. On the way home they heard on the car radio of the assassination of Martin Luther King, Jr., in Memphis. Tom said: "There is a restaurant in Bardstown, operated by a black friend of mine, Colonel Hawks. It is important that we go there." A picture taken at the restaurant showed the Canon and Merton and the colonel at a table on which stood a picture of John F. Kennedy.

August 27, 1968

September has nearly come around and alas, no Wales. First of all the General Chapter is not until next March, and second Fr. Abbot has

decided (and I agree) that there is no point in my going to it. I am going—
I hope—to the Bangkok meeting but that will not bring me anywhere
near Wales.

Perhaps some other time I may get a chance to be in Europe: this
time it is Asia, and frankly I am quite excited by the prospect. Please
pray that all may be as it promises to be—very interesting.

Delhi, India
November 10 [probably], 1968
. . .The Indian journey has been fine so far, fine talks with the Dalai
Lama and others. I am now trying to get permission to return via England
in May. Can we do Wales then?

To Edward Deming Andrews

*Edward Deming Andrews (1894–1964), with the help and encouragement of his
wife, Faith, dedicated much of his life to a study of the history, beliefs, craftsmanship, and way of life of the United Society of Believers in Christ's Second
Appearing. This sect, better known as the Shakers, had its origin in eighteenth-
century England with Mother Ann Lee and emigrated to the United States in
1774. Thomas Merton found a kinship between the Shakers and his own Cistercian
Order in the ideals of honesty, simplicity, and good work for a spiritual motive.*

*Though always adhering to the most exacting standards of scholarship, Mr.
Andrews was no detached observer; he grasped the spirit of these people and
wrote about them with clarity, sensitivity, and enthusiasm. Mark Van Doren has
said well: "He knew the Shakers, because he loved them: not sentimentally, nor
nostalgically, but with an abiding respect for the ideas their entire life expressed.
And he knew how to write of what he so perfectly understood." His books include,
among others,* The Gift to Be Simple: Dances and Rituals of the American Shakers
(1940), The People Called Shakers *(1953),* Visions of the Heavenly Sphere *(1969),*
Religion in Wood, *with an introduction by Thomas Merton (1982). The story of
the Andrewses' many years of involvement with the Shakers is simply and charm-
ingly told in* Fruits of the Shaker Tree of Life: Memoirs of Fifty Years of Collecting
and Research *(Berkshire Traveller Press, 1975).*

December 12, 1960
It was indeed a pleasure to get your kind letter. I had been thinking
of writing to you myself for some time, as I know several of your fine
books on the Shakers and indeed have the two most important ones here.
(I take it that *The People Called Shakers* and *Shaker Furniture* are among
your most important studies.) So first of all I want to express my gratitude
to you for the fine work you have done and are doing. I shall certainly

have to depend very much on you, if I do any work at all in this field, and I am grateful for your offer of assistance.

It is quite true that Shirley Burden and I have discussed the possibility of a book on the Shakers. My part would not be precisely a study of their religion, if by that is to be understood their doctrines, but of their spirit and I might say their mysticism, in practice, as evidenced by their life and their craftsmanship. To me the Shakers are of a very great significance, besides being something of a mystery, by their wonderful integration of the spiritual and the physical in their work. There is no question in my mind that one of the finest and most genuine religious expressions of the nineteenth century is in the silent eloquence of Shaker craftsmanship. I am deeply interested in the thought that a hundred years ago our two communities were so close together, so similar, somehow, in ideals, and yet evidently had no contact with one another. I have seen the buildings of the Shaker colony near Harrodsburg here, and of course it speaks volumes to me. There is at present a plan on foot in which you will be interested: some friends of mine in university circles in Lexington are trying to buy the buildings and preserve them in some form or other, perhaps as a study center. If you are interested I can have them get in touch with you, they are having rather a hard time and you might be able to help them. In fact it might be wise eventually to coordinate the various efforts to save the different Shaker communities everywhere. I wrote a little letter to the Shakers at Canterbury, N.H., and got a sweet letter back from one of the old ladies, but I have not pursued the correspondence. I ought to try to write to them for Christmas, though.

But in any case, your letter inspires me to pursue further my studies of the Shakers. I will not rush at it and I will try to profit by their example and put into practice some of their careful and honest principles. It would be a crime to treat them superficially, and without the deepest love, reverence and understanding. There can be so much meaning to a study of this kind: meaning for twentieth-century America which has lost so much in the last hundred years—lost while seeming to gain. I think the extinction of the Shakers and of their particular kind of spirit is an awful portent. I feel all the more akin to them because our own Order, the Cistercians, originally had the same kind of ideal of honesty, simplicity, good work, for a spiritual motive.

Now I do want to take advantage of your kind offer. I am still far from getting down to the study I want to do. But if you have any interesting books that are not too precious to lend, which speak of the Shaker spirit in work and living, I would be very happy to borrow them and take care of them. But more urgent than that: I wonder if you could let me have any reproductions of your Shaker inspirational paintings? I would like to use two or three if possible in a book on religious art which is ready for publication. I think certainly some of the trees of life, etc., would be most suitable (these I have seen in reproduction) but I do not know about the others. Perhaps there is among them something with a special spiritual quality. I would be glad to use anything you can let me have . . . I am very interested in your project to save the Hancock community and shall pray for its success . . .

January 17, 1961

This morning I received a good long letter from Shirley Burden in California and some pictures he took of the Shaker buildings and graveyard at Harvard. I was very glad to hear from him after a long silence, and to know that he was still interested in our project. He told me also of the proposed exhibition that is being planned by the Museum of Modern Art for 1962 which will include photographs and probably furniture, etc. I am sure you know all about this.

Today therefore seems to be a good time to answer your kind letter of December 19th and to thank you for the two charming little booklets. The one on herbs and herbalists is particularly charming, and again it brings to mind the similarity of ideals and practices which bring Shakers and Cistercians closer together. Unfortunately we do not grow our own medicinal herbs today at least in America, but St. Bernard wanted the monks of Tre Fontane near Rome to do so. Or rather, to be more exact, he wanted them *not* to "seek out doctors and swallow their nostrums" but to "use common herbs such as they are used by the poor" . . . The study of the use of herbs by the medieval Cistercians would be quite interesting, I am sure.

. . . Certainly a Cistercian ought to be in a good position to understand the Shaker spirit, and I do hope that with leisure, study and meditation I will eventually be able to do something on this wonderful subject. I would like to borrow the volume you suggest, Elders Wells and Green's *Summary View of the Millennial Church.* The trouble is that I lack so much of the background of what one might, for want of a better term, describe as the "gnostic" element that came down through unrecorded, oral traditions and eventually reached people like Mother Ann. I did my thesis on Blake when I was in the graduate school at Columbia, and this would count as a start, but it was long ago.

. . . Before I go any further I want to say that you have my full permission to quote from my letter about the importance of preserving Shaker craftsmanship. If anything I have said can be of the slightest help, I will be delighted. Also I do not think I answered a question you asked in your first letter: as to whether the monks here were reproducing Shaker pieces of furniture. No, indeed we are not. We are very busy with a big job of renovation in our old buildings and our carpenters are all engaged in this. We have one very good cabinetmaker but his work is nothing like Shaker furniture. I know that one of our Brother carpenters is very interested in Shaker work, however.

The closest we are getting is that a friend of mine, a layman, is copying an old Shaker school desk from a reproduction in the book on New England pine furniture, for me. This I hope to use in a hermitage in the woods. It is just possible that some rumor about this got around, and led to your surmise that the monks were now reproducing Shaker pieces. But we are not.

. . . As to the contacts between our Fathers here and the former colony at Pleasant Hill, there is quite a distance between us and in those days I hardly think any of the monks would have had much occasion to go over that way. I should say it was about sixty miles over hilly country. I can imagine one of our Breton founders perhaps having to go to Lexington through Pleasant Hill, and being somewhat perplexed as he drove through in his wagon. The language barrier would in itself have created an obstacle if nothing else. It was a long time before our first monks became naturalized so to speak, and Americans did not join the community until the end of the nineteenth century.

I have not been in touch with Barry Bingham, but I might discuss the Pleasant Hill project with him later on. The people who are interested in the idea, in Lexington, tell me that the owners have banded together and put up such a big price that there is no hope for the moment of anything being done. Perhaps one or another of these friends of the Pleasant Hill colony may get in touch with you. I hope it will eventually be saved. There is a wonderful character of solitude and loneliness about the hilltop site looking out over rolling country. I was deeply moved looking out of the attic of the old guesthouse through the branches of a big cedar at the quiet field in which they used to dance (Holy Sion's plain). Incidentally, in an offprint of Coomaraswamy, I ran across a lovely old carol, about the "dancing" of God with man in the mystery of the Incarnation. I think here there may be an important lead. The carol is an ancient English one. In it, the Lord speaks of His coming at Christmas in the following words: "Tomorrow is my dancing day . . ." I do not have the text at my elbows, one of the other fathers has borrowed it.

Your study on the "Visions of the Heavenly Sphere" sounds very absorbing and I hope I shall one day see it in print . . .

I have seen your book *The Gift to Be Simple* referred to in many places, and that too I want to read someday. I shall not borrow it now, since I may be able to get it in town. And in any case, it must wait a bit.

In working on the Shakers I would certainly not make any sense if I let myself be hurried and crowded and confused by multiplicity. But I hope to continue my reading and study in the things I have on hand to keep up with the Shakers at the same time. Eventually, at the right time, the two lines will converge and something will result. Meanwhile I am very happy to be in touch with you, and I want to keep in touch . . .

August 22, 1961

It is a terribly long time since you last wrote and since you sent the little book on the *Millennial Church*. I should have answered you long ago, and I should also have returned the book by this time. I am at last answering and it is in order to accuse myself of slothfulness and lethargy, and ask your indulgence so that I may keep the book a little while longer.

To excuse myself, I can point to the condition of our times, which no one, not even a monk, completely escapes or transcends. I have allowed myself to be involved in more tasks and interests than I should, and the one that has most suffered has been the study of the Shakers. It is in a way so completely out of the theological realm with which I am familiar, although their spirit has so much in common with ours. This makes me hesitant to plunge in deeply, and so I turn to other things in which I feel I can accomplish something . . . I am hoping that I can get back to this kind of study of the Shaker sources later in the fall.

Yet perhaps some of my other interests may remotely cast a light on this study. I am currently very interested in Clement of Alexandria, one of the earliest Christian "Gnostics," and his spirit has much in common with that of Shaker simplicity and joy. Then too I am acquainting myself with the magnificent work on primitive religions that has been done by Mircea Eliade. In reality I think he is the one most qualified to give a complete, well-rounded appreciation of the Shaker doctrines, practices and spirit . . . It is very certain that the Shakers preserved many many deeply important religious symbols and lived out some of the most basic religious myths in their Christian and gnostic setting. I cannot help feeling also that the very existence of the Shakers at that particular moment of history has a very special significance, a sort of "prophetic" function in relation to what has come since.

How are the last Shakers up in New Hampshire? I often think of them. I have intended to write to the Eldress but I have so little time to write letters that have to be written that none is left for those that would be mere luxury.

I was happy to see your allusions to Mark Van Doren and to Coomaraswamy in your last letter (as understanding reviewers of your fine book on *Shaker Furniture*). Mark is coming down to Louisville in the fall and I hope he will be out here . . .

The carol "Tomorrow will be my dancing day" is to be found in any good collection of English carols, I believe. My reference was to a little introduction by A. Coomaraswamy to a translation of the Hindu religious play the *Taking of Toll*, printed in London in 1915. If you cannot trace this carol I will be happy to send you a copy of what I have of it, which is incomplete.

Everything regarding Shakers is always of great interest to me. I think often of them, of the extinct colony that was so near here: I think of their simplicity and their mystical fervor. It is always to me a deeply significant thought, and I feel deeply related to them in some kind of obscure communion . . .

The copy of the Shaker schoolboy desk which is in our hermitage is a pure joy . . .

[*Cold War Letter 12*]

December 21, 1961

Forgive please this very long delay in thanking you for the copy of *Shaker Furniture* which will remain a highly valued possession in the novitiate library. I believe it is of the highest importance for the novices to see these things, and get used to this wonderful simplicity. This wordless simplicity, in which the works of quiet and holy people speak humbly for themselves. How important that is in our day, when we are flooded with a tidal wave of meaningless words: and worse still when in the void of those words the sinister power of hatred and destruction is at work. The Shakers remain as witnesses to the fact that only humility keeps man in communion with truth, and first of all with his own inner truth. This one must know without knowing it, as they did. For as soon as a man becomes aware of "his truth" he lets go of it and embraces an illusion.

I am so glad you liked Clement. If it ever gets printed, I will gladly send you a copy. New Directions is not in a hurry to decide because we are working on a more urgent project, a book of articles against nuclear war.

Speaking of Clement and Alexandria, you know of Philo Judaeus, the Jewish Platonist who flourished in that city. He has a very intriguing book *De Therapeutis* (which I have not yet found and read). In this book he speaks of Jewish monastic communities in Egypt in which there are some similarities with the Shakers. Particularly the fact that they were contemplative communities of men and women, living separately and joining in worship, though separated by a partition. It would seem there might be many interesting facts in this book, and I recommend it to your curiosity. Alexandria remains a fascinating place, and I am sure that more study of the intellectual and spiritual movements that flourished there will prove very rewarding.

. . . My prayers and good wishes to you and Mrs. Andrews . . . It was a very great pleasure to have you here with us for an afternoon and I hope you will be back again one of these days.

September 20, 1962

Probably my silence is the result of a more or less frantic effort to preserve some simplicity in my exterior life by only writing letters when I can think about them. Or rather, by trying to convince myself that it is possible to do this when, in reality, it is not possible. So I write business letters under pressure and leave the things I would really like to write until it is too late to write them. Thus I am afflicted with the modern disease, which you perhaps have escaped better than I, although I am supposed to be a monk.

The Gift to Be Simple is a book of inestimable value to me. It has in it so many things that move one by their clarity and truth. The "Gift to be Simple" is in fact the "Gift to be True," and what we need most in our life today, personal, national and international, is this truth. Some of the songs are naïve, all of them are charming by their honesty, but there is one which contains great power: "Decisive Work." There is more in this than just a pious song.

I shall continue to enjoy these songs and ponder over them. How beautiful is the Meeting House you have moved over to Hancock [Shaker village]. I wish I could be there for its dedication: or at least to see it some time. Perhaps I will.

The story of the Shirley Meeting House is filled with conflict and paradox. At this, one need not be surprised, because the law of all spiritual life is the law of risk and struggle, and possible failure. There is something significant in the fact that the Shaker ideal was to most people all but impossible, and that therefore it was inevitable that many good men should fall crashing out of the edifice they had helped to build. God alone understands those failures, and knows in what way perhaps they were not failures. Perhaps somewhere in the mystery of Shaker "absolutism" which in many ways appears to be "intolerant" and even arbitrary, there is an underlying gentleness and tolerance and understanding that appears not in words but in life and in work. It is certainly in the songs. Some of us only learn tolerance and understanding after having been intolerant and "absolute." In a word, it is hard to live with a strict and sometimes almost absurd ideal, and the ambivalence involved can be tragic, or salutary. More than anyone else, the Shakers faced that risk and the fruitfulness of their life was a sign of approval upon their daring.

No, I have not settled down to the photo essay. If I did it now, it would be too superficial. I must read and think more . . .

December 28, 1962

I was touched at your thoughtfulness in sending me the music for the song "Decisive Work." It is what I would have expected, and I have learned it now, so that I can sing it to myself from time to time when I am alone. I am still deeply convinced that it represents a most important insight into our own time. And of course it is for us in our own way by our faith and obedience to all of God's "words" to attune ourselves to His will and to join in His work, according to our own humble capacities. The Shakers saw this so well, and saw that their work was a cooperation in the same will that framed and governs the cosmos: and more governs history.

I am so glad you liked "Grace's House" [see *Collected Poems of Thomas Merton*]. I thought you would. If you would like more copies I can send them.

. . . I have not seen Pleasant Hill [i.e., Shakertown, Kentucky] since the work has been going on, and I have no idea what it is like. There does not seem to be a great deal of enthusiasm over the project in this part of the country.

. . . Did I ever send you a mimeographed book of mine on Peace [*Peace in a Post-Christian Era*]? I will put a copy in the mail. It is not, unfortunately, being published.

January 29, 1964

Thanks for your most recent letter, as well as for the previous one which I put off answering until I thought you might be back from your trip. Thanks also for the book in its new edition, which I am very glad to have. I don't know whether I had written to you saying I was quoting you in the article now in *Jubilee* [January 1964], but in any case I hope you do not mind my going ahead and using your material. The funny thing is that I took for granted that the "sermonettes" were drawn from something by you. If they are not, then they must be from something in the University of Kentucky Library, on material from Pleasant Hill. I think there are a couple of books I used there which were printed locally about forty years ago, and this probably comes from one of them. I still want to do a little work on the material that is down in this part of the country, such as it is, but do not have time yet. I have a copy now of the memos of Benjamin Young's* journey down here, and that should prove interesting.

Now as regards your new book, I would really be delighted to try an introduction. I love the Shakers and all that they have left us far too much to be able to say no, though I have taken to refusing prefaces lately. But in this case I really want to do something. Could I have a look at some of your material when the time comes to write this up?

One thing I have been meaning to consult you about. I am finishing a little book on *Art and Worship* and would like to include a couple of Shaker prints, at least the Tree of Life. Can you possibly furnish me with pictures of these that will reproduce? I mean one of the Tree of Life and perhaps examples of one or two others (I do not know them well enough to specify which). Also I understand it is now possible to have colored reproductions of the Tree of Life. I would like very much to get one of these to put on the wall. Do you know where I could do this?

---

* A Shaker from Watervliet community, and a missionary to Ohio and Kentucky.

. . . I am happy about the federal aid granted to the Pleasant Hill project, that is to say happy in principle. It is good that they have two million dollars, provided that they do the right thing with it. Sometime I will send you some of my photographs of Pleasant Hill (the two in *Jubilee* were mine), you might like to have them on file. I must get prints made. I still cherish slight hopes of doing a little book on Pleasant Hill someday. It will take time. I know that I need the gift to be simple and am inclined enough toward it, so that when I start to get complicated in my projects, I grind to a stop, and have to get the work untangled before it starts up again. I don't think an ambitious Shaker project would fit in with my other commitments at the moment. But someday perhaps . . .

March 13, 1964

The Tree of Life has arrived, and indeed has been on the wall [in the kitchen of the hermitage] for some time. It really brightens up the room and fills the whole place with its own light. I am very happy to have it, and deeply grateful.

Our Lent proceeds quietly but a little hectically as there have been floods near here. The monastery was not affected by them, as it is on high ground, but we had lots of rain, and I always manage to be busier than I would like to be. In the contemplative life one imagines that one would spend all the time absorbed in contemplation, but alas this is not the case. There are always innumerable things to be done and obstacles to getting them done, and large and small troubles.

Did I tell you I got a very interesting set of notes from a Benedictine nun at Regina Laudis, Bethlehem, Conn., about a visit she and another nun paid to the Shakers at Sabbathday Lake? I am sure you would be very interested. If you do not know Regina Laudis you ought to get to know it. A quite exceptional convent. You should perhaps try to have a conversation with this Sister Prisca, and the Prioress, Mother Benedict, is also a very fine person and would be most interested, I think, in speaking to you about the Shakers.

Easter approaches and I keep you and Faith in my thoughts and prayers. May the light and the joy of the Risen Lord shine in your lives through and through.

. . . In a new book I am bringing out [*Seeds of Destruction*] I am using sections from letters I had written at one time or another and I want to use a bit out of one of my letters to you about the Shakers. Is that all right? Your name will be mentioned as the recipient of the letter but of course there will be nothing personal in it.

To Mrs. Edward Deming Andrews

July 20, 1964

Some time ago a rumor had reached me that Ted had suddenly been taken from you and from us. I was not able to verify the rumor until recently and I find that it is actually the case. I am shocked and saddened at the news. This is of course a great loss to all of us. He was a bit older than he looked, but I was expecting more work from his pen on the Shakers. Unfortunately that has been cut short.

There is no question that his vocation was to keep alive the Shaker spirit in its purity and mediate that to the rest of us. I feel personally very much in debt to him for this. I realize more and more the vital importance of the Shaker "gift of simplicity" which is a true American charism: alas, not as fully appreciated as it should be. Ted was faithful to his call, and his work has borne more fruit than we can estimate on this earth. His reward will surely be with those angelic ones whose work and life he understood and shared.

You are perhaps wondering what has become of the preface I was asked by him to write for *Religion in Wood*. I have been delayed, by a variety of tasks and chores. But the preface is now finished and needs only to be retyped. I will get it in the mail to you perhaps this week, perhaps later. But in any event I will be as quick about it as I can.

In the preface I have been bold enough to bring in quite a lot about William Blake. I hope you will not think this too venturesome, but I thought it would be worthwhile to write a preface that was an essay in its own right, and I hope it will add to the book. The text which Ted sent is very clear, interesting and even inspiring, as was all that he wrote. I am most eager to see the new material in the illustrations.

To Reza Arasteh

Born in Shiraz, Iran, on September 27, 1927, A. Reza Arasteh received his bachelor's and master's degrees at the University of Teheran (1948 and 1949) and a Ph.D. at Louisiana State University (1953). Acquainted with both Eastern and Western psychology (in Western psychology he has worked with Erich Fromm and C. G. Jung), he is principally concerned with the way in which one becomes a fully integrated human person. This, he believes, entails a transcultural outlook which can lead to peace both for the individual and for the human community.

The two books of his that especially attracted Merton were Rumi the Persian: Rebirth in Creativity and Love *(1963) and* Final Integration in the Adult Personality: A Measure for Peace *(1964). Merton wrote two reviews of the latter work—one of which is a key article in* Contemplation in a World of Action: *"Final*

Integration: Toward a 'Monastic Therapy.' " *Merton also found Dr. Arasteh's*
writings helpful in preparing the lectures he gave to the Gethsemani community
on Sufism. Dr. Arasteh, who for some years has lived in Bethesda, Maryland,
became an American citizen in 1976.

December 18, 1965

It is a great pleasure for me to have your book on Rumi. I am reading
it with great interest as I like the Sufis and admire them. In fact I will
shortly be lecturing on Sufism to the novices and young monks here.
Your book will help me in this.

I think your book would be even more interesting and valuable if
there were allusions to other mystical writers and traditions by way of
comparison. You might be interested in some of the works of St. John of
the Cross, a Spanish mystic who is thought to have been influenced to
some extent by a Moroccan Sufi, Ibn Abbad. Though this hypothesis of
influence is very shaky, there are many points in common. In connection
with Rumi, it would be worthwhile to examine some of the mysticism of
pure love among the Flemish mystics of the fourteenth century and thereafter. Of course there is always Eckhart too.

Meanwhile I hope you have received my little book on Chuang
Tzu . . .

December 27, 1965

I am interested in your book [*Final Integration in the Adult Person-*
ality], which I am sure will fill a great need in this country. The subject
is important and it is one which I would gladly preface. Unfortunately,
however, I have written so many prefaces in the last few years that my
publisher finally took me to task and said that it would not be advisable
to continue on such a scale. I promised that I would not undertake any
more prefaces for a good while, and so I am unable to accept your offer.
I wish I could.

This does not mean I am not interested in the book, and I would be
happy to look it over some time, perhaps when it gets further into the
process of publication. Do you take up the question of psychedelics? I
think this is important, because it seems to me to raise the whole question
of the validity of mystical experience. And the real purpose of interior
transformation by love. Love cannot be incited by a drug . . .

December 30, 1967

Thanks for your very charming card: certainly the most beautiful and
most "spiritual" I have seen this Christmas. It reminds me very much of
a charming and "visionary" Tree of Life done by a member of the Shaker
sect a hundred years ago, which is reproduced and hangs in my kitchen.

. . . Now I have a favor to ask. I am planning on editing a small literary magazine [*Monks Pond*], at least temporarily. It will be printed here without special cost and distributed more or less free. It is to include poetry and other creative work, but also religious and mystical texts, particularly from Asia. I wonder if you could help me in that regard: can you furnish me with anything from Persian Sufism, particularly something hitherto untranslated? Or any texts that you feel would be particularly interesting, poems, letters, aphorisms, etc.? I would be very happy to have something like this from you—or a short piece of your own perhaps. The character of the magazine is more literary than scientific and academic . . .

January 26, 1968

Your book is very fine and I am giving it a slow and fruitful reading. I find it very interesting and illuminating and perhaps if occasion offers I may review it somewhere. My compliments on it.

. . . You refer in your book to an unpublished article: "Succession in Identities." Do you have a copy of this I could borrow? I should be interested in reading it.

I am also still very anxious to get little known and perhaps hitherto untranslated Sufi texts from various sources—and will also look up many of the books you refer to, material I had not known of before . . .

March 22, 1968

I am sorry I have not written for so long. It was a disappointment not to see you, but I hope we can look forward to a visit later. Meanwhile I have been extremely busy and have let my correspondence fall behind.

I have finished your excellent book and have written a long review article [for *Monastic Studies*, Vol. 6, 1968], which I will send along in due course . . .

I also enclose a copy of something I wrote last fall ["Rebirth and the New Man in Christianity"]* which will show that I was already in complete agreement with you. It may also give you some introduction to the idea of rebirth which is so important in Christianity—just as it is in Sufism.

I am using your unpublished article on Sufism in my magazine, but I do not have space for the notes, so I am presuming it is all right to omit them, not only the ones at the end but also many of the footnotes. The article should appear in the second issue of the magazine . . .

April 2, 1968

Many thanks for your letter. April 12 is a difficult day in some respects as it is Good Friday, and there are special ceremonies in the afternoon.

---

* *This was a revision of what was originally a preface to the Japanese edition of* The New Man. *The revision was published in* Love and Living *(1979).*

However, I am free until about two o'clock. The morning is quite free. Could you come for lunch (11:30 a.m.) at the monastery and I could meet you after lunch, namely about 12:15. That would give us time to talk a little. If you come about 10 a.m. that would be even better. So let us put it this way: I am free until about two and look forward to seeing you when you can make it. Please let me know ahead, so that I can be there.

I shall take up the question of a paperback edition of *Final Integration* with one of my publishers. If you want to use my article, that's fine. That is the preface to the Japanese translation of one of my books. I'll look it over and modify it if need be. Any suggestions? . . .

May 22, 1968

Here is the reworked piece on "Rebirth in Christianity." I have been somewhat delayed in sending it as I have been away.

I was in San Francisco where I mentioned your book to the publisher of City Lights Books, Lawrence Ferlinghetti. You might send him a copy of *Final Integration*, though I think you could find a publisher who would give you more extensive readership . . .

To Abdul Aziz

Ch. Abdul Aziz, whose letters sparked Merton's interest in Sufism, has lived all his life in Karachi, Pakistan. Educated at the University of Karachi, where he achieved high honors and the degrees of M.A. and LL.B., he spent much of his life in government service. In 1974 he retired as the Collector of Customs.

More important to him than his work, however, are his spiritual aspirations that have moved him to a lifelong study of mysticism and especially Sufism. His first contact with Thomas Merton came through his reading of Merton's Ascent to Truth, *which he purchased in 1952. His favorable impression of the book was confirmed by Louis Massignon, well-known French Orientalist and specialist in Islamic studies, who in 1959 came to Karachi. Mr. Aziz asked him for the name and address of some genuine Christian saint and contemplative mystic. Professor Massignon gave him Merton's name and address, describing him, as Mr. Aziz recalls, as "simurgh" (the king of the soaring birds, in Persian mythology).*

Abdul Aziz first wrote to Thomas Merton on November 1, 1960. "This," he states, "was the beginning of our most useful correspondence and candid and fraternal contacts on mysticism and comparative studies of religion. We never met in person. We exchanged books and ideas on a reciprocal basis." It was this correspondence and his study of the books Abdul Aziz sent him that inspired Merton to give a series of lectures to the monks at Gethsemani on Sufism.

November 17, 1960

It was a pleasure for me to receive your good letter and I am certainly grateful to our mutual friend Louis Massignon for referring you to me. Thank you for your very kind words concerning the *Ascent to Truth*. As you expressed some interest in the things I write, I have sent to you under separate cover two packages of books of mine which I hope you will accept as a gift. They include most of those you ask for. The *Seven Storey Mountain* is the original edition of *Elected Silence*, and it is a longer, more complete version. There are some passages on contemplation in the later sections of *The Signs of Jonas* and I also included two little books on monasticism. I hope you can find something in these books that may be of interest to you. As to *Seeds of Contemplation*, the reason why I have not added this to the others is, frankly, shame. The book was written when I was much younger and contains many foolish statements, but one of the most foolish reflects an altogether stupid ignorance of Sufism.* This I have many times regretted, now that I know much better what it is, but I could not bring myself to send you a book containing such a lamentable error. You will pardon me. If there is to be any further edition of the book I shall have the error corrected and then you will receive the book . . .

Yes, I am indeed very interested in Husayn Mansur Hallaj,† that great saint and mystic, martyr of truth and of love. I am also well acquainted with Jalalu'l Din Rumi, who is to my mind one of the greatest poets and mystics, and I find his words inspiring and filled with the fire of divine love. I am also tremendously impressed with the insights into the mysticism of Islam that I have been able to attain through the medium of Louis Massignon's writings. I believe that it is of the greatest importance for these writings to be studied and made known everywhere and I am sure your work is one that will be blessed with great fruitfulness. I should be very glad indeed to make known to you any possible sources in Western mysticism. In return, if you can help me to widen my knowledge and understanding of Sufism I would be deeply grateful to you . . .

In regard to St. John of the Cross, I think we have here some paperback editions of his main works and I have asked them to be sent to you. I might also refer you to the life of St. John of the Cross, in French, by Père Bruno de Jésus-Marie, which has some interesting pages on the possible influence of Sufism in the mysticism of St. John of the Cross. References will lead you further along these lines. I forget the name of the French publisher, but any one of your correspondents in France can

---

* *See page 87 of* Seeds of Contemplation *where Merton speaks of "the sensual dreams of the Sufis" as a poor substitute for the true contemplation that is found only in the Church. This book was written in 1949.*

† *A Muslim saint about whom Massignon had written a great deal.*

inform you. I wonder if Father Paul Nwyia still has another offprint of his article on Ibn Abbad and St. John: I would be very interested in reading it as I do not know this mystic. In fact my ignorance in this field is very great.

Some important books which I recommend to you can be obtained from Harper Brothers . . . They are publishing an interesting little volume, the *Centuries* of Thomas Traherne, which you ought to have . . . They print something of Fénelon, I believe. Also a fine book by John Ruysbroeck, the *Adornment of the Spiritual Marriage*. You should also get to know the anonymous *Cloud of Unknowing*. St. Bernard of Clairvaux, one of the early fathers of the Cistercian Order of which I am a monk, has some very important mystical writings. Perhaps the best way to get to know him would be to read the *Mystical Theology of St. Bernard* by Etienne Gilson.

These are only a few of the things that might be of interest and importance in your researches. Do please feel free to call upon me for anything else. I will try to answer any questions in these matters. Or look up any book that you may want . . .

One question you can perhaps answer for me. Recently in a [Cincinnati] museum I came across a most remarkable and sacred Islamic work, a beautifully designed cloth that was once spread over the tomb of a holy man, Imam Riza. There was on this cloth a Sufi poem, fortunately translated into English on a notice nearby. I was deeply moved by this sacred object and poem and felt a profound sorrow and distress that it had come so far to be reduced to a purely secular function. Yet I thanked God that I was able in this way to come into contact with a great spirit. I would like if possible to know something about him. All I know I have already told you: his name only. Of course he was from Persia, and a Sufi. The cloth was a thematic representation of paradise, with various animals and four angels. There were also in this same museum fine prayer cloths. It was inexplicably saddening to see these sacred things reduced to the status of mere anonymous objects which no one understands, though the heads of the museum are indeed sensitive and intelligent people and treat everything with great understanding and respect. Yet one is shocked by the awful secularism of our day which has become a pestilence of the spirit.

As one spiritual man to another (if I may so speak in all humility), I speak to you from my heart of our obligation to study the truth in deep prayer and meditation, and bear witness to the light that comes from the All-Holy God into this world of darkness where He is not known and not remembered. The world we live in has become an awful void, a desecrated sanctuary, reflecting outwardly the emptiness and blindness of the hearts of men who have gone crazy with their love for money and power and with pride in their technology. May your work on the Sufi mystics make

His Name known and remembered, and open the eyes of men to the light of His truth.

January 30, 1961

Your admirable letter of December 20th reached me promptly and I was deeply touched by your understanding and charity. I value most highly the prayers you have offered and, I hope, continue to offer sometimes, for me at the hour of dawn when the world is silent and the new light is most pure, symbolizing the dawning of divine light in the stillness of our hearts. I am sure that much good has come to me because of your prayer and I have also prayed for you at that same time, which is the time when I offer Mass in the silence of an isolated chapel in a remote part of the monastery, with rarely more than two or three novices present. This represents for us the moment of the nearest presence of God in our lives: He is present at all times, but we believe that at this time His mercy and His bounty express themselves most fully towards us. I wish then to share all this bounty with you, and do not fail to do so in so far as I can.

There is no question in my mind that the mercy and bounty of God are very clear in the inspiration which has brought about our correspondence, and His angels certainly have their part to play in this. Let us then in joy and humility take the unknown good which He is offering us in this increased understanding of our faiths. I have been trying to read a little here and there about Moslemism and Sufism and realize the great importance of this study and this understanding. I look forward very eagerly to receiving any books and articles you may have sent. I hope that the package that started out from here well over a month or six weeks ago may perhaps be arriving by this time . . .

I am very interested in your explanation of who Imam Riza was.* I can send you a partial copy of the English text of the poem which I picked up when I was in the museum. I do not know if there is anyone there capable of copying out the original, but I can inquire if you wish. In any case I can get you the complete English text from there. Meanwhile, perhaps the partial text I enclose may be of some value to you. I was probably in error in saying it was a Sufi poem, since I was very vague about the nature of Sufism then. I presumed that any Persian mystical poem was necessarily a Sufi production. In any case I do not think the poem was written by the Imam.

. . . One other thing I can send you at the moment is a magazine with a study I did of Chinese thought: it may interest you, though it is outside the area of our previous discussions. I find in Taoism something

* Imam Riza, eighth imam (religious head) of the Shias, died A.D. 834. His tomb at Mesad in Iran is a place of pilgrimage for the Shias.

of the same spirit that is so central to all the other mystical movements everywhere.

Louis Massignon is a very fine man for whom I have the deepest love and respect. His understanding of Islam is a precious gift and one that has an importance that perhaps not everyone has yet understood.

You ask for some information about our life here . . . This monastery is a contemplative community, that is to say we are monks who live strictly enclosed within our monastery and do not go outside into the world except for very exceptional reasons. We keep a strict rule of silence, not speaking to one another except when it is essential. Our life is devoted to prayer, and we live under a relatively strict discipline of poverty and obedience. Of course, like all Christian monks, we are obligated to chastity. I say our poverty is relatively strict: we possess nothing at all, but the standard of life in the monastery would not appear poor to a resident in Pakistan though it is relatively poor in America. That is to say we lack many of the comforts and conveniences that American people regard as necessities, and we live by our manual labor and the produce of our farm. Our clothing is poor and simple, and our food also. The diet is vegetarian.

As a community, the monastery is chiefly cenobitic in its spirit. Emphasis is on the choral prayer, which consists mainly of recitation of psalms. We rise at two o'clock in the morning and chant the night vigils until about four. Then we have other prayers or readings and meditations, alternating with work and study throughout the day until evening when we retire at seven.

Some of us in the community, and I am one of these, have aspirations for a more solitary and meditative form of prayer life. Our situation is a little difficult, but it is possible to obtain permission for a certain latitude in this respect. Thus I am allowed by the Father Abbot to spend a certain part of the day, often an entire afternoon, in a little house in the woods where there is complete silence and isolation, and it is possible to give oneself completely to meditative prayer. I feel that in some respects our situation is a little analogous to that of the Sufis in their relation with the orthodox Moslem community with its emphasis on legal observance.

You ask about Our Lady of Gethsemani: the monasteries of our Order are dedicated to Mary. The meaning of this dedication may be understood in different manners by different types of monks. For my part, I consider that each monastery dwells so to speak surrounded and protected by the maternal love of Mary, and by her prayers in heaven. If we are dedicated to the mystery of Gethsemani, it means to say that we are in particular to be mindful of the Blessed Virgin's solitude and sorrow of heart in her compassion for the suffering of Christ in the Garden of Gethsemani where He was abandoned by all who loved Him and was betrayed by one of His disciples. I think then that this means our life as monks is lived especially under the sign of a kind of inner solitude and dereliction, and I know from experience that this is true. But in this solitude and dereliction we are united with others who are alone and solitary and poor. As for Our Lady of Fatima I believe that this is a very mysterious title. Mary is believed to have appeared at a village in Portugal called Fatima: but this name certainly derives from the time when the area was under the Moslems and the village must have been named after the daughter of the Prophet. Hence there is a mysterious joining of Christian and Moslem elements in this devotion to Our Lady of Fatima. L. Massignon has studied the relationship in a very interesting way . . .

I must close this letter now, but I will write in more detail about these things. I am very interested to know if there is an interest in mystical prayer and spirituality among Moslems at the present day. I know that Islam has been enjoying a gradual revival of spiritual strength and fervor, as has also Christianity, since the "doldrums" of the nineteenth century, and I am very interested to know of the latest developments in Moslem thought and spirituality . . .

May 13, 1961

It has been a long time since I received your good letter of March 8th. The books took a great while to get here and did not reach me until well after Easter. Besides this I have been taken up with more numerous classes for the last three months, but this is now ending. I will send you the notes of these classes in mystical theology when they are ready. Meanwhile some time ago I ordered the full set of works of St. John of the Cross for you and I hope that by now you have received them . . .

But now first of all and before everything else I want to thank you for the remarkable books you sent me. I have been tremendously impressed by Titus Burckhardt on Sufism, which is the book I have read first. It is one of the most stimulating books I have read for a long time, and I realize that there is very much in it for me. In a sense it is one of those books that open up new horizons that I have been waiting for. I am tremendously impressed with the solidity and intellectual sureness of Sufism. There is no question but that here is a living and convincing truth, a deep mystical experience of the mystery of God our Creator Who watches over us at every moment with infinite love and mercy. I am stirred to the depths of my heart by the intensity of Moslem piety toward His Names, and the reverence with which He is invoked as the "Compassionate and the Merciful." May He be praised and adored everywhere forever.

It is because of this spirit of adoration and holy awe which is at the root of Sufism that the tree can reach such great heights and bear such bountiful fruits of love . . . I want to say how much I liked your article on Islam as vision and wisdom. The concept of wisdom as "Din" is very close to our monastic view of life, in which the wholeness of life itself, lived in prayer and in the understanding that is conferred by symbols, liturgy and contemplation, is a living wisdom and a constant communion with God the Source of all Wisdom. It is in all truth a union of shari'a and haqiqa. Your analysis of the shahada was also impressive. The whole article opened up great new perspectives and it is easy to see why we agree in so many things . . . I am going to read the Burckhardt book a second time to get all the riches that there are. I have not yet got very far with Sir M. Iqbal, but I realize already that I like the book . . .

You ask me again about the address of E. Allison Peers. I regret to say that he died a long time ago, about ten years ago at least. I remember writing to him once or twice. He was a good translator and wrote a little book on the Spanish mystics which is in the same "Wisdom of the East" series as the two you sent me. (I like Arberry and what I have seen of Al-Ghazali is very akin to our monastic life.)

I especially appreciate what you said about remembering me in prayer on the "Night of Power" since I have read about this in Burckhardt. I have been remembering you in prayer as the days go by, and will keep you especially in mind on the feast of Pentecost, May 21st, in which we celebrate the descent of the Holy Ghost into the hearts and souls of men that they may be wise with the Spirit of God. It is the great feast of wisdom . . .

. . . After reading Burckhardt, I have glimpsed many interesting relationships and problems. The question of Tawhid is of course central and I think that the closest to Islam among the Christian mystics on this point are the Rhenish and Flemish mystics of the fourteenth century, including Meister Eckhart, who was greatly influenced by Avicenna. The culmination of their mysticism is in the "Godhead" beyond "God" (a distinction which caused trouble to many theologians in the Middle Ages and is not accepted without qualifications) but at any rate it is an ascent to perfect and ultimate unity beyond the triad in unity of the Persons. This is a subtle and difficult theology and I don't venture into it without necessity . . .

One of the chapters I like best in Burckhardt is that on the renewal of creation at each instant, and also that on the dhikr which resembles the techniques of the Greek monks, and I am familiar with its use, for it brings one close to God.

. . . Let us in any case have great love for Truth and open our hearts to the Spirit of God our Lord and Father, Compassionate and Merciful. He alone is Real, and we have our reality only as a gift from Him at every moment. And at every moment it is our joy to be realized by Him over an abyss of nothingness: but the world has turned to the abyss and away from Him Who Is. That is why we live in dreadful times, and we must be brothers in prayer and worship no matter what may be the doctrinal differences that separate our minds.

Would you tell me something about yourself? Are you a university professor? Or a theological student? What do you do? I will describe our life in more detail when I have more time later.

September 24, 1961

It is a very long time since I have had a letter from you and I am beginning to think that something you wrote may have gone astray. The last letter I received was, I think, back in March. Meanwhile, however, some books recently arrived from you, so I know that you have not forgotten me. I imagine that perhaps a letter announcing the books did not reach me. Whatever God wills.

Meanwhile I want to thank you for the books. I especially like the one on *Truthfulness*. This is a splendid ascetic treatise which confirms me in my deep sympathy for Sufism. It is highly practical, realistic, profoundly religious and set in the right perspective of direct relationship with the All-Holy God. Our conduct is based on His relation of Himself, not on mere ethical systems and ideals. This is the basic principle shared by all the "people of the book." We should rejoice together in this light of truth which other religions do not fully understand.

Henry Corbin is an author in whom I am greatly interested and think that his book on Ibn Arabi is going to be very important for me. I like very much the first pages of it and the approach that he takes. This is an aspect of mysticism that I have not studied so much: that of the intermediate realm of what the Greek Fathers called *theoria physike* (natural contemplation) which deals with the symbols and images of things and their character as words or manifestations of God the Creator, whose wisdom is in them. I hope sometime to send you a little thing I have written on Wisdom (Sophia). It is being printed in a very limited edition on a hand press by a good friend of mine. It will be very rare.

. . . In a few days I hope to send you an article of mine on the English mystics, and if the books referred to there interest you, I can get hold of them for you. Also I am sending under separate cover a mimeographed piece, written for a friend in Latin America, a poet, Cuadra [see Merton's *Emblems of a Season of Fury*]. The theme of this open "letter" is the international situation and the deplorable attempts of the great powers [pictured in the letter as Gog and Magog] to threaten one another and the world with nuclear weapons. There is no question that in these maneuverings of power we see a dire evil force at work, a force which is spiritual and more than human. It is my belief that all those in the world who have kept some vestige of sanity and spirituality should unite in firm resistance to the movements of power politicians and the monster nations, resist the whole movement of war and aggression, resist the diplomatic overtures of power and develop a strong and coherent "third world" that can stand on its own feet and affirm the spiritual and human values which are cynically denied by the great powers. What is your opinion of this? What is the thought on this situation in Pakistan? Naturally in the monastery I am not very well versed in politics, but I feel that a certain spiritual outlook does have some value after all. It gives a perspective which is not available to those who think only in terms of weapons and money and the manipulation of political groups. May the Lord give us peace and spare us to serve Him in joy and understanding. May He bless us in wisdom and may the light of His countenance shine upon us. I remember you very often in prayer before Him, "the compassionate, the Merciful." It gives me joy to think you also remember me in prayer.

[*Cold War Letter 67*]

April 4, 1962

Finally I must answer your letters, at least briefly. A brief answer will be better than none at all. If I wait until I can do full justice I will wait too long . . .

I am glad you appreciated the letter about the Giants. This has been published in England, Argentina and Central America, perhaps also in Germany, and has been well received. I looked up in the Quran the references to Gog and Magog and found them to be extremely significant.

The magazines containing the excellent essay on Sufi religious psychology reached me and I have read the essay with the greatest interest. It confirms me in my realization that there is much in common, on the level of experience, between Sufism and Christian mysticism . . .

St. Basil, whom you are probably reading by now, is an ascetic who adapted Egyptian monastic practices to the Greek world. He stressed community life and manual labor, also humility and obedience. He had a strong influence on St. Benedict, who took many of St. Basil's ideas and adapted them to the Roman world, and thus founded the monastic order to which I belong. St. Basil is very interesting but yet there are deficiencies in him. He was an active "organizer" rather than a contemplative and there is little or no mysticism in him. One feels a certain coldness and lack of deep inner spirit, though his faith was strong and his ascetic tendencies were virile and well ordered. In a word there is a bit of the formalist in him.

We are about the same age, perhaps almost exactly the same age [Abdul Aziz had written that he was forty-six years of age and unmarried]. I am now forty-seven. I was born in France, educated in France, England and America. My outlook is not purely American and I feel sometimes disturbed by the lack of balance in the powerful civilization of this country. It is technologically very strong, spiritually superficial and weak. There is much good in the people, who are very simple and kind, but there is much potential evil in the irresponsibility of the society that leaves all to the interplay of human appetites, assuming that everything will adjust itself automatically for the good of all. This unfortunately is fatal and may lead to the explosion that will destroy half the world, of which there is serious danger. I entered the monastery twenty years ago, and am the novice master here. I believe my vocation is essentially that of a pilgrim and an exile in life, that I have no proper place in this world but that for that reason I am in some sense to be the friend and brother of people everywhere, especially those who are exiles and pilgrims like myself . . . My life is in many ways simple, but it is also a mystery which I do not attempt to really understand, as though I were led by the hand in a night where I see nothing, but can fully depend on the Love and Protection of Him Who guides me.

. . . Do not forget me in your good prayers, as I remember you often, particularly at dawn. The whole world, however, is going into darkness and I think there are difficult times ahead. I want to write a book against nuclear war and am engaged in this now. I do not think this will make life any simpler for me, and may rouse enmity, but it must be done.

In a letter of December 18, 1962, Abdul Aziz writes that he had replied to Merton's letter of June 21 and had raised a number of questions for which he still hoped to receive answers. He speaks of the death of their mutual friend, Louis Massignon, on October 31, 1962.

December 26, 1962

It is certainly true that I deserve your mild and kind reproach for being a poor correspondent. When I see that you have waited more than six months for an answer, I am deeply ashamed, and I must try to offer some kind of explanation. First of all, it is unfortunate that I have a much greater volume of correspondence than is in keeping with my monastic state of life. Further, I do not have a secretary, except one who can handle purely routine matters on his own initiative. I do not dictate letters or anything like that. There are always quite a few letters demanding immediate attention and most of these do not get what they demand. In the end, I put off the letters which really interest me so that I will have time to give a thoughtful reply, and then I end by not replying at all. This is a sad situation and I know it does not fully excuse me.

. . . Now to more immediate concerns: yes, I received your two books safely—the Saints and Shrines and the Biographies. I am especially interested in the latter, which are in many cases remarkable. I thank you very much for these two books. The "Shrines" will answer many future questions about holy places and pilgrimages in Islam, a most absorbing topic.

The departure of Louis Massignon is a great and regrettable loss. He was a man of great comprehension and I was happy to have been numbered among his friends, for this meant entering into an almost prophetic world, in which he habitually moved. It seems to me that mutual comprehension between Christians and Moslems is something of very vital importance today, and unfortunately it is rare and uncertain, or else subjected to the vagaries of politics. I am touched at the deep respect and understanding which so many Moslems had for him, indeed they understood him perhaps better than many Christians.

The book I wrote on nuclear war [*Peace in a Post-Christian Era*] is not being published, but I will send you a mimeographed copy of it. I hope it may be of some interest. I find that as a matter of fact the circulation of mimeographed copies is in a way more effective in topics of this kind, because thus the books directly reach those who are likely to be interested. The general public is unfortunately apathetic and the whole issue of nuclear war is not at all understood as a religious sign, of awful and prophetic import for man who has forsaken his faith and his right relation to the All-Holy One. I will also send a homily on the Virgin Mary which may not be in all respects relevant to you but you may find one or two common points of agreement here and there. I hope so. I know that Mary is treated with the greatest reverence in the Koran and have read these passages with deep emotions.

I am not surprised at your great interest in St. John of the Cross. The question of detachment depends it seems to me first of all on self-knowledge. Or rather the two are mutually interdependent. One must know what are the real attachments in his soul before he can effectively work against them, and one must have a detached will in order to see the truth of one's attachments. In practice, the events of life bring us face to face, in painful situations, with the places in which we are attached to our inner egoism. Exterior detachment is easier: it is a matter of re-nouncing comforts and gratifications of the sensual appetites, and this renunciation is of course essential. It has, however, a certain measure which differs in each person, according to his condition and his needs. One must handle this question with prudent discretion. But inner de-tachment centers around the "self," especially in one's pride, one's desire to react and to defend or to assert "self" in one's own will. This attachment to the self is a fertile sowing ground for seeds of blindness, and from this most of our errors proceed. I think it is necessary for us to see that God Himself works to purify us of this inner "self" that tends to resist Him and to assert itself against Him. Our faith must teach us to see His will and to bend to His will precisely in those points where He attacks the self, even through the actions of other people. Here the unjust and unkind actions of others, even though objectionable in themselves, can help us to strip ourselves of interior attachment.

Also St. John of the Cross makes much out of the purifying effect of aridity and helplessness in prayer: which is very beneficial to us if it leads to an increase of faith. I think here the important point is now to discuss the relation between the concept of faith for a Christian and a corresponding concept for a Moslem. This is probably where a deep divergence may be found, though perhaps not as deep as I anticipate.

I will be interested to hear from you further on this point, and will also keep it in mind myself.

. . . Now I must close: yes, I have remembered you most particularly in prayer in this season of prayer and hope you also will remember me in the holy season of Ramadan and on the Night of Destiny . . .

June 2, 1963

. . . Thank you for your brief outline of the Moslem faith. I can certainly join you with my whole heart in confessing the One God (Tawhid) with all my heart and all my soul, for this is the beginning of all faith and the root of our existence. Without this faith we are in deep night and do not know where we are going, and this precisely is the source of all the evils in the world. I believe with you also in the angels, in revelation, in the Prophets, the Life to Come, the Law and the Resurrection.

As you say, the differences begin with the question of soteriology (salvation).* Personally, in matters where dogmatic beliefs differ, I think that controversy is of little value because it takes us away from the spiritual realities into the realm of words and ideas. In the realm of realities we may have a great deal in common, whereas in words there are apt to be infinite complexities and subtleties which are beyond resolution. It is, however, important, I think, to try to understand the beliefs of other religions. But much more important is the sharing of the experience of divine light, and first of all of the light that God gives us even as the Creator and Ruler of the Universe. It is here that the area of fruitful dialogue exists between Christianity and Islam. I love the passages of the Quran which speak of the manifestations of the Creator in His Creation.

Yes, I know the *Way of the Pilgrim* very well. It is a fine book. The Russian mystics are too little known. I believe that the "Jesus Prayer" has parallels with certain Sufist methods of prayer: I have read about this somewhere. I would be grateful for any information that occurs to you about Sufist ways of prayer and contemplation.

. . . I am about to make a week of solitary retreat in the woods near the monastery and I shall pray for your intentions during this time. I greatly value our friendship and the simplicity and sincerity with which you express your thoughts about prayer for me is of great significance. I am sure you will be greatly blessed by God in many ways. I am sure too that He will be pleased that we pray for one another's spiritual progress, and these prayers surely have special value in His sight because they

* In a letter of April 4, 1963, Abdul Aziz had detailed the beliefs of Islam. It inculcates, he said, "individual responsibility for one's actions and does not subscribe to the doctrine of atonement or the theory of redemption."

proceed from a humble and disinterested fraternal charity, and not from merely human and social ties such as unite those who belong to the same society and same city. We must strive more and more to be universal in our interests and in our zeal for the glory of the One God, and may His Name be magnified forever in us. I will send you an essay I did on the Name of the Lord in the Bible. I do not know if it will be of special interest to you, but you might find a few points in it.

October 18, 1963

The delay in replying to your letter is due to three things: first, my desire to read the books you sent. Secondly the fact that I have been ill in the hospital (nothing important, but it interferes with my typing), and third, that I find it difficult to reply to questions about Christian belief in such a way as to be able to present the ideas comprehensibly. This takes a great deal of understanding and ability, and I realize that, like so many other Christians, I am perhaps not equal to the task of making clear what I believe in such a way as to satisfy one of a different religion. It would of course be quite easy simply to state baldly the dogmas of our faith, but this would not make them comprehensible and would in fact perhaps make them more incomprehensible. I will try to return to that later.

First of all, thank you for the remarkable book on Ahmad Al-'Alawi [Martin Lings, *A Modern Saint of the Twentieth Century; Shaikh Ahmad Al-'Alawi*, 1961]. I want to say how deeply moved and impressed I was with this book, from beginning to end. I had a chance to read it at leisure and thoughtfully in the hospital, and I am convinced that this is certainly one of the major religious figures of our time. I am very open to the vigorous clarity and the depth of his religious vision, and I must say that there is little in the book that I cannot heartily accept, I look forward to reading it again more slowly and meditatively. I am surprised that Louis Massignon made so few references to Ahmad Al-'Alawi.

The first thing that must be said about this "encounter" with present-day Muslim mysticism is that it is quite obvious that with someone like Shaikh Ahmad, I speak the same language and indeed have a great deal more in common than I do with the majority of my contemporaries in this country. In listening to him I seem to be hearing a familiar voice from my "own country" so to speak. I regret that the Muslim world is so distant from where I am, and wish I had more contact with people who think along these lines. Martin Lings seems certainly to have done a fine job. I hope to hear more about Ahmad Al-'Alawi.

I have just finished reading the [Frithjof] Schuon book on Islam, in French. It strikes me as one of his best books. Its interest for me was a little uneven, and I wonder if he is not interpolating here and there a lot of his own gnostic ideas. It is so terribly difficult to do a really good job of combining the different traditions among themselves. I know the school of Schuon and [René] Guénon well, and read them with interest, but at times I do get the feeling that they are vanishing into the mist. Then they come clear again. I think they deserve all credit for their efforts to bring East and West together. I must say I enjoyed this book on Islam, especially some parts of the chapter on the Prophet and on the Way . . .

Here I think I can take an example that may enable you to approach the idea of the Trinity. I note that Ahmad Al-'Alawi thought that the Trinity could be made comprehensible to Moslems, but the book did not say how. My approach would be this. Just as you (and I too) speak with reverence of Allah Rahman and Rahim,* so I think you can see that speaking of Father, Son and Holy Ghost does not imply three numerically separate beings. The chief thing that is to be stressed before all else is the transcendent UNITY of God. Now as this unity is beyond all number, it is a unity in which "one" and "three" are not numerically different. Just as Allah remains "one" while being compassionate and merciful, and His compassion and mercy represent Him in different *relations* to the world, so the Father and Son and Holy Spirit are perfectly One, yet represent different relations.

But there is of course a distinction: Rahman and Rahim are "attributes" and "names" of God, but not subsisting *persons*. Here the trouble comes in the definition of person. The idea of "person" in God is by no means the same as the current and colloquial idea of "person" among men: where the "person" is equivalent to the separate individual man in his separateness. This is of course where the confusion comes, in speaking of the "Three Persons" in God. This naturally conjures up an image of three separate beings, three *individuals*. The idea of Person must not be equated with that of individual. And, once again, "three" is not to be taken numerically.

The one thing which we must absolutely confess without any hesitation is the supreme transcendent Unity of God, and the fact that there is no other with Him or beside Him. He has "no helper." The work of creation and of the salvation of man is entirely His work alone. The manner in which Christianity preaches salvation in and through Christ must not obscure this fact which is basic to the Christian faith, as it is to Islam. The fact is that we believe, as you know, that Christ is not a being outside of God who is His helper. It is God in Christ who does the work of salvation. But here we come to the enormous difficulty of stating in technical terms the Incarnation without making Christ something separate

* *Rahman means the mercy of God as it exists in himself as limitless; Rahim, the mercy of God as manifested in creation.*

from God, when in fact the humanity of Christ is "an individual" human nature. This is beyond me for the moment, but I will try to think about it in terms that would be meaningful to you. I note only that in his chapter on the Prophet, Schuon is talking exactly as we do about Christ, except that he formally excludes the incarnation. But in point of fact, to judge by that chapter, there seems to be much in common between our idea of the working of God in and through Christ and your idea of God manifesting Himself to the world in and through the Prophet. I must leave this to future consideration. The one technical difference of a doctrine of the incarnation is of course enormous.

I perfectly agree that any man who in his heart sincerely believes in God and acts according to his conscience, with all rectitude, will certainly be saved and will come to the vision of God. I have no doubt in my mind whatever that a sincere Muslim will be saved and brought to heaven, even though for some reason he may not subjectively be able to accept all that the Church teaches about Christ. There may be many extrinsic reasons which make it impossible for him to understand what the Church means. This also applies to Jews, Hindus, Buddhists and in fact to all sincere men. I think that all men who believe in One God Who is the Father of all and Who wills all to be saved, will certainly be saved if they do His will. This is certainly the teaching of the Catholic Church, and this is being brought out clearly now, in connection with the Council. But it was also brought out a hundred years ago at the time of the First Vatican Council.

I know well the two collections of texts from the Philokalia. I like them very much, and some of this material is used and taught here in the monastery.

As to my time of Khalwa [or Kahliva, solitary retreat]: I slept in the monastery and took my meals there, or rather two meals a day. A couple of times I missed meals or took some bread and water with me. I went to the cottage at about four-thirty in the morning and stayed until the evening. My time was divided between the recitation of the "Office" (Psalms and so on) which took about an hour or two (divided up according to the different canonical hours, said at different times of the day), meditation, also for over two hours, meditative reading, study, and a little work. I hope to do this again some time soon. It is very profitable indeed.

I will try to have a copy of some texts from Simeon the New Theologian sent you from Paris . . . Hesychasm is to me very interesting and I think you will find it the point of contact between Christian mysticism and the Sufis.

Now I must stop, I will try to answer more of your questions in a future letter. I assure you of my deep friendship, and I believe that our friendship is a blessing from God that will bring much light to us both, and help Him to be made known through us. All glory and praise be to Him Who shows Himself in all things infinitely merciful and a lover of all that He has created . . .

June 28, 1964

Only now I am getting around to answering your fine letter of last November or December. I know you have patience with me, so I will try to make amends. I know there are many questions you have asked that I have not answered, and truly I am so much behindhand in this that it is difficult to know where to begin.

In your letter of last August you referred to a statement of Pope Pius XI about the question of the salvation of non-Christians.* I do not know if I ever commented on this, but I think I did. In any case, it should be perfectly clear that Christian doctrine on this point is in accord with common sense and the ordinary religious feeling of all believers: obviously the ultimate destiny of each individual person is a matter of his personal response to the truth and to the manifestation of God's will to him, and not merely a matter of belonging to this or that organization. Hence it follows that any man who follows his faith and his conscience, and responds truthfully and sincerely to what he believes to be the manifestation of the will of God, cannot help being saved by God. There is and can be no question in my mind that every sincere believer in God, no matter what may be his affiliation, if he lives according to his belief will receive mercy and, if needed, further enlightenment. How can one be in contact with the great thinkers and men of prayer of the various religions without recognizing that these men have known God and have loved Him because they recognized themselves loved by Him? It is true that there are different ways to Him and some are more perfect and more complete than others. It is true that the revelation given to the "People of the Book," Christians, Jews and Muslims, is more detailed and more perfect than that given through natural means only to the other religions.

. . . This year I have not been able to renew a week's Khalwa because it is necessary for me to be with the novices, and I have had more time out in the hospital (not serious). However, I am taking a day at a time, once or twice in each month.

The program of Khalwa which you outline is excellent, and I hope that someday I may obtain permission for a forty days' retreat of that kind. Actually this is never practiced in our Order where everything is concentrated on the common life, and permission to do this would be granted only with extreme difficulty. But I am in hopes that as time goes on the value of such solitary retreats will become more and more evident

* Abdul Aziz refers to a statement of Pope Pius XI, contained in a book Merton had sent him. Pius XI said to the apostolic delegate to Libya: "Do not think you are going among infidels. Muslims attain to salvation. The ways of Providence are infinite."

and we will gradually begin to be able to have these advantages, beginning with a few days and so on.

Actually the best I can do is spend the day in the hermitage, having to return to the monastery at night to sleep as it is strictly forbidden to sleep outside the enclosure walls (unless in the hospital or on a journey). I know the Muslim custom of fasting is different from ours. In the Christian context the time of eating, whether in the day or night, is not important, though the tradition is that on a fast day one does not eat until sundown. That tradition has been modified to one meal taken earlier in the day. I think the idea of fasting until sundown would be very practical in solitude. This would be practical too if some meal were taken before sunrise. It is unfortunate that fasting has become less and less practiced among Christians of the West, though the Orthodox are still very strict.

Our silence is always quite strict and there is no difficulty in spending a day without talking. If I could get permission to stay in the hermitage, the problem of solitude would be easily solved. Meanwhile, this is something to work toward, as I have to live in obedience to the Superiors and cannot undertake anything they would not permit. I hope someday there will be changes in this question of solitude.

. . . You probably have received the wonderful new edition of Louis Massignon's *Opera Minora*. Excellent. I will see that you get them if you do not have them already. Please tell me. Meanwhile I think I will write at least a note of review about Dr. Lings's book on Ahmad Al-'Alawi which I want to reread. I am incidentally supposed to provide notes on Islamic mysticism from time to time for the magazine of our Order. This is a new step, and a promising one.

I am sorry to be such a bad correspondent to be so little help in getting things and answering questions. Actually we are so far away from the center of things here and I am so out of touch with the sources and libraries, not to mention bookstores, that I really am not able to give satisfactory answers. Probably the books I have not been able to find are still available. I might be able to get you the addresses of stores that would inform you more helpfully, but I note that it is hard to get unusual books unless one is right on the scene and keeps after the booksellers until they dig up what you want. I will in any case keep praying for you to the All-Merciful One, in whose hands we all are and upon whose infinite and loving wisdom we all totally depend. Let us grow in this realization of dependence and obedience to Him; this should be our great desire, to obey His truth and His love in everything and thus give Him great glory in His world where men in their madness do not know Him.

December 9, 1964

It was a pleasure to get your letter this morning. Certainly I hope to write you a long reply with many thoughts and to speak in more detail of all the interesting points you raise. I am certainly happy to hear about some of the books you mention, and will want to go into them more deeply. I do wish the one on solitude could be translated. It is a pity that I do not have any contact with a scholar in this country capable of doing it . . .

Recently I sent you two small books on Boehme, his confessions and another. I like his confessions. Unfortunately his work is so full of abstruse terminology borrowed from alchemy, etc., that I find it hard to follow him. But when I do make contact with his mind, I like his spirit very much indeed.

I have also sent you my own latest book, *Seeds of Destruction*. You will note that in the last section of the book, consisting of letters written by me to various friends, I have presumed to include part of one of my letters to you, without mentioning your name. Some of the letters are identified, others not. The ones identified are to people who are writers or public figures of some sort who would not mind their names being mentioned. Naturally I have not put anything personal in the letters except where I have asked the permission of the ones involved.

 . . . Now I must close, and will try to write you a decent reply after Christmas. I have good news. I am now able to sleep in the hermitage and may perhaps be able to arrange something like a decent retreat, if I can get a whole day and night free from other disturbances. With the novices I have a constant series of classes and other sessions, and I am still expected to be at the offices in choir most of the time, but now happily the way is open to a better adjustment and I hope to have at least a short retreat, unbroken by any distraction. The point you make is very true: there must be no interruption.

I close with my blessings and best wishes for Christmas and the New Year. When is Ramadan in 1965? I would like to join spiritually with the Moslem world in this act of love, faith and obedience toward Him Whose greatness and mercy surround us at all times, and Whose wisdom guides and protects us even though, in the godlessness of the world of men, we are constantly on the edge of disaster. We must humble ourselves truly and seek to see our state, and strive to pray with greater purity and simplicity of heart. I see more and more clearly that even the believers are often far short of having true faith in the Living God. The great sin remains idolatry, and there is an idolatry of *concepts* as well as of graven images. The minds of men are made vile and corrupt by the images which they worship under the pretext of "science," "politics," "technology," etc. . . .

November 7, 1965

Yesterday, two days after sending off my letter to you, I received your letter. I was very happy to hear from you again, and I certainly agree with you that we lose much by not keeping in touch with each other. On the other hand, I admit that it is my fault for not answering your letter of last December in detail. It is not possible for me to do so now because when I moved out of the monastery to the hermitage I discarded all letters and files. Actually here I am in a much worse position to write. Our monastic rule frowns on much letter writing and being in the hermitage I must give more time to prayer and study than before, naturally. Also I do receive quite a few letters that have to be answered immediately, usually from people in urgent spiritual trouble . . . Please understand my situation and I in my turn will do my best to reply at least briefly and in substance to whatever you ask that is within my power to answer without research.

On the other hand I am quite sure that at least one letter of mine must have gone astray. I am certain that I wrote acknowledging the gift of Arberry's translation of the Koran which I find excellent, and I even gave an explanation of why I thought it would not be right for me to chant the Koran daily, as I do not know how this ought to be done properly, and I would not want to simply go in for improvisation in so serious a matter. It seems to me that here again, my task is rather to chant the sacred books of my own tradition, the Psalms, the Prophets, etc., since I know the proper way of doing this. But on the other hand I read the Koran with deep attention and reverence. Also, I am sure that in the same letter I spoke of Ibn Abbad, by whom I was very much impressed, and later I even did some adapted versions of his thought, in semi-poetic fashion, based of course on the French version. These will be published next year in a book with other things of mine, about June. If at that time I have not sent you the book, you must remind me, please. On the other hand I am sending you now a mimeograph copy of the renderings, to make sure that you have them. With this I will send the review of Martin Lings's book and other matters that may interest you. I have also sent a copy of the book about Chuang Tzu as I mentioned in my letter of the other day.

. . . I like very much the Practice of the Presence of God, and Meister Eckhart. I have not read Malaval, but I think he must be very interesting. St. John Climacus is a bit exaggerated but he is a classic guide for monks and a great standard, especially for monks in the Eastern (Orthodox) Church. There is great enthusiasm everywhere now over Teilhard de Chardin. I would be interested in your impression of him. I have not read him very thoroughly yet myself but his best book is *The Divine Milieu*, as far as I can see. Would you like me to get this for you, or do you have it already? . . .

Well, my friend, we live in troubled and sad times, and we must pray the infinite and merciful Lord to bear patiently with the sins of this world, which are very great. We must humble our hearts in silence and poverty of spirit and listen to His commands which come from the depths of His love, and work that men's hearts may be converted to the ways of love and justice, not of blood, murder, lust and greed. I am afraid that the big powerful countries are a very bad example to the rest of the world in this respect.

Yes, you are right that the Catholic clergy are usually so caught up with tasks and rituals that they do not have time or interest to get involved in deeper contacts with those who are not members of the Church. The great trouble today is that with the increase of communications and the greater number of people there is so much to be done that few have time to do anything properly, at least in the West. At least I hope to devote myself more fruitfully to the opportunities I have at present. Without ceasing to write letters, I hope to get in three or four hours a day of meditation besides my other Office prayer, and the work I have to do . . .

January 2, 1966

I have your two kind letters of Dec. 1 and Dec. 20th and once again I will try within my capacity to answer at least some of the points you raise, though I may not be able to cover everything in this one letter. I will do what I can, at the cost perhaps of brevity here and there.

First, I deeply appreciate your suggestion for a full-length book on prayer. It accords with my own desires and ideas. I recently told my publisher that I hoped to spend about a year studying and meditating in view of such a book. This will not be possible until I have cleared the way. I have several articles to write, and some other chores. The trouble is that I am always being asked for articles and reviews and I always manage to see the importance of the requests, and this keeps me from getting down to a more continuous piece of writing. Your idea, however, is excellent and I really hope that I will be able to do this. At the same time, I have written such books in the past. I will have a copy of one of them, the *Ascent to Truth*, sent to you. I believe you already have *Seeds of Contemplation*. I will send also a mimeographed work on monastic prayer which contains quite a few typing errors, but you will I am sure be able to make it out . . .

. . . If you have not sent *The Phenomenon of Man*, please do not send it as we have copies here. I have not read it yet, but I have read another book of Teilhard which I like very much, *The Divine Milieu*. I will see if I can send you something by or about him. The market is swamped with books of his now. You might like his *Hymn of the Universe*. I will see about getting a copy for you . . .

. . . The main thing I can tell you without difficulty is the outline of my daily life in the hermitage.

The hermitage is ten minutes' walk from the monastery in a hidden place in the woods. No one comes there so the solitude is very good and appropriate for prayer, especially at night.

I go to bed about 7:30 at night and rise about 2:30 in the morning. On rising I say part of the canonical Office consisting of psalms, lessons, etc. Then I take an hour or an hour and a quarter for meditation. I follow this with some Bible reading and then make some tea or coffee and have breakfast if it is not a fast day. Breakfast consists of bread and tea or coffee, with perhaps a piece of fruit or some honey. With breakfast I begin reading, and continue reading and studying until sunrise. Now the sun rises very late, in summer it rises earlier, so this period of study varies but it is on the average about two hours.

At sunrise I say another Office of psalms, etc., then begin my manual work, which includes sweeping, cleaning, cutting wood, and other necessary jobs. This finishes about nine o'clock, at which time I say another Office of psalms. If I have time then I may write a few letters, usually short (today is Sunday and I have more time). After this I go down to the monastery to say Mass, as I am not yet permitted to offer Mass in the hermitage. Saying Mass requires an altar, an acolyte who serves the Mass, special vestments, candles and so on. It is in a way better to have all this in the monastery. It would be hard to care for so many things and keep them clean in the hermitage. After Mass I take one cooked meal in the monastery. Then I return immediately to the hermitage usually without seeing or speaking to anyone except the ones I happen to meet as I go from place to place (these I do not ordinarily speak to as we have a rule of strict silence). (When I speak it is to the Abbot, whom I see once a week, or to someone in a position of authority, about necessary business.)

On returning to the hermitage I do some light reading, and then say another Office about one o'clock. This is followed by another hour or more of meditation. On feast days I can take an hour and a half or two hours for this afternoon meditation. Then I work at my writing. Usually I do not have more than an hour and a half or two hours at most for this, each day. Following that, it being now late afternoon (about four) I say another Office of psalms, and prepare for myself a light supper. I keep down to a minimum of cooking, usually only tea or soup, and make a sandwich of some sort. Thus I have only a minimum of dishes to wash. After supper I have another hour or more of meditation, after which I go to bed.

Now you ask about my method of meditation. Strictly speaking I have a very simple way of prayer. It is centered entirely on attention to the presence of God and to His will and His love. That is to say that it is centered on *faith* by which alone we can know the presence of God. One might say this gives my meditation the character described by the Prophet as "being before God as if you saw Him." Yet it does not mean imagining anything or conceiving a precise image of God, for to my mind this would be a kind of idolatry. On the contrary, it is a matter of adoring Him as invisible and infinitely beyond our comprehension, and realizing Him as all. My prayer tends very much toward what you call *fana*. There is in my heart this great thirst to recognize totally the nothingness of all that is not God. My prayer is then a kind of praise rising up out of the center of Nothing and Silence. If I am still present "myself" this I recognize as an obstacle about which I can do nothing unless He Himself removes the obstacle. If He wills He can then make the Nothingness into a total clarity. If He does not will, then the Nothingness seems to itself to be an object and remains an obstacle. Such is my ordinary way of prayer, or meditation. It is not "thinking about" anything, but a direct seeking of the Face of the Invisible, which cannot be found unless we become lost in Him who is Invisible. I do not ordinarily write about such things and I ask you therefore to be discreet about it. But I write this as a testimony of confidence and friendship. It will show you how much I appreciate the tradition of Sufism. Let us therefore adore and praise God and pray to Him for the world which is in great trouble and confusion. I am united with you in prayer during this month of Ramadan and will remember you on the Night of Destiny. I appreciate your prayers for me. May the Most High God send His blessing upon you and give you peace.

December 28, 1966

Your good letter reached me in this season of holy days and I have not failed to keep you in my special prayers. Also when the Night of Destiny comes I hope to be united with you in fervent prayer.

You are right, I have not written since March. That last letter was sent to you just before I went to the hospital for a rather serious operation. Though the operation was successful, I was slow in recovering and I still have some trouble, but of course I can type and so on. However, when I got out of the hospital I was very slow in catching up with correspondence. I also read the book on Al-Junayd in the hospital and was greatly impressed by it. He is surely one of the great mystics. In the hospital I found it rather difficult to read however, and I will go through the book again to get full profit out of it and to know this great mind better. I knew you would not like Zaehner. I do not think he is consciously hostile to Islam, but he is just a characteristic Western academic mind. Such minds are really not attuned to the ancient traditions and you will find in them a certain apparent lack of respect which is not due to ill will but to the scientific atmosphere in which people are trained today. This gives an objective view of things and also a distortion of perspectives, a lack of certain kinds of appreciation which are vital for a true understanding of the saints of Islam. This is regrettable indeed, for he has access to much knowledge.

My life in the hermitage continues to be quiet and simple. In fact I find that I can no longer carry on the same kind of routines as I did before. It is frankly impossible for me to keep up consistently with letter writing at fixed times and my correspondence has suffered badly. There are some business letters about writing that I have to take care of and after those I find it almost impossible to write about more or less personal matters, I seem to have nothing whatever to say. In fact this Christmas I am simply having a single letter mimeographed and am sending it to all the many correspondents to whom I cannot reply, they are too many. I will enclose a copy, you can judge my situation from it . . . My time in the hermitage is divided between study and meditation. Since the operation I have not been able to do much manual work. The silence of the woods is perfect. I go to the monastery once or twice a day but not for long. Once in a while I still have to go to the doctor in town, but I think that will stop soon, even if I have to have another operation. But these operations if I have any more will perhaps be less complicated.

Sometimes I see a visitor to the monastery and this autumn I was most privileged to meet an eminent Sufi master from Algeria, Sidi Abdesalam, who is the heir to the tradition of Shaikh Ahmad Al-'Alawi. We had a very pleasant conversation through his interpreter and I feel he is a true friend. He has of course returned to Algeria. He was in this country briefly, brought here by some university people. If you wish, you can write to Dr. Bernard Phillips of Temple University, Philadelphia, Pa. (that is a sufficient address), who is a professor interested in Sufism and a friend of Sidi Abdesalam. But these professors are not great letter writers. Still, he might be able to give you information you would need about things in this country and put you in touch with out of the way publications. You might ask him for instance about the R. M. Bucke Society in Montreal, Canada, which puts out an interesting newsletter. There are Sufi studies going on there. [See letters to Raymond Prince and Linda Sabbath.]

And now, my friend, trusting your kindness to pardon me for being a bad letter writer, I take my leave of you again with warm good wishes for the future, and may you receive every blessing, peace, and joy. Let us continue in faith and in the service of the All-Merciful One who has deigned to look upon us insignificant creatures and to grant us a little of His light. May He be forever blessed and glorified.

January 16, 1968

I was happy to receive your letter of December 18th. Also especially thank you for your greetings for Christmas and New Year and your prayers during Ramadan. I had not expected it so early, and I was not too sure when the Holy Night of Destiny occurred. I did, however, unite my prayers with yours in the days following Christmas as I believe it came about that time.

Yes, I know well the books of the Carthusian Dom Pollien. They are quite well liked here. Also Caussade is a classic, and those who guide themselves by his principles of abandonment can be sure of inner peace. He comes close in many ways to the ascesis of Sufism.

For about a year I have been giving conferences on Sufism here to the monks, based largely on books you sent me in the past. I have found Al-Hujwiri especially useful. I know another book of Dr. Nasr, but would be delighted some day to receive *Ideals and Realities of Islam.* I suppose the Suez problem affects us both, but I have a small paperback edition of the *Cloud of Unknowing* so I will send that air mail. I hope it reaches you safely soon.

About reading in solitude [this in reply to Abdul Aziz's question whether reading is a hindrance to interior detachment for one living a solitary life], I have the following remarks to make:

First, it is true that one who is learning to meditate must also learn to get along without any support external to his own heart and the gifts of God. Hence it is good for such a one to have to remain in silence without reading or even using vocal prayers sometimes, in order to come to terms with the need for inner struggle and discipline. On the other hand this is not a universal rule. There are times when it is necessary to read, and even to read quite a lot, in order to store up material and get new perspectives. In the solitary life, however, though one has a lot of time for reading, it becomes difficult to read a great deal. One finds that in a couple of hours he reads only a few pages. The rest of the time is spent in reflection and prayer. It becomes difficult to absorb more than this. Someone in solitude who would read voraciously all the time might perhaps be considered in the wrong place. Moderate reading is, however, normal. Provided that more time is spent in prayer and meditation than in reading . . .

April 24, 1968

I want to say that some time ago I received the book of Seyyed Hossein Nasr safely and that I am now reading it. It seems to me to be one of the very best books on Islam. I like it very much. Thank you for sending it.

I will send out today two books on Zen Buddhism which might interest you, including one which is printed in Taiwan and would normally be almost impossible to obtain, but fortunately it is by a friend of mine and I wrote the introduction to it. You might be interested in this. I have been doing considerable work on Zen Buddhism. Did you ever receive my book *Mystics and Zen Masters?* . . .

Some people with whom I am in contact in this country say that Dr. Nasr is likely to travel here and perhaps I may have a chance to meet him.

For more than a year now I have been giving weekly talks on Sufism to the monks here. I have been enabled to do this by your kindness in sending books, and want to express once again my gratitude. Do keep me in mind if anything of special value comes up: I would appreciate it even if you could just give me a name or reference to some books or articles. I am always most interested in Islamic mysticism.

Apart from this, there is not much news. The state of this country is not reassuring, neither is the state of the world. Men without deep faith live as it were with no center and no heart, and consequently one can only expect violence, injustice, confusion and chaos. But we can continue to hope in the mercy of the Lord, that He may give light and peace to men and help them make the necessary efforts to recover peace and wisdom.

To James Baker

James Thomas Baker, born February 5, 1940, in Clarksville, Texas, became acquainted with Thomas Merton while a student at the Southern Baptist Theological Seminary in Louisville. His church-history class had been invited to the Abbey and Merton spoke to them. When in 1968 he was looking for a topic for his doctoral dissertation at Florida State University, he chose to write on Merton. This dissertation, completed in 1968 and entitled Thomas Merton: The Spiritual and Social Philosophy of Union, *was published in 1971 by the University Press of Kentucky, Lexington, under the title* Thomas Merton, Social Critic. *Dr. Baker then joined the history department of Western Kentucky University in Bowling Green, Kentucky, only ninety miles from Gethsemani Abbey. There was to be only one more visit. On September 4, 1968, Dr. Baker visited Merton, at his invitation. Shortly after, Merton left on his journey to Asia.*

September 19, 1967

Thanks for your letter. As I have not made any firm commitments as far ahead as next March, I leave you to pick a date convenient to you, though Sundays are not too good for me. Also the week immediately preceding Easter is not convenient. Let me know, and I will make arrangements for you to stay, and will make a note of it for myself.

The main problem in dealing with your tortuous subject would probably be to keep track of the material that is printed in out-of-the-way places or of things that are circulated in mimeograph. I am sending you under separate cover a hotchpotch of material of this kind. It is picked out more or less at random, covering all sorts of territory. If there is something specific you may have heard of and want, I will try to unearth a copy.

Recently I had an exchange of views with Martin Marty in the *National Catholic Reporter* [see letter to Martin E. Marty] which might be relevant. Also there is an interview in the latest *Motive* which I may have mentioned before. Do you see the *Catholic Worker*? I have had several things in that recently.

When you are in this part of the country you might find something in the large collection of mss., mimeographs and general junk which is accumulating at Bellarmine College, Louisville. In a word, your problem will not be lack of material, but finding some kind of sense in all of it . . .

October 16, 1967

Fine, I'll keep February 28th for you. Let me know when you will arrive, and whether you will want overnight accommodations . . .

I have not been able to find a copy of the *Jubilee* article on "Sacred Art." Doubtless Bellarmine College could send a Xerox. I have a carbon of the "Religion and Race" material, and would appreciate your returning it when through.

I have dug up a few other things which might be of use and they are on their way to you. I hope they arrive safely. Did I send you the mimeograph on the "Hot Summer of Sixty-seven"? This is to appear shortly in *Katallagete*—do you know this small magazine?

March 28, 1968

. . . My pamphlet on Camus's *Plague* is now out (Seabury)—I'd send a copy, but I have run out of author's copies already.

Ran into some trouble with a certain set of conservative Catholics in Louisville, recently, for supporting a conscientious objector who refused draft induction. There was some correspondence about it in the *Record*, the diocesan paper, but I don't have that either. One good man said he was about to burn my books. That is one way of disposing of them . . .

I look forward to seeing you in the summer and hunting up Shaker material in Bowling Green . . .

June 11, 1968

In the past couple of weeks I have hardly had time to answer any mail at all. Things have been more busy than usual: groups of nuns to give conferences to, other visitors, and so on. But I do want to acknowledge receipt of your dissertation and reassure you that it arrived safely, and that I am going through it with attention. Also to say I am glad you will soon be in the neighborhood.

You have really done courageous work! I never take a census of how much I have written, and always think in terms of much less than is actually there. Your "fifty books" is a figure which does, admittedly, embrace pamphlets, but even then it is a shock to me. You have really had to struggle through a mass of stuff, and I think you have done a very good job of organizing it and tracing lines of development: where I find myself wondering about the material it is almost always because I am disagreeing with some of my own ideas. The only "corrections" I would suggest would be matters of insignificant detail. For example it was in 1965, not 1966, that I got permission to move out into the hermitage full-time. And you have spoken of *A Man in the Divided Sea* as a journal (it is verse). These are just small slips. In the main, I am astonished that you were able to make sense out of such a variety of materials.

Naturally I want to thank you not only for the care you have taken with the work, but also for the insights which it can provide for me. It is very useful to me to see an evaluation of my work as a whole. It gives me some perspective on it, and I suppose the thing that strikes me most is that I have said so much that was premature, provisional, and in many ways inadequate. I am surprised that people have received those ideas, on the whole, with more respect than they deserved. I have certainly had unfriendly critics, but on the whole my work has been accepted with sympathy. And of course I do feel it to be significant that much of the sympathetic understanding has come from Protestants—and that the first dissertation is by a Baptist . . . As a matter of fact a Quaker friend of mine [June Yungblut; see letters to her] in Atlanta is also thinking of writing something on my work, in comparison with several others, a Jew, a Buddhist and a Protestant. I feel that Catholics have tended to be either too uncritical or too critical of me, and I appreciate the more objective and balanced view of my work that is sometimes taken by those outside the Catholic Church. Inside it, I seem to get either total adulation or total rejection. Or at least I have that impression sometimes.

In any case, I value the help your dissertation is giving me in getting some perspective on my own work. I must admit I really wish I had never written most of it. And it is quite possible that I will finally be able to write less now and concentrate on the kind of things I really want to do, both in writing and otherwise: more creative work, less topical comment, more meditation . . . I am always promising myself this, and yet I do feel obliged to meet certain requests and needs that seem unavoidable. Another contradiction. Or just the ordinary dialectic of life.

. . . Thanks again for sending me the dissertation, and may God bless you and your family.

July 25, 1968

In your letter you mention the cool summer: it has got hot enough now! I have thought often of you and have been meaning to write, but it has been hard to make definite plans. I have a trip to Asia coming up in the fall—naturally I am very excited about something so unusual, and I am at present getting the shots, visas and all. Hoping of course to get a closer look at Buddhist and other forms of monasticism.

September would be a good time for you to drop over: preferably during the week, as weekends are more likely to be crowded up. I suggest you come over, if possible, during the first week, say on the Wednesday or Thursday. You can bring your wife if she wants to see Gethsemani— we can always get together outside, either in the gatehouse or under the trees or by a lake.

You need not be nervous about my reaction to the dissertation. Did you get a letter I sent some time ago to the college saying I liked it? That must have been a couple of weeks after I got the ms.

You certainly did a lot of work on it and went through a lot of material which I think you have summarized objectively and fairly. Naturally such an account has to be a very simplified one and I sometimes feel a bit oversimplified. But that is probably partly my own fault too, as I never manage to say fully all that I want to say. There is always something overlooked, some other aspect that needs to be remembered. I certainly did not find you too critical: you are most benign, and I think your work does help to get a real understanding and perspective of what I am trying to do. The idea of striving for unity and reconciliation of opposites is certainly one that I think is central in my work, and I think you have brought out well my idea that that is what "Catholic" really ought to mean (but still to a great extent does not) . . .

To Daniel J. Berrigan

Daniel J. Berrigan was born in Virginia, Minnesota, on May 9, 1921, the fifth of six sons of Thomas and Frida Berrigan. The family moved to Syracuse, New York, where he received his early education and to which he returned, after his ordination as a priest in the Society of Jesus, to teach at Le Moyne College (1957– 63). After a trip to Europe, he became associate editor of Jesuit Missions *(1963– 65). His radical involvement in the peace movement (he was, in 1964, one of the founders of the Catholic Peace Fellowship) resulted in a period of "exile" in Latin America. On his return his antiwar activities took him to Hanoi to bring home three prisoners of war, and later to Catonsville, Maryland, where, with his brother Philip and seven others, he participated in the burning of draft records (May 17, 1968). Convicted in October 1968, he went underground for a time, finally being apprehended by federal agents in August 1970. In February 1972, he was paroled. Today, still very much involved in the cause of peace, he resides in New York City. The many letters he exchanged with Merton attest to their warm friendship and their common commitment to the cause of peace and social justice.*

November 10, 1961

I am very glad to hear that the Pax movement is getting started in this country and that you are part of it. So am I. We are perhaps very late. Nor should it be regarded as much of a consolation that we are able in some way to salve our consciences by doing something at this hour, even though ineffectual. We must desire to be effective. The greatness of the task is appalling. At moments it seems we are in the middle of a total apostasy, an almost total apostasy from Christ and His teaching. It is not comforting to read the prophets in our night Office these days.

With New Directions I am trying to get up a little paperback anthology of good strong articles by all kinds of people about peace. Can you suggest anything? I am getting together things like that Jerome Frank article on "Breaking the Thought Barrier," something by Erich Fromm, Lewis Mumford. I wonder about the whole article on Ottaviani, part of which was in the recent *Pax Bulletin*. Are there some good Catholic pieces? . . .

We are going to have to keep in touch with one another. I don't have eyes and ears down here and others have to do my seeing for me. Don't hesitate to clip something and send it down if it seems at all significant. I will be getting the *Catholic Worker* now, I think, and perhaps *Commonweal*, but not much else.

Next year you and some other peace people must come down, and we must get together a bit. Do you think you can do this—in the spring, perhaps, or the early summer?

. . . The great problem is the blindness and passivity of Christians, and the way they let themselves be used by crypto-fascist elements who get stronger and stronger every day. I have just realized that, as Catholics, we are almost in the same position as the Catholics before the last war in Hitler's Germany.

Sometimes too I think we have about five years left to work in, and after that *venit nox*, in whatever form . . . maybe the total *nox*. This one does not go around saying, it seems so foolish. And we are so far from reality. As if the Lord were bound to give us hundreds more years to get some sense in our heads.

December 7, 1961

Thanks for your very fine letter and all the other things. I have not yet had a quiet moment in which to read the play about Charles de F[oucauld]. Or rather I have not been able to get to it, though in spite of all, I do have an occasional quiet moment. Perhaps tomorrow's feast will provide the opportunity. I am so glad you like him, he is a great sign to our age. A pity he was still so limited by the outlook of his time, but who of us is not?

I have written to Tony Walsh and not yet heard back, but Gordon Zahn came back fast and enthusiastically and is working on something for the paperback. Lewis Mumford is very cooperative and so is Erich Fromm. I hope I can get the young English Catholics who wrote the book on

Nuclear Weapons and Christian Conscience. I am trying to get the whole book in my collection. It has splendid stuff in it.

. . . I have asked Father Abbot if we could have you down to give some talks to the novices and students next summer. He said yes. Hence I am inviting you to come down and give us three talks at least, one a day, on perhaps the main problems confronting the Church in America at the present moment. And what ought to be done about them . . .

Whatever happens I am getting out an ingenuous, wide-eyed article on peace in the Christmas *Commonweal.* It may have some effect. I have been asked to write for *The Nation,* and may perhaps do something on "Christian Ethics and Nuclear War." Laying down a barrage all around, and then when the smoke clears we'll see what it did. Probably not much. All I can hope to do at the moment is make quite clear that total nuclear annihilation is definitely a crime and that the Popes have clearly said this in a way that cannot be honestly got around. But then the natural law can always find a way of being dishonest in honor of the Gospel. To save the Church. Yes, that's what the dear old Church needs: the protection of natural law, or even, who knows, of gang law? At any rate, protection. She simply can't get along anymore with this Christian stuff about charity, it's plain ruinous and utterly against the moral theology manuals. So let's wipe out the reds with a first strike. This will really put the Gospel message of peace across to the backward savages in those uncultivated and unciv- ilized countries where they still kill with spears. (Haven't caught up with the more sophisticated angles of double effect.) . . .

January 15, 1962

We will look forward to your advent in August, around the 10th. By all means bring some of your friends. I have been in touch with Gordon Zahn who has written a fine contribution to *Das Buch.* The publisher is going to be down here the next few days and we hope to get everything settled. I am so swamped with mail, especially Christmas mail, that I don't know where to turn. Well, I do know where to turn. I have turned to a couple of the novices and they are batting out acknowledgments for gifts, Masses, etc. When I think of the people who could really use those dollars, and I can't lift a finger to do anything about them because of a vow of poverty . . .

Slowly and laboriously some of the things I write about peace try to get past the censors . . .

March 10, 1962

My correspondence is a kind of Sisyphus act: rolling the boulder up the hill and then having it roll down again. The boulder is way ahead of me at the moment and I am only just getting around to your letter(s). . . I am preparing a bunch of talks on the Prophets and in doing this I am getting much deeper into the Bible. Frankly I have been inhibited by the fact that for a long time there was nothing but

Catholic material on the Bible around the monastery. Now that we have much of the best of Protestant books available, it is a different story.

I am glad you like *New Seeds* and will look forward to seeing the review. Your poems [*Encounters*] arrived. They are tremendous. You have great energy and discipline. I mean especially discipline of your poetic emotion and experience. Discipline in the art can and must only flow from a deeper discipline like this. I would be hard put to it to say what I like best, but I do think "Tasks" is exceptionally good . . .

I find I have reached the stage where I involuntarily wince when I come upon another poem by a priest called "Vocation." But yours is fine, and I hope you mean all the ambiguity that is packed into the last line. Are Jesuits always happy? Are they always human? I cannot say that Cistercians are invariably one or the other or both, and the systematic canonization of inhumanity does nothing to help the situation either with us or, I dare say, with you. I am glad your censors like the book. I wish our censors liked my peace articles.

In case you don't know, I have been in contact with John Heidbrink for some time and hope he will be coming down here. Douglas Steere was here and we had a good talk. A lot of guys from the *Catholic Worker* were here also, went home enthused and are now in jail. I feel bad about it.

I am not sure I know what you mean about the Benedictine approach in prayer. If you mean liturgical . . . but I think you do not. Maybe you do. If you mean the Cassian-like desert solitary stuff, this is Benedictine in its way, Cistercian in its way, I don't know what it is. But really it is Oriental and when seen in the Oriental context, I think such objections as you may have to it, vanish. There is an absolute need for the solitary, bare, dark, beyond-concept, beyond-thought, beyond-feeling type of prayer. Not of course for everybody. But unless that dimension is there in the Church somewhere, the whole caboodle lacks life and light and intelligence. It is a kind of hidden, secret, unknown stabilizer, and a compass too. About this I have no hesitations and no doubts, because it is my vocation; about one's own vocation, after it has been tested and continues to be tested, one can say in humility that he knows. Knows what? That it is willed by God, insofar as in it one feels the hand of God pressing down on him. Unmistakably . . .

June 15, 1962

Probably by now you are in the middle of your retreat with the Protestants at Mount Saviour. May God bless all of you. I am sure it must be a wonderful experience. A great deal can be done in these meetings, not in the human or organizational sense, but just in the order of charity, and that is what really matters.

I have been reading a new book about my favorite Jesuit, Matthew

Ricci [1552–1610]. I am convinced that he had the right idea about the Christian apostolate to the civilizations that have not known the Gospel. But few agreed with him. The first book he wrote in Chinese was, if I am not mistaken, his book on friendship. It would be very interesting to read it. Does it exist? Have you ever seen it? . . .

Here is the point of the letter. Can you please let me know for sure in a day or two exactly when you are coming and how many are coming with you? Our guest quarters are more limited this year as there are alterations going on in the buildings, and we have to make reservations a good way ahead to make sure, especially if you are coming on a weekend. If you can avoid the weekend it will be better. A wonderful Rabbi friend of mine [Zalman Schachter] is coming down about the 4th of August I think, or maybe the 7th. I am not too sure. Hope you can meet him. It would be great if you all got here together . . .

My peace writings have reached an abrupt halt. Told not to do any more on that subject. Dangerous, subversive, perilous, offensive to pious ears, and confusing to good Catholics who are all at peace in the nice idea that we ought to wipe Russia off the face of the earth. Why get people all stirred up?

So that is that. I knew it would be along sooner or later, and it was better later than sooner. I finished the peace book and a copy went off to you yesterday—the stencils were just finished when the order came in. The order only refers to publication. I wish our censors were as nice as your censors, but they aren't, though I must say they vary. Some are pro and others con. This book, however, didn't even get to the censors. The thing that was finally forbidden was "Target Equals City."

The anthology seems to be cooking nicely, and ought to be out in a month or so, perhaps two months.

Yes, I saw Phil's study of segregation in the *Catholic Worker* and am eager to see him, I hope he comes with you . . .

June 29, 1962

This is a quick one to confirm your arrangements. I will get a note into the guesthouse quick, and we will expect you sometime August 13.

The talks will be three of them to the novices and students. These are alert and not easily shocked and interested in all that concerns the Church. So give them what you think most important.

Father Abbot will certainly want you to say something to the community as a whole: this is a bigger and slower group. Anything that gives a good perspective of the Church's needs today will be appreciated by them, however. In a word, anything that can help them participate more intelligently in the life of the Church today . . .

Looking forward to seeing you . . .

September 2, 1962

. . . Your remarks about Gethsemani were moving and comforting. I certainly agree with you completely about the value of small groups and personal contacts. My own feeling about the "big movement" sort of thing is so negative that I do not trust myself to comment accurately on them. I am extremely suspicious of all the totalitarian compulsions that inevitably enter into the "movements" and destroy their Christian quality or pervert it.

Things like the Little Brothers, and small ventures like Damasus Winzen's monastery strike me as being the real thing. Perhaps some of the aspects of what goes on at Gethsemani may have reality, but other aspects definitely not.

. . . Guess what, the censors of the Order are now objecting to my essay on the _Jesuits in China_! On what grounds I do not know. Isn't that something? I will tell you more when I know more . . .

He had written Merton asking him for a recommendation for a grant from the Guggenheim Foundation.

November 27, 1962

Just got your blanks from the Goggenbuch Stipend House. I will write you up a litany of praises that will knock them off their chairs. I will tell them you are Scipio, Cicero, John O'Hara and twenty-five other people, including Berrigan. Your last book of poems deserves half a dozen Guggenheims. It is really splendid, you have really got in there now: the others I always felt were sort of tending in the right direction, now you are on your beam. I didn't find any clichés anywhere, and that in a book by a Catholic and a religious is a major miracle. It is terse and even Zen-like, and it is the integrity of the experience that above all comes through. Great, man, great.

What little I have heard about the Council sounds good. Especially that debate on the sources of Revelation . . .

As for Cuba, well thank God we escaped the results of our own folly this time. We excel in getting ourselves into positions where we "have to" press the button, or the next thing to it. I realize more and more that this whole war question is nine-tenths our own fabricated illusion. How clear it is that we are purely and simply building up "just-war" arguments so that if we feel that we need to use the "weapon" we will have a "just cause." Motivated by fear and hate? Not we! Hate a little place like Cuba? Heck no, this is for their own good. Etc., etc. I think Kennedy has enough sense to avoid the worst injustices, he acts as if he knew the score. But few others seem to. However, it seems that for the moment there is a lull, time out for another tranquillizer, then back with renewed zest to the fray. Fortunately Khrushchev is falling over himself to prove that he is really and in deadly earnest anxious to be just another American-style manager in a country of happy TV-viewing consumers, which is the truth: for our two materialisms, given time, will happily merge in an abyss of total secularism. But then there will be those Chinese and those Africans and those Indonesians and those Indians and those . . . etc. Hungry: can you beat that? And in the free world, too, some of them. Angola, for instance.

. . . Dorothy Day's articles on Cuba have been moving in their honesty and earnestness and in their wonderful Gospel sweetness. So rare . . .

Bob Lax is in Greece and in the same mail as yours came an application for a Guggenheim for him too. All my friends are after Guggenheims. Marvelous. Hope you all hit the jackpot.

Berrigan's deep involvement in the civil rights movement upset some of his Superiors. It was decided that he should take a sabbatical in Europe.

February 9, 1963

I have not yet thanked you for the clipping from the [Le Moyne] college paper with your exorbitant statements about me. One at least I will accept: the Spanish look. I look like a Barcelona hotelkeeper. Maybe it would be a good thing if I were one. But thanks for your charity.

. . . I envy you going to France. Say hello to Chartres for me. I was working on the school of Chartres until this year I got all the novices, brothers and choir together and am trying to make sense of the combination. Actually it is very good. But I also have a lot of junior professed in my classes. Pray that I may weld it all together rightly and for their good.

Did you get the Guggenheim? I hope so. Hope Bob Lax got his too. He is still in Greece . . .

In a letter of June 14, 1963, Berrigan wrote of his desire to go to Birmingham, Alabama, to take part in a civil rights demonstration. His Superiors were opposed to his going. In the letter he muses about the question of civil disobedience and Church disobedience. "Is this wild talk?" he asks.

June 25, 1963

This will come to you as a conscience-matter letter, so that I can deal with your question freely. Remember that our mail here is strictly censored and the Abbot reads it, sometimes quite carefully. Whether he read your letter or not, I cannot say, but he probably glanced at it at least. I don't think you would have wanted that. So be warned.

First of all, the same idea has come to me many times. I am still not able to give a final and satisfactory answer one way or the other. I think that such an answer is not yet possible. We are going to have to grope our way with a great deal of prudence (the supernatural kind) and attention to grace. I will just jot down some of the different aspects of the matter as they occur to me.

1. Most important of all: you do have to consider the continuity of your work as a living unit. You must be careful not to rupture that continuity in a violent and drastic way without having an exceptionally grave reason and a rather evident sign that this is required precisely of *you*. By this I refer to the fact that a violent break with Superiors would tend to cast discredit on *all* the initiatives you have so far taken and render them *all* suspect as part of a dangerous process leading inevitably to radicalism and defection. If you allow this to happen (of course it might have to happen in some cases) you must consider that you are turning adrift those who have begun to follow you and profit by your leadership. And you are also at the same time wreaking havoc in the minds of Superiors, who were perhaps timidly beginning to go along with you.

I don't mean this in a cozy way, now. I mean it as a response to the serious reasons for thinking that in your present work you are following the call of God, and that to follow His call further presupposes (unless there are clear signs to the contrary) continuity in the same line, and the completion of what you have begun.

2. What are the reasons for wanting to get in there with the movement for racial justice? Setting aside the obvious and indisputably valuable ones which stem from personal conscience and the need to affirm an honest and loyally Christian position, there is also the matter of bearing witness to the fact that the Holy Roman Catholic Church is not, much as one might be tempted to think so, ossified and committed to the status quo, but that she is really alive and means to do something about justice. Very well. But if you get yourself censured or kicked out or something, even though a benevolent bishop may eventually with many signs grab you just before you hit the left field fence, you will spell out too unmistakably for comfort that the Church is plenty conservative and still profoundly asleep in some areas where she ought to be most awake. Now of course there are moments when one feels that maybe this is necessary. I don't know. It is in any case a very serious problem.

3. Certainly I think that the only thing to do is to scout around and canvass the best Catholic opinion in Europe. Get in touch with Fr. Régamey, O.P., who has been slapped down a lot about the peace issue and is into non-violence and probably civil disobedience. Remember that isolated and oddball action on your part will cast discredit on honest efforts made by people of his type who are clinging to a relatively tenable position and are just tolerated. If it turns out that there are workable ways of proceeding, these people can let you know. For instance I know that the

Goss-Mayrs are looking for someone to do non-violent action with them in Brazil. Did I tell you this? . . .

4. One has to consider that no matter how far one goes now, it is not going to be far enough. I mean that the racial movement is entering a revolutionary and perhaps soon violent stage. Hence to build your hopes around the kind of actions that would have been fully valid up to recently, when they involve a very drastic separation, is to cut yourself off when you need to be able to hang on to something. We need to see what is coming next, I am afraid. I don't mean prosperity about the corner. I mean violent revolution around the corner. Of course, in a way it would be well to be further left than we are now, and in an evident way. But I wonder if in six months all these positions will seem meaningful at all. I really think that at the present moment you can do more by talking and writing than by anything else . . .

And now about the monastic life and ideal, in relation to the world. Look, I hate to be vulgar, but a lot of the monastic party line we are getting, even where in some respects it is very good, ends up by being pure unadulterated ——— crap. In the name of lifeless and graven letters on parchment, we are told that our life consists in the peaceful and pious meditation on Scripture and a quiet withdrawal from the world. But if one reads the prophets with his ears and eyes open he cannot help recognizing his obligation to shout very loud about God's will, God's truth, and justice of man to man. I don't say that this has to be done in a journalistic way or how, but it has to be done somehow. I don't say it is the dish of every individual monk, but certainly it is incumbent on some monks. I don't say it necessarily means going out of the monastery but I don't say that one can rightly confine the monk completely to his monastery in the name of a literalist and antiquarian concept of the contemplative life.

I have gone through the whole gamut in this business. In the beginning I was all pro-contemplation, because I was against the kind of trivial and meaningless activism, the futile running around in circles that Superiors, including contemplative Superiors, promote at the drop of a hat. They will have the whole monastery humming with kindergarten projects and assure everyone that this is "contemplation." But try anything serious, and immediately you get the "activism" line thrown at you. Or rather, I have been told (they cannot very well call me an activist, because they know how much time I put in to non-active pursuits) that I am destroying the image of the contemplative vocation, when I write about peace. Even after *Pacem in Terris* when I reopened the question, I was told: that is for the bishops, my boy. The bishops meanwhile are saying, "That is for the theologians," and the theologians are evidently pussy-footing around as you say Courtney Murray is doing. What a tragedy! I know however that they wanted to get me over at West Baden (of course the Abbot never told me this, but I heard it in roundabout ways) but I will never be allowed to go . . .

Obviously the monastic life is nothing if it does not open a man wide to the Holy Spirit. In actual fact, the head-in-the-ground type of monk is usually in practice the most damnable fascist you ever saw. This was true of Solesmes and of Maria Laach: the one was Action Française and the other pro-Hitler, so I am told.

In a word, it is all right for the monk to break his ass putting out packages of cheese and making a pile of money for the old monastery, but as to doing anything that is *really* fruitful for the Church, that is another matter altogether.

What is the contemplative life if one doesn't listen to God in it? What is the contemplative life if one becomes oblivious to the rights of men and the truth of God in the world and in His Church? Answer: listen to the Superior and shut up because the Superior is God. My own Abbot always manages to show just enough good will and tolerance on the crucial issues to keep me hesitant about the next drastic step: but I think that in my own case everything indicates my staying put and waiting. Nothing else is definite enough, and writing does get someplace. When it gets past censors, or around them.

Keep in touch and let me know what comes. Europe is obviously the next step, because over there you may find out what's what. And you need to. When you do, let me know . . .

November 15, 1963

I am glad to have your letter and cards from Paris. I was not sure where you were going to be and so hesitated to write. If that is an excuse. I also was in the hospital with a bad back and they are still mumbling under their breaths about operations unless I behave myself, so that held things up a bit too. But it is nothing serious, only a nuisance . . .

In a way I envy you in Paris and in Europe . . . If you see Fr. Danielou when he gets back from Rome, say hello from me.

. . . If you see the Goss-Mayrs tell them our Abbot General died and that there will be a new one. If they speak to him about my writing for peace, it might produce an impression. The old one was a great man, but some monolith, I tell you. Total unbending loyalty to de Gaulle and the *force de frappe* [France's nuclear arsenal], convinced that I was a dangerous pacifist and Red, etc. etc. But a good friend in his own way. This is perhaps not a useful suggestion as you won't see them for a while. But anyway give them my love. What I envy you most is going to Vienna and meeting them . . .

After a visit to Eastern Europe, Berrigan had hopes of being appointed a Vatican observer at the Christian Peace Conference that was to be held in Prague in the summer of 1964. He did not receive this appointment. He did go to Prague, however, and it was there in a meeting with Jim Forest and John Heidbrink that the decision was arrived at to form the Catholic Peace Fellowship. Following the Prague meeting, he visited the Soviet Union. He returned to New York City, by way of Africa, to become associate editor of Jesuit Missions.

February 23, 1964

Your letter from the Budapest was wonderful. Got to me long after Christmas, however, and I did not write to Rome because I could not have reached you there. However, I was not surprised that your hopes were dashed to a great extent. Does that mean however that all hope of going is shot? Or only the hope of going as Vatican representative? So you have got deep into the great mystery of paralysis which we are. I feel it is like a sickness, as though I were some kind of an addict that has been through impossible and incredible things and does not know whether he is out or in. A lot of the time now I find it impossible to move or think, when one gets into the area where motion and thought are imperative. Obviously because any movement will be blocked exteriorly. But I suppose I have finally internalized the official prohibitions. It is like a bad dream. Out of this, of course, some moments of lucidity come and I can reach out with an article that is *near* but not *on* the forbidden target.

I don't know what I can do to help you. You must think I have influence. I might have, if I had contacts . . . I have come to the conclusion that the only thing for me is to speak out when I can, to sing on my own perch, and if they don't like the song it will take them a little time at least to get all the way down to me to shut me up. They too are busy after all. But if I go try to sing in their offices . . .

What did the Goss-Mayrs have to say? Anything good? John Heidbrink sent stuff about non-violence in Latin America. Too late, but it has to be done anyway. I am so sorry he is not well, will write at once.

. . . My book on Black Revolution is coming out in Paris very soon. The same, plus all the peace articles I was permitted to do in magazines, is to come out in NY in the fall, I hope . . . Incidentally Fr. Haring has read the Peace book ms. and apparently likes it. Bishop Wright also. And our General died, but I have no better hopes from the new one and I am convinced that it would be a very wrong move to make my first contact with him a request to get the ban on this book lifted, at least to do this myself. Just get in the doghouse for good, from the start . . .

I think that in the next year Latin America is going to burst into flame in six or seven different places and who knows but that the Pentagon people may decide that these ought to be brushfire wars to keep democracy safe like in Vietnam. I do not foresee any improvement in the situation . . .

. . . Have been reading and reviewing Rahner's latest book and agree with him about what he calls the diaspora situation. It is what we have to face, especially where we think we are not in it. Even the Church is to some extent its own diaspora. Though the fact that I often feel alien in the Church is no new thing and proves nothing about the Church, I suppose.

I send you a message I wrote for a bunch of poets meeting in Mexico. I think Henry Miller read it to the meeting, and I think it was published in a paper in Mexico. I don't know. I may be able to find out when one of them comes by here. That is all I do. Throw stones in the air, and if somebody yells I know the stone came down.

I hope the trip to South Africa will be fruitful.

. . . Do not be discouraged. The Holy Spirit is not asleep. Nor let yourself get too frustrated. There is no use getting mad at the Church and her representatives. First there is the problem of communication, which is impossible. Then there is the fact that God writes straight on crooked lines anyway, all the time, all the time. The lines are crooked enough by now. And we I suppose are what He is writing with, though we can't see what is being written. And what He writes is not for peace of soul, that is sure . . .

May 18, 1964

. . . I have tried to get up a little book on Gandhi, part introduction by me and part texts of Gandhi himself. Pray that the wild boars do not totally rend it. Also did a piece on "Mercy" for a collection got up by a Catholic abbé, friend of the Goss-Mayrs, for Schweitzer. I hope this will pass. In other words I am trying to say indirectly what will be of some use, and frankly am not fretting over the inability to get tied up in the strategy concept of it. In the long run, I think that would be sterile. Someone connected with the boys at Georgetown Strategy Center (I understand of course that the SJ's are running the Pentagon really) wants me to get involved with *that.* Can you imagine? I will have to tell him more or less why I can't. The moment one starts from the supposed axiom that war is reasonable, the conclusions cannot be made completely Christian in the present context. Other day a group of Hibakusha, survivors of the atomic bombing at Hiroshima, stopped here. Such good, beautiful, beat-up people. I think they are being well received on their peace pilgrimage but really the thinking of this country has not changed one bit. Johnson is good in many respects, but who or what can prevent him acting just like Truman if an analogous situation arose? And how easily it could, if not a worse one.

Your Polish tape arrived, was played, and passed on. Many thanks. It was excellent. Did you say there was a South African tape on the way??? I got your letter from down there . . .

I have decided that I have to have a very clear position on solitude and so on. Though I don't get permission to travel in any case, I think I ought not even to consider asking them, not out of pique, but simply because non-traveling and staying put in the woods have come to be essential to my whole life and vocation. This also means keeping contacts with the outside on a certain informal plane and always non-organized and offbeat. I told John Heidbrink this when he wanted to organize the visit of the peace guys as a formal sort of conference. If they come in November, it would be just a visit. Hope you will be with them. We can sit around and discuss things as we did before. I don't know what he will answer but I am sure he will understand. The Latin American poet who organized the meeting where my message was read came through here back in Lent. A very fine fellow plenty open and very alive. I have more hope for the intellectuals of South and Latin America than for almost anyone. There are great hopes of life and truth there and a real freedom of spirit, a real "spirituality" and not this phony curled-up-in-the-shell stuff.

I have a new job for the magazine of the Order. Am responsible for reports on the best stuff written each year on Islam, Buddhism, Hinduism and—Anglicanism, what a mixture. Obviously I can't do it well, or cover the territory properly. But as far as I go it will be interesting. It will be pretty patchy though.

All the best to you. I hope things are getting ironed out with the censors but am not fool enough to think that you will have no more trouble with them. This thing is only beginning. There is a priest in California Wm. Du Bay who may write you. He is a friend of Dewart's and is groping around for answers.

June 30, 1964

One of the things that you can do for Latin America is get in touch with the poet Pablo Antonio Cuadra, *La Prensa*, Managua, Nicaragua. My good friend, you remember from the *Letter on Giants* maybe. He is doing first an anthology of Christian poetry XXth cent. and would like suggestions and leads. Then he is also running this fine little magazine of his and is broadening out to make it a really worldwide thing. Up to now, it has been strictly Central American (Indian and Spanish stuff) apart from me. If you can think of some good lively minds in Europe, tell them to contact him too. Mostly literary approach, poetry especially, but commentary also, essays, etc. And Christian all through . . .

I just finished *The Pilgrim* by Serafian, on the Council. It is really a smasher, much better than the gossip columns of Xavier Rynne, much deeper, much more serious and much more sobering. I had not realized what a beating [Cardinal] Bea took at the last session and what this really represented. This curial thing is really disastrous, and it threatens the whole structure of the Church, and maybe, one thinks, this is providential

. . . I wonder if we are really going to have to get along without a structure one of these days. Maybe that will be good, but Lord it will be rough on most people. Maybe less rough on you and me, with all the welts we have acquired in the machinery. More and more I come to think we are living in one great big illusion. Centuries of triumphalist self-deception. The late Middle Ages, with all their sores, were more real . . . Everything is all twisted up and the worst thing is the façade of smoothness over all the busted iron and the fragments of a building that has perhaps fallen in. But where it has fallen God will build and is building. The front is man's work and that will really cave in. Who worries about that? We must learn not to, and even, when necessary, give it a good shove. Mitres, croziers, rings, slippers, baubles, documents, seals, bulls, rescripts, indults . . . Have a good time on your trip.

August 4, 1964

. . . When you come down in the fall, the purpose will be for you to give us a talk on South Africa, and also another one on anything else you like, religious life, aggiornamento, etc. Would you want to talk at Loretto? They are eager to have you.

I forget what news I have to give, if any. I don't think it is much hotter in Africa than it is here. I have a book coming in the fall with a big chunk of peace stuff in it after all. That is nice. I look forward to seeing you and John H. and a few others in October but let's make it purposeless and freewheeling and a vacation for all and let the Holy Spirit suggest anything that needs to be suggested. Let's be Quakers and the heck with projects. I am so sick, fed up and ready to vomit with projects and hopes and expectations.

Let me write about this for a moment, even at the risk of being neurotic about it. It is of course not God's will that a religious or a priest should spend his life more or less in frustration and defeat over the most important issues that face the Church. But you and I know that, in fact, this is what a lot of people have to face. I have a great deal less reason to complain of it than most. I have been extraordinarily fortunate in chances to speak, much much more than one would expect in a Trappist monastery of all places, so that really I have been blessed with special graces. So I should complain. However, at the same time I realize that I am about at the end of some kind of a line. What line? What is the trolley I am probably getting off? The trolley is called a special kind of hope. The streetcar of expectation, of proximately to be fulfilled desire of betterment, of things becoming much more intelligible, of things being set in a new kind of order, and so on. Point one, things are not going to get better. Point two, things are going to get worse. I will not dwell on point two. Point three, I don't need to be on the trolley car anyway, I don't belong riding in a trolley. You can call the trolley anything you like,

I have got off it. You can call the trolley a form of religious leprosy if you like. It is burning out. In a lot of sweat and pain if you like but it is burning out for real. The leprosy of that particular kind of temporal hope, that special expectation that young monks have, that priests have. As a priest I am a burnt-out case, repeat, burnt-out case. So burnt out that the question of standing and so forth becomes irrelevant. I just continue to stand there where I was hit by the bullet. And I will continue to stand there, saying Mass. Not that Mass doesn't mean a thousand times more. You know what I mean. But I have been shot dead and the situation is somehow different. I have no priestly ax to grind with anyone or about anything, monastic either. This has got a bit of burning out to do yet, though. The funny thing is that I will probably continue to write books. And word will go round about how they got this priest who was shot and they got him stuffed sitting up at a desk propped up with books and writing books, this book machine that was killed. I am waiting to fall over and it may take about ten more years of writing. When I fall over, it will be a big laugh because I wasn't there at all.

I do not propose this as a paradigm for anything or anyone, it is just something that happened (or did not happen, verbs are deceptive) to me (pronouns are even more deceptive than verbs).

I am sick up to the teeth and beyond the teeth, up to the eyes and beyond the eyes, with all forms of projects and expectations and statements and programs and explanations of anything, especially explanations about where we are all going, because where we are all going is where we went a long time ago, over the falls. We are in a new river and we don't know it.

With this spiritual nosegay I declare myself your happy and insouciant Kentucky friend, and no wonder Henry Miller says I look like an ex-con and like him and like Genet. Actually, though, it is only Picasso I look like which is deceptive: he got money.

September 19, 1964

Got a good letter from John Heidbrink today and he said you were back, also told me where to find you though you had told me before. Are you going to be coming down in November with the rest of them? I am sure you still intend to, and I have at least arranged for you to give a talk at Loretto. Bellarmine College is all booked up they say. And you can give a talk to the novices, etc. etc., who will be eager to hear what was not heard when the first tape from South Africa failed to get out . . .

About the time you all may come down I ought to be having a showing of abstract drawings in Louisville. Maybe that will be later, though. I am not sure yet.

What news? I am still here, plugging along. There is going to be a meeting of all the abbots and novice masters of the Order in North America here in October. Unusual for us, though it is the sort of thing you are used to. I hope I can say something that makes sense, it has to be about the background and thought with which "they come to the monastery." Actually an important and complex topic, and one which we have always oversimplified, loading the answers in our own favor to explain why so many wash out. I am sure they are really looking for what is really here, but we are organized in a way that, "they" being what they are, the things that are supposed to be helps become insuperable obstacles in many cases. This is a funny life. I suppose it is to some extent the same in all Orders. What is the Society doing about aggiornamento? Do you have a vocation problem? Are you doing something new about religious formation? I don't know, perhaps those questions do not really matter as much as they seem to. I am not totally convinced of the importance that is attributed to them.

I just got through writing a short article on Flannery O'Connor, you probably knew she was dead? A wonderful writer. Writing along, I don't seem to get to write the things I really want to. But a lot of peace stuff is finally getting into my new book, did I tell you? In the end I had to do some rewriting and the result was that I stated much more clearly and directly all the things that had previously been objected to and they got through . . . I am looking forward to seeing you in November. All the best. God be with you.

November 9, 1964

. . . I have been planning to have no plans and to go along quite informally. I hope they are all in a position not to be disconcerted at this and to expect a very freewheeling and unorganized approach. However, if you and I are both prepared with ideas, it will do no harm. I hope, however, that it will be a real authentic opportunity of awakening and new directions for us all and am praying for that.

November 11, 1964

Could you be prepared to more or less lead a discussion at one of the sessions? General topic: spiritual roots of protest. Take any angle you like. I will give it from monastic-desert viewpoint.

The freewheeling meeting took place at Gethsemani from Wednesday, November 18, to Friday, November 20, 1964. It was apparently a bit more structured than Merton originally intended. The guidelines he eventually proposed included: (1) the topic: "Our common grounds for religious dissent and commitment in the face of injustice and disorder"; and (2) a structure for the meeting: "It is suggested that at each of our meetings someone act as leader of the discussion, after himself starting off with a talk on any aspect of the question that seems relevant to him." E.g., Wednesday morning: T. Merton, "The Monastic Protest: The Voice of the

Desert"; Thursday morning, A. J. Muste; Thursday afternoon, John H. Yoder; Friday morning, Fr. Daniel Berrigan, S.J.

February 26, 1965

. . . I have not even been able to type up the stuff from last November. Actually if it were just a matter of sitting down and typing it would not be so bad, but I have forgotten what I said and the notes aren't much help, so really I will have to start all over again. Which I will, perhaps, in Lent. . .

Things are moving along quietly and in a certain amount of confusion, but with the Holy Spirit I hope making sense underneath it all. It is definite that I am to be allowed a chance to try a crack at real hermit life. That will be after I have finished out the year as novice master. Meanwhile I am in the cottage a lot more, and actually living pretty much as a hermit right now, except to come down for work in the novitiate and for some of the offices. I know I can cook, anyway. So provided enough cans of beans are sent my way, I can probably survive. No worry on that score. Gets pretty cold out there in zero weather. One thing is sure is that most of the statements made about the solitary life are sheer nonsense. I can't think of anything less likely to make a person indifferent to other people. Quite the contrary. I think that the business of herding people together is what makes them hate and misunderstand each other, or teaches them indifference. Just the fact of being on the same electric line as all the poor farmers (I am on the rural cooperative which serves people back in out of the way hills, which the utility co. refuses to do because there is no money in it), just that is solidarity too.

Later there are chances I might be able to move to a real wild place five or six miles away. A completely hidden valley where nobody but hunters ever go, and the thing about it, two things—quite symbolic— first, slaves used to live there and second, the SAC plane goes over sometimes five or six times a day real low so you can look right up at the bomb bay and get your mind on what you are there for. Composition of place made easy. This is perhaps where I may end up, but meanwhile the cottage is going along good.

This Vietnam thing is sickening and just about as stupid as one would imagine possible, but I have an odd feeling that it is not going to get any more intelligent as time goes on. This country seems to be bent on giving everyone for all time a clear lesson in how to miss all one's opportunities to make a good use of power.

I haven't been writing much. One thing about living in the woods is that you have plenty to do just keeping the place clean and warm. Lot of wood to chop but it is good exercise . . .

Your statement on Vietnam was really fine! Very strong and right on target.

May 18, 1965

. . . I guess my visits are now really at an end. This is good and bad, but anyway good from the viewpoint that I am moving out of the novitiate and into the hermitage next month sometime. I don't know what the mail situation will be, but I am pretty sure visits will more or less completely end, except for Hildegard Goss-Mayr whom I have promised to see in October. Will you pass this info on to Jim? I wouldn't want anyone to come all the way down hoping to see me and then have to go away.

Here are some notes on the Schema for *Commonweal*, maybe. Perhaps after the bishops see them the hermitage will be the best place, though I certainly don't think they are in the least radical nor should they be regarded as in any way strange. Have sent copies to Bishop Wright, Bishop Flahiff, et al. Jim Douglass is also sending out a few. It was wonderful having you three here back when, and Jim was out the other day with Sally.

Pray for me through my "novitiate." A new kind of novitiate, with no novice master and no novices. But the postulancy has been pretty good and I am looking forward to the rest of it. Me and the birds . . .

May 19, 1965

Glad to get your note. I would be delighted to see you and Jim [Douglass] if you can get out on the 29th, morning or afternoon. Let me know. I will get the permission and fix things so you could come direct to the hermitage . . . I think the Administration is just plain nuts, and they are doing more to strengthen communism in Asia and Latin America than anyone else on earth. They couldn't do a better job if they were paid. Hope to see you, let me know, and let me know also if you will be in the guesthouse, v. g. for a meal. If coming middle of the day, why not bring some chow and we can have lunch at hermitage.

On October 15, 1965, David Miller, a young Catholic Worker who had been a student of Berrigan's at Le Moyne College, defied the Selective Service Law and burned his draft card. Less than a month later, on November 6, 1965, Roger La Porte, also a Catholic Worker, immolated himself on the steps of the United Nations Building as a protest against the war in Vietnam. Merton was very disturbed by this "suicide" and sent telegrams to Jim Forest and Dorothy Day. In the telegram to Jim Forest he asked that his name be removed from the list of sponsors of the Catholic Peace Fellowship. (Merton later regretted this and retracted his overly hasty decision. See James Forest letters.) Daniel Berrigan celebrated a memorial service for La Porte, describing his action as a proclamation of life. Under pressure from Cardinal Spellman, Berrigan was "exiled" to South America.

November 19, 1965

Today your letter came, with one from Jim and also one from Dorothy Day. It was a great relief to hear your human voices. I don't think you have any idea what a distorted and kooky picture of things I have been getting here. More than ever I am dependent on fragments and bits of gossip that blow in the window, and what had been blowing in lately came on winds of much alarm from people who were very disturbed by everything. On top of that the tragic death of Roger La Porte. I will write to Jim and tell him of the things I am sorry for having done, the first being the very unreasonable act of immediately sending that telegram, as a kind of emotional reaction. It was a reflex of shock.

I am very sorry indeed to hear about you being shipped out. If I can think of a reasonable thing to say to your Provincial this afternoon, I will enclose a copy with this letter. But if you go to Latin America it may be all to the good, in some long-range plan. I could perhaps put you in touch with some good people, depending where you go.

To return to my telegram and letter to Jim: inevitably I was very unclear about the problem. It is bound up chiefly with the particular problems of my own life, living now my third month in more or less complete solitude (going down to the monastery for Mass and a meal and often seeing hardly anyone, let alone talking to anyone). If I was talking about devils in the peace movement it is probably because I get too much devilish static down at this end. One of the things about living alone is that you suddenly find yourself thinking, perfectly plausibly, thoughts that turn out to be in themselves schizoid. It is not that one is nuts, but the situation of removal from reality and contact does that. This poses a real problem, and in order to cope with it one has to get pretty simply organized and stick with rather rudimentary and well-united elements in one simple picture. And work with that. The fact that I have always been so spread out and so scattered does present a problem. Consequently when something like the news of Roger La Porte's death came it was pretty hard to fit into any context that made sense, and I guess I just didn't cope with it right.

In any case let me be clear about this: I really don't mean to blame the Catholic Peace Fellowship or to "blame" anyone. Jim's letter and enclosures threw a lot of sane light on the situation, and cleared up a lot of my questions. Certainly it never was and never will be a question of a personal repudiation of Jim, Tom, etc. Why should it be? Why should what I said be interpreted that way? Yet inevitably it has been. My problem is different from any of yours by the simple fact that you are, or have been up to now, *there*, fully informed, fully aware, fully involved. I am at the other extreme and I felt that I was not intelligently involved in something that was developing in a way I knew nothing about and which I could not seriously participate in. This still remains a problem.

However, I do not want to do anything abrupt about it, especially if it is going to be interpreted as a personal break which is the last thing I want. I am just trying to get my own life organized in such a way that I can cope with it and do what God seems to be asking of me. This may mean throwing out very many things that don't fit. But I will take time to think it out so that I don't hurt anybody else. I will write more about this to Jim. Thanks for your letter and for the moving, difficult words at the liturgy for Roger. Don't think I am blind to the great spirit of charity and understanding that is evident in all of you, in all this. It is really very striking. It gives me hope that you can bear with me in my own difficulties and lunacies. And really I think you don't need me that much. I am pretty sure that I have outlived my active usefulness and that I can serve you much better by being a halfway decent hermit. In any case it is the job I have to do now, and I must try to do it properly. I can use prayers for that end. I keep you all in my prayers and in Christ's love.

February 14, 1966

Some event, hearing from you. Letter came today, dated Feb. 6th in Argentina, and I don't know how long it will take this to get to Ecuador, sure hope I don't miss you there. If you see a Padre Cardenal among the Jebs there, say hello, I know his brother very well. Probably not there, though. No matter, anyway. You are probably not going to Nicaragua, who does? But if you do, look up at all costs Pablo Antonio Cuadra who is editor of the main paper *La Prensa* in Managua. And give him my regards. Very good friend and fine guy. Looking at your letter, it says you fly home from Bogotá. Oh well. I used to know some Jebs in Bogotá.

For one I have never managed to get awful sorry for you going to Latin America: it is where everything is going to happen, and I guess a lot of it will have to happen without or in spite of the U.S. rather than with. We have no savvy about Latin America, I think. Why it is so important for someone like you to get in contact . . . I have been asked, begged and pleaded with to come to Latin America but naturally can't get loose from the rock-bound establishment here, and hence I feel jealous of you, to tell the truth. Wish I knew how you did it.

Man, you are one of the most popular priests in the U.S. You are all over the front of *The Critic*, you have a fine piece in *Jubilee*, you are teamed up well with that wild great nun Sr. Corita and it is a good team, you got all the cats eating out of your hand. And you ask why you are shipped out? Nothing but good can come to you from it. Your prose book is out, I just got it the other day and haven't gone into it yet. The poems in galleys I liked and I saw they used a quote in an ad. Both these books will certainly do well. You are news, man. The CPF seems to be really jiving. I get good letters from Tom and Jim . . . Certainly I think you will run into friction and the hate types will be yelling about you. I think that the conscience of the country is thoroughly bad by this time, hence the need for so many to convince themselves they are right by hating and hunting people down but I don't think they are going to do anything but bark and yell. On the other hand, the honest people of which there are still plenty are really going to want to know what the score is. Even with the brainwashed state of the mass media this country still wants to know the truth about an obviously absurd and evil business—and so much else that seems to go along with it.

Way it looks to me is this: you are going to be able to do a great deal of good simply stating facts quietly and telling the truth quietly and patiently. With so much obvious truth on your side and with enough honesty around to keep people open and interested, you should not have too much trouble. With the hate people, I don't know what you will run into, but they are people too and I suppose there must be some way of keeping communication open, which is important. When the communication by word and reason stops entirely, then we're in trouble. With your bosses, my guess is that probably your Provincial wants to keep himself off some kind of a hook, and will probably look the other way as much as he can, which is what I would let him do if I were you. All I know is that one can eventually reach *modus agendi* with these people in which, as long as they do not feel that they are too involved, they will put up with a lot that they would not otherwise tolerate and think they are being generous about it. Also when people get thoroughly used to you being a bad boy, they will expect a certain amount and will not complain too much. My suggestion then would be to proceed quietly, coolly, firmly with whatever is obviously right, and back yourself up with obvious directives of Council, etc., and though they may not like it they cannot stop you. On the other hand I would say don't needlessly get involved in big symbolic confrontations. Later, however, such things may arise. I say later because I think of the big explosion of the obedience-authority crisis that is sure to come. Then there will indeed be symbolic confrontation and there will be a lot of chips down and a lot of people getting hurt. And maybe some institutions cracking wide open into the bargain. You are going to be one of the central figures in this, along with Bill Du Bay (who is incidentally thinking of starting a priests' union, which I think is wacky, put that way, but there is a germ of truth and good in it nonetheless). So I would say go quietly and don't rush, you have a long road ahead of you and in any case nobody is going to stop the Vietnam war for a long time, it seems to me . . .

The problem of authority and obedience has to be handled with delicacy and understanding. For many reasons. First of all there is a lot of emotional power pent up in lay people and just ordinary frustrated religious and it is looking for an outlet. Just an outlet. And this is not enough. What is demanded is a real renewal, not just an explosion. So the problem is to see that these pressures, which include real needs, should end up in renewal and not just in a big bang and a lot of fallout. The explosion would be the easiest thing in the world. The reason why I stress this in writing to you is that without any trouble at all this force is centering on someone like you (and to some extent on me, but I am trying very hard to get disengaged from such possibilities, whereas you have a different job to do). The forces working for explosion simply try to line everything up in a plain black-white opposition, four legs good, two legs bad, subjects good, Superiors all crazy.

While in fact there are a lot of Superiors who think themselves infallible, and are absolutely incapable of understanding what it means to really find out what their subjects need and desire (they consult only yes-men or people who have made the grade by never rocking any boats); there is a new bunch coming up that sincerely wants to help change things, but obviously can't do everything they would like to do either. And then there are the good Joes who want to go along wherever the Church seems to be going even if they don't really understand what it is all about. If all these are treated as if they were purely and simply reactionary tyrants, then there will be a real mess for sure. In your position, if you really clarify a true and indisputably Christian position, these openminded Superiors will give you credit for it, even though the others may play every kind of dirty trick in the book. The moment of truth will come when you will have to resist the arbitrary and reactionary use of authority in order to save the real concept of authority and obedience, in the line of renewal. This will take charismatic grace. And it is not easy to know when one is acting "charismatically" when one is surrounded with a great deal of popular support on one side and nonsensical opposition on the other.

The business last fall persuaded me definitively to renounce all illusions about a charism of leadership in any form whatever, in my own case, however remote. It could too easily become a very silly game. With you the case is entirely different because you are in the middle of things. In either case let us work for the Church and for people, not for ideas and programs. For my part I can see after six months that the hermit life is anything but a hermit idea. It is a life with its own kind of problems and benefits, sometimes bitter and disillusioning, but something I cannot doubt as being what I need: it is so much more to the point than anything I ever ran into in the community, and above all it is good to get out from under the stifling mentality of the establishment . . .

March 23, 1966

Very happy to have you back! Glad things have cleared. I thought they might. Go to it, man! Maybe with this dirty war the nation will learn a few things about itself and grow up.

Meanwhile I am off to the hospital for a back operation and also have a tumor to be investigated. Pray. Best to all the gang.

Operation coincides with days of protest. My part!

Holy Saturday [1966?]

It was good to get your letter. The operation worked out fine, but it was a little rough for a week. However, I am going home today—a fast comeback—due to everybody's prayers. Will be glad to get back into the bushes, though I can't live in the hermitage for a while. I have a kind of feeling that the Abbot is using the hermit pitch as a pretext for imposing complete silence as regards not only events but even basic principles. However, I think I can always manage to say anything I really need to say. I have no idea where this Vietnam thing will lead us, but cannot help feeling there is a big war ahead—perhaps a few years away.

The real job is to lay the groundwork for a deep change of heart on the part of the whole nation so that one day it can really go through the metanoia we need for a peaceful world.

September 18, 1966

. . . Congratulations especially on the prize and vigil: of course I knew nothing about either, glad you told me. So you drove Vagnozzi out into the bushes. That at least is something. Anyway, I am very happy that some Catholic outfit [Sodality gathering in Washington, D.C.] saw fit to give you a peace prize . . .

Thanks for your last letter which has been waiting around for an answer too. I think we need to talk a lot about all of it, and it would be really great to have you here mid-October . . .

I always loved New York and once when I was back there secretly a few years ago, it really turned me on good. All the old days came back in a big mad choking rush and I loved it, just talking to the guys, bartenders and whatnot and people all around at Columbia, man it is a *city*. You know what rural means when you get back out here. However, I probably have got so far out of it now that I wouldn't be able to survive it. Louisville is bad enough for me now. One day in Louisville and I can't sleep when I get back out here with all the excitement, seeing buses and mad things like that batting around.

. . . Have been reading a lot of Camus and writing on him: did an article on him and the Church which I sent to Dorothy for the *Catholic Worker*. But already so much water has gone under the bridge since Camus.

As you know I am supposed to be cut off as to communications from M. but maybe you could take care of the enclosed—I'd be most grateful. Going back to the possibility of your coming down, I see the 13th is a Thursday and I was thinking in terms of weekend. But if you are here Friday 14th that will be great. Stay over Saturday too if you want . . .

February 22, 1967

Thanks for the laurel note and the clipping on A.J. [Muste]. He certainly was one of the notable people, really notable people, of this time. We can ill afford to lose someone like that. Looks as though the ones coming up don't equal his measure but that is what people have always thought. I have great confidence in Jim and Tom and the younger ones . . .

Tomorrow I go to the hospital, St. Joseph's Infirmary, Eastern Parkway, Louisville. Will be in five or six days I guess. They are going to get this bursitis out of my elbow I hope. Nothing much, but still something I guess. Sorry about your ulcers but my only surprise is that you didn't have them long ago. Like my own churned-up gut, except I am churned up and eaten away at the other end of it. Crazy society makes us beat ourselves up inside as its delegates. We are our own concentration camp. Too damn docile if you ask me.

This afternoon I will try to get some sort of statement to Jim about Vietnam (help to the destroyed who have had to be the victims of our obsessions). That will be about the last thing I can get out before I take off . . .

March 7, 1967

Just got your new book yesterday. It looks great. Will report soon as I can type again.

I just got walloped with a terrific idea: a happening that could be possible down here. A get-together of extreme people to talk of community and particularly on the most radical level the prophetic and monastic type community and in what terms monasticism is even tolerable as a Christian concept any more. To be *against* would be Rosemary Ruether and Vahanian. To be in the middle and for a quasi-monastic type thing, Dorothy Day and Dave Kirk. To be for at least a kind of continuity with traditional monasticism, Dom Jean Leclercq and myself—and then you and perhaps Jim Forest as free-floaters. Wonderful too if we could get Corita.

Are you going to the forum in the spring? We could talk about this. I think it would be groovy. Right now (still night and snow swirling all around hermitage) it feels like great fun. But I get these ideas at this time in the morning.

Let me know what you think and I can begin working on it.

Get Joan Baez too maybe . . .

In April 1967 Berrigan was invited by the Fellowship of Reconciliation to be part of a group who would go to Hanoi with symbolic medical gifts. His Superiors were unwilling to let him go, but the issue became academic when the plans to ship the medical supplies fell through. This did not happen, however, until some time after Merton wrote the following letter.

April 15, 1967

Sounds as though this is it, doesn't it? I find it hard to organize clear thoughts but you will make the best of the jumble that follows.

1. The one real clear thought I have is that obviously sooner or later it is going to be a question of obeying God or obeying man. Do they really have the right to forbid you to follow your conscience in this? Sooner or later they reach the point where they think they have to cut you down in favor of their institutional view of the Church. And you can't accept. Maybe this is the time. But are there any questions and reservations?

2. Is the issue as clear as you put it? Are they throwing you out if you go to North Vietnam without approval? Is it clear to everybody? Should you simply make this known and see what happens? In other words, is the best, clearest, simplest, cleanest thing just to go to NV and let them do the terrible and dirty thing they want to do? I feel very sorry for these people. But if this is a situation where they are so clearly in the wrong, maybe that is when to go ahead. On the other hand . . . I don't know. I'd say if it's clear, then go. Is *your* gesture that clear to everyone? It has to be. It must not be obscured in a case like this. What I would *not* want to see would be just a confused, stupid, lying mess come out of it, and that could very well be the issue.

3. When Fr. Perrin quit the Society, he worked it out with them that he was certain in advance to do things they would not approve of so he might as well quit before that time came. Should you work it out on that basis? I don't know, times have changed, this is an entirely different situation, the lights are full on, and everybody knows what is what, whereas in his case everything was only beginning and was very obscure.

4. There will be plenty of people standing by you. Also churchwise you are in a much stronger position for having obeyed and gone to South America the other time. What will come? The Holy Spirit will take care of that. But be careful of the way people will exploit it: this is no Sunday school picnic.

In short, Dan, if you think this is it, then go ahead. And let them heave you out. And don't worry about the consequences: but just watch yourself in the mushroom cloud that follows, be sure in all things you are really trying to do it in God's way as a real Jesuit (because sometimes the real ones are the ones on the outside of organizations). I'll certainly pray, God knows. I don't know how useful that'll be, better get someone who is slightly holy to do some praying for you if you want results maybe (but it isn't really like that, I guess).

. . . Keep chin up. Are they really threatening to throw you out or are they putting you in a position where you will have to put yourself in the wrong and then they will more easily be able to throw you out? To keep your own position strong maybe you should announce they have forbidden you to go to NV under pain of throwing you out . . . But this is a political interpretation and I am not smart. But you'd better be because this is an angle. Do you know a good canonist, just in case?

July 13, 1967

You will probably hear of this through the FOR [Fellowship of Reconciliation] but since people in France have been writing to me about it I had better write you. They—some Protestant pastors, Catholic priests and some of Lanza del Vasto's group, are planning an international, ecumenical seven-day fast in December and want some "American churchmen" to be there and join in. I'd go if I could, but obviously there is no hope. I presume you might be interested and would know who else to invite. The idea is for this to be a central and public group which could draw plenty of attention to the fast. Others could join in in various ways, and I guess I could try the fast here, without it being in any way public. I'd just go along with the big fast as best I could. I don't suppose total fast for seven days in a hermitage is the smartest thing in the world: easier to do it with a bunch of people around, but I could probably do it on liquids (bourbon excluded). Anyway, that is not the point. Are you interested in the one they are planning at Geneva?

Could you write, if you are, to Pasteur Jean Lasserre, 42 Cours Fr. Roosevelt, Lyon 6, France. And if you can think up other people who ought to go . . . I am sure the FOR will take care of it.

. . . I wrote a pamphlet on Camus's *Plague* for Seabury Press and thought I'd dedicate it to you, so here is a copy of it. I know you like the *Plague*. So do I . . .

In the fall of 1967 Berrigan was invited to become associate director of United Religious Work at Cornell University. He was asked to teach a seminar on nonviolence and religious traditions. He wrote asking Merton for help in planning this seminar.

September 16, 1967

Here is some stuff I dug out of the pile. Not much, if any, about non-violence but some on Zen and so on. I'll have the bookstores send along *Mystics and Zen Masters*. Not much specifically on non-violence there but one essay is kind of background for it and might be of use: "Pilgrimage to Crusade."

Zen was somewhat tied up with samurai fighting, but Suzuki in Zen and Jap culture has a good chapter on Zen swordsmanship in which there is no hate and no "violence." The swordsman is just so cool that the sword kills people all by itself. Hm! But anyway it should probably be taken into account in connection with non-violence. Zen was anyway not bloodthirsty and very economical, none of this overkill stuff, I think it could be called "defensive" and simply using the aggressor's aggression to destroy the aggressor. That's a point. Turning violence back on itself.

. . . I'm glad you're at Cornell. It's a good place. Stay away from Catlicks, they are poison.

Too bad about Hanoi but something better will turn up.

Pray for Ad Reinhardt, some fine guy he was. Found dead in his studio after heart failure. First of our immediate gang to go: I guess my whole bunch won't outlast sixty. The ones I've seen lately all look pretty wrecked and all have bad hearts. And I feel pretty moth-eaten myself, but I guess the woods will prove too healthy.

Come down this way when you can . . .

Dan's brother Philip had proposed the need for the peace movement to move in the direction of violence against "idolatrous things." This he and three other persons actually did, when on October 27, 1967, they poured blood into the files of the Selective Service offices at the United States Customs House in Baltimore. Several weeks before this, Dan had written to Merton asking for his thoughts on the issue.

October 10, 1967

Reaction to the airmail special about Phil and the group that wants to get violent. This will help me clarify my own ideas too. We are all in a position now where some kind of important choice of direction is called for. What I am going to put down now is just my own way as it more or less appears to me at the moment.

1. First to size up the situation as I see it—dimly and at a distance. Perhaps I'd better formulate it in questions rather than statements.

a. To what extent is the new revolutionism, centered mostly on black activism, simply irresponsible, capricious, idiotic, pointless, haphazard and inviting disaster? To what extent do these people realize they are so disoriented that at the moment all they can think of is systematic unreason and disaster—acceptable insofar as precipitated by themselves? And more acceptable if a bunch of docile whites come running behind, bleating friendship noises. And go over the cliff with them. Or even ahead of them.

b. A lot of talk about Che and Debray. I think that in Latin America there may be something real behind all this, but in the U.S.A. I think it sounds so far like just noise. Hence I wonder if it makes sense to treat the thing as a serious revolutionary option in the first place? In Latin America I think a priest and a Christian might have a serious question to face. I don't think it is like that here—I mean in choosing for the Molotov cocktails.

c. The obsession with being "with it" whatever "it" may turn out to be. It seems to me that the indifference with which the radicals and some liberals are now non-violent, now flower power, now burn-baby, all sweetness on Tuesday and all hell-fire on Wednesday, reflects sheer mindlessness and hopelessness. Can it be that this is the surest and most disturbing sign of pre-fascist mental chaos, the kind of thing that makes some kind of fascist totalism, police state, etc., *inevitable*? Is it even a kid reaction that unconsciously invites the support and security of a police state? Is radicalism *asking* to be put down? Looks like that to me. Then why get involved in that, especially as people are most certainly going to get killed. Needlessly, without meaning, and without message, in a way that will only confirm the squares in utter squareness. Is this a real view of it?

2. Should we then, CPF [Catholic Peace Fellowship] and Catholic left, etc., try to be less naïve, try to go it more on our own, have a more or less firm and consistent position, is our best contribution to the whole mess a kind of relative clarity and consistency and firmness that *stays with* a clearly recognizable Christian and Gospel position? Have we ever even begun to explore what real non-violence is about? Is this just the testing that is essential before we even get sorted out enough to *begin*? Are we now ready for a novitiate? In my opinion the answer is to close ranks with people like King—insofar as non-violent: I don't know what his politics are right now. To become recognizable as committed to very clear limits on the violence thing? At least to take up enough of a basic position to be able to go on from there to decide whether yes or no we can be violent "against property." That is outside the Gandhian thing right away. My opinion would be some of us ought to stay with Gandhi's end of it until we have at least gone deep into it and seen what was there (as King has). (As maybe the SNCC guys also have, I don't know. Here I talk and they were getting shot two and three years ago.)

Summarizing my feelings on this then:

a. Ethically and evangelically we are getting toward the place where we have to be able to define our limits. I don't say violence against property is off-limits. It certainly seems to me that killing people *is*. But if it comes to burning buildings, then people are going to be in danger and whoever is involved is going to be partly responsible for people getting destroyed even on his own side in a way that the non-violent resister would not be responsible. (They—fuzz—have no right to kill a non-violent person but they certainly think they have a right to kill a violent one.)

b. Politically: are we just getting involved in a fake revolution of badly mixed-up disaster inviting people who are willing to do anything absurd and irrational simply to mess things up, and to mess them up especially for the well-meaning "idealists" who want to run along proving that they are such real good hip people.

c. Psychologically: how nuts is the whole damn business?

In my opinion the job of the Christian is to try to give an example of sanity, independence, human integrity, good sense, as well as Christian love and wisdom, against all establishments and all mass movements and all current fashions which are merely mindless and hysterical. But of course are they? And do we get hung up in merely futile moral posturing? Well, somewhere we have to choose. The most popular and exciting thing at the moment is not necessarily the best choice.

I don't say any of this comes anywhere near applying to the situation Phil speaks of, I have no real idea whether that is sane or nutty: I am just talking in terms of the whole situation judged by the smell of the smog that reaches me down here.

Cornell sounds good. Keep in there slugging . . .

In November 1967 Berrigan wrote asking Merton to support a proposed cable to be sent to the Pope asking for a Vatican condemnation of the war in Vietnam. Further, he asked Merton to be one of a number of clergy of various religious faiths who would invite thousands of Catholic, Protestant, and Jewish young men to send them their draft cards at Christmas time.

November 27, 1967

. . . Here's about the two proposals. Inevitably, to me down here it looks more strange than to you who are in it. I do get the feeling that a great deal is popping and that the CPF is on the crest of a wave—and this is all good. It may really be a kind of kairos, a moment of breakthrough. Of this I am not so sure but I know I simply have no way of knowing.

The text of the proposed cable has not reached me yet. I'll keep any decision until I see it. Probably sign it, but the question arises: is this ambiguous? I mean I know how I feel about people who appeal to Church authority to condemn something. And the old Church/state thing. Still, it is probably a good idea nevertheless. Nothing is that clear these days anyhow. One must make do with a relatively light fog.

About being one of the receivers of draft cards. First, since I would not be able to be there with the others on that or any other occasion, it is rather futile. All I can see it would mean here would be more mail, a lot of which could get lost. But that is not the decisive point for me now. Here is a little background on present conditions here. The present Abbot is retiring. No idea who the next one will be, but I want to give him every possible chance to be different. In particular I want to see if he will not be a lot more open than this one about letting me get a little more freedom of movement, which I could certainly use to advantage.

Like I was invited to take part in a meeting with the Vietcong, by the American Friends Service Committee, which is the sort of thing I really ought to be doing. At the present moment, if I get involved in some public manifestation of something or other, it will unduly complicate matters and guarantee more years of doghouse, without any real need to do so. And with no particular advantage to anything or anyone. Thus at the moment I am planning to stay out of any public demonstrations and civil disobedience until I see if I can't perhaps move into a slightly wider area of action, so I will not take on the business of receiving draft cards.

. . . Trouble about the Abbot who is retiring here is that he will stay around and continue to influence things indirectly. He has a very snappy-looking hermitage going up on a distant hill. It is out in moonshine country, too. Place where the local boys have orgies, and you find all the bushes full of beer cans with bullet holes through them. Abbot won't be invited to these, of course, unless perhaps they take to cannibalism or something. Anything can happen. They might eat him. But the problems down in the monastery would still remain. Meanwhile I am bent on refusing if they elect me, which they almost certainly will not . . .

February 8, 1968

. . . The new Abbot [Dom Flavian Burns] is a real good man, perhaps the best we could expect in the circumstances . . .

As to getting out and around. [He] will certainly let me have any freedom of movement that is normally recognized in the Order. In other words he will not tighten the normal rules in order to keep me especially immobile and out of circulation. The old one of course did not even allow me the freedom of movement that most monks in most monasteries could expect. But as far as the Order goes, the normal freedom of movement is not all that much. In other words, I can hope to get to other monasteries and to participate in conferences of monks, etc. Perhaps also I may harvest a few secondary gains going and coming, be able to see some friends, etc. Now this is already a big step forward, and without pushing and shoving too much. I am sure I can and will get in circulation at least this much. That is what I hope to do in due time, when he gets settled. And of course the trips will remain rare and occasional. But he has assured me that when the occasion arises he will be favorable.

When it comes to appearing on campuses, Catholic or other, speaking at public conferences, and doing anything that happens outside a monastery, we have a different kettle of fish. The sentiment in the Order even now is heavily against, so that doing this would involve a major operation and would take me far beyond my Abbot . . . is something that would demand changes in the legislation of the outfit. Whether or not such changes ought to be made is of course a matter of reflection. And I guess they'll have to face that sooner or later.

Looking at the thing from my own viewpoint, and having given it some thought: if I had a choice and had to decide it myself, I would also be against any form of public appearance. It is not consistent with what my life has been and has become. I have become committed to this solitary pitch, and to start running round talking would only make it very ambiguous—besides really messing up what I am trying to do. I have enough trouble getting things done as it is. I mean work, etc., as well as my own job of figuring things out. I think it is necessary for me to stay out of the lecture circuit and campus appearances, much more some of the other things (N.Y. appearances, etc.) that would necessarily follow. I don't think I can do what God and the Gospel demand of me personally unless I maintain the special kind of conditions I have been chosen for, that have been wished on me, and that I myself have chosen and prefer . . .

As regards peace movements, etc.: my job continues to be putting it on paper as best I can, I think, and, by letter or otherwise, helping individual C.O.'s with advice. In this last connection I want to maintain a kind of clarity, focussed on the right and duty of a priest to give such advice even to people who "resist" the law, and that giving such advice does *not* constitute civil disobedience, but the ordinary job of any priest. It seems to me that this point is very important indeed and it may be in danger of getting lost. One of my own functions, as I see it, is to keep it from getting lost. That helping a man form his own conscience is a priest's duty, and how the man forms his conscience even if it is formed in a way that is socially unacceptable, does not alter the right and duty of the priest to help him follow his conscience. And that society has no business whatever interfering in this area. Which is why it must remain clearly a private and personal affair.

. . . Well, can't write more. The day I got your letter I heard you were going to NV to pick up prisoners, and that same day Malcolm Boyd appeared here by surprise. Are you back now? I hope and suppose you are.

Berrigan did go to Hanoi in February 1968 with Howard Zinn of Boston University to obtain the release of three prisoners of war.

March 18, 1968

Here's the little booklet on *The Plague* I told you about. No one deserves the dedication better than you. Even those who oppose you have to admit it.

I'll send along a copy of my new magazine *Monks Pond* some time soon in the hope you can send me a poem or above all a *fable* or two. Or just an outcry of some sort.

No more for the moment. Things may change here but very slowly, and day after day brings confirmation that I can't get involved in anything public outside of here (talks, etc.). As soon as the Abbot is convinced I know this, I may get a little freedom of movement. Well, I know it. Have been having a little trouble with the John Birch element on *this* campus (mostly our ex-Jeb, Fr. Raymond, who is threatening to have me burned). But nothing of any consequence . . .

A month later, on May 17, 1968, Daniel and Philip Berrigan and seven others broke into the Selective Service offices in the Knights of Columbus building in Catonsville, Maryland. They seized the 1-A files of potential draftees from several cabinets, carried them to the parking lot, and burned them in wire baskets with napalm made from instructions given in a military manual.

The nine were imprisoned, then released on bail. The trial was set for October 5, 1968. Phil Berrigan wrote to Merton—who was in Alaska at the time—asking him to be present as a witness at the trial.

To Philip Berrigan

September 30, 1968

Your letter finally caught up with me in Alaska, but I am moving on.

Impossible to get to trial. I am going to India in October and am busy raising money for it now. I wish you all luck.

Hope you enjoy your new Trappist vocation. But don't get too much of it. Enough is enough.

At the Catonsville trial (October 5–9) the nine defendants were found guilty of destruction of government property and interference with the Selective Service Act.

On November 27, 1968, Daniel Berrigan wrote to Merton in India saying that The New Yorker *was doing a profile of the Berrigan brothers and the writer wanted to complete the picture with the story of Merton's association with them. She would be willing to fly to India to interview him. Was he receptive to the idea? Merton received the letter, probably in Singapore. He wrote to Wilbur H. Ferry that he had no interest in giving such an interview. There probably would not have been time: the letter to Ferry was postmarked December 5, 1968, five days before Merton's death.*

To Sergius Bolshakoff

Sergius (Serge) Bolshakoff, a Russian Orthodox scholar, was born in St. Petersburg in 1901. His early training was as a civil engineer. Later he studied economics and sociology. Upon receiving a doctorate in philosophy at Christ Church, Oxford, he became involved in the active promotion of Christian unity. He traveled a great deal, visiting monasteries, staying at times with the Cowley Fathers in Oxford, going to Rome and to Greece to contact ecclesiastics in high places in both the Roman Catholic and the Orthodox Church. He was personally acquainted with John XXIII, Patriarch Athenagoras, Archbishop Temple of Canterbury. He was also on friendly terms with Dom Gabriel Sortais, Abbot General of the Cistercians.

He has written a number of books and articles on orthodoxy and on mystics of the Christian East. In 1962 he published I Mistici Russi, *an Italian translation of a book he had originally written in English. Dr. Bolshakoff sent the original English manuscript (written in longhand by Bolshakoff) to Merton, asking if he would correct the English and send it to a publisher. The book was not published in English till 1976, when it was put out by Cistercian Publications.*

December 28, 1962

Thanks for your two kind letters. I was interested to hear of your visit to the monks at Tolleshunt [see letter to Archimandrite Sophrony]. I hope you will remember me to them and ask them to pray for me. I think of them often and believe that they will do a great work for the glory of God . . .

My work with your *Russian Mystics* proceeds slowly as there are many other duties to be performed. I am now in the last part, where the pages are smaller and the writing is more concentrated: hence it is harder to make corrections. I am happy that the whole typescript will be gone over carefully. I am afraid that in many cases where I was trying to make the text more easily readable, I may have altered the sense. This will have to be carefully checked. Then of course someone well versed in Oriental theology will also have to correct more carefully the passages which I have left to a great extent untouched, on prayer, etc.

The first half of the ms. is already in the hands of the Benedictine monks at Collegeville, who are typing it. I will send the rest along in a few weeks. Meanwhile I am giving my novices a few classes on Russian mysticism, using notes drawn from your ms. as well as from Fedotov and other sources. I think St. Seraphim is still my greatest favorite, but now I am glad to make the acquaintance of the great Startzi of Optina. I am much impressed with them, as of course I expected to be after reading *The Brothers Karamazov*. You should do an anthology of the writings of Optina.

Our library has a rather small budget for periodicals and I was not able to get your newsletter included in the subscriptions: however, I did ask Fr. Abbot if, on this one occasion, he would consent to send you a small present on behalf of the Abbey, as a contribution toward your expenses in the coming year. I enclose it herewith. I hope that this once you will do us the honor of accepting.

I am deeply grieved and worried at the serious illness of Pope John

. . . He has done a great and providential work at the Council and is a very great Pope, one whom I personally love and revere as a true Father, and indeed I may say there is no man on earth for whom I have a deeper veneration, not only because of his office but also because of his personal qualities. I hope that if you chance to write to him or to see him you will tell him this on my part and express to him my most devoted filial affection, asking his blessing for me.

Let us then, my good friend, proceed in faith, trusting in the unfailing help of God our Father and in the intercession of so great a "cloud of witnesses," including the great monks and contemplatives of Russia . . .

January 29, 1963

You will be glad to hear that I have finished all the work on the revision of your manuscript and it is now being typed. The Benedictines at Collegeville expect it to be finished within a month. They ask me where to send it, for further reading and correction? You will want to have the copy sent to you, no doubt, and then you will pass it on to someone, perhaps at Chevetogne, who can bring everything to perfection in what regards Oriental theology. Will you write to them at Collegeville and inform them of your wishes? . . .

I will write the preface and perhaps an article based on the book, when I have the typescript in my hands. I have got a very good picture of Russian mysticism from your fine work. I am especially glad to learn about Theophane the Recluse, a magnificent figure, and his spirituality appeals to me very much indeed . . . These nineteenth-century mystics appeal to me greatly and I am indebted to you for bringing me close to them. I have spoken to my novices about them on many occasions . . .

Thank you very much indeed for the kindness which prompts you to send your ms. on Staretz Alexander of Gethsemani.* I shall receive it with joy and gratitude, and read it avidly. Your thought of a *jumellage* between Gethsemani (here) and Zagorsk is certainly a great inspiration. What would be a tactful way of going about it? I spoke to our Father Abbot about this and he is pleased with the idea. Of course it must be discreet and there must not be any "American publicity" . . .

November 11, 1963

. . . I wonder how your book is coming along. I hear word occasionally from St. John's and they tell me it has been for some time at Chevetogne. I hope that Dom Theodore is doing a good job of revision, because mine

---

* *Bolshakoff had sent Merton a French manuscript he had written on Staretz Alexander of the Russian* skete *of Gethsemani. This skete is no longer in existence, but it had been a dependency of the great Russian monastery of Zagorsk. Bolshakoff suggested the possibility of a formal union of prayers* (jumellage) *between the Abbey of Gethsemani and the Zagorsk monastery.*

was certainly inadequate. When I see the final copy that is going to the printer, I will write my preface. It is a very worthwhile book, and I look forward to seeing it in print.

It was of course a joy to learn that Russian observers were at the Council. This is a great step forward. I imagine also that the clarification of the "collegiality of bishops" was a welcome one. I am very drawn to the Russian idea of *sobornost* [the doctrine of the Spirit acting and leading the whole Church into the truth] which seems to me to be essential to the notion of the Church, in some form or other. I do not know how this can be gainsaid. Collegiality is a step in that direction.

I was grateful to God for the test ban. As a matter of fact a group of professors in Massachusetts, who have an organization working for peace, gave me a peace prize this year, which was encouraging, though I am not able to continue writing in favor of peace . . . I shall send you a magazine with an article of mine on the terrible race question in the U.S., which is closely connected with the problem of peace. Even though the test-ban treaty is signed, there is still not complete security by any means. There is a terrible quality of restlessness, suspicion and nervousness about the mind of this nation; and this, coupled with enormous destructive power, is not something that one can accept peacefully. It does not give complete confidence for the future. Hence the need for earnest prayer, in the monasteries of both our countries. I do not know how the idea of *jumellage* developed, but it would certainly be a good thing to have monks on both sides explicitly united in a common prayer for peace . . .

October 28, 1964

Thank you for your recent letter, as usual full of interesting news of your amazing activities and visits to many monasteries. I am always glad to hear of your achievements and travels. May God bless your good initiatives.

I am very sorry that I have not written for some time. Is it really as long as that? I thought I had certainly written in the spring. Perhaps some letter or other of mine has been lost. This often happens. But in any case I am sorry. The last time you wrote about your book, I wrote at once to Fr. Colman Barry but never received any kind of reply. I do not know what the trouble is. I know he feels that the manuscript needs more revision from the point of view of English style, but I thought it had been arranged that a monk at St. John's would take care of this. I have not heard whether this was ever undertaken. That is probably what is holding the book up. The delay is certainly very regrettable.

The Council progresses, and much that is heartening has taken place. I am hoping that the statement on world peace will be retained in its strength and even strengthened. It seems quite excellent, at least for a start. It is a timely document, Schema 13, and the one which I personally find most interesting and important, though it has less theological impact than the decisions on collegiality and on revelation.

We live in difficult times, but we are in the hands of a merciful and wise Father. He guides our destinies, He brings salutary medicine for our sins. The world faces much suffering. May we all be faithful to His grace . . .

December 13, 1964

As Christmas approaches once again, I want to send you my best wishes and a token of our friendship here in the monastery. Fr. Abbot has graciously consented to let me give you this small token in our name, hoping that it will contribute a little to your expenses as you go about doing good and spreading the message of unity and peace.

I still have no further news of the translation of *Russian Mystics*, which remains in the hands of the monks of St. John's. It ought surely to have been in print by now. I do not know what is the matter.

. . . We have often spoken, you and I, of the possibility of spiritual *jumellage* between Gethsemani and a Russian monastery. As time goes on, and as the situation in Russia remains always uncertain, I think it would probably be most prudent to forget this idea, which might in the long run mean only trouble for the Russian monks who became involved in it. One can quietly and unofficially pray for one's brethren without any need for a formal organization of anything, and this is what I do . . .

June 9, 1965

. . . I am in perfect agreement with your hesitations in approving the new trends on the part of some monks toward activism. I readily grant that the motives are good, and that the desire to help the Church is most laudable. But it seems to me that whatever may be the value of the means chosen, they are foreign to monasticism. Hence it seems to me that if Trappists want to go and live as Little Brothers, let them by all means leave the monastic Order and live as Little Brothers. But it is a confusion to assert that this is a new form of monastic life. On the contrary, what I have heard about the experiments in trying to combine a contemplative life on the Trappist pattern with factory work strikes me as completely inauthentic and ambiguous. It is neither honest factory work nor serious contemplative solitude. It is simply a naïve and well-meant game without too much relation to the realities of the age or the exigencies of the monastic vocation. It seems to me that if we want to take our true place in our time then we must recognize that our place is that of *monks*. And the more perfectly we try to live in the monastic tradition of simplicity, solitude, prayer, silence, etc., the better we will justify our existence in the world, though there is no need for us even to think of "justifying ourselves." God is our only justification . . .

For a very long time I have heard absolutely nothing from Fr. Colman Barry about anything, including your book . . . I do not know if he has given up the idea of publishing your book, which still, according to the publisher, requires some revision as regards style. I am very sorry that this has not made better progress.

December 8, 1965

First of all I am taking this occasion to send you a Christmas present from our community. I hope perhaps this will enable you to help defray some of the expenses of your operation, or whatever else you may need . . .

At the present time I am still striving to consolidate, so to speak, my position in solitude. That is to say, while everything goes well in the hermitage I still have to break off contacts with some rather active groups in the world which are still using my name. In so doing, they give the impression that I am actively involved in their projects and controversies and this causes repercussions for me here. This is particularly true in the case of the peace movement. It is true that I regard the Vietnam war as highly dubious morally and something that ought to be protested against, but it is not for me to involve myself any more in political forms of protest, especially since I cannot keep up with the news and do not attempt to. But they keep involving me without my own initiative or consent. This is being taken care of, I think. You are perfectly right that I have no further need to be writing on these topics that have a political aspect. Too many people think that the Christian conscience in social affairs needs to be expressing itself by all kinds of active demonstrations, and an infinite number of petitions and declarations. All of this is perhaps all right for those who are in the thick of such activity, though I question whether it has any real value. But for me it has and can have no value whatever.

I suppose that it will take a little time for this appearance of "engagement" in such movements to fade away. But I am at peace in the forest here in any case, and I see more and more that there is but one thing necessary. The exterior silence of the forest makes interior silence at once imperative and easy . . .

April 26, 1968

I am afraid I owe you a deep apology: I have not been able to get your Easter letter to the Sobesedniks [people bonded together by prayer and consultation with one another on matters of the spiritual life] mimeographed. I am terribly sorry for this, but there has been a considerable change in the situation here. First of all, with the new liturgy (we have a completely new experimental English liturgy in the monastery) there have been innumerable new texts and the work of putting these out has absorbed all those who were originally doing this kind of thing here. Thus my own material is no longer able to be mimeographed here. It just happened that a friend elsewhere ran off my Easter circular letter for me. Hence I cannot rely on the services of my brethren to put out even my own material.

As a result of all this extra work, the young monk who fell heir to the mimeograph machine has been overburdened and has finally asked to be relieved of the job. Others will doubtless carry on with the work that is to be done, but I have decided that I cannot impose on them, and will leave them to do the liturgical and other community work. The new Fr. Abbot is intent on reducing the activity in the community and thus giving the monks more taste for a deeper contemplative life. I know you will sympathize with this. All of us here are hoping to cut down on extra activity. I myself will write less. It is of course already necessary for me to cut down on correspondence. Hence, as you can deduce, it will no longer be possible for us to send out your letters. I am sorry to disappoint you in this, but I know you will understand. I am returning your copy of the letter, in case you wish to modify it and have it run off by someone else as a Pentecost letter perhaps.

The situation in this country grows darker and more tragic, so that I think even the most insensitive must begin to realize that there is something radically wrong. What is wrong is the indifference to God and to authentic religious and moral values, even among those who call them-selves Christians—who are sometimes the worst in regard to things like racism, injustice, intolerance, hatred. At no time was it more evident that prayer and repentance were necessary here. Yet the Catholics are, some of them, going off on a tangent of activism and exterior worldliness—and basic indifference to deep religious values—in the name of progress.

Never was a real renewal of the contemplative and monastic life more necessary. In union of faith and charity, in Christ Jesus.

To Cameron Borton

When he wrote to Thomas Merton on May 12, 1968, Cameron Borton was pastor of a Congregational Church in Winchendon, Massachusetts. He had read a num-ber of Merton's books and also St. John of the Cross. He was drawn toward St. John of the Cross, yet at the same time repelled by his seeming harshness and the almost superhuman demands that his spirituality seems to call for. Can the teaching of John of the Cross have any meaning for people who do not live the monastic life and especially for people who are married and raising a family? Did John of the Cross ever laugh?

May 23, 1968

Thanks for the confidence you show in me, in presenting your questions about John of the Cross. I cannot take them up in detail, but I will enclose a mimeographed piece in which I refer to him, and this may be of some use.

In general, I would say this: John of the Cross, like some of the Asian mystics, takes a standpoint that is so to speak on the "other side" of attainment. He speaks from the fullness of fulfillment, and from the experience of the completely *positive* underside of what appears to be a merely negative cloud of darkness to us. It is from this positive experience of the Christian truth that he who loses his life for Christ saves it, that John of the Cross can be so apparently ruthless about the business of losing it. This of course appalls us since we see nothing but the losing, and don't experience the gain.

Actually, he was not a forbidding person at all. He was very kind and simpatico, and he was in fact in strong reaction against a much more fanatical group in his own reform who wanted extreme asceticism. Note that he never advocated this kind of extremism: only a total interior detachment—which he thought would liberate and release our affectivity to love and enjoy everything, but in God.

On the other hand, I agree that the social context of Spain in his time cannot help but make him look a bit grim. It is perhaps a good thing for us to counterbalance him with someone as human as Bonhoeffer or with the warmth of Buber's Hasidism.

To Jeanne Burdick

Jeanne Burdick has worked for over twenty years in communications rehabilitation in a number of institutions in Kansas. She has also been involved in the teaching of theology and has written poetry and stories. She has a B.A. in religion from Andrews University (Michigan), an M.A. in speech pathology from the University of Southern California, an M.A. in spirituality from Creighton University, and a Ph.D. from Kansas City University in administration. Her contact with Merton began with her reading of The Seven Storey Mountain. *Merton became a kind of spiritual director for her by mail, though only the two letters that follow are available.*

[*Cold War Letter 15*]

December 26, 1961

For several weeks I have wanted to find an opportunity to answer your letter with its one very important question. For when such a question is asked, I am of course obliged to answer, if I can. I know you will understand that it is not easy to find time or words for such a thing.

Christmas is a good time, however. We then write letters to our friends and family, and "the disinterested love of God" does make itself more real than usual. Though the Christmas cards have done a pretty good job of concealing it.

What I said in *The Seven Storey Mountain* about the disinterested love of God represented my interest, at that time, in the medieval Platonic tradition, running through St. Augustine and Duns Scotus, and including the Cistercian monks of my own Order. A monastery is supposed to be a "school of charity" (i.e., disinterested love). A school of *agape* rather than *eros*. Disinterested love is also called the "love of friendship," that is to say a love which rests in the good of the beloved, not in one's own interest or satisfaction, not in one's own pleasure. A love which does not exploit, manipulate, even by "serving," but which simply "loves." A love which, in the words of St. Bernard, simply "loves because it loves" and for no other reason or purpose, and is therefore perfectly free. This is a spiritual ideal which also had secular counterparts in the courtly love of the Provençal poets, and there is a whole interesting literary tradition, which finally gets lost in the sand.

The ideal of disinterested love is one that in one form or other crops up in all mystical religion. It is, in a very intellectual form, found in the offprint on Zen which I sent you. It is found in a wonderfully rich and charming human expression in the mysticism of the Hasidim, Jewish tzaddiks of Poland and Central Europe (read Buber).

The way I would express it now is in purely religious and symbolic terms. That we should "love God" not merely to convince ourselves that we are good people, or to get a warm glow of peace, or to fit in with an approving group, or to get rid of anxiety, but to throw all that to the winds, and anxiety or not, even though we realize the utter depth of our inadequacy, to realize that this simply does not matter in the "eyes of God" for, as we are, with our misfortunes and needs, "we are His joy" and He delights to be loved by us with perfect confidence in Him because He is love itself. This is of course not capable of being put in scientific language, it is religious symbol. But if you will be patient with it, and stay with it, I think you will find it is the most fundamental symbol and the deepest truth: at least I am trying to express that which is deepest and most essential. My own symbol may be very poor. But that is the way I would put it. It is not that we have to sweat and groan to placate an austere Father God in our own imagination, but rather to realize, with liberation and joy, that *He is not that at all*. That in fact He is none of our idols, none of our figments, nothing that we can imagine anyway, but that He is Love Itself. And if we realize this and love Him simply and purely in order to "please Him," we become as it were His "crown" and His "delight" and life itself is transformed in this light which is disinterested love.

Freud did not think much of a mysticism which was described as "an oceanic feeling" and I think in a way he was rather right in his suspicion of it, though he was a great old puritan that man! Oceanic feeling is not something that has to be rejected just because it might suggest a danger of narcissism. But pure love, disinterested love, is far beyond the reach of narcissism and I think even old Freud would have caught on that this was an equivalent of mature and oblative love in the ordinary psychophysical sphere.

I hope these few words from me will be of some help. The rest may be found perhaps in the offprint. Dr. Suzuki is an interesting and splendid mind, and a great Buddhist. And I enjoyed trying to keep up with his Zen, which after all does have some parallel in the Western tradition. Disinterested love opens a way to the understanding of both.

June 11, 1962

I was happy and surprised to get your good letter, and very glad for you. Certainly the dimensions that faith gives to life are absolutely necessary for us to find our true selves and lose our false selves. I am glad that light and liberation have come into your life, with the Holy Spirit. Do not be surprised however if he also sometimes brings darkness and crisis. Crisis is both necessary and fruitful and the religious view of life makes crisis more fruitful, and truly so.

The situation in our time is baffling and when one comes into the Church at a time like this one can definitely have the feeling that one is scrambling up the gangplank into the ark. And sometimes one can also be tempted to wonder if the ark itself is going to leak or even founder. But God is the one to worry about that.

If you come into the Church you come with work to do, and you should have a sense that the Catholic laity are an important, very important part of the people of God. The Church is not just an institution for the benefit of priests and nuns, with lay people around to fill in the background. The coming Council may, we hope, give light and direction on these things.

I can at least, give you a list of names of authors you ought to keep in touch with: Guardini, De Lubac, Danielou, Régamey, and of course the Maritains, Gilson, and others like Congar and Bouyer. Then there are magazines you should know about, like *Commonweal* and *Jubilee*, also *Cross Currents*. With these windows in the ark I think you should be able to understand both the ark and the storm better.

In any case, I send you all my blessings and I join you in your happiness. I am glad to have had some small part in God's work for you.

To Dom Helder Camara

Dom Helder Camara was ordained a priest in 1931, and in 1952 was appointed Auxiliary Bishop of Rio de Janeiro. It was as Auxiliary Bishop of Rio that he attended the Second Vatican Council. Before the Council sessions were over, he was made archbishop of one of the poorest and least developed regions of Brazil— the archdiocese of Olinda and Recife in the northeast of the country. While in Rome he met Jean and Hildegard Goss-Mayr, who later came to work with him at Recife in training people in the strategy of non-violence. (See the letters to the Goss-Mayrs.) Dom Helder Camara, a bishop of the poor and the marginalized, believes that unjust and inhuman structures, which deprive people of the ability to produce for themselves and paralyze their freedom of decision and action, are caused by human selfishness and can be transformed only by love and truth and human determination acting in a non-violent way. Revered by some as a saint and despised by others as a radical, he was concerned not only to relieve poverty but also to eliminate its causes. The reactions to him are perhaps best summed up in his own words: "When I give food to the poor, I am called a saint; but when I ask, 'Why is it that the poor do not have food?' then I am called a communist." The following letter, written in French, was translated by the editor.

April 8, 1967

I am very moved by your gracious words and I thank you very much for them. I am even more grateful to you since, as you can imagine, I am never sure of being understood either by the right or by the left. Like Camus, whom I greatly admire, I take a stand that is more or less my own and I end up getting on everybody's nerves. Which doesn't matter, provided I am faithful. But am I faithful? At any rate your words are very reassuring. Thank you.

Thank you too for your lectures at Cornell and Princeton. They are much needed. I am very much afraid that our bishops here in the United States are dominated by too deep a respect for our government and for our "establishment" in which as a matter of fact they play a significant part. The inevitable is going to happen and it will be terrifying, for surely judgment will come and it will be painful for the Church.

As for Maritain's book [*Le Paysan de la Garonne*, 1966], yes, I will speak to him about it. His criticism bears, above all, I believe, on philosophy not on politics, since he continues to remain in agreement with his radical friends, such as Saul Alinsky. Concerning Cardinal Roy [Archbishop of Quebec City], I am not as well informed as you think, since I do not know what it is about. But I did write to Dorothy Dohen, because her book has been criticized unfavorably by a writer who is nevertheless himself a liberal.

The conference on *Pacem in Terris* [in Geneva, Switzerland]—well,

I have been invited [see letters to Wilbur H. Ferry], but it is impossible to obtain permission from my Father Abbot for this kind of travel or, to put it bluntly, for any kind of travel. I have received a very interesting invitation from a Muslim master [A. Reza Arasteh] to come to meet with his students [in Bethesda, Maryland] and speak to them, which would be quite a novelty! But I am not allowed to do such things, not even "incognito," not even with the utmost secrecy. And of course *a fortiori* I am not allowed to attend conferences, though actually I am afraid that if I did go I would be letting people see me as the jackass I really am. In any case, if Church authority should ever ask me to go some place, I will go. Especially if it is in Asia or Africa or Latin America. I will tell you more about it another time perhaps . . .

To Amiya Chakravarty

Dr. Amiya Chakravarty, Indian poet, philosopher, and world scholar, was born in Serampore, West Bengal, India, on April 10, 1901. After studies at the University of Patna, India, he earned a Ph.D. at Oxford in 1936. In the United States he has taught at Boston University, Smith College, and the State University of New York at New Paltz. It was while he was at Smith College that he was in touch with Thomas Merton.

Dr. Chakravarty served as advisor to the Indian delegation at the United Nations in 1952 and was for several years a delegate to UNESCO. As a young man he was literary secretary to the Indian poet Dr. Rabindranath Tagore, whose works he anthologized in 1961 in the Tagore Reader. *He marched in peace demonstrations with Gandhi and knew and admired Gandhi's successor, Jawaharlal Nehru. He visited Albert Schweitzer in Africa, and in 1959 traveled to Moscow to see Boris Pasternak. During his residence as a fellow at the Institute for Advanced Studies at Princeton, he knew Albert Einstein, whom he came to admire not only for his scientific genius but for his humanitarian concerns.*

The correspondence was initiated by a letter of September 28, 1966, in which Dr. Chakravarty says that he is taking the liberty of sending two copies of Raids on the Unspeakable, *which he asks Merton to inscribe, with a blessing, for two Smith students: Gabriel Maria Muncker (from Germany) and Sally Conley (of Pittsburgh). A month later he writes that only one of the books had arrived.*

November 4, 1966

Many thanks for your letter. I sent the book off in the special delivery envelope: unfortunately the other one must have been lost somewhere. The mail gets very mixed up around here, especially as we do not go direct to the post office ourselves. I will meanwhile look forward to hearing if and when you may be coming in December and will make arrangements accordingly. The Gandhi piece is part of a small book which I am sending you. Thanks for expressing an interest in it, and my most cordial good wishes.

Dr. Chakravarty visited Merton on December 18, 1966, at Gethsemani. He had requested the meeting for personal reasons.

January 10, 1967

I am very grateful for your kind letter and for the other package of books. I am especially glad to have the ones on India, and I am bent on continuing to read about Hindu thought and deepening my appreciation of it. I am particularly glad to have your *Tagore Reader*, which seems to me to be much better than another collection of his that I have.

Thanks above all for Loren Eiseley. It is splendid to have a scientist whose wavelength I can get on. It turns out of course that in addition to science he has also wisdom. I think there are probably quite a few like that around and they are really worth listening to . . .

Your good news is comforting. I shall continue to pray for your good friends, and it is always good to have someone like yourself come here and really appreciate what the place is for. It reminds us what we are here for too. So please be sure that you are always welcome.

In January, Dr. Chakravarty requested Merton to write a preface for a "sensitive and original paper on Marcel and Buddhism" written by Sally Donnelly (née Conley). The article, "Marcel and Buddha: A Metaphysics of Enlightenment," with a preface by Thomas Merton, was published in the Journal of Religious Thought, *Howard University, Vol. 24, no. 1, 1967–68. Merton's preface, under the title "Nirvana," was also published in* Zen and the Birds of Appetite. *Dr. Chakravarty also wrote that the Smith students would hold a "Merton Evening" at the college in March.*

January 21, 1967

. . . I have written a preface for Sally's essay on Marcel and Buddha because I think that in the past I had more or less committed myself to do this. Unfortunately the typist has rather massacred it. But I think it is all right in the main. I have felt it worthwhile to expand a little on some points. I hope there will be no serious objections.

. . . Thanks for letting me know about the discussion at Smith. I feel honored—and also I am not humble enough to take these things gracefully and therefore I am also a little confused. It is perhaps not necessary to do so, but I would like to say that I hope it does not take on the aspect of a personality cult. I think the girls at Smith are wise enough to avoid that. Besides, I think I have always been frank enough about my limitations for people to be fully aware of them. So, apart from that, I am happy with the idea, and it is to me a way of being in contact with others like myself, with kindred interests and concerns, people who look for something more in life than plenty of food, comfort, amusement and money. In fact I suppose that some of them feel as I do that American life can at times take on the aspect of an appalling wilderness. I am certainly not one of those who, on supposedly "Christian" motives, preach submission to this state of affairs. What does matter, however, is not just protest and discontent, but the love which is beyond all that. May that love grow in all of us. It is the one thing necessary. Give them, then, my love.

Chakravarty suggested offering to New Directions a book that would include Sally Donnelly's article and Merton's preface, together with an address of his own on Pacem in Terris.

February 15, 1967

. . . I have written to J. Laughlin, as you suggested. Publishing gets to be more and more difficult and he will probably be anxious for this to be a coherent and unified book rather than just a collection of pieces "thrown together" at random. That is the only problem I see. I think that there will be some editorial questions and we will have to proceed with some care. If the book does indeed correspond to the title, then I think we will have no problem eventually. I will soon have another paper that might well fit into it, on "The New Christian Consciousness," the first draft of which is done, and which I hope to correct and enlarge if we eventually see it will fit into the book. In any case, I am sure J. will be interested.

Thanks too for your piece on Buddhism and the Vietnam war. I could wish that Cardinal Spellman had not so far lost all moral sense as to be blind to these obvious facts. We must frankly admit that one of the great problems of the Church today is that so many of those in power are simply blinded by their power, think themselves in all things infallible, and never listen to any view that does not coincide with their own. This is a disastrous situation, really. Above all, disastrous for the Church which they think they are "defending" . . .

March 27, 1967

Thanks for your letter of the 9th and the enclosure from J. Laughlin. About your proposed book: I do not know if Naomi Burton has been in touch with you about it yet, but she generally tries to restrain me from being involved in too many projects. I assured her that I was not actually collaborating with you in the sense of writing a book together with you. At the same time too she wants to make sure that too many books do not appear with me apparently as author or co-author, apart from the ones that regularly appear with Doubleday or New Directions. This will let you know what her attitude will be with regard to my relation with your book. It will have to be clearly a book of *yours* with a paper contributed by me and Sally's contribution . . .

I hope the [Merton] session at Smith on March 14th was a good one.

Things are very much like summer down here now, but no doubt we will have cold weather again. Things are rather busy at the moment. I have a full quota of visitors coming and will be glad after that to get back to a quieter and more normal life when I can get some work done.

On March 29 Chakravarty wrote: "We had the great evening. It began late in the afternoon, but the students and faculty carried on till past dinnertime. We were immersed in the silence and eloquence of your thoughts and writings . . . The young scholars here realize that the absolute rootedness of your faith makes you free to understand other faiths . . . Your books have the rock-like inner strength which sustains the Abbey of Gethsemani, which can challenge violence and untruth wherever they may appear."

April 13, 1967

I have put off answering until a moment of quiet, an afternoon that is almost as hot as summer. And I am answering more than your letter describing how it was when you all talked and read about the monastery and about some of my ideas. I was so moved by the two very understanding letters—from Miss Eck and Mrs. Wilson. And of course by yours too.

For a writer there is surely not much that can be more rewarding than the fact of being really read and understood and appreciated. After all, the great thing in life is to share the best one has, no matter how poor it may be. The sharing gives it value. Often when I reread things I have written I find them so bad that I am irritated with myself: of course this is only vanity. But once I realize that they have meant something to someone they acquire something of the other person's value and meaning. What you read and liked of mine I shall like better now because you have all enjoyed them: I will like them because of all of you. I will like them because they are more yours than mine.

It is not easy to try to say what I know I cannot say. I do really have the feeling that you have all understood and shared quite perfectly. That you have seen something that I see to be most precious—and most available too. The reality that is present to us and in us: call it Being, call it Atman, call it Pneuma . . . or Silence. And the simple fact that by being attentive, by learning to listen (or recovering the natural capacity to listen which cannot be learned any more than breathing), we can find ourself engulfed in such happiness that it cannot be explained: the happiness of being at one with everything in that hidden ground of Love for which there can be no explanations.

I suppose what makes me most glad is that we all recognize each other in this metaphysical space of silence and happiness, and get some sense, for a moment, that we are full of paradise without knowing it . . .

I am sending along a poem ["A Round and a Hope for Smithgirls"]. It is not about this exactly, but it is somewhat along the same lines. But the poem was written before I got the letters and it supposes much younger and more confused people.

Janice Wilson mentioned Ecclesiastes: and of course this is one of the books of the Old Testament I like best. It is in some places almost Taoist. I lectured to the monks about this a long time ago and lost the notes or I would send them.

Well, this is an attempt at answering all of you and saying that I am so happy that you enjoyed reading things I had written. May we all grow in grace and peace, and not neglect the silence that is printed in the center of our being. It will not fail us. It is more than silence. Jesus spoke of the spring of living water, you remember . . .

April 25, 1967

. . . I feel most fortunate, to have been able to join with Sally Donnelly in her study . . .

I am grateful to you for bringing me in contact with so many new friends at Smith. I am touched by their response and feel very close to them and grateful to them. Living alone in the woods, I am more appreciative of friendship than ever before. The least I can do is sign a few cards, though that seems very little. I will also look around and see if there is something else I might share. I have a new essay they might enjoy.

As to the poem, it was rather inadequate, as it had in mind people less mature, but still no matter how mature we are we need to know that we are not as helpless as we may sometimes feel. I very much appreciated Lindsay Jones's words on silence. I read them several times, and thank her for them.

I enclose a snapshot of myself which was taken by a friend recently. The main purpose of this is to dispel any illusion that I am an ascetic and unearthly being and to show that I am a very ordinary Kentucky farm type. I am rather afraid you have created an impression that I am half angelic or something. I cannot think of anything they need to send me, or anything that I myself need, though I would really appreciate seeing some photos of them, to know what they look like. That is if they have any snapshots lying around. I am human enough to want to see the people I have come to know through you . . . Also I'd enjoy having a couple of copies of the campus paper that reprinted the poem.

. . . I have not seen any papers lately, but the serious escalation in Vietnam and the fact that an American plane was shot down by Chinese have got through to me. This looks bad indeed. I am very much afraid that the protests in this country have only hardened the people in Washington who want the war to go on and want it to be serious enough so that they can really clamp down on any form of dissent. Hence another reason for them wanting to get involved with China. But if they do, they will give us all reason for great regret for a long time to come. I hope the worst can still be avoided. Let us do what we can, anyway.

May 25, 1967

After I had mailed my note to you the other day, your letter arrived with the photos and the enclosed letter of Janice Wilson . . . The photos were, as I expected, of people who are all very alert and alive, and I am happy to feel that somehow a bond of friendship will continue to unite us all, even though they may scatter to the four winds. Please assure them that they are always welcome to turn this way if there is ever anything I can do for them . . .

Thanks for all you have done in this regard. I hope your future work will be as fruitful and half as pleasant as your year at Smith seems to have been.

I have not had much news of the Arab–Israel crisis in the last couple of days, but it is not comforting because these are people who seem to be more willing to fight than to bluff, and a war there could be a big and dangerous step toward the world war that always looms over us. If I thought that only human efforts could preserve us from war I would not have much hope: fortunately, there is always the Power that is too easily forgotten. But in the end, the willfulness and stupidity of men can elect to go very far . . .

I wish you a fruitful Asian trip. I cannot think of anything to ask you, specifically I know that if you run across something new that I should know, you will feel free to send a clipping or something on the chance that it may reach me. The chances are generally fair. I would certainly appreciate information on good new books about Asian traditions in contemplation and philosophy.

August 21, 1967

I just got your card of the Zen monk and the sand garden. Very tranquil and pleasing. You mention having written a letter from Kamakura. This, alas, I did not get. But often items of my mail never reach me, though I think most of them do. I am sorry to have missed that one. I was glad to hear you mention Miss Okamura. Is she still at Dr. Suzuki's old place? Are they publishing any of his unpublished papers? I hope we will have some more of his work to read.

The offprints of Sally's fine article reached me, and I am very grateful. Also I was happy to get your various cards from the Pacific, and have vicariously enjoyed your voyage, while remaining in the peace of my own woods here . . .

Will this reach you in Saigon? I don't know. In any case I am sure it will be forwarded somewhere. Meanwhile we continue to pray for peace and for an end to the gigantic and costly misunderstanding that is becoming more and more involved in Vietnam . . .

October 11, 1967

Thanks for your letter: I am glad to know you are settled in America again, and now I will know where to write to you, though as you know I am not a very reliable correspondent.

I think that in the end I did get all your cards, some of them very entrancing, from the South Pacific, Japan, and SE Asia. One of the most beautiful of all was the card of the Seine at Paris, most precious because of the words and signature of Gabriel Marcel. I am most grateful. Actually, I have never written any articles explicitly about Gabriel Marcel, though I have referred to him here and there in passing. I do not know exactly what to send him. I could at any rate send him a copy of *Conjectures*. I believe he is referred to there a time or two . . .

Of course I was interested and gratified to know from you that Dr. Radhakrishnan knew and liked my work. It is always a joy to me to feel that my writings have made friends for me in Asia. More and more I feel that Asia is in so many ways more congenial to me than the West. I am happy that the first offer for a translation of *Mystics and Zen Masters* has come from Japan. The Japanese edition will concentrate on Asian essays, plus one or two others that were not in the book. Dr. Wu's book on Zen, meanwhile, is appearing in Taiwan. He himself is in this country now. You might perhaps run into him, as he is in New Jersey . . .

March 6, 1968

Yesterday I was reading in the *Forum* of the ICIS both your note on Iqbal and Diana Eck's marvelous article on Krishnamurti. The latter was really a most unusual article and I am glad you saw that it got published. It was a pleasure to read both these items. Where is Diana Eck now?

As you will see, I am editing a magazine myself [*Monks Pond*]. It is only temporary, mostly literary, but I am anxious to get good Asian religious texts. When you see it, perhaps you might get an idea of something that would belong in those pages. I would very much value any suggestion—something of yours, something of Diana's, some Indian text, the only restriction being that if it is prose it can't be too long. I don't have much space.

It is Lent, and at moments appears to want to be spring. But it has been a hard winter and I don't believe too easily that spring is here yet. Toward the end of the year I hope to bring out a little book of essays mostly about Zen [*Zen and the Birds of Appetite*]. I hope to make use of the foreword I wrote for Sally Donnelly's essay on Marcel and Buddha. Could you clear that for me with her, please, as I do not seem to have her address . . .

How are you? I haven't written for a long time as I have so much mail to take care of—and do not manage to do it. But I am always most happy to hear news of you and of your work.

Meanwhile, things do not improve in Asia, and everywhere they seem to become more ominous. I have been invited to a meeting of (Christian) monastic Superiors in Bangkok in December—but doubt if Thailand will be at peace in December. Meanwhile I am having a hard time getting this unusual permission to travel. My Abbot doubts that one of his monks ought to go so far—he is a new and young Abbot. Perhaps if someone at the UN wrote him a note suggesting that this might be *important* (possibility of talks with Buddhists is obviously very much a consideration), it might help him make up his mind. Though what he really needs is stimulation from Church Superiors—which I hope may be forthcoming.

March 28, 1968

Thanks for your very good letter. It took some time for your own Shibayama book [Zenkei Shibayama, *A Flower Does Not Talk*] from Yale to reach me but I sent it back as soon as I got it. I hope it has safely reached you. I was speaking yesterday with a man from Vanderbilt University who entertained Shibayama Roshi at Nashville and liked him very much. I still have faint hopes I might meet Shibayama sometime.

Sally Donnelly wrote me a very nice letter and I must answer when I get a chance. I will also write to Diana when I am a little less pressed. Thanks for your judicious remarks on Thailand and on the proposed meeting of Catholic abbots there. I feel more and more that by December the situation will be so aggravated as to make the meeting impossible. Unless of course it is held somewhere else. Besides that, as an American, I feel very hesitant to go to Asia at the moment, presenting myself as a representative of Christianity. I am afraid I would be so ashamed that it would be terribly uncomfortable. There is still the question of my Abbot not having given permission—though he has not refused it either. In other words, it is all in the air and I shall wait patiently to see more clearly what really fits the situation and what ought to be done.

In any case, it all depends on what happens in the next six months— or perhaps also on the election. I feel we are in for a serious crisis. I hope you received and enjoyed the copy of *Monks Pond* which I sent.

June 14, 1968

It was nice of you to send a check for the magazine. The second number is on its way to you. Hope you like it. The next two will be larger—and then finish. For all things must have an end.

My book *Zen and the Birds of Appetite* (which contains the introduction to Sally's "Marcel and Buddha") is now in the press. It contains essays mostly about Zen, from one aspect or other. All Asian in other words. I thought it might be appropriate to dedicate the book to you so, if you permit, your name will appear on the title page or somewhere. It will be an honor for the book. And it will give me some small opportunity to express my friendship, thanks, and esteem for you.

And now, good news. Though it is not certain that I shall attend the meeting at Bangkok I have received permission to go and preach a retreat at our Cistercian monastery in Indonesia. This will give me also an opportunity to visit some non-Christian monasteries in SE Asia and in Japan. That is what I'd like to plan. In Japan I want most of all to visit Suzuki's friends and associates. They are presumably at Otani University. Have you any suggestions? And I'd like to see a couple of good Zen monasteries and meet some Roshis. Do you think there is any hope at all of my getting into Rangoon? Is there anything you know of at or near Singapore? Anything you know of in Java (which is where our monastery is)? It is good to think that even if I don't get to the Bangkok meeting (to which I do not attach excessive importance) I may yet see the things I ought to see and meet some of the people I ought to meet. I hope you can give me some good suggestions. (I am not planning on going to India this time, though if it were possible to make a retreat in the Himalayas I'd certainly be most tempted to change all plans and go there. But as I am too arthritic to be a caveman, it would have to be in a cottage of sorts!!!)

Utopian to talk in such a strain when the whole place may be in flames by the end of the year. Nobody knows. I find myself almost inarticulate in the presence of the *usualness* of assassination . . .

June 24, 1968

Many thanks for your letter and card. This is just a brief note to give the tentative plans I now have made. The whole thing centers around the Bangkok meeting planned for the first week in December. At present I am thinking of going to our Indonesian monastery before the meeting. Now I have just realized that the rainy season begins in Indonesia in November. It might be good to go there in October, and leave November for possibly Burma (hope!!) or somewhere else in SE Asia (or even conceivably India). I think you are right though about the Temple of Understanding Group. Anyway I didn't think of meeting a group at this time. I want to avoid groups if possible but unofficially visit traditional communities as a monastic brother of another faith, and just quietly discuss things behind closed doors, and join in some meditation.

It is altogether possible then to plan the Indonesian part of the trip for October, November for somewhere in SE Asia, then Bangkok, then on conceivably to Japan. Or alternately I could go somewhere after the meeting, that is in December. The plans are flexible . . .

Perhaps my calculations on the rainy season are irrelevant. Maybe after November it rains all over the place out there!!

I will write more when I am more definite about Indonesia, for instance. But any suggestions of yours would be valuable. In particular it would be worthwhile making any adjustment for the chance to get to Burma.

August 31, 1968

I am most grateful for all your help in providing addresses. I am getting in contact with the ones who will be helpful for India first of all. It is possible that my visit to Japan may be put off until spring (the nicest time there, I understand) and hence I will reserve the Japanese addresses for winter and write there then. I have been especially anxious to meet Dr. Hisamatsu. Roshi Ogawa is also someone I must meet, and I want to see his monastery and others. It is possible I may get help from Miss Okamura or Miss Kudo in translating in Japan.

Meanwhile things seem to be shaping up very well for India. I have, I think, a good chance of entrée to some of the Tibetan Buddhist monasteries and hope to stay at Darjeeling after the meeting to see those in that area. I hope to go to Nepal and also to go over and meet the Dalai Lama at Mussoorie. I don't think I will have time to see Dr. Radhakrishnan. Originally I had hoped to go to Ceylon if Burma was not available, but it now it looks as if I will have plenty to occupy me in India. However, there is always a chance of going back to Burma or India after the meeting in Thailand . . .

Meanwhile I look forward to the Darjeeling meeting and I am sure that there we will find many new openings. So I am once again deeply grateful to you for your kindness and your concern. I keep you in my prayers and will also keep in touch. I am leaving soon for the West where I have a meeting on the Coast before going abroad. And I have other commitments there too. Personal mail will be forwarded from here: just mark it personal—please forward. I will contact you en route when I have further available addresses.

Merton met Chakravarty in Calcutta in October 1968. In The Asian Journal *Merton writes (October 22, 1968): "Yesterday I drove with Amiya Chakravarty . . . to the home of the painter Jamini Roy . . . Amiya bought a Christ which he will take to the nuns of Redwoods."*

To Richard S. Y. Chi

Richard S. Y. Chi, born in Peking on August 3, 1918, studied first in his native China, where he received a B.S. at Nankai University and then in England, where he holds Doctor of Philosophy degrees from both Oxford and Cambridge. For a brief time he lectured at Oxford and Cambridge and served as curator of the Oriental Art Gallery in Bristol, England. In 1965 he came to Indiana University, where he now holds the rank of professor. He has written on Oriental logic, art, calligraphy, etc., and is the editor of the journal Buddhist Philosophy.

In the fall of 1967 he was put in contact with Thomas Merton by a mutual friend, Lunsford Yandell, who wrote to Merton about a translation of Shen Hui done by Richard Chi. Merton read the manuscript with great pleasure and wrote to Dr. Chi.

December 26, 1967

As you know, Lunsford Yandell has forwarded to me the excellent ms. on Shen Hui,* and I am reading it with real pleasure. At the moment, with the pressure of Christmas mail, I do not have leisure to discuss it, but I would like to get in contact with you at least and say the following things.

1. I have ideas for possible publishers if the Indiana Press does not accept it.

2. Sometime I hope you can come to Gethsemani. If you drive, then it is simple. If you do not, then I have a friend who teaches there and who comes down by car: you might come with him . . .

3. I am starting a small magazine—mimeographed, non-commercial—of poetry and creative work, in which also I would love to publish some Asian texts. I would like very much to make a selection from Shen Hui to use in the magazine. Would you permit me to do this? . . . In addition, I have a friend who has a small printing press and who might be interested in doing a pamphlet of a few of the texts, a small book which would be nicely done (hand press) and would be worth having. I hope someday we can talk over these things . . .

January 9, 1968

Just a brief note in response to your welcome letter. I have written to my friend Dr. Denis Goulet at Indiana U. suggesting that we could combine our visits and he could drive you down on the 26th or 27th (or thereabouts). He will get in touch with you or you can call him and decide on the time. He is in the Department of Government at the university.

I look forward to seeing you at the end of the month. As to your book, let me only say that I thought the preface excellent, and just what is needed to counteract the mindless word chopping that ruins so much academic study of religious texts. Or Zen texts (not quite the same thing!) . . .

---

* *Successor to the Sixth Zen Patriarch Hui Neng as the leader of the Southern (sudden enlightenment) school of Ch'an (Zen) Buddhism. He is a figure of decisive importance in the development of Chinese Ch'an Buddhism.*

January 21, 1968

. . . I have made a fairly short (a dozen pages) selection of material from the Shen Hui dialogues for the first issue of my *Monks Pond*. I hope to use more in a later issue, before the book appears. I am happy to be able to present this important material even though to a very limited audience mostly of poets. Still it is a *Monks Pond* and there will be some who will be intrigued.

The fact that you have done other translations from the "Finger Pointing to the Moon" interests me very much. I'd like to see even the old ones if you have no more recent ones available, I could reprint something that had appeared in England . . .

I hope we will speak more fully of all this Saturday. About a possible introduction, I make a practice of saying no but I also make a practice of making exceptions for something like Zen, and all we need to find out is whether a preface by me would add anything. If you think so, I can give it some thought . . .

On January 26–27, 1968, Richard Chi and his colleague Dr. Denis Goulet visited Merton at Gethsemani.

February 6, 1968

Many thanks for your letter and for the additional pages completing the "Humorous Dialogue." I like it very much indeed and want to run it in the second issue of *Monks Pond*. I have gone through it with a green pencil and jotted down a couple of places where I thought I might help it to read more smoothly, and perhaps reinforce your meaning. But you must look it over and see if I have helped or hindered your purpose. Just mark it as you please (cross out anything of mine you don't want) and return the pages to me . . .

. . . I hope in the future we can talk more about things of mutual interest. Your visit was indeed a pleasure and my only regret is that we were not able to spend more time in serious conversation.

February 28, 1968

Very many thanks for the revised Zen dialogue. It is fine. I am saving it for the third issue of *Monks Pond* as the second is now full . . . I hope to send you a copy of the first issue in the course of next week. Other copies to follow later . . .

Congratulations. I am delighted to hear about Shen Hui. It will be a very important contribution to Zen literature. I must begin to think about my preface. Have you anything about Shen Hui that I could consult for background? I don't really know him except through your ms. and through references in Suzuki.

March 14, 1968

The preface to the "Humorous Dialogue" is very good indeed, and though I really do not have space to spare, I will use it nevertheless. I'll face the problems involved when I come to them: that will be in the fall issue.

I am grateful for your contribution—surely you have done so much for the magazine already! Shen Hui gives this issue its most serious content and claim to importance. But your kindness is appreciated.

Thanks too for the material on Shen Hui. My preface is crystallizing out, and I hope to get it on paper in a little while . . . Meanwhile, I wonder if I should not read Hu Shih's article from *Philosophy East and West*, 1953. I have Suzuki's reply. If that is available in the U. of Indiana library, maybe you could borrow it for me? If not, I will get our library to borrow it somewhere on interlibrary loan.

The more I consider Shen Hui the more I see his importance and the more I like his Ch'an. Much as I find Zen appealing, I think the early masters of Ch'an are the best.

April 3, 1968

I am grateful for the Xerox of Hu Shih's article. It was just what I needed to make everything fall into place. The draft of the introduction is finished and it is now being typed. A very enjoyable and interesting task. However, I shall count on you to correct my glaring errors in scholarship and in Zen: there must inevitably be quite a few. I shall send you the fair copy as soon as it is typed . . .

April 7, 1968

Here is my attempt at a preface. Naturally, as I said before, I expect you to find in it things that ought to be corrected. Meanwhile, I would be most grateful if you could get three or four Xerox copies made, for my own files etc. I do hope it is all right. I very much enjoyed writing it.

July 25, 1968

I am sorry I was not able to see you and Denis back in May. Due to my trip to California and to meetings on my return, I was impossibly crowded then. It is the busiest time of year. Perhaps I can see you in September—in October I am to go to Asia for three months. I would like to talk to you about it.

Meanwhile, I am wondering about the text of the "Humorous Zen Stories." I have two here I think, and you said you might be doing another. Is either of the texts here all right for publication? Can I just take the one that will fit in best? Or do you want to make sure I have exactly what you think best? If so, could you send me a text you definitely want me to print? I'd be much obliged.

How is the Shen Hui book coming along? . . .

Darjeeling, India
November 21, 1968

I have been having a very fruitful trip in Asia. I have been in India over a month, mostly in the Himalayas, and have had good conversations with the Dalai Lama and with many others high in Tibetan Buddhism—including some extraordinary mystics. Now I am going on to Thailand, Indonesia, and eventually Taiwan and Japan. I wonder if you know of anyone I should see, especially in connection with Ch'an and Zen. If you can think of a few names and addresses, write to me at the following address: % Pertapuan Cisterciense, Rawa Seneng, Temangguny, Java, Indonesia.

I should be interested to hear how the book is coming and when it appears I can send some addresses of people in India who would be interested in receiving copies—including the Dalai Lama.

During my stay here I have added a bit to my knowledge of Madhyamika.* I am eager to reread Shen Hui in the light of this study and look forward very much to seeing your book [still unpublished]—or any other studies you may be doing on Buddhist topics.

In any case I would be glad of suggestions, some people to see, especially in Taiwan.

With my best regards. Hoping you are in good health.

Dona Luisa Coomaraswamy

Dona Luisa Coomaraswamy, born in 1905 of Jewish parents in Argentina, came to the United States at age sixteen. In 1930, when she married Ananda K. Coomaraswamy (AKC), she was a Boston society photographer; her husband was already well known as an authority in art history and as a writer on Hinduism and Buddhism. In 1938, at the suggestion of her husband, Dona Luisa spent more than two years in India studying Sanskrit and popular folklore. Upon her return, she was able to act as his secretary, and after his death in 1947 began the task of putting together a definitive collection of his writings. (She was working on this collection during the time she corresponded with Thomas Merton.) She died in 1970, before bringing this project to completion, but in 1977 two volumes of selected papers of Ananda were published, edited by Roger Lipsey.

* School of Mahayana Buddhism developed by Nagarjuna in the second century A.D. It stressed the notion of emptiness: "Everything is the void."

January 13, 1961

It was a great pleasure to learn that Graham Carey had spoken to you about my project [to write on AKC] and an even greater one to receive your letter, with the books also. I think that, as you say, by far the most important thing now is the exchange of ideas between us. Certainly I have no intention of rushing into a kind of absurd journalistic exploit without meaning or without the possibility of genuine fruit. I do not intend to print anything at least until the appearance of the definitive work of AKC in the Bollingen Series. But I do think that a reasoned and meditative study on my part at that precise time, coinciding with the issue of the first volume, might be of some use.

First of all, Ananda Coomaraswamy is in many ways to me a model: the model of one who has thoroughly and completely united in himself the spiritual tradition and attitudes of the Orient and of the Christian West, not excluding also something of Islam, I believe. This kind of comprehension is, it seems to me, quite obligatory for the contemplative of our day, at least if he is in any sense also a scholar. I believe that the only really valid thing that can be accomplished in the direction of world peace and unity at the moment is the preparation of the way by the formation of men who, isolated, perhaps not accepted or understood by any "movement," are able to unite in themselves and experience in their own lives all that is best and most true in the various great spiritual traditions. Such men can become as it were "sacraments" or signs of peace, at least. They can do much to open up the minds of their contemporaries to receive, in the future, new seeds of thought. Our task is one of very remote preparation, a kind of arduous and unthanked pioneering.

I certainly feel that I owe very much to AKC as his book *The Transformation of Nature in Art*, when I was doing my thesis on Blake years ago, was decisive in leading me to take the right turn in life and to set my feet upon the spiritual road, which led to the monastery and to the contemplative life. Renewing my contact with his thought here more recently, I have found in it all the riches, and more, that had first delighted me. I really want to continue my study not just of his life but of his many works . . . Perhaps you could offer a few suggestions of titles which you consider to be most important and which would be of greatest use to me, which you would not mind lending me. I would take the very best possible care of them.

I am not making any promise of great results, that is in the way of "production," but I do promise what is more important and what, I think, would have been pleasing to AKC: namely that I will meditate long and happily in silence upon these things, and enrich my life with the symbols, the "mysteries and sacraments" in which he has shown us so many manifestations of God in His world. It is not that I want to write about AKC but rather that I want to enter contemplatively into the world of thought which, as you so rightly say, is for all of us, is not any private property of his, but which nevertheless had to be opened to us by him. In other words, Dona Luisa (may I call you what all his friends call you?), I am speaking not as a writer but rather as a monk.

Such writing as I do (when I work I manage to write quickly) is not any part of a career, nor do I even conceive of it as an apostolate. It is simply a way of meditating on paper. If others wish to share in it, they are welcome, because I too have no proprietorship over these thoughts which are not "mine" and which if they are given are not given just "to me." I think I have learned to distrust the appearances of the "I" that we must nevertheless use in our everyday speech for want of a better understanding.

The study of AKC will be reserved for a very pleasant hermitage among the pine trees, looking over the valley, a place which I think would have appealed to him and where I now spend much time, when I can . . . Please feel perfectly free to refuse me anything, to take your time in answering any letter, and do not be disturbed if my requests may accidentally and unintentionally seem importunate. I do not want to badger you or impose on your kindness, and really what is important is not that I be able to "get information" or "borrow books" but rather that I may have the joy and the privilege of a living contact with you and thus with AKC and his world of thought. I cannot help but feel that his "world of thought" is also mine, and that in any other realm today I am purely and simply an exile. Forgive me then, all I really ask is an opportunity to feel myself a citizen of my true country.

. . . The material that most interests me is the later work that has been characterized as "theological and prophetic." I have tried in vain to get (in this part of the country) *Am I My Brother's Keeper*. If this has been recently reprinted will you please let me know the publisher. Otherwise, could I perhaps borrow it from you? And *The Dance of Shiva*? . . . I shall be most grateful for your help, your charity and your patience.

If there is anything I can send you or do for you, please let me know. The best my friendship can offer you is prayer, during the psalms at night, in my Mass at dawn. (I have a rare privilege, unappreciated and unthought of by almost all priests even here, of saying Mass just at sunrise, when the light of the sun falls on the altar, and powerfully lights up the mystery of the divine presence spoken of in so many, many prayers for "illumination," like this morning's postcommunion: "Come to meet us always O Lord with the heavenly Light everywhere, that we may discern with clear mind the mystery of which you have made us partakers, and that we may enter into it with awe and love.")

February 12, 1961

Many thanks for your two very rich and stimulating letters, and the additional notes. So many wonderful openings for new thought, study and meditation. I have meanwhile returned to you the things you lent me first: the memorial volume and the two or three magazines . . .

We have here a record of some Indian religious music, in the Folkways series, and I enjoy it very much, especially some of the popular legends, like the one about the Black Parrot. But the chanting of the Vedas, of which a sample is given, was the thing that really first opened up the Upanishads to me. The *way* in which the words are chanted shows the spiritual character of Hindu singing and reflects the spiritual understanding of breath that is exposed in the Upanishads. I am now finishing the Brihad Aranyaka Upanishad and it is tremendous.

Yes, I have read Marco Pallis [i.e., *Peaks and Lamas*]. We do not have it here, I borrowed it from Victor Hammer's wife (he met AKC once and has some offprints of his). I copied out some of the best bits about Tibetan art and craftsmanship (I make no distinction).

A friend of mine, Louis Massignon, one of the great scholars of Moslem mysticism, is passionately devoted to Abraham and his mystical life is all under the sign of Abraham and of the sacrifice of Isaac. Massignon is one of the few Christians I know who has really deep and warm contacts with Moslems. Through him I have met one very ardent soul in Pakistan [Abdul Aziz]. You are right about the Sufis and about the need for Christian equivalents of the Sufis. This kind of need is not something that man thinks up and then takes care of. It is a question of God's honor and glory and of His will. Men do not choose to be Sufis, least of all Christian Sufis so to speak: they are chosen and plunged into the crucible like iron into the fire. I do not know if I have been so chosen but I am familiar enough with the crucible, and I live under the sign of contradiction. Would that I might so live gently, non-violently, firmly, in all humility and meekness, but not betraying the truth.

But there is certainly a great need of an interior revival of truth, religious truth. There are everywhere movements which more and more seem to be simply evasions. Collective evasions, with an enormous amount of publicity and false front, with great numbers of speeches and conferences and publications and no one knows what else. And little or no interior fruit, simply a multiplication of addicts and proselytes. Like you, I hate proselytizing. This awful business of making others just like oneself so that one is thereby "justified" and under no obligation to change himself. What a terrible thing this can be. The source of how many sicknesses in the world.

The true Christian apostolate is nothing of this sort, a fact which Christians themselves have largely forgotten. I think it was from Ananda that I first heard the quote of Tauler (or maybe Eckhart) who said in a sermon that even if the church were empty he would preach the sermon to the four walls because he had to. That is the true apostolic spirit, based not on the desire to make others conform, but in the desire to proclaim and announce the good tidings of God's infinite love. In this context the preacher is not a "converter" but merely a herald, a voice (*kerux*), and the Spirit of the Lord is left free to act as He pleases. But this has degenerated into a doctrine and fashion of "convert-makers" in which man exerts pressure and techniques (the awful business of "modern techniques of propaganda") upon his fellow man in order to make him, force him, bring him under a kind of charm that compels him to abandon his own integrity and his own freedom and yield to another man or another institution. Little do men realize that in such a situation the Holy Spirit is silent and inactive, or perhaps active *against* the insolence of man. Hence the multitude of honest and sincere men who "cannot accept" a message that is preached without respect for the Spirit of God or for the spirit of man.

. . . [AKC] just was a voice bearing witness to the truth, and he wanted nothing but for others to receive that truth in their own way, in agreement with their own mental and spiritual context. As if there were any other way of accepting it. But no, this awful mistake of the West, which is certainly not a "Christian" mistake at all, but the fruit of Western aggression, was the idea that one had to "convert" the East and make it change in every way into a replica of the West. This is one of the great spiritual crimes of man in its own unconscious way and we are only beginning to reap the fruit of it in China, the Congo, etc. Have you read a wonderful book called the *Dark Eye in Africa* by Laurens Van der Post? He is another remarkable person, and on primitive man he also wrote a splendid book about the Bushmen of South Africa, *Lost World of the Kalahari*. Several other interesting books about these Bushmen are appearing here and there. Most important insights into the reality of primitive man. What you quote AKC as saying about the underlying resentment and contempt in the attitude of men like Frazer and Lévy-Bruhl is terribly true.

Thank you for your quotes on Hebrew forms of prayer. I wish I knew Hebrew. My languages are all Western. Someday I will have to start on an Oriental one but I dread it, our time for concentrated study is very short. Yet perhaps I may do it.

. . . The books you said you would send, including *The Dance of Shiva*, will be most welcome when they arrive. I am profoundly grateful and look forward to them. It is good of you to put yourself out for me . . . What would you say AKC would have thought of abstract expressionism in art? It has much to be said in its favor, but as a fashion it is a bit obnoxious. What did he think and say about people like Picasso, who is undoubtedly a great genius . . . but perhaps that is the trouble.

Eckhart I know. We have here a popular edition of him, and I have something in French of his. I like him, and Tauler and Ruysbroeck. Do you know St. John of the Cross? He is less metaphysical than the others.

I am sending you an article of mine on Chinese thought, which Graham Carey has read. He may already have spoken to you of it, as he wrote to me about it. And a book of mine on the Psalms which goes somewhat into the different senses of Scripture you spoke of before. Yes, I agree that much ought to be done on symbolism and typology and I hope to get at it sometime . . .

March 8, 1961

This is just a note to ask you a question and a favor.

Victor Hammer, of whom you know, and who knew Ananda, is considering some more work on his hand press at Lexington near here. He has asked me to think up something and I have for a long time been considering that it would be very worthwhile perhaps to do a small volume of sayings and aphorisms of AKC. This would consist, for instance, of some of the remarks quoted from conversations with him in a book like the commemorative volume. Also one could include some short texts taken here and there at random from his essays. It would of course be a very small thing, privately printed, limited edition, limited circulation, copyrighted (I hope) and surrounded with every care. I would perhaps write a short introductory essay.

I have come to the point of considering it very seriously, though not in a hurry, and have mentioned it to V. Hammer who, I am sure, will like the idea. Meanwhile, however, I want your reaction. If you have no objections to the plan, I would of course submit everything to your inspection and approval, and no doubt if the project pleases you, you would think of things to be included.

I am sure that this would be something very timely, important and salutary. There are so many aphoristic sayings of AKC that could be used that would be of great value to man in his modern predicament . . .

May 1, 1961

. . . I liked very much "On Being in One's Right Mind" and I think it is really fundamental, one of AKC's very best. Recently I have received a lot of interesting books on Islam, but have not begun them yet as I must take one thing at a time and not be lured by the Western folly of trying to do everything and ending by doing nothing. I have been working only on the Chinese philosopher Chuang Tzu, besides my classes. I am doing no writing at the moment, though I plan an article on the English mystics, in review of a new book on them by David Knowles.

Graham Carey thinks a selection of sayings by Ananda, printed privately by Victor Hammer, would be a good idea. Hammer himself is interested in this. Are the possibilities good enough for me to get together a tentative selection and submit it for your approval? If you say yes, I will try to get this done in the next couple of months . . .

. . . You can call me Fr. Louis or Tom as you please! No formality about titles.

August 27, 1961

It is months since I have heard from you. I have been intending to write and have not had time for the really thoughtful letter that I like to write to you. Nor will this really be it. But I do want to give some sign of life and at last to return some of the offprints you sent me.

The last time I wrote I was wondering whether or not there would be some possibility of Victor Hammer printing on his hand press a little volume of selections from AKC. And that is where we stopped. Since then I have made no headway with this idea, although I still think it is a good one. And it could always be done quietly and gradually. And I am still not quite sure what you think. In any case I have no clear idea where you are with the definitive edition of his works. Perhaps sometime later on this little book might be worthwhile.

In returning these offprints I want to say that I particularly enjoyed the one on Satan. I think it is full of deep wisdom and opens up many very illuminating insights in new directions. Certainly this is an important truth and a vital one for our time and I think it is approached in the right way . . .

I have been reading a really remarkable book on Eckhart, by Vladimir Lossky, in French. It is very difficult in parts but it is one of the finest studies on the Meister. I highly recommend it. Published by Vrin. It is unfinished, as Lossky died. He was a great man, wrote a very fine book on the mystical theology of the Oriental Church which you should know.

Also I just finished Mircea Eliade's *Myths, Dreams and Mysteries*. This too is very rich. He refers incidentally to Ananda and in the final pages has some very good things on Maya . . .

The article on "Being in One's Right Mind" is, I think, one of Ananda's very finest. I assume you want this copy returned. However, I have not yet gleaned the quotes from it that I might use in a possible selection (nor have I done this with the Satan piece either), so I am holding on to these two pieces for a little while yet. Please let me know if you want them returned in a hurry.

. . . Please do not think I have forgotten you, or that I have lost interest in Ananda. Quite the contrary. He always impresses me more and more, the deeper I go into his work. I must really try to get the *New Approach to the Vedas*.

By the way, about addressing me, why not be included in the circle of those who for simplicity's sake call me "Tom." These are the writers and intellectuals with whom I deal, some Catholic and some not, and it is much more feasible to have just a plain name, which in any case I prefer. The custom of taking a formal and special monastic name with a handle to it is very late, fifteenth and sixteenth centuries. One's baptismal name strikes me as being the one "new" name that is sufficiently new to include everything else . . .

September 24, 1961

Certainly you are right about "doing nothing" and all things coming out of it. And that we ought not to be preoccupied with doing "things." This thing and that. I am certainly going more and more in that direction. I am deliberately concentrating (wrong word, I don't mean concentrating at all), orienting my life or letting it be oriented in a direction in which I will write no more books, and write nothing except what writes itself unsystematically and spontaneously. I shall turn my face away from writing and write nothing except what can be written by the right hand without the left hand knowing what it is doing. I am forty-six and it is getting time for vaprastina (my memory is bad and I am almost sure that is the wrong spelling). It is time to start unweaving the outer social self and stepping out of it into the joy of emptiness. Not that this "ought to be" (you are right) but that in the organic growth of life the time has come.

. . . I am sending still another thing (which you can also keep). It is an indignant letter to a friend of mine, a poet in Nicaragua [Pablo Antonio Cuadra; see *Emblems of a Season of Fury,* 1963]. I have translated some of his verse by the way and will send that too, but I don't want to burden you with a lot of useless paper. The "letter" which is a little long is irate (more than it should be) about the merciless stupidity of the Great Powers and power politicians. I am, like you, indignant with the pharisaism of the "West" along with the Russian variety of the same. This question of standing by while they prepare manipulations that could easily lead to the destruction of the human race is not my idea of honesty. Hence I feel that something must be said and I am starting in Latin America, where it may still be listened to. What I say for the U.S. has to be a bit more cryptic and poetic, like the Auschwitz piece. You might like some of the later pages of this letter, the theme of which is that the Christian missionaries in South America came with their eyes closed by pride, unable to see Christ in those whom they "discovered" and seeking only to impose their own beliefs which meant their own "culture." Thus they did and did not preach the Gospel. They were and were not true to Christ. This awful ambiguity has been the tragedy of Christianity since the Middle Ages. It has been part of the rise and decline of the West, and contributed fatally to the terrible split in the world.

. . . The world is lying inert under a huge weight of spiritual torpor and heaviness, with conscience gone dead and all awareness extinct. And the disaster hangs over all men. This is indeed the time for purity of heart, compunction and detachment, to embrace the truth. I still do not see clearly what to look for!

. . . You must understand by now that I do not entertain formally conventional notions of the Church. I certainly believe with all my heart in the Church, none more so. But I absolutely refuse to take the rigid, stereotyped, bourgeois notions that are acceptable to most Catholics and which manage in the long run to veil the true mystery of Christ and make it utterly unattainable to some people. You can pull my leg all you want, it stretches indefinitely, and we both understand quite well the way in which you belong to Christ. We both belong to Him in His mercy which is inscrutable and infinite and reaches into the inmost depths of every being, but especially of all who, with all their deficiencies and limitations, seek only truth and love, as best they can. I do not understand too much of any kind of Church which is made up entirely of people whose external conformity has made them comfortable and secure, and has given them the privilege of looking down on everybody else who is automatically "wrong" because not conformed to them. This does not seem to me to have a great deal to do with the message of Christ. The Church is indeed visible, yes, but it depends what you mean by "visible." Not Cadillacs, surely.

. . . Thank you for sending the offprints. I shall treasure them. I have not "lost interest," but the time is not ripe at the moment for a little collection of AKC. First, my printer is busy with a long job. And I have a tiresome task to complete for an encyclopedia.

Please tell me if you would approve of my doing a small collection of sayings of Ananda (as planned—with introduction) to be published by New Directions instead of privately printed. Or would you prefer it to be privately printed? In either way it would be slow, as both of my friends take their time.

December 18, 1963

This Christmas note gives me a chance, with much confusion, to return an offprint of AKC that you lent me some time ago, it must be two years or more. I am very sorry indeed. It got buried under some other things. But I was very grateful for it and enjoyed reading it which I did, as usually, with deep agreement.

It is a shame that I have not had a chance to do the work on him that I was hoping to do. But one must be realistic and take one thing at a time, and there is always something closer at hand. I do hope, however, that I will always work with something of his spirit. I often think of you and whenever I have a chance to reread something of his it gives me joy, light and peace. I do hope that more of his great work will be available in print as time goes on. One of his very best things is the one "On Being in One's Right Mind" and this has always made a deep impression on me, and I am thankful for it . . .

To Jean Danielou

Jean Danielou (1905–74) was born in Paris. He entered the Society of Jesus in 1929, after having completed a doctorate in letters at the Sorbonne. He was ordained in 1938 and upon receiving the degree of Doctor of Theology at Lyons, he began in 1944 what was to be a long and distinguished career as professor of primitive Christianity at the Institut Catholique in Paris. He is the author of many works. Merton found especially helpful his Platonisme et théologie mystique: Essai sur la doctrine spirituelle de Saint-Grégoire de Nysse *(1944). Many of his books have been translated into English, e.g.,* God and the Ways of Knowing *(1956),* Holy Pagans of the Old Testament *(1957),* The Scandal of Truth *(1962),* The Development of Christian Doctrine before the Council of Nicaea *(1964),* The Infancy Narratives *(1968). Danielou was made a cardinal by Pope Paul VI.*

April 21, 1960

. . . Louis Massignon strikes me as a grand person. He has been writing about all the causes in which he is interested and I am going to try and do a little praying and fasting in union with him on the 30th of the month when there is to be a demonstration outside Vincennes prison—even Gabriel Marcel participating. This is one way in which I can legitimately unite myself to the *témoignage* and work of my brothers outside the monastery! . . .

Your work in Sweden is very interesting, also the work for Africa. If any of the people you meet in this connection turn out to be very interested in our kind of approach, and come to America, it might be possible to persuade them to come here and we could have a little colloquium in the monastery. I have received permission to begin this kind of work in a very small way, and already this spring I shall have a couple of meetings with Protestant theologians teaching in seminaries in this part of the country: more in the nature of a kind of colloquium-retreat. It is a new experiment [see letters to Pope John XXIII]. My attitude is that if we get together and discuss the word of God and prayer, then the word being "announced" among us as a group, we are in a certain quite real sense united in Christ, and there is a beginning of reunion. Also there will be other groups: the faculty of a nearby Catholic college will come for a colloquium-retreat in which we will consider their aims in humanistic education. Later perhaps some writers and publishers and art critics from New York might come down.

Other contacts by letter seem to be promising. But my big care is to keep from plunging too vigorously into this kind of thing and not trying to start a "movement." At best I think it would be enough to have twelve or fifteen such meetings a year. I have to keep to my own silence and solitude—and keep up my reading too . . .

About the vocation problem. At the moment it is no problem because the decision of Rome is clearly the will of God, and I am perfectly at peace. I shall simply keep myself alert to catch any indication of a change. I got another letter from Cardinal Larraona in which he said that actually nothing had been said about [Gregory] Zilboorg [psychiatrist whom Merton had consulted in 1956], and airily dismissed the whole thing with a pleasant Spanish proverb: *De poeta y de loco tenemos todos un poco* ["We all have a bit of poetry and a bit of madness in us"]! So there my suspicions overshot the mark. Meanwhile I have consulted the psychiatrist in Louisville, who tells me that I am not neurotic and that my problem here in the monastery is quite a natural reaction to the situation. He feels, as you did last year, that it would help me to get away from the monastery now and again and renew my perspective. He also suggested the possibility of my withdrawing to the mountains of Kentucky to found a small annex to my own monastery for the purposes I had originally, remarking that since the "glory" of this would redound on the monastery there might be less objection to it. I have not given the matter much thought because I don't think the proposal would be well received, and at any rate I am not prepared to make it at this time as I have no plan, and do not feel like making one. I shall just continue with things as they are, for they are passable, and the work I am doing is clearly God's will. (Even the Holy Father has had a word of approval for it, as was confidentially told me by his private secretary.)

One thing, though: I wish someday I could get away on a really useful trip—something that would contribute to my monastic education and life. For instance to Mount Athos for the millenary celebration. Or perhaps to Oxford for the International Patristic Conference, or something like that. I would prefer it to be a monastic journey, especially in the East . . . But I do not dare even to suggest such a thing. Later the man in Louisville is going to suggest this himself to Father Abbot. I shall not try to push my own ideas. . . . I will close this long letter, which it has been a pleasure to write.

To Dorothy Day

One of the truly influential persons in the history of American Catholicism in the twentieth century, Dorothy Day (1897–1980) was received into the Roman Catholic Church in 1927. In becoming a Catholic, she did not repudiate the radical social and political convictions that she had shared with socialists, anarchists, and communists; indeed, she found much that bolstered those convictions in the Gospel.

For half a century she exercised a prophetic role in the American Church, combining a radical position on social issues with a conservative and unquestioning theology of Church and sacraments. Her deep concern for the poor and the needy and her total commitment to non-violence and pacifism were a source of inspiration for many (Thomas Merton among them), as well as a cause for discomfort and even open opposition to her on the part of others. She wrote constantly and traveled, but when she returned home it was to the Catholic Worker soup kitchen in New York's Lower East Side. She lived as one who was poor among the poor. "Poverty for Dorothy Day," Merton wrote for the jacket of her book Loaves and Fishes, *"is more than a sociological problem; it is also a religious mystery."*

Dorothy Day was an able journalist and essayist. In her regular column in The Catholic Worker, *"On Pilgrimage," her persuasive, anecdotal, Gospel-inspired style was at its best. Besides this regular column, which she wrote for many years, she produced a number of books:* Union Square to Rome, *the story of her conversion;* The Long Loneliness, *which continues her autobiography; and* Loaves and Fishes, *which tells of her meeting with Peter Maurin and their founding of the Catholic Worker movement. Merton's letters to her show the special respect, even reverence, in which he held Dorothy Day.*

July 9, 1959

It was a pleasure to get your letter, and of course I keep praying for you and for *The Catholic Worker*. The purpose of this note is to let you know that we have again been given some sweet-smelling and -tasting toothpaste and that I will be sending along a consignment to *CW*, for the glory of God and for Cistercian simplicity such as it still may be, what's left of it.

Again, I am touched deeply by your witness for peace. You are very very right in going at it along the lines of Satyagraha. I see no other way, though of course the angles of the problem are not all clear. I am certainly with you on taking some kind of stand and acting accordingly. Nowadays it is no longer a question of who is right, but who is at least not criminal. If any of us can say that any more. So don't worry about whether or not in every point you are perfectly right according to everybody's books: you are right before God as far as you can go and you are fighting for a truth that is clear enough and important enough. What more can anybody do?

Once again I came upon a copy of *CW*. The one with the piece about the Hopis in it. Again, same reaction. You people are the only ones left awake, or among the few that still have an eye open. I am more and more convinced that the real people in this country are the Indians—and Negroes, etc. . . .

The reason I mention the Hopis is that (this is in confidence) I think more and more that the only final solution to my own desires will be something like getting permission to go off and live among Indians or some such group, as a kind of hermit-missionary. Obviously the hopes of gaining such a permission, humanly speaking, are very low. But it is not for us to go by hopes that are merely human. I do very earnestly and imploringly ask your prayers for this . . .

February 4, 1960

. . . Thank you for your last letter, and for the offer of Cassian. Yes, we can certainly use it. We do not have him in the novitiate, except some translations we ran off on a pale purple machine, which are not too legible. I am going to be lecturing on him shortly. Your offer is providential.

Perseverance—yes, more and more one sees that it is the great thing. But there is a thing that must not be overlooked. Perseverance is not hanging on to some course which we have set our minds to, and refusing to let go. It is not even a matter of getting a bulldog grip on the faith and not letting the devil pry us loose from it—though many of the saints made it look that way. Really, there is something lacking in such a hope as that. Hope is a greater scandal than we think. I am coming to think that God (may He be praised in His great mystery) loves and helps best those who are so beat and have so much nothing when they come to die that it is almost as if they had persevered in nothing but had gradually lost every-thing, piece by piece, until there was nothing left but God. Hence per-severance is not hanging on but letting go. That of course is terrible. But as you say so rightly, it is a question of His hanging on to us, by the hair of the head, that is from on top and beyond, where we cannot see or reach. What man can see the top of his own head? If we reach it—this we can do—we stand a good chance of interfering with God's grip (may He forgive us).

O Dorothy, I think of you, and the beat people, and the ones with nothing, and the poor in virtue, the very poor, the ones no one can respect. I am not worthy to say I love all of you. Intercede for me, a stuffed shirt in a place of stuffed shirts and a big dumb phony, who have tried to be respectable and have succeeded. What a deception! I know, of course, you are respected too, but you have a right to be, and you didn't jump into the most respectable possible situation and then tell everyone all about it. I am not worried about all this and am not beating myself over the head. I just think that for the love of God I should say it, and that for the love of God you should pray for me . . .

August 17, 1960

Your good letter of June 5th has been waiting for a reply and before that the Cassian came, for which I do not believe I have yet thanked you. It has been a very welcome addition to the novitiate library, for I have been working on the Conferences with the novices. It is in a sense our only real manual of ascetic theology. I love Cassian, though I cannot always be as tough as he is.

. . . Dorothy, what you say about the disturbed family moves me deeply. I was in Louisville at the Little Sisters of the Poor yesterday, and realized that it is in these beautiful, beat, wrecked, almost helpless old people that Christ lives and works most. And in the hurt people who are bitter and say they have lost their faith. We (society at large) have lost our sense of values and our vision. We despise everything that Christ loves, everything marked with His compassion. We love fatness health bursting smiles the radiance of satisfied bodies all properly fed and rested and sated and washed and perfumed and sexually relieved. Anything else is a horror and a scandal to us. How sad. It makes me more and more sad and ashamed, for I am part of the society which has these values and I can't help sharing its guilt, its illusions. Whether I like it or not I help perpetuate the illusion in one way or other—by a kind of illusion of spirituality which tends to justify the other and make it more smug on the rebound. And I am not poor here. I wonder if I am true to Christ, if I have obeyed His will. I have obeyed men, all right. I have perhaps been too ready to obey them. I am not so sure I have obeyed my Lord. The equation is sometimes temptingly oversimplified. Do please pray above all that I may really and from my deepest heart obey Him, it is crucially important now.

Yes, I too love Dostoevsky, very much. Staretz Zosima can always make me weep and a lot of the beat people in the books also. I love the little Jew in *The House of the Dead* (the one with the prayers, the weeping, the joy) . . .

We should in a way fear for our perseverance because there is a big hole in us, an abyss, and we have to fall through it into emptiness, but the Lord will catch us. Who can fall through the center of himself into that nothingness and not be appalled? But the Lord will catch us. He will catch you without fail and take you to His Heart. Because of the *prayers of the poor*. You are the richest woman in America spiritually, with such prayers behind you. You cannot fail even if you try to. The mighty prayers of the poor will embrace you with invincible strength and mercy and bear you in spite of everything into the Heart of God. Those prayers are His own arms. I have immense faith in the prayers of the poor: ask them for me too please. God bless you, in Christ . . .

July 23, 1961

. . . I can see where people would be discouraged these days. We have still got the habit of thinking in terms of Christian civilization and when the civilization(?) of our time fails more and more to measure up to what we have accustomed ourselves to expect, we are tempted to despair. We have got to keep up our trust in Christian civilization as an ideal, and our hope in God as the One Reality. I can imagine CW would be a place where really sincere people come to the end of the line, that is to say they seek there the last resort of truth and hope to be able to do something, and see how helpless they are. This frustration is terrible, but I hope salutary. And at CW one at least can and doubtless must face it. Here too, but with a whole lot more cushions. In a way it is nice to be able to think that one's prayers are invisibly effecting great things: you don't have to look then. It is not our prayers or our works either that do good, but God only. But we can be glad if He chooses to use us, and if we are able to perceive it in some way.

I become more and more skeptical about my writing. There has been some good and much bad, and I haven't been nearly honest enough and clear enough. The problem that torments me is that I can so easily become part of a general system of delusion. From the moment we are labeled as Catholics and the "Catholic position" also has a label, even our sincere rejection of falsity can be used in the service of falsity, since our label is associated with the system that wants and intends to defend itself—and the glory of God—with bombs. But all the systems are in the same boat, it seems. I find myself more and more drifting toward the derided and probably quite absurd and defeatist position of a sort of Christian anarchist. This of course would be foolish, if I followed it to the end. But it is no less foolish to hang in midair halfway to it. But perhaps the most foolish of all would be to renounce all consideration of any alternative to the status quo, the giant machine. These words on the Sunday of Christ's tears over Jerusalem . . .

August 23, 1961

. . . I still don't know what the censors think of it [Auschwitz poem], but there are very good chances that their judgment will be entirely negative: not because of "faith and morals" but because a "Trappist should not know about these things, or should not write about them, etc."

This, Dorothy, is sometimes a very great problem to me. Because I feel obligated to take very seriously what is going on, and to say whatever my conscience seems to dictate, provided of course it is not contrary to the faith and to the teaching authority of the Church. Obedience is a most essential thing in any Christian and above all in a monk, but I sometimes wonder if, being in a situation where obedience would completely silence a person on some important moral issue on which others are also keeping silence—a crucial issue like nuclear war—then I would be inclined to wonder if it were not God's will to ask to change my situation. Of course I do not plan this and I know it would be impossible (because I have already tried). I also know that somehow God always makes it possible for me to say what seems to be necessary, and hence there is no question that I am completely in His hands where I am and that I should therefore continue as I am doing. But why this awful silence and apathy on the part of Catholics, clergy, hierarchy, lay people on this terrible issue on which the very continued existence of the human race depends? . . .

. . . As for writing: I don't feel that I can in conscience, at a time like this, go on writing just about things like meditation, though that has its point. I cannot just bury my head in a lot of rather tiny and secondary monastic studies either. I think I have to face the big issues, the life-and-death issues: and this is what everyone is afraid of . . .

If you have anybody there who wants to make a retreat, certainly I am sure I can arrange for them to do so here. Just write to me. If the letter reaches me, the chances are fifty-fifty, I will make sure that things are arranged. It is in a place like this that CO's and sit-ins and all sorts of people who are struggling hard to swim against the stream ought to be able to find silence and rest and understanding. Only trouble it is so far away . . .

September 22, 1961

Just a quick note. The attached article ["The Root of War"] IS for *The Catholic Worker* and it IS censored. So if you want it you can go right ahead with it.

Actually it is a chapter from *New Seeds of Contemplation*. This is a rewriting of the old *Seeds* which preserves practically all the material that was there before and adds a whole lot more. Most of this material is new, though there are a few paragraphs from the old version. I have just added on at the end a page or two which situate these thoughts in the present crisis. I think it would probably be better if this last part were actually printed at the beginning, as an introduction to the rest. You can easily spot it by the change in the typewriter ribbon.

I have to give a conference to the novices now so I close, and will write more later. I have some other things to say. In any case let us be united in prayer and trust and work for the abolition of war in any way that we can, even if there seems to be slight hope of success. Our faith demands it, and you have been one of the few that have really responded to God. One shudders at the mentality of so many American Catholics, feeding their minds continually with hate propaganda in the name of religion. May God have mercy on us.

The December issue of The Catholic Worker *carried an article by Thomas Merton called "Shelter Ethics" (see James Forest correspondence). Merton had been informed that Dorothy Day had not agreed with the approach he took in the article. The following is his attempt to clarify.*

[*Cold War Letter 11*]

December 20, 1961

I have read your latest "On Pilgrimage" in the December *CW* and I want to say how good I think it is. In many ways it is about the best thing I have seen that came out of this whole sorry shelter business. What you say in the beginning is clear and uncontrovertible. You make one unanswerable point after another, though I don't claim that people are not going to answer you, and some may get quite hot about the fact that you want to point out that Castro may have good intentions and may have been in actual fact less wicked than our mass media want him to have been. People who are scared and upset use a very simple logic, and they think that if you defend Castro as a human being you are defending all the crimes that have ever been committed by communism anywhere, and they feel that you are threatening *them*. But as Christians we have to keep on insisting on the distinction between the man, the person, and the actions and policies attributed to him and his group. We have to remember the terrible danger of projecting on to others all the evil we find in ourselves, so that we justify our desire to hate that evil and to destroy it in them. The basic thing in Christian ethics is to look at the *person* and not at the *nature*. That is why natural law so easily degenerates, in practice and in casuistry, to jungle law which is no law at all. Because when we consider "nature" we consider the general, the theoretical, and forget the concrete, the individual, the personal reality of the one confronting us. Hence we can see him not as our other self, not as Christ, but as our demon, our evil beast, our nightmare. This, I am afraid, is what a wrong, unintelligent and un-Christian emphasis on natural law has done.

Persons are known not by the intellect alone, not by principles alone, but only by love. It is when we love the other, the enemy, that we obtain from God the key to an understanding of who he is, and who we are. It is only this realization that can open to us the real nature of our duty, and of right action. To *shut out* the person and to refuse to consider him as a person, as an other self, we resort to the impersonal "law" and to abstract "nature." That is to say we block off the reality of the other, we cut the intercommunication of our nature and his nature, and we consider only our own nature with its rights, its claims, its demands. And we justify the evil we do to our brother because he is no longer a brother, he is merely an adversary, an accused. To restore communication, to see our oneness of nature with him, and to respect his personal rights and his integrity, his worthiness of love, we have to see ourselves as similarly accused along with him, condemned to death along with him, sinking to the abyss with him, and needing, with him, the ineffable gift of grace and mercy to be saved. Then, instead of pushing him down, trying to climb out by using his head as a stepping-stone for ourselves, we help ourselves to rise by helping him to rise. For when we extend our hand to the enemy who is sinking in the abyss, God reaches out to both of us, for it is He first of all who extends our hand to the enemy. It is He who "saves himself" in the enemy, who makes use of us to recover the lost groat which is His image in our enemy.

It is all too true that when many theologians talk about natural law, they are talking about jungle law. And this is no law at all. It is not natural either. The jungle is not natural. Or rather, perhaps the true primeval life is natural in a higher sense than we realize. The "jungles" which are our cities are worse than jungles, they are sub-jungles, and their law is a sub-jungle law, a sub-sub-natural law. And here I refer not to those who are considered the lowest in society, but rather those who exercise power in the jungle city, and use it unscrupulously and inhumanly, whether on the side of "law and order" or against law and order.

And yet, as a priest and as one obligated by my state to preach and explain the truth, I cannot take occasion from this abusive view of natural law to reject the concept altogether. On the contrary, if I condemn and reject *en bloc* all the ethical principles which appeal to the natural law, I am in fact undercutting the Gospel ethic at the same time. It is customary to go through the Sermon on the Mount and remark on the way it appears to *contrast with* the Mosaic law and the natural law. On the contrary, it seems to me that the Sermon on the Mount is not only a supernatural fulfillment of the natural law, but an affirmation of "nature" in its true, original Christian meaning: of nature as assumed by Christ in the Incarnation. As a remote basis for this, we might consider Colossians 1:9–29, noting especially that we humans who were at enmity with one another are "reconciled in the body of His flesh." Christ the Lord is the Word Who has assumed our nature, which is one in all of us. He has perfectly fulfilled and so to speak transfigured and elevated not only nature but the natural law which is, in its most basic expression, treating our brother as one who has the same nature as we have. Now here is the point where our ethical speculation has gone off the rails. In the biblical context, in the context of all spiritual and ancient religions that saw this kind of truth, the good which man must do and the evil he must avoid according to the natural law must be based on an experience or a realization of connaturality with our brother.

Example: if I am in a fallout shelter and trying to save my life, I must see that the neighbor who wants to come into the shelter also wants to save his life as I do. I must experience his need and his fear just as if it were my need and my fear. This is not supernatural at all, it is purely and simply the basis of the natural law, which of course has been elevated and supernaturalized. But it is *per se* natural. If then I experience my neighbor's need as my own, I will act accordingly, and if I am strong enough to act out of love, I will cede my place in the shelter to him. This I think is possible, at least theoretically, even on the basis of natural love. In fact, personally I am sure it is. But at the same time there is the plentiful grace of God to enable us to do this.

Now to approach casuistry: if the person who threatens the life of my children, say, is raving mad, I have a duty to protect my children, it may be necessary to restrain the berserk guy by force . . . etc. But my stomach revolts at the casuistical approach to a question like this at a time like this.

My point is this, rather, that I don't think we ought to simply discard the concept of the natural law as irrelevant. On the contrary I think it is very relevant once it is properly understood. Matthew 5:21–26 is, to my way of thinking, a vindication of human nature because it is a *restoration* of human nature. I admit that this view of nature is perhaps not that of the scholastics but rather that of the Greek Fathers. But it is to my way of thinking more natural, more in accord with the nature of man, to be non-violent, to be not even angry with his brother, to not say "raca," etc. But we cannot recover this fullness of nature without the grace of God. In this peculiar view, then, the natural law is *not merely what is ethically right and fitting for fallen man considered purely in his fallen state:* it is the law of his nature as it came to him from the hand of God, the law imprinted in his nature by the image of God, which each man is and must be in his very nature. Hence the natural law is the law which inclines our inmost heart to conform to the image of God which is in the deepest center of our being, and it also inclines our heart to respect and love our neighbor as the image of God. But this concept of nature is only comprehensible when we see that it presupposes grace and calls for grace and as it were sighs and groans for grace. For actually our contradiction with ourselves makes us realize that without grace we are lost and condemned to a sub-natural law.

In a word, then, I want with my whole heart to fulfill in myself this natural law, in order by that to fulfill also the law of grace to which it leads me. And I want with my whole heart to realize and fulfill my communion of nature with my brother, in order that I may be by that very fact one with him in Christ. But here, as I said in the beginning, I must rise above nature, I must *see the person* (this is still possible to nature "alone") and I must see the person in Christ, in the Spirit.

These words are to explain and apologize for the totally insufficient tone of my last article in *CW* which seemed in so many ways to fall short of your editorial standards. Yet any statements made there about self-defense were based entirely on the only practitioner of non-violence I have read in detail, Gandhi . . .

March 21, 1962

. . . I am sorry to hear that you are having your usual interminable troubles with the well-meaning young men that join the *CW* and that some have had to leave. I was glad to meet Jim Forest [in February 1962] who seemed to me to be exceptional. But the impression I got from all of them that were down here was that *CW* seemed to be a temporary phase with them and that their hearts were really in something different.

The literary aspirations they feel certainly seem to be a little offbeat with regard to CW. I think they have good possibilities as poets and so on, but I don't know if they are all what you are looking for in your work there. But I do say this, I think that it is fine that you are able to have such a flexible and wide open setup there. CW certainly seems to me to be a real sign of life and to be full of a certain truth that one looks for in vain in many other quarters. I hope your book is coming along well, and pray that it will be very meaningful. And I hope your health is good and that God's grace will be with you in all things more and more. Please pray for me, as I need light and guidance badly. I especially do not know what precisely Our Lord expects of me in regard to the world situation and peace, but I am sure that I must be careful not to overdo the activity and try to write too much about it. This is taking on something of the character of a temptation and I know I must be careful . . .

Some of the young staff people at the CW *had put out a risqué magazine on the press of the* Worker. *Dorothy dismissed them. These are the "troubles" mentioned in the preceding letter and the "situation" referred to in the following letter.*

April 9, 1962

Many thanks for your letter. There were certainly a lot of things I needed to know. And I am glad to be enlightened, though sorry to know them. You are right about the peace movement. It is so small and helpless in itself, and now to find it eaten up from the inside. It is really almost nothing. It is a good thing that we are able to put our hopes in God and not in movements. What is being done by men seems almost meaningless. And yet we can do what we can, and say what needs to be said, and I suppose suffer what needs to be suffered.

The situation you refer to at CW, when they would have so little sense and so little compassion as to create a problem for the poor people coming there for help, shows how poor these dedicated ones really are. It has been that way all through my lifetime, I can remember it at Friendship House also. I suppose all the way through there is an attempt to escape from the real struggle into a mixed-up idealistic, sexy, pseudo-mysticism. Poor people. I feel sorry for them. I am most sorry to hear about J. marrying J.; I am sure it will not work out and he will just get fouled up by it.

. . . I am trying to get all the material I have done on peace together in a book. Do please pray that the obstacles to this and the various difficulties may smooth themselves out, by God's will. I think at any rate the picture is rounding out and I am getting clear on what to say.

One thing is bothering me: what about the American Pax? Was Jim the one running that, and if so has he completely dropped it? What is happening? A couple of people have written to me about it, and are interested. I hope it will not just die stillborn. Please let me know what is being done and who is in charge, if anyone . . .

. . . I am enclosing a copy of the Ladies' Jail poem [see Forest correspondence], which however is not yet censored, but it is for *CW*. I will let you know when it is cleared by the censors.

And so here we are in the middle of the mystery of the Passion. Our Lord has certainly had to do it all by Himself. We have not been much help to Him, ever, and perhaps we cannot be. And now with this tremendous destructive power, and with our incapacity to handle it, and our inability to think straight, and our best efforts going astray: it would be sad and discouraging, if we did not remember that the Cross itself is the sign of victory. But victory is one thing and "success," in the dimensions familiar to us, is quite another. You are so right about prayer being the main thing: it is the realm that cannot be closed to us and cannot be got at. There we are strongest because we are frankly centered in our helplessness and in His power, not obsessed with fictions and trivialities . . .

[*Cold War Letter 86*]

June 16, 1962

. . . It is true that I am not theoretically a pacifist. That only means that I do not hold that a Christian *may not* fight, and that a war *cannot* be just. I hold that there is such a thing as a just war, even today there can be such a thing, and I think the Church holds it. But on the other hand I think that is pure theory and that in practice all the wars that are going around, whether with conventional weapons, or guerrilla wars, or the cold war itself, are shot through and through with evil, falsity, injustice, and sin so much so that one can only with difficulty extricate the truths that may be found here and there in the "causes" for which the fighting is going on. So in practice I am with you, except insofar, only, as a policy of totally uncompromising pacifism may tend in effect to defeat itself and yield to one of the other forms of injustice. And I think that your position has an immense importance as a symbolic statement that is irreplaceable and utterly necessary. I also think it is a scandal that most Christians are not solidly lined up with you. I certainly am.

. . . Yesterday I mailed to you a copy of the book which is not to be published, *Peace in a Post-Christian Era*. My Superiors, having been alerted by zealous individuals in this country, felt that I was "going too far" and getting away from the contemplative vocation into "dangerous ground," etc. etc. The book has not even been censored, just forbidden. I accept this with good will and I think humor, because there is a lot of irony in it after all. Have you seen the news release about the fallout shelter which our monks in upper New York [Abbey of the Genesee, Piffard, NY] have built for themselves? What a grim joke that is! In all their innocence. Where is the "prudence of serpents" that sees through the lies and nonsense with which the world surrounds and seduces us, especially the Catholics who are so lamentably involved in worldly interests? The fallout shelter at that monastery is to be seen in the light of the "monks bread" ads. It is the same monastery which gets royalties from the bread formula which is used by some big bakeries in the East. It all hangs together, doesn't it? It becomes part of the same "image" (that fatuous, unintelligent monk-face in the ad, and the fatuous shelter in which the monks say, with all seriousness, "No, we will probably not have the Blessed Sacrament there permanently"). Monks bread. Bl. Sacrament temporarily in the shelter with the monks etc. One shudders a little.

I am so happy you are going to Brazil [to join the Goss-Mayrs]. Amoroso Lima is the translator of one of my books, and I met him some years ago. Is Aimee his wife? If so I met her also, and she is charming, as also were their children, then quite young. I saw one of his sons recently, with his wife. They are a lovely family and wonderful people of whom I am very fond, but he has an altogether exaggerated idea of my powers as a writer I am afraid. Do be sure to give them my most cordial messages. In fact, before you go, please let me know and I will send you a couple of things to take to them. I have an awful time trying to get things through to Brazil by mail.

I will be sending you a copy of the *Cold War Letters* too. Since I am not writing anything about war anymore, I have gone back to the Fathers, to Cassiodorus, Cyprian, Tertullian etc. . . .

It is no use speculating too much about the world situation, but it is certainly a very risky one. The whole world is under judgment, and one feels it keenly. Without saying that I think something is going to happen, I think I can say reasonably that there is just no reason in the world for it *not* to happen. I think the evil in us all has reached the point of overflowing. May the Holy Spirit give us compunction and inner truth and humility and love, that we may be a leaven in this world . . .

All blessings to you, Dorothy, and to all at the *Worker*. Your presence and your example are precious to all of us, and especially to me.

July 12, 1962

The poem about the Ladies' Jail has finally, after five months, been passed by the censors of the Order. The fact that it took five months was due to an accident, the censor's letter was lost. In reality it took only three and a half months to censor this three-page poem. But in any case it is now censored and it is all yours to print if you want it. And if not, then please let me know and I will send it elsewhere.

. . . When are you going to Brazil? I will send along some extra copies of these mimeographed things for you to take to Alceu Amoroso

Lima. Anything that comes unaccountably like that and that you already have yourself, please take to him. I don't want to overload you however.

With all blessings and good wishes, especially for your trip to South America. I just read the report written by Jean and Hildegard Goss-Mayr and it was one of the most deeply moving documents that has come into my hands for a very long time.

August 11, 1962

You might be interested in the copy of the letter I sent to Hiroshima. A couple of extras in case you want to share it with anyone. It really says nothing, but I wanted to make at least an inarticulate gesture of some sort, with the Russians dropping their bomb on the very anniversary of the destruction of Hiroshima. The persistent erosion of all compassion, all human sensitivity, all awareness of human and moral values, goes on and on. I can see no good end to this.

. . . I am sorry that Pax is not shaping up to anything. I suppose it is a manifestation of our confusion and helplessness. We Catholics are so frustrated and passive that we no longer know how to begin to do the things we really ought to do. It saddens one: I should talk, you must be much more saddened by it than I could ever be, since I am away from most of it.

Let us keep praying for one another. I see clearly the futility and misdirection of my own life. But God can accept waste, I suppose, if it is well intended. My gift of zero. Yet we must not simply do the futile on purpose and that is where the problem comes, perhaps . . .

September 5, 1963

The other day a packet of mimeographed articles emanating from here went out to you. I hope you like some of the things, but please note: *none of it is for publication* in *CW* because most of the items have been accepted elsewhere, and those that have not are not for publication anywhere. I was glad though that you were able to use the Danish Non-Violence bit under a pseudonym. [It was published in *CW*, July–August 1963, under the name Benedict Moore.]

You know by now how much I enjoyed your book [*Loaves and Fishes*]. Am reading James Baldwin's *Go Tell It on the Mountain* which I find very moving.

You often mention my perseverance: I am no stronger than anybody else, but it seems to me that I am almost bound to stay here even for the worst motives, let alone the best. Here is one place where they will have me and feed me and tolerate my presence permanently. How do I know I would find the same charity elsewhere? Tramp as I am, I think this is sufficient inducement, even if there were not the question of heaven to which I am not, I think, insensitive. If people are fussing about my being as they think somewhere other than here, that is their affair. I am here and unless the Lord pulls me out by the hair of the head (and there is no hair left) I will probably remain here, as far as I know. I have no other plans. Bless you, Dorothy, and pray for me your least brother.

December 4, 1963

Fr. Charles passed your letter along from the hospital, and I write immediately to say that you will certainly be most welcome to come down here and I earnestly hope that you will, because I have been wanting to see you if you were out this way. Fr. Charles will be very anxious to see you too. He will probably be going home a little before Christmas. Can you get down in the meantime? Please let us know at once and we will plan on it. I do hope you can.

I have not been able to get over to the hospital to see Fr. Charles, although others did. I had to be content to wait until his return, so I hope to have a talk with him which has been long delayed. He had his heart attack the day he was supposed to see me, and I was waiting around for him wondering what had gone wrong. Only later did I learn that he was in the hospital, and wanted to get over, but things always seemed to work out so that I was not permitted.

The events of these recent days have been shocking enough to wake the dead. As though we were being bombarded with significant and terrible warnings. I learned only from your letter that Fr. La Farge and Huxley were dead too. May they rest in peace . . .

July 16, 1965

I was very glad indeed to get your letter. It came at a good time, I had just been reading and enjoying Karl Stern's new book, *The Flight from Woman*, which is excellent. And I am always very glad to hear from you. I think often of you and pray often for you and the CW. Jim Douglass and his wife were here the other day speaking of you.

When you wrote, I had been thinking of some texts from St. Maximus you might like, so I decided to write them up as a whole article. You can have it for CW if you like [published September 1963]. I think the texts are very striking and hope I have helped make them understandable to Americans.

The Church is going through difficult and I believe hopeful times, but the question of the bomb getting back into Schema 13 is a bit disturbing . . .

November 22, 1965

This is just a note to thank you for your warm, wise letter. You are well experienced in this kind of upset, over the years, and I was grateful to hear your human voice simply stating what you know, and not magnifying it any further.

It might help to explain my telegram—I do not try to justify it—a rather ill-considered and immediate reaction to the sad news of Roger La Porte. I think the intensity of the reaction was due mainly to the fact that I am not properly informed and very much isolated now, naturally, since I am living in solitude in the woods near the monastery. I am aware that I cannot make adequate judgments of such things and hence my obvious reaction would be not to judge at all but simply to pray. Unfortunately Jim Douglass has been very anxious for me to write or say something about what has been going on in the peace movement. I have tried to persuade him that I am not in a position to speak intelligently, but he insists. On top of that, my Superiors have told me not to write on current events, controversial events, what have you. The prohibition is not very precise, so the way is still uncertainly open for perhaps a statement of principle, but I am very unsure. All this adds up to a very messy situation for me.

My main reaction has been to try to withdraw further from the peace movement and from the appearance of being publicly involved in it, and this too was unfortunate, because Jim Forest and above all John Heidbrink interpreted this as a knife in the back, and so on (since I said I would prefer to be no longer on the list of sponsors of the Catholic Peace Fellowship). They think I am doing this out of fear, and I know I cannot really expect them to take the slightest interest in the peculiar problem I have trying to live an authentic life of solitude (which I certainly think will do more for the peace movement than anything I write). However, we will work this out quietly I hope, and come to some conclusion. John Heidbrink by the way in a long letter argued that my whole monastic life was a pure evasion, that I ought to be back in the world leading a life of authentic involvement like himself, etc. etc. Don't worry, I have heard enough of that to know what I think of it. I am more determined than ever on my present course, in spite of what they may think about it, in fact their opposition is to me another reason to continue obeying God rather than man.

One point remains: Jim Douglass's insistence that I write something. Actually I think I am in an even worse position than before, since if I do say anything it will be that I personally do not agree with card burning, and I would much rather not say this since once again I am not "there," I cannot really judge, I have not discussed it. And by my request to resign from CPF I have put myself clearly in a position where anything I say will be automatically mistrusted. Hence I hardly plan to write anything for *CW* at this moment on this subject. But I do have an opportunity to make some statement on it in another connection. It will be general enough and constructive enough, I hope, to be of some use. But I honestly realize that my function now is *not* to try to be a voice in the peace movement. I feel that such an attempt would be clearly false on my part, playing a role God does not now ask of me (unless in some particular situation it becomes evident that He does require me to speak. But this is not that situation.)

This therefore is an apology for anything disturbing or untoward that may have been in my telegram, and also a request for your good prayers. I keep you and all your intentions in my own prayers and am very much with you especially in these times of tension when you are threatened by upset people and when we must depend more and more on truth and faith and support one another by love . . .

December 20, 1965

Thanks for your very good letter. I reached what I thought would be a fair solution with the CPF: I would continue to be their sponsor insofar as I heartily approve their pastoral activities for objectors, etc., and it would be understood in some way (by a statement or something) that I did not make myself responsible for every political act of theirs. I haven't heard, but I should think that would be acceptable. It is more and more clear to me that if I pretended to keep up with politics here and tried to utter profound judgments from my solitude I would be deceiving myself and perhaps others. You are right, and I see that my solitude has to be completely genuine, otherwise what use is it?

About Dan Berrigan: I guess you and I are a bit old-fashioned, but I agree with you. I wrote a quiet letter to his Provincial, not protesting the decision but just saying that I had full confidence in Dan as a fine priest who was doing much good, and got a courteous reply. Quite possibly there was a little string pulling behind the scenes to get him out of NY but I don't see that he will suffer much from the transfer and will probably come back better than ever. I have had enough in twenty-four years of monastic life to know that even if certain measures of Superiors may be a little unfair, one never loses anything by obeying, quite the contrary, and God sometimes reserves special gifts and an extra fruitfulness for us, something we could not have gained without this sacrifice. I hope Dan is taking it well and I am sure he is. As you say, his silence will say much, and probably a great deal more than a lot of noise by his friends. However, Superiors will also have to learn by experience that the Decree on Religious, in the Council, meant what it said: that subjects are to be trusted more and given more latitude in important matters. Maybe some will learn the hard way. But I agree with you, the religious himself should obey and trust God. There is no better way. If there were, Our Lord would have shown it to us. His example led to the Cross.

I liked Jim Douglass's talk very much and am glad you are publishing it. By the way, I am not too well informed but I think poor Jim has some trouble at home and I hope you will pray for him. I think he is suffering considerably. I know you do pray for him but he needs extra prayers I think . . .

December 29, 1965

. . . To me *The Catholic Worker* stands for something absolutely unique and alive in the American Church. It would be hard to put into words how much it means to me, for so many personal reasons: it stands for my own youth and for the kind of influences that shaped my own life thirty years ago. It happened that I went to Friendship House [in Harlem] rather than *CW* because I was at Columbia, FH was just down the hill and so on. But *CW* stands for so much that has always been meaningful to me: I associate it with similar trends of thought, like that of the English Dominicans and Eric Gill, who also were very important to me. And Maritain. And so on. *Catholic Worker* is part of my life, Dorothy. I am sure the world is full of people who would say the same.

True I do not always get it, and sometimes I glance through it and set it aside to read more at leisure and then don't get to it, as so often happens with many things. But naturally I made a point of reading the November issue, which reached me only a few days before Christmas. It is really an historic issue of the paper, deeply moving and very enlightening on many points. It gave me a much clearer view of the motives behind the burning of draft cards. (I was not at all clear about the law that is really being "disobeyed." I thought it was the draft law itself, which I do not consider manifestly unjust, as long as one can be a conscientious objector: but the other law about not destroying the card is, it seems to me, quite a different matter. Here I agree that some protest and civil disobedience may be perfectly right. I would just say that while Tom C. and Dave Miller were right, I am sure, I would not be prepared to say anyone and everyone who burned his card was necessarily doing a good thing.)

If there were no *Catholic Worker* and such forms of witness, I would never have joined the Catholic Church.

. . . I will keep you in my prayers in the New Year, and in this rather chilly solitude. Still, when one has to break the ice to wash one's face one feels a little more like a monk, though I must admit that I have never been much of one. I was very moved by your account of the fast in Rome, and was happy to get the card that all the fasters signed. Let's hope and pray now that the message of the Constitution on the Church in the World will really get through to the Church, especially in the U.S.A. . . .

September 12, 1966

I have not sent you anything for the *CW* for quite a long time, and I have been meaning to. So I wrote this study on Camus for you. I hope you will like it and find it relevant. It is a little contribution to your great work which always remains so important to the Church in our country.

Thanks for the notes you have written me in the past year or so. I may not have answered them all, because in the spring I had a back operation and that slowed me down for the summer. Things are back to normal now more or less. I have taken a permanent commitment to live in the hermitage for the rest of my life, insofar as I can (of course if I get incapacitated I can go to the infirmary). So please pray that I may carry this out as God wants. When one is entirely on his own, I find that curious mistakes become possible. But with the guidance of grace and normal good will they do not have effects that are too terrible. Pray for me, then, and I keep you and the *CW* in my prayers and thoughts always.

You mentioned the fact that in the zeal for new things, many are losing all sense of proportion. I agree with you, and this will certainly cause a great deal of confusion and even do harm before we are through: yet the Holy Spirit remains with us and I have no doubt that through it all we will learn much—maybe even become more humble by our mistakes. I hope so.

February 9, 1967

Thanks so much for your good note of January 29th. I have read your piece in the latest *CW* on Cardinal Spellman and the war. It is beautifully done, soft-toned and restrained, and speaks of love more than of reproof. It is the way a Christian should speak up, and we can all be grateful to you for speaking in this way. It *has* to be done. The moral insensitivity of those in authority, on certain points so utterly crucial for man and for the Church, has to be pointed out and if possible dispelled. It does not imply that we ourselves are perfect or infallible. But what is a Church after all but a community in which truth is shared, not a monopoly that dispenses it from the top down. Light travels on a two-way street in our Church: or I hope it does . . .

Yes, Lent is a joy. And we do not have to be worried about relishing the cleanness of it. It feels better not to be stuffed. A little emptiness does one good, and I think it is better now that it is something one can simply choose without any sense of legal obligation. More of a gift. Not that I am a terribly strict ascetic myself, I assure you. Far from it. In any case I am going to have a little penance mapped out for me when I go to the hospital in a couple of weeks for a minor operation (bursitis on the elbow) . . .

I wrote to Marty some time ago about the possibility of my doing a little piece on that last California Indian, Ishi (the last "wild" one). Do you know that beautiful little book? Have you ever had anything about that in *CW*? Maybe Marty did not get my letter. The mail situation here is always rather unpredictable I am afraid.

August 18, 1867

. . . The hermit life is no joke at all, and no picnic, but in it one gradually comes face to face with the awful need of self-emptying and even of a kind of annihilation so that God may be all, and also the apparent impossibility of it. And of course the total folly of trying to find ways of doing it oneself. The great comfort is in the goodness and sweetness and nearness of all God has made, and the created isness which makes Him first of all present in us, speaking us. Then that other word: "Follow . . ."

Has anyone decided to go to the seven-day fast in Geneva? I wish I could try it but of course can't go. May do what I can about it here in the woods . . .

September 19, 1967

. . . Recently I offered to go to our foundation in Chile, largely because I thought it would be a way of renouncing my citizenship and becoming a citizen of a country that does not have the bomb and probably never will have it. My Abbot is inexorable on keeping me here where the image of Gethsemani won't suffer. It is odd to think that I am supposed to be an edification: I am glad people don't know me! I'd rather be a disedification, and do something worthwhile. Naturally, I am only joking. The solitude that has been granted me here is certainly a precious gift and I value it most highly. The long hours of complete silence are the best thing in the world and I appreciate them more than I can say. Pray that I use them well!

As I go on, and as friends die (Ad Reinhardt, the abstract artist, one of my close friends, had a heart failure and died in August) (please remember him), I think more seriously of the deep value of a repentant life. And working on things like the Auschwitz piece, I see the triviality of all possible monastic efforts at "penance." The thing is just so deep and so serious. Well, one just laughs a lot less. And the running around, the superficiality of so many well-meant efforts at making things new seems quite pitiful at times. So beside the point. You have seen so much more than I have, and understand it all so much better. Fortunately, one also sees the greatness of God and His immense mercy. Then there comes a way of just being quiet, just "shutting up" and minding one's own business which is to listen.

In this context it is a joy to send things to the *CW*, precisely because it is a simple, humble, honest paper that goes its own way and cares nothing for anybody's establishment . . .

July 25, 1968

. . . It is quite touching that you have all those families of imprisoned protesters there at *CW*. Another of the quietly eloquent things so typical of you. I have to get busy and write to some of those in jail.

I am always happy to write something for *CW* when I get a chance. But in the last couple of months I haven't had a chance, having had quite a few meetings, visits and what not. But I did send Eileen Egan a little paper she asked for for the Pax conference these days, and if she does not need it for her magazine you are welcome to it in *CW*.

I pray for the conferences to be a success. And for all of you. Please pray specially for me: I have a big thing coming up. I am to go to Asia as peritus for a regional meeting of abbots and also to attend a meeting of leaders from non-Christian religions. I hope this may mean a deepening of understanding and a chance to enter more deeply into the mind of some of the Asian monastic traditions. Prayer will be the most vital help.

To Dom Francis Decroix

Dom Francis Decroix, abbot of the Cistercian monastery of Frattocchie near Rome, received in 1967 a request from Paul VI for a "message of contemplatives to the world." The Pope suggested that Thomas Merton might be one of the monks asked to compose such a message. Accordingly, Dom Francis in a letter of August 14 requested a statement by the end of the month. Merton wrote his statement* on August 21, the very day he received the abbot's letter. He mailed it the following day with an additional statement.

August 21, 1967

This morning I received your letter of August 14th and I realize I must answer it immediately in order to get the reply to you before the end of the month. This does not leave me time to plan and think, and hence I must write rapidly and spontaneously. I must also write directly and simply, saying precisely what I think, and not pretending to announce a magnificent message which is really not mine. I will say what I can. It is not much. I will leave the rest of you to frame a document of good theology and clearly inspiring hope which will be of help to modern man in his great trouble.

On the other hand I must begin by saying that I was acutely embarrassed by the Holy Father's request. It puts us all in a difficult position. We are not experts in anything. There are few real contemplatives in our monasteries. We know nothing whatever of spiritual aviation and it would be the first duty of honesty to admit that fact frankly, and to add that we do not speak the language of modern man. There is considerable danger that in our haste to comply with the Holy Father's generous request, based on an even more generous estimate of us, we may come out with one more solemn pronouncement which will end not by giving modern man hope but by driving him further into despair, simply by convincing him that we belong to an entirely different world, in which we have

---

* *This letter was published in* The Monastic Journey, *edited by Brother Patrick Hart (Sheed, Andrews and McMeel, 1977), pp. 169–73.*

managed, by dint of strong will and dogged refusals, to remain in a past era. I plead with you: we must at all costs avoid this error and act of uncharity. We must, before all else, whatever else we do, speak to modern man as his brothers, as people who are in very much the same difficulties as he is, as people who suffer much of what he suffers, though we are immensely privileged to be exempt from so many, so very many, of his responsibilities and sufferings. And we must not arrogate to ourselves the right to talk down to modern man, to dictate to him from a position of supposed eminence, when perhaps he suspects that our cloister walls have not done anything except confirm us in unreality. I must say these things frankly. I have seen over a thousand young men of our time, or rather nearly two thousand, enter and leave this monastery, coming with a hunger for God and leaving in a state of confusion, disarray, incomprehending frustration and often deep bitterness: because they could not feel that our claims here could be real for them. The problem of the contemplative Orders at present, in the presence of modern man, is a problem of great ambiguity. People look at us, recognize we are sincere, recognize that we have indeed found a certain peace, and see that there may after all be some worth to it: but can we convince them that this means anything *to them*? I mean, can we convince them professionally and collectively, as "the contemplatives" in our walled institution, that what our institutional life represents has any meaning for them? If I were absolutely confident in answering yes to this, then it would be simple to draft the message we are asked to draw up. But to me, at least, it is not that simple. And for that reason I am perhaps disqualified from participating in this at all. In fact, this preface is in part a plea to be left out, to be exempted from a task to which I do not in the least recognize myself equal. However, as I said before, I will attempt to say in my own words what I personally, as an individual, have to say and usually do say to my brother who is in the world and who more and more often comes to me with his wounds which turn out to be also my own. The Holy Father, he can be a good Samaritan, but myself and my brothers in the world we are just two men who have fallen among thieves and we do our best to get each other out of the ditch.

Hence what I write here I write only as a sinner to another sinner, and in no sense do I speak officially for "the monastic Order" with all its advantages and its prestige and its tradition.

Let us suppose the message of a so-called contemplative to a so-called man of the world to be something like this:

My dear brother, first of all, I apologize for addressing you when you have not addressed me and have not really asked me anything. And I apologize for being behind a high wall which you do not understand. This high wall is to you a problem, and perhaps it is also a problem to me, O my brother. Perhaps you ask me why I stay behind it out of obedience? Perhaps you are no longer satisfied with the reply that if I stay behind this wall I have quiet, recollection, tranquillity of heart. Perhaps you ask me what right I have to all this peace and tranquillity when some sociologists have estimated that within the lifetime of our younger generations a private room will become an unheard-of luxury. I do not have a satisfactory answer: it is true, as an Islamic proverb says, "The hen does not lay eggs in the marketplace." It is true that when I came to this monastery where I am, I came in revolt against the meaningless confusion of a life in which there was so much activity, so much movement, so much useless talk, so much superficial and needless stimulation, that I could not remember who I was. But the fact remains that my flight from the world is not a reproach to you who remain in the world, and I have no right to repudiate the world in a purely negative fashion, because if I do that my flight will have taken me not to truth and to God but to a private, though doubtless pious, illusion.

Can I tell you that I have found answers to the questions that torment the man of our time? I do not know if I have found answers. When I first became a monk, yes, I was more sure of "answers." But as I grow old in the monastic life and advance further into solitude, I become aware that I have only begun to seek the questions. And what are the questions? Can man make sense out of his existence? Can man honestly give his life meaning merely by adopting a certain set of explanations which pretend to tell him why the world began and where it will end, why there is evil and what is necessary for a good life? My brother, perhaps in my solitude I have become as it were an explorer for you, a searcher in realms which you are not able to visit—except perhaps in the company of your psychiatrist. I have been summoned to explore a desert area of man's heart in which explanations no longer suffice, and in which one learns that only experience counts. An arid, rocky, dark land of the soul, sometimes illuminated by strange fires which men fear and peopled by specters which men studiously avoid except in their nightmares. And in this area I have learned that one cannot truly know hope unless he has found out how like despair hope is. The language of Christianity has said this for centuries in other less naked terms. But the language of Christianity has been so used and so misused that sometimes you distrust it: you do not know whether or not behind the word "Cross" there stands the experience of mercy and salvation, or only the threat of punishment. If my word means anything to you, I can say to you that I have experienced the Cross to mean mercy and not cruelty, truth and not deception: that the news of the truth and love of Jesus is indeed the true good news, but in our time it speaks out in strange places. And perhaps it speaks out in you more than it does in me: perhaps Christ is nearer to you than He is to me: this I say without shame or guilt because I have learned to rejoice that Jesus is in the world in people who know Him not, that He is at work in them when they think themselves far from Him, and it is my joy to tell you to hope though you think that for you of all men hope is impossible. Hope not because you think you can be good, but because God loves us irrespective of our merits and whatever is good in us comes from His love, not from our own doing. Hope because Jesus is with those who are poor and outcasts and perhaps despised even by those who should seek them and care for them most lovingly because they act in God's name . . . No one on earth has reason to despair of Jesus because Jesus loves man, loves him in his sin, and we too must love man in his sin.

God is not a "problem" and we who live the contemplative life have learned by experience that one cannot know God as long as one seeks to solve "the problem of God." To seek to solve the problem of God is to seek to see one's own eyes. One cannot see his own eyes because they are that with which he sees and God is the light by which we see—by which we see not a clearly defined "object" called God, but everything else in the invisible One. God is then the Seer and the Seeing, but on earth He is not seen. In heaven, He is the Seer, the Seeing and the Seen. God seeks Himself in us, and the aridity and sorrow of our heart is the sorrow of God who is not known in us, who cannot find Himself in us because we do not dare to believe or trust the incredible truth that He could live in us, and live there out of choice, out of preference. But indeed we exist solely for this, to be the place He has chosen for His presence, His manifestation in the world, His epiphany. But we make all this dark and inglorious because we fail to believe it, we refuse to believe it. It is not that we hate God, rather that we hate ourselves, despair of ourselves: if we once began to recognize, humbly but truly, the real value of our own self, we would see that this value was the sign of God in our being, the signature of God upon our being. Fortunately, the love of our fellow man is given us as the way of realizing this. For the love of our brother, our sister, our beloved, our wife, our child, is there to see with the clarity of God Himself that we are good. It is the love of my lover, my brothers or my child that sees God in me, makes God credible to myself in me. And it is my love for my lover, my child, my brother, that enables me to show God to him or her in himself or herself. Love is the epiphany of God in our poverty. The contemplative life is then the search for peace not in an abstract exclusion of all outside reality, not in a barren negative closing of the senses upon the world, but in the openness of love. It begins with the acceptance of my own self in my poverty and my nearness to despair in order to recognize that where God is there can be no despair, and God is in me even if I despair. That nothing can change God's love for me, since my very existence is the sign that God loves me and the presence of His love creates and sustains me. Nor is there any need to understand how this can be or to explain it or to solve the problems it seems to raise. For there is in our hearts and in the very ground of our being a natural certainty which is co-extensive with our very existence: a certainty that says that insofar as we exist we are penetrated through and through with the sense and reality of God even though we may be utterly unable to believe or experience this in philosophic or even religious terms.

O my brother, the contemplative is the man not who has fiery visions of the cherubim carrying God on their imagined chariot, but simply he who has risked his mind in the desert beyond language and beyond ideas where God is encountered in the nakedness of pure trust, that is to say in the surrender of our poverty and incompleteness in order no longer to clench our minds in a cramp upon themselves, as if thinking made us exist. The message of hope the contemplative offers you, then, brother, is not that you need to find your way through the jungle of language and problems that today surround God: but that whether you understand or not, God loves you, is present in you, lives in you, dwells in you, calls you, saves you, and offers you an understanding and light which are like nothing you ever found in books or heard in sermons. The contemplative has nothing to tell you except to reassure you and say that if you dare to penetrate your own silence and risk the sharing of that solitude with the lonely other who seeks God through you, then you will truly recover the light and the capacity to understand what is beyond words and beyond explanations because it is too close to be explained: it is the intimate union in the depths of your own heart, of God's spirit and your own secret inmost self, so that you and He are in all truth One Spirit. I love you, in Christ.

August 22, 1967

Since the letter I wrote yesterday was too late for yesterday's mail, I am sending this one which may perhaps be more succinct and more useful. I thought of destroying yesterday's letter or entirely rewriting it, but I send it as it is, in the hope that there may still be some point in it.

First of all, I want to say how touched and grateful I am that the Holy Father should remember me, and I will write to him myself to express my gratitude and devotion.

About the message he asks of us: I should say first of all that it is not our place to write anything apologetic. Thus I am sure we all agree that it is not for us to spell out proofs for the existence of God, but merely to bear witness in our simplicity to His universal love for all men and His message of salvation, but above all to His presence in the hearts of all men, including sinners, including those who hate Him. Without going into technical distinctions of natural, supernatural, and so on, though emphasizing grace later on.

The important thing in our message should it seems to me be prayer and contemplation. But we must be careful not to present prayer as a mere formal duty or to emphasize prayer of petition. We should bear in mind that Marx taught an interesting doctrine about religious alienation, which is a consequence of regarding God as distant and purely transcendent and putting all our hope for every good in the future life, not realizing God's presence to us in this life, and not realizing that prayer means contact with the deepest reality of life, our own truth in Him. Also we should perhaps point out that prayer is the truest guarantee of personal freedom. That we are most truly free in the free encounter of our hearts with God in His word and in receiving His Spirit which is the Spirit of sonship, truth and freedom. The Truth that makes us free is not merely a matter of information about God but the presence in us of a divine person by love and grace, bringing us into the intimate personal life of God as His Sons by adoption. This is the basis of all prayer and all prayer should be oriented to this mystery of sonship in which the Spirit in us recognizes the Father. The cry of the Spirit in us, the cry of recognition that we are Sons in the Son, is the heart of our prayer and the great motive of prayer. Hence recollection is not the exclusion of material things but attentiveness to the Spirit in our inmost heart. The contemplative life should not be regarded as the exclusive prerogative of those who dwell in monastic walls. All men can seek and find this intimate awareness and awakening which is a gift of love and a vivifying touch of creative and redemptive power, that power which raised Christ from the dead and cleanses us from dead works to serve the living God. Which should remind us also that the monastery must not be a place of mere "dead works" and that faith is the most important thing in our lives, not the empty formalities and rites which are mere routines not vivified by the living presence of God and by His love which is beyond all legalism. It should certainly be emphasized today that prayer is a real source of personal freedom in the midst of a world in which men are dominated by massive organizations and rigid institutions which seek only to exploit them for money and power. Far from being the cause of alienation, true religion in spirit is a liberating force that helps man to find himself in God.

I regret that time does not permit me to write more on this. I feel it is useless to try to convey these ideas on paper when it would be much more worthwhile to be able to discuss them with you in living words and work out with you and the other Fathers just what ought to be said. I will in any case pray that you may arrive at something corresponding to what the Holy Father really wants.

To James Douglass

As theologian and writer, James Douglass is perhaps best known for the thoroughness of his commitment to a life of unconditional love and of non-violent resistance to evil, especially to what he considers the greatest man-made evil of our times: nuclear weapons. Douglass has taught at Bellarmine College (Louis-

ville), the University of Hawaii, and the University of Notre Dame. His first meeting with Merton came while he was teaching at Bellarmine College. He served from 1962 to 1965 at the Second Vatican Council as theological advisor to some of the bishops on questions regarding nuclear war and conscientious objection. He has written three books on the theology of non-violence: The Non-Violent Cross *(Macmillan, 1968),* Resistance and Contemplation *(Doubleday, 1972), and* Lightning East and West *(Sunburst, 1980).*

Since 1973 Douglass has been actively involved in the anti-nuclear movement. He helped found Ground Zero Center for Non-Violent Action alongside the Trident nuclear submarine base near Seattle, Washington. Ground Zero is not only devoted to resistance to nuclear weapons, it is also a center for exploring the meaning of non-violence as a way of life. His thinking and writing have been strongly influenced by the New Testament, and by the writings of Gandhi and of Merton. The fact that he named one of his children Thomas Merton Douglass is perhaps as much a sign of his hopes for his son as it is a tribute to Merton.

May 26, 1965

Your letter just reached me. I will be delighted to see you and Dan [Berrigan] next Monday . . . So I will expect you . . . at the hermitage . . . I can make myself responsible for providing some simple items like bread, oleomargarine and such . . . It will be fine to see you.

I had no idea you had been in Louisville since January. Apparently you wrote to me about it and the letter did not get through, a common occurrence . . .

You may be interested in this copy of a letter I sent to Pope Paul. I think he will sympathize, but I will not be at all surprised if the boys in the Secretariat of State end up by writing a letter to the Abbot telling him to shut me up and see that I do not concern myself with these base worldly issues. They have done this before. Anything can happen. There is no question at all that some rather representative portions of the U.S. Church have simply identified the Pentagon line with Christianity and are blind to the moral consequences of such an attitude. This is a fact which I can only regard as apocalyptic, much as I hate to be dramatic about it . . .

For our part, I think that we can still do something, and perhaps the European bishops can still exert their power. A news item like the one you sent me is good, because it alerts people in time. Much better that they should be a bit scared and get up in arms about it, than to have it happen by surprise at the last moment. I am convinced that at the moment the fact that those who protest against total war are regarded as pacifists creates a certain amount of confusion . . .

November 6, 1965

Thanks for your two letters, and the clippings. I got both, and I must admit that I agree with you. These are disturbing developments, and I cannot claim to understand them. More and more one sees that there is no longer the old kind of "logic" behind events but a new and more monstrous kind of pattern. This is so, or seems so, insofar as we are really changing more and more rapidly and no one knows quite where we are going. We are getting into a kind of political vertigo that could be in part demonic in origin, I suppose. On the other hand I don't think the more frantic reactions are the only proof of this: the deepest symptoms are still those of the massive and official irrationality which provokes everything else.

The awful death of the man [Norman Morrison]* burned in front of the Pentagon is something that will take a little time for me to absorb. I admit I am a bit dazed by it. Of one thing I am sure: the people who saw it must have been shaken up to the point of perhaps momentarily questioning the whole setup. Momentarily, but on the other hand, psychological defenses are so strong and the general voice is there to support them and drown out any new tones. Anyway, whatever else it had, it was an incontestable statement about the Vietnam war . . .

Again, I don't know what I think about the burning of draft cards. At first sight my reaction would be to say that this is an act of provocative violence, a moral aggression which is not justified as the draft law is "just." On the other hand, since I have not discussed it with any of the people involved, I have no way of seeing what they see in it. Personally I remain highly dubious.

You say I should write about all this, and certainly I will say something about the basic principles that may be involved when I can, as I can. But more and more I see that I am simply incompetent to comment on events, as such, or to contribute much that has any immediate value in understanding them. I am too out of contact, never hear of anything until it is all over, almost never have a chance for reasonable discussion or debate, and when I have made up my mind about something I discover that the whole situation has radically changed and calls for a new decision. Hence I am confined to questions of more or less abstract principle, if anything.

The root of all the trouble is the lack of rationality and of clear objective in our whole social system. The massive use of huge technological resources with no long-range plan and no clear objective ends up in a kind of motiveless violence, which is where we now are in Vietnam. We have no ideal, and the pseudo-ideal provided by the hope of better

---

* *Ironically, the day Merton wrote this letter was the very day that Roger La Porte immolated himself in front of the UN building in New York.*

refrigerators for more people, plus a few clichés about faith and liberty etc., do not serve to cloak our essential emptiness. It is this emptiness that is the great danger. And the speed at which we are going makes it impossible to get people to consider the relevancy of the fact that we are going nowhere, just plummeting through space. No wonder we are a bit dizzy at times . . .

November 11, 1965

Today I sent telegrams to Dorothy Day and Jim Forest. To Jim I had to send one asking to remove my name from the list of sponsors of the CPF. Here is a copy of the first draft of a letter I sent him as a follow-up. These are the only ideas I have at the moment. Where and how to write them up I don't know. Send information and suggestions. And any ideas you may have on this. The situation smells very bad and very crazy indeed to me. This suicide business is surely demonic. God help us.

November 24, 1965

This [the article "Peace and Protest"] is an attempt only. Needs correction perhaps. The Catholic Peace Fellowship and Fellowship of Reconciliation are quite mad at me about my letter and attempt to resign as sponsor of the CPF and Heidbrink told me I had no business trying to say anything about the peace movement. Hence I think I would only antagonize them still more if I sent this to *CW* and I don't think *CW* would ever publish it.

Honestly I think I ought to wait, especially as the main parts of this will probably be used in the [Louisville] *Courier-Journal* in an article that is being written about me. For this time, I think this is the best place for it—also maybe some diocesan papers?

December 3, 1965

. . . I thought Bishop Mussio's letter was classic (the typing) but was glad to get the information. I had a very similar one (better typed) from Archbishop Flahiff. I am glad Bishop Wright took the stand he did and shut up Hannan. We owe God thanks for the wonderful way things have turned out. But it remains to see how the modi [i.e., amendments to Council documents which bishops could submit] affect the section on conscientious objection.

After another letter from Jim Forest I decided that there was no real need for me to resign as sponsor of the CPF, provided that it could be made clear that I was not automatically in favor of everything they did. I mean, if they decide on some kind of demonstration, then hand out a news release of it and conclude with the statement that I am one of the sponsors of the Fellowship, people will naturally conclude that I am sponsoring the demonstration if not actually in it. I don't think that is a fair use of my name. But I think we can come to an understanding on this point.

Jim said if I would send a statement he would work it into a story, and thus I think all will work out satisfactorily for everyone . . .

I have not heard from [John] Deedy, but may today. Thanks for handing him the article [Deedy published "Peace and Protest" in the *Pittsburgh Catholic*, of which he was editor.]

December 14, 1965

I think your piece on Vietnam [in *Catholic Worker*, December 1965] was really first-class. Dorothy wrote a good letter saying she likes it very much and is using it. I am delighted. It is really clear, one of the best things you have ever done . . .

Nothing from Jim Forest yet but I am not concerned. I think we have reached a solution and that is that. It will work out. But it is quite clear to me that as a hermit I am no longer in a position to make political judgments in matters of detail myself. I am going to write a piece for Hildegard [Goss-Mayr] (she asked for one) on "humility." Things of a general nature I suppose I can try to speak about . . .

As to the other matters: I certainly keep your problem in my prayers. It is a shame that when there is so much anguish in the world one cannot find a refuge of peace at home, but only more anguish there. Still, that is the nature of the world we are living in. Another indication that our great need is peace, peace everywhere . . .

December 26, 1965

First of all, thanks for the letter and for the Council text . . . The book sounds like a good idea.* I will send along the Gandhi book. I thought you had it. Didn't I ever send it to you? . . .

What about the truce? I have heard something very vague about its possibility, nothing more. Did it ever come off? At least it would be something positive, instead of all this negative and truculent stupidity. I could write to the President if I knew what the situation was . . .

All things considered, the Constitution [on the Church in the Modern World] is good. The mere fact that conscientious objection is recognized is already a great deal, and the firm condemnation of total war is as clear as can be. Anyone who follows the Pentagon line does so now with a bad conscience if he is a Catholic and can read. And understand. But of course it is easy not to see things one does not want to see.

---

* *Douglass was making plans to move from Louisville to Hedley, British Columbia, where he would spend the next two years writing* The Non-Violent Cross, *which at this time was only an idea.*

I was amused at the paragraph about "if you are a freedom fighter you are ok."* Aren't we all freedom fighters always? . . .

March 24, 1967

Ping Ferry sent me what is evidently a chapter of a new book of yours and I just want to say how much I have been stimulated by reading it [Chapter 3 of *The Non-Violent Cross*, "From Gandhi to Christ"]. Certainly you are now getting into your full stride and this is far and away the best and most important thing you have ever written, or that I have seen of yours. I am glad to see someone make the right qualifications about technology while fully accepting secularity as it must be accepted. The trouble with the "secular" Christianity more or less in fashion now, at least among Catholics, as far as I can judge, is that it is simply bustling to catch up with the status quo: affluence, gimmickry, the Muzak-super-market complex and all that. The net result of all this is merely that Los Angeles is the New Jerusalem. There has to be an element of further-looking protest if the absent God is somehow to be realized as present in the supermarket. You bring this out very well.

One thing that struck me in reading your chapter. Not a criticism, but just thinking along the lines you open up and looking forward. There is no question that Gandhi is in the end non-modern. His whole basis is in the Indian tradition and metaphysics. Like Camus, he is essentially a "conservative," in the sense of consciously keeping alive the continuity with a past wisdom stated in contemporary terms. Since I am pretty much in the same boat, I cannot but approve and sympathize. But on the other hand, looking at the thing coldly, I begin to wonder if we are not moving very fast beyond all this and beyond what we still comfortably accept as future. For instance I wonder if the "politics" to which you appeal have the firmness your argument supposes. If we are in the post-Christian era (and we are) are we not also perhaps in the post-political era and post-historic era? Or soon about to be? Is it any more relevant to preach politics to the teenage kids than it is to preach God? Is not the present situation in regard to Vietnam in reality the death of American politics? In a word, instead of tentatively and surreptitiously (and very provisionally) slipping history and politics into the old base position once occupied by meta-physics, as Dewart and Co. seem to do, will we not soon have to face the fact that *all* of it has died on us and is one big embarrassing corpse? The danger is that in accepting the provisional historicism etc. and sociologism as religious areas of reality we may in the end just contribute to the big slide into technical totalism. These are just reflections that have been surfacing lately. What I think is called for is a radical rethinking of politics

---

* *The reference is to a sentence in the Constitution on the Church in the Modern World which tells members of a country's armed forces that they are to be considered "agents of freedom."*

and political relevance, to find something else besides the brutal authoritarian manipulation of the establishments and the quietism or nihilism
of the minorities.

What do you think?

April 17, 1967

Thanks for sending the new chapter (which I return). I like it, and
find the last part especially powerful and convincing. But I find it more
uneven than the other . . . It needs to be tightened up . . .

The long quote from Webb Miller of the non-violent march on the
salt works* is dreadful and perhaps essential. But there are difficulties.
This kind of massive beating down of wave after wave of marchers will
tend for many reasons to make your message quite ambiguous not only
because it is so "Asiatic" and so remote from what we conceive to be our
kind of experience (though not as remote as all that), but because (1) the
human *personality* of the individual marchers is totally lost in the mass
effect, they become cattle, though certainly they were not by any means.
But the reader can't help looking at them as remote, cattle-like, less than
human, and consequently can hardly identify with anyone there (while
he can very easily see the point of Gandhi's fast because there is a *person*
right in focus). (2) When the suffering is not only passive but massive, it
ceases to be really comprehensible by a critical Western reader (acceptable only to the one who forces himself to say, "This is the right way").
Without questioning the undoubted heroism of these people, *was* it on
all their parts a real, fully developed non-violence? Was it in other words
completely and maturely personal, or did they in fact move as a mass,
impelled by the will of a leader? This is one of the great difficult questions
of Indian non-v. and it raises its head here. I am being perhaps overfussy
about this, but I do think that this quote here will not really help your
thesis on voluntary acceptance of suffering. I think it would be much
better to get examples of individuals or very small groups. There it will
be abundantly clear to Americans, and these are the ones you must reach.
The Webb Miller example will be repudiated lock stock and barrel by
SNCC† and the Negro movement in general. The thing has come around
in a circle in this country. In the South, to let yourself be beaten does
not convey the message of human dignity so much as the message that
you are a Negro and therefore naturally take a beating, thereby proving
you are inferior . . . etc. For all these reasons I would suggest being

---

* *The UP report by Webb Miller described the Gandhian march into the Dharasana salt
works in India on May 21, 1930, in which row after row of marchers were beaten by the
police.*
† *The Student Non-Violent Coordinating Committee, which at this time was beginning to
repudiate Martin Luther King's approach and leadership.*

careful about the long quote, though certainly it has to be brought out somewhere in your book I suppose . . .

June 30, 1967

I am returning the two chapters with thanks. The one on the Council is really first-rate, one of the best things in the book full of valuable information and perspectives. And it is really sobering to read! For the first time I have clearly felt to what an extent the Constitution on the Church in the World is an admission that the Church cannot pretend to talk to the world in that way: that she just can't claim to have answers the world really needs to listen to. The efforts of those people to tell everybody what God's mind about the bomb is are just a little shocking, though so many of them did try hard. They were honest and so on. It is getting clearer and clearer that the institutional Church does not measure up to the tasks that she believes and proclaims to be hers, and it is a wonder more people are not fully aware of that. I guess a lot are . . .

Blessed Are the Meek, as you probably know, is coming out as a CPF pamphlet pretty soon. I think it will at least be good-looking! Yes, someday I hope to pursue the distinction between person- and nature-oriented thinking in ethics . . .

October 3, 1967

I am doubly sorry for having delayed about your chapter—the last one ["Christians and the State"]—because now I haven't got your new address and I know you have moved: to Hawaii, no? I hope it will be all right if I send this to B.C. and ask them to forward it.

This last chapter is one of the best and makes some splendid points. You have stated better than anyone recently the whole point of the "render under Caesar" business and I think your final sentence caps it perfectly. It is a very good chapter, but I do have one complaint about it. It seems to me that there is one very thin patch, around p. 21, when you slide over the Constantinian transition with the greatest of ease. A thousand and two thousand years of history are it seems to me dismissed with little hint of their enormous complexity. I don't say "dismissed" fairly, of course, because you cannot be expected to go into all that. Yet it is central to your argument. At the same time, do we really yet know what really went on, what kind of a shift really took place in the thinking of the Church, when "Christendom" went into business? I think it yet remains to be studied. And then too there are so many subtleties about the Dark Ages, about the "truce of God" in the tenth century, about the First Crusade as a means of *peace*, by uniting warring Westerners not in an attack on Jerusalem but in defense of Byzantium (thus helping reunite the two Churches then breaking apart). And all that. I think your treatment needs to at least hint at all these complexities which make the thing more mysterious and more real at the same time. Will we ever really understand it? . . .

To William Du Bay

William H. Du Bay, born in 1934 in Long Beach, California, was ordained to the Roman Catholic priesthood for the archdiocese of Los Angeles in 1960, after completing his studies at St. John's Seminary, Camarillo, California. He was a priest committed to the struggle for black rights in civil society. The archdiocese was especially repressive of priests who dared to defy the Cardinal's ban on all preaching about discrimination and civil rights. Despite the ban, Du Bay did preach on the rights of black people. The result was that he was transferred three times in four years. Finally, in 1964, his frustration at not being allowed to preach what he considered an essential element of the Gospel moved him to send a cable to Pope Paul VI asking that the Cardinal be removed from office for "gross malfeasance" and "abuses of authority" in failing to exert moral leadership against discrimination and for conducting "vicious programs of discrimination" against priests, seminarians, and laymen who showed leadership.

As was the custom when a priest had disobeyed the Cardinal, Du Bay was required to renew his promise of obedience. On June 9, 1964, before two hundred priests on retreat, Du Bay knelt before the Cardinal and repeated his promise of obedience. He had submitted; but he had also made his point and the whole world had heard. This reconciliation with the Cardinal did not last long. In 1966 he published a book without proper clearance in the form of an imprimatur from the archdiocese. In the book, called The Human Church, *Du Bay proposed a labor union of priests and called for other radical reforms. On February 25, 1966, he was suspended and forbidden to exercise his priestly functions in the archdiocese. He appealed in vain to the Pope, and some time later departed from the Los Angeles area.*

May 14, 1964

Thanks for your book which, it seems to me, does not need to be safely publishable, only to be used. It can be used in its present state, or in some other such form, can't it? After it has been used a while and after adjustments have been made, maybe someone will publish it. Naturally with the liberty you have displayed you will meet opposition and publication might mean giving up something somewhere. That is normal. We have to be content with humanity as it is, even though we recognize that we must be helping to change things. We change by pressing on what is there.

Yes you are absolutely right about rights within the Church. The right to have an opinion as a member of the people of God, a right to participate in the life of the people of God, and not just by hymn singing. This is one of the most important things about renewal. Without it, no real renewal. The fact that along with Vatican II there has been a lot of discussion and new ideas have reached a lot of ordinary Christians, this is already something, but not much. It is not just a matter of ideas "reaching ordinary people" but recognizing that "ordinary people" may have some ideas of their own which may be important for the whole Church. And they are entitled to something more than misinformation or withheld information, or tricky and deceptive information. I agree with you that the Catholic liberal is content to make pious statements about "roles" to be assigned and to avoid the issue of changing structures.

. . . Now: why I don't overtly go joining more clubs, at least for the present. In the organizations which I have joined (the Fellowship of Reconciliation, for instance) my membership is more or less symbolic, meaningless. I do not find it easy to keep in contact with things of which I am a member. Contact can be broken at any time. All my mail is censored. Some gets through, some doesn't. I am repeatedly getting in situations like this: I commit myself to something important, get out on a limb, and then suddenly everything goes black. An important letter does not get through and there is one hell of a mess lying around by the time I finally discover what happened. In such circumstances it is impossible to function intelligently. The only way I can be sure a letter gets through is to put it on the "conscience-matter" level and even then I am not sure. This all goes to prove the necessity of the kind of thing you suggest. I agree, but to be effective in my case it has to be at work within the Order itself and using channels of communications which are accessible to us. So I think the only thing I can do for you is start my own end of the tunnel and work in your direction without sending up a whole flock of signals in all directions. In other words, permit me to stay quiet, because I can't yell anyhow.

You should be in touch with Fr. Dan Berrigan, S.J., of Le Moyne College, Syracuse . . .

February 17, 1965

I owe you two letters at least, and I have been wanting very much to write. The thing is though that I have finally reached the point where it is coming to a form letter. I have written one that will have to make do this Lent. But you deserve an answer, and I have not written you since before you became famous [because of the cable to the Pope regarding Cardinal McIntyre], so here goes, for what it is worth.

The book idea sounds fine. I am glad you are writing on war and peace. With the present mess in Vietnam the subject needs treatment, and it is very ambiguous indeed. It seems to me that what needs treatment is something more than nuclear weapons or total warfare, but above all the fact that now Catholic moralists are to a great extent accepting a completely pragmatic and unprincipled moral code in international affairs. There could be no clearer and more obvious example of immoral and aggressive action than the bombing of North Vietnam recently in reprisal for raids carried out by South Vietnamese rebels. The trouble is that the truth of the situation is consistently distorted, and it is to the interest of the Pentagon and the arms manufacturers to see that it is distorted because a bigger war is to their advantage. They are obviously not getting anywhere with the guerrilla kind . . .

. . . You have to be careful that you don't handle the issue in such a way that it can be easily discredited by right-wing types. From that point of view, you have to be especially careful since they have got you typed. You are already a stereotype of the rebel priest, and that puts any cause you defend at a disadvantage since it will be prejudged every time. I would say be as objective and as straight as you can, and don't be unnecessarily provocative, in the interests of truth and peace . . .

August 21 [probably 1966]

Ping Ferry sent me some documents concerning your case and your dealings with the Curia. I have sent them back to him with remarks that are disjointed, superficial and useless. I think a lot about this situation and am very concerned about your struggle, concerned above all that your suffering bravely and sincerely undertaken may not be fruitless. I don't claim to have any profound or far-seeing answers, but I want to say something anyhow, as a brother, something besides the evident fact that all of us who have anything at all are being put through the same kind of wringer in one way or another. It is to our common interest to organize our ideas and our hopes along more effective lines. What I offer now are simply a few remarks that occur to me, that might orient things helpfully . . .

First of all, in studying the documents in terms of a kind of political judo, I notice that the curial types had a tremendous advantage by the fact that they *limited* themselves entirely to the minimum of effort but concentrated at the point of greatest power. You were not "concentrated" in this sense, but dispersed in the sense that it is not quite clear what you want of them.

Second: it seems that this lack of clarity comes from the fact that you are trying to use the thinking and tactics of the civil rights struggle against a Curia that has never heard of that struggle or its thinking and tactics. At the same time you have made a sketchy attempt to translate that thinking and tactic into the language of the Curia, but not in such a way that they have seen what you meant, or even realized what kind of pressure you were trying to put on them. All they seem to know is that you are mad about something, they are not quite clear what, but it is enough for them to write it off as being mad at your Cardinal . . .

Third: at this point they have now to their entire satisfaction and probably also to that of the general public, crystallized the issue in their own terms: you are simply a priest who is mad at his Superior, and mad enough to get out rather than agree with him. From a certain point of view they have won this round, and I think you must take time to consider carefully what you intend to do next. Whatever it is, I think it ought to be directed toward breaking this image of the situation and restating it all in terms that bring the iniquity of the Cardinal and the Curia back to light: iniquity in the old rockbound essence of the impregnable innocence of those who have firmly decided to take no notice.

Fourth: I think your only real hope now is to get seriously in with those bishops who might be inclined to agree with you and help you, and having quietly got back into a diocese and worked at something solid for a while, you could start over with a phalanx of people who all say the same thing as you, some of them with the power to say it and be heard in Rome.

. . . Forgive me butting in like this but as a brother I wanted to say something anyway. I have a few troubles of my own I ask you to pray for. It is rough for all of us, but what I think now is that we can at least avoid hurting ourselves more than we need to, and to no purpose. I think we owe it to ourselves and to God and the people we love to keep ourselves in the fight and not get knocked clean out of it.

God bless you, Bill, and I will certainly keep you in my prayers always.

To Heinrich Dumoulin

Born in 1905 in Wevelinghoven, Rhineland, Germany, Heinrich Dumoulin was ordained a Roman Catholic priest as a member of the Society of Jesus. He has a doctoral degree in philosophy and a licentiate in theology and has been for many years professor of religion and Oriental thought at Sophia University in Tokyo, Japan. He has also served as secretary of the Commission of the Catholic Church in Japan for dialogue with non-Christian religions. He has written The Development of Zen after the Sixth Patriarch *(1953) and* A History of Zen Buddhism *(1963). He has also contributed to the* New Catholic Encyclopedia *and to* Monumenta Nipponica.

July 20, 1964

It is a great pleasure to receive your letter and to be in contact with you. Needless to say, it makes me happy to be able to tell you directly how much I have enjoyed your book on Zen. It is most valuable, and besides that, it has been presented in a most attractive way.

. . . The exchange of ideas I had with Suzuki was in *New Directions 17*, but I don't have a copy here and I cannot give you the date. It is an annual which is put out by New Directions . . . I will ask them to send you a copy. I am afraid it is very avant-garde and I have not read most of what is in it, but I do not recommend it as spiritual.

As to my criticism of your thoughts on Hui Neng. First of all, I am in no position whatever to take issue with you on a scholarly basis, and you realize that this was not my intention. As to my saying that you thought Hui Neng's Zen was on the level of the empirical ego, then perhaps I misinterpreted the English translation.

But, puzzling over the English and the German of the text you cite in your letter, and speaking of it purely in terms of Zen, at least of Zen as I understand it—and this may be no understanding at all—it seems to me that even as you explain it in your letter, it does not fit the Zen of Hui Neng. I am speaking now only of the words. But words like "concentration" and "Konzentrationsübung" strike me as completely foreign to the Zen of Hui Neng. I cannot get anything from your words except the fact that Zen is the suppression of concepts by concentration and effort directed precisely to suppression. There is a mind from which concepts are to be removed, suppressed, eliminated. Then the mind is left in its pure mirror-like activity which is emptiness. I am unable to see how this can be the Zen of Hui Neng, when this is what Hui Neng says Zen is not. When he declares that prajna and dhyana are the same, he seems to me to be saying also that the step from mind-with-concepts to mind-without-concepts is not a step which is taken, but that on the contrary Zen is the realization that the mind-with-concepts is empty and that the concepts themselves are emptiness. This may be pure madness on my part, and as I say, it is only my own understanding of Zen, so I cannot even claim that it is a correct interpretation of Hui Neng. But it does seem to me to be the meaning of Hui Neng's verse, as opposed to that of Shen Hsui.

Since I may be completely wrong in this, the best thing for me to do is to promise that I will carefully revise my article if it is ever published again in another form, and I will in any case try to make it less negative as far as you yourself are concerned. In other words I will concentrate on making clear what I think is Hui Neng's Zen. If this only confuses everyone, then the blame will be mine.

. . . Meanwhile, Father, it is a joy for me to be in touch with the Jesuits of Japan who are interested in Zen. I hope to keep in contact with you and learn from you. And I hope, too, that when you come to this country you will be able to fit Gethsemani into your itinerary . . .

September 24, 1964

Your letter of the 16th was a very agreeable surprise, and I must say I was delighted to get it. The idea of going to Japan is not something that

I had ever seriously dreamed of, but I had long been perfectly aware that I could not hope to make sense writing about Zen if I did not know the Zen life as it is lived in Japan, and did not know some Japanese. Hence it is clear that your suggestion is very timely and practical, and it seems to me to be perfectly in accord with the Spirit now sweeping through the Church, especially when there is much genuine concern about relationship with non-Christian religions. The mutual understanding of East and West also presents itself as one of the great spiritual tasks of our time.

Now the main difficulty is that of getting my Superior's permission for such a journey. I mentioned it to Father Abbot yesterday, and he promised to take the question up with our Father General in Rome, for the permission of the General, though not strictly necessary, I believe, if I were going to another monastery of the Order, would really be required in this exceptional case.

Father Abbot seemed a bit shaken by the totally unusual nature of the request, and I cannot say I think he wants me to go to Japan under any conditions. But I have asked him to look at it objectively and give it his serious consideration, which I know he will do. It seems to me that the best thing is to try to let you see how my Superiors will be looking at this.

1. Father Abbot's chief concern is about my being out of the monastery and traveling around, also about the possibility of my being asked to give talks, lectures, etc., outside monasteries of the Order which, he fears, would lead to more and more invitations and to situations that might be difficult to get out of gracefully. Hence the first thing to set his mind at rest would be some kind of guarantee that I would be leading as fully a monastic life as possible, and exposed to only a minimum of "the world." But naturally there would be no purpose in making the trip if I did not have full contact with Zen students and communities. I think Fr. Abbot would regard Zen communities as equivalent to our own monasteries. As long as I would be "monastic," his objections would be to some extent allayed.

2. The other point is that our Superiors here are not too aware of the meaning and importance of Zen. They know it exists, but they regard it as a curiosity without too much importance, and hence they would tend to feel that a long journey to Japan could not really be justified. Father Abbot's first objection was that the Japanese monks of our Order ought to do this, and not an American. I tried to explain that the Japanese monks were perhaps in quite a difficult and in any case ambiguous position.

3. Then the Superiors would also be very anxious at the thought of this journey receiving any notoriety.

You see the difficulties. But I think that if it were clear that this experiment would be of immense use to my own interior life, and would indirectly redound to the advantage of the community here and of the

Order: if it were seen that I would be close to the monastic life either in communities of my Order or in other equivalent places, and if it were understood that this would not lead to involvement in "active work" as a consequence (even if only a matter of giving talks here and there) they might be ready to look favorably on the proposal.

What do you think, then, of dropping a line to our Father General on this subject, and making known to him your precise thoughts and your feeling as to why this trip ought to be undertaken. . .

You see that your suggestion, so normal in your own society, is so unusual in our Order that all kinds of consequences arise from it. But I still personally feel that your inspiration is something that ought to be regarded as something desired by the Church and by God Himself at this time. Precisely because it is so unusual, and requires such an original view, it seems to be in accord with the needs of the moment, and ought to have very far-reaching effects. As far as I am concerned, I would regard it as an immense grace to be able to come to Japan and meet you and your colleagues who are engaged in this most important work, in order to get a firsthand acquaintance with Zen and be able to be more of a contemplative myself. I believe that the grace of this opportunity could be something quite unique and decisive in my life and so I want to do whatever I can to cooperate with it.

Naturally, my Superiors must decide and I leave the ultimate solution in their hands, in a spirit of faith and detachment. But thank you most warmly for thinking of me, and please keep the issue in your good prayers . . .

November 29, 1964

You have perhaps guessed the reason for the long delay in a final answer to your proposal for a trip to Japan, to see Zen at firsthand. Our Abbot General was very busy at the Council. However, with the end of the session he reached a decision. Of course, the decision was really up to our own Abbot in any case, but the General submitted his advice to the latter and between them the answer is no. I am surprised that the project was rejected so categorically, since your persuasive letter seemed, at least to me, to show that there was a definitely good reason for the idea, and that it might be for the good of the Church.

However, from the terms in which the proposal was rejected, I must conclude that it was not really understood, and that it will be perhaps many years yet before such a plan will be really acceptable or even comprehensible . . . I would of course have profited much by the experience, but I naturally renounce it willingly and without afterthought. What troubles me more is the failure of understanding, which I seem to be able less easily to forget. However, religious life is made up of these things, and indeed so is the whole life of the Church, particularly in these times of more rapid evolution. But still, I must admit it is rather wounding to be told that such a project "is not from God." Paradoxically, it is Zen itself which gives the most practical perspective by which to see and accept all this: So with this final element of humor, I put the whole thing aside, not without once more thanking you for having such a kind and brilliant idea. Perhaps someday it will still become realizable, who can say? . . .

To John Tracy Ellis

A historian of note who has helped to form a whole generation of scholars specializing in the history of the American Church, Monsignor John Tracy Ellis may well be called the dean of American Catholic historians. Born in Seneca, Illinois, in 1905, he received his formal education at St. Viator College and at the Catholic University of America. His long and distinguished teaching career has been associated largely with the Catholic University of America, where he taught from 1935 to 1964 and from 1976 to the present. His one other teaching position of some duration was at the University of San Francisco, where he taught from 1964 to 1976.

His many scholarly articles and books have told the story of the Catholic Church in the United States; but they have done more: they have often challenged the Church. Thus, in his 1955 essay "American Catholics and the Intellectual Life," he summoned Catholic institutions of higher learning to a self-examination of their academic commitment. As a highly respected scholar whose interests cover the whole ecclesiastical scene in America, he has had far-reaching influence in the academic and religious fields.

October 10, 1961

Dan Walsh passed on to me your articles, including the very kind review of *The Seven Storey Mountain*, for which I am warmly grateful.

But above all I want to express my enthusiastic appreciation for the splendid article on "American Catholicism in 1960." This is one of the best and most encouraging things I have read in a long time. I must confess that sometimes I let the problems and limitations inherited from our "ghetto" days get me down. And of course I do not enjoy a perfect perspective in my cloistered life here, where only distorted echoes occasionally reach us. Your article and your talks here were a most welcome and salutary exception.

If there are any suggestions you can offer me as to how I can help further this work of God in America, they will be most welcome . . .

[*Cold War Letter 6*]

December 7, 1961

A quiet morning on the Vigil of Our Lady's Immaculate Conception gives me a few moments to answer your kind and thoughtful letter which already dates back nearly two months. And first I want to thank you for all the things you kindly sent. Those that could possibly be posted on the novices' bulletin board were put up and enjoyed . . .

. . . The thing that strikes me is that at a time when there are formidable and very basic issues at stake, some of our official minds can waste time and create confusion over things that are quite secondary: and yet thereby divert valuable energies that could go into more constructive work. It is absolutely crucial for the Church in America to have enough freedom of movement to deal with the unique and large problems of our country in a healthy and productive way. As you know, one of the things that most bothers me is the attitude of so many American Catholics to nuclear war. They make no distinction between out-and-out pacifism which refuses to serve even in a "just war" and the Christian obligation, pointed out by the recent Popes, to avoid the criminal tragedy of nuclear annihilation of civilian centers, even for the best of causes. Apparently much popular thought in this country simply goes along with the immoral and secularist attitude that since communism is evil, we can do anything we like to wipe it out and thus prevent it from gaining ground and overwhelming us. This awfully short-sighted and completely un-Christian attitude may well result in complete disaster for the Church. For one thing, the result might be that Russia and the U.S. would knock themselves out and leave the whole world at the mercy of Red China. The West of Europe would of course evaporate into the bargain. What would be left of Christianity? What would be the attitude of conscientious non-Christians toward the survivors of a Body that had urged such a crime in the name of religion? The hour seems to me to be extremely grave. I have been asked to write about it for the Christmas *Commonweal* and have done so, perhaps forthrightly and ingenuously, and not everyone will be pleased. I hope you will be a bit of a weather bureau for me there in Washington. If you hear anything I ought to know, I hope you will pass the word along. I mean especially about reactions to what I write on this subject.

. . . Finally I am doing a paperback on peace for New Directions [*Breakthrough to Peace*]. It will be a mixed bag, Catholic and non-Catholic, all pretty solid and sure in showing that nuclear war is a tragedy to be avoided and that there must be every insistence on negotiation before all else.

The chief reason why I am doing this is that the general silence of Catholics, especially the hierarchy, on the war question is a grave scandal to very serious and thoughtful non-Catholic minds . . .

[*Cold War Letter 29*]

February 4, 1962

. . . Thanks for your remarks on the *Catholic Worker* articles. There is one in *Commonweal* this week ["Nuclear War and Christian Responsibility," February 9, 1962] which you may have seen by the time this letter reaches you. In this *Commonweal* article I may perhaps give a wrong impression by some rather sweeping statements, and I have re-written the article. You will see the longer version eventually. One of the main points I am trying to make is that I think our theology ought to stand above political issues a little more than it does, and that we ought to be making every effort to clarify the moral principles instead of to explain them in such a way that they seem to favor some altogether limited and immediate political purpose that seems to us to be good. I think this is the case with some of our American theologians and nuclear war. I note in *Theological Studies* in the last couple of years that they seem to be wanting in every possible way to squeeze around the traditional lim-itations of the "just" war, in order to show that by Catholic standards a preemptive nuclear attack is really only defense.

Now this seems to me to be quite fatal both to theology and to political sanity. Actually it seems logical on a certain level, but only because on that level we have already abdicated from a really Christian and traditional view of war and accepted the unprincipled opportunism of the secularist. In fact what we are trying to do is to find pretexts for nuclear attack, and if that is the case, then I think it is a very grave defection . . . It seems to me quite gratuitous to assume that a war will be a limited nuclear war, when all our policies are built on all-out war, and then what happens is that we proceed to justify limited war, in order without explanation or justification to slide right into all-out war and assume that it too has been justified.

This is the way moral thought seems to have evolved in World War II. You start out by saying that a given situation is morally acceptable. This leads to all sorts of consequences which should have been foreseen but were not. These consequences, by traditional standards, are immoral (e.g., Hiroshima) but they are accepted as an accomplished fact, and then justified post factum.

It seems to me we are doing that now. We are arguing that a limited nuclear war is licit. We realize that a nuclear war might become an all-out war of annihilation, but we hope that it won't, and at the same time we prepare for the fact that it might by saying that it after all might be justified too. Meanwhile, the Pentagon has not consulted us anyway. And having conditioned our people for a limited war, we then precipitate them into an all-out war. And we refuse them any appeal to their own con-science. They have to abide by the decisions of "legitimately constituted authority." The results are likely to be terrible . . . I am glad the Holy Father has fixed the date for the Council. He evidently seems perturbed about the international situation and wants to get the Council under way before it is too late . . .

I am sorry to say that the pessimism of your friends in Rome rings a bell with me too.

I am certainly going to keep a lid on any sanguine hopes for the Council. I know of course that the Holy Spirit will bring much good out of it, but there are all sorts of other factors to be taken into consideration. And the chief one is the awful inertia of the Curia, and of some of the bishops. However, the German bishops are alive and the bishops of some of the new countries may also bring unexpected fresh air into the discussions. Or am I too hopeful?

Certainly, though, I fear that it will be difficult to get down to the most important issue of all, which, it seems to me, is the question of war and peace . . .

[*Cold War Letter 53*]

March 10, 1962

. . . Clearly the issue is the practical one, the interpretation of strategy and of the implications of political action at the present moment. This is most serious and difficult. The main difference between my position and that taken by these theologians, as well as by most theologians in this country, it seems to me, is one of standpoint. It is a question of two radically different perspectives, and the perspectives depend on where you start out. They start out by accepting all kinds of assumptions which I do not accept. They accept, uncritically, it seems to me, all the viewpoints that are taken for granted by the mass media in the cold war. In other words they start out to view a deeply disturbing and serious Christian problem with fundamentally secular presuppositions. They take as axiomatic the highly debatable questions of strategies and issues in the cold war. And in so doing they seem to me to accept without any question the rather pragmatic scale of values implied by the cold-war policies of our nation. This of course they are free to do, and there is no way of proving that they cannot start from such a position and end up with a position that is after all Christian. But it seems to me that this way of approaching the problem, while it may lead (with difficulty and danger) to an acceptable moral solution of the nuclear war problem as a *casus*, simply makes it impossible for the theologian to help others see their way *beyond* the cold-war impasse.

On the contrary, what this approach tends to do is to *dictate* as a "Christian solution" the one way out which the whole country is insensibly and irresponsibly coming to adopt along with the mass media and the military-economic managers; that if we seem to be losing the cold war, then the way out is a hot war, with perhaps a preemptive first strike on Russia.

It is my opinion that theologians who are in a position to influence the President's thinking, and help him form his conscience on this most crucial of all questions today, are going to be advising him that such a preemptive strike is not unacceptable to Christian morality. In point of fact this is precisely what one of your moralists says. Do please tell him to consider the necessity of taking a more detached view of this awful problem. I feel that it is our duty as priests and "theologians" (I put quotation marks insofar as I dare to include myself under that heading) to do much more than simply bless a pragmatic decision which may have frightful consequences, even though it may in some sense be technically "right." We must try as far as possible to open the way for a new and positive solution, something that will help us all work towards a peaceful and constructive issue from the nuclear dilemma. This means not an immediate answer on a case, but a whole preparatory job of rethinking the approach to the problems of our time in such way that we can gradually prepare the way for a solid and lasting peace, meanwhile staving off the imminent danger of hot war. This danger is, I believe, much more imminent than most people would like to think, and I do not believe that all the aggressiveness is on the Russian side, necessarily.

As you say, a permissive and even encouraging attitude on the part of moral theologians would be an abdication of responsibility in this crisis.

The apostolic constitution on Latin [*Veterum Sapientia*] was read here in the refectory. It is very very strong. The writers seem to find unusual zest with which to suppress all efforts at vernacularism. It is this more than the actual measures decreed which strikes me above all. The gusto with which they go about stamping out the flames of this small fire which bothers them. Can this be an encouraging sign before the Council? I mean the fact that something that is so ardently desired by so many and with understandable reasons would simply be put down with such total and uncompromising force? Certainly I can see the validity of the measures and of the reasons offered and have no difficulty in continuing myself with this kind of policy in teaching, but once again, it is the "state of mind" reflected that is disturbing. And I think this "state of mind" is there and everywhere and it is going to have tremendous power in the Council . . .

. . . Poor Bride of Christ, and poor Bridegroom of the Bride. We all contribute something to her wrinkles.

You must by now have had a look at the new Hans Küng book, *The Council, Reform and Reunion*. If you have not, then do by all means get it as fast as ever you can. I think it is not out but I have a review copy. It will really gladden your heart. It is one of the most forthright, direct and powerful statements of our actual condition and problem that I have ever seen. It is a most remarkable book and it will have a terrific impact. What the results will be, no one can say, but it is in a lot of ways a portent . . .

[*Cold War Letter 55*]

March 19, 1962

Many thanks for your kindness in sending me the editorial from the Washington *Standard.* It was very important and helpful for me to see this editorial, from many standpoints. Naturally my writing from a place like this means that I suffer certain lacks of perspective, and being out of contact with opinion, and even to a great extent with events, is a most serious handicap.

For a while I toyed with an idea of writing to the editors of the *Standard,* but on reflection I realized that this might only confuse matters still further. In any case I do want to share my reactions with you, and I would appreciate your advice. Obviously I don't want to antagonize more people than I can avoid antagonizing, and since I tend to express my convictions with vehemence, naturally anyone who does not agree with them is liable to come back explosively. I recognize this to be largely my own fault.

I also recognize that my choice of words was careless and unfortunate when I sweepingly said "governments" were explicitly thinking of wars on an all-out scale and had practically said so. This could naturally be interpreted as a very unjust slam at President Kennedy. This was of course far from my intention. I fully recognize and appreciate the deep sincerity and obvious solicitude with which the President is trying to handle his most onerous responsibility. I do not envy him his position at all, and I regret very much having given the impression that I was simply dismissing his Administration offhand as a bunch of potential war criminals.

At the same time, though I may be much mistaken or may be misled by my lack of contact with the outside world, it certainly seems to me quite clear from what I have read that there is no question that the military, in the U.S., have been building for many years a policy that involves the "massive" use of nuclear weapons, and that this has been made quite explicit. One quote occurs to my mind: doubtless not from one of the highest officials, but certainly representative enough: "We are not going to reduce our nuclear capability. Personally I have never believed in nuclear limited war. I don't know how you could build a limit into it when you use any kind of a nuclear bang." This is ascribed to Roswell Gilpatric, who is Deputy Defense Secretary and is doubtless not a Catholic. The statement needs to be interpreted, and in any case it is an off-the-cuff personal opinion. But I repeat, it seems to me quite clear that this is the way the Pentagon thinks, and is probably indicative of much more strongly expressed views which do not get out in public. People who hold these views are, it seems to me, in a position to exert a decisive pressure on the President and in fact I believe they eventually will do so.

Understood in this light, I do not think my conclusions are altogether "gross" though I admit they were stated much too loosely in my article.

. . . Finally, I think the writer of the editorial, in the heat of his indignation, misread my true thoughts about war. To begin with, I am not an absolute pacifist and I am in no sense trying to claim that the Church has forbidden war as such, or even that the Church has formally denied that there can be a "just war" with the use of nuclear weapons, provided of course that use is limited. What I am contending, and I think this is abundantly clear from the documents of the Popes, is that the Church definitely frowns on and forbids an all-out use of nuclear weapons on a massive or indiscriminate scale, where civilians and cities are concerned. The rest is a question of the interpretation of scientific and political fact; *can* a total nuclear war be kept within the bounds of justice, and is it in fact the intention of the strategy makers to keep the war within such bounds? I recognize that there is a very respectable body of opinion which states that in practice we have to build our hopes and our policies on the optimistic estimate that if nuclear weapons are used at all they will be kept within limits. But to me this opinion rests on pious hopes and not on solid prospects of actual realization. To guide our moral thought on such unsteady lines seems to me to be folly.

I think, finally, that the writer of the editorial did me an injustice by stating that I was guilty of a "startling disregard of authoritative Catholic utterances" which almost seemed to imply a rebellious and independent attitude with regard to the Church. I think I appealed very frequently to authoritative Catholic utterances in my article, but they did not happen to be the ones which the writer of the editorial felt were important. I submit that I could claim that *he* did not quote the authoritative Catholic utterances which supported my side of the question, but of course this would be childish. He evidently believed that when I said it was the mind of the Church to hope that all governments would work for the *abolition* of war I meant that the Church was formally condemning all war. This is certainly not the meaning of my words.

The fact remains that we live at a time when we are faced with a stark choice between disastrous all-out war, or the abolition of war. Both are essentially possible . . . If we simply let ourselves be hypnotized by immediate military solutions to our problems we are never going to seriously consider other solutions . . .

Certainly I feel grieved that I have given the impression of being a rebel against the Church. But equally certain I do not feel that my conscience seriously reproaches me in this regard, at least as far as my own personal subjective dispositions are concerned. I am always of course extremely grateful for advice, criticism and enlightenment, especially from well-informed and authoritative sources . . .

To Sister M. Emmanuel

Sister M. Emmanuel de Souza e Silva, born in Rio de Janeiro, was the daughter of an officer in the Brazilian navy. She attended schools in England and France, as well as her native Brazil. After spending a number of years doing social work in the slums of Rio, she entered the monastery of the Virgin Mary in Petropolis. In 1955, when the International Eucharistic Congress was held in Rio de Janeiro, Sr. Emmanuel wrote to Merton asking if he would do the English translation of the official prayer for the Congress. It was this letter and Merton's reply that initiated their correspondence. Sr. Emmanuel later did most of the Portuguese translations of Merton's books.

February 28, 1955

A letter from a cloister, written on the feast of my beloved St. Romuald, and asking for a service to be done for Jesus in the Sacrament of His Love—how could a priest who longs to live for Jesus alone refuse such a request? I only wish the translation were worthy of the occasion. I enclose it. Father Abbot, you guessed, was glad to give the permission.

I will not reproach you with making me break a Lenten resolution not to write letters. I foresaw I would have to write some. God, the legislator, has asked for the letter and the resolution is not broken.

I had heard of the Eucharistic Congress already and had been keeping it in mind in my prayers. The Holy Spirit prays in us, in these days, with groans, *inenarrabilibus gemitibus*, as we consider the poverty and superficiality of so much that is called "devotion"—including devotion to the Blessed Sacrament. Nor am I surprised that you wondered, for a moment, on hearing that there was such a thing as contemplation in the United States. It is not growing on naturally propitious soil, our contemplation. But God is at work in souls. Many desire and seek Him. May many learn to find Him in the Sacrament of His Love, and learn, at the same time, that the thing signified by this Sacrament is the Whole Christ—the Body of all those who eat of One Bread . . .

February 3, 1959

First of all, thank you for your generous and careful work in translating the two books you have sent and working on the others. I am very pleased with the presentation of these translations and thank you especially for taking the trouble to get such distinguished introductions. Please thank the writers of them in my name. If Alceu Amoroso Lima* is in this country, I certainly hope to see him some time.

Do not apologize to me for the difficulties you have had with the censors. I ought rather to apologize to you. I can at any rate say with all

---

* *Alceu Amoroso Lima (1893–1983), one of Brazil's distinguished literary figures who, besides his teaching and literary career at home, lectured widely in Europe and the United States. In 1951 with his two sons he visited Merton at Gethsemani.*

simplicity that the censorship situation in our Order is utterly beyond all reason. It is an enormous penance for all concerned . . .

. . . The best I can do is to try to see that the foreign editions do not get all mixed up. One thing I can say in this regard is that the short works you mentioned, "Basic Principles of the Monastic Life," "What Is Contemplation?" etc., are being translated for Agir.* They have also been kind to me and I wished them to have something to show for it: do not begrudge them some of the crumbs. Vozes* has the majority of my books by now.

. . . It is unfortunately not true that we are planning a foundation in Brazil. I certainly wish it were true and would like very much to be the one selected to go there. It does not seem to be the will of God. However, there is no harm in praying for this intention, and I know you will do so . . .

October 24, 1959

I have received your nice letter and the copies of *Martha Mary and Lazarus* and *What Are These Wounds?* I am very grateful for the care which you have taken even with [the translations of] these minor works— I am very pleased. For they are beautifully done. I am not angry with the cover of *MML*, though it does somewhat suggest a vacation at the beach. But above all, I don't know how I can be sufficiently grateful to Alceu Amoroso Lima for his indefatigable patience in writing excellent prefaces. Surely it is a sign that he is full of unfailing charity . . .

. . . I am growing more and more disturbed by the events and the psychology of the United States. The mentality of this country, its blindness and I might add its willful perversity grow more and more disturbing from day to day. It is undoubtedly the effect of centuries of complacency and undisturbed success in materialistic enterprise. But this has become a blind and sick nation, without realizing it. To my mind the situation is becoming crucial. The nonsense that is going on between the U.S. and Fidel Castro is a case in point. Obviously Fidel is not infallible, and he has real limitations. But the whole situation makes me realize that the U.S.A. still has no real appreciation of its relationship with Latin America and its obligations toward Latin America. Still less of how much it needs Latin America, in the right way (that is, culturally and spiritually). But enough of that—I cannot claim to really know all that is going on . . .

. . . The Benedictine Oblate you refer to sent me the latest collection of the works of Jorge de Lima and I am enthusiastic about it. I am going to do some translations of some of the poems and perhaps a short article on him. He is to my mind a very great poet, unfortunately I do not

* *Agir (Rio de Janeiro) and Vozes (Petropolis) were the two principal publishing houses that brought out Merton's works in Portuguese.*

understand the best poems, the Negro ones. Too much specialized slang. I think I am going to be very interested in his great long poems . . .

I want to write to Amoroso Lima. But while I am waiting for time to do so, please convey to him my warm thanks and sincere regards. I remember with happiness his visit and his happy sons, and for the whole family I cherish affectionate memories. I keep him also in my prayers, along with *you* and all my good friends in Brazil. I want you please to pray for a very special intention of mine at this moment . . .

God bless you, Sister, and your beautiful Brazil which I love so much. And all the people in it.

July 28, 1960

This is terrible. How many months have passed since I received your last letter? And I still owed you another from May. Please forgive me. I have been very busy and it is really impossible for me to keep up with my correspondence. I know you are very patient.

First of all, *Art and Worship* has been very much delayed. It is still not finished. I am waiting to get more modern material. The Desert Fathers book is being printed, but slowly. It was designed by a famous typographer in Verona, Italy, and this has complicated matters. But there are other things forthcoming.

One is a book which I think Agir ought to have. They have been asking so long for a full-length volume. This is full-length with much new material, articles on Pasternak, totalitarianism, Mount Athos, aspects of sacred art, and many things of that nature. It is called *Disputed Questions*. I hope I can send you a copy in the fall.

. . . Who might be willing to do some of my poems in Portuguese? I think it is time a selection of them was translated, perhaps with the essay on poetry and contemplation. I will have the *Selected Poems* sent to you. But don't try the poems unless you are sure of yourself with them. I do not know to what extent you are a poet.

Alceu Amoroso Lima's son was here with his charming wife and we had a little conversation that was very pleasant. I feel sorry that A. A. Lima is leaving his other multiple works to translate a whole book of mine, though it is wonderful to have such an eminent and capable translator. I feel I am imposing on him. I wrote to him a little while ago.

I have not yet had a chance to translate any Jorge de Lima. This too will require time and thought, but I wish I could get to it. Certainly the Brazilian poets appeal to me tremendously. I would enjoy going into a real translation project and doing a lot of their work. Unfortunately this is not possible. I still have the novices of course, and many problems in that connection.

Do keep praying for my intentions. The Lord has been very good and yet I still fight my way through the forests. That is to be expected.

I can depend less and less on my own power and sense of direction—as if I ever had any. But the Lord supports and guides me without my knowing how, more and more apart from my own action and even in contradiction to it. It is so strange to advance backwards and to get where you are going in a totally unexpected way. How is your nephew? I pray for him. You cannot push him. I am sure there is in him a very genuine religious sense. It must be allowed to grow quietly in its own way. God will lead him . . .

December 2, 1960

This is certainly *your* season—Advent. Emmanuel da Virgem. I shall remember you especially when we read Isaias, and as we prepare for the coming of God with us. Thank you for your letters. If you have not yet received the copy of *Disputed Questions*, it is due to difficulties which Farrar, Straus has been creating [about contractual rights]. I got rid of Curtis Brown [the literary agency] because they would not do what I wanted them to do, and now my publisher is even worse than the agent was. I have had the monastery send you a copy of the book, and you will get it soon.

. . . I can hardly think of a better translator for the poems than Manuel Bandeira. But I do not think I deserve anyone so good. I will be highly delighted if he should decide to do some of them. I like his poems very much and have them here. I am myself translating a lot of Latin American poets and will probably do some of his when I get time. I still have not got around to translating any of Jorge de Lima, though I have been promising myself this pleasure for nearly three years. Some Spanish American poets that I have translated are being represented in various anthologies here.

For a long time I have not done any drawings and that is why I did not send you any. But now I send a few. St. Benedict, the Holy Face, the Blessed Virgin and St. John the Baptist. They are very modern and sketchy and you may not like them . . .

. . . The special intention I once asked you to pray for is still a matter of prayer though it has partly been fulfilled in an unexpected manner. I owe this to the prayers of many good and holy friends. I had hoped I might someday get away to Latin America and start something new, but apparently this cannot take place. However, an experimental venture here which involves more solitude for me has been partially approved. It also involves special retreats for Protestant theologians, Jewish scholars, and all kinds of unusual groups like that. So please keep the whole thing in your prayers, above all that I may be able to use the special little retreat house that has been built for the purpose but which is not yet fully and finally approved by higher Superiors.

There are many things we must pray for, and above all world peace.

I think the United States badly needs prayers: the hour of opportunity came for this nation and seems to be passing by without effect: through lack of spirituality and insight. It is a great, rich, blind, absurd nation, stiffnecked with pride in its own money and accomplishments, vulgar in its assumed simplicity, complacent in its imagined innocence. Yet there is still much sincerity and good will and a kind of inexplicable humility, readiness to change, which one misses in the older nations of the world. I say readiness to change: but the constructive changes never come.

My special prayers for all of you, for all my dear friends in Brazil, for Brazil itself which I regard as a very warm collective friend . . .

March 9, 1961

The Abbot General has sent us here the *imprimi potest* for your translation of *Thoughts in Solitude*, which has been sent off to you. Or rather your manuscript has been sent already. I am now sending you the *imprimi potest*. The General was evidently not sure of your address.

The Behavior of Titans and *The Wisdom of the Desert* have now both appeared. Perhaps you already have received the former of these. It may not be easy to translate.

I will soon send you the very fine translation in Spanish of a selection of my poems, by a Nicaraguan poet who was a novice here for nearly two years [Ernesto Cardenal], but who went to the Benedictines in Mexico. It is illustrated by Armando Morales. It would be interesting to do an edition in Rio with the same illustrations, if we only had a translator . . .

August 9, 1961

. . . I *have* enjoyed so your (2) letters, but have not had time to write! I have been very busy. I am so grateful to all of you for all that you are doing, especially to Alceu Amoroso Lima, and for all those who are *so* generous as to write prefaces.

We are going through difficult times and I think it is going to be worse, from a human point of view. But we have to realize the full supernatural dimension of our life in Christ. Let us at least pray for true peace, and that we may be faithful to Christ in everything. I thought the latest encyclical, *Mater et Magistra*, was certainly one of the greatest. Here we see the truth. Let us hope that we can live up to it . . .

I will send you under separate cover a very lugubrious poem about Auschwitz that I wrote, but it is simply a florilegium of statements from official documents and other declarations, for the most part. That makes it even more terrible.

But Christ is Risen and has conquered death. Let us live in His Spirit, and be loyal to His merciful love and to the truth in everything. I think your president, Quadros, is a fine person and a good president. It is very important that there be men of principle and honesty, not dominated by pressures from great power groups and in your case not subservient to more dominant nations and their influence. The hope of the world is in the "Third World" that is not yet completely dominated by Russia or by the U.S.A. Unfortunately they seem to be tending more and more towards Russia. As for us, our misfortune is to have just a little more conscience than the Russians and just a little less political acumen. Hence the U.S. can be accused of iniquity when it is, in fact, simply hampered by its own lack of unscrupulousness. Russia can go forward completely committed to any action, however dishonest. We have to at least justify ourselves in our own eyes, and this causes fatal hesitations! Hence we can be hated by all for at least attempting to be straightforward, while those who are frankly dishonest and tyrannical gain more respect. Perhaps in the long run theirs too is a kind of honesty. But I don't think it is the kind that makes for a safe world to live in, or for peace. Maybe in twenty years society will have reverted to cannibalism . . .

[*Cold War Letter 22*]

January 16, 1962

. . . I am especially occupied at the moment with an anthology of short things about peace [*Breakthrough to Peace*]. The situation is grim enough to make the publisher think it urgent to get this book into print soon. I do not see that hurry is going to stop a war, but it is urgent to make clear statements, anyway. And I want to do this. These articles are by various authors. Some will be excellent. I also have written a few things on this subject myself. I will send you a small collection of such articles which might make an interesting book, and if you like it, and Agir for example wants it, you can go at it before it has finally appeared in English. I will put several of these articles in the mail today.

The poems of Dom Basilio* are *quite charming*. The Advent one was particularly good. But I have not yet read them all, nor the clippings that you sent. I have them still. I *hate* to rush through things, and I have so much to read at the moment. One has to read much in order to be able to think at all clearly on the problems of the time, and they are very great. There is so little said, people seem exhausted with the labor of coping with the complications of this world we live in. Yet it is absolutely necessary that we do so. We have got to take responsibility for it, we have got to try to solve the problems of our own countries while at the same time recognizing our higher responsibility to the whole human race. It is in a time like this that we are forced to have a Christian view of society at the risk of failing to be Christians altogether. And yet I remain a contemplative. I do not think there is a contradiction, for I think at least some contemplatives must try to understand the providential events

---

* *Dom Basilio Penido, O.S.B., Abbot of the monastery of Olinda (near Recife), admired Merton's works and wrote prefaces to some of Sr. Emmanuel's translations of them.*

of the day. God works in history, therefore a contemplative who has no sense of history, no sense of historical responsibility, is not a fully Christian contemplative: he is gazing at God as a static essence, or as an intellectual light, or as a nameless ground of being. But we are face to face with the Lord of History and with Christ the King and Savior, the Light of the World, who comes forth from the Father and returns to the Father. We must confront Him in the awful paradoxes of our day, in which we see that our society is being judged. And in all this we have to retain a balance and a good sense which seem to require a miracle, and yet they are the fruit of ordinary grace. In a word we have to continue to be Christians in all the full dimensions of the Gospel.

I know that this is a very critical time especially for Brazil. I hope that the crisis will be weathered and that those who have given themselves so generously, at last, to the task of Christian social action will not be frustrated and deprived of their hopes. Meanwhile here we are trying to start a small Catholic movement against war. It is hard to say whether the danger of nuclear war is really as great as it seems, but in any event there is no doubt whatever that a most destructive cataclysm is possible and perhaps even probable . . .

Certainly there is a great danger everywhere of extreme movements. Here in the U.S. also there are many people who are upset and tormented and who think they have to allay their anxieties by looking for communists everywhere except where they are, and as a result they make life very unpleasant and difficult for the more liberal-minded people who still stand for peace and for a reasonable way of solving the problems of the country. I would not be terribly surprised if in a few years this country found itself under a dictator of some sort. I think Kennedy is all right, and his brother is a good man. I know his brother's wife. They are reasonable people, and probably as good as anyone we have at the moment. In a word I think Kennedy is fairly capable, but that is perhaps because he presents a favorable contrast with Eisenhower who, with his whole Administration, was a complete failure and did much harm to the country. Though Eisenhower himself is a very fine person, as a President he was zero. However, let us hope that Kennedy may be able to rise above his own level and grow into a great President, for we certainly need one. Some of his cabinet are pretty good men too. But the task is enormous, and the dangers are very great. I do not at all like the mentality of this country at present. People are trying to convince themselves that nuclear war is reasonable and that it makes sense to consider it as a real possibility, not just as something inconceivable. This is a very dangerous step, for if this country comes to accept nuclear war as a reasonable solution to anything, we are very likely to have one. This would be disastrous for all of us. In which case we might just as well prepare for the end of our civilization and of all that it stands for.

These next few years are going to be quite crucial. However, I think we have to be *careful* what we say about developments, careful about the guesses we make in public, *careful* about the possibilities we consider. We are going to need to learn a *prudence* which does not belong to the mass mind . . .

June 18, 1962

I am glad some of the books finally reached you. I also sent copies of *Blackfriars* magazine with the "Letter to Cuadra," registered, to both you and Alceu Amoroso Lima. Then more recently I sent a big package of all the more recent editions of the peace articles, except for one which has appeared just now in *Blackfriars*. Also finally I sent the mimeographed manuscript of the book *Peace in a Post-Christian Era*.

But be careful, this book is not for publication. The Abbot General has decided that it must not be published, and so that decision is final as far as I can see. I had asked for a clarification and he made it quite clear that this book was not to be published. And he also gave a very general directive that I must stop publishing on peace and such matters which he feels have nothing to do with monks. So that is the situation at present, and I believe this is permanent.

This raises a question concerning the peace articles which have already been published with approval in this country. I do not know if they will be permitted in translation. I do not know if the General's prohibition extends to translations of articles already published. It would seem to me that it probably does not. But I am not at all sure . . .

. . . I hope everything is in order. Your friend Lilian [May], I have her letter but have not answered it yet, I have an impossible dream of getting in the clear so that I can answer letters reasonably and at leisure. But something has to give way somewhere, hence I compress the letters into a short period every morning, and do what I can. The rest have to wait, but I will try to get to her soon. In any case I do not have the letter here, but I know where it is. Also I am not absolutely sure of Dom Basilio's address as I failed to copy it in the address book. Negligence. Sorry. I will send him the notes.

. . . Things are quiet. I am reading Cassiodorus and other early Fathers, and preparing later on to do a book on Cassian, which ought to be peaceful enough.

November 2, 1962

First, don't worry about the censorship, or any reaction. I have no doubts about the unreasonableness and unfairness of the decisions: however, I do have a vow of obedience and hence I have to accept unjust decisions too. At times I feel it necessary to make known my views and there is a little discussion. But the General is very set on maintaining a most rigid control over the writing in all forms and especially the peace articles. In fact the latest decision he has handed down is that they cannot even *begin to be translated* without an explicit permission from him. Hence if you want to translate any of them, you must first contact him and find out what he wants. "Original Child Bomb" was already translated and ready to be published in French (in fact the type was set up) and he prohibited it, though it had been permitted in English. Felt it was not nice for France. I suppose he is one of those people who is convinced that France has to have the bomb and maintain her honor with the *force de frappe* . . .

Well, it is All Souls' Day, cold and rainy. We had our procession in the cemetery. This year is nearly over. With that Cuba business it nearly turned out badly, but thank heaven Kennedy was at least clear and kept his wits about him. I do not know what will develop next.

So let us keep praying for the Council, and for one another. We are starting some big changes next year, amalgamating the brothers and the monks in one group, and I will have the two categories in one novitiate. The brothers will continue their usual life, with modifications, but will have a vote, and the same habit, etc. It may mean problems of adaptation so I will need prayers.

May 22, 1963

As to your letter about the photos, no—it would be better if this picture were not used for "promotion." We never do this. So neither Agir nor Vozes can have a picture to use. However, if it is a question of giving a few copies to friends, you may have some. It is just that they must not be printed for commercial promotion.

I am glad all the books are coming along well. Thanks for your photo. It is so small I will have to get a magnifying glass to see you. Haven't you a larger one? You look lively!

August 22, 1963

It would be a pleasure for me if you could be the translator of *Life and Holiness* which is to be published by Herder and Herder of São Paulo. I do not know if they have made previous arrangements themselves. Maybe they have. But I certainly encourage you to get in contact with them and see.

Please forgive this scribble. I am writing in a hospital in Louisville where I have been treated for a cervical disk. It's still not well, but I am slowly improving. It will possibly slow down my work . . .

Thanks for your picture in "in desert places." You are *just* as I would expect you to be, a lively and open person. May God preserve you in joy and zeal!

January 17, 1964—St. Anthony

. . . I hope you had a nice visit with Eileen [Curns], and hope she is doing well. It is possible that I might publish some of the *Cold War Letters* in a book, along with the *Black Revolution* and some peace articles. I would probably include the ones to Eileen and AAL, so if you run across either one of these persons please mention this to them and tell them to alert me if they have any objection. I think I will send *you* an extra copy of the *Letters*, you might be able to use it.

. . . The visit of Pope Paul to Palestine was a shattering and wonderful event. Especially the first day in Jordan, the Pope in the midst of a crowd most of whom were not Christians and who were gripped by indescribable feelings. It was an amazing sign, and certainly a rough experience for the Pope. It shows what the Church in the world is coming to be. No longer the edicts from the Ivory Tower, but a frail body in the midst of pressures without reason, and hopes full of incomprehensible anguish!

The Kennedy assassination has almost been forgotten, as far as I know, though the family itself was shattered and has barely recovered. It was especially rough on Bob and I doubt if he will try anything special in politics. It will be a long time before he runs for President. As for Johnson, I think he is a well-meaning but inept goof. He may be able to handle the situation much as Truman did. And Truman was the one who sanctioned the bomb . . .

May 31, 1964

As usual I have several letters that I have not answered. This batch goes back to the days when you had the flu. If the flu produces poems you ought to have it more often. I liked "Rosas e sangre" very much. I sent you immediately the things you asked for, "Monk in the Diaspora," etc. I hope you have them. I was much criticized by some in the Order about "Monk in the Diaspora," for seeming to question the solidity of our façade in full view of the public. Actually I think most of our problems here are in the mind, and in the way we insist on thinking about ourselves. The situation could be a lot worse, and we could certainly make use of what we have in order to enter deeply into the mystery of the monastic life. Instead we are so insecure that we get involved (a) in useless activity, (b) in useless projects and revolutions, (c) in useless theorizing about our state and (d) in useless self-justification. So I with my theorizing have collided with them in their self-justification. But it worked out all right. I think that if all goes well, we will normally and naturally simplify our own life. On the other hand, there are all those projects . . . What we want is not Trappists working in factories but Trappists who are monks, and real monks, not just sustainers of a monastic edifice which is very impressive to the world and very "regular" and well organized within.

. . . I am going to revise *Climate of Monastic Prayer* [i.e., the mimeographed booklet] thoroughly and put a lot more in it. It might almost make a little book by itself. If I did not send more copies it is because the first edition is run out and I want to leave it until I have made changes before running off more. But I will try to remember to send several copies of everything. The monks in Curitiba sound interesting. That was the place where I thought of a foundation, if there had ever been a possibility of our founding in Brazil. I think that possibility is gone forever and frankly as far as I am concerned I can see that I will not, or should not, go on any foundation. I am getting too bogged down in the nonsense of middle age, bad back, etc., and I really need the solitude and the time to think that are here but would not be on a foundation . . .

. . . Here is a poem I read to some survivors of the bombing of Hiroshima when they came through here. "Paper cranes" are little folded birds they make as the symbol of their peace movement.

What else? I have been busy, mildly productive, am sending copies of the latest things separately. Did I send the little booklet of the *Letter by Guigo,* which the Stanbrook nuns printed for me? I think I did.

My feeling is that this will probably cross with a letter from you reproaching me for my silence and telling me a thousand interesting new things! Keep well, give my regards to all my friends, AAL, Dom Timoteo, Dom Basilio and all of them . . .

June 10, 1964

Since I last wrote you, Kabir has arrived. It is a totally precious book beautiful in every way, full of magnificent things, *I shall treasure it.* Last Sunday I was reading it in the forest, in a truly paradisiacal spot, a high moss-covered bluff of rock and shale over a quiet stream. Perfect for Kabir's message. Tagore's translations are wonderful. Thanks so much for this book!

. . . There is one thing perhaps someone in Rio could get for me: I have run across the Portuguese poet Fernando Pessôa, who also wrote under three or four different pen names. Octavio Paz has translated selections from him into Spanish. I would like very much to have him in Portuguese, and I think his works are obtainable in Rio, for one edition was published there. Could you give someone the good idea of finding them for me? . . .

It seems that at last I may be able to get out something on peace. There seems to be a chance, anyway. Please pray that it gets past the Abbot General . . .

July 28, 1964

Your long letter arrived yesterday and I will try to do something about it before all of it has drained out of my mind . . .

. . . Now about business: first the *Black Revolution*: this I am not sending, because it will be wiser to publish in Brazil the whole book as it is to appear in N.Y. I have approval for the material on peace in this book. The title is *Seeds of Destruction*. Patience, it will be there before the end of the year. It also contains a longer version of "Monk in the Diaspora," and I would wait to translate from that.

Is it true that the articles on peace are being translated and published? THIS MUST NOT GO THROUGH. I am absolutely forbidden to republish any of those articles, in any language, even though they were published before. Do, please, see to it that they do not get into print. No harm in copies being passed around from hand to hand, or in mimeograph, but even that is not advisable. The new essay on peace in *Seeds of Destruction* is permitted and should cover the ground well enough . . .

. . . I spoke to Dr. Suzuki, the Zen master [during their visit at Columbia University], about Pessõa and translated some poems of his for S. (from the Spanish of Octavio Paz) and S. was delighted. Said it had a great Zen quality. I think so too.

. . . Yes, you may use mimeographed material here and there, in magazines etc., provided it is not specifically marked "not for publication" and provided it is not some of the old stuff about the H-bomb.

Yes, you can translate "Monk in the Diaspora" but I suggest waiting for the complete version.

Thank AAL for yet another preface. He outdoes himself. All you say about Dom Basilio is wonderful. To me it is a great sacrifice to be unable to do anything concrete for the monastic revival in Latin America. But with the great blessings on Dom B.'s monastery someone like me is not needed. How great a grace that is.

Now I must stop, but God bless all of you. *Let us keep united in prayer* . . .

August 23, 1964

Thanks for your latest letter, in all its ramifications. And for the clippings of Alceu A. L. He outdoes himself in generosity and once again I am convinced that his own charity has made him exaggerate. It is more to his credit than to mine that he can say so many good things about me.

I was moved by Dom Basilio's little poem on St. Brendan's Island. I have been working on the *Navigatio* of St. Brendan and may do a little study of it. It is in reality a document connected with monastic reform in the area of Treves in the ninth or tenth century, where the Irish were numerous. The islands St. B. visits are all more or less monastically perfect. It is a beautiful story, anyway.

. . . I am sending you an article on Gandhi, which is to be part of the book *Seeds of Destruction*. This might be used in a magazine perhaps while waiting for the book?? I have an enormous set of proofs of the book which I could send you, if you want it, but it is very heavy and ought not to go airmail, and it would probably be lost by sea mail. I wonder if anyone could bring it to you? It makes a very big package. Perhaps you had better wait for copies of the finished book.

This is all for the moment. Under separate cover, the *Reader* will go to you, also the Gandhi article and a couple of new things.

Best wishes and blessings. I *often* pray for all of you and for all Brazil and all South America.

. . . I love Brazilian music—can you play Bossa Nova??

September 10, 1964

This will have to be short. Poison ivy has taken the skin off my hands and if I type long my fingers start bleeding. This is not just to elicit your tears of sympathy, I haven't a chance to write a decent letter!

Your long good letter arrived today. I will take care of everything. Pessôa not here yet. You can by all means go ahead with the Gandhi article. There is no problem. It is sold for English-language rights in U.S. and Canada. That is all.

Today I am sending part of the proofs of *Seeds of Destruction*. I do not have a complete set to send you now. I am sending the part about race. The rest will come later, on war, etc.

I am also sending a complete small book: selections from "Gandhi on Non-Violence," with a long introduction I wrote. I think this little book could be quite important. Naturally for the Gandhi rights the Indian publisher would have to be consulted, but do not go direct to them, do it through Robert MacGregor, New Directions . . .

December 2, 1964

You get a brand-new ribbon. It brings you my *best* wishes for Advent and Christmas . . . Meanwhile, here is an urgent request.

Some friends of mine, very fine people indeed and very prominent in European Catholic circles, Jean and Hildegard Goss-Mayr, activists in peace movements and non-violence, have been working in the Brazilian Northeast. They are very interested in the Gandhi book and eager to have it come out soon in Brazil, as it will help their work tremendously. Can *you* meanwhile send them the ms.? I hope you can get it to them. I hope also that any publisher, Vozes, anyone, can get moving with it soon. I think this is important. I cannot send the American edition because it is not yet out and not yet even in proof. It may appear early next summer. But we cannot wait that long. The French edition is in the works now.

. . . I liked the letter of Br. Christiano [young artist in the Benedictine Olinda community], very touching and simple, and of course gratifying for me. I am sure he owes you much, and all his praises of you are probably well justified. I will see what material on art I can send. I am going to send along some notes on an exhibition of drawings of mine being held in Louisville, but this stuff is *very* abstract, I warn you. I don't know how it would be liked there, though Brazil is great in abstract art. If anyone is really interested, not just curious, I might send a few drawings and perhaps they could be framed and hung up somewhere. Do you have any friends who like abstract art? I don't want to make it too much of an operation however.

I must close now, but please send the ms. of Gandhi to the Goss-Mayrs. After the new year they will be in São Paulo . . .

February 17, 1965

. . . I have been extremely pressed. Gandhi book is in proofs here now. I hope everything will go well with it in Brazil. The Goss-Mayrs have been pushing it, and that is fine with me. *Thanks so much* for having it copied!

I hope to write you a *decent* letter soon! Will send a few papers, but there is not much new at the moment, except that we are working along on the hermit proposition which seems hopeful!!

July 11, 1965

I will not multiply lamentations about the mail situation. It gets worse and worse, since I get more and more letters and spend less and less time trying to answer them, since I have less time to spend. I am not yet completely in the hermitage, but when I am, certainly it will be impossible to handle most of it. Naturally, I will remain responsible for mail like *yours* that deals with business matters of importance, but perhaps there may be delays. Also I do not have all the mimeographs you would like but I have sent off some, and some new ones. The copies of *Life and Holiness* arrived, and I am very happy that the Gandhi book is coming along well. I have sent the article you requested to Dom Basilio, and a couple of new ones. It is splendid that he is doing so well. He has more novices than we have now. I think that though things are quiet here now, our Order is in for a lot of trouble. There are many articulate desires for change, and there is much going on (certainly it was a great step that the General Chapter formally acknowledged that hermits were permissible in our Order). But on the other hand there is much confusion and in-comprehension, and personally I do not think that the grave situation can be met even with some much needed changes. The confusion of motives and ideas is still too great and the monks for the most part are not stable enough or mature enough (in the U.S. at least) to assimilate what is going on and make good use of it. Basically, they do not really know what they want, but they are sincere in their seeking. I think it will come out all right, and have not time to worry about it anyway. I have my own job to do, and will have plenty to think about doing it.

. . . We have concelebration on Sundays and Feasts now, and will probably have it every day as soon as we get the conventual Mass rearranged so that all can come to it, daily, including brothers. I am wondering whether the monks here who want to go on without being priests will see their desires respected. People seem to approve the idea in theory, but in practice they push the young ones into the priesthood and I am afraid that this may create complications later on.

. . . I am delighted that I look Latin American to your friends! I feel very much like a Latin American and have always maintained that my poems look better in Spanish than in English.

I am always very much in contact with poets in Venezuela, Nicaragua, etc. etc., and get along very well with them. I have not only the face of a South American but also the heart, and I firmly believe that without South America there is no America. It is because the U.S. has never been able to see this that there is trouble ahead for this country (witness the pure nonsense in Santo Domingo and the even more fatal nonsense in Vietnam, which seems to most people here quite reasonable).

I shall certainly keep you in my prayers, and I know you will also pray for me. The religious life is not going to get any easier or less confused and we are going to go through more of a crisis than we have yet seen. But in the end, this will bring us, if we like, to a more radical obedience of faith. After all what matters is not simply to be a monk or a nun but to be a Christian and a perfect disciple, open in heart and mind to God's word. The trash will be thrown out of our lives, and God knows there is plenty of trash in them. But we will absolutely not see any real peace and perfection in religious life in the next ten or fifteen years. That need not prevent us from being happier than we ever were. I am not concerned with the perfect realization of monastic ideals any more. I see that there is really nothing much I can do about it. The system is too big and too clumsy and too much of a system . . .

December 14, 1965

I am really sorry to be such a bad correspondent, but in the hermitage it is worse than ever now. In the novitiate I used to have regularly an hour or so each morning in which to answer mail. In the hermitage the time is much less. Twenty minutes or so, and some days nothing at all. I just write notes most of the time. And really it is hard to write letters. My mind is empty of the things one says in letters.

. . . Today I will send you the new book that is out recently, *Seasons of Celebration*, and also the Chuang Tzu book which is one of my favorites. They will go by sea mail. Or did I send Chuang Tzu before? If you get an extra copy it won't hurt, I know you will give it to someone who can use it.

Finally, I send you all my *warmest and best* wishes for Christmas. I will certainly remember all my Brazilian friends on that great feast, Don

Alceu, Dom Basilio, Dom Timoteo and all. *God bless you always,* and may everything be joy and peace in your community.

April 17, 1966

Thanks for your birthday–Holy Thursday letter. And forgive my handwriting. I have recently got out of the hospital where I had a serious operation on my back and am recovering slowly. I am in the infirmary, though now I can get up to the hermitage in the daytime—usually the afternoon.

First the most important question—as to the essay on "Christianity and Humanism"—yes I will do this. It seems to me very important and I have not too much to stop it, though I will be busy. I will try to get it to you by the beginning of August. Is that all right? Of course I know the *Jornal do Brasil* and appreciate the significance of the series. How long should the article be, please?? . . .

. . . Thank you for your good letter. I *always appreciate* your letters and your news of Brazil. You give me a very living and warm contact with a country I love—and for which I pray now in serious concern.

June 13, 1966

Here is the article for the *Jornal do Brasil.** It was finished a couple of weeks ago but the typing around here is getting slow. This copy is corrected and comes to you airmail. Other copies will come by sea mail. I hope it will be all right. I leave you and Alceu Amoroso Lima the care to see if it needs to be checked over by a friendly theologian.

We have our hot weather here now. I have been slowed down in my work by a bad arm, but there is no need to be frantically turning out new articles every minute. I have an unanswered letter from Dom Basilio that I want to answer today if I can, and also one from one of the monks in Rio.

There is a great deal of noise in the monastery. The church and cloister are being renovated and I can hear the machines all the way out here at the hermitage. The new church will be simple and modern and I suppose it will be acceptable to most of the community.

I have a new book coming out this fall, *Conjectures of a Guilty Bystander,* which I think *you* will like. It is not exactly a sequel to *The Sign of Jonas,* and it is not really a journal, but consists of personal notes in the same style, but a great deal of current comment, etc. Before that, *Raids on the Unspeakable,* a collection of prose pieces and prose poems, is appearing as a paperback with New Directions. I will send you a copy as soon as I have one.

* *"Christian Humanism." Also published in English in* Love and Living *(Farrar, Straus and Giroux, 1979).*

We had a Buddhist monk from Vietnam here, a very fine person, one of the leading Buddhist intellectuals there, a Buddhist existentialist and Zen monk. Thich Nhat Hanh is his name. I was very impressed with him. Pray for him.

October 6, 1966

First, many things have arrived: *Seeds of Destruction* and *The New Man*. Everything all right, but if you can possibly prevail on these publishers not to print my picture in the book, I would be much obliged. There is still a statute prohibiting this on the books of the Order and I would be the last to take any interest in having the statute repealed. Photos not in or on the book of the author are all right apparently. But I would not encourage that either.

Nhat Hanh is in France, has written a book on Buddhism in the world, and I expect to see it soon and write a preface. He has been advised not to return to Vietnam. Had a long private audience with the Pope. Maritain is coming here this evening and I hope to have a good but short visit with him before he goes East again. Probably his last trip to America.

. . . My new book *Conjectures of a Guilty Bystander* ought to be out soon. I don't know if you ever got *Raids on the Unspeakable*. Let me know. I will put a copy in the mail just in case. *Conjectures* is fairly important. A piece of it was published in *Life* and raised a lot of reactions . . . You should be getting the mimeographs as they come out, but I think a lot of these never got sent out. I do not take care of it myself any more. I don't really know what happens to a lot of this material. I assume you are receiving what you should get but perhaps you have not. You have not mentioned getting it. Articles on Camus, for instance.

I know I am becoming a worse and worse correspondent, but I have a hard time keeping my mind on business, except for the most immediate matters involving a new book and so on. Otherwise I simply do not retain things in my memory. Effect of living in the woods I guess! The weather is quite nice now though the nights are colder . . .

May 4, 1967 (Ascension Day)

Your letter came yesterday and I was delighted to hear you are now Benedictines.* Welcome into our family. I know of course the monastery

* *The community to which Sister Emmanuel belonged was at first an independent contemplative enclosed community that had been founded in Rome at the request of the Pope. The Mother-foundress, a young Brazilian woman of aristocratic lineage, died in the late 1930s, after which the community closed the Rome monastery and came to Petropolis. After Vatican II and the renewal of religious life that it encouraged, the sisters after three years of reflection, prayer, and study became juridically and canonically Sisters of the Order of St. Benedict.*

of NS das Graças. You are in good company. I feel much closer to you all now.

It is getting more and more impossible for me to keep up with letters, for all kinds of different reasons. First, there are just too many. Second, if I take time to write letters I do not get my writing work done. Third, there is just something about the mentality of the hermit life that makes systematic letter writing very difficult, it is no longer spontaneous. I hate to write artificial letters. Now the best I can do is send out mimeograph letters—except of course where business demands a reply, or charity does. Certainly if Dom Inacio [Abbot of Benedictine monastery in Rio] writes and if things work out I will reply, but it is a risk. I never know when I will really be able to write a coherent answer. I am trying to answer you now because if I don't . . .

I am glad to hear the article on "Christian Humanism" has been published. I was afraid perhaps it had been suppressed . . .

As to the title of *Conjectures,* I leave that to you. I have no idea how it might sound in Portuguese . . .

I am terribly sorry to hear of the sufferings AAL has had to go through. I will keep him and all his family in my prayers. I am glad he is not angry with Jacques Maritain's book [*The Peasant of the Garonne,* English edition, 1968]. Progressive Catholics in this country are already furious even before the book is out. But after all, Maritain has some valid criticisms, and if we are such mature and adult Catholics as we claim to be, then we ought to be able to listen to them with equanimity. What irritates me about the reaction here is that it does not fit in with all the noisy claims that these people make about themselves. If they are supposedly fair-minded, then let them demonstrate the fact.

I had to have another operation in February and now I am seeing doctors about a peculiar food allergy which has been giving me some trouble but really this is not anything important, it is just a nuisance, and having to go to the doctor takes up more time that could be better spent in some other way. In general I can say my health is all right . . .

May 30, 1967

. . . What you say about the Benedictine monasteries in Brazil sounds always very good. You have good people there and more vocations than we are getting here now. I think now there are only ten novices, or less. I am more and more reserved about the chances of real monastic renewal within the strictly institutional structures that we have. But I don't say much about it. The changes that are taking place in our Order seem well enough meant, but superficial, and the real issues are not properly understood. Great triumphal gestures are made, however, and some people remain quite happy. Others just leave.

Yes, I did get the check from *Jornal do Brasil* and also a copy of the article. They did a very attractive and interesting supplement. I am happy to hear my Teilhard article is now permitted at least in Portuguese. I guess it is probably out-of-date for the U.S.A. by now, and I will not try to revise it. But thanks for getting it published there. At least!

Did you ever get my book *Redeeming the Time* published in England? It is partly what was in *Seeds of Destruction*, but the first part is new. This might be useful as a very short book for Vozes. I forget if I ever sent you a copy. I'll send one now.

July 31, 1967

. . . I wish I had time to write to Dom Basilio, but my mail is far beyond my capacity—so is his no doubt. One day when I get a free moment I will write to him. I got a letter from Dom Helder Camara a couple of months ago and wrote back to him.

Bad situation in this country. I have expected it for a long time, but the violence is now serious and could easily reach the proportions of a civil war. If the Vietnam war gets worse and if China gets involved and trouble continues at home, the consequences could be very unpleasant. Pray for us. But all this is to be expected. Yet people are astonished, as if they cannot explain to themselves such happenings. They do not use their eyes. Perhaps they do not want to know unacceptable facts.

. . . At the moment I am beginning to do some work on primitive messianic and prophetic cults in Africa, Melanesia, etc. If there is some good information on the cults currently going in Brazil I'd be interested. Don't go to a great deal of trouble, but if there is some one source that is exceptionally good, I'd like to see it. The Cargo cults of Melanesia are a fantastic eschatology. Very revealing.

Nothing much new here. I enjoy the quiet of the hermitage and am saying Mass here now, which is very beautiful at least for me. I did not realize it would mean so much. I have two authentic ikons over my altar, one Bulgarian and one Greek, both from good periods, and also two good copies of Russian ikons. I pray for you and think of you often.

October 30, 1967

Here are some photos of the ikons. I think you can get some idea of how beautiful they are from this. Also the hermitage—perhaps you have seen views of it before, but these are recent.

Many thanks for the addresses of Mestre Didi* and the other Afri-canists. They all sound wonderful. I have not written to any of them yet because I have yet to decide on the questions and other points I want to raise. To tell the truth I am not yet at Brazil in my study of the "move-

---

* *Specialist on Afro-Brazilian culture, living at Bahia, a center where the Portuguese once imported black slaves from Africa.*

ments"—still in Melanesia and Mexico. It is not precisely "Africanism" but apocalyptic movements and Cargo cults. That would include the sort of thing in *Os Sertoes* (which I have not yet read I am ashamed to say— and I fear it would take too long in Portuguese). I did get the "paradise" book and sent a note to the author at the address suggested: but perhaps he never got it. I am most grateful. I have not gone all through it yet because I am not on the paradise theme at the moment, but will be again (that is part of the picture—I don't know what I'll end up with)! I am very happy to have these books and contacts and I know much that is fruitful will come of it all.

Look, it is hopeless to try to get me to Brazil! But I will offer at least one suggestion. DO NOT attempt anything now, anywhere, even in Rome! The Abbot is resigning. The new Abbot may be a different matter. This Abbot is obsessed with the fear of my going elsewhere and not coming back, as if that would be bad for the "image" of Gethsemani—or bad for business, in other words. It is ludicrous, but I can't do anything about it. Give us a couple of months and things will probably be very different.

. . . A zombie is a dead body moved by evil spirits. The expression "zombie" in my books refers to the alienated, stupid, bourgeois or other mass-man. There is probably a real good Afro-Brazilian word for it! *Un fat*—would be a weak substitute, but OK. Mass media: surely there is a current Portuguese word for it! Covers all forms of communication, papers, big magazines, radio, TV etc. . . .

March 4, 1968

. . . I have a new book out which is probably untranslatable—*Cables to the Ace*. Will send one with this. Later, *Faith and Violence* might be useful there. I don't know if I spoke of this before but the new version is quite different. I have started a small (temporary) magazine and will send a copy. (Literary only, no piety.)

March 18, 1968 (Gethsemani)

Just a quick note to send you my congratulations and prayers and best wishes for the 25th. I'll say Mass for you on the day of your Jubilee and ask the Lord to bless you in every possible way. I owe you a lot and am truly grateful for all your devoted zeal.

Above, by the way: a picture of the hermitage in a very non-Brazilian pile-up of snowdrifts. At the moment a small addition is being built off to the left, where the sunlight strikes, I'll be having a little chapel where I hope I can (old-fashionedly) have the Bl. Sacrament. I am enclosing as a present a copy of the new pamphlet on Camus which just came out. I will have the brothers send *Mystics and Zen Masters*. Please give my warm regards to AAL, and to all my friends whom you will see at the Jubilee festivities. I will be with you in spirit. Certainly tell AAL he has my permission to do whatever he wants in the way of editing some of my material. I trust his judgment completely. It is possible that under the new Abbot I may be able to visit Brazil—if I can do so very quietly, without publicity, and without having to appear in public for talks, etc. Not this year, however. It might be done if I am sent to our foundation in Chile for some work, temporarily. However, my request to be transferred to Chile permanently was refused. My Superiors are very definite in wanting to keep me here, and I can see their point. I do not frankly think there is any chance of my making an ecumenical foundation or any other foundation in Brazil. I am definitely not going to become the head of a community of any kind, as I do not feel this is my vocation at all, and I belong where I am in solitude. (Even if I went to Chile permanently it would be only as hermit.)

However, it may someday be possible for me to travel and visit different countries in a quiet way, to see communities and people, but not to get involved in anything public.

Anyway, that is all very conditional and depends on many other things. I just want to wish you joy and peace on your feast, and to assure you of my prayers. God bless you.

To W. H. Ferry

Wilbur H. Ferry, born in Detroit in 1910, was vice-president of the Center for Democratic Institutions at Santa Barbara from 1954 to 1969. He had received his undergraduate degree from Dartmouth College, and was the recipient of an L.H.D. from Starr King School, Berkeley, California. In October 1968 Merton flew to California on the first leg of his trip to Asia. He wanted to search out a possible site for a hermitage and, with this goal in view, "Ping" Ferry drove him along the Pacific coast on a trip of several days. Then on October 15, 1968, he saw Thomas Merton off on the plane that was to take him to Asia.

I visited Wilbur H. Ferry at his home in Scarsdale, New York, in August 1983. He was most gracious with his time and most helpful in what he had to say about Merton, as the prodding of his memory relighted the obvious joy he took in his friendship with the monk of Gethsemani. We spent a couple of quickly passing hours in his nicely equipped garage-office, whose walls display memorabilia of his many years' involvement in the social issues (especially the war issue) of the time. There are many reminders in his office of Thomas Merton, who had hoped to find the Center a source that he could look to for information about the issues of the day. He found what he was looking for ("Ping" was most faithful in sending books and articles to him); but he found more: a cherished friend, whose visits to Gethsemani he looked forward to.

September 18, 1961

For a long time I have been meaning to write this letter to you, ever since my friend and publisher, James Laughlin, of New Directions, has spoken to me about the work you and Dr. Hutchins are doing at Santa Barbara. Through his intervention and by your kindness I have now received many of the pamphlets published by the Center and have read many of these with great interest. I knew before this the one called "Community of Fear," which is certainly one of the most pointed and articulate statements of our present danger. I am at the moment reading the one on Cuba and Latin America, which seems to me to be also very accurate and sane in its approach to a problem that ought not after all to be so complex. That we have made it so is real cause for concern, to put it mildly. It seems to me that our deep-rooted addiction to the kind of narcotic thinking induced by mass media has gone very far in blinding even those who are supposed to be in a position to see, understand and decide our destinies. It seems to me that the situation is altogether *extremely* grave and that the work of your Center has come too late for you to be heard. God grant that I am wrong in this.

In any case, as one who is at the same time a priest, a member of a monastic Order, and a citizen of the country which still prides itself on being the model and defender of democracy, I believe it is a moral issue of the greatest importance which faces me along with everybody else: and that most of us are not even regarding it as a moral issue at all. As if politics and ethics had nothing whatever to do with one another, and indeed as if ethical considerations were completely irrelevant, or at best subjective, only, in their relevance. However that may be, it is certainly a personal ethical question, a question of conscience for me to enter to some extent actively in the work that goes on around this central problem of our time. I feel that too few of the religious spokesmen of our time, and every minister is such a spokesman, have faced the question of war and peace, except in a very general way. "Peace is desirable." On the other hand, under the avalanche of words and statements, some of them extremely ambiguous, that pour on us from all sides, I also well understand the confusion, the desperation and the frustrated silence which possesses so many men who ought, by their vocation and office, to have something very definite to say.

I want first of all to say that I am very interested in the work of the Center and would like to participate in it in any way that I can. I am grateful for all the things that have been sent and I look forward to receiving all you mail out. Finally, since I cannot come out there to discuss things with you, I would like to extend to you and Dr. Hutchins, or any other member of your staff, or anyone you would consider likely to be interested, to come to the Abbey for a couple of days. As Laughlin probably told you, I often have guests here for the purpose of dialogue and discussion. There have been lots of Protestant theologians, some writers, and so on. This simply means that a contemplative monk should have a quiet though articulate place in the discussions of his time, when the time is one like ours. I am sure you agree.

. . . One thing that seems to fit my situation [we might discuss is] the contemplative approach to the present world situation. There is one, and it is by no means the least horrifying: yet there is comfort in it also, and I don't mean "inspirational" comfort.

In any case I assure you of my deep interest in the work you are doing out there and my very best wishes for its fruitfulness and success.

November 18, 1961

J. Laughlin is probably writing to you about our idea of a paperback of articles on peace. I especially liked the Lewis Mumford talk you sent and want to use it . . .

Your letter was very fine and I hope you had a good time in Greece. You did it rather quickly, but that is the way things go today. I am so pleased you will come and see me here and I look forward to having some good talks with you . . .

Merton was continuing his search for contributors to the book that would be published as Breakthrough to Peace *the following year.*

December 6, 1961

. . . How will I get in touch with Sir Robert Watson Watt? I would like very much to have a piece by him. I am hesitant to ask people to sit down and *write* one because J. is in a hurry, and so am I, and so perhaps is the world. But he may well have an article or a speech lying around. Abba Lerner sounds interesting too . . .

So far we are doing well. Lewis Mumford has sent a longer article, that was in the *Atlantic* Oct. 1959 and it is superb. Erich Fromm is letting us have something brand-new . . . I would like to use both Piel and Christiansen. Have also asked Gilson, maybe Maritain. And Gordon Zahn has given us something. He is quite good . . .

December 21, 1961

. . . I am having a bit of censor trouble. This makes me think that one way of getting some of my stuff around would be to let you people mimeograph it and circulate it with your material. Would you consider this in some cases? This would not require censorship. I have, for instance, some copies of letters to people—to make up a book called *Cold War Letters*. Very unlikely to be published (!). I'll get them typed up and you can judge whether you would think it worth circulating some of them. Happy New Year to all of you.

Don't forget good resolutions to come to Gethsemani . . .

January 18, 1962

You will probably be hearing soon from J. who left here yesterday for Florida and for some amazing transactions which he described to me. We had a good two days and got the book into very fine shape, I think. I had not seen before the thing of yours which we are printing, the one on *Disarm and Parley*. This is very fine indeed . . . We have some Norman Cousins from the *Saturday Review*, at least one Mumford piece, a new one by Gerald Piel, Mayer's "Tomb," a couple of things I scared up in *Liberation*, and a fine piece by Gordon Zahn, the Catholic sociologist, on Catholics in Hitler's war. Very compelling and not too pleasant. All that remains is for me to get busy on the preface which will tie it all together . . .

Under separate cover I am sending you several mimeographed copies of new articles I have done, and these you can give to anyone you feel would be interested. I will be glad of any comment. I have been in touch not with John Courtney Murray, but with Fr. Ford, who is a close associate and who thinks like him. I gather they are in a rather quixotic abstract position saying limited nuclear war is fine but all-out nuclear war isn't, and therefore we just have to see that we don't go beyond a limited one. This is very logical according to the tradition in which they find themselves sitting, but the only trouble is that the tradition in which they sit, that of the post-Tridentine casuists, is a boat that has slipped its moorings and is now floating off in midocean a thousand miles away from the facts. But within that boat everything is logical all right, and in apple-pie order . . .

. . . I do feel that there is a lot of point in sending around copies of things in a small circle of interested people. This to me is a significant activity, all the more meaningful because it lacks that mass, anonymous, stupefied quality that everything else has. So too with those ads put out by committees of intellectuals in the papers, and the sudden realization that letters to the editor make sense . . .

I painstakingly explained to J. that when I said I was going to circulate uncensored mimeographed letters or copies of letters that this was not in any sense a wild subversive activity. There is no censorship ordinarily demanded for material circulated privately or as the phrase has it *"pro manuscripto."* The articles I have sent you are in any case being censored for eventual printing, but meanwhile they can be of interest to a circle of thinking people and may arouse worthwhile comment . . . I have sent you ten copies or so of the pieces done recently. Tell me if you can use more and let me know the names of people who might want more.

Don't forget you are planning to come through here some time. Meanwhile we are just on the point of starting a week's retreat. This is really a kind of vacation when everything stops dead, and we get special talks to revive our pristine fervor, and we meditate more and read spiritual

things more. So I will forget the war, more or less, for a week. I hope
the war forgets me. And you and all of us.

I have given up guessing what will happen soon. I have little confidence in Kennedy, I think he cannot fully measure up to the magnitude
of his task, and lacks creative imagination and the deeper kind of sensitivity
that is needed . . . What is needed is really not shrewdness or craft, but
what the politicians don't have: depth, humanity and a certain totality of
self-forgetfulness and compassion, not just for individuals but for man as
a whole: a deeper kind of dedication. Maybe Kennedy will break through
into that someday by miracle. But such people are before long marked
out for assassination. He does not strike me as so marked. At least not
for that kind of reason.

. . . J. was also horrifying me with tales of the sedate gambling places
at Lake Tahoe, the ones that are prim and country-clubbish and which
cater to decent people, with dealerettes in prim black dresses, and soft
Muzak, and nary a drunk on the premises, and the nice old ladies coming
up to gamble in busloads from the cities of the plain. I am utterly dis-
heartened. What has happened to good old sin? Here I am behind these
walls doing my bit and counting on the world to do its bit, with barrel-
house piano and the walleyed guys in eyeshades, with long cigars, raking
in the pieces of eight, and the incandescent floozies lolling over the
roulette wheels . . . Tell me, Ping, am I wasting my time? Is all that
utterly gone? I am shaken. How can I go into a week's retreat if all has
. . . GONE? But maybe there is still plenty of evil in other fields. I take
heart again and get back to the sackcloth . . .

. . . What distresses me most is the aspect of Europe and of course
Algeria: and the fact that Khrushchev, far from being the nastiest Red,
is really the nicest and most amiable. There are others so much worse.
And here at home, how many millions of abject crazies. With power to
make their madness felt where it hurts most.

Yes, as you say, Happy New Year . . .

[*Cold War Letter 26*]

January 30, 1962

I have just received your two letters and the other items. I have just
read the article you indicated in *Worldview*. We have our Catholic Herman Kahns and I think they are the majority. As far as I can see, this is
the more or less accepted view of many theologians and perhaps of the
majority in the U.S. It is stated with much more subtlety and humanity
by John Courtney Murray, and there is one Jesuit, Fr. John Ford, who
takes exception to it and is more over our way. But this man Fr. Mahon
is a cruder and franker expression of all that lies behind the suave surface
of Murray's arguments. Here are my remarks, without much preparation,
and spontaneously.

1. Fr. Murray has a good, reasonable, clear mind, makes all kinds

of clear distinctions, is learned in his theology. Underlying his thought is a basic assumption that somehow everything is quite reasonable, that military men are not extremists really, that we are all human, sensible and tolerant, that we all mean pretty well. And that the Reds don't mean pretty well at all. Hence what we need is to make it quite clear that we are ready at any time to engage in a *limited war*, a reasonable war, a nice kind of war, in which the limits set down by Catholic moral theology and Pius XII are respected by the Pentagon. The Pentagon will always be ready to give Fr. Murray and any other Catholic full assurance that they have no intention of doing anything that is not "limited" in some way or other.

2. The emphasis is on limited war as a military possibility. Of course it is possible, isn't it? It is what the government intends, isn't it? Well, the reason for that is if a war is limited then no Catholic can possibly object to it in conscience. The Popes have said strong things about all-out war, they have even called it a sin. Hence there might be trouble if one started out right away on an all-out basis, wouldn't there? But it is clear that a limited war is licit, hence every Catholic has a moral obligation to support it, hence *that* is in the bag. Just let's remember please that this war is going to be limited. Limited to countries. Some of the continents will not be directly hit, they will only get the fallout. But the effects of the bombs will not be beyond control. On the contrary, we will know very well that when we explode a bomb over or near Leningrad, the blast and fire will affect Leningrad while the fallout will affect Helsinki, Riga, Warsaw, Berlin, etc. etc., or, if the wind is wrong, well, Archangel, etc. We have full control. This is a limited war. And this Fr. Mahon, he likes to look at it principally as the destruction of *property*. If you think of the destruction of property, the ruin of buildings, then one who objects to the destruction is nothing but a pragmatist, he puts material things (buildings) before spiritual things (the spiritual desert which will result under communism). This is in line with the primitive Christian ethic which stated that one should at all costs destroy the potential persecutor of the faith. One should under no circumstances allow oneself to give witness to the faith by suffering persecution. This must remind us to put aside "romantic notions of the Church of silence," etc. He definitely prefers "a world of smashed buildings and smashed skulls, to a Soviet World without God or freedom." That is a lovely touch, isn't it. Smashed skulls. We are not fighting with H-bombs, only with clubs. Real limited war, isn't it? Limited to clubs all of a sudden. There is a kind of magic in this kind of moral theology, don't you think?

3. The real thing they are all getting at is the justification of preemptive first strike. The game is this: Traditional Catholic morality about the just war says that under no circumstances can a war of aggression be accounted just. At best it must be a war of defense. But of course the

missile armed with the nuclear warhead gives overwhelming advantage to the man who strikes first. Consequently we have to have that first strike at all costs, and the Christian thing to do is to adjust traditional moral teaching so that it becomes licit for us to attack if we want to. We have to be able to take "anticipatory retaliation" if we are "sufficiently provoked."

This is the beauty of the new theories. Gone forever is all this nonsense about patiently sustaining injuries, which is not even good for the individual Christian any more, and never was any good for the state (even though Pius XII said the state was just as much obliged to practice charity as the individual was). One does not have to be attacked. One just has to be "provoked." Who decides what constitutes provocation? The standard, our Fr. Mahon frankly admits, is sufficient as long as the one provoked is "subjectively" certain that he has been provoked. I take it this means all we need is to feel provoked. Hence the thing to do is to drop all cultivation of any kind of virtue that would make us suppress feelings of provocation. Let us realize that anger is virtuous, and that it provides us with a sensitive barometer that registers provocation a whole lot sooner than patience would. This will bring our moral teaching and practice right up to the minute. "The combatant must be subjectively certain of the justice of his fighting and of its efficacy."

4. Justice and efficacy. Ah, now we come to the heart of the new theory. Traditional teaching on war taught that a condition for just war was the moral certitude that one could actually achieve something by going to war. This meant two things. One that there was no disproportion between the destruction on one hand and the good achieved on the other, and that there was really after all some good to be achieved. The modern Popes have of course said that they did not think war was a just and reasonable means of settling international disputes, and declared that we should not resort to it any more. That it resulted not only in great physical evil (even conventional weapons did this) but greater spiritual evil.

All this goes by the board with the new theory. Efficacy? Sure, what is more efficacious than ICBMs armed with H-bombs. Here you really have efficacy for the first time in all its purity and simple strength. Naked, streamlined efficacy, no? This is what the Pope wants. "It is interesting to note that he speaks of *efficacious* self-defense," says our mentor. "May we not assume then that in using the expression 'efficacious self-defense' in the year 1956 he is using the term in a modern context?" Not only may we assume this, but as loyal followers of the Papal teaching we go right ahead and declare it. The Pope, ahead of his times as always, was looking forward to the theory of counterforce and preemptive strike, counterforce with bonus, you know, ten percent of the missiles take out the chief cities . . . This is what is necessary to make the thing efficacious.

5. We will, in short, prove our obedience to the Holy See by twisting the words of the Popes around to make them mean exactly what they did not mean, and doing exactly what the Popes wanted us not to do. We will be blindly loyal to our Christian obligations and we will get in there with the nuclear first strike and wipe Russia off the map. Then our troubles will all be over, we can sit back and Christianity will have the whole world at its feet. And all as the result of an innocent little limited war fought with a preemptive club.

The funny thing about this reasoning is that it makes me vomit. Possibly I am not a good Catholic. I guess that is really the trouble. I haven't learned how to go into this kind of mental gymnastics yet. But I guess they are going to want to teach me after they see the article I have in *Commonweal*. I will have to beef that up a little more, as it is to be in the book. Already one of the censors in horror has denounced me as a pacifist, just because I don't believe in all-out war. The Pope too is a pacifist, except of course he can get away with it, being old and probably soft in the head, the way he comes out with sentimental nonsense about having absolutely no recourse to violence. But patience, nobody listens anyway. Nobody even knows he said that, and really few care . . .

[*Cold War Letter* 39]

February 17, 1962

I envy you the sunny, dusty lanes [of Mexico], but why go spoil it with Jules Romains? Anyway I hope you are having a nice rest.

The main purpose of this letter is to say that certainly the second week in April will be fine . . .

I am stimulated greatly by the little book on the problem of abundance, and also by your essay on justice in economic life. Certainly your essay is completely "Catholic" in the best sense and it seems to me to fit in perfectly with *Mater et Magistra*, which is a document full of good sense. There is no Catholicity without this basic good sense, and where it is lacking, or where it is evaded, under the pretense of being "more human" or (usually) more "realistic," then everything begins to split open and fall apart . . .

Certainly the greatest danger today is to assume that we have to accept society and its ills as a divinely given and final reality to which our thinking must be adjusted, without any attempt to change anything according to deeper standards. That way, we just let "society" push us along, and we forget that we are society. That if we do not strive to build and guide society according to reason and to conscious principles, then it will lead us and sink us by the power of our own unconscious forces, with a little help from the devil.

. . . Dusty lanes of Sonora! Well, enjoy them!

[Cold War Letter 48]

March 6, 1962

Thanks for your good letter from Mexico and the one sent on returning, with its enclosures. I wonder why you chose a place where you would be surrounded by squares in the first place. There must be lots of other places. But as I understand it now, the squares are all over and there is no island left where one can escape them. Indeed they have come to specialize even in the nicest islands.

That reminds me, we have in the novitiate now a West Indian Negro postulant from St. Lucia and he is refreshing indeed. I am picking up from him bits of the charming French patois they speak on the island. Its religious undertones are warm and moving. It seems to be pretty much the same sort of thing that is spoken in Haiti, as the island was once French.

Time does not permit more of this pleasant kind of thing. Criticism comes in about the *Commonweal* article which you perhaps saw. It was doubtless oversimplified. The standard tactic of the defenders of the status quo is to say that all moral criticism of the bomb is prompted by "fright" and is a manifestation of "emotionalism." The people who want to use the bomb are, on the other hand, qualified as objective and unemotional thinkers. True virtue is on their side, etc. etc. It is the basic aberration of cold-war thinking . . .

The first and greatest of all commandments is that America shall not and must not be beaten in the cold war, and the second is like unto this that if a hot war is necessary to prevent defeat in the cold war, then a hot war must be fought even if civilization is to be destroyed. Once this is accepted, and of course it depends on how tight one hangs on to it, then other assumptions are not even considered, other possibilities are rejected as unreal and put aside without even a thought. The one great "reality" is the threat of communism, and all else is illusion, fantasy, speculation, theory or what you will . . .

I have to close now. Really it is vitally important that we now work at keeping the way wide open for thought, for discussion, for investigation, for meditation: and the thing that most blocks this is getting oneself permanently identified and so to speak classified as the holder of one or other set opinion. And, by implication, as loyal or disloyal to our side in the cold war. Even to question the primary importance of this kind of loyalty is itself regarded as disloyalty and immediately disqualifies all that one says from further consideration. We have got to keep thinking and asking questions. And the mere ability, once in a while, to raise the right question ought to be regarded as an achievement. May we learn to do this and keep at it. What did the Fathers of the Church say about Socrates being among the saints? And there are also the Prophets.

March 16, 1962

. . . If you arrive toward the evening of April 10, Tuesday, and stay over 11th and 12th, that would be very fine. The details will depend on where you go from here.

Usually the most convenient thing is to hire a car at the airport and drive out yourself, which is what J. always does. Then you are not tied down to bus schedules . . .

The top brass in the American hierarchy is getting wind of my articles and is expressing displeasure. An editorial in the Washington Catholic *Standard*, evidently by a bishop, takes very strong exception to the *Commonweal* article and I am strongly reproved for a "startling disregard of authoritative Catholic utterances and unwarranted charges about the intention of our government towards disarmament."

In actual fact the editorial twists and misquotes my own statements, trying to make me out an absolute pacifist and trying to make it appear that I said the Pope had taken a stand which was a condemnation of all war.

So you see it is beginning. The whole line taken by this editorial is the official Pentagon line. Russia's attitude is the real obstacle to peace. It is implied that I am unjust to our government by my "gross conclusions" which say that indiscriminate destruction is what is intended in the use of nuclear weapons . . .

This is a straw in the wind and I guess in a little while there will be more than straws, there will be pine trees. Which may make it difficult or even impossible to bring out the book on peace I was hoping to do. But if the separate bits can get out here and there as articles, that will be something. And of course there is no harm in my sharpening up my use of theological statements and trying to make them more foolproof. I wish I were more of a professional, for the sake of peace.

Well, anyway, I hope you will be here April 10th and that we will have some good quiet talks. Until then, God bless you, and all the best of wishes.

Ping Ferry visited Merton on April 10, 1962. On May 7 he wrote that he was sending to Abbot Dom James a triptych of the Last Supper done by a Santa Barbara artist.

May 8, 1962

How long is it since you were here? I forget, must be almost a month already. There have been so many things to do, and so many unwritten letters to worry about and leave unwritten . . . It was good to hear from you, that you were back, and to hear echoes of your passing through the cities of the East. I got a letter from H. S. Hughes and sent him the *Cold*

War Letters. I think by now you should have received a fair packet of the same.

One of my main troubles is with the censors, again, always, maybe now in a final and exasperated tussle which may end with the war book getting shelved and most probably, in fact almost certainly, means that I must put and leave in wraps the *Guilty Bystander* . . .

Talk about strident. I do not realize how strident I have been until I get into print. The one in this month's *Jubilee* ["Religion and the Bomb," *Jubilee* 10 (May 1962): pp. 7–13] will set a whole lot of people right on their ear, and I guess it is my fault. I could after all have been more circumspect and moderate, and there are smoother ways of saying the same thing. I lash out with a baseball bat. Some professor of non-violence I am. Oh well . . .

J. is worried about "Original Child Bomb" [Merton's grim poem on the bombing of Hiroshima] not getting any attention and finally it transpired that the bookstores were putting it with the juveniles, Peter Rabbit, etc. My comic book.

. . . The weather here has been great, perfect spring, a little hot, rain once in a while to freshen things up. The yellow tulips came out in front of the hermitage and made it very nice all over. Such yellow too. The valley is most beautiful . . .

May 22, 1962

. . . I got a letter from one of the ladies [Valerie Delacorte] in the women's strike for peace and that is a good one too. Have those kids got off in that twenty-five-foot boat for Christmas Island yet? One of them wrote me, as I think I told you. That is a stirring and heartwarming effort if ever there was one.

For the rest I have no news about anything, I know there are tests but that is all, I hear nothing. People say my stuff is being quoted and discussed but none of it gets to me. If you see or hear anything I know you will let me know.

Very hot around here now, hot as the middle of summer. I am still trying to finish the peace book and as I think I told you *Conjectures* will probably not get permission to be published . . .

[*Cold War Letter 77*]

June 4, 1962

. . . Your Marina triptych I saw yesterday in the library, so it has acquired a home. I have delayed in sending back the transparencies but they go off to you today.

That little bit about Fort Detrick was an eye-opener all right. Did you ever get a debate going? Surely there is no more debate: it is wonderful for science to create these grand new mutants that carry disease and resist all forms of insecticide. They even fly in more than one direction. Like for example they are launched so that they fly toward Russia, and lo, they can turn around and fly back where they came from. I think there is a great significance in this new leap of science. Hurray for the resistant mutants.

Did I tell you that the decision of the higher-ups has become final and conclusive? *The Peace Book* (I mean the one I just wrote) is not to be published. Too controversial, doesn't give nice image of monk. Monk concerned with peace. Bad image. Monks in NY State [at the Abbey of the Genesee, Piffard] have fallout shelter paid for with monks bread as advertised with pictures of subhuman monks in NY *Daily News:* good image of monk, fine, go ahead. Hurray for the resistant image, the non-mutant.

I am not sore, not even very much interested any more. I did what I thought ought to be done and that is that.

Have been going back to Origen and Tertullian, where I belong. What do I find? Preaching non-violence. Christians never kill with the sword, these characters say. They haven't heard that this is a bad image. Father of the Church, bad father image. But well, we all know what everybody thinks of Origen and Tertullian (if they have heard of them). Augustine came along and fixed up the image OK. The war of the merciful fought for love, he says. Nice image. Non-mutant resistant. You can pour anything you want on that image and it won't change, it is official.

So let the merciful non-resistant mutants resist and travel. Let them pack up our troubles in their old feedbag and kick off for anyplace. Our mutants will come home to roost.

The anthology (it has a couple of sporadic title changes since I last wrote but it is a non-mutant and it keeps coming up as *Breakthrough for Peace*) this is going through . . .

July 13, 1962

. . . By the way, talking of books: Jules Romains. I don't care what he thinks about the Church. It is just that years ago when I read the first volumes of the *Men of Good Will*, I came to the conclusion that he was almost as pedestrian as Zola, which is saying a lot. I just think him a complete bore. Maybe he has got better lately, I don't know. If you really think I ought to be converted on this point, I am not averse to trying my best.

Are you the one who sent the little mimeographed thing about Jean and Hildegard Goss-Mayr in South America? That is probably from the FOR. I was most impressed by it. You ought to see some of their stuff: Catholic peace movement in Austria, Pax, FOR, etc. . . .

What else? I am sending you a piece on the English mystics. I don't know if that is what all your companions are thinking about, but there are several copies anyway . . .

August 30, 1962

Am in the hospital for some tests—nothing special. Brought Everett Gendler's ms. of Rabbi Tarnaret so as to read it here. It is really very fine. The deep principles, the sources of non-violence in Exodus, are right down in the root of everything. This is very fine, very convincing and I am grateful to have a chance to meditate on such salutary truths.

. . . *The Merton Reader* is a big 500-page thing Harcourt, Brace is putting out this fall—with all the most outspoken stuff concentrated in one place so that if they didn't know before, the Squares will know now I am on the other side of some fence.

In a letter of October 30, 1962, Ping Ferry described himself as the corresponding secretary "sending your stuff to the Merton Club of south California."

December 31, 1962

Good to hear from you. Thanks for the stuff. Just been reading that fantastic James Baldwin article in *The New Yorker* about the Negro situation. It is shattering, very fine, except that by implication he does what everyone does in such a situation and ends up with the same error in reverse (the whites are scum because they are whites). Still it is a very important statement. The [Xavier] Rynne letter also about the Council, the second one especially, is very fine.

. . . I think the *Reader* came out nicely and hope people treat it well. I was glad the *LA Times* gave such space to the *Breakthrough* piece. As you say, I am happy that the book gets around at all. Now of course that we have shown our "power" with Cuba, there is every reason to believe we will be confirmed in the delusion that this is the ideal way to settle problems. Hence the situation is not less dangerous than it was, from this point of view. But if the explosion of threats did end in easing tension temporarily (if that means anything) we can be glad. (Glad?) I ponder those funny words, "we can be glad." They are strange things to have put down on paper . . .

Have you seen the whole book of Lax's poems? Fantastic, some of them. I will use my influence to get you the book if you have no way of getting it. Lax is in Greece with the Eliots (who are they?) and is trying to get a Guggenheim. If Guggenheim ever sees that book, he will throw away the glowing paper I wrote for Lax. But it is a wonderful book . . .

January 12, 1963

. . . I got a nice card from Henry Miller saying he reads the *Reader* with joy. That's good.

I am just reading Rachel Carson's *Silent Spring*. Have you read it? You must. It is very enlightening, because it shows that the disease is everywhere. The same type of absurd logic that drives us to nuclear adventures is driving us to spray thousands of acres with something that does not effectively eliminate the insect we are getting at, but does eliminate the birds that would otherwise eat the insect we don't like. It is very instructive, and the book hits hard chapter after chapter. Very important to get this idea around, it is not peripheral at all.

. . . Have translated some poems of Raïssa Maritain, and have had some fine letters from Jacques, retired, teaching philosophy in France to a special outfit of little brothers, very holy, very poor, very zealous. I will send the poems of Raïssa along when they are typed . . .

March 20, 1963

. . . "What Price for Peace" is terrific. I wish you had written it about a year and a half ago, and we could have put it in the book. I am sure plenty of people are taking it seriously, but they are probably people who cannot do anything anyway. There I suppose is where the politics of despair comes in. The people who are able to think aren't in a position to act, except to write letters to congressmen or to perhaps take one aside and talk to him for ten minutes. Then what? The people with the power don't do that much thinking, or they are too influenced by people with more power who do even less thinking. I understand there is a continued and serious push for invasion of Cuba . . .

I got a good letter and article from Theodore Roszak, and want to write to him about them when I get time. Friend of mine [Jim Forest] is doing a good job on the new look *Liberation.* Have you seen it?

June 12, 1963

Thanks for the letter and the packets of things. I was especially glad of the little Pelican on *Mysticism* [by F. C. Happold]. It looks great, so far . . .

You are right about the race thing. Whatever may be going to happen, this is for *real.* That alone is comforting. The reality may turn out to be frightful, but it is a relief at least after the mouthings and the tepid steam of the mass media, which are absolutely meaningless and totally out of touch with any reality but that which they themselves have manufactured. There is going to be an awakening. But a lot of people do not want that kind of awakening, I am afraid. Still, it has to come. I too am afraid there is going to be a real revolution and real violence. There already is a revolution. Martin Luther King started it off, and in a way that was admirable. But the less admirable ways are certainly going to take over, and the confusion is going to be tremendous. But as you say, it may well keep us from the bomb, and make us realize that there are more real problems than those of international power: that there are problems of people, and that we are the people with the problems. This will be something new for a change: I mean for us to have problems that are objective and not just in the head. A great blessing of God, though it may be bloody . . .

It is understandable that they should now be taking the Muslim line more and more. After all, the Muslims have done more than anybody else to give them what a human being really needs: a chance to help himself and improve himself, an increase in self-respect and in the sense that his life has a meaning. What have the rest of us done in that way? The terrible thing about white liberalism has been its awful benevolence, the benevolence that assumes, without possibility of appeal, that the Negro is utterly incapable of doing anything really significant for himself, and therefore that he is not fully human. I can see precisely why they are so mad: it is more honorable to be shot at like an animal than to be treated as an incurable infant . . .

I am very glad you want to come in the fall. October and November are good, but not September. We will be planning on it. All the best to you.

September 11, 1963

. . . Fr. Haring, who is one of the big theologians at the Council and was very close to John XXIII, as he is to Paul VI (I would not be surprised if he had a hand in *Pacem in Terris*), was here and urged me to continue writing about peace. When I told him the situation, he said he would intervene with the General in Rome, so that may happen and I may get back on my horse . . .

Have a very bad arm and shoulder, bursitis or something. It is really knocking me out and cutting into the work. Today I am to go to town to see a specialist about it.

October 28, 1963

I was awfully sorry you did not get here. Hope everything is all right and that all is calming down in the East. Come some other time.

The paper on the "Still Point" idea was very fine indeed. Where did it come from? Was it one of the Princeton talks? I am very sympathetic to that kind of thing, and always incline toward something of the sort here, on a very small scale, say once in a blue moon. We really ought to think of a small special group getting together for a couple of days. The trouble is that this is so out of the way for most people. And then I can't get involved in too much: something like this could easily grow into a project that was beyond handling. Still, we might keep it in mind.

Do you see *Ramparts* magazine? It is evidently out now with my long piece on the Negro affair, and I can send you a couple of extra copies, or you can get a few from them. It is going to be in *Blackfriars*, brought more up-to-date, and I think it is being done in French for a small book . . .

March 23, 1964

Your latest consignment contains many good things. "Triple Revolution"* is urgent and clear and if it does not get the right reactions (it won't) people ought to have their heads examined (they won't). (Even if they did, it would not change anything.) We are in for a rough and dizzy ride, and though we have no good motive for hoping for a special and divine protection, that is about all we can look for. I have recently been accused again of pessimism because I refuse to equate hope in God with an unbounded trust in our economic structures. How is it that so-called Christians (and they are perfectly sincere, even devout, nay holy) are totally convinced that the promises of God to Abraham are now totally invested in our spiritually and mentally insolvent society? One cannot question this first and basic truth without being hustled at least spiritually toward the stake . . .

April 4, 1964

Thanks for everything, especially for renewing IFS [*I. F. Stone Weekly*]. By the way I assumed that you sent that card from that tantalizing French restaurant in the middle of a dinner with IFS. The card arrived on the hungriest day in Lent and I thought feelingly of the cuisine. I was with you in spirit.

"What Price Peace" is one of your best. Stinging, and for my money irrefutable. A brilliant piece of writing and full of sense to which few will attend. Have you a few more copies of the offprint? I could use about a dozen if you have them. It ought to get around. You are so right . . . I read a hair-raising piece by some French general on the philosophy of nuclear war. Terrorize them. Keep hold on your own nerves just a few minutes longer than the other fellow and you will not have to destroy more than a few cities, he will quit. Some philosophy. He blandly admits it can be two-sided but does not seem to realize that this may have consequences.

. . . The thing that is worst about the whole involvement of so-called Christians in the cold war is the way it is assumed that Christian hope and optimism are built around the survival of the Church as a plush and privileged establishment in the affluent society. If this isn't a spiritual apostasy, I'd like to know what it is. The war theology of the Churches ought to be sufficient demonstration of the fact.

Have you heard about the very interesting letter of Cardinal Tisserant, dug out of some files which the Nazis took from the chancery office in Paris during the war? It was a personal letter in which he spoke of efforts to get

* The title of a letter (written by Ferry) sent to President Lyndon B. Johnson by the ad hoc Committee on the Triple Revolution. The three revolutions cited in this long letter are: the Cybernation Revolution, the Weaponry Revolution, and the Human Rights Revolution. The letter concentrated on the changes needed to meet the first of these revolutions.

Pius XII to speak out against terrorism against Poland (before the final solution of the Jewish question) and to declare that the individual conscience had a duty to disobey abusive and absolutist state authority. The Pope said nothing, though later remarks about conscience, notably in the 1956 Christmas message which the cold-war pundits all quote, because it said a Catholic must defend his country in a just war: but here the Pope immediately adds a reference to the rights and obligations of conscience. This is significant, in terms of the vagueness and allusiveness of such documents, and it stops up a cold-war loophole for the war people, strictly qualifying the statement of obligation to serve (in a just war only) etc.

Keep us in mind. Visit beautiful Kentucky. Romp in the fetid Knobland. The open door is open . . .

May 27, 1964

. . . I am sending various mimeographs, including a poem I was able to read to the Hibakusha [people from Hiroshima on a peace mission] when they were here. That was a short but impressive visit and I found it very moving. Also I felt that they were people I was really interested in meeting and talking to, as if they were in some sense more actual than a lot of the visitors who float in and out. Too many of them these days.

Still fighting censors, and publishers. I am hoping that my new book (with the race stuff and other material like the "Monk in the Diaspora" article that was in *Commonweal*) will eventually get moving. It is now blocked in four or five ways. I am getting a bit sick of all this nonsense, but not in the sense of wanting to get in there and raise a cloud of dust. It is to a large extent futile anyway.

I wrote an article like on [Henri] Perrin* and perhaps it will get published but I don't want it in one of the larger Catholic magazines as it will arouse comment and I have not cleared it with the censors. However, here are copies. I like the book very much. Very moving and gives a good idea of what the real situation is . . .

Have you been in touch with Archbishop Roberts? One of the only Catholics who will dare to come out wholehearted and flat-footed for your *Pacem in Terris* convocation. I can imagine the political intricacies of the planning by this time! . . .

June 8, 1964

This is a rush note, to say that unfortunately I am tied up on the 18th. Too bad. But John Heidbrink is plotting something for the fall, and perhaps you might be able to get here with a few others (I want to keep it small) in November. So we will have to skip it this time . . .

---

* *His original draft, "The tragedy of a worker-priest," became "A Priest and His Mission," a review of Perrin's autobiography. The review appeared later in* Continuum, Spring 1965.

About the piece on *Pacem in Terris:* as it is short, I think I ought to be able to do it, except that I have made nine hundred resolutions not to take on any more articles or prefaces for a while. But if this project gets rolling and I am in the clear, certainly it should not be too much trouble and it seems that I am now allowed to write about *peace* provided I don't write too much about *war*. This seems to mean that I can radiate sweetness and light but not condemn the bomb. How much sweetness and light can you stand?

July 1, 1964

. . . It was good to have you here, and I hope the rest of your trip was fruitful.

One book you must read if you have not already is *The Pilgrim* by Serafian, about Pope Paul and the Council. Thesis that Pope Paul's curial instincts took over and he sacrificed Bea and the Johannine drive to the conservative pressures against them, then went on pilgrimage as a surrogate for the non-achievements of the second session. In a way it is a curious parallel to *The Deputy,* though not of course as rough. What impresses me is that wherever we turn we come back to this baroque image of the Papacy, more than an image, an idol, of which curial power is an essential element. The conservatives see it better than the liberals. The thing is now so constructed that perhaps the Papacy has come to depend to a great extent on machinery like that of the H. Office, and the Office crowd is serenely convinced that it has to arrogate to itself all the powers of the Pope even against the Pope himself, becoming in the end the real seat of infallibility. This means of course that infallibility becomes organized and to some extent anonymous (no longer a charism but an institution) and of course that means one thing: totalism and the monolith. But if that is it, then what happens to the guys down the line? Do they suddenly acquire rather frightening obligations to dissent? There is going to be quite a crisis one of these days . . .

P.S. I am sending you some rather poor Freedom Songs I was asked to write. Forget if I told you about that.

August 31, 1964

Thanks for many other things, including the picture of St. Francis, which I probably did not acknowledge yet. It is very sober and striking and just right for a monastery. Thanks for it. And for all the other "items." I am reading the one on the potato famine and it is tremendous. A great job of work and a revelation. So like the civil rights crisis, too.

I am glad people are liking "Perrin." I ran off a few more and am sending them ·. . . I have added a couple of new items, one on the race situation for a magazine in France . . . I am glad that everything is set for the *Pacem in Terris* piece and for the meeting. My book is clear, or did I tell you? This is a kind of miracle. Should be out in January . . .

October 17, 1964

Your note and packet just came in. The FOR group is supposed to come here for November 18 to 20, most of them arriving, I expect, on the evening of the 17th. I do hope you will be able to make it. I especially want you to meet Fr. Dan Berrigan, a very live young Jesuit with great potentialities, and perhaps also his brother Phil who is the only priest I know who managed to get himself on a freedom ride. I am not sure who is coming. There was a possibility that Martin Luther King might, but now that he has the Nobel Peace Prize and is just out of the hospital I suppose his time will be taken up getting ready for Sweden [sic]. But really that award of the Peace Prize to him is one of the greatest things that has happened in recent years. Most encouraging, and it ought to have a great effect for all the American Negroes . . .

One man I just thought of for your PIT [*Pacem in Terris*] conference is Giorgio la Pira, Mayor of Florence, very prominent Catholic politico in Italy, close to Paul VI, knows Adlai Stevenson well, etc. etc. He was here yesterday and is going to see Stevenson today. I think he would be a good man for it. Speaks little English, however. Is ebulliently Christian, but I think a very good head too.

No more for the time being. Let me know if we can expect you in November.

On October 20, 1964, Ferry wrote that he would attend the peace meeting scheduled for November 18–20, 1964. He was only able to stay for the first two days.

December 5, 1964

Yes, I am long overdue with these scribbles. It took time to get back on the rails after our wonderful meeting, which everyone really liked. You contributed very much and I appreciate it. I think the whole thing worked out exceptionally well, and it was all real from beginning to end. Retreats do not always achieve this unusual distinction.

Thanks for your letters and geometric swirls. You are a hidden Santa Barbara Mondrian. (I have a suspicion that some of your colleagues are mandarins but I don't know just how to work these two words into a funny pun, so I will let it all go.) Like I said, you have the Mondrian touch. Why not do some of that in color? I like the ones that lead you into a funnel. There's where you have been putting your secret spirituality, you old Christian . . .

With the coming year and the business of stepping back into the shadows of the pine trees I am perhaps going to have a gradually increasing communication problem, but I do hope Fr. Abbot will let me stay in contact with you, while he gaily cuts the lines to everyone else, I would like a few reminders of civilization (they are not exactly too plentiful here). I mean of course the benefits of civilization as well as its horrors: or to combine the two: the benefit of some sane comment and protest around about the horrors.

Here are some artifacts with names. One is called "Ebbing and Emerging" and is perhaps my favorite picture of my own, the Ebbing in question is not Krafft-Ebing. You picked with unerring accuracy the best one in the exhibits Signature III. I think it is marked at $275. The reason for this outrageous pricing is that I hope to make the monies that accrue to me (how you like that business stuff?) the nest egg so to speak for a scholarship so to speak for a Negro girl student at Catherine Spalding College. All this is very much so to speak. I don't expect to sell many in Louisville. How would the Santa Barbara cats like to have the exhibit out there, for the cause?

Well, I am off to the races. Be good, keep well, happy Christmas, hope you are getting the cheese all right. Fr. Abbot would not let me accept an invitation to Japan to see the Zen people, said the higher Abbot thought that this request, coinciding with an interest in the solitary life, was a manifestation of a "dual personality." Meanwhile Fr. Abbot is off to Norway, for the blessing of a bishop friend. A Cistercian . . .

On December 14, 1964, Ferry wrote: "I met some marvelous people at Gethsemani and will never forget those two stunning days."

March 19, 1965

I have just written to Mr. Leavitt at the museum saying I would be delighted to send the drawings out there for September. Thanks for bringing them to his attention. They are at present in Milwaukee, and have been treated more or less kindly everywhere except in transit, when some frames have been broken. Rather the glass, but that is enough. After June there is nowhere lined up in the East (except perhaps NY) but I am not sure. I was planning on Atlanta for June but have not heard definitely. Can you suggest other people on the Coast who would be interested? Someone in San Francisco for example? I might arrange to get them over there for the summer.

. . . Fr. Goffield, formerly of LA, in voluntary exile in Chicago, came through here last evening on the way back from Selma with some firsthand information about it. It sounds both terrible and inspiring and now I understand today there is a real march and a breakthrough, one of the biggest in the whole struggle. I guess the white South is going to have to recognize that there are things that can no longer be done in broad daylight in front of TV cameras, but there is still the night. But really, I hope it will be a big step forward. And certainly if the Negroes can vote, it is going to be the end of a lot of political careers that should never have begun . . .

April 30, 1965

. . . It is very exasperating at a time like this for me to get nothing but secondhand news, allusions, vague gestures in sign language, and then the straight dope ten days after it has happened (when Izzy Stone throws his lifesaver my way). But in a general way I know what you mean. It seems to me that the U.S. is looking for any "justified" reason or pretext for laying into China and knocking out the Chinese industrial centers and the places where they would be likely to have or to make the bomb. And I am quite sure that they intend to do this as soon as they conveniently can, and that it will certainly be the beginning of World War III and of one huge mess. Having just finished Flannery O'Connor's new book [*Everything That Rises Must Converge*], I can easily believe that this country has got seven devils in it and a few more perhaps besides, and that the American illusion of innocence and universal messianism is now about to unleash THE worst war that ever happened, maybe the final one. It seems to me that only some kind of direct intervention of Providence can prevent it. But since God is on the side of the poor, it is quite possible that rather than let us wreck so many innocent people, he might intervene and let us blow up some of our own stuff and have an accident that would set us back hard enough to shut us up for a while. Since reason has ceased to have any operative part in the proceedings, I don't think we can expect salvation from any other quarter, and of course we have no right whatever to look for it there either.

To think that one has grown up to the distinction of belonging to the beast of the Apocalypse: food for thought. Not that any of the other beasts are much better . . .

Well, I wish I could end with some sort of cheerful message, some smile of confidence, some genial priestly guff. Nor on the other hand have I a sufficiently cogent image of gloom to sum up the situation and make some sense out of it . . .

Apart from that, there is good news. I am expecting J. Laughlin in a couple of days, and will find out how the Gandhi book is coming, and will talk about the Chuang Tzu versions (under sep. cover they come to you) and some crazy photos of roots I have been taking (again) . . .

July 20, 1965

Thanks for the latest consignment which came in this morning. I will go through it at leisure and comment (if I am left articulate enough to do so) . . .

I will send you the latest things which are just coming off the mimeo. I think I sent the notes on Schema 13, no? They were sort of a shotgun blast, because I did not know any more than anyone else (except bishops and periti) what is in the new draft. Actually I think that from the way it seems to stack up (the report from Jim [Douglass]) what is the real nerve center of the new draft is not the bomb but conscientious objection. Massive destruction is deplored, or even condemned, I hear. But while objection is timidly nodded at, in the last analysis the presumption of justice rests with secular authority, and that is that. There is the real pinch because that can be used to squash all genuine objection. All the bishops have to do is recognize that the war is just, and off we go.

Well, we'll see. I sent the bit on St. Maximus on non-violence to Dorothy Day for the *CW*. Later, a preface I have written for Herder and Herder to Régamey's excellent theological and pastoral study on non-violence, which should be invaluable at this time if anybody buys it and reads it. I glanced at the Mindszenty group's letter and this is the solid Catholic thinking of the American Church, by and large: there are two swords of God, He has one in each hand: the spiritual might of the Church and the military might of the U.S. This is what most of the American bishops probably think, in the last analysis, though they might not admit it. Pretty spiritual, what? Just like the Gospel.

The Chuang Tzu book is finished, censored, in the hands of the lads at New Directions. A book called *Mystics and Zen Masters* has just been delivered to Farrar, Straus and Giroux. With this all off my chest, on August 20 I am officially retiring to the hermitage and will not be seen very much around the monastery, will not be novice master, will have very few visits. About that, however, I am sure there will always be exceptions, which will be up to Fr. Abbot, but I think he would make an exception for you occasionally. You can ask. Your mail will also get through. I am not sure what will finally happen about mail in general but I will see to it that the important contacts are not broken, and I think that will be respected.

Actually, the decision has been great. I am here almost all the time anyway, but now that it is official and final, everything makes more sense. This is what I came here for, and I think it will be, as it already has been, very fruitful. I realize that I am extremely fortunate to be able to do exactly what I am supposed to do in life: a thing which few people ever manage to get around to doing, and there is something pretty wonderful about it. I hope to continue writing, of course, in a leisurely way . . .

September 20, 1965

. . . All I can say about the life in the cottage is that it makes immense sense, and does not necessarily imply any kind of serious break with reality: quite the contrary, I am back in touch with it. Certainly a most healthy and peaceful existence, lots going on, I finally got back to hit *Conjectures of a GB* and it is going to be a very lively book I think, much wider and more varied than the little bit I had a few years ago . . . Did J. send you the Gandhi book? He should have . . .

Your remarks on the Center do not surprise me. I often wondered how much of a community they thought they were anyway. When communities work out to be less communal than they think, the last man to be surprised is J. Easy for a hermit to say this. I am convinced that most of man's troubles come from his illusion that he can only live in hives.

The letter to Jim Forest referred to below was prompted by Merton's concern over the implications of the self-immolation of Roger La Porte. See Forest letters.

November 11, 1965

Here is a copy of a letter I had to send to Jim Forest today. I may be wrong in my judgment of the situation, but since I cannot keep properly in touch I thought there was nothing else for me to do. Will you look it over, tell me what you think some time, and return the copy? Thanks. The situation is awful.

November 30, 1965

Thanks for all the things that have been coming in. I hope you have not been worried about the letter to Jim. Things are working out all right. We are understanding each other. I do regret a bit the fact that the CPF is in the middle of a great deal of improvisation which it does not sponsor but—well, it is in it. I obviously can't keep track of all this or know what it is, and naturally I have questions about it. I think for instance that it has been responsible for Dan Berrigan being shipped out to South America, which is a shame. But I am in no position to analyze these things, and as I say, we are understanding each other . . .

January 26, 1966

. . . Glad you like Chuang Tzu. I certainly do. That is my favorite book. I mean of my own. Most of my own books I can't stand. This one I really like. Marshall McLuhan interests me from what I have heard about him, read an article here and there. If you get anything more on him, shoot it along . . .

What you say about Fr. Du Bay [priest of the archdiocese of Los Angeles] is no surprise. Certainly I haven't written about that aspect of the priest's problem! I am in no position to. I will just put down what comes to my mind. Certainly, in the situation where we now stand, something like this is bound to happen. I mean by that that even in the Council it was spelled out that the relations with ecclesiastical Superiors were not what they should be, and it was also said, in traditional terms, that the Superiors ought to get down to the business of mending their ways. The trouble is of course that they can't. They don't see the problems the way subjects do, especially if they have been in a Chancery Office for years, twenty, thirty, forty, some of them. And think of those characters who have been in the Vatican since they were teenagers practically. They just have no idea what the score is, and they don't know how to look squarely at the problems of subjects, especially they do not and cannot understand the difference between the real problems of creative initiative and the neurotic kid problems that, in fact, they generate in subjects and unconsciously like to perpetuate. The relations of Superiors and subjects, in religion and in the secular clergy, are very often completely puerile, centered on artificial and illusory problems which are almost deliberately kept going because they create an illusion of important decisions being made. All this nonsense could be avoided with a minimum of maturity.

Now the big question is not whether or not there is a problem: that is obvious. It seems to me that the priests of Fr. Du Bay's and Dan Berrigan's generation are saying, Hell, there is this problem and the Superiors are never going to solve it themselves. On the other hand, the Superiors respond only to pressure. And we cannot get higher Superiors to bring pressure on lower Superiors, they are all in cahoots like a gang of thieves, and all support one another in tricky procedures, secret power plays, cheating, etc. etc. Hence the only thing to do is to bring pressure from the secular arm so to speak. In Dan's case, the "secular arm" was an ad in the *Times*, or so I am told.

In my opinion, I think that the risks of this approach should be studied objectively. Not by Superiors, obviously, their answer is a foregone conclusion. But by the people who are starting this. Personally, I think that it will do a great deal of harm to the Church, if it is not handled with extreme tact and care, and I don't think Fr. Du Bay, for all that I have great respect for him, is tactful. Maybe tact is not what will help this kind of ploy to get anywhere. But I think nevertheless, theologically and biblically, we have to ascertain whether the Church is the kind of body that can stand such a thing as a priest's union without getting into schism. I think that the fact that they start out uncritically making no distinction between a labor union and a "priest's union" shows that there is danger of being wrong from the beginning, because, however you look at it, the relation of a priest to his bishop is not that of an employee to an employer. Hence the problems that arise between them, and the very real question of the priest's rights, need to be expressed in a different form. To baldly state the problem in terms of unions, and presumably picketing strikes etc., is to say that the priest, considering his bishop as his boss, employer, is free to get the support of people outside the Church in pressuring the bishop to settle matters that are Church business after all. I know that this principle of not washing dirty linen in public etc. has been abused time and again by Superiors in order to silence criticism and keep problems hidden and ignored. But nevertheless there is a problem.

I am going to have to do a great deal more thinking about it, and would appreciate any information. One thing is certain, I am not going to get personally involved in this *at all*.

The only thing I have written about this problem is the piece on Fr. Perrin. He settled it in the best way he could, and I think with the cooperation of right-minded Superiors. In the Jesuits he foresaw that in the future his vocation as a worker priest and his really creative initiatives would run into unreasonable obstacles, and having discussed this with his Superiors he decided to get out.

My frank opinion on this is that instead of forming a priests' union and causing public pressure with a lot of noise in the press, priests should form a kind of private association for settling their problems in the more or less "regular" way, and it would be understood that instead of appealing to outside pressure they would make it understood that if they continued to get the runaround they would simply get out, get secularized, and use their talents in some other way where they would be less obstructed. The need of priests is considerable these days, but is presented in artificial statistical sort of language which is really bypassing all issues. Yet it scares the bishops. If they realize that they are just not going to have any decent priests left, and that they will be stuck with aged cranks, creeps, seventy-year-old infants and so on . . . they may think things over.

I think Fr. Du Bay is certainly the type who would do a good spearheading job, but I hope he won't do it in such a way that it simply wrecks the lives of a lot of people and compounds the incomprehension of the stuffy.

As I say, keep me posted, but I have no intention whatever of becoming associated with this, though I will always be glad to express an opinion . . .

As to Jim Forest, I think he is a most promising person and I have a great affection for him. I think he will do a great job. I am glad he was out there . . .

March 11, 1966

Thanks for the info about Fr. Du Bay. I am afraid that the kind of collision course with authority that he advocates is not going to get anywhere really. The whole situation is already so vitiated with politics that his ideas will only make it ultra-political. The whole source of the authority problem in the Church is precisely that Superiors act too much as politicians and manipulate subjects for purely institutional ends. Du Bay's course seems to point to an even worse kind of institutionalism in the long run. John Leo's column brought that out. But I am sorry for the guy, he has a real grievance and wants to do something that needs somehow to be done. God knows, I don't have any answers. Nor am I terribly optimistic about the whole situation . . .

I am afraid my back has finally got to the stage where it has to be operated on, so I am heading for the hospital in about ten days. It is a nuisance and I wish I could have avoided it. This mania for surgery does not impress me. But the doctor is a prudent man and would not do this unless I had to have it . . .

On June 28, 1966, Ferry came to Gethsemani at Merton's urgent request. Merton wanted to discuss a deep relationship that had developed with a nurse who had attended him at the hospital.

June 28, 1966

Thanks for your very good visit today—most enjoyable and most helpful . . .

July 15, 1966

. . . This thing here on Buddhism* I have sent to *Cross Currents*, with no notion whatever whether they will want it.

I am sending one of my last two copies on the dialogue with Dr. Suzuki. Hope I can get it back eventually, though if more are printed it will not be so necessary. I just heard the other day that Suzuki died. If you see anything about him in print, please clip and send. He was a very great old man. A real Zen master . . .

It was really great to have you here and I certainly enjoyed it. A fine day. Come again any time. Though if you were here now, you would not enjoy it much. Thermometer up to a hundred several days in a row, in fact above a hundred. The hermitage is impossible by the time afternoon comes around. I just take to the woods and look for a corner where there is a breeze . . .

July 23, 1966

. . . Do you have any dope on or anything by Edwin Muir [an English poet]? I have to review his collected poems for *Sewanee Review* and they will want something thoughtful. I do not really know him very well, have just run into him here and there, and know enough about him to know I am interested. That's all.

Did I send you this piece on Buddhism with the page on Nhat Hanh? If not here is a copy. More available, naturally. I sent it to *Cross Currents* but don't know if they will take it. If they don't *Jubilee* will. By the way, you don't know someone who would want to help *Jubilee* out? They are in a hole again, as usual. It's a wonder some Catholic millionaire hasn't decided to take them under his wing . . .

* "*Buddhism and the Modern World*," *published in* Cross Currents (*Fall 1966*) *and in* Mystics and Zen Masters, *1967.*

July 27, 1966

. . . Thanks for sending back the Suzuki dialogue. Hope Mrs. Carlson is interested in printing it as I can use umpteen copies. It was a good little exchange. Too bad he died. I understand he was at work at his desk. Just what one would expect of him.

It looks as though I will be very much in touch with his followers who are around this country, or some of them. Some will visit here. I am planning some articles for their magazine. You will see them in due course, I hope.

Still hot here but not so bad. My bursitis is really damnable now. Acting up badly. I have tried some manual work and that has aggravated it. I can see I have to adjust myself to a radical change of life in the sense of not being very active physically, or not as active as I would like to be. Nothing to stop me from going for long walks, so I will have to take it out that way. I will try to get some sun on me, there seems to be an abundance of that around. Nights are still stuffy. Just have to put up with all this, I guess. I am going in for a cortisone shot day after tomorrow. That usually helps . . .

Ferry writes that he is sending Merton the collected poems of Edwin Muir, though he knows nothing about him.

August 20, 1966

. . . Thanks for letting me see the Du Bay file. It is tragic. I do not know quite what to advise or what to say. It takes a canonist. My own reaction is that Bill Du Bay and the Curia are playing in two different ball games. It was Bill's obvious intent to try to communicate in some way with Rome, but he has quite evidently failed to get anything across at all. I think he was willing to get axed provided he could say something in the process: but assuming that this was something like dealing with a corporation, he thought it was enough to threaten. But threaten what? What can a cleric really threaten against an outfit that has such complete power over him? Unless he wants to threaten from outside, and then his position is entirely different. And he forces everyone to close ranks against him. I wish I knew of some effective way in which he could do what he really means to do as far as the hierarchy is concerned. If on the other hand he gives up trying to communicate with them, then how is he going to use their response to him as a means of communicating effectively with others that he wants to reach?

My general feeling is that the whole issue of the relations of the subject with ecclesiastical authority has here been brought up in a rudimentary sort of way that cannot lead to any real conclusion, and cannot really clarify anything. Perhaps that is too sweeping a judgment, and perhaps something has been prepared for the future. I don't know. But I do know that authority in the Church still has no concept of the kind of level of dialogue that Bill Du Bay is trying to initiate. It will always remain the dialogue of a grandpa with a six-year-old grandchild, because that is the way they think. Eventually they may begin to see it differently, I don't know. Doubtless some of the younger bishops do now . . .

As I say, it is tragic. I wish there were more help I could offer . . .

August 21, 1966

I keep thinking of the Du Bay case, and just in order to help a little I thought I might write him a conscience letter on the subject. I don't know where he is now, so will you please pop this in an envelope and shoot it on to him? I'd be grateful. I hope it will help him get straightened out with the boss. There is no use in a man like this just wrecking himself and confusing important issues while doing it.

August 25, 1966

McDonald essay on Du Bay just came in. I am afraid that when I read the dossier (which should have reached you several days ago), my eye did not catch that particular phrase about him not being entitled to appeal to his own conscience. That is appalling. I do not quite know what it is supposed to mean, or what the canonical catch is. (When you are in public conflict with the Church, you are no longer allowed to appeal to your own conscience?) (Is [Cardinal] McIntyre the Church?) What about Joan of Arc? This question really needs to be cleared up! I am sorry that not having paid attention to this enormity, what I wrote to him is not really to the point. Please pass this on, with my deep sympathy.

September 17, 1966

Thanks for the *Life* letters and for the latest batch of stuff, including above all your PEP. The latter is powerful, a great punch in the American gut, and I predict that it will really offend and madden the readers of *The Saturday Evening Post* (but of course you will get a lot of good reactions). It is inexorably Swiftian, brilliantly sharp and keeps the bright light focused right on the unacceptable point. My prediction is this: the power of it will so awaken them to the horror of our weapons that they will blame *you* instead of the weapons. That is to say that the indignation they should feel against the government and the military—and themselves the citizenry—for making and using such things will be turned against you for revealing the facts: as if the revelation of the horror were equivalent to its perpetration. That is the way the mind works in our day. But on the other hand you will certainly bring home inescapably to a whole lot of people the existence of these things they don't know about. I wish you luck with it: the piece is one of your best. And maybe it is just so strong that it will silence them, stun them . . .

You mention coming back this way: sure, when you are likely to come and have a little time, send up a rocket or something and I'll let you know if it's OK with the boss for you to come . . .

As I am no longer getting I.F. Stone through regular channels (it has been blocked on me) maybe you can slip it in with the batch when a batch comes. Also I would much appreciate good, gaudy, noisy *ad* material. I am getting conscious of the wacky material there is to exploit in ads. Send also the most smart and subtle ads, the ones that people really admire and get involved in by identification. I need to see some of the ads that everyone is looking at. I think this is even more important than reading the day's news. I mean for feeling what is in the air . . .

October 4, 1966

. . . Yes, for petesake no tearsheets from *Playboy*. I am very grateful to you for the advertising material I needed, which came in the form of *Fortune*, etc. But enough! It was all I could take. Am still retching. Weak stomach, getting old. Too long in the woods. Can't handle *Esquire*. Old gut won't hold it. This will be quite enough to produce the long poetic retch I was planning. More than enough.

Not having much news, I had not realized how far things were going in VN, but I agree with you, from everything I see they are warming up to the big game with China . . .

Here is uncorrected bit on Muir,* thought you would like it. His literary essays are very fine and as a poet I like him very much too, though he is a bit bumpy at times. A great man. If you have never read his ·autobiography I think you would greatly enjoy it.

. . . If and when you whirl by, you are always most welcome. Just shout in advance. All the best. Will keep the light burning in the window in case you are around this fall . . .

On December 1, 1966, Ferry wrote to Merton that he had just talked with Ira Sandperl and Joan Baez and had contacted the Abbot about their seeing Merton. The next day he wrote that Merton would be hearing from them soon.

December 9, 1966

Joan and Ira were here yesterday—got here late and had all too little time, but it was wonderful to have them, and I enjoyed every minute of it. Thanks again for sending them. I think they got something out of being here and I know I profited greatly from meeting them and having them here to talk to. Joan is a person of total integrity and purity of heart: one of those rare people who keep things from falling apart. I don't know

---

* "*The True Legendary Sound: The Poetry and Criticism of Edwin Muir,*" *draft dated September 1966, published in* Sewanee Review, *Spring 1967, and in* The Literary Essays of Thomas Merton, *1981.*

exactly how I can help them but I can at least send them some of the stuff we crank out around here. They can help me just by being around: they are an inspiration.

. . . Lots of rain here. Have been more or less holed up in the hut, which is not bad at all. Proofreading, writing, just looking at the rain, thinking . . .

January 4, 1967

. . . I hope things will not turn out as bad as they promise to in the "happy" New Year. Since I cling to the mad belief that God can and will override the follies and cruelties of men, even of believers, there is still perhaps some hope. On the other hand, he does let people get what they want so they will be in a position to see what it was they wanted and if possible amend their wants. There is where I don't see much hope. There is a terrible pharaonic hardening . . . power does grim things, and there is a lot of it around. It certainly dehumanizes more effectively than anything else under the sun . . .

Best of everything to you. Let's at least survive the New Year. I hope.

Ferry wrote that he would probably not get to Gethsemani until April. He confessed to being somewhat depressed and liking the things he wrote less and less.

January 19, 1967

OK, April or any time. What is this about you not liking the stuff you are putting out? To me it is better than ever. But I admit one easily gets tired of one's own jazz. Too close for comfort. A little rest and perspective always help.

Thanks for the *Observer* piece on or of Fr. [Charles] Davis. As far as I can see, his points are unassailable. Authority has simply been abused too long in the Catholic Church and for many people it just becomes utterly stupid and intolerable to have to put up with the kind of jackassing around that is imposed in God's name. It is an insult to God Himself and in the end it can only discredit all idea of authority and obedience. There comes a point where they simply forfeit the right to be listened to.

On the other hand, I regret that poor D. had to get pushed so far. It doesn't help the rest of us much. If everyone with any sense just pulls out, then that leaves the curial boys in full command of the field with the assurance that they are martyrs to justice or something. The real problem remains the reform of the Church people who remain inside. And if there can only be a little agreement on a more reasonable and free approach, something can be done. With super-organization and over-control, the whole works is doomed . . .

In a letter of February 17 Ferry wrote that Joan Baez "has been taking lots of whacks from Al Capp and others." (Al Capp referred to her as Joannie Baloney.) He also expressed the wish that he might flee the country and escape from "Johnson's War."

March 14, 1967

Many thanks for the chapter from Jim Douglass: Bonhoeffer-Gandhi. Very fine indeed. He is now doing most valuable work and this looks like a splendid book coming up, saying things that really need to be said, and making qualifications that some of the naïve secular city theologians are not making. I want to write to him about it when I get a chance . . .

I can understand how you feel about wanting to get out and be in some other country that can never own a bomb, never afford genocide, and lacks the joys of American know-how in alienating the rest of the universe. But wherever we might go we would take our America with us: there is no escaping that responsibility or that trauma. We are stuck with it. Might as well stay where the guilt is. I periodically yearn to become a citizen of Ecuador or of Costa Rica, so I know how you feel.

. . . Still hoping you will parachute in here one of these days. Let me know if there is any hope. I told Ed Rice to write you, and hope he did.

Ferry wrote on March 24: "We are wound up for the PIT meeting. Wish you could be with us in Geneva." This was a four-day conference on John XXIII's encyclical Pacem in Terris. *The conference, sponsored by the Center for the Study of Democratic Institutions, was held in June 1967. The Center had held an earlier conference on* Pacem in Terris *in New York City in 1965.*

April 10, 1967

. . . Does not look as if the bursitis operation worked out. It is still much bother and X-ray shows some calcium still there. Also the back is acting up. Last night I must have turned over the wrong way but woke up with a real good jab of pain such as you get with these things. Got into traction and it went away, however.

Sending a couple of things. The celibacy statement is self-explanatory. The Catholic bishops are meeting this week. No one expects anything from them. More and more movement seems to be taking place just underground and with no concern for these people. Did you see Dan's lovely fables in *The Critic*? One about death and the bishop was pretty timely . . .

Incidentally, got a very warm letter from Helder Camara, who is a live bishop and not a rack for episcopal robes. He urged me to get myself invited to the PIT conference. I assured him there was no chance of a permission to travel.

April 11, 1967

I just finished your excellent piece on corporations (in the Hamilton alumni mag.). Really first-rate. I am starting some reflections on "War and Meaning," and your reference to Steiner and the decay of the German language due to its being used as weapon impressed me. Can you provide more on that? Who is Steiner? Where? Etc. My thesis will probably be that as language loses its meaning, war tends to supplant it as a much more "sure" means of communication. (Language of escalation, etc.) But it is unilateral: it only communicates its message to those who have already accepted the message. By bombs we try to convince ourselves.

I really ought to go over to Ft. Knox and get to know the military we have so close to home. I can hear bigger and better explosions all the time. It would be worthwhile to see what is going on and to observe what is supposed to be the purpose.

Naturally I will be eager to hear what is said at the PIT conference.

May 4, 1967

This may perhaps get you before you take off for Geneva. Thanks much for all the hippie stuff which came in. I have read it with great interest. Thanks too for G. Sykes's book which I will return or give you when you pass through next. I look forward very much to seeing you after the PIT binge. Good in fact that you are not coming the 9th as I am again involved with going to the doctors over an allergy in the gut now, which is old stuff.

Have a good time in Geneva and may the conference prosper and give out light. Good luck. Blessings.

A card from Geneva, with no date, arrived for Tom: "We have Helder Camara on the final program here. Great man. The South Vietnamese are making it very bad for us. Ping."

July 18, 1967

Thanks for your note: I was relieved, I thought something might have happened to you. It was a pity you could not come, but once again I have been overvisited anyway: so perhaps we can hope to get together some other time when I am not so swamped. One visitor a week = swamped in my language. But I haven't been able to keep up with anything really, barely getting out my work, failing to meet up to correspondence, etc. I should have written you in Europe, but I did not know how long you would be at the Geneva address. But anyway I am sure PIT must have done some good, wars and rumors of war notwithstanding . . .

August 11, 1967

. . . Of course I am delighted that you gave the drawings around: that was what they were for. I still have one of your Agendas, I think, the one with Basil Bunting, whom I like tremendously. David Jones too I like, and would like to see. Will faithfully return the agendas. Glad Steve Allen has one of the drawings. Sure I'd like to see him very much. I have been pretty swamped with visits this summer, but things are letting up and I am keeping spaces in the fall for you and J. and could fit Steve A. in. September is bad though because the guesthouse is full of priests during the week and they don't like to have others in at that time—see the good fathers supposedly making spiritual exercises and really playing poker or something. Tsk tsk.

. . . I have written a tirade on the hot summer riots, perhaps irresponsible, not for publication, but anyway a blast of breeze. I will be interested to see what you say about Detroit. I guess it is just about inevitable this way, and somehow deep down I trust a basic vein of sense in the American Negro, and maybe, maybe he just knows what he is doing, and maybe it will be a bit wild but if whitey doesn't turn into a Nazi damn fast it might work out. Whitey doesn't have to do much turning to become a Nazi. I heard about two Detroit cops shooting down Negroes in cold blood in a motel where there wasn't a sign of any riot . . . nice . . .

I don't know about making a difference. In a way we can't help making a difference of some sort, but when it gets to be the kind of difference that stops Johnson's war, that is another matter. I don't think we can expect that much. But the fates have their own ways of intervening. The thing is to be on one's toes when they come snip-snipping at the threads . . .

More later. Have interesting new friends with out-of-the-way mags in England, and a little girl in Cal. [Susan Butorovitch, Campbell, California] who says she is running an underground paper and is obviously very young and very innocent.

August 22, 1967

. . . Was invited to go to NY to talk over some business with Cardinal Koenig (atheist-secretariat). No soap. Maybe the Abbot considers me a prominent atheist, which is what Koenig is apparently here to see.

Main thing is I'm sending along this tape with some of my new far-out poetry stuff on it. I think it sounds OK, but it is only a couple tracks of stuff to see how it comes out. Mostly for my own interest, it helped to play it back a few times. However, maybe Teo Savory and Elaine and others out there would like to hear it. I send it to you and you do what you think best, so long as eventually it gets back to Bellarmine College,

or better, in this case, Sister Therese [Lentfoehr]. She has a collection
of my stuff . . .

September 5, 1967

Thanks for your comments on "Hot Summer." I have incorporated
them or will incorporate them in new corrected version, and it will be I
think printed in *Kattalagete*. More copies are on their way to you. They
need not be regarded as confidential. The enclosed is a bit pitiful, but is
a piece of homework done in response to a request from Rome no less:
concerning a proposed "message of contemplatives to modern world" [see
letters to Dom Francis Decroix]. In my private opinion the contemplatives
are a bunch of dolts and squares—at least the Catholic ones, and they
have nothing to say to the modern world at least until such time as they
wake up and come alive. However, I have dutifully done my homework
and written this draft which will be torn up and put together again over
there by others . . .

Looks like J.L. is not stopping by after all. This has been a bad year
for the visits I like: the indifferent ones have come through but alas . . .
I do hope you'll get a chance to get by here in the fall. I'll look forward
to seeing Steve Allen.

September 14, 1967

The David Jones *Agenda* is a real event and revelation. As I told
you, I did not know him at all. This has me felled. It is just what I have
looked for so long: better than Bunting. With Jones, Bunting and Zukofsky
we have the real poets and I wonder where they have been hidden. Of
course it is no problem to keep a poet hidden from me as I don't see
most of the mags. (a subscription to *Poetry* was given but the Boss would
never let it through).

Anyway, I am happy with the discovery and want to go into it much
more. Also—could I ask you for this? Can you dig up for me the paperback
of *Finnegans Wake* and I'll swap you a drawing for it. I need it bad with
Jones here. I'm trying to get *In Parenthesis* [by David Jones] etc. to do
a chronicle for *Continuum* on him. Maybe won't be able to round it up.
Where does one get Jones? I'd borrow yours but I want to get my
own . . .

Did they ever record Dylan Thomas's readings (broadcast) of *In
Parenthesis?*

In a burst of something or other I tried to get myself transferred to
Chile, to live as a hermit in the Andes and get out from under this
goddamn overkill society. The permission was indignantly refused (was
told to stay and save the society from within—i.e., to bust my skull against

the impossible). Doesn't matter that much, really. Wherever one is, one is only an ambassador of affluence and napalm . . .

September 24, 1967

I am so glad you liked the tape. Perfectly OK for you to make copy. Right now I don't have the poems on paper except in my scrawl in the notebook where I am building the *Geography of Lograire.* So I can't yet send typescript, mimeo or anything like that. Later. And if you like I'll pass on more tapes of this kind of material, if I make them . . .

But I am having fun with the *Geography of Lograire* and it will develop into something quite lively as well as complex: my summa of offbeat anthropology. Let's hope anyway. Edifying *Cables* in the works with ND right now, galleys went back Saturday. New title, which I hope J. accepts: *Cables to the Ace.* Does it sound good to you? Have the old timbre? Better than the other anyway . . .

September 26, 1967

The books arrived yesterday. It is sheer joy to get back into *Finnegans Wake* again after all these years. The lightness and freedom of it is a huge relief after all the piles of heavy junk one gets buried under. All the messages, all the media, all the mustaches—for the medium as we know is the mustache.

I have gone right into *The Anathemata* [of David Jones] and it is a fine poem: curious from the Catholic viewpoint right at this time! I hope at least one or two Catholics read it one of these days and keep their sense of continuity with the past. He says everything. And has the sap and solidity of Romanesque sculpture, too . . .

September 27, 1967

Got a bright idea. As I go on with the *Geography of Lograire,* I could make tapes while it is still in the rough—could send tapes to you and you could take copies if you liked and send original tape to Bellarmine. It would be a long time before I finally got to typing it and thus the material would be available in some form—and if I drop dead or something, a publishable text, even though imperfect, would be got from tapes. How does it sound?

December 1, 1967

I am just sending off the benefaction to Bob Lax. He will be very happy. Did I say he is coming back to this country for a while? Probably arriving about now. It will be good to have some money to get by on for a while. I thank you very much in his name and will let you know when I hear from him . . .

December 21, 1967

Just a quick note in the massive confusion of Christmas, when I no longer know which end is up. First I enclose Lax's letter of thanks to Santa. Please return when you have finished with it . . .

Thanks for materials for *Lograire*. One that worked out best was the "Polar Journal" from Dartmouth. Got a nice North section out of it. Have not fully got into the others yet. Indian material from your friend in Washington or Vancouver is buried in shuffle at moment, but I am most grateful for it and all and will pursue when I can again run . . .

December 26, 1967

Christmas rush: I hope over. Nice bright sun, I want to get out into the woods, just a few hasty letters.

First, Mrs. Carlson's offer of Vedanta books—most welcome, most acceptable, I hasten to say yes on behalf of our monastic library. If any place should have the books, we should, though there may be some of them on reserve for proven yogis. Anyway, the people here ought to have access. I would much appreciate anything that can be done.

Very fine of her to start such a project. I am in contact with a man [Dr. Richard S. Y. Chi] who has translated some very important Zen texts (Shen Hui) and is trying to find a publisher. Any suggestions? . . .

Now for the Christmas cracker: guess what I am doing: editing a magazine. Probably mimeographed only, and certainly will be restricted to four issues (at least that's my plan, unless the tumult of encores is so vast that it drowns out everything else). Poetry, creative stuff, Asian relig. texts, or other unusual material (Hasidic stories, etc.) . . . Can you stir up other poets and creative types? And how about some sharp comment from you about something? . . . Already have some fine poetry from good people. It's grooving. Will put bits of *Lograire* in it too. Outlet. Lot of fun.

Only problem may be the boys in the back room here. There is one little fellow who is quite censorious and turns me in when my material does not meet his nice sensitivities. Some of my artisti may come up with four-letter words . . . First issue should be ready for the press in three weeks.

Title of the magazine so far is *Monks Pond*.

No more now, I have to go out and look at a pond and perhaps photograph it, anyhow study it carefully, so as to imitate faithfully. Basho's frog.

January 25, 1968

Thanks for letter from plane: good rundown on black self-determination. I agree—and I for one am not offering anyone advice! I don't see how an enormous mess can be avoided, however.

New Abbot is a very good man: young, but willing, definite, open, with solid monastic ideas not crackpot ones.

Old Abbot still in no hurry to rush off into the freezing woods. Is around getting his "papers together" for a few weeks.

Monks Pond swims along nice: have a first issue in the works now and it is quite presentable I think. Keep hunting up poets for me, I am eager to get all I can . . .

Finally, the books from the Vedanta crowd arrived and I want to write and thank Mrs. Carlson: can you please give me her address? It is a fine batch of stuff, very glad to have it, and the librarian is over-joyed . . .

February 21, 1968

J. Laughlin was down lately and we had a good visit, got a lot done with the Literary Trust and with the general publishing work. I spoke to him about the *Anti-Letters Mertonlax*. Neither he nor Doubleday wants to publish same. The suggestion he made was that perhaps it would be a good thing to send it to someone like Unicorn Press. I have a feeling, naturally, that both ND and Doubleday would like the book to be slightly obscure and for "special" readers. Which would be right for Unicorn. So I have sent a Xerox to Teo Savory . . .

Thanks for all good suggestions re *Monks Pond*, *Lograire*, etc. Much appreciated. *Monks Pond* is ready to go, first number. Only thing holding it up is a bloody great logjam of liturgical material going through our machinery. I didn't realize this was in the works, or I wouldn't have started a magazine. But actually the mag. is going to be very nice—if I can get it out.

I'm having a small addition built on to my place. When the workmen get through, I hope to hole in for a good part of Lent. Then maybe I'll get a couple of things done I want to do—and even work on *Lograire* which I now and then do anyhow, but it goes slow. Which is only right. *Cables* ought to be out any day and I will send a copy pronto.

March 20, 1968

Fine, April is great. I'll put down April 27th, as Saturday is best for me. I'll hope Jim can bring you over about lunchtime. We can have the afternoon together anyhow.

Bob Lax is dickering with Farrar, Straus and Giroux about the *Anti-Letters*. I told Teo this and maybe they are waiting to hear further. I don't think FSG will take them. I'm sure they'll eventually go to Unicorn. Anything you do in their regard will be appreciated much.

Am sending 10 *Monks Pond*. There is no price, but if you want to donate some monies to the mag. fund that will dispose the local management in favor of the mag. and give the impression we are real.

Much banging on the part of workmen putting an addition on to the hermitage.

May 6, 1968 (on "friendly skies of United")
I must admit that drinking champagne over an entirely invisible South Dakota is something I find refreshing. Will be at Abbey of the Redwoods, Whitehorn, California, until May 14. Best.

Merton left Louisville on May 6 and arrived at Our Lady of Redwoods Monastery, Whitehorn, California, the following day. He was in San Francisco on May 15 and in Albuquerque, New Mexico, on May 16. From May 17 to 20 he visited the Monastery of Christ in the Desert, Abiquiu, New Mexico. On the 20th he returned home.

May 24, 1968
New *Monks Pond* just out. Here (over) is a spot on the Cal. shore I am in love with. Certainly do hope to return. Kentucky is muggy and stuffy and unprepossessing right now. Saw Ferlinghetti in S.F. and drank some espresso with visionaries. New Mexico was great. Met Jon Devereux, Peter Nabokov, etc. The monastery is fine—chapel getting back in shape.

. . . Good to talk to you when I was out there.

June 1, 1968
Eight copies of the new *Pond* are on their way. I'm also sending to Jon Devereux. I miss Cal. and New Mexico. Have some fine shots to remind me however.

A wonderful idea to get a place on the Pacific—too bad you aren't further north, you c'd buy Beau Harbor. But probably there are many equally fine places down at Big Sur—except I always wonder if that isn't too well known now. One very lovely place near the convent is obtainable, but lacks view of the sea. Very high up, lovely, well-protected little ranch. All around there, full of great places.

I am fully set on spending any time I can on that shore and wish I could move out for keeps. More later.

June 6, 1968
The first (single) *M. Pond* was because I had only sorted a few. Then I sent five, and am now sending five more. If you need more

I still have some. More *Lograire* in the next one as soon as I get grooving.

I miss the Coast! Understatement of the year . . .

June 16, 1968

Well, I really do take seriously the idea of exploring the Pacific Coast with you. There is no question that I really need a top-secret hideout where nobody will know I am there and where I can be alone with a lot of wind and sea for long periods—perhaps indefinitely.

Practical question: when would be the best time? My outgoings are still rare here, but I think the next one will be the right one to tie in with this project. This too is secret as yet. I am going to Indonesia, God willing, in November. That is the one thing definite about Asia so far. Bangkok still undecided. Doesn't matter. Indonesia is a good start, and I presume after that at least Japan.

It seems to me that the best thing would be for me to come out to Santa Barbara before my flight to the Indies and we could take a week or so to look at the Coast. Then perhaps when I came back I could hole in for that retreat I am hoping to make early next year. That's the way it seems to make sense at the moment and the way I think the Abbot would tolerate it. If I ask to go out for a special trip, he isn't going to be too happy about that. But since he has already given green light for this other, I think the two can be combined. I could come any time after Nov. 1st or even before if necessary. Wd probably need to take off for Asia around Nov. 18 or 20.

In Indonesia, by the way, the idea is that I give a retreat to a monastery of our Order. Will prob. have to do same in Japan. Fine with me.

If I can't swing it on the way out, I can make our exploration on the way back. What do you think?

First draft of *Lograire* is going to be typed up shipshape. Still much to do but now there is a strong unit, book-length.

Dom James went to the Kennedy funeral, which puts me in a good position in regard to his dogma that hermits never travel.

July 8, 1968

Thinking of you at Ghost Ranch.

Plans are maturing for my Asian trip—Japan, Indonesia, Thailand. I plan to leave a little earlier than I anticipated. Beginning of November. Could we think of our exploration of Pacific Coast right at beginning of November or end of October? Abbot is interested in something on Coast. I am hoping it will really develop eventually—but he might be amenable to my settling down in Cal. for a while (in isolated spot) on return from Asia—like January. Wonderful! Can I count on getting together two or three weeks earlier than originally planned? Let me know.

Come by here if you get chance!

July? 1968

. . . Sure, keep original ms. of *Lograire* all you want. No rush. I have mailed back four books you lent. Hope they arrived OK. Will be happy to get the typescript whenever, glad to have time to go over it. Good—let's hasten on to Mendocino when the time comes . . .

Monks Pond III just out, on its way soon. I think it is the best of the four (IV is in the works).

Can't wait until we get on that Coast. Was in Washington last weekend meeting a marvelous guy, the Indonesian ambassador, who will line up all sorts interesting contacts for me out there.

July 11, 1968

Many thanks for the card from Ghost Ranch. You probably by now have my scrawl that I will go sooner to the Coast. The plans I have now call for flight to Tokyo on *Nov. 1*. And full month in Japan before meeting in Thailand, after that Indonesia. Any suggestions for people to see in Japan?

In October I may probably have a brief workshop and meeting with a bunch of nuns in Redwoods. When in October wd be good for yr trip? I am not sure when workshop is, no plans yet, but much will depend on nuns.

Busy getting things finished and out of the way for fall. Knopf alas said no to the *Anti-Letters* but Holt, Rinehart and Winston seems interested. My early novel was finally accepted by Doubleday with hesitation. I guess you never saw it. Maybe I can get a copy to you.

No more for the moment. Very hot here. I'll get ready for a stuffy night, I guess.

July 20, 1968

Fine, I think things are clear enough now to begin to plan something for October. Let's suppose I land in LA (nearest to Santa Barbara I presume) on Oct. 14 ready to go on from there wherever you think best— and for as long as you can afford time. I suppose I should be at the Redwoods convent about Oct. 23. And perhaps on the way should stop at the one at Vina (but we'll see). Meanwhile, my own idea would be to see as much of the actual coast as one leisurely can, probably following route 1 all the way up to Fort Bragg and then cutting over to get to Vina (near Redding).

For my part I'd like to spend some of the time just sitting around on a point meditating and listening to the waves: maybe we could stop here and there and you could watch birds meanwhile. But my main objective I guess is to explore around for a possible hideaway where I could get some real solitude someday, temporarily or permanently. In other words the Abbot—Fr. Flavian—is seriously thinking of setting something up out there one day. But he seems willing to let me move out there on my own quite soon. Even this winter, when I get back from Asia. I imagine it would mean being on land near the nuns at Redwoods, or else squatting on somebody else's territory. That is the real serious intent I have in mind. Probably I'll end up in the north near the nuns, as that is the most practical thing to do (re food etc.) but it would not hurt to look at the southern coast around Lucia–Big Sur, and also perhaps get back into the Zen place at Tassajara spring and see other such places in those mts.

The early novel—I'll send a copy. Unfortunately the typist got the chapters mixed up, but I'll see if I can get a copy straight. (Worked over two, one for publisher and one for myself.) . . .

July 22, 1968

Here we go again—moving it up another couple of weeks. I have to fly to Asia Oct. 17—and participate in another meeting—this time at Darjeeling, India. I'd like to have a few days at the Redwoods Abbey before going—like to get there around the 12th.

Supposing I fly to LA on Sept. 30th—will be free from then until 12th and we can plan whatever is convenient to you there?

OK then, between Oct. 1st and 12th?? . . .

July 28, 1968

Here is *The Geography of Lograire* ms. which I hope to have typed by the time I leave for Asia. Need one carbon, I guess. It should not be too hard, and since it is verse, shd go fast. I hope it is not hard to find someone who will fight through it for me . . .

July 28, 1968

Great! Will fly to Santa Barbara I hope on Sept. 30 and will let you know when my flying saucer touches down. As to the trip—yes I do plan to stay at the Redwoods convent when I get there, as I have a meeting of nuns (and will have to be there abt the 9th I guess). But fine if your wife comes along. Addition of feminine wisdom will doubtless help find even better hideout.

No plans need be made for meeting people, except maybe a poet or two in SF, and I may stop at the Esalen inst. in Big Sur as they are hoping I'll give them a conference some time. I'll be slow to let any monasteries know I am around, but will have to stop here and there for Mass, I guess. But I'll fix all that. Looking forward most eagerly!!

I have run into a frustrating problem with typing again. *Geog. of Lograire* first draft is complete and I sent to typist a good six weeks ago or more, hoping it wd be finished by now. But she had sent it back with the first few pages typed on two different machines (utterly unlike each other) and has said she is so ill she has to give up. Which once again leaves me up a tree. The whole thing has to be typed, and I'd like to have it safe on paper before I leave for Asia if possible. Can I send it out to you? Would someone there be able to fit it in? Can pay normal rate and all that. So in fact, the urgency being urgent, I am sending it . . .

All full of vaccinations, and busy hunting visas.

August 6, 1968

Very glad Jo will come and I think Rogue River is a great idea. The further north we get, the better for me. I'd think then if we get past San Francisco the second or third day and then slow down up on the Mendocino coast and reserve the best of dawdling for the north—unless you have some search to accomplish in the south: that wd be great.

Today I am mailing out the mimeograph of *Journal of My Escape from the Nazis*—the old novel. The chapters of the first half are all fouled up but I have a list of the right order, identified by first lines of each chapter . . .

September 4, 1968

Good idea about having people in for a drink. I sure wouldn't want to trek around all those houses. And of course I do owe it to many good friends to say hello. Yes, Cogley, Laucks, and any one or two others you think—certainly not a whole mob. Right now somehow can't place anyone in LA—probably one or two. I don't think I'll hang around SF talking to anyone. Hate cities. Want to scram out after ten minutes. But will contact Milosz. Maybe ought to go say Mass at SF Carmel the morning we get out of there.

Moving fast up coast fine with me. A couple of days around the ins and outs between Mendocino and Eureka good. I'm all for the desolate mists and the nords. Might be somebody in Eureka ready to give or lend an acre of sandbar or something. I'll find out, but it needs to be done with much discretion I guess, so's not to set off a great chain of firecrackers all over Cal.

As a matter of fact, the latest is that I am hauling out of here next Tuesday the 10th and heading down to Abiquiu because there is a good Indian fiesta the 14th–15th and I'd like to be there (Apaches). Then off on a whirl various places. On way to Cal.

I'll look for the ms. of *Geog.*, hope it gets here before Tuesday but someone can send it on to J. if it doesn't.

Many other things I have to skip—must write Dan—does mail reach Phil? I am under impression mine doesn't. I sent him a book (*Faith and Violence*—did you get that, by the way? I'll send one to make sure). Don't think he got it. Dedicated to him and Jim F.

September 6, 1968

There will come some mail for me there probably between now and 30th. This will include a mysterious (and mystic) package addressed to Rabbi Vedanta, care of you. Have no fear. 'Tis only I under the beard. For security reasons, since as yet no news is out here about my going. Or I hope not. Am sending the Rabbi some books to read on the shore after I get rid of the ones I hope to have read that far.

My journey before Santa B. takes me, guess where, to Alaska. I have been assigned an impossible flight with a three-hour wait at Los Angeles. I'm going to look into that when I get out, and fix myself up with a direct flight to San Francisco and maybe a layover, then a direct from SF to Santa B. Back over that again, it's most unclear. I have a flight to Santa Barbara via Los Angeles from Anchorage. After all day in the plane from Alaska I sit during the best shank of the evening in LA airport. Nix on that. I'll thumb the airline schedules when I get loose. I'll try to fix it so I get in Santa B. direct from some civilized place and during the day. Preferably morning. Or noon . . .

Final preparations in full swing. Packing next.

On September 11, 1968, Merton flew to New Mexico and then on to Anchorage, Alaska. He arrived in Santa Barbara on October 3.

September 25, 1968 (Anchorage)

I am due to arrive in Santa Barbara on United flight 899 at 10 a.m., October 3rd. All set. The country here is *marvelous*—never saw the like— flying all around in bush planes; this is a wild, grand and exciting country. More soon.

September 26, 1968 (Anchorage)

Your note of the 24 just reached me here in the Chancery Office of the Archdiocese of Anchorage, where I am wrestling with the mysteries of an electric typewriter. Since the Archbishop is using to the full my potential for shooting off my crazyy (yeeow what a word) mouth I see no reason why I shd not seek to pick up a shilling or even a half crown in Santa Claus Barbarossa. The only stipulation would be no immediate press publicity. I can perhaps think up material for a "paper" on something— at least something to do with what I am about to do in Asia. In fact, probably the best thing would be to present some informal ideas as to how everything looks about the trip now, and then a report of how it went when I come back. Before and after, so to speak. It could be quite interesting . . . As I wrote yesterday I plan to sail into Santa Barbara on United Fl. 899 from San Francisco on the morning of October 3, 10 o'clock.

This would give me practically two days in yr villa, and as I said before I am going to be very anxious to lie around and read and think a bit. There will also be time to meet the folks and so on. If our exploration of California is a bit shorter, it won't affect much my original purpose because I have found enough lonely spots here in AZlaska (zow that's a grand word) to last any hermit until Judgment Day. It is quite possible that if and whenever I get back from Asia, I may end up here. Local bishops xtreley (extremely) friendly and gene   rous (generous) and everybody very helpful. Lots of little lost islands and spots like fishing villages with two Catlick families who'd be glad to have Mass on Sundays, wonderful lost towns with no road to them only reachable by plane or boat, places turned upside down by tidal wave and earthquake and moved to another spot etc. The mountains are the finest I have ever seen anywhere. It is a GREAT land. Today off to Juneau and SE Alaska and then back to Anchorage for the nunnies. Before I go on Wed. I will get a look at the west end down toward the Aleutians, where there is a lost lake amid tundra that sounds fab. (Near the usual fishing village for food.) Have eaten moose but not yet bear.

Could run on forever. Plans excellent. Will hold forth Oct. 4 and glad of any small shillings to take to farthest Ind. See you Oct. 3 at Santa B.

Best of everything to all. Hope Rabbi Vedanta's books arrived not to mention pants from New Mexico.

On October 15 Merton flew out of San Francisco to begin his journey to Asia.

October 28, 1968 (Delhi, India)
Calcutta was busy—depressing—starved. Everybody should have to see that city! Delhi much better. Many good contacts and interesting talks. Heading for the mountains in a couple of days. They looked wonderful from the plane, in the distance. Enormous! I'm sick of hotel life— hoping for a bit of quiet in the mountains. All my best to all of you.

November 11, 1968 (Oberoi Grand Hotel, Calcutta)
Hastily sending back the transcript which I only received today. Hope changes are OK. I had a marvelous eight days at Dharamsala in the Himalayas—three long talks with the Dalai, who is a great guy. All pure gold. And met many other lamas; also they are all on to something deep, which must not get out! Very good stuff. Great people.

Will write more in detail later. The Indian Oly* is horrible, but I am getting by on gin and tonic which is expensive so I do hope Mrs.

* Oly—i.e., Olympia—a beer brewed in the state of Washington that Merton became very fond of when he visited there. He now uses "Oly" for any brand of beer.

Carlson will buy the notebooks which are getting to be quite a literary curiosity. (If I may say so!) No more news from Bellarmine, so maybe they've given up.

Will look if Cameron point of departure. I am glad (sorry?) that I have spread the Oly gospel ever so little. But I repeat, Indian Oly is fatal. The rest of the Indian trip, apart from a bout of dysentery, has been marvelous. I love Delhi, love the Himalayas and now—second time round, am crazy about this wild city, Calcutta. (The quintessential city—just people and poverty and dirt and no masks that hide anything any more) . . .

On November 27, 1968, Daniel Berrigan wrote to Merton that a writer for The New Yorker *wanted to come to India to do a profile on him to add to the story she was writing on the Berrigans.*

December 5, 1968 (Singapore)

Money OK—no need of loan.

Thanks for letter and the clippings that were waiting here today. I am sitting down with a fine big bottle of Singapore Oly which is vastly superior to the venomous Indian variety (made of swamp water). Just came from Ceylon which is the loveliest spot on earth—you must get there someday!! Too bad about Corita—and Dan too. *New Yorker* profile idea is a gas. I don't want to meet no NY ladies no place.

Next address—RAWA SENEG—TEMANGGUNG—JAVA.

To George Bernard Flahiff

Born in Paris, Ontario, in 1905, George Bernard Flahiff became Archbishop of Winnipeg, Manitoba, in 1961 and was made a cardinal of the Roman Catholic Church in 1969. He studied in Canada (St. Michael's College) and in France (the University of Strasbourg and the Ecole Nationale des Chartes, Paris). In 1935 he became professor of medieval history at the Pontifical Institute of Medieval Studies at the University of Toronto. In 1961 he was named Superior General of the Basilian Fathers, a position he held until his appointment to the archdiocese of Winnipeg. After participating in the Second Vatican Council, he was made a member of the Sacred Congregation for Religious.

July 17, 1965

I am not sure the U.S. bishops will appreciate the enclosed, which I have sent to *Commonweal*. If *Commonweal* does not print it, I will try elsewhere. I have not seen the new draft of Schema 13 and the article on nuclear war, only the report that said there was now a favorable judgment of nuclear weapons.

In any event I thought I would let you see the notes I wrote about the Schema ["Schema XIII: An Open Letter to the American Hierarchy"], and I think you are probably one who will agree that the article on war is really a sort of exposed nerve in this whole operation of Christian renewal. If we are going to get anywhere in the modern world, obviously Christians are going to have to make new judgments in new situations, and in order to do this they must be free to protest, in the name of Christian conscience and of the Gospel, when mere acceptance and submission might in effect mean cooperation with a power structure showing demonic tendencies (as in the case of Hitler Germany). Where, as in the case of Germany again, the whole thing was decided beforehand by Church authority, the Christian conscience was silenced and men simply had to submit to what was objectively a great wrong, and they participated in this wrong, thinking they were obeying God.

I think this is much the same kind of problem we face with Schema 13: and the most important thing, it seems to me, is not necessarily to lay down a hard-and-fast rule this way or that, even about the bomb, but rather to make clear that there must be plenty of leeway for new and creative decisions, and hence also for protest and for resistance (of a nonviolent and pacific kind) when the power structure arrogates to itself decisions which are not acceptable to the Christian conscience . . .

In any case, I thought I would share these ideas with you. If, as I understand is possible, the Council might implicitly or explicitly approve new methods of war in a way that might seem to open the door to anything and everything, it would really torpedo the whole work that has been done so well, and at such cost, up to now. Forgive me for adding to your heavy burden of correspondence. I am grateful for the kind word you sent via our Fr. Timothy, who will be off to complete his studies in Rome soon.

Archbishop Flahiff wrote on July 29, 1965, thanking Merton for his letter and encouraging him to continue to speak out. He enclosed with his letter the section of the revised Schema XIII that dealt with war and peace and asked for comments.

August 13, 1965
I was delighted to get your kind letter, and especially happy to have a chance to look at the revised text of the section of Schema 13 *de Pace Promovenda*. It was much more positive than I had been led to expect, and my feeling is that on the whole it is excellent. I do have reservations on a couple of points. Besides being still doubtful as to the wisdom of giving an official blessing to deterrence, I am, as you guessed, still not sure that what has been said about conscientious objection is really of any use. It is then on this point that I will gladly take your invitation to express my ideas.

1. Certainly I think that everyone should be perfectly free to follow

his conscience, and that even in a case of a doubtfully just war one should certainly be permitted to fall in with the decisions of the government conducting the war. My problem is not precisely with this, but with the rather more somber fact that, to begin with, almost all wars are of very dubious justice today (the one in Vietnam is a very glaring case in point) and secondly, the way this is phrased on p. 80, n. 101, lines 17 ff. seems to *bind* the conscience of the faithful to submit to the decision of authority in case of doubt. I believe that this simply makes the right to object illusory. The government will always insist that it is conducting a just war, and will add that it is acting on classified information, etc., which cannot be questioned. The phrase about the government being obliged to act with the greatest prudence and according to the moral law would be all very well if there were a few Christian governments around which could be counted upon to take this seriously . . . I believe that this section in fact, instead of really guaranteeing the right to protest, as it stands simply binds the Christian conscience to give the benefit of the doubt to a government which, according to all laws of probability, will be certain somewhere to violate the laws and the principles of morality. Again, the Vietnam war confronts us as a horrible example. How can one who realizes what is going on and what the issue is, really give the benefit of the doubt to the Johnson Administration? (I admit of course that those who are not adequately informed and who cannot be adequately instructed on the point can perfectly well go to fight in Vietnam, but that is not what this section is saying.)

2. I do think the wording of lines 22 ff. is weak. *Sat conveniens* is perhaps not strong enough. It seems only to tolerate the scruples of a tender conscience, and to recognize the exceptional case. That is already something, but it falls short of the spirit of *Pacem in Terris*, don't you think? Also *ex sincero fastidio* is unfortunate, because it seems by implication to accept the cliché that pacifism is for people who are emotionally indisposed to fighting. I would perhaps suggest a positive statement, "Those who are morally convinced of the necessity of non-violent conflict resolution, and who reject war as a solution which will hardly be reasonable in our time" (using the language of *Pacem in Terris*).

3. The suggestion I would most urgently make would be this practical one. In the U.S.A. currently, Catholic objectors are now facing difficulties with draft boards because the claim that one cannot conscientiously accept an unjust war is not recognized. The draft law here is framed in such a way that the only conscientious objection it recognizes is that of one who belongs to a Church which formally rejects all war. That is to say that today the draft laws are being more and more explicitly interpreted to recognize as objectors only men who belong to the so-called peace churches, like the Quakers, Mennonites . . . Will the wording of these lines be enough to support a Catholic objector in this situation?

With these points in mind, I would suggest perhaps the emendation of lines 17 ff. as follows. I am afraid I don't dare attempt this in Latin at this stage, but if you are interested I could go over it and draft it in Latin later, after more thought. Here is what I would suggest as worth considering:

All, both individual citizens and governmental authorities, are bound to take the greatest care lest the laws of God be violated in an unjust use of force. This objection particularly binds those who *rei publicae rationem moderantur et qui jussa impertiunt. Praesumptio quidem iuris auctoritati competenti agnoscenda est, eiusque jussis est parendum.* But since it is more and more difficult to guarantee that secular governments will in practice comply with moral laws, which are only confusedly or ambiguously recognized and understood, the right of the individual citizen to refrain from active participation in violence which may be gravely unjust must be guaranteed. It is therefore most opportune that laws should *positive eos respiciant qui vel propter* METUM OFFENDENDI DEUM IN EXERCITIO INJUSTO VIOLENTIAE *vel propter testimonium lenitatis Christianae, vel propter reverentiam erga vitam humanam vel* out of sincere conviction that non-violent methods of conflict-resolution are to be preferred to the use of force, *ex conscientia servitium militare etc. . . . recussent.*

How does that strike you? I hope it is not too much to add or change all at once, but perhaps you might see in it some merit, and might find some way of making use of it, without too much difficulty. I would say that the few Latin words I have contributed in capitals might perhaps fittingly be added, because they represent the real heart of conscientious objection. If this could be added, and the *sincero fastidio* bit could be taken out, it would already be something. But I do also believe it is important to make a positive recognition of the need for non-violence. We must by all means get away from the "pacifist" who just wants to avoid the nasty business of war, and get back to the real truth of *Christian resistance to evil on a non-violent basis . . .*

December 30, 1965

It was a delight to get your long letter from Rome and to breathe a little of the atmosphere of the historic Council which is now over. These have been four great years to live through and the work done has been magnificent. How many reasons for thanking God and His bishops, and the Pope He has given us.

I have seen now not only the section on peace but the whole Constitution and in fact I have finished a longish commentary on it or about it* (it rambles a bit about modern so-called religionless religion, the Bonhoeffer set) for Burns Oates. I am having it typed up now and will send you a copy when I have one available . . .

* *"The Church and the 'Godless World,' "* in Redeeming the Time *(Burns and Oates, 1966).*

My only sorrow, not very bitter, is that the bit on conscientious objection was not finally spelled out clearly. But anyway it is there, and the deterrent is properly treated, and total war is condemned as it must be. Now there is, as you say, a great task: that of getting it through to the Christian people particularly in this country. There are all sorts of problems involved in this. And indeed there is much to be done to develop the ideas that are only in germ in the Constitution. I don't think the Constitution goes much into the problem of the technological culture we live in and the revolutionary assumptions that underlie it: for one thing, these are not yet at all clear. The clear insistence on the human person in the Constitution is splendid: but does not technological culture itself tend to be more and more anti-personalist and even anti-humanist? This is a debatable matter, but all hangs on this central question. The question of war seems to be more and more whether conflict is decided in terms of mechanical efficiency or in terms of human beings. I am afraid that in Vietnam it is above all a technical problem and people come last.

It is a pity too that some of the pacifist protest has taken place in ways that seem to me both irrelevant and offensive to a lot of perfectly well-meaning and open-minded people. I have been in a bit of an argument with the Catholic Peace Fellowship [the Roger La Porte incident] of which I am a sponsor and we have come to an agreement on the matter. There is a temptation for everyone to want to be "prophetic," which is to say spectacular and dramatic, and that is not the answer just at the moment. There are a great number of good Christians who recognize that the war in Vietnam for example is all wrong and yet who don't want to take a "pacifist" position. They are right. But who is going to help them take any meaningful position at all? And then there is the question of the fact that any statement that sounds "political" is neutralized by that very fact. A pastoral issue in something so hot and so political is then no easy matter.

Forgive me for thinking out loud on all this. I just wanted to thank you . . .

For my own part I have been living as a hermit in the woods for over four months now and am settling down at it. It is an amazing life, and it certainly empties one out. At times I am a little dazed by it, and I can see one needs enormous grace to keep at it. But I think God asks this of me and I hope I can fully respond . . .

On February 28, 1966, Archbishop Flahiff wrote that he had been appointed to the postconciliar commission for religious. The task of the commission, he said, was to translate the principles of the Council regarding religious life into a few norms slightly more practical. He expressed the hope that "we do not fall into the pitfall of the too concrete before much study, reflection, communication and prayer intervene."

May 15, 1966

Recently one of the contemplative Superiors of women who is associated with Mother Angelica, P.C., in trying to form an association to discuss the problems of contemplative women, wrote to me and asked if I would be willing to give a short retreat to a group of these Superiors some time in the future after one of their meetings. I wrote and told her that I certainly would, but that the policies of my Superiors would probably make this totally impossible. However, I suggested that she might ask higher Superiors about it. That is the occasion of this letter.

My intention is to expose to you what seems to me to be one of the most serious problems in the renewal of the contemplative life, as it is understood here at Gethsemani. This problem also has a special personal import in my own case which, though I usually hesitate to discuss the matter at all, ought perhaps to be considered.

I don't suppose I am deluding myself when I say that a lot of people who are otherwise reasonable and apparently endowed with good sense seem to think that I might be able to contribute something to discussions about the contemplative life, its problems, their possible solutions, new perspectives and so on. I am frequently invited to participate in seminars, discussions and so on, some of them quite important like the one at Collegeville (an ecumenical panel) last September. Hence it does seem that many people believe I could make an active contribution to the work of renewal. I do not personally want to get involved in a great deal of very active work, but I am bound in conscience before God to say that I am deeply disturbed by the fact that I cannot ever in any way do what seems to me to be my small part, at least by discreetly participating in closed meetings, giving small retreats or occasional conferences.

Therefore, in all humility, and recognizing that I may be simply deceiving myself, I feel it my obligation to make the situation known to you and to say that I frankly believe that in this matter my Superiors are following a line of thought which is detrimental to the Council's policy of renewal, harmful to the real interests of our Order and of the contemplative institutes, and I think also in some way harmful to me, though I do not worry about that and I leave my own growth and development in God's hands. The basic question seems to me to be one of a *correct understanding of the contemplative life*.

My own Abbot, Dom James Fox, in very many ways a highly competent and justly respected Superior, not closed to all new ideas by any means, but basically conservative and not, I think, really sympathetic to the new trends in their real implications, pursues what one might call a policy of negation and suppression in regard to anything that would bring monks into any kind of contact with the world (exception made for the brothers engaged in selling cheese and promoting material business) and anything "apostolic." Note that "the world" here includes everything outside the monastery walls and that means even other contemplative monasteries. His view, to put it frankly, is that as long as the monks are all kept locked up in the monastery and as long as contacts of any kind with anyone outside the monastery are cut off, the monks are "contemplatives" . . .

This Superior is so set on keeping some of us from going out to other monasteries and entering into contact with other communities, discussing problems and so on, that he was for a while a standing joke among the American abbots of our Order. When there was a question of holding a meeting of novice masters of our American houses, at the time when I was novice master here, he refused to let the meeting be held anywhere else than Gethsemani, so that I would not go out to another house! I do not pretend to understand his motives in this matter, but the case is typical. Naturally, he has absolutely refused to let me even consider the following very interesting invitations at a fairly recent time, which I think would have had a great effect at least in improving my own knowledge and capacity to be of service.

1. Invitation to the ecumenical panel of theologians on the spiritual life at St. John's Abbey, Collegeville.

2. Invitation to an important meeting of the board of editors of the official magazine of our Order—I am on this board—to discuss the renewal and revamping of the whole policy of the magazine.

3. Invitation from Fr. Dumoulin, S.J., member of the postconciliar commission on relations with non-Christian religions, to come to Japan and spend some time in observation and discussion in Buddhist monasteries. (I have been doing some work on Zen Buddhism in which the Buddhists themselves have manifested very much interest.)

Not only were all these refused, but the Abbot refused *even to discuss* the mere possibility of any such thing with me. The basic principle he stated was: "We are contemplative monks and contemplatives do not go outside their own monastery." Period. I of course accepted all these decisions in the approved spirit of obedience, but I am convinced that mere passive acquiescence is not what the Council is asking of us. It seems to me that simply to let this sort of thing continue indefinitely would short-circuit much of the energy that could help bring about a renewal of the contemplative life. And God knows, it needs renewal. From experience in this house, where I have been four years master of scholastics and ten years master of novices, I can say that we are not really forming contemplatives at all, that there is a great deal of unrest and questioning, and that the monks themselves feel that this kind of policy of suppression is merely stultifying and sterilizing. That it cannot do any good whatever. At the same time, there is no use trying to discuss this with our Abbot. He is open on other points, in fact so open on the question of vernacular liturgy that he is completely ignoring the desires of Rome in regard to monks retaining the Latin liturgy (and I agree that the English liturgy here is excellent, and we should go on with it if possible). But he will hear absolutely nothing that savors of an "apostolate" in any form whatever, even an apostolate *within* contemplative monasteries and ordered to the improvement of the contemplative life.

In this connection I might mention some of the legislation we have on our statute books, in our Order, to prevent nefarious "contact with the world."

1. Letters sent out without the complete control of Superiors, except of course those to Higher Superiors, are forbidden under pain of mortal sin.

2. Phone calls are considered on the same plane as letters and a phone call made without permission of the Superior is a mortal sin. (Parvity of matter admitted. Nice of them, isn't it?)

3. Remaining outside the monastery after dark, without legitimate permission, at least presumed, is a mortal sin. In some circumstances (to be decided by the Superior) to leave the monastery during the day without permission can also be a mortal sin.

I respectfully submit that this kind of legislation represents a most harmful and stupefying mentality, and also it is the kind of thing which many monks today simply ignore. Which of course is not much help.

There would be no point to continuing the litany of such things. I just wanted you to have a fair sample of what we are up against. I would say that, in my own frank and private opinion, the chief reason why my Abbot wants to keep me within the walls and prevent me from attending meetings or giving retreats is purely and simply that he does not wish me to express views with which he does not agree, or to influence thought in directions he does not approve.

I am certainly grateful that I have been granted permission to live a modified form of hermit life. One reason why this permission was granted is certainly that this would be one further reason why I should not in any way actively participate in the kind of thing to which I am frequently invited. Yet personally I believe that one could live a life of solitude, and yet quite reasonably and legitimately participate in something like the retreat suggested by this Superior of whom I spoke.

Concretely, then, without drafting a possible statement of principle, I would like to be on record as saying that I believe that before God I should be in a position to do the following type of thing, if it is asked of me, and of course within reasonable limits:

1. Preach closed retreats to contemplative communities in certain exceptional cases, or at least to groups like that of the contemplative Superiors.

2. Attend certain conferences and seminars on renewal of contemplative life, at least when these are not on a large scale and highly publicized.

3. Attend meetings devoted to the study of special problems in Latin America. (I was invited to Msgr. Illich's place in Cuernavaca and this I did not even attempt to ask about, knowing it was hopeless.)

4. Accept an exceptional invitation, such as the one to Japan mentioned above. Fr. Dumoulin is still eager to do something about this and I mention it to you as something I believe would be very worthwhile.

All this is simply for your information, and as a kind of manifestation of conscience, which of course you are perfectly free to use in any way that may be of help in the work of implementing the Council's desires for the renewal of the Religious Life.

. . . Forgive me if any of this is out of line. I have tried to write with sincerity and objectivity as far as possible.

June 7, 1966

Many thanks for your kind and encouraging letter. I certainly appreciate it, and I am glad you agree on the urgent need for renewal among contemplative religious. You now know that I feel bound to help in any way that I can and am always willing to undertake anything that can throw light on the problems of contemplatives.

About the meeting of the Superiors of contemplative nuns: if they simply ask Archbishop Paul Philippe [head of the Sacred Congregation for Religious], and he merely transmits their request to the local Superior, nothing at all will come of it. He will simply say that it is not possible for me to do this.

It seems to me that it is important to clarify, at the very top, a certain point of principle. I think that if someone could discuss this point with Archbishop Paul Philippe and if he could then (if he agreed) impress upon our Abbot that he thinks this is the true mind of the Church, then I think something might be accomplished.

This principle which is being *mis*applied here is that "contemplatives are not supposed to leave their monasteries to undertake any form of active work and this must be jealously guarded at this time since some are trying to lure them out into the active ministry." It should be perfectly clear that to extend this so far as to make it impossible for someone like myself even to participate in necessary work for the implementation of the Council's wishes concerning religious, particularly contemplative, is an abusive interpretation. It is self-defeating and leads only to inertia and stagnation in the contemplative life. This stagnation is in fact one of the problems we confront. The stifling effect of rigid formalities is still very evident in many contemplative monasteries.

I think then if someone discussed this with Archbishop Philippe (perhaps if several approached him from different angles with this question), he would then be willing to take up the matter personally with our Abbot and stress the fact that he thought it advisable and necessary for me to be allowed, in exceptional cases, to do something along the lines that have been suggested—for instance this retreat to contemplative Superiors conducted within a religious community and without publicity at all.

The trouble with contemplative renewal is that principles can be misinterpreted and misapplied, especially in what concerns the difference between essentials and accidentals. This difference is by no means clear, and if it is so far reduced that antique customs and interpretations are still regarded as "essentials," then renewal is impossible. I would say that the whole question of communication with the outside world and information about the outside world on the part of men contemplatives (women too) is a case in point. Some are still considering that men have to be so strictly cloistered that they never go out, except in case of grave illness, never participate in study sessions, conferences, which might be of great use to them, etc. etc. Certainly there ought to be great liberality in letting them visit other monasteries, to broaden themselves.

If you can think of some way in which it might be fruitful for me to draw up some notes on the subject of contemplatives, and to whom these notes might profitably be sent, I would be glad to take a crack at it . . .

To James Forest

James Hendrickson Forest was born in 1941 in Salt Lake City, Utah, and educated first in California, and later at Hunter College in New York City. In 1961 he was discharged from the U.S. Navy on the grounds of conscientious objection (that same year he had become a Roman Catholic). He joined the staff of the Catholic Worker, a pacifist group who run a house of hospitality for unemployed and homeless persons and also publish a pacifist magazine. This was for Forest the beginning of a lifelong commitment to peace and non-violence.

He served briefly on the Committee for Non-Violent Action (CNVA) and for the Catholic Relief Service (CRS). In 1964 he became one of the founders of the Catholic Peace Fellowship (CPF), an affiliate of the Fellowship of Reconciliation (FOR). From this time on, his ties with the FOR grew. After a thirteen-month stay in prison for his involvement as one of the "Milwaukee Fourteen" in the burning of military conscription records, he became in 1973 editor of the monthly magazine Fellowship. *In 1977 he assumed the office of General Secretary of the International Fellowship of Reconciliation (IFOR), with the responsibility of serving FOR branches in twenty-nine countries, as well as editing the IFOR* Report *five times each year.*

I visited James H. Forest in 1983 at Alkmaar, Holland. He is a person of gentle manners and a gracious host. We went over the many letters he exchanged with Thomas Merton. It was exciting for me to have the vicarious experience of living through the ups and downs of the Catholic peace involvement in the 1960s.

Jim Forest's first contact with Thomas Merton came through Dorothy Day in the summer of 1961. The fact that Merton had sent a poem for publication in the Catholic Worker *("Chants to Be Used in Processions around a Site for Furnaces") offered Forest the opportunity of initiating a correspondence that would continue on a regular basis for eight years. He wrote thanking Merton for the "Auschwitz poem," saying that it would be published.*

August 9, 1961

There are complications about that Auschwitz poem. First of all, if it is to get published at all it has been promised to Lawrence Ferlinghetti in San Francisco, some kind of a magazine he is starting. Secondly, it is not yet through the censors of the Order and they may very well say no. They are like that. So please don't go running it in *CW* just yet. You can have it *after* Ferlinghetti has run it, whenever that may be. I will let you know later . . .

I see you say in your letter that the *CW* is coming out "next week," which puts it right about now. If you have appeared with the poem complete, well, OK, nothing can be done about it. I hope you haven't, at least for Ferlinghetti's sake, as he wants it bad. And I'd like to help him get started. Kind of a beat magazine, called "Journal for the Protection of All Living Beings," I think.

This morning I said the Mass in Time of War. Might as well face it. It is a very good formulary. Nowhere in it are there promises of blessings upon the strong and the unscrupulous or the violent. Only suggestions that we shut up and be humble and stay put and trust in God and hope for a peace that we can use for the good of our souls. It is certainly not a very belligerent Mass, and it asks no one to be struck down. But it does say that we don't have to worry too much about the King of Babylon. Are we very sure that he has his headquarters in Moscow only?

Best wishes to you and everyone at CW. Let us pray that we may some day learn the meaning of peace, and the prerequisites for it.

The "Auschwitz poem" was published in the August issue of the Catholic Worker. *On September 22, 1961, Merton sent an article to Dorothy Day for publication. Entitled "The Root of War," it was a chapter from* New Seeds of Contemplation, *a revision, just approved by the censors of his Order, of an earlier work. To the censored text Merton added three fairly long paragraphs (not censored!) which, as he put it, "situated these thoughts in the present crisis." In this augmented form, it was published in the* CW *in October 1961. In the uncensored paragraphs Merton had fantasized about the possibility that people might one day sit in their air-raid shelters with machine guns to prevent their neighbors from entering. Meanwhile, unknown to Merton, this "fantasy" was presented as a defensible theological position in an article by L. C. McHugh, S.J., an associate editor of* America, *in the September 30 issue of that magazine. The* CW *issued a press release contrasting Merton's view with that of Fr. McHugh. Merton then sent*

them an article, "The Machine Gun in the Fallout Shelter," which appeared in
the November CW as "Shelter Ethics." Thus, in the course of four months, Merton
had published three pieces on war. The publicity these articles engendered was
apparently not lost on the censors. The frustration Merton experienced from an
ever more restrictive censorship becomes only too evident in these letters.

October 21, 1961

Your letter of the 17th or rather 18th reached me today. I had not received the previous one to which you refer, and so was a bit in the dark, though I did hear about the *America* article, which seemed to me to be in many ways completely scandalous. Not that men renounce the right to defend themselves, but it is a question of emphasis and viewpoint. Are we going to minimize, and fix our eyes entirely on the lowest level of natural ethics, or are we going to be Christians and take the Gospel seriously? This is a matter of extreme importance, because never has the Church and the Christian world (so called) been so grimly and terribly under judgment. Now is the chance for us to be Christians, and it may be the last chance. If we let this go, the world may be destroyed or, more likely, it may be handed over to the secular messianism which will take over the task we have let fall from our hands and perhaps accomplish it with grim and inhuman efficiency, producing universal peace at the price of liberty, intelligence, faith, spirit, and everything that is valuable in man, reducing us to the level of ants and robots.

The big question is indeed to save the Christian faith, but if we strive to save it with bombs and nuclear submarines we are going to lose it. If we are going to save Christendom, there must be some Christendom to save, not just nominal Christianity.

I do not deny that at the present juncture we have to, as a nation, use political methods to stave off our own destruction. I do not deny that when one is not able to practice non-violence, violent defense is legitimate and even necessary. But what I do assert is that the Church, the clergy, the Catholic lay apostle, the Catholic teacher, the Catholic intellectual have a serious obligation today to investigate the meaning and the feasibility of non-violent defense not only on the individual but on the national level. If we fail in this obligation we are very probably lost. And we *are failing* in it.

. . . Note I am not denying a man the right to defend himself and his children, but I am just saying that to look at the problem with that kind of false perspective is not only futile but fatal. We have got to see things the way the Gospel sees them, the way the saints see them, the way the Church sees them, not just from the viewpoint of natural ethics, without further qualification. It is greater to sacrifice your life, on occasion, than to defend it. Christians need guidance in this respect. They are not able to think for themselves. They were never more passive. We have got to lead them in the ways of peace, not expect them to find those ways all by themselves.

Please let me have about twenty copies of the October *CW*, and keep in touch with me . . .

October 29, 1961

I want to get this text [of "The Machine Gun in the Fallout Shelter"] to you so that you can at least read it. I am trying to get it through the censors if possible for the November issue. I have begged them to be cooperative if possible, but this means nothing. I don't think most of them have the slightest idea of the import of what is taking place, or if they do they have perhaps cultivated a kind of holy callousness that does not seem to me to have much to do with the Gospel of Christ or the spirit of the Church. Let's not blame them, however, but pray and hope they will come through. Do not of course print this until the *nihil obstat* comes through. Where is Dorothy, still in NY? I will send a full corrected text when approval is given.

November 2, 1961

Thanks for your letter and for the enclosure. I will make good use of it, as the article I sent you will really lack point unless it implies a real understanding of McHugh's piece. I am all in favor of my article being both in *CW* and *Jubilee*, and I think that would be the best way to run it.

Commonweal has asked for an article for the Christmas issue. I have written it and am sending you a copy. You might want to reprint it in the January *CW*.

The censors have not come through with approval for the "Machine Gun and Shelter" article, but they have returned it fast and so news ought to come from Rome before Nov. 10. I will amend the article, hold it as long as I decently can in case changes have been suggested, and send it on to you next Monday or Tuesday. I hope you can hold the issue for a day or two in case approval is delayed . . .

November 5, 1961

Here is the revised article. It is a little longer. I have beefed it up quite a lot. I will let you know at once when the approval arrives—give me until the 13th (in the morning)—can you do that? I will send a wire . . .

All right about the permissions [for "Root of War"]. But all should give credit line to New Directions, and say it is from the book *New Seeds of Contemplation*.

November 8, 1961

Today Father Abbot will probably be answering your telegram. No approval yet but you can set the thing up at least, or so Fr. Abbot has said.

He also said it would be all right for me to be a sponsor of the Pax movement in America. I think this is very important and I am very eager to help out. You understand my inevitable limitations, however . . .

As for the article, I leave it to you to use it as you wish and to give it to anyone you see fit for second publication. Whether to *Jubilee* or *Commonweal*, or however else you want to do it. As long as it gets around. This refers of course to the article on "Shotgun in the Backyard Shelter" . . .

November 14, 1961

The telegram announcing the censors' approval of the article was sent the other day. We made it this time because one of the censors was Fr. Charles English [former *CW* staff person]. The big delay was in Europe. It is utterly futile to have letters chasing the Abbot General around all over Europe, trying to find him when there is a matter like this to be settled. However, that is the way it goes . . .

As you see, the censorship situation is very absurd and idiotic. For that reason I cannot be getting too many things jammed up in the censors' offices all at once because that will make things even worse than they already are. At the same time I want to try to remain moderately articulate at a time like this when I simply have to speak, as so few others are saying anything.

There is one loophole in the censorship statute that leaves me a little liberty of action. When a publication is very small and of very limited influence (and this is not defined), articles for it do not need to be censored. Father Abbot has decided that we can regard the publication of the FOR as falling under this category. Also Bob Lax's things, Pax. There may be one or two others around like that. For some articles, then, the obvious thing is to get them published in one or more of these very small publications. However, even if you wanted to pick them up after that for *CW* there would probably still be need of censorship. But there is another possibility. You could write a short article reporting on the appearance of my article and quoting bits from it, if you wanted to do so. I think this is a feasible way of handling material that would otherwise just get jammed up in the censorship machine forever.

I am enclosing a piece that I sent to Heidbrink at the FOR. He will probably print it in something of his (*Fellowship?*), and if you are interested you can follow the procedure I outlined above. Anyway, you can look it over . . .

November 29, 1961

Thanks for the letter, the copies of the paper, and all the other clippings, etc. You have been very generous with your time and trouble.

I am especially glad to hear of the news of the formation of Pax in America and how it is going along. I am glad too to know about the people who will be active in it.

Are you planning a separate publication like the Pax *Bulletin*, for this country?

Do not worry about the change of title for the article [from "The Machine Gun in the Fallout Shelter" to "Shelter Ethics"], I understand all right. No problem, as far as I am concerned. I can also understand that since my viewpoint was not precisely that of the editorial policy of *CW*, Dorothy might want to clarify somewhere along the line. Technically I am not a pure pacifist in theory, though today in practice I don't see how one can be anything else since limited wars (however "just") present an almost certain danger of nuclear war on an all-out scale. It is absolutely clear to me that we are faced with the obligation, both as human beings and as Christians, of striving in every way possible to abolish war. The magnitude of the task cannot be allowed to deter us. Even if it seems impossible, we must still attempt it. This demands of course a spirit of faith. Without the religious dimension, even pacifism and non-violence are relatively meaningless. One cannot have non-violence that makes sense if one does not also have faith in God. This of course complicates matters tremendously, because of the scandal that so many who claim to believe in God enlist Him in their wars. God is always the first one to be drafted, and this is a universal stumbling block.

I haven't heard from *Fellowship* about the "Red or Dead" article, but it makes no difference. I also sent it to the Mennonites just in case they might want it. I like those Mennonite people. They have sent a very kind letter and some literature. I feel very close to them, as I know you must do there also.

Fellowship is a very good little publication and the FOR, about which I knew nothing, impresses me as a living and efficacious movement . . .

The latest issue of *CW* has very good things in it. I was moved by Karl Meyer's last article on the peace walk and their experience in Russia.* It is clear that everywhere we are up against a brass wall of organized stupidity and prejudice, the monumental institutionalism that says no to all truth that is inexpedient. To be without God is to be condemned to a cult of expediency.

. . . I am trying to get in touch with Gordon Zahn. I don't see him on your list of Pax names. Did I tell you I am doing a paperback anthology of articles on peace for New Directions? So far [I] have Lewis Mumford,

---

* CNVA *(Committee on Non-Violent Action) had organized a walk from San Francisco to Moscow. The marchers made it to Red Square.*

Erich Fromm (I think), the Jerome Frank article you printed (I hope), and then I want to get that whole English collection edited by Walter Stein. This is first-class. It represents exactly the stand I take myself, so I suppose that is why I like it. I also got a letter from Archbishop Roberts, in which he placed much emphasis on his tussle with the higher-ups and told me to expect the same kind of treatment.

The letters in reply to the McHugh article are really good. I enjoyed reading that page of *America* [issue of November 25, 1961, giving reactions to the McHugh article], and it made the air seem a little fresher. The off-key note in McHugh's reply, which shows he is a "realist" and thinks the Sermon on the Mount after all sentimental, seems to cinch the argument as far as I am concerned . . .

As to the Cuba question, I think *CW* there too is taking a healthy position. Our "realists" have been sadly unrealistic in their foreign policies always. Everything they do to put across the American way of life or defend it against the "inroads of communism" is so uncomprehending and so misinformed that it has just the opposite from the intended effect. If we acted as Christians we would be far more successful and it would paradoxically also be more expedient for us to do what seems inexpedient but is recommended by the counsels of Christ. I may perhaps write Kennedy's sister-in-law that we ought to (a) recognize and (b) feed Red China. Little do we know what a tremendous good we could do for ourselves as well as for our fellow man by being Christians in regard to Asia and not counting the cost or seeking a cut out of it.

December 20, 1961

This ["Christian Ethics and Nuclear War"] is being sent to *Jubilee*, and they will possibly want to print it. If *CW* wants it also, OK with me . . .

Good news. Fr. Abbot said if I wrote a *letter* at any time, it could go in without censorship. This does not mean a flood of eight-page letters, but anyway if I do have anything special to say, you can quote any letter without further formality. This simplifies matters. The book is coming along fine . . .

January 5, 1962

Are there still one or two copies left of the October issue of *CW* with "The Roots of War"? That is the only complete text, and I have given away all the copies I had. Of course the FOR is supposed to be coming along with the pamphlet. I haven't heard much from them.

In a day or two I will finish a short thing on Fr. Max Josef Metzger, with some quotes from him. You know his life of course. I am sending it to *Jubilee*, and if they want it and you also want it you can both use it as far as I am concerned. I am just not signing it. That way, since it is mostly his material anyway and not mine, I just do not need to get it censored at all. That makes things simpler, for matters of this kind.

It is really necessary for me to try to work out something sensible on this absurd censorship deal. It is completely and deliberately obstructive, not aimed at combing out errors at all, but purely and simply at preventing the publication of material that "doesn't look good." And this means anything that ruffles in any way the censors' tastes or susceptibilities, including social susceptibilities. Fr. Charles is just one of the censors and there are a lot of others . . .

Commonweal asked me for an article for Christmas. I sent it to the censor in October. It still hasn't been passed. One censor vetoed it, and it has been in the hands of a third for some time. Just said that peace was a good thing, and that nuclear war added up to mass suicide which didn't seem to me to be exactly Christian. This is dangerous doctrine, I guess. That is the kind of thing one has to try to be patient with. It is wearying, of course. However, it is all I can offer to compare with what you people are doing to share the lot of the poor. A poor man is one who has to sit and wait and wait and wait, in clinics, in offices, in places where you sign papers, in police stations, etc. And he has nothing to say about it. At least there is this element of poverty for me too. The rest of what we have here isn't that hard or that poor.

How is Pax coming? . . . All I have read about the San Francisco–Moscow walk impresses me very much. In human and worldly terms it adds up to about zero. Spiritually, I think it means quite a bit. They are all concerned about the fact that their own human failings and incompatibilities came out a bit. That is all right, though. It has to be that way. Another form of poverty that we have to accept. We have got to be instruments of God and realize at the same time that we are very poor and defective instruments. It is important to resist the feelings of resentment and impatience we get over our own failings because this makes us project our faults onto other people, instead of bearing their burdens along with our own . . .

The following letter was brought to Jim Forest at the scene of a strike for peace at the AEC (Atomic Energy Commission) building. He read the letter to some of the other demonstrators.

[*Cold War Letter 25*]

January 29, 1962

It is really quite providential that the Peace article ["Nuclear War and Christian Responsibility"] I wrote for the *Commonweal* Christmas issue was held up (by the censors) and is now appearing this week [February 9, 1962], in conjunction with the General Strike for Peace. I do hope it helps even a little bit. Anyway, my heart goes with it, and I am with you all in spirit. I am glad that in that article I explicitly mentioned the point that all people, the ordinary people, the ones who don't want war, the ones who get it in the neck, the ones who really want to build a decent new world in which there will not be war and starvation, these should know the power of their witness against war, and the effect they can have by protest and refusal of cooperation in immoral war efforts.

Of course the tragedy is that the vast majority of people do not understand the meaning of this kind of witness. In their pitiful blind craving for undisturbed security they feel that agitation for peace is somehow threatening to them. They do not feel at all threatened by the bomb, for some reason, but they feel terribly threatened by some little girl student carrying a placard, or by some poor workingman striking in protest. Somehow they feel that it is after all possible for people to change their mind and revise their whole attitude toward a setup that has its enormous disadvantages but—at least it is "what we are used to, and please God don't ask us to get used to something else" . . .

My Mass on February 1st, the Feast of St. Ignatius Martyr of Antioch, will be for all of the strikers everywhere in the world and for all who yearn for a true peace, all who are willing to shoulder the great burden of patiently working, praying and sacrificing themselves for peace. We will never see the results in our time, even if we manage to get through the next five years without being incinerated. Really we have to pray for a total and profound change in the mentality of the whole world. What we have known in the past as Christian penance is not a deep enough concept if it does not comprehend the special problems and dangers of the present age. Hairshirts will not do the trick, though there is no harm in mortifying the flesh. But vastly more important is the complete change of heart and the totally new outlook on the world of man. We have to see our duty to mankind as a whole. We must not fail in this duty which God is imposing on us with His own hand.

The great problem is this inner change, and we must not be so obsessed with details of policy that we block the deeper development in other people and in ourselves. The strike is to be regarded, I think, as an application of spiritual force and not the use of merely political pressure. We all have the great duty to realize the deep need for purity of soul, that is to say the deep need to possess in us the Holy Spirit, to be possessed by Him. This takes precedence over everything else. If He lives and works in us, then our activity will be true and our witness will generate love of the truth, even though we may be persecuted and beaten down in apparent incomprehension.

About the *Commonweal* article: you can have this in *CW* next issue if you want, but I am going to work it over a little and beef it up, clarifying here and there. Let me know right quick if you want it. Thanks for the issues of last month's *CW*. Did I thank you for the Christmas letter? The singing outside the ladies' jail warmed my heart,* I wish I had been there with you. Small things like that have very great Christian meaning, so much more than a lot of more formal and pompous gestures.

. . . God was seemingly never more absent from the world and yet His Christ, the Word, is walking about all around us all over the face of the earth, and in a terrible hour . . .

Jim Forest was arrested at the AEC demonstration, but afterward released.

February 5, 1962

. . . If you are not in jail, you maybe got the telephone [message] about not yet printing "Christian Ethics and Nuclear War." Censors are still working it up. I am sending a rewritten version of the one in *Commonweal*. This you can use. You will probably want to divide it as it is too long to use all at once. Anyway here it is, minus a couple of prefatory pages . . .

Above all don't put my name on the Metzger piece, as it has never been sent to the censors. God bless you. Tell me about the strike.

[*Cold War Letter 31*]

February 6, 1962

Today is Dorothy's feast and I am remembering her in a special way. Do please give her my congratulations and best wishes. Also Dorothy Steere, who, with Douglas Steere, was here yesterday. I had a very fine talk with them and they spoke of being at *CW* recently.

I was very moved by your account of the civil disobedience at the AEC. It must have been very significant indeed for you. I am extremely happy that the letter reached you right there, and that too seems to me significant and a great grace for me. At the same time, when you speak of the violence and resentment of the bureaucrats leaving work and making a point of kicking people out of the way, this is no surprise and also it raises certain questions.

One of the most problematical questions about non-violence is the inevitable involvement of hidden aggressions and provocations. I think this is especially true when there are a fair proportion of non-religious elements, or religious elements that are not spiritually developed. It is an enormously subtle question, but we have to consider the fact that in its provocative aspect, non-violence may tend to harden the opposition and confirm people in their righteous blindness. It may even in some cases separate men out and drive them in the other direction, away from

* *The reference is to the caroling outside the women's House of Detention in Greenwich Village that had become an annual custom. The event inspired Merton's poem: "There Has to Be a Jail for Ladies."*

us and away from peace. This of course may be (as it was with the Prophets) part of God's plan. A clear separation of antagonists. And perhaps now we have to see that this may be all we can do: simply clarify the issue.

Anyway we can always direct our action toward opening people's eyes to the truth, and if they are blinded, we must try to be sure we did nothing specifically to blind them. Yet there is that danger: the danger one observes subtly in tight groups like families and monastic communities, where the martyr for the right sometimes thrives on making his persecutors terribly and visibly wrong. He can drive them in desperation to be wrong, to seek refuge in the wrong, to seek refuge in violence.

The violent man is, by our standards, weak and sick. Though to us at times he is powerful and menacing in an extreme degree. In our acceptance of vulnerability, however, we play on his guilt. There is no finer torment. This is one of the enormous problems of the time, and the place. It is the overwhelming problem of America: all this guilt and nothing to do about it except finally to explode and blow it all out in hatreds, race hatreds, political hatreds, war hatreds. We, the righteous, are dangerous people in such a situation. (Of course we are not righteous, we are conscious of our guilt above all, we are sinners: but nevertheless we are bound to take courses of action that are professionally righteous and we have committed ourselves to that course.)

This is not for you so much as for myself. We have got to be aware of the awful sharpness of truth when it is used as a weapon, and since it can be the deadliest weapon, we must take care that we don't kill more than falsehood with it. In fact, we must be careful how we "use" truth, for we are ideally the instruments of truth and not the other way round . . .

In February of 1962 Jim Forest visited Merton at Gethsemani. While there, he was called back to New York City for a further demonstration at the AEC. During the demonstration he was arrested and sentenced to a short prison term on Hart's Island in the East River.

March 21, 1962

I owe you a lot of letters, and I want to get this one off in a hurry to say I will at least be praying for you when you go on trial tomorrow. From what I hear, it is likely that demonstrators will be sentenced. If so, I wish you courage and patience. Being in jail is part of the whole business of non-violence. I imagine it is not the easiest part. One has to learn to see the significance of one's apparent uselessness and not be driven to frustration by it. The uselessness, the inactivity, the frustration are deliberately assumed as an important part of non-violent resistance . . .

Let me know how the trial came out and if there is anything I can send you. If you get in jail, you ought to be able to do some reading and writing, anyway, and study up on the non-violence too.

[*Cold War Letter 61*]

March 28, 1962

Your note just arrived and put an end to my wondering about the sentence. I too had hoped it would be suspended. Since you have fifteen days at Hart's Island, then there is meaning in it. It is part of the plan and part of your training. It is an experience and a trial that you will need, and by which I pray that you will profit. You have been completely right in following your convictions, and I am sure that you have taken care to express them in a way that was true and direct, in order to make clear that you were defending a strictly moral issue that could not otherwise be made fully clear.

. . . The peace movement needs more than zeal. It certainly needs to be organized on a very clear basis, and it is necessary for the people who know what they are trying to do, to be formed into a coherent nucleus who can make things clear to the others. It is not going to do any good for a lot of excited people to mill around without purpose and without definite means of making their protest clear and intelligible. Especially if a lot of them are not too clear themselves what they are protesting about. The movement is really only beginning and a lot of groundwork has to be done. I admit that there may not be much time.

I have got a better idea of the Cuba project [CNVA was sending a boat to Cuba loaded with children's toys] and I see more clearly what it means. It strikes me, however, that this project is premature. I don't mean for Cuba or for peace, but for the people likely to be involved. It is too big and still too ambiguous. I wonder if it takes sufficient account of the political realities. That is important. There is further ambiguity provided by the fact that Castro is now apparently on the skids. He has evidently reached the last stage of the processing which he has lent himself to and which will end with his own discrediting and rejection. For CNVA to get involved even indirectly in that situation, and perhaps be used also in it, would be a fatal mistake. But if you go there you are bound to do so on terms that will imply movement. Of course I am not well enough informed to talk about this, but this is just my impression . . .

What you say about the prisoners is important. At a time like this, a jail sentence can be very meaningful even to the person who undergoes it. At the same time you need inner strength. The deep good in these dopesters etc. is also tangled up with deep misfortune and tragedy. And this can subtly affect you also. But I only mean by that that you need lots of grace, and need to realize your need, and if you make mistakes don't say they are not mistakes. One can go from defending the health in these people to defending the sickness also. You know what I mean.

But on the other hand the clergy tend to be altogether too scared of trouble, and take refuge in meaningless gestures, not even of righteousness but just of legality. Pfui.

. . . Keep your chin up. I am reading Brendan Behan, also in jail. A fine writer and a good guy. Hope your jail is better than his . . .

After serving his jail sentence Forest took a job with the CNVA. One of his first responsibilities was to organize a peace march from Nashville to Washington, D.C. While he was in Nashville, he married his co-worker, Jean Morton. The marriage was sudden, not carefully thought out, and was to end in separation.

[*Cold War Letter 69*]

April 29, Low Sunday, 1962

First of all, I ought to have congratulated you and Jean long ago. The reason why I didn't was twofold. First I thought you would probably be in Nashville on the walk, and waited to hear you were back in NY. Then also I have been trying to finish my book on peace, and have succeeded in time for the ax to fall. So congratulations. I hope you will be very happy. It seems everything is happening at once in your life. Jail, marriage, peace walk, eviction, and what else? Don't let it become an avalanche. You want to keep your footing and be able to look about you and see what you are doing. The trouble with movements is that they sweep you off your feet and carry you away with the tide of activism and then you become another kind of mass man . . .

But I bless you and pray for you both. You say I know Jean, but really I don't: except that I think she is a good poet.

. . . Now here is the ax. For a long time I have been anticipating trouble with the higher Superiors and now I have it. The orders are, no more writing about peace. This is transparently arbitrary and uncomprehending, but doubtless I have to make the best of it. I am hoping to get the book through on the ground that it is already written. Of course the order does not apply to unpublished writing, but I have to be careful even with privately circulated stuff, like the mimeographed material. So, for one thing, please do not under any circumstances publish anywhere anything I write to you on this subject or on non-violence etc. It will only make it impossible to do whatever still remains possible. Besides, the order is not yet absolutely beyond appeal and I can perhaps obtain some slight modification of it. But in substance I am being silenced on the subject of war and peace. This I know is not a very encouraging thing. It implies all sorts of very disheartening consequences as regards the whole cause of peace. It reflects an astounding incomprehension of the seriousness of the present crisis in its religious aspect. It reflects an insensitivity to Christian and ecclesiastical values, and to the real sense of the monastic vocation. The reason given is that this is not the right kind of work for a monk, and that it "falsifies the monastic message." Imagine that: the thought that a monk might be deeply enough concerned with the issue of nuclear war to voice a protest against the arms race, is supposed to bring the monastic life into *disrepute*. Man, I would think that it might just possibly salvage a last shred of repute for an institution that many consider to be dead on its feet . . .

. . . The monk is the one supposedly attuned to the inner spiritual dimension of things. If he hears nothing, and says nothing, then the renewal [of the Church] as a whole will be in danger and may be completely sterilized. But these authoritarian minds believe that the function of the monk is not to see or hear any new dimension, simply to support the already existing viewpoints precisely insofar as and because they are defined for him by somebody else . . . The function of the monk . . . then becomes simply to affirm his total support of officialdom. He has no other function, then, except perhaps to pray for what he is told to pray for: namely the purposes and objectives of an ecclesiastical bureaucracy. The monastery as dynamo concept goes back to this. The monk is there to generate spiritual power that will justify over and over again the already predecided rightness of the officials above him. He must in no event and under no circumstances assume a role that implies any form of spontaneity and originality. He must be an eye that sees nothing except what is carefully selected for him to see. An ear that hears nothing except what it is advantageous for the managers for him to hear. We know what Christ said about such ears and eyes.

Now you will ask me: How do I reconcile obedience, true obedience (which is synonymous with love), with a situation like this? Shouldn't I just blast the whole thing wide open, or walk out, or tell them to jump in the lake?

Let us suppose for the sake of argument that this was not completely excluded. Why would I do this? For the sake of the witness for peace? For the sake of witnessing to the truth of the Church, in its reality, as against this figment of the imagination? Simply for the sake of blasting off and getting rid of the tensions and frustrations in my own spirit, and feeling honest about it?

In my own particular case, every one of these would backfire and be fruitless. It would be taken as a witness *against* the peace movement and would confirm these people in all the depth of their prejudices and their self-complacency. It would reassure them in every possible way that they are incontrovertibly right and make it even more impossible for them ever to see any kind of new light on the subject . . .

I am where I am. I have freely chosen this state, and have freely chosen to stay in it when the question of a possible change arose. If I am a disturbing element, that is all right. I am not making a point of being that, but simply of saying what my conscience dictates and doing so without seeking my own interest. This means accepting such limitations as may be placed on me by authority, not merely because it is placed on me by authority, and not because I may or may not agree with the ostensible reasons why the limitations are imposed, but out of love for God who is using these things to attain an end which I myself cannot at the moment see or comprehend . . .

. . . Once again, please don't print anything of mine in a letter or anywhere else about peace, or about anything else as a matter of fact, and above all don't print any of this one . . .

May 17, 1962

Yesterday I received a very moving letter from Hal Stalling telling me about *Everyman* [CNVA boat sailing into atomic testing area in the Pacific] and about his sailing today. I had also seen a copy of the bulletin about it (it is on the novices' notice board now). Tried to reach him by telegram to say my prayers go with him. I am saying Mass for the three in *Everyman* this morning. In about three hours from now. It is at present still early and dark and the birds are waking up.

There is something ominous about the title Operation Dominic [name of AEC's test in the Pacific]. The AEC is identifying itself no doubt with the (Dominican) Inquisition. The final payoff will probably be called Operation Ignatius—the destruction of Europe and America.

I think the courage and the alertness manifested in the building and sailing of *Everyman* is significant in a high degree. The CNVA is alive as few organizations are. This is the moment of truth—or close to it. And yet the project is also inevitably very much of an improvisation. You must be careful of that, because the temptation to multiply improvisations as if they were miracles may be dangerous to the CNVA eventually. What you need is that ashram, and deep roots from which these things grow more slowly and firmly. But one may say this is no time for anything to happen slowly . . .

June 14, 1862 (more or less)

. . . It is good to see you are settled somewhere and that you have a new job [with the Catholic Relief Service] which sounds good. I think it makes a lot of sense, and that you are better off out of the main whirl at CNVA. I was not surprised at what happened to *Everyman* [captured by the Coast Guard]. Although it seems to me that the action has no legal basis whatever, it is purely and simply an arbitrary act of power, because we are getting more and more into a situation where power has supplanted law, and the precise effect of a protest like *Everyman* is that it brings this out one way or another. Besides, in a way, I think it is a good thing that they had to arrest the men, or drag them back, with such a preposterous statement of charges and reasons. Perhaps too the voyage would have ended in an accident before they ever got out there. It is a pretty-looking little boat, but I doubt if it would ever weather a real Pacific storm . . .

I appealed the case of my book to the General of the Order, but he repeated his order firmly and clearly: I am to publish nothing more on war and peace. I was denounced to him by an American abbot who was told by a friend in the intelligence service that I was writing for a "communist-controlled publication" (the *Catholic Worker*). You didn't know you were communist-controlled, did you? Maybe George [Joseph Johnson, *CW* staff member] is really Khrushchev's nephew. Meanwhile, though I look in all my pockets, I cannot find that old card.* Must have dropped out when I was mopping my brow in the confessional.

Someday soon I will send you a mimeo copy of the book [*Peace in a Post-Christian Era*] but man you got to be careful with this. I don't mind who you show it to but don't let anybody go print any of it . . .

Here is poem about Lee Ying [Chinese refugee child pictured in a *Life* article]. This is not for publication . . .

Forest wrote that he thought Merton, in his efforts to please the censors, was bending over backward and not really saying what he meant.

July 7, 1962

Thanks for your long letter, and the remarks on the book. That just goes to show what a mess one gets into trying to write a book that will get through the censors, and at the same time say something. I was bending in all directions to qualify every statement and balance everything off, so I stayed right in the middle and perfectly objective, and so on, and then at the same time tried to speak the truth as my conscience wanted it to be said. In the long run the result is about zero.

Certainly if I ever get to work over the book again, I will bear in mind all your requests. At the moment, the best I can probably do is make a few new stencils and run off some more copies of what is there already. I have about a dozen copies left available and was more or less holding on to them in case special requests came in from people who had no chance of borrowing a copy. I was not planning to run off any more. At the moment, I think it would be prohibitive to try to make a decent revision and then run off more mimeo copies when I have so many other things to do that have a chance of getting somewhere.

My feeling is that it is not worth the trouble to do anything more with this book. Let it die. There is plenty of good stuff coming out now . . .

Gordon Zahn is quite right about it being the layman's responsibility,

* *Merton, while at Columbia, had for a brief time been a card-carrying Party member.*

and about the fact that laymen have the leeway. After all, there is not that much the bishops can do to you guys . . .

[*Cold War Letter 101*]

August 27, 1962

Thanks for all the letters, poems, etc. I will comment on the latter when I have more time. There have been people visiting and when that happens there is no time left for anything else, so I haven't been writing letters.

The parish [St. Theresa's, Manhattan] sounds fine, I will send the books along. I think it is especially important for you to be working in and with the parish at the moment. The Church is after all a reality, and the central reality: though her members have failed shockingly in their Christian responsibility in many areas, and though there may be a great blindness and weakness pervading whole areas of her life, nevertheless she is indefectible because God lives and acts in her. And this faith must live in us and grow in us, especially when we are tempted against it as we are now. I think you will get a great deal out of this effort . . .

I think the peace movement is a great potentiality, yet I think also that it remains terribly superficial. But then everything is superficial now. And I am in no position to prescribe means of deepening everything, least of all the peace movement. The fact that I am really unable to keep it in right perspective, in spite of all the help I get from friends sending things, is evidence of the fact that I am really out of the game and can't do much in the ordinary way.

The book *Breakthrough to Peace* (which I edited) is now out. I will try to get copies sent to you and others in the mvt. . . . .

September 22, 1962

Thanks for letting me know that the people at SANE [National Committee for a Sane Nuclear Policy] are mimeographing my book [*Peace in a Post-Christian Era*]. I had heard absolutely nothing about this, and I have no idea who gave them the book for this purpose, though I may have sent a copy to Steve Allen, or perhaps a friend of mine on the Coast gave them a copy with a suggestion that I wouldn't mind if they made more. But I haven't heard from them. On the other hand, I am never sure whether a letter came and never reached me.

I have no real objection to their doing this, as long as they are discreet and don't get me in a jam with the authorities (Church) which would affect my other writing. I don't think there is anything whatever wrong with the book from the Church's official point of view, but if it raises a lot of discussion in the wrong place, among stupid people, who complain to bishops, then it will inevitably get back to my Superiors and they will want to know what's all this, who do I think I am, and will I permanently shut up about everything except the Rosary.

. . . We are mimeographing an enlarged edition of the *Cold War Letters,* and I will send you a few. No objections to it going to Europe where people are more intelligent about the peace issue, generally, than here . . .

I am joining the FOR officially, anyway, as a rather obvious thing to do. Reading a ms. of Father Delp who was killed by Hitler. A tremendous document. It will come out next year, I think, and you will see.

As for *Breakthrough,* it was (as far as my contribution is concerned) approved before the ax fell. I have not gone around publicizing the fact that I edited the book. Officially there is no one named as editor . . .

November 7, 1962

I am happy to hear about your visit to Regina Laudis [Benedictine monastery in Connecticut]. I have never met Mother Benedicta but I respect her highly from what I know of her, and RL sounds like one of the few really fine convents that are around. I shall send her some things . . .

I have just received a fine new book, just a small one, in French, by Père Régamey and another Dominican on the CO stand. It is very well done, clear and ordered to the practical purpose of moving the legislators into action in France.

Certainly for my part I believe this is a most essential issue, one of the cardinal moral issues of our time, one on which the witness of the Church will depend. The fact is that the ambiguity of so many Catholics on the war question, or worse still the frank belligerency of the majority of them, is a very serious symptom of spiritual sickness in our society. It is a mark of the failure of Catholics to meet the spiritual challenge of the times. They have failed to meet it not because the Church as such has failed, because the clear statements of the Popes are there. But these statements have not been effectively interpreted or put in practice. On the contrary they have been left as a pure dead letter except for clauses that give a loophole for militarists. One of these of course is the statement by Pius XII that a Catholic could be obliged in certain circumstances to fight for his country. Obviously this brings in the old question of the just war, for the Catholic certainly cannot be obliged to fight in a war that is not obviously just.

Then arises the question of how to judge the justice of the cause, when the facts are not known, or when they are distorted by mass media. In the latest Cuban crisis, for instance, the immediate setup was such that any priest would have urged any Catholic to fulfill a strict obligation to get in there and fight because it was a cause of *defense.* Obviously if one puts on blinkers and is extremely selective about what facts he considers, and takes into account only the President's speech declaring the blockade etc., with the facts alleged in it, the pictures of the weapon sites etc.: well, then there is no choice according to the position taken by most of the clergy.

The real issue is then the recognition of the individual conscience to assess the *facts* of the case, as well as the principle of the just war. To say that the clergy can tell the laity they are obliged to fight because the Pentagon or *Time* magazine says so, this is to me a total default of Christianity, a surrender to the worst kind of secularism, a handing over of the Christian conscience in servitude to nefarious and anonymous secular power. And we have good reason to believe that in the exercise of that power the morality to which we hold is ignored and sometimes derided. It is certain that some of those who have the greatest power, some of the button pressers, frankly consider the moral issue "irrelevant" in nuclear war. All that matters is to "get them first." To make the Christian conscience subservient to the decisions of such people is a crass betrayal. This is intolerable. It is also a travesty of democratic principle . . .

. . . Blessings and love to you and Jean and to the new one on the way, the Benedictine addition to the family. [Jean and Jim had decided to name their child Benedict if a boy.]

December 8, 1962

. . . It seems to me that the basic problem is not political, it is apolitical and human. One of the most important things to do is to keep cutting deliberately through political lines and barriers and emphasizing the fact that these are largely fabrications and that there is another dimension, a genuine reality, totally opposed to the fictions of politics: the human dimension which politics pretend to arrogate entirely to themselves. This is the necessary first step along the long way toward the perhaps impossible task of purifying, humanizing and somehow illuminating politics themselves. Is this possible? . . . At least we must try to hope in that, otherwise all is over. But politics as they now stand are hopeless.

Hence the desirability of a manifestly non-political witness, non-aligned, non-labeled, fighting for the reality of man and his rights and needs in the nuclear world in some measure against all the alignments . . .

January 17, 1963

How many letters of yours haven't I answered? First I must get in my congratulations and blessings for Benedict. That is wonderful. May he have all the grace and courage he will need. And you and Jean with him. It is possible that the ones who are coming into the world now will have great trials and sorrows, but they may also turn out to be terrific people. As I said before, your generation is a much better crop than what came between mine and yours. And of course my generation: the Kennedy generation, hah? Maybe the less said about us the better. I have the feeling of being a survivor of the shipwrecked thirties, one of the few that have kept my original face before this present world was born . . .

We are mimeographing an enlarged edition of *CW* letters so this will reach you someday but not soon. It is quite a lot bigger and fuller, and we are doing a lot of copies . . .

. . . I think it would be good if the non-violent movement could get a more and more solid foundation, and deeper roots, spiritual roots. I know you have them already, but an immense amount of work needs to be done by us all. We have really got to work on the theological and spiritual bases for ahimsa and tie them in with the Gospel in a way that leaves no doubt as to the Christian *obligation* in this regard. As long as these deep foundations are not there, I think you *can* very well be used or misused by political elements that have nothing to do with you, whether you like it or not . . .

March 27, 1963

. . . *Liberation*: I am glad you have the job [editor of *Liberation* magazine]. I think it is a good one for you and you will get somewhere with it. I am glad you have some funds to work with, and I guess the pictures are a good idea. The full page of the Negro kid was impressive. That a man should walk up and down in front of the White House with a sign saying "Gas the Jews" is to me incredible. I mean incredible. I think this is no joke at all, it is very serious. That such a thing should happen and be accepted without a batted eyelash, without a murmur, without a surprised expression, as part of the normal landscape (it evidently is) points to a degree of moral anaesthesia that I had not thought possible. In effect, there is no longer any such thing as a serious public opinion worthy of the name. There are just passive reactions . . .

. . . Hence the importance of non-violent people who are really conscientious objectors not only to nuclear war but to *everything* that leads to it or goes with it in the same general atmosphere of violence and criminality. I think the perspectives of the non-violent have to be enlarged in all directions, so that it becomes a genuine and profound spiritual movement, and a force for *life* in a really rotting and corrupt world. How badly this is needed.

. . . People in Austria (the Goss-Mayrs) wondered if I wouldn't join them in a non-violent project in Brazil; I wish to heaven I could, though I don't think I'd be much help . . .

April 17, 1963

Here is a poem which you can perhaps use in *Liberation*—only wait for the censors please! I am happy about the encyclical saying clearly that it is "impossible for war to be an instrument of justice" in the context of nuclear armaments. The Pope is lucky he does not have to be approved by the censors of our Order, he would never get by them!

Hope you and Jean are well. All the best to everyone.

The thing on Danish non-violence I sent to *CW*, but I don't know if they want it. It is not to be printed over my name.

April 26, 1963

Quick note . . . H. Stuart Hughes, up in Boston, has some organization that has awarded me a Peace Prize. Well, well. Me and Pope John. I am glad they thought of me, though, and appreciate it, though there is still not much I can do. But I think I told you I wrote to the Abbot General and said it is a good thing Pope John didn't have to get his encyclical through our censors: and could I now start up again? I will let you know what happens. The General is probably impregnable in his serene conviction that he really wants me to preserve the contemplative silence of our mystic order, and that is really his "only motive." Not de Gaulle's *force de frappe*, no, only contemplative silence.

Things have been pretty busy, I am hoping to make a couple weeks' retreat early in June, however, and catch up on the ability to think, if I ever had it.

June 7, 1963

. . . By the way, this ["On Danish Non-Violence"] is being printed in the *Catholic Worker* sometime, I believe, and *without my name*. If you do prefer to use a name, for this item, will you please use the pen name of Benedict Lemoyne? [The name actually used was Benedict Moore.] Many thanks, Jim.

In printing the "Chant for Furnaces," will you please mention that this forms part of a new book of poetry mostly on themes of the same kind, to be printed by New Directions this fall. The title of the book is *Emblems of a Season of Fury*.

Yes, the loss of Pope John is great, but he did an astonishing work in four and a half years. The Holy Spirit really moved in him, and I hope this will be true at the conclave and in the next Pope, whoever he may be. I have always liked Montini, but I suppose he has had people against him from way back. Lercaro might be good. But I think it would probably be best if we got another like Pope John, a dark horse who was not thought to be too progressive. I'll settle for another of the same! I sure wish old Maximos of Antioch could get it, but of course he doesn't have a chance . . .

Preparations were in progress for the March on Washington that was to take place in August. Bayard Rustin was one of the organizers of the March. It was during this demonstration that Martin Luther King gave his famous "I Have a Dream" talk.

June 10, 1963

Thanks for the terrific Rustin piece. Clear and definite and saying what is what. I am glad this issue is getting real clear; I think there is going to be a hard time ahead for everybody, because this is going to reach right into the heart of *everything*. But this is the work of God, and the finger of God is in it everywhere. He knows what He is going to do in it all. But I am more hopeful than I have ever been: it may mean the salvation and survival of America. The power elite cannot do anything but ruin the country. The Negroes may save it—but through fire.

Here is a poem ["And the Children of Birmingham"] I was not thinking of giving to *Liberation*. I thought it would be better someplace else where everyone might not agree. But if you want it real bad, tell me. It is being censored and is not yet cleared.

June 24, 1963

Thanks for the last two letters and enclosures. About the business in Miss., the murder of Evers and the rest. I have a friend or acquaintance if you prefer down there, a crusading small-town editor P. D. East who wrote a book called *The Magnolia Jungle*. He has fought the racists all by himself for years, and now finally it looks as though they might have started to get tired of having him around. I don't think his life is absolutely safe down there.

He is a good writer and could do a lot of good stuff for *Liberation*, I believe, though he is more an editorialist and satirist than a newsman or anything like that . . . Be careful, they are probably working over his mail. The Land of the Free, hah? I repeat, his life is probably not worth too much. Also he is flat broke, since running an anti-segregationist paper has not proved popular in Miss. He is not read there. So far they have just ignored him, while occasionally spitting in his eye. But this seems to be moving into a new phase . . .

About this sex question: here I get off the train. It is not that I am not interested, but this really is a question beyond my competence. I mean, this calls for someone who has been doing work in parishes with married people, or in college or something, or a moral theologian in the field itself. There is an awful lot of Byzantine technicality that one needs to know in order to handle this issue in a way that will pass muster with Catholic theologians. And in any case I think there is so much sheer crap written about it by Catholics and non-Catholics alike that I don't want to get into such a pile of confusions. This is just not my line, and while I think I must speak out, insofar as I can, on things like war and races, when it gets down to other issues like sex, birth control, etc. etc., I must pass it by. I can't keep up with the literature and with the state of the question . . .

I will write P. D. East and tell him about you all.

I read the proofs of Dorothy's book [*Loaves and Fishes*] and gave it a good boost for *Harper's* . . .

June 29, 1963

Thanks for the letter and the *Libs*, also for the Cuban book. I always like to see good stuff from Spanish America, may uncover some good poets to translate. Incidentally I thought A. J. Muste's piece was one of the very best things in the last issue and a very good summary of the problems facing the peace movement . . .

The other thing is that I don't have that many real Catholic contacts of any value around Kentucky. You don't know how out of contact I am. I could inquire from friends in Lexington, but they don't seem to be too aware of the strike either.

The Governor came out with a broad decision that should, on paper, help integration in this state. I don't know how serious it is or what it will mean. Have you heard any comments on it? . . .

July 15, 1963

. . . Thanks for all the stuff on Hazard [coal miners' strike in Hazard, Kentucky]. I will go over it carefully. I really want to do something about it, and the chief reason I did not last time was that I forgot and then assumed that the whole thing was over because I was hearing nothing about it. As far as Kentucky is concerned, it might as well never have existed, no one seems to know or say anything about it, least of all in the monastery. It must be up in eastern Ky. I know conditions are terrible there . . .

July 19, 1963

Here are some copies of "Letter to Papal Volunteer." Thanks for the Hazard stuff, in case I didn't thank you before. It doesn't exactly explain to me what is going on, but it makes me see that it is immensely complex and that this is a kind of symptom spot, where something is beginning the breakout that is going to break out all over. Anyway, as you say, these are certainly our neighbors, though eastern Ky. is a somewhat different area and we have very little to do with them. In fact, I am not sure that us busting in there with cheese, even, is going to be well understood: those people are generally fundamentalist Protestants, and probably think of us as having horns. It may take a little thought. Really it would be good to know of some priest out there who is known to the miners and has their confidence and we could work through him . . . I'd like to follow this up as best I can, without giving the impression of barging in where not wanted.

October 19, 1963

The main reason why I have not been answering is that I was for some time in the hospital, and if I got out of the hospital by special pleading, earlier than anticipated, it was because I was expected to keep up the hospital treatment and regime more or less in the monastery infirmary. I haven't but things are getting along better anyway. Problem: a cervical disc, which interferes with some of my usual activities, and cuts into the amount of time and energy available for work.

But I have been grateful for all the material you sent, particularly that about Alabama. I think I told you I was writing a long article for *Ramparts* on the race situation. They are now publishing it, but unfortunately I have not been able to add anything on recent events and there is nothing in it later than July . . .

I am having to cut down on blurbs, prefaces, and various minor statements, for the obvious reason that I am just snowed under. And also Superiors are getting rather testy again about things that seem to them to get far out of the monastic field . . .

I think in the long run it is best for me to shut up in this particular realm (of blurbs and prefaces) (at least outside the specifically "contemplative" sphere) for my own good. I have got to consider the impact of the chief work I am trying to do . . . if I ever get time to do it. In other words, I think it is essential that I get back to saying what I have to say in books, and in books that are more than collections of essays. For this I am going to have to shut up awhile and read and get thinking again.

. . . What I will send you is some strictly safe abstract art. This I am not hindered in, and I can say what I want perfectly freely because nobody knows what any of it means anyway (for the simple reason that none of it has that kind of a meaning). Meanwhile, the prefaces and statements that I have indulged in to date will probably keep coming down like fallout for the next year, so don't be surprised . . .

December 19, 1963

As usual I have been very bad about writing and cannot promise to get better. Next year it is going to be necessary to cut down somewhat on contacts, but I will keep writing to you anyway. Just be patient. I value very much all the ideas that come from you and the things you send. Don't apologize ever. Jean's poems, too, are always very welcome and they get better all the time. I respond very much to them. As for the calendar and desk book of all the peace etc. organizations, I am delighted to have it: it gives me some information I need.

However, there can be no question that I have got to simplify my life to a great extent and not get too actively involved in things which I cannot properly do. I will keep trying, however, to do what I can in a way that makes sense, at the right time, and with as much impact as I can provide with God's help. But the best thing I can do is keep my mind to some extent clear of dust, even when in the midst of it. Or is it dust after all? One has to be able to tell.

I have kept forgetting to send you scrawls. I am doing these calligraphies and they may or may not look good. I think they make sense for me to do, and I am sending a few, so you can make what use of them you please.

You mentioned in one of your letters that you knew indirectly that Oswald had been connected with racists in NY. I think this is extremely important information, and I would like to communicate it privately to Robt. Kennedy. Can you tell me some details that would be relevant, and do you think there is anything wrong with my telling him? I certainly think I should. It seems to me that this whole investigation thing is inadequate (haven't heard much anyway), and I think that all Dallas stinks to high heaven with corruption, racism and the rest. It would be ridiculous if they simply accepted the idea that Oswald was "excited" and Ruby even more so. I am convinced that there is much more to it than that. What do you think?

I am getting along OK except yesterday I slipped in the snow and fell on my can, which shook up the back a bit and might start trouble again. May end up on my back in traction some more, who can tell? But I hope not.

. . . Jack English was here for several weeks, because he got a heart attack when visiting the place and had to be hospitalized. He left for Georgia today. I had some good talks with him. He was hoping Dorothy might come down and so was I. Glad to hear the farm is moving to a good place and I am completely in agreement about the quasi-monastic character that peace mvts. ought to have. And monastic movements ought to learn from the peace and race groups too. SNCC for instance has things that monks ought to know about and ought to practice. CNVA too. Things seem to be quiet on peace front since the ban, I wonder if this is illusory. Or have they just worn themselves out shouting? . . .

February 7, 1964

. . . We are finally getting next to the Hazard affair here. There was a good piece in the local paper, in fact a supplement with lots of pictures (Louisville *Courier-Journal*) and then I also dug up a good article by Dan Wakefield in *Commentary* which I have (I hope) persuaded Fr. Abbot ought to be read in refectory. Then finally we have found out there are a couple Franciscans down there, and we are going to send food and money and hope the Franks get them to the right crowd. This should have been done long time ago, but you know how it is . . .

My stuff on "Race Question" is coming out in a small book in France almost any time now. In America, God alone knows when. I am in a bad tangle with publishers and everything is just so damn stupid you can't see straight. By the way say hello to Betty Bartelme if you know her, I think you do. She was an innocent bystander in this veritable Kentucky feud that started between me and Farrar, Straus when I inadvertently, in an off moment, sold a book to Macmillan . . . There were apparently some letters I didn't get, and the rest. That is what happens. Just when things are getting real hot on some issue, a key letter goes to Ceylon or somewhere instead of coming here. Or it comes here and gets into sour mash for the bourbon . . .

There is a little girl in Virginia called Karin Myrin wants to join *CW*; if she ever comes to NY and knocks on your door and says Uncle Louie sent her it's me, it's OK. I only know her by letter. She wants to join Little Sisters of Jesus eventually maybe.

February 27, 1964

. . . I am awfully sorry John Heidbrink is in bad shape. I dropped him a brief line the other day and will keep him in mind. The [Catholic] Peace Fellowship sounds good but I hate to see things multiply when one ought to be able to do it. I suppose Pax just isn't. I haven't had much contact with them at all and have really no idea what is going on there if anything. However, without a lot of membership and organization there is something to be said for it, and the fact of putting out good literature, study kits and so on will be very valuable. Where are you getting your financial support? FOR? . . .

March 16, 1964

. . . I am in trouble with the new General already. I wanted to republish in a book some of the peace articles that had been permitted in magazines. There was a misunderstanding about this, and now he wants to prevent even the republication of articles that were permitted.

There is an interesting guy from Argentina in the country, Miguel Grinberg, poet and publisher of a good magazine, very lively, starting a movement of poets all over the place. I have given him your address. John Heidbrink would be interested too, I think. I think that this movement, which is also peace-oriented, can be a great force for good and intelligence, and for communication on a serious level between people in the different countries. For sure there is going to be much trouble in Latin America largely because of the stupor and lack of understanding on the part of the U.S.; when we could be doing so much for progress—other than naïve gestures which are easily frustrated by the people who want to continue to make all the money they can out of those countries.

I enclose some calligraphies. Perhaps one thing that could be done with some of them would be to use them in Lax's new book of poems which I am supposed to be helping to edit, but I am so busy that I cannot get to it seriously. And it is not easy to edit either.

And then again, how about an exhibition in some gallery, small, back alley, or something? Or in a place where they drink espresso and look at calligraphies, or something of the sort? If you think this is a good idea and anything gets sold you can have half. Someone would have to be interested enough to mount the pictures in some way, and I could take care of any expenses involved in that. If you think this a good idea I will send the best and subtlest of the calligraphies which are all on a kind of very thin Japanese paper.

May 20, 1964

. . . A group of Hibakusha [Hiroshima victims on tour for peace] came through here Saturday. I had them up at the house and we talked a bit but they were rushed away before we could really get down to anything interesting. Yet they are the people I have most enjoyed meeting for a long time. Rare ones that seemed to be worth talking to. I read them a poem (of which I do not yet have copies but I will send one when I do) and one of them, an old lady, very sweet and quiet left me a folded paper crane. I loved them.

. . . I am reading some fantastic stuff on Islam by Louis Massignon, and Buddhist books which I now have to review for magazine of the Order. I am reviewer in chief of Buddhist, Hindu, etc. etc., bks. Something I would not have expected from our magazine a few years ago, and who knows it may yet get sat on. We shall see. I like the job. The Hinayana (pardon, Theravada) group is getting into the picture with books now, Ceylon etc., they have the advantage of being clearer and less cloudy than Mahayana, serve as good starting points. Walpola Rahula real sharp.

I still have a huge pile of mss. of Lax which he wants me to edit, but it is impossible to edit Lax. Got to print all or nothing, but how print a thousand-page book with little one-word-a-line poems running down the middle of the page? Did they ever find out anything more about Oswald? *Black Revolution* book is going over great in France and being done in Italy, Spain, Germany, all bogged down at Farrar, Straus, etc., however, not their fault but the Order's. Stop now. Lots of love to you both . . .

In June–July 1964 Jean and Jim Forest went to an international peace conference in Prague. On July 20, after his return, Jim wrote a long letter detailing his impressions of the Church in Prague. He was especially impressed by the vitality of the Protestant churches. During the Prague meeting Jim discussed with Daniel Berrigan the possibility of forming a Catholic Peace Fellowship.

July 22, 1964

Thanks for the letter. Glad to hear the trip was a success. Time moves fast and you have covered ground. I believe what you say about Prague. One of the most impressive Christians I have ever met is Jan Milic

Lochman from the Comenius there. He was here this spring. I got a warm card from him the other day. I feel I have much more in common with him than with many American Catholics.

Thanks too for the paper. The thing gets inexorably more grave, but what else can anyone expect? Causes are not removed, effects continue, and we have reached the time of their proliferation. Of course I know about Goldwater and the nonsense we can expect in that quarter. I am not one of those that think he won't carry anything but Arizona. I think he will take the South and a lot of other places, but the East might still outweigh him. Still, Johnson is as much of a fire breather as he is when it comes to Vietnam, and that is what is most tragic. There is not a shred of justification for war there. It is a pure power play, without necessity, a brute piece of stupidity and frustration on the part of people who have no imagination or insight and no moral sense. Because a few people in America want power and wealth, a lot of Vietnamese, Chinese, and Americans have been and will be sacrificed. It is a complete travesty of justice and right and liberty. I do not think it can meet any of the requirements of the traditional "just war." Please keep me posted on this.

I have to get ready for class, so this is all for the moment. Keep in touch. I look forward to articles on your trip. Love to you and Jean. Pray.

September 1, 1964

Thanks for the letter and the big packet of things. I am very grateful as always. I need this kind of information and it was well chosen. Most of it will do well on the board. I especially liked your article on Vietnam. It was one of the clearest and best summaries I have seen and I hope the *CW* will take it. I strongly suggest you send it to Ted Roszak, who is the new editor of *Peace News* . . . He is a friend of mine and is looking for stuff. A couple of things of mine are supposed to come out there, including a piece on race which I wrote for a magazine in France. I think he would like this piece on Vietnam, though I suppose the ending might be somewhat adjusted. Why not try him with it?

I know the situation in Vietnam is completely poisonous. In a way it makes me much more disgusted and depressed than the tests and so on did because here the folly of it and the crass, brutal untruth of it is spelled out so much more obviously because in so much more human detail. The injustice of it is so flagrant and so absurd, and what is worst is the *refusal* to see it. Even an uninformed person, you might think, would be able to tell, reading between the lines of the *Post* article, that the whole thing stinks to heaven and that the people of Vietnam themselves are completely free of any delusions about fighting for freedom, etc. Naturally they don't want to fall into the arms of Red China, but there are other possibilities, and if we were as noble and objective as we pretend to be, we would be helping them to get set up as a neutral and self-sustaining free government instead of as a corrupt satellite of ours, full of graft etc. . . .

On September 10, Forest wrote asking Merton if he would agree to be one of the sponsors of the Catholic Peace Fellowship that was being founded.

October 2, 1964

Thanks for the letters and all the things sent. I am sorry I forgot about the name business. I was thinking about it, and actually I want to help, so I suppose you might as well use my name for the Peace Fellowship along with the others if it is any use. The only thing is that I do agree in feeling that it is sort of a useless gesture. Sure, it is what is done, and it helps. But I think this will probably be my last time at it. It is true that if one has that illusory thing, "a name," it might as well be used for its illusion value. And yet I don't know if that really makes sense either. Anyway, I think this had better be the last illusion of this particular kind. But go ahead and put my name on the list.

I have been thinking a lot lately about my efforts to speak out and participate in some way in the noises of the public conscience. It all gets to be a bit ambiguous. However, I have at least made some sounds, and if now I make fewer (because it is hard enough to keep up with things enough to know whether one makes sense), it will not bother me or anyone else so much.

With Dan and Phil and people like that getting in there more, and with small hopes popping up (I know how really small though) perhaps I can just be more of a monk . . .

Do you by the way have any contact with Fr. Du Bay? Maybe you should. He has now been put in a John Birch Siberia parish, but is batting away manfully and wearing down the Birchite pastor and assistant he is with. Though they are probably wearing him down too . . .

October 21, 1964

. . . I have no more copies of *Peace in a PCE*, but the essence of it is going to be in my new book, as also most of the *CW* letters, or a lot of them. Hence there is no need to mimeograph these. I will send some copies of *CW* letters that you can use, however. I may also dig up a few other items. I will see what I have lying around.

. . . I am so happy about Martin Luther King [getting the Nobel Peace Prize]. That is magnificent and I think it will do much for the race situation, in that it will restore a lot of confidence in his leadership. Or at least I hope so . . .

From November 18 to 20 a meeting took place at Gethsemani for leaders in the peace movement. Forest was among those present for the meeting. (See Berrigan correspondence for details.)

December 9, 1964

Thanks for the letters and clippings. The stuff on the bomb was hallucinating. And all the rest too. These are the monks of the twentieth century: the fellows cloistered in the bomb silo, with their communal life, their silence, their austerity, their separation from the world, a monasticism in reverse. The monk is supposed to dig into the earth to find the sources of life in hiddenness, and these dig into the earth with the power of death. They become seeds like the seeds of hell that are in people's minds. Living more in solitude I see more clearly how real it is that there are so to speak nests in our minds, where death hatches all kinds of eggs. One of the great and awful realities of the time is this infestation of man by a very active and very prolific force of evil. The scholastic idea of evil as a mere negation has lulled theologians into a sleep where they not only fail to see this, but cultivate it, and as a result produce an "infested" theology. I can say nothing else of the interventions of Hannon and Co. in the Council, on Schema 13.

I got a nice letter from Fr. Haring on my book . . . I will seriously try to get something on paper [about the November meeting]. I found my notes of that afternoon's talk, so I guess I can piece it all together, though it will obviously not be the same. I think it is a fine idea to get all that stuff in one book. Published? Not sure. Mimeographed anyway.

By the way, if I were you I would not mention, even in a confidential mimeograph, that you intend to mimeo and distribute things by me that are (it is implied) not able to be printed. All it needs is for some kook to get hold of a sheet like this and send it to the General and I will be under an explicit prohibition to mimeograph anything.

The Abbot (now in Norway) is probably going to make it difficult for me to keep providing this sort of material, but anyway I will look through the old stuff and send some along. It is very definite that my contacts with people are to be cut down, and the ecumenical talks and dialogue have been definitely stopped. I think it would be better to warn people not to expect to get to see me, and I don't know what will happen about mail, though I think we will be able to keep the lines open for CPF, etc. I hope. More later. Blessings for Christmas, New Year, love to all.

March 8, 1965

I thought you would like to see this letter to *Commonweal* which they may or may not print. If you want to mimeograph it—OK with me. The other bit is for *Peace News. Negro Digest* did a longer version of the

Gorilla bit. I liked *NCR* very much, it is the first copy I have seen. No time to type that talk yet. It must wait.

The letter to Commonweal *was Merton's first public statement on Vietnam.*

March 13, 1965

Thanks for sending along the clippings about Selma. There does not seem to be much hope of very encouraging news these days. I suppose this sort of thing is going to drag on for a long time, now here and now there. As to Vietnam, the Pentagon crowd really seems to want a regular war out there, but there is not much taste for it among the people as far as I can see, so this may be holding things back a little. All we need is the sinking of the *Maine* or another Pearl Harbor.

However, I am beginning to have no trust at all in my judgment of trends and events. It is certainly true that I just can't see things in perspective from here, though I may come out with an occasional intuition about the general climate. It seems more and more that I have to just shut up and try to do my own part, which is that of a monk, and which amounts to nothing much in the external way, and maybe nothing much in any way at all. It is one thing to be somewhat dramatic and quite another to be pertinent. And it is always easy to talk, but not always easy to say something that makes real sense (instead of just sounding reasonable). Thus far my Lenten meditation for the day.

But I do have something good for you. This piece is written by Jean and Hildegard Goss-Mayr. They sent me the English translation to look over and correct and pass on to someone. I leave it to you to decide who is to have it. First I suppose you will want to mimeograph it yourself, and then it should certainly go to *CW* if not to *Liberation*. I think it is a really excellent piece, and one which is *not* dramatic and *does* say something and *is* (not merely sounds) significant. I turn this piece over to you. Let me know what you do with it and send me copies, I will see that the Goss-Mayrs get them.

Keep sending stuff. Best wishes to everyone.

May 16, 1965

Here is a first draft of a letter I am hoping to send off to Paul VI tomorrow. I was shocked but not surprised to hear (after considerable delay) that Phil had been silenced. Nevertheless I think much has been gained by the fact that his case is right out in the open and everyone has to think about it. It raises the question just how long religious Superiors can evade responsibility in grave issues like this, while refusing to let others speak out according to their conscience and in line with what is obviously indicated by the Holy See, even.

You can tell Phil and Dan. I don't know where Phil is now. Don't worry about the style of the letter to Paul VI. You have to write like that or the secretaries won't give it to him.

August 20, 1965

Thanks for the letter and for letting me see the statement [in the *National Catholic Reporter* on war in Vietnam], which is very good. Is it too long? Should there be a line or two to say that though we advocate peace, this by no means indicates a willingness to submit passively to the threat of communism and that, on the contrary, the blundering violence of the current war is actually doing much more to strengthen Asian communism than to weaken it? I think this would be an important addition . . .

I hesitate to suggest changes when I am not signing the document myself. Now that the hermit project is getting under way, I am especially restricted and have to watch everything I do that can be construed as looking back to the wicked world, such as thinking thoughts of peace, etc. etc. I think the Abbot's main fear at the moment is that I will keep too many contacts open and will remain involved in activities which he questions, and the letters coming in complaining about it are of course increasing, so they influence him, I guess. Thus, in order to maintain my real responsibilities, I have to remain out of the public eye for a while at least, while sounding off when I can. I don't know what is becoming of the Schema 13 letter, but neither *Commonweal* nor *Jubilee* wants it and I have suggested sending it on to *National Catholic Reporter* at Douglass's instigation.

The hermit project has been voted and approved officially by the council of the community and is accepted and understood by most everyone. It begins officially tomorrow . . .

[*Telegram*]

November 11, 1965

Just heard about suicide of Roger La Porte. While I do not hold Catholic Peace Fellowship responsible for the tragedy current developments in peace movement make it impossible for me to continue as sponsor for fellowship. Please remove my name from list of sponsors. Letter follows.

November 11, 1965

This is a bitter letter to have to write. This morning, after receiving the news of the suicide of Roger La Porte, which I heard of quite by chance, I had to send you a telegram asking to remove my name from the list of sponsors of the CPF. I know of course that the CPF is not encouraging people to burn themselves up. Unfortunately, however, the CPF is in the middle of a peace movement in which, rightly or wrongly, with good intentions or not I don't know, there is something that looks to me to be a little pathological.

As you know, I am not sufficiently well informed to make clear judgments of this or that policy, for instance the burning of draft cards. Certainly protest is called for, and it may very well be that this precise form of protest is what is called for at the moment. I do not know. Maybe I am wrong in thinking that it is harming the peace movement rather than helping it, and that it is in fact fanning up the war fever rather than abating it.

But this suicide, coming on top of the other one in Washington and of so many other things which are disturbing and equivocal, leads me to make the regretful decision that I cannot accept the present spirit of the movement as it presents itself to me.

It seems to me that there is something radically wrong somewhere, something that is un-Christian, though I am not questioning anybody's sincerity and good will, or even the objective rights and wrongs of the clearest cases. But the whole thing gives off a very different smell from the Gandhian movement, the non-violent movement in France and the non-violence of Martin Luther King. Jim, there is something wrong here. I think there is something demonic at work in it. This suicide of a Catholic ex-seminarian (I was told) does not make sense in terms of a Christian peace movement.

I repeat, I know you are not encouraging such things, that you are as shocked and opposed as I am. It must seem arbitrary and pitiless of me to withdraw at a moment like this. But I am in a different position from you, and also in a different position from Dan and Phil. I am strictly out of touch with what you are doing, and yet my name is being used, and by its use kids are likely to get drawn into something that seems to me to have something very bad around the edges of it. I have no way of helping anyone to stay with what is good and avoid what is bad, I cannot be there and talk or advise. Hence there remains only one thing for me to do, that is to withdraw my name from the list of sponsors. So please take me off the list.

The spirit of this country at the present moment is to me terribly disturbing. To you too, and to everyone, no doubt. It is not quite like Nazi Germany, certainly not like Soviet Russia, it is like nothing on earth I ever heard of before. This whole atmosphere is crazy, not just the peace movement, everybody. There is in it such an air of absurdity and moral void, even where conscience and morality are invoked (as they are by everyone). The joint is going into a slow frenzy. The country is nuts.

For people to avail themselves of their right to conscientious objection which the Council has, thank God, finally acknowledged: that is what ought to be done. Instead, this business of burning oneself alive. What in heaven's name is the idea of that? It will only neutralize all the work that has been done and all the gains that have been made. What on earth are the American bishops going to make out of that?

I am sorry, Jim, I must ask you to take my name off that list. Naturally I will do anything I can to be of help, if you need me for anything. This does not mean a complete repudiation of the CPF or anything of the sort.

This morning I offered Mass for the peace movement and I shall certainly keep it in my prayers, particularly you and everyone associated with you. God bless you, and forgive me this hard letter.

November 19, 1965

I am really grateful for your long letter. Also for the enclosures. The whole package was a very great help indeed. I was happy to read Tom Cornell's lucid statement [*Commonweal*, November 19, 1965], which is the first real information I have had on the positive arguments for card burning. I have been getting a very partial and rather alarmed set of reports on everything down here and my perspective has been way out. Your enclosures were very encouraging and I am happy about all that.

Let me first of all apologize for the following things:

1. For sending the telegram as a more or less emotional reflex, without really thinking the whole thing out.

2. For insinuating that the whole peace movement, including CPF, was operating in a climate of pathology. You are right, of course: the whole current reality has a lot of pathology in it, but the country is not nuts and the peace movement is not nuts either. You are making a lot of sense.

3. For blasting at you with what is really a personal problem of my own, at a time when you certainly had enough difficulties of your own to contend with. It was selfish of me and I am sorry.

I can see from your letter, the enclosures and from letters of Dan Berrigan and Dorothy Day, that really God has used all this and His love has not been idle or refused in your hearts, in this very tragic and difficult trial. As for Roger, the picture I get of him is a very positive one. I am very sorry he had to do what he did but I am sure that as far as he is concerned nothing has been lost. He was not, by the way, a Trappist. These are the other Cistercians in Wisconsin.

Now to get back to my own difficulty. I suppose I was wrought up enough for it to take on the air of a formal public repudiation of CPF, but that is not really what I intended. I certainly don't want to make things difficult for you, and I would hardly want to interfere with the fine work you are doing for conscientious objectors.

My chief problem is, as I said before, personal. I am so to speak making my novitiate as a "hermit" of sorts and I have my hands full with this. It is a full-time job just coping with one's own damn mind in solitude, without getting wrought up about what appear to be the vagaries of others. Let's face the fact that my usefulness to CPF is at best purely symbolic, but it does nevertheless imply a heavy responsibility. There is no question that people, at least in this area, tend to hold me responsible for what you guys do. I know this because I am told it. It is of course more gossip, but they are associating the card burning with my ideas about peace. This certainly does not make life simple for me since I am not quite sure that I agree with card burning (though I accept Tom's arguments for his own position). At the same time it is not easy for me to find out just what the scoop is. This leaves me hanging on a hook not of my own choosing. Jim Douglass, who also is apparently not too sure about how he stands in this regard, is asking me to write about it, which I would rather not do. It is mainly due to this sort of pressure that I got a bit wrought up about Roger. And it may be necessary for me to make some kind of statement that I do not personally *advocate* burning draft cards. If I do, I will try to make it in such a way that I do not condemn anyone else or interfere with your witness.

If I thought of getting my name off your list of sponsors it was chiefly because of the embarrassment caused me by the inevitable fact that I am automatically blamed for whatever is done in your area of the peace movement, which means in practice for anything done by a Catholic Worker member too.

I am perfectly willing to leave the thing hanging in the balance for a while, so as not to create the impression that I am publicly denouncing you or throwing a wrench in your good work. But in any case I must sooner or later get in a position where it is clear that I am *not* accountable for what my friends do, and that I don't necessarily advocate all that is done by them.

Do you see my position? I think it would be clear and acceptable to all if it were understood that I was withdrawing from all such involvements, formally, without repudiating anyone personally. And without repudiating the movement.

I am in no rush to do this, and I am willing to consider different possibilities. But now I must end this letter, and I do so hoping you understand that it is simply a personal matter of my own, not a "political" move of some sort. I would appreciate it if we could work this out some way.

Again, I appreciated your letter very much indeed. It made a lot of sense. And what you are doing is great. I admire the courage of Tom, of Dave Miller and all those who are going through the struggle you are going through. I keep you in my prayers, and I hope it is possible for me to say these things frankly without you getting the impression that I am betraying you. I have enough confidence in your friendship to hope that you will not interpret it in such a way.

December 3, 1965

I was glad to get your letter of Nov. 26. Before I received it I had reached the conclusion that perhaps if I could make a statement of some sort on the subject, I could define the terms in which I was sponsor of the CPF and remain a sponsor. I have written such a statement, and it appears to me reasonable, though I am beginning to wonder about that. The telegram seemed quite reasonable at the time. If you think this statement is absurd, well, let me know. But I do think it makes sense, and if you will use it all, working it into a story or however you like, and get it into print so that people know what I think, then there is no further problem about my being a sponsor. All I ask is that people should never be led to assume that I am personally behind a specific project or demonstration inspired by a recent event of which I may have no knowledge. In other words, I am behind the pastoral aims of the CPF all the way, and insofar as you are implementing the teaching of the Church on peace, I have no reason to differ with the CPF. Where differences might come, in the realm of political action and in the decisions regarding this or that specific policy, then I cannot obviously be with you if I don't have sufficient information or perspective, and even then, as you say regarding other sponsors, I am liable to differ. Hence I do not want people to assume that I am personally behind every move you make. Still less, of course, the personal acts of individual members. But in point of fact, when Tom burned his draft card, people were holding me personally responsible. Which is of course absurd, but all is not reasonable in politics. The point is that this does create situations which are a bit too much for me to handle in my particular spot, I mean in this hermitage, where I am likely to be totally without perspective (as the telegram showed).

If you will respect my curious decision to live this form of life without being called upon to make political noises, then I will gladly give you all the moral support I can for your pastoral work which is, I think, the really essential job of CPF. Of course, when there is question of an immoral war, then the moral decision is obviously tied in with politics. But even then, I think it is extremely important not to come out with some gesture that strikes the average Catholic as a needless provocation and drives him back into the arms of conservatism and inertia. In my opinion the job of the CPF is not so much to make a strong impression in the press of being a very radical group (I don't say you are doing this, just that you might) but to reach the ordinary Catholic as far as possible, or at least the ones who are most open to the new look, without being very radical themselves. It is this that is going to make the big difference. Anything else may make a splash for a moment and then vanish forever . . .

Anyway, here is the statement. I think it adequately covers the points I want to make, and I cut it short so as not to get too involved. I did not make it a pronouncement on card burning. I appreciate Tom's reasons and think that in his case he did right as also Dave Miller probably did. I do not want to condemn his act at all. I just question whether it had all the desirable consequences. Certainly it got a very good press, and its impact will be positive in certain areas, no question about that. But did it also result in Dan's Superior's decision to ship him out? I don't know. In any case, I am certainly for Tom and Dave in the sense that I respect their action and its meaning and am even glad they did what they did. But I would not want to start a chain reaction among a lot of kids whose motives might be much less positive and clear.

Note that in my statement I have started out with the rumors that I have left, etc. This seems a convenient hook to hang the message on, since probably one reason why people think I am "out" is that I appear to be so active in various movements. Or at least some are getting that impression. It would be good to counteract that. It is one of the reasons why my Superiors would like me to pull out of the CPF, though they do not demand this and they are tolerating my decision to continue as sponsor.

. . . Well, I hope that we are out of the woods. Let me know how the statement strikes you and go ahead with the story as you see fit. I hope it will do some good for all concerned. Again, I am very sorry this mess arose. I was simply taken off guard when I ought to have been more attentive. I hope I have learned from it and I regret having caused trouble for all of you. Forgive me and pray for me, as I do you . . .

December 29, 1965

Your letter, statement, Christmas wishes and all reached me yesterday, no doubt held up while officially scanned, and then also it is the Christmas rush. But I was glad to get all of it. No objection to any slight change in the statement, no problems. I liked your covering letter. I am glad that if and when this is a story in the press we will both have contributed something and it will be for the benefit of CPF and also a churchly act—wherever two or three are gathered together in my Name . . . etc. So everything has worked out fine so far.

As a matter of fact I have finished quite a long commentary on the Constitution on the Church in the World. Had to do it for Burns Oates, they are bringing out the peace part of *Seeds of Destruction* only, in England, and this needed to go with it. When I get a mimeo I'll send it along . . . I think the Constitution is great, but the English translation is abominable, murky, heavy, it stupefies the reader, is not the language of modern man, etc.

I am very glad you are going to do something about this. This is crucially important. Here the Church has spoken as clearly and as authoritatively as one would want, and it is an obvious apostolic duty of everyone to get down to work and interpret and apply the Constitution. Obviously, the Hannans and Spellmans are not going to do much with the parts that have any bite and call for any substantial change of thought. This is a big job of the CPF in the Church of America: it is what you are called to do now. I think for one thing you ought to publish something: perhaps a collection of comments and statements from bishops and theologians. I'd be glad to do a leaflet which you could mimeograph or anything you like, simply spelling out the Council teaching on war. And when you get my long commentary, you can use it insofar as you don't conflict with any magazine who might need it first (I have already mentioned it to *Continuum*) . . . The commentary goes over the whole Constitution and stresses the basic principles, personalism and the unity of the human family, on which the whole thing is built up.

You want to get to the colleges, the seminaries and the clergy, and maybe you will need three separate approaches. I am not too smart about all that, so I won't suggest anything. You will know. I am personally convinced that this is the big chance for CPF to really do something important for the Church. Much more important than *CW* can do. I mean it. I share your immense respect for *CW* and its prophetic quality, but precisely because it is prophetic it remains more or less a symbol that everyone admires and stays away from. Your more colorless and less dramatic job is apostolic: simply reaching a lot of people and helping them to change their minds. You will at this present juncture be much more likely to have a deep transforming effect on the American Catholic Church than the *CW* ever will, if you use your opportunity. I think you need to get all your priests on the job in their milieux. The thing about this particular task is that it is not in the least ambiguous, it is straight teaching of the Church which everybody is bound to listen to or else. Of course there will be all kinds of attempts at evasive interpretation. I think your job is in this case simply to get the Constitution across, not even worrying about whether or not it gets CPF better known and so on. Just get people thinking in terms of that Constitution. That alone will be enough to justify any one man's existence in this life. Any help I can give, I will gladly give, within my limitations.

An important point in your letter: the question of "provocative" witness. That calls for clarification, I think. Maybe I did not use the right word. Here is what I mean by it.

1. By provocative actions I mean actions that have an aggressive, challenging nature *over and above* the simple question of conscience that is involved. For that reason I do not consider Jaegerstaetter's refusal of military service provocative. It was straight business: a refusal to commit a crime. Naturally this had an aspect that could not help but be regarded as "provocative," but this did not flow from the essential nature of the act. It did not have a provocative character and intention. Also I would

say that the Peace March in Washington in November, from what I heard about it, was not in any sense provocative, though it was a determined statement against the war in Vietnam.

2. Certainly there must be some provocative witness, especially now in a serious moral situation. I have changed my view of the draft-card burning in the last weeks since only now am I fully informed. Before I had no idea of the existence of the law that one had to carry the card, etc. I thought that the burning was just a protest against the draft law as such. It is much more easy to see that the law about having to have that card is unjust and repressive, and aimed at silencing protest. The law itself is an example of provocative use of authority. It is a challenge, and if someone takes up the challenge, that is understandable. In this sense I think the card burning was right, and I would go along with it in the case of one or two reasonable people. But I still would not (as you would not) back an irresponsible resort to card burning by a bunch of kids who want something to do to prove themselves.

3. I still do not think that the dramatic and provocative type of witness is what we most need now, in the sphere of Catholic peace witness. On the contrary, I think what we need is massive and undramatic apostolic work to clarify the Church's teaching and get it thoroughly known. In this I think we should avoid as far as possible any dramatization of conflict between conservatives and liberals, subjects and Superiors, and so on. The more we can work along on the assumption that the whole Church is united (until someone *provocatively* proves otherwise) the better chance we have of getting this Constitution understood, and making the first step toward an abolition of war or a renunciation of the war mentality by everyone. The job is titanic, and I think a few dramatic demonstrations that simply get people excited will not do much to start it, at this point.

At the moment, you know it better than I, the country is full of sincere people who are honestly bothered by the killing in Vietnam and cannot see it as a just war, yet cannot identify themselves with a specifically pacifist protest. These people are morally in no-man's-land, under pressure from both extremes. These are the ones who need help in articulating their objections in terms of the Church's teachings. I think they must be reached in such a way that their refusal to be identified as pacifists is fully respected, above all because the Constitution's position is simply Catholic, and nothing else. No further label is required. People should understand this first of all. The next thing is I think to begin a study of the pervasive violence that is everywhere in our thinking. This is the thing that I think is most dangerous, and humanly speaking I think it makes one almost despair of this nation being a peaceful one: we are a nation addicted to images of violence, brutality, sadism, self-affirmation by arrogance, aggression, and so on. That is another reason why the "provocative" is ambiguous as soon as it gets into such a context. On the other hand, behind all this aggressiveness is fear. Once these people are sure they are not being attacked, undermined and ruined, they are willing to listen to reason. The job is to get a hearing, a real hearing.

. . . God bless all of you, and peace be in your hearts anyway. Ping Ferry seems gloomy about the war outlook. I don't have much of a picture of Vietnam except diffuse horror and inhumanity: but the sinister thing is that both the Chinese and the Pentagon concur in wanting this crime to continue without hindrance, and the Chinese for their part are making a great point of brave little Vietnam doing it by herself, which is pretty sad. If only somewhere there were a government one could really respect. I see no hope from that quarter. The Church is really in a position to do something now. So let's trust and do what we can. God bless you again.

Jim Douglass is moving out to British Columbia and will write a book on non-violence.

January 17, 1966

I want to get this off to you before our retreat starts tomorrow. The pamphlet for objectors is very good I think, makes good use of the Council Constitution. The sensitive spot is that on non-cooperation. I think you should go over that paragraph carefully. As it stands, there is nothing to enlighten the average priest for instance about the legitimacy of such a position from the Catholic viewpoint. I think specifically Catholic arguments should be stated somehow. It should be stated clearly that non-cooperation with a law that one considers unjust is legitimate; and reasons why the selective service law might seem to some an unjust law. The way you state them, the reasons are very vague. On the other hand it is hard to go into details. Perhaps the one sentence that counts is the one where it says that the law does not really provide effectively for different forms of objection. I think there it should be stated clearly that: "The selective service law as it now stands was framed with members of the traditional 'Peace Churches' in view, that is to say for those who believe, as part of their religion, that all war is always immoral. Hence it fails to provide for those who discriminate between just and unjust wars, as many Catholic objectors do." Something like that. Of course you may have other cases in mind. I think that particular paragraph ought to be quite clear, anyway. Your next sentence, however, doesn't fit in with what I just said: I guess there are a lot of angles. You were probably thinking of the non-religious objectors.

Here is a piece ["Blessed Are the Meek"] I wrote for Hildegard Goss-Mayr . . .

I have confusing reports about Johnson's peace offensive. Some good, some not. In any case, I hope something may come of it, though it appears nothing will. Personally I think that in his own way he is quite sincere, but that the situation is too big for him to handle. Besides, I think the

Chinese really want the war to go on, and as a result neither side can get far enough toward the middle to have a meeting of minds. It will be tragic if this fails, because then the Pentagon boys will surely run away with the game. And God knows what may come of it . . .

Is Dan [Berrigan] back yet? Probably nothing will stop him when he does get back.

On February 15 Forest wrote that he was in a bleak mood; no one seemed to be listening to CPF. "I feel like an ant climbing a cliff, and even worse, for in the distance there seems to be an avalanche . . . Perhaps you have some thoughts that would help?"

February 21, 1966

Thanks for the letter and for the awful, and illuminating, enclosure. I can well understand your sense of desperation. And the "bleak mood." And also I am glad that you wrote about it. As you say, there are no clear answers, and you can guess that I don't have magic solutions for bleak moods: if I did I would use them on my own which are habitually pretty bleak too. But that is just part of this particular life and I don't expect much else.

Actually, I would say one thing that probably accounts for your feelings, besides all the objective and obvious reasons, you are doubtless tired. I don't know whether you are physically tired or not but you have certainly been pouring your emotional and psychic energy into the CPF and all that it stands for, and you have been sustained by hopes that are now giving out. Hence the reaction. Well, the first thing is that you have to go through this kind of reaction periodically, learn to expect it and cope with it when it comes, don't do things that precipitate it, without necessity (you will always have to).

And then this: do not depend on the hope of results. When you are doing the sort of work you have taken on, essentially an apostolic work, you may have to face the fact that your work will be apparently worthless and even achieve no result at all, if not perhaps results opposite to what you expect. As you get used to this idea you start more and more to concentrate not on the results but on the value, the rightness, the truth of the work itself. And there too a great deal has to be gone through, as gradually you struggle less and less for an idea and more and more for specific people. The range tends to narrow down, but it gets much more real. In the end, as you yourself mention in passing, it is the reality of personal relationships that saves everything.

You are fed up with words, and I don't blame you. I am nauseated by them sometimes. I am also, to tell the truth, nauseated with ideals and with causes. This sounds like heresy, but I think you will understand what I mean. It is so easy to get engrossed with ideas and slogans and myths that in the end one is left holding the bag, empty, with no trace of meaning left in it. And then the temptation is to yell louder than ever in order to make the meaning be there again by magic. Going through this kind of reaction helps you to guard against this. Your system is complaining of too much verbalizing, and it is right.

This country is SICK, man. It is one of the sickest things that has happened. People are fed on myths, they are stuffed up to the eyes with illusions. They CAN'T think straight. They have a modicum of good will, and some of them have a whole lot of it, but with the mental bombardment everybody lives under, it is just not possible to see straight, no matter where you are looking. The average everyday "Catlick" is probably in worse shape than a lot of others. He has in his head a few principles of faith which lend no coherence whatever to his life. No one has ever sought any coherence from him or given him the idea that he needed any. All he has been asked to do has been to measure up to a few simple notions about sexual morality (which he may or may not quite make, but anyway he knows where he stands—or falls on his face) and he has been taught that the cross and sacrifice in his life mean in practice going off to war every twenty years or so. He has done this with exemplary, unquestioning generosity, and has reaped the results: a corresponding brutalization, which is not his fault and which he thinks has something to do with being a real human being. In this whole area of war and peace, no matter what the Council may have said about it the average layman and the average priest are all alike conditioned by this mentality. Furthermore, when it is a question of a kind of remote box score of casualties which gives meaning to life each day, they no longer think of the casualties as people, it is just a score. Also they don't want to think of them as people, they want *casualties*, they want somebody to get it, because they have been brutalized and this is a fully legitimate way of indulging the brutality that has been engendered in them. It is not only for country, it is even for God.

You can be as indignant as you like about this: and it is sickening, but being indignant has its disadvantages. It gets you into the same damn-fool game. Take the myth of "getting results." What is the driving power behind the massive stupidity in Vietnam, with its huge expense and its absurd effects? It is the *obsession* of the American mind with the myth of know-how, and with the capacity to be omnipotent. Once this is questioned, we will go to any lengths, ANY lengths to resolve the doubt that has thus been raised in our minds. The whole cockeyed American myth is at stake in Vietnam and what is happening to it is obvious, it is tearing itself into little shreds and the nation is half nuts in consequence. The national identity is going slowly down the drain in VN and a lot of terrible things are happening in the process. We are learning how bestial and how incredible are the real components of that myth. Vietnam is the psychoanalysis of the U.S. I wonder if the nation can come out of it and survive. I have a hunch we might be able to. But your stresses and strains, mine, Dan's, all of them, are all part of this same syndrome, and it is extremely irritating and disturbing to find oneself, like it or not, involved in the national madness. The fact that you and I and our type have a special answer which runs counter to that of the majority seems at first to make us sane, but does it really? Does it save us from being part of the same damn mess? Obviously not. Theoretically we understand that, but in fact our hearts will not admit it, and we are trying to prove to ourselves that (a) we at least are sane decent people, (b) sanity and decency are such that *our* sanity and decency ought to influence everybody else. And there is something to this, I am not preaching a complete anomie. Yet the others think the same way about themselves.

In a word, you have said a lot of good things, you have got a lot of ideas across, it has perhaps caused some good reactions among the bad and what has it achieved in terms of the whole national picture: precious little. The CPF is not going to stop the war in Vietnam, and it is not even going to cause very many Catholics to think differently about war and peace. It is simply going to become another image among images, in the minds of most Catholics, something around which are centered some vague emotional reactions, for or against. Nevertheless, you will probably, if you continue as you do, *begin* the laborious job of changing the national mind and opening up the national conscience. How far will you get? God alone knows. All that you and I can ever hope for in terms of visible results is that we will have perhaps contributed *something* to a clarification of Christian truth in this society, and as a result a *few* people may have got straight about some things and opened up to the grace of God and made some sense out of their lives, helping a few more to do the same. As for the big results, these are not in your hands or mine, but they can suddenly happen, and we can share in them: but there is no point in building our lives on this personal satisfaction, which may be denied us and which after all is not that important.

So the next step in the process is for you to see that your own thinking about what you are doing is crucially important. You are probably striving to build yourself an identity in your work and your witness. You are using it so to speak to protect yourself against nothingness, annihilation. That is not the right use of your work. All the good that you will do will come not from you but from the fact that you have allowed yourself, in the obedience of faith, to be used by God's love. Think of this more and gradually you will be free from the need to prove yourself, and you can be more open to the power that will work through you without your knowing it.

The great thing after all is to live, not to pour out your life in the service of a myth: and we turn the best things into myths. If you can get free from the domination of causes and just serve Christ's truth, you will be able to do more and will be less crushed by the inevitable disappointments. Because I see nothing whatever in sight but much disappointment, frustration, and confusion. I hope we can avoid a world war: but do we deserve to? I am not thinking so much of ourselves and this country but of all the people who would be killed who never heard of New York and of the U.S.A. even, perhaps. It is a pity that they should have to pay for our stupidity and our sins.

The real hope, then, is not in something we think we can do, but in God who is making something good out of it in some way we cannot see. If we can do His will, we will be helping in this process. But we will not necessarily know all about it beforehand.

I got a letter from Dan in Argentina and he may be back in New York by the time you get this. He expects to be home right at the beginning of March anyway. I hope he got the letter I wrote him in Quito. I don't think really he has lost much by being down there, though this was a rough time for him to have to go. He will get back in a better position than ever, I think. Certainly he has gained a lot of sympathy and attention from this business and people will be very ready to listen to him. He will meet opposition, but I think he will have a lot of effect.

. . . Returning to the idea of pacifist: I think the word is *useless* for our purposes. It does not in the least describe what CPF is trying to do, it seems to me, and only gives a false impression. To speak of pacifism today gives people an excuse for bellicism: it implies that there is an alternative. One can be a pacifist or a bellicist. But there is no alternative, and it is not a question of some ethical ideal or some cause, but as you say of the plain, basic human justice, the old natural law . . .

. . . Can you give me Dave Miller's address? I ought to write to the poor guy. And I could send him stuff to read, anyway. Has he been sent off to the penitentiary? Naturally I am keeping Tom's trial in my thoughts and prayers.

May 27, 1966

I am shocked to hear of the violent death of Addison Wilkins [shot to death in Richmond, Virginia, because he wore a peace button and was opposed to the Vietnam war] but from your account he is a martyr in the cause of peace and probably can do better praying for us than we can praying for him. Still I will offer my Mass for the repose of his soul tomorrow, the Vigil of Pentecost. And will pray for all of you, for we all need the Gift of the Spirit more than ever today. Tomorrow John Heidbrink is to stop by here with a Buddhist from Vietnam [Thich Nhat Hanh]. Am looking forward to it.

September 21, 1966

It was rather an eerie experience a few weeks ago to receive a Vietnamese translation of *Seeds of Contemplation* and a request to write a preface for the Viet translation of *No Man Is an Island*. The whole thing brings home the futility of so-called spiritual literature in this day and age. Who is going to have time for pious meditations with the whole place getting showered in napalm? Maybe someone in a plush apartment in Saigon . . . I tried to say something, and to say it non-politically. Don't know if it makes any sense. I was too embarrassed. I guess being embarrassed is a luxury too. Everything is. Life is.

Did you ever see the "Freedom Songs"? This singer [Robert Williams] is probably going to present them in Boston this fall. He owns the songs and they are for a foundation for African students. I have never met him but he sounds like a sweet and serious guy. Is originally from Kentucky.

Every once in a while someone writes me about being a CO and I refer them to the CPF . . .

November 16, 1966

. . . About "Blessed Are the Meek": certainly you can publish it but I thought FOR was going to. The magazine that is supposed to have published it is *Cowley* at Cambridge, Mass. Fr. Wesinger is the man to contact.

Sure you can sell drawings if you can sell them and if anyone will buy them. The ones you have aren't so hot, though. I'll sign a few if you like but I may send some other better ones. I'll see what I can dig out. Also have to share them out with a magazine in Venezuela. But let me say at once I would be utterly delighted to have Sr. Corita design the booklet of "The Meek." Also to foot the bill I might try to twist Abbot's arm and get us to put a few pennies in the kitty. After all, we are stinking rich, we ought to do something for peace . . .

You are right, Jim, about all the "hate LBJ" stuff. The thing this Vietnam war is proving is that this whole country is rotten with violence and hate and frustration and this means the peaceniks as much as anybody else. We just don't know what peace and love *mean*. The only ones who have really done anything are Martin Luther King and those who worked so hard at it in the South—and a few others who have tried here and there in various ways and for various causes. And now that is being discredited. Of course Dorothy is there to remind us with her unfailing wisdom what it is all about too.

At the same time, the more I think about the card burning the more I think that you, Tom, are utterly right before God. I don't think that a lot more card burnings will do anything, but this business of drafting kids to get killed in a war to inflate Johnson's political ego and power is simply tragic and disgusting: to appeal to the idea of "defending one's country" in such a case is pure charlatanism . . .

November 21, 1966

Here is a collection of shapes, powers, flying beasts, cave animals, bloodstains, angelic mistakes, etc., that can perhaps have some visual effect on the local bisons. I suggest selling them for around ten bucks apiece to the art lovers who can get them fixed up in any way they please, quantity not quality and so on. I have signed them but that isn't fair because the buyer should not be dictated to in any way as to which way he wants the shape to be up. Maybe this will bring in a few pennies to print the Meek . . .

February 13, 1967

It is true, I do have files and I do keep copies of letters. But I can never find anything in the files, and I don't know what happens to the copies of letters. I guess my head is so addled with Zen and Sufism that I have totally lapsed into inefficiency, and am rapidly becoming a backward nation if not a primitive race, a Bushman from the word go, muttering incantations to get the fleas out of my whiskers, a vanishing American who has fallen into the mythical East as into a deep dark hole . . .

. . . Can you please give me John Heidbrink's address? If I do happen to rob a bank or something, I will want to send the money quick before it burns a hole in my hand. At best it will probably buy a few lollipops for those pretty kids.

Tom sent a wire that A.J. [Muste] died. I was able to get him in my Mass today and will offer the Mass for him Wednesday. God rest his soul: a great and saintly old guy and I am happy to have had the privilege of meeting him: thanks to you . . .

February 22, 1967

Here is mere raw material for a statement [that CPF was preparing, calling for aid for the war victims in Vietnam], nothing more. It is a hasty first draft, not even corrected. I will go over it and have one of the kids mimeograph a corrected version and I will send you a batch of them in a few days, maybe a week or more. Meanwhile you can think of this one and use it to work on, drafting something better for yourself.

The reason why I am getting this off now is that tomorrow I go into the hospital for an operation and I will be out of commission for a while. Nothing serious, but since it is bursitis of the elbow I may not be able to type for a while. We'll see. In any case I want to get something to you while I still can . . .

February 23, 1967

One more note before I take off for the hospital. I have been through (rapidly) the dossier you sent about CPF. A lot of good ideas there. What is most encouraging is the evidence of real interest. I am convinced that now is the time for CPF to really catch on if it is going to. This is the kairos. It must not be missed. This is the moment to connect with the people all over the place who are potentially interested and get them doing something.

Get them specifically talking and acting where they are, and explaining the fundamental of a Catholic peace movement in the simplest and most universal terms: *Pacem in Terris*, the Council on war, Jaegerstaetter, Pope Paul, etc.

A good newsletter is most important. The kind of exchange you sent out is fine: the newsletter should give a good proportion of space to exchange (until it gets to be a pure logjam) (then control it and use only what keeps things moving). In the CPF everyone should feel that his initiative and ideas mean something—and be willing also to adjust them to the movement and growth in the ideas of others.

From the "education" viewpoint: there ought to be a very clear, simple history of the growth of violence in the modern world, and the reply of non-violence. Objective, not preachy, with the facts and with understanding (VG showing how the U.S. exercises *violence* on nations it claims to be helping—hence the petty dictators, the opposition of the people, and why the U.S. is hated). But above all fair, overall picture: the big powers exercise intolerable violent control over everyone else, or try to. And the facts, in clear schematic form, about the death camps, about World War II, both Coventry and Dresden—about the bomb, about napalm, etc., in Vietnam, about the development of CB weapons, etc. etc.

And then the moral issue spelled out: this is a world in which power rules by indiscriminate nihilistic terror and depends on the cooperation of "ordinary decent people" to do it, and the "ordinary decent people" come through with flying colors, giving their docility and even their lives, in order that brutality may continue and grow worse—threatening the survival of the human race itself.

I don't know who could do this, I could try my hand at part of it, but I don't have material here. Maybe when I get back from hospital, I'll try an outline at least. FOR ought to have a lot of factual material on file.

But whatever you put out it has got to be readable stuff. I see a lot of these newsletters that one just does not even bother to look at. The appearance of the page is enough to put you off . . .

In his letter of October 1966 Forest had indicated that after nearly two years of discussion he and Jean were seriously considering separation because of vocational incompatibility. In April 1967 they were quietly divorced, with the hope of possibly getting the marriage annulled. On May 14, 1967, John Heidbrink witnessed the marriage of Jim Forest and Linda Henry. Dorothy Day opposed the wedding and felt that Jim had forfeited his right to continue as head of the Catholic Peace Fellowship. It was several months before Jim and Dorothy were again reconciled.

March 21, 1967

Your letter about Dorothy's offer to resign as sponsor has waited ten days for an answer. I want to get to it finally, sorry for the delay. I have been held up by trips to doctors and by a long visit of an old friend. When visitors come here all work stops for me: not possible to combine the two.

The problem is terribly difficult. Naturally I cannot hope to disentangle most of it, as I do not know the facts. This is the first I heard of any special problem at all, though I knew you and Jean had broken up.

My first thought was perhaps an ironic one. I was reminded immediately of my own attempt to resign when Roger burned himself up outside the UN. At that time I think Dorothy was quite angry with me. Yet I think the problem of what others interpret as suicide is on a par with the problem of what others interpret as "immorality." I might say once that I do not in any way judge your relationship with Linda, and I think I take a much more flexible view of it than Dorothy does, though I am no "underground priest." In other words I am much more prepared to concede that before God you are perhaps doing no real moral wrong. But as I say, God alone knows that, and there will still be many who will judge otherwise.

Dorothy is a person of great integrity and consistency and this hits one between the eyes in the way she sums it up, hard as it may be. I can see where she is in a sense quite right in demanding a like consistency from others who act as "Catholics" formally and explicitly in the eyes of the whole world. Perhaps it would be desirable for everyone to be as she would desire, and as the traditional Church position would demand. Yet we have to face the fact that this inflexible position is called into question not just by mavericks and radicals: there are enormously serious unsolved questions being debated in the Church, especially in the area of marriage, by the most reputable theologians, and the situation is such first that everyone outside the Church is quite aware of it, and second that it is no longer completely possible and fair to impose the old inflexible (though I think better and truer) position as a matter of strict obligation on everyone without further appeal. At least *in foro interno* (forgive the old lingo). On the other hand, I do agree with her that quite apart from the question of sin, it would be better for the head of the Catholic Peace Fellowship to have made the kind of sacrifice she speaks of, and that a lot of us have to make in one way or another.

Nevertheless, all that having been said, I do not think that it is quite fair of her to make it an either/or. Either you resign or her name drops from the list of sponsors—or you give up Linda. In the new situation where many might be willing to concede that you were not in the wrong and when scandal is not given (possibly) in the way it once would have been, I don't think it is fully just to be so categorical. On the other hand, there is so much I do not know about the case that I offer this opinion only with some hesitation. There is so much more to it, and once again I realize that my isolation makes it impossible for me to see clearly. One thing I will say: now I am talking in terms of the traditional and accepted theology which Dorothy herself must accept. IF there is some way you can continue living with Linda, in which, according to the judgment of a reputable authority—even one with whom Dorothy does not necessarily agree—you are not "in sin" (and here the boundaries may be far wider than Dorothy herself would impose), you preserve every right to maintain your position and she does not have any right to question it, except perhaps insofar as "appearances" may need to be "saved" and there I assume she is no more intolerant than any other normal person.

In other words the Church grants you the right to follow your conscience as formed with the approval of a reputable theological opinion or arbiter. This is not new, this is *old*. No one can question it. It is of course quite possible that the situation cannot be saved in this way.

If not, I still think Dorothy should regard it more as your own personal business, be content to offer you charitable advice, and stop short of withdrawing her name from the list of sponsors. But that is just my opinion.

It might, ideally speaking, be better for you to resign: but in practice if this means the collapse of the CPF, which it well might, then you should not do so. Let her withdraw her name if she must. But this in turn will be a grave blow.

So on this practical level it turns out to be one very nice mess. If in the end it were possible for you to consider the thing in terms of sacrifice, this of course would be ideal and admirable. I do not urge this on you, certainly not as an obligation. I only say that in the abstract, and in terms of Catholic tradition and the lives of the saints, this is theoretically "the best." Yet I simply cannot evade the fact that this "best" is very much under fire today from people whom I cannot dismiss as morally irresponsible.

My own monastic vocation is constantly being called into question on these grounds, and if I hold on to it, which I certainly do, it is no longer on the grounds that it is "best" but on more existential grounds: "It may be absurd, I may not understand it, it may look like madness in the eyes of all these cats, but it happens to be what I am called to, and this is what I am going to do."

Ultimately, I think it is on this level that all our decisions have to be made today. What does God ask of ME?

So I pray that you may see what God is asking of you, really and truly, and that he may give you the strength to do just that, as best you can. Pray for me too, Jim. I hate to see anyone in such a bind. God love you. Happy Easter. My love to both you and Linda whom I don't know.

June 17, 1967

. . . Thanks for your last letter. I am glad everything went off all right, and I was with you in spirit on Pentecost which was a big day down here as my old friend Dan Walsh was suddenly ordained, in his sixties, with all sorts of dispensations, and there was a lot of celebrating. In fact I celebrated on too much champagne, which is a thing a Trappist rarely gets to do, but I did a very thorough job. At one point in the afternoon I remember looking up and focusing rather uncertainly upon four faces of nuns sitting in a row looking at me in a state of complete scandal and shock. Another pillar of the Church had fallen.

I do hope everything is forgotten, with Dorothy and so on. Thinking back to my letter, I realize how inadequate it was and in any case I had only the very vaguest notion of what was happening. I tried to say things that even Dorothy would have to accept. I hope everything is now fixed up and that you are at peace and that God's blessing is with you both— and that people will mind their own business in the future.

Here it is getting good and hot now. A rough time of year, when it is hard to get much work done. But I am as usual pretty busy. The Abbot is now away but I get vague storm warnings that when he gets back I am going to be in trouble. Something about the Apostolic Delegate objecting to my activities. We'll see. I couldn't care less. Except it is a little stupid being involved in this elaborate organization that constantly trumpets its successes and advances, but takes one step forward and one step back— if not two. Our mail was uncensored for about six months but I now hear that it will be opened for inspection again . . .

. . . I am getting some idea of the extreme complexity and nastiness of the Near East thing from friends in France who know a lot about the Moslems. If anyone thinks anything has been settled they are crazy. It is a really tragic business. And as usual this country looks at it entirely in a rose-colored one-dimensional view. Bad as Vietnam is, the Near East situation worries me as much more dangerous for everybody. But maybe there is time . . .

June 26, 1967

Many thanks for the proof of the cover [of the pamphlet "Blessed Are the Meek"]. Very handsome indeed: wonderful structural quality, very rich, very alive: admirable. It is good to look at it just in black and white to get that particular quality out of it. The color too will be great, I am sure. I am glad the pamphlet is on the way and that it will not cost too much.

One thing I have been meaning to write about, and keep forgetting,

I want a *dedication* somewhere, wherever it can be fitted in, in the front. Is there a little spot, where you might put: For Joan Baez. Joan was down here last December and I had a good talk with her, like her very much, as does everybody (except creeps like Al Capp). Could you fit that in? I hope so.

I like the "monks" letterhead, and would love to have a few more. I'd be grateful to Linda (Hi, Linda!). Only thing is I wonder if the monks are moving. Everything I do gives me scruples about being identified with this stupid rhinocerotic outfit that charges backwards into the jungle with portentous snuffling and then busts out of the canebrake with a roar in the most unlikely places. Still, the letterhead will I think be read as it ought to be read, and I won't be identified, I hope, with Gethsemani farms. Thus I think it will help my morale. I could use a few and will enjoy them: like I have struck up a contact with some kids on the Coast who are running what they consider to be an "underground paper" and who have good taste. They will enjoy it.

One of our latest one step forward, two steps backward moves: censorship of mail was called off in December here, and has been called back on again. I understand. Just waiting for the announcement and for the loss of several interesting correspondents . . . I guess it means my being cut off from the NAPR (priest-marrying outfit), of which I was on board of advisors in a purely decorative capacity.

Love to you and Linda and to everyone.

Enclosed with the following letter, addressed to Linda, Tom sent a picture of himself for her and Jim.

November 18, 1967

Many thanks for the letter and the cards. The cards are handsome and stark, and I'll probably shout for some more as Christmas draws near . . .

In return I am sending you a photograph of a supernatural event such as (of course) occurs around here at every moment and even more frequently than that. In between the moments. You have to duck all the time to keep from being brained by a supernatural event. I also have a picture of Meher Baba which says "Meher Baba loves you" but I can't find it. Probably swiped by some desperate soul who needs to be loved by Meher Baba. Otherwise I would have sent it. It is frightening. Looks like Stalin.

Thank Jim for his letter too. And as for you not being able to last through one of the local anti-liturgies, I would say that shows you are a good Christian . . .

December 20, 1967

I can't find a copy of *Peace in a Post-Christian Era*. If I do I'll send one. Essentially the same material is in the peace section of *Seeds of Destruction*.

Also I haven't replied yet about Dan's telegram to the Vatican. Maybe it is too late. I've lost the card you sent.

I hesitated because I wanted to think over the business of running to Father figure for condemnation of bully in White House. And also because of U.S. allergy of Papal interference. There are angles that I am not thoroughly at home with.

However, if it is not too late, sign me on with a YES. But it is probably too late by now. I am sorry to have let it go. I have been terribly busy and it just got out of sight for a couple of weeks. At one point (as I told Tom) I had decided on no, but I changed my mind again. Anyway I am afraid the telegram won't get anywhere and I don't think there is much chance of the Pope doing anything—or of it making any difference if he did . . .

December 31, 1967

Just a hasty note. I have written a letter for Gary [a C.O.], enclosed. Edit it as you see fit. I think the monastery ought to contribute something and I'll try to hit the retired Abbot for some dough: he is still running the place until the election which will be in a couple of weeks. For heaven's sake pray. There are some local conservatives who might conceivably get it: extremely rigid, unimaginative people, some going all the way over close to John Birch Soc. views. Their man is a mindless, honest and narrow character who understands nothing much about what is happening but has a strong will and an inclination to ulcers. There are fortunately others who are quite good, but nobody with a really broad view of everything. As for me, I have made it clear that I will never under any circumstances accept an abbatial election, to the point where some people feel that I have insulted the community. In any event, my ship is sunk and lies peacefully on the bottom of the ocean, even before the fleet sets sail.

Don't know what the future holds in store for me. I might be transferred to the monastery in Chile, and that would be quite OK with me—I tried several times to get there anyhow and always got refused. I could be a hermit there in the Andes and help out slightly with classes, etc.

Linda: thanks for the extra cards and for everything, letter, all. I keep you both in my prayers. If I'm still around here later in the year why not both get down this way, if you can!?

That's all for the moment. Happy New Year. Joy and peace in the Lord.

February 27, 1968

I received your two telegrams. Funny part of it was that I got the second one first. They phoned it in from Bardstown and did not phone the first which I received only by mail. So I learned you [and Thich Nhat Hanh] were not coming before I heard that you were . . .

Very sorry not to see you and Nhat. I have thought often of both, especially Nhat, knew vaguely he was around. I still hope he can come down and give a couple of talks on Buddhism.

One other thing I have meant to write about: I am dedicating my new book *Faith and Violence* to you and Phil Berrigan. Before, it was to Dan and Phil, then I suddenly remembered that I had just dedicated a pamphlet on Camus to Dan. It should be out any day—the pamphlet. The book is due in summer sometime.

Our new Abbot is a very good understanding young guy, but he clearly will not let me go out and speak in public which is all right with me. I think it would be foolish. I hope he will be more liberal about other (incognito) traveling and he assures me I'll get down to our monastery in Chile at least briefly sometime. To teach a course or something, and maybe see a little of Latin America. Nothing is certain yet.

Meanwhile I'm digging in for Lent. If you think of coming down, let's plan it sometime after Lent—and let me know ahead because I have one or two things scheduled. But I hope you can make it with Nhat.

April 6, 1968

Sorry I didn't send *Monks Pond* before. Am doing so now. I have had to put it together myself and haven't had time. Many interruptions. It's nice to have visits but they throw everything off, work gets messed up and behind and then I can't catch up and everything goes wrong. Last week especially busy and fouled up . . .

Terrible about Martin Luther King [assassinated April 4]. But I guess it was expected. I almost have the feeling he *wanted* it: even get the temptation to think that in a kind of desperation he realized that martyrdom was the most efficacious thing left for him. That the March wouldn't work.

As to Johnson I don't trust his withdrawal at all. I think it's another gimmick in his power struggle. I think he is totally dedicated to power for himself and his bunch.

July 20, 1968

Well, I was on the road for a while and will be on the road again in a while. Right now I'm trying to get my mind together and catch up on accumulated back work. When I got back here had meetings with sisters, visits of lots of people like Lax, and haven't been able to do much.

About the preface to the WRL Gandhi book calendar.

It is obviously the sort of thing I'd like to do. But I have had to make up my mind on this business of prefaces. In the last couple of years I have done so much in the way of prefaces, reviews, blurbs—including five or six introductions to or contributions to books that never even appeared—that I have simply had to wise up and stop. I have just been dissipating my energies with this petty shotgun stuff, and I have to get back and concentrate on the work I am really supposed to be doing, which is creative work. What doth it profit a man to write all the prefaces in the world and suffer the loss of his poetry? And/or more fundamental statements.

So I'm sorry, I just can't do it. I have to add this to the other refusals I have been sending out lately. Also I've been getting lots of invitations to talk, which all have to be refused too.

Now for the main thing: can you please send me the address of the jail where Phil now is? And Tom too maybe? (Is he in or out?) Where's Dan? Out or in? Why do so many people all of a sudden become Trappists (at the expense of the federal govt.)? A flood of vocations, comparable perhaps to that which hit our monasteries in the early fifties.

Nice issue of the bulletin. Tell Tom I liked "Penny a Copy" very much. A fine job . . .

August 5, 1968

Steamy hot here now, and I have to try to catch up on some mail. All will have to be brief.

. . . *Monks Pond* II is out for some time and I'll have to get busy and send you a copy. III is now in the works and will be the best of the lot. IV will be the end of it. Putting the thing out has been great fun and a good experience but it has also meant a logjam and blocking of everything else, so I have to quit. Money not really needed. Contributions have helped to make the thing seem serious in the eyes of our accountant, that's all. We're in the clear now anyhow.

I don't think there is the slightest chance of my getting to N.Y., but thanks for the invitation. My goings-on and getting-around remain entirely monastic. If I get to some monastery in the East I might or might not stop off in N.Y. Trouble is I am so completely allergic to cities that I avoid them if I can.

I'd be interested in your piece on the spiritual roots of revolution. For my part—as usual I am half in touch and half out of it—I hear a lot of political talk about revolution coming in and it sounds highly irresponsible and calculated to do nothing but get a lot of people's heads knocked off for no purpose whatever. More and more I see the thing in terms of a kind of post-political eschatology which in any case I cannot articulate. Of course I know this would be most unacceptable to the people who are convinced they can get somewhere with direct action. To just up and say we are under God's judgment, well, I guess that doesn't cut ice with anyone. However, that's where we are. And maybe we're going to find out something about it.

From Redwoods, California
September? 1968

We are at the meeting at Redwoods in an atmosphere of love and peace. Thinking much of you and praying for you. Pray for us.

To Erich Fromm

Erich Fromm (1900–80), psychoanalyst, philosopher, and anthropologist, was born in Frankfurt, Germany. He received his Ph.D. in 1922 from the University of Heidelberg and was trained as a psychoanalyst in Berlin. In 1934 he left Nazi Germany and came to New York City. He taught at several universities there before becoming in 1951 professor of psychoanalysis at the National University of Mexico, Cuernavaca. While he was teaching in Mexico, he came to his New York City office for two months each year.

One of his chief concerns was the adjustment of individuals to society. Departing from the Freudian view that one's social character was determined by instinct, Fromm followed the lead of Karl Marx (for whom he had profound respect and who he felt was misunderstood) in believing that cultural factors are decisive in shaping individuals. Fromm was especially concerned with the estrangement of modern men and women and the fact that so many had lost any sense of meaning in life. His strong opposition to modern warfare resonated with Merton's view on this issue.

His concern for the dignity of the human person was strong and deep, though not in a theistic context. He acquiesced when Merton described him as "an atheistic mystic." Yet, in an interesting letter (December 8, 1954), he confessed that he was shocked by the blending of alleged religious teaching with the profoundly irreligious spirit of the modern business world. (He specifically referred to what was being done by Billy Graham, Dr. Norman Vincent Peale, and Bishop Fulton J. Sheen.) Fromm's works include Escape from Freedom *(1941),* Man for Himself *(1947),* Psychoanalysis and Religion *(1950),* The Sane Society *(1955),* May Man Prevail *(1961),* War Within Man *(1963),* You Shall Be as Gods *(1966). The letters exchanged by Erich Fromm and Thomas Merton are fine examples of true dialogue and an honest meeting of minds despite the existence of fundamental differences.*

October 2, 1954

Some time ago when I was reading your *Psychoanalysis and Religion* I thought I would write you a letter. Now that I am in the middle of *Man for Himself* and am hoping to get *Escape from Freedom*, I think I shall put a few of my thoughts on paper and send them to you.

The chief reason for my writing is that, since discovering Karen Horney, I have been reevaluating my originally rather premature judgment of psychoanalysis. Now that I am in contact with what is best in the field at the moment, I would like to say that I notice a profound agreement between the psychoanalyst and the Catholic priest on some very fundamental points. I believe that this agreement ought to be noticed and emphasized, because I feel that our two vocations in a sense complete and assist one another. I also feel that there is much in Christian tradition that fits in very well with the general tendency of writers like Horney and yourself.

The reason for this is that Christianity is fundamentally humanistic, in the sense that its chief task is to enable man to achieve his destiny, to find himself, to be himself: to be the person he is made to become. Man is supposed to be God's helper in the work of creating himself. *Dei adjutores sumus.* Salvation is no passive thing. Nor is it an absorption of man into a kind of nonentity before the face of God. It is the elevation and divinization of man's freedom. And the Christian life demands that man be fully conscious of his freedom and of the responsibility it implies. I am in full agreement with your basic thesis on the humanistic conscience. I also observe with satisfaction that you emphasize the mystical element in religion. In fact, Christian humanism and Christian mysticism coincide. "Where the Spirit of the Lord is, there is liberty."

At a time like the present, when over vast areas of the earth systems of thought and government are tending to the complete debasement of man's fundamental dignity as the image of God, it seems to me important that all who take to heart the value and the nobility of the human spirit should realize their solidarity with one another, and should be able to communicate with one another in every way, in spite of perhaps grave doctrinal divergences. I know indeed that in France Catholicism and psychoanalysis are not now considered to be in any way mutually exclusive. In fact there are priests who are practicing psychoanalysts—though this should not be regarded as normal. There are congresses in which the priest and the analyst join in giving papers and conducting discussions that further the spiritual life of Christians. I believe that there is an association of priests in this country interested in psychiatry, but I do not know any of them.

As spiritual director of some thirty monks in this Trappist monastery—monks in the crucial period of their formation, who have been in the monastery between two and six years—I fully realize the wisdom of what you have to say about types of conscience and modes of conscience formation and malformation. You can well realize that I run into all kinds of difficulties and problems, precisely where an "authoritarian" conscience is allowed to have its way. It is pitiful to see the harm that can be done in potentially fine monks by the pettiness and formalism they can get into as a result of making their whole life depend entirely on the approval of another.

If you have read the Rule of St. Benedict, you can realize that I seem to be faced with an insoluble problem. But I do not think the position is as bad as that. It is true that the Rule of St. Benedict presupposes a long period of formation in which the whole spiritual life is summed up in the two words "obedience" and "humility." I know that it is also true that men who are in your terminology "authoritarians" can wreak havoc on themselves and others by a narrow and absolute view of what St. Benedict means. Obedience for its own sake, humility for its own sake. However, familiar as I am with ancient monastic tradition, I am convinced that it is possible to take the true Benedictine idea just as it stands and make it the foundation of a life of spiritual freedom and "humanism" and "mysticism" in the best sense. I am sure that is what St. Benedict intended. The function of obedience, in his context, is not merely to bring the monk into submission to authority as if the authority were everything. It simply presupposes that in the beginning he does not know how to go about living the monastic life and needs to be told, and that the more he is willing to be open to suggestion and formation, the better off he will be. But if we consider the rule closely we find that the mature monk is a very capable and many-sided person, completely integrated, leading a life of freedom and joy under the guidance of the Holy Spirit rather than out of servile fear. In fact, servility is the exact opposite of the Christian and monastic spirit.

I think that in your treatment of obedience and authority you are perhaps too absolute—but this is quite natural, since you have in mind Nazi authoritarianism, than which I can think of nothing more abominable. But in the monastic life I think we are quite entitled to "escape" from certain responsibilities—those of worrying about how to plan meals, what to wear, when to get up, when to go to bed, how to plan our social life, etc.—in order to be free for something better.

Finally, on one point I think you are definitely wrong. I do not see how you can consider that mystical religion is indifferent on the question of the objective existence of God. Jnana yoga and perhaps Buddhism are more or less atheistic, but the majority of true mystics stand or fall with the existence or nonexistence of God. Besides there is, it seems to me, the absolute ontological impossibility of anything existing if God does not exist. However, I have argued on that point long and uselessly enough not to start it again. I think what you are really saying is that true mysticism does not know God after the manner of an object, and that is perfectly true. God is not experienced as an object outside ourselves, as "another being" capable of being enclosed in some human concept. Yet though

He be known as the source of our own being, He is still *das ganz Andere*. Surely you know Rudolf Otto's work. And do you think God was not real to the Prophets?

However, I did not write to emphasize our differences. I simply want to take this opportunity to express my appreciation of your work, and to thank you for the thoughts you have suggested, which have been of great value in my own work. I hope I can someday do the same for you.

March 18, 1955

Even though I am answering your letter at the earliest opportunity, I do not suppose that I can catch you in New York, although I believe it would be there that it would be most reasonable to reach you with my reaction to your declaration [statement on the Far East situation, prepared by the Committee for Reason].*

I distinguish in this declaration two main objectives, the one ethical and the other political. As regards the first, I feel that the blindness of men to the terrifying issue we have to face is one of the most discouraging possible signs for the future. At a time like this, fear has driven people so far into the confusion of mass-thinking that they no longer see anything except in a kind of dim dream. What a population of zombies we are! What can be expected of us?

It seems to me that the human race as a whole is on the verge of a crime that will be second to no other except the crucifixion of Christ: and it will, if it happens, be very much the same crime all over again. And then, as now, religious people are involved on the guilty side. What we are about to do is "destroy" God over again in His Image, the human race. It is to me a thing of plain evidence that any person who pretends to love God in this day, and who has lost his sense of the value of humanity, has also lost his sense of God without knowing it. I believe that we are facing the consequences of several centuries of more and more abstract thinking, more and more unreality in our grasp of values. We have reached such a condition that now we are unable to appreciate the meaning of being alive, of being able to think, to make decisions, to love. We have been trying for so long to turn ourselves into machines that we have finally succeeded. The logical consequence is to destroy everything.

It seems to me that there are no circumstances that can make atomic war legitimate. The axiom *non sunt facienda mala ut eveniant bona* (evil must not be done even for a good end) applies here more than ever

* *This statement urging opposition to war and work for peace was accompanied by a letter asking for signatures for the statement and advising that the statement would be published in a full-page ad in* The New York Times. *The statement was signed by Erich Fromm, John C. Bennett, and Norman Thomas.*

before. In such a position as ours, even the risk of atomic war cannot be legitimately taken because where an issue of this magnitude is before us, we have no right to risk disaster. We are obliged to take a safer course, and if we do not do so we will be responsible for grave evils, even though the disaster itself may not happen. The mere possibility has to be guarded against.

Therefore, I am entirely with you on the issue of atomic war. I am opposed to it with all the force of my conscience.

However, when it comes to signing the declaration, I find myself in the presence of difficulty. I know nothing whatever of the political situation because I am not informed at all. We never see a paper or a magazine, or hear a radio. Consequently I do not feel that I can commit myself to any public statement regarding political policy. Besides, even if I knew what it was all about, I would still be hampered by the fact that anything I say would register as coming from my monastery, my religious Order, and would involve others who might perhaps not agree entirely with my position. Finally, I believe my Superiors would probably discourage my signing a declaration anyway, because it has been their policy in the past to keep me out of all such things . . .

The liberal Catholic I would think of suggesting to you is Jacques Maritain, but he is not a priest. And here again I am rather at a loss. I do not really know very many priests well enough to call upon them for a thing like this—and I do not know precisely how they might react . . . I have heard that Bishop John Wright of Worcester, Mass., is a very straight-thinking and broad-minded sort of person, however, but I do not know him.

I shall be very interested to hear what comes of the declaration and I hope you will keep me informed. Even though I cannot sign, I am perfectly willing to let it be known (unofficially) that I am absolutely opposed to atomic war, and I don't mind you quoting anything I may have said on the subject, as long as it does not have an official look about it, and preferably not in print, although that is all right provided it is not, as I say, too "official"-looking. In other words I am certainly glad to have my personal attitude on the matter known, but I do not want to involve my monastery or my Order in anything that looks like a stand on some particular detail of political policy with regard, for instance, to China or Formosa.

No Man Is an Island is out now. I would be delighted to send you a copy if you have not already bought one . . . Are you publishing the lectures you mentioned? I mean on the development of religion? They sound very interesting. I still think you might be interested in my *Ascent to Truth* which might have something along the lines you mention. So I am sending you a copy, but it is rather dry reading in patches and badly put together . . .

September 12, 1955

I am about halfway through *The Sane Society* which I received some time ago. I am reading it with the greatest interest and profit, and taking my time, for I believe it to be your very best book. I thank you for having written it and for having been so kind as to send me an inscribed copy.

Once again I would like to tell you how closely I agree with your main conclusions, that I have read so far, and especially with your admirable analysis of man in our present society. The long passage about the Chicago suburb, in the section on anonymous authority, made my blood run cold. In a way that sort of thing is more terrible than Nazism, because it is so much more insidious. It is certainly what we are up against—everywhere. I am glad too that you are showing up the danger, so great now in America, of the psychiatrist becoming just another expert who helps industry to manipulate its employees.

I certainly agree with you that we ought to scrap the notion that mental health is merely a matter of adjustment to the existing society— to be adjusted to a society that is insane is not to be healthy. The trouble is that those who are not adjusted to it, even for the right reasons, have a rather hard time too . . . As a priest and a man dedicated to God in a monastery, I am bound to say that I am deeply worried by the falsity, the superficiality and the fundamental irreverence of what is so often hailed, nowadays, as a "return to God." People have resurrected a lot of "words about" God and a lot of concepts of religious things, but it sometimes seems to me that they—we—are not too anxious to find the Living God. At the foot of the mountain, we prefer our golden calf but we do not even have the honesty to invite a Moses to ascend for us into the smoke and communicate with God and receive His messages. I think, incidentally, that your page on idolatry (121) is a most acute observation, along the lines that you have already indicated in your other books.

I also like very much your pages on work. In giving some lectures on art to my students last year I went into Eric Gill's thoughts on work, which are very similar to yours. I am sending you the mimeographed notes of which I have plenty, in the event that you might feel like glancing through them . . .

There are one or two other points on which I disagree with you. It seems to me that your statements about the history of various religions are often rather sweeping and arbitrary. For instance it is by no means certain just *what* original Buddhism is—atheistic or theistic. Then in your note on page 55 you are certainly wrong in saying the original idea of Christ was the adoptionist one. After all, how about the Gospel of St. John: "In the beginning was the Word . . . and the Word was made flesh." You could easily find plenty of Christian thought that would substantiate your idea of the dignity of man. Most of the Fathers of the

Church looked at the Incarnation in that light, and Duns Scotus, for instance, is always speaking of the Humanity of Christ as the *assumptus homo*, the man who was taken up by God. This is far stronger than adoptionism, for it says that the Man Christ was not only "adopted" but the true Son of God—"true God and true man." All our ideas on the dignity of man, all our "humanism" really flows from the right understanding of the mystery of the Incarnation and of the recapitulation of all in Christ. If you are interested in a good exposition of this idea, De Lubac's *Catholicism* brings it out very well in the first couple of chapters.

I have just finished giving some lectures on Ecclesiastes, comparing it in the end with Lao Tzu. It was a fascinating study for me. The Pope, you may know, has come out rather strongly in favor of psychiatry and even (implicitly) of psychoanalysis, and in passing he recommended the Catholic psychiatrist to reread the sapiential books of the Bible for the light they throw on man's psychology. To my mind, Ecclesiastes is the best from this point of view, with its rejection of arbitrary, a priori and wishful rationalizations about life and its insistence upon a real adaptation to reality, much of which comes to us as unknown and unpredictable— hence also the acceptance of risk and the avoidance of dogmatism and of extremes, the humility of faith, the recognition of our own limitations, the ability to cooperate with others in a common endeavor, etc. Your book *The Forgotten Language*, which I read last May or June, also interested me very much.

Did you, by the way, receive *No Man Is an Island*? I hope you did. Probably you would not be interested in all of it. For my part I think the last few chapters are the most important ones, together with the prologue and the principles given in the first chapter . . .

Once again, if you will permit a personal observation, it seems to me that your writing shows you to be one who has a very real sense of the God of Abraham and Isaac and Jacob, the Living God Who is defiled by the images and concepts which we so easily allow to become idols and projections. Your book would not be comprehensible without an implicitly religious foundation, without an implicitly *monotheistic* foundation.

My Superiors are considering letting me stop writing and go into a kind of retirement—perhaps even in the woods, I don't know. If they do, they will probably desire me to sever the contacts I made as a writer, but nothing has been said about it so far, and I trust I will be able to hear from you until something definite is said on the subject. But I would like to repeat that I have profited very much by reading your books and by our letters and want to express my gratitude. No matter what the future may bring . . .

September 30, 1960

Under separate cover a new book of mine is on its way to you: *Disputed Questions*. This is one I particularly want you to have, and I think in many places I am indebted, in it, to our stimulating dialogue. Anyway, I think you will feel at home with it.

In regard to the business I proposed in my last letter, writing something to go along with me and Suzuki: as I have not heard from you, I can understand that you were probably a bit hampered in trying to deal with it. But whatever may have been your hopes and intentions, and the obstacles in the way of them, it seems the whole business is finally settled in a simple way. It has been decided by others than myself to add nothing to the two articles but to run them together, in the New Directions *Anthology* that is to appear soon . . . I would still be interested in your reaction, however, and do hope you can find time to drop me a line about it . . .

Recently I have been deeply impressed and moved by the wonderful work of Abraham Heschel. I have no doubt that you must know it. It is singularly authentic religious material. For the first time I have been going into Niebuhr too, and I find his outlook very sane and good. It is clear to me that I need to broaden out in my social thinking. This business about the U.S. and Latin America is especially sickening: to think that we could be so stupid and so naïve in our dealings with Cuba, for instance, and then get so upset at the absurd results. But it is too enticing, this business of being naïve. It still seems to serve as a cloak for so much injustice. Unfortunately it hides us only from ourselves and not from the rest of the world.

September 26, 1961

Your latest book [*Sigmund Freud's Mission*] has reached me and the material is very interesting. The texts you have presented for the first time in English seem to me to be important in the highest degree, and I like your analysis of them. This is a very revealing book. Reading it one wonders at the torpor that has kept us from paying more attention to this material before the present moment. I can understand how it would be rejected as "idealism" on the other side of the Iron Curtain also. Among us it is rejected a priori for purely authoritarian and dogmatic reasons, I mean here in America. It is un-American. That is enough.

The concept that seems to me to be at once the most operative, the most suggestive and yet also the weakest in these papers of M. is the idea of man's "species being," his *wesen* . . . I think Marx needs a little clearer kind of personalism to fully clarify his idea of unalienated man. This is the realm of investigation that seems important to me. Especially since the only society so far more alienated than that of the Marxists is our own, where, however, we like to talk of personalism. Actually, all we are is individual natures running around irresponsibly, cozy in our reliance on the big hypostasis of nature which is the anonymous crowd.

The international situation, or what news of it filters through to me, is serious and sickening. There is no point in being either bitter or disgusted, but I have written a rather angry tirade and sent it to a friend of mine in Nicaragua [Pablo Antonio Cuadra]. I am sending you a copy as I have done to other friends of mine whose intelligence I respect and who, I feel, may be in a position to sympathize. This at least gives me the chance to express myself, which I think is a human need at such a time, and a need which is not easily fulfilled in a society of open-mouthed and passive TV watchers.

At the same time I am sending an offprint of the exchange of views with Suzuki which has finally appeared. I think you may be interested in it. It deals with the old theme of the Fall again, which is certainly a very important symbolic expression of our condition.

Hoping that you are well and that life is a bit saner in Mexico than it is here.

November 14, 1961

Your new book *May Man Prevail* has reached me and I am reading it with the greatest interest. I think it is a really sane and sound book. It is a very noticeable contrast with the kind of thinking that is so general everywhere here today. I wonder what hope there is of getting the country at large to see this point of view. The situation certainly seems to be very discouraging, from the point of view of peace.

One thing I want to ask you now and I hope you can let me know the answer very soon: can you let me have some article of yours, already written or published, to include in an anthology of articles on peace, which New Directions wants to bring out? I was thinking of your piece on unilateral disarmament, the one from *Daedalus*, but if you have something more recent, and perhaps something which condenses many of the same ideas as your new book, I would be very grateful to be able to use it. This anthology is to be a paperback, and I am hoping to have such authors as Lewis Mumford, yourself, Jerome Frank of Johns Hopkins, who did a good piece on "Breaking the Thought Barrier," and several other things of the same type.

Catholics in the United States are very silent and inarticulate on this most urgent question, but a small Catholic peace movement is at least starting. I am one of the sponsors, though I don't have much freedom of action where I now am. In Europe Catholic thought has been much more articulate and Cardinal Ottaviani, who is very high up in the Roman Curia and is in fact the head of the Holy Office (and something of a shellback, to tell the truth), has pronounced very strongly for the total abolition of war, asserting that nuclear war is not just a more intense form of the traditional warfare but a new species of war which does not admit to any of the conditions that make war morally permissible. To tell the truth, I believe the Holy See ought frankly to pronounce a condemnation of nuclear war. Whether this can be expected or not is another matter. I don't think Pope John would hesitate if it were up to him alone. The irony of it is that the integrist faction in Rome, which is most insistent on Papal infallibility, is actually against the Council, which gives more importance to the ideas of the bishops as a body. And the Pope himself is the one who wants the Council. A paradoxical development of Vatican centralism.

You may see a translation of the *Letter to Cuadra*, which I believe I sent you: it is appearing in Spanish in Mexico one of these days, also in Nicaragua . . .

Do let me know if you have an article available for the paperback project. Best wishes to you always, and God bless you . . .

[*Cold War Letter 5*]

December 1961

I am deeply grateful for your two letters, and glad to hear the new book [*May Man Prevail*] is coming along so well. Indeed it is to some extent heartening that there is such a current of sanity welling up on all sides. Yet not as encouraging as it might be, because though people in general have preserved a great deal of the old energy and health in striving for a society based on truth, the sickness is awfully deep-rooted, and most of all in those who make everybody move in the direction they want. I am more and more baffled by the mystery of this great insidious force that has the whole world by the neck and is forcing it under water in spite of all its good and self-preservative reactions. The situation certainly makes the psalms we chant in choir each day most eloquent. Erich, I am a complete Jew as far as that goes: I am steeped in that experience of bafflement, compunction and wonder which is the experience of those who have been rescued from tyranny, only to renounce freedom and in confusion and subjection to worse tyrants, through infidelity to the Lord. For only in His service is there true freedom, as the Prophets would tell us. This is still the clear experience of the Jews, as it ought to be of the Christians, except that we were too sure of our freedom and too sure we could never alienate it. Alas, for hundreds of years we have disregarded our sonship of God and now the whole world is reaping the consequences. If only Christians had valued the freedom of the sons of God that was given them. They preferred safety and the Grand Inquisitor.

The Catholics in the peace movement we are now starting are not the most influential in the country by any means, quite the contrary. Some of us are of an already notoriously pacifist group, the Catholic Worker, tolerated by all as a sign that we can find a mansion for beats in the Church as well as for the respectable. There are few priests, no bishops. The English Catholics are more articulate. There is a fine little book which I hope to include in toto in the paperback, by Catholic in-tellectuals in England, edited by Walter Stein . . .

Incidentally we very much want you to send us the article you are finishing now for *Commentary* [on civil defense]. That would be much better for our purposes anyway than the *Daedalus* one, though we do need a good piece on disarmament. Can you suggest any? What we lack is a good article on the positive and constructive side, a suggestion for a possible policy of peace, what to *do*.

Today I received a curious letter from a priest in Italy to whom I had sent an article on Christian pacifism and the obligation to resist this pressure toward war and disaster. He sent it back, or rejected it for the magazine to which I had sent it, saying that in Italy there was a kind of war psychosis and everybody was easily depressed by this sort of thing, and it was better to keep them optimistic by showing them the bright side. I am not condemning him, because they have been through horrors I have been spared, and they are doubtless quite aware that they can do *nothing* themselves, for they cannot change our policies. Yet I am disturbed by this prevalent attitude in Europe. I wrote a poem about Auschwitz which was just the truth, awful as it is. A good French Jesuit friend of mine simply couldn't read it, and another told me that a Jewish friend of his who had been in the camps would never write like that, but would just turn to love "stressing the positive side of things." I am perfectly willing to admit that when things have a definitely positive side to them, it should be stressed. They told Jeremiah to stress the positive side of things, too. It seems to me that there has never been such a black avalanche of negation in human society, and that if there is evil someone should point to it. It is not that I mind sentimental people telling me I am a pessimist, but people whose judgment I otherwise respect in many ways, say I am too much of a pessimist. Perhaps there is much in what they say, but at the same time I cannot feel quite easy with the attitude of so many Christians, priests and monks included, who at the present time are totally occupied in small points of patristic theology, of liturgy, of changing forms of observances etc. Nor can I be satisfied with the happy-making attitude of my friend's magazine in Italy. There the whole idea is to stress the warm, expansive, positive aspect of Catholic life, the charity, the fraternal unity of Catholic actionists, their hopeful approach to problems: but what problems? Secondary ones mostly. Or if they approach the big ones, it is in a secondary sort of way. "There ought to be peace." In the long run I find the whole thing smells slightly of the engineering of consent we are used to over here. The creation of the hopeful image, the optimistic cover story.

Again, I think people have wholly failed to take into account the objectively evil force (I say objectively with reservations, meaning that it transcends subjective good will), which makes use of and manipulates the best intentions of optimists and turns them to evil, in spite of the hopeful image they have created for themselves. I would call this for want of a better word a demonic force. People ignore it completely because they know that they themselves, subjectively, want only "the good." They do not realize that the good they want is rooted in negation and injustice, that it depends on the vast cruelty of an alienated society that is *kept* alienated with deliberation.

The other possibility is that by being "pessimistic" and looking at the dark side, pointing to the evil, I am only helping the process of evil along by collaborating with it, getting people used to it in some new way, perhaps even my pessimism equals a kind of acceptance of the worst disasters as a foregone conclusion when there is still a clear way out. All these questions float about in my mind, but my personal conviction is that when everybody else in my Church (except the Popes who have after all spoken quite clearly condemning nuclear annihilation bombing) seems to want to stay silent and perplexed, or worse still encourages nuclear war as the "lesser evil," it has become my clear duty to speak out against this crime and to denounce the steps taken to perpetuate it, while refusing all cooperation and trying to get others to do the same. If there is anything positive I can do, I wish I knew what it is . . .

The poem of Yevtushenko moved me very deeply. I have already come in contact with him, and this poem ["Babi Yar and Anti-Semites"] represents a distinct growth. It is a great crime when, in our day, so many men are feeling in their hearts this warm and profound need for identification with "the stranger" everywhere, governments should deliberately stifle the little spark of human love and enlist all our psychic energies to fill their mass movements, perverting and crushing our souls when they could and should grow so freely and so well. It is a world in which there could and should be a universal state, and if the men who made the policies wanted it, a world government could be created. They don't want it. What can you do?

February 16, 1962

I was sorry to hear you had been ill, and glad to hear you had been finishing the article on civil defense. Do not forget that you said we could have it for the collection of essays that is now going to press. The publisher is holding up the book in the hope of seeing your essay. Do please send a copy along to me as soon as you possibly can . . .

I am glad that we have a lot of good material anyway. Here is a little article of mine for fellowship, which I think you will enjoy and agree with. I have also been sending along mimeographed texts of some of the other stuff I have been putting out. It takes a terribly long time to get some of it through routine censorship of the Order. Sometimes because the censor has rigid and fanatical views, and sometimes because he just can't face the possibility that a monk should be interested in a public issue. We are supposed, no doubt, to be in a permanent moral coma.

The Yevtushenko poem on Babi Yar [where the Nazis killed thousands of Jews] is profoundly significant. I feel very much as he does, too. The Jews have been the great "sign" of an apocalyptic age. A sign for the dissolving "Christian society" and the waning culture of the West. A sign for all religious people, including yourself. We are heading for a bleak age in which, if we survive, our religion and our humanism are going to be stripped down to appalling neediness and reliance on the utterly essential, without the merciful protection of all that is accessory and devised to make life more human. I say, if we survive . . .

Early in 1962, Fromm formulated his concept of necrophilia (the "death wish") and applied it to violence in war. He sent the manuscript to various friends for their critique, including Jerome Frank, Roy Menninger, Hans Morgenthau, Paul Tillich, Pitrim Sorokin, and Thomas Merton. Fromm replied to their comments. (Merton's comments may be found in Faith and Violence, *Notre Dame, 1968, pp. 111–18). The original manuscript with the comments and Fromm's reply was printed in 1963 by the American Friends Service Committee, under the title* War Within Man: A Psychological Inquiry into the Roots of Destructiveness.

In a letter of September 10, 1963, Dr. Fromm refers to the Friends' publication and writes to Merton: "I just want to express to you personally what I have written in my answer to the discussion, and that is how deeply I enjoyed your statement and how much I feel the common bond between us." He expresses his regret that he would not be able to speak at the occasion in Boston of Merton's receiving of the award by Pax.

He mentions that he has just returned from Europe, where he attended a meeting on the topic "Man and Modern Society" organized by Yugoslav philosophers. He speaks of the joy of meeting philosophers from Yugoslavia, Czechoslovakia, and Poland. He mentions, too, that he met a number of Roman Catholic theologians: Diaz Allegria of the Papal University in Rome, Jean Danielou, and Karl Rahner. He writes: "It seems that there is a growing understanding for what you might call, in psychological terminology, an unconscious faith in God which you might find in the atheist and an unconscious lack of faith which you might find in a practicing Catholic."

October 8, 1963

It was good to hear from you again. I am sorry for my long silence, but I have had a hard time keeping up with correspondence which gets heavier all the time, and recently I have been in the hospital with a cervical disc . . . But I did feel that our exchange in the Friends booklet was a kind of correspondence. I appreciated the opportunity to join in the discussion and when it was all over I was sorry to see that most of the other participants had not done much to participate at all. I suppose it is understandable that each one sits in his hutch and barks out the door without moving from his position these days. It must be very hard to preserve much sensitivity in the midst of all the racket. But I do agree with you that we are certainly trying to see things in the same sort of way. I know more and more that mere narrowly partisan positions in religion or philosophy or anything else are simply useless today, and I refuse to take such positions. It is the duty of man to try to focus on the truth whatever it may be, and not to deceive himself by trying to make the "truth" conform to what keeps him happy. Of course the first truth of all is that we cannot do this perfectly and that if we think we can we are not going to take the first step. But surely there are better ways than following the mass media or some approved "line" in academic or political circles. You and I certainly agree in being dissenters first of all, and in having much the same kind of dissent: in favor of basically human values. Since to my mind man is made "in God's image" it is impossible really to dissociate these human values from the "worship" of God, and this is one of the central truths of the Gospel.

I am glad you feel the way you do about the Yugoslav and Polish "revisionists." I think there is much hope there. The Polish poetry I have read in translation strikes me as very alive these days. I do not know Allegria but Danielou is a very good friend of mine, and as for Rahner I respect him very much. His brother Hugo is a most interesting and important writer, I think you would like his books even better than those of Karl. I recommend them. He has always been active with that Arcona group, the Eranos circle, which interests me.

I agree with you perfectly about the "unconscious faith" of so-called atheists and the unconscious infidelity of supposedly religious people. This of course is the great thing a priest has to contend with, not only in others but also in himself. The key is of course, as Kierkegaard saw, the question of conformism and security. When one becomes a "believer" in a well-established and accepted group, he no longer needs the concern and the risk of freedom that are demanded in real faith. Fortunately for us in the Church, there is that other element, the Holy Spirit's action and grace, which keep working to break the institutional crust.

. . . I am happy to have got the Pax award and am sending you the statement a friend will read for me there, because I can't go. Just as well that I don't travel or I would be able to do even less work and writing . . .

January 15, 1966

I was glad to get your note. You are right, I have not written for a long time, but I think of you and run into people you know: for example I had a brief exchange of notes with Reza Arasteh, who has sent me his little book on Rumi. I am glad someone is doing work like that.

The other day I sent you my new book on Chuang Tzu. I had hoped my publisher would send you a copy but evidently he did not. I also sent you the booklet on Gandhi and an essay on Zen. I hope you like them.

You will be interested to know that I have moved out of the monastery to live in the woods as a hermit, remaining under the jurisdiction of the monastery. I go down once a day, take one meal there, and give one class a week on anything I like. At the moment I am giving conferences on the poetry of Rilke, but I cover a lot of other areas and hope to give a few lectures on Sufism, then Celtic monasticism and so on. As to the solitary life, it is to my mind a very valid experiment. It seems to me at any rate much more serious and in some ways more exacting than the life in community, where relationships are to some extent stereotyped anyway. I use a bit of Zen out here too, though I am not cracking my head with it. It is a good life, a bit chilly at the moment . . .

April 27, 1966

The other day I finished your *Heart of Man* and found much good in this expansion of the former short work.* Most helpful. Am temporarily not sleeping in the hermitage, as I am recovering from an operation for cervical disk. But I work and meditate there in the daytime when possible. Be sure that I am not exaggerating this project or being fanatical about it; but I need this delving into reality, this sweating out of illusions and desires . . .

On August 25, 1966, Fromm sent this interesting comment: "I understand very well about your need for meditation and delving into reality. I try to do this in my own much more limited way, and to meditate an hour each morning, and remain sensitive all day to what is essential, and even in this relatively small effort I find tremendous rewards of new insights and new strength; I am sometimes surprised how, even at my age of 66, and after so many years of being occupied with the analysis of others and myself, I still discover the many veils and blindfolds and the increasing happiness when more and more falls off."

October 13, 1966

I have been hoping to answer your letter of late August and now your new letter with the poems of Carmen Blumenkron and your superb ideas on a Papal peace conference has reached me. Let me take the last first.

The idea is a splendid one [Fromm's call for a meeting on peace to be called by the Pope] and I am sure Pope Paul would consider it very seriously. My own reactions are these. First of all, I think it would be better in ways if it were not in Rome. But that all depends. To my mind it ought to be in Latin America perhaps, say Mexico City itself. This

* *The short work was the booklet, referred to above,* War Within Man. *Fromm incorporated this material into* The Heart of Man.

would be impressive and would perhaps serve to underline the fact that the conference would be entirely free of the influence of any great power bloc. But of course there may be reasons for having it in Rome. But does Rome mean to everyone just what we would like this conference to mean? I think too your title—a conference "on solutions to the present dangers to the survival of mankind"—is very telling. It could almost be a kind of secular "Council" following up and implementing what the Vatican Council barely suggested in some lines: and if we consider *all* the dangers to survival there could really be quite a program . . . but best to restrict it to the very great and immediate danger of global war . . .

In any event, I am heartily in agreement that it would be very effective indeed for the Pope to call this conference, and I think this should somehow be done with such authority and force (moral not juridical) that the U.S. would be shamed into slowing down its escalation and holding back from an invasion of North Vietnam and China. This in itself would be an achievement. Then perhaps the conference might be able to bring the whole affair to the point of negotiation and the next world war be averted. It would be a tremendous thing, and I think there is a very real hope. Do keep me posted . . .

Carmen Blumenkron's poems [she was a neighbor of Fromm's in Cuernavaca] are deeply moving and very beautiful, and their matter is very impressive. The form does suffer a bit though not only because it is traditional (that is not in itself an obstacle to publication) but because the vocabulary in it seems to me general and weak—the words used are outworn ones which do not lend themselves to the mediation of creative fire, though the fire is certainly there, with deep religious power. There are certainly magazines which would publish these poems, I think, but it would be hard for me to say just which ones. But publication of poetry in book form is very unpopular now: publishers refuse excellent poets until there is some indication that they may sell, and there are hundreds of others sending in manuscripts that are not even looked at. With poems of this type the best thing is private publication for one's friends and for a restricted public, and this can often be done quite nicely and without too much expense. Much of the best verse today is published in a way that is, so to speak, semiprivate.

I am very interested in what you said in your other letter about Dr. Machovec [a Marxist writer and a former Catholic whom Fromm met in Prague], and hope you will keep me informed about his forthcoming book. Don Milani [a priest who worked with poor children in a village near Florence and was committed to the struggle for the poor] of course I know. I saw a translation of his protest, or a copy of the protest, I am not sure which, but it came to me via Elizabeth Mann Borghese last spring I believe. It was most impressive.

Your own book on the Old Testament [*Ye Shall Be Gods*] interests me greatly: and I am sure that is just what the OT needs: a radical interpretation. That in fact is what the early Christians did, though their radicalism did not last long and has had to be revived from time to time—by people like St. Francis.

The book you refer to that I must now send you (I keep forgetting) is my little book on Chuang Tzu. I must see that a copy gets off to you right away. I have asked the publishers to send you my new book that is due to appear any time now, *Conjectures of a Guilty Bystander*.

. . . I am thriving in the hermitage: it is the ideal milieu for me, out in the woods, plenty of silence and inner freedom. I am not cut off in an artificial way from other people: occasionally I have a visitor for a day or two at the monastery and can keep human that way, and I also participate a little in some of the monastery activities, giving a course on this and that—for a while lectured on Marx. Now I am talking on modern poets. Really I feel much more human and natural on my own than when tied up in the routines of an institution. Here I don't have to play any part at all, and that is very delightful. I just live.

To Jean and Hildegard Goss-Mayr

In August 1983 I had the pleasure of meeting Hildegard Goss-Mayr at the Fellowship of Reconciliation headquarters at Nyack, New York. This petite, quiet-mannered woman lights up when she talks about the Gospel message of love. The peace movement and the Gospel stance of non-violence have taken deep root in her person. Born in 1930 in Vienna, she was strongly influenced by the peace activities of her father, Kaspar Mayr, who had been converted to non-violence during the First World War and became editor of a small but influential journal, Der Christ in der Welt. Hildegard's husband, Jean Goss (a Frenchman), while a prisoner of war during the Second World War had experienced a deep religious conversion in which he came to see Jesus Christ as "Absolute Love." He met Hildegard in 1955 and they were married in 1958.

The following year, John XXIII announced that the Church would hold an ecumenical council and invited suggestions on agenda. The Goss-Mayrs took him literally and came to Rome in 1961 with a dossier of materials and a series of proposals on modern war and Christian conscience. Cardinal Ottaviani, a well-known conservative but a strong opponent of war, listened sympathetically to Jean and put him in touch with Sebastian Tromp, S.J., who was in charge of the preparatory theological commission. Thus the Goss-Mayrs were able to get their materials on war and peace to the theologians and the Council Fathers.

The Goss-Mayrs have been active in promoting the non-violent message of the Gospels and in teaching non-violent strategies in both Eastern and Western Europe, as well as in Latin America. In 1965 Hildegard came to the United States and, in company with Jim Douglass, went to see Thomas Merton at Gethsemani.

Their correspondence began in 1961 (probably December) when Hildegard wrote to Merton telling him of the work for peace that she and her husband had been involved in, and also about the peace dossier they had prepared, which she sent to Merton for his reactions.

[*Cold War Letter 19*]

January 1962

Your very welcome letter has been received and I have been waiting for some time to get the documents which were sent under separate cover. I have not yet received these but at least I want to send a word of acknowledgment for your letter. It is very good to be in touch with you. I will send you a few things which you may or may not be able to use in *Der Christ in der Welt*. I can read German sufficiently well to profit by this if you send it.

It is sometimes discouraging to see how small the Christian peace movement is, and especially here in America where it is most necessary. But we have to remember that this is the usual pattern, and the Bible has led us to expect it. Spiritual work is done with disproportionately small and feeble instruments. And now above all when everything is so utterly complex, and when people collapse under the burden of confusions and cease to think at all, it is natural that few may want to take on the burden of trying to effect something in the moral and spiritual way, in political action. Yet this is precisely what has to be done.

At times it seems almost humanly impossible, in the fluid, obscure and ever-changing movement of words and secular ideologies, to find stability and clarity, and even to formulate the problems we face. I think your efforts to state the questions clearly and place them before the Church, particularly before the Council, is of the greatest importance. The fact that the Church, while opposing war in a general way, says nothing very definite about the acute and present problems is to many people quite disconcerting. Of course they do not realize how complex the problem is, nor do they know that the Church does not always have to proceed by formal definitions in everything that she does.

I believe it is very important for Catholics to take a clear stand for nuclear disarmament, on some practical basis. But there again we get into the political maelstrom.

One of our great problems is to see clearly what we have to resist. I would say that at the moment we have to understand better than we do the cold-war mentality. If we do not understand it, we will run the risk of contributing to its confusions and thereby helping the enemies of man and of peace. The great danger is that under the pressures of anxiety and fear, the alternation of crisis and relaxation and new crisis, the people of the world will come to accept gradually the idea of war, the idea of submission to total power, and the abdication of reason, spirit and individual conscience. The great peril of the cold war is the progressive deadening of conscience. This of course is a process which was already well under way after World War I, and received a great impetus during the second war.

No one knows what this year will bring. The mentality of this country is deeply disturbing. But in the past year, the awful nonsense about the fallout shelters has finally awakened resistance and articulate opposition on the part of many intelligent people. This is a healthy reaction, but I do not know where it will go. The book I am editing will, I hope, contain very many interesting and compelling articles . . . I rely very much on your help and friendship. Send me anything you think will be of service to the cause of peace, and pray that in all things I may act wisely . . .

John Heidbrink gave the Goss-Mayrs the good news that Merton had joined the FOR. "We are happy for this," she wrote Merton, "because now you are profoundly united with us in the belief in the absolute power of love as revealed by Jesus Christ." She asked him for suggestions about what American bishops to consult. In addition, she asked him to write a brief leaflet for their magazine, Der Christ in der Welt.

October 14, 1962

I am actually expecting John Heidbrink here today or tomorrow, and we will speak of you. Of course I will send along a little page of material for the leaflet, with great good will. It will go to Vienna during the course of the week, and I will also send with it an article, actually an introduction to Fr. Delp's *Meditations*, to be published here. You may use a translation of this as an article in the magazine if you like, subject to the censorship of the Order (they can handle that at Engelszell) . . .

I think I will send a copy to you in Rome by surface mail, just in case it may reach you there. I am glad you are there at the Council, and that your proposals will have a hearing. Archbishop Roberts tells me he is hoping to get an official approval for conscientious objection. I think this is a very good approach, and most important. It is absolutely terrible that Catholics today should be forced into wars that are almost certain to be immoral, just because the hierarchy may be willing, if not eager, to accept the lies of the military as to the probable character of the war. In this country now everybody is calmly accepting the morality of what is called "counterforces" warfare. It is all very simple. Our missiles will aim at their missile bases and knock them all out before they can aim at our cities. This is considered to be the acme of morality. Of course there are not lacking those who are willing to equate this with the traditional just-war morality, since in this case attack is the "only valid defense." Of course they conveniently overlook the fact that either side may strike first, and either side may have a few missiles left over for the key cities of the enemy, because obviously any missiles that are left will be useless against missile sites that are now empty . . . And so it goes on.

But the great problem is that with the regressive official thinking of many moralists, the Catholic is likely to be forced to participate in an unjust and criminal war with no recourse to his own conscience. In point of fact, however, this would be a case where the conscience would have to be the last court of appeal, but how many Catholics would have the courage or the sufficient knowledge to realize this?

I do not know what other of my articles on peace are available to you. One has just appeared in *Der Seelsorger*, I am told. I sent several to a friend, Miss Elsa Englander, a teacher in Linz . . . who translates them and gives them to people who are interested. She has probably printed things in small journals . . . which you would be able to use in *Der Christ in der Welt* if you want to. I suggest you get in contact with her for my other peace articles.

Material in the magazine would have to be censored. Other things in mimeographed bulletins etc. need not be censored. You can always quote from letters, I should think, without further censorship. The thing of mine in Pax bulletin, last issue, is not officially censored in that form, but can be used in things of limited circulation like mimeographed bulletins.

About the American bishops: I have not much information. Most of them would simply not understand the problem, I am afraid. Archbishop Flahiff of Winnipeg, Canada, is a bright and understanding new bishop, and a friend of good friends of mine. He is a good prospect. You must see him. Also Fr. Stransky on the Secretariat for Christian Unity, whom I know. Also Bishop Wright of Pittsburgh, very good. Perhaps Cardinal Ritter of St. Louis, who was a pioneer in race relations here. I think he is open-minded. I don't know if there would be much point in seeing the theological advisor of our own Archbishop. This is my friend Msgr. Horrigan, president of a college near here. The Archbishop is too timid and conservative to understand the problem aright, though he is a good man (Archbishop Floersh of Louisville, whom you can see anyway, but don't expect anything much. But he will be delighted you are a friend of mine and will gladly speak to you. I am very fond of him, he ordained me. But he does not see those new issues, I believe. Don't please tell him that I am a member of FOR. He is very upset about what he thinks will confuse the clear lines of demarcation between Protestant and Catholic) . . .

Another priest from Louisville is the scripture scholar, Fr. Barnabas M. Ahern, C.P. He will be very nice and friendly, though I don't know what he can do for you. Incidentally I suggest you go see our Abbot General, Dom Gabriel Sortais, and give him a strong push in favor of my writing about peace. He is reasonable enough, but is also under pressure from a lot of silly and unreasonable people . . .

You might at least ask the General if he would not permit you the use of something I have written on war that has not been censored in English, and might pass the censors in German. There is no harm in trying. He is better to handle when he meets you directly rather than by mail. Please don't discuss anything about me and the FOR with him. I regard the question of the FOR and myself as a personal matter of conscience, which does not involve any rights of the Order one way or the other, as the Order is not involved. John H. has promised to keep the Order entirely out of it and to make no kind of publicity.

I hope God will bless your work at Rome. And all your work. I am glad you are going to South America with Dorothy Day, or rather she with you. I must write about Latin America some other time. I have not heard from Dorothy since she went to Cuba. I hope she is safe. I am glad to hear news of Fr. Régamey. Is this book on conscientious objection something new, or is it the one on non-violence which appeared several years ago?

November 30, 1962

Thank you so much for having John Heidbrink pass on your letter to me. It had many good and encouraging things in it. I am especially delighted to hear that your work is having good fruit and that there is a possibility of the question of nuclear war being discussed later in the Council.

This is a rather hasty note to bring to your attention a most important book. It is by a nuclear scientist, and is factual, but with a deep moral concern. It is called *Kill and Overkill,* by Ralph E. Lapp. I will ask John to send you a copy of this most important book.

The reason for its importance is not of course that it makes any kind of theological statement, but on the contrary, that it reveals crucially important facts about the whole status of the question.

As you know, the real issue about nuclear weapons is not so much the matter of moral principle, which after all does not change with the megatonnage of weapons, the principles are clear. But in applying these principles, there are enormously important problems and questions of *fact.* These facts totally alter the circumstances and even essentially change the very *rationality* involved in the use of these destructive weapons.

It seems to me that the arguments about the morality of nuclear war by Catholic theologians, even by the Popes, all seem tacitly to assume that the atom bomb or the H-bomb are simply bigger and more powerful versions of what we already know. Those who have said that this constitutes an "essentially new kind of war" have doubtless used this phrase more rhetorically than theologically. But as a matter of fact the entire rationale of war is completely altered by the present state of arms production and the arms race.

This crucially important book shows quite clearly that already the buildup of nuclear weapons has gone far beyond the point where it constitutes a reasonable defense or even a rational deterrent. It is not only supremely dangerous and harmful but also completely useless, except as a means of terrorizing and demoralizing people still further—or else annihilating the civilized world. This latter cannot be considered by any stretch of the imagination a rational end, let alone a moral one.

The facts in this book demonstrate that already the production of nuclear weapons is of such a nature that it no longer comes under the heading of a valid and rational form of "self-defense" and therefore to construct arguments in favor of nuclear war, conscription in such war, and the rest, on the basis of the "right and obligation of self-defense" is in fact pure fantasy and has nothing to do with the real facts. I feel it is extremely important for these facts to be made quite clear to those who will eventually discuss the morality of nuclear war. It seems to me that the policies of the cold war are already in themselves to a great extent criminal, just as the war economy of the United States at the present moment is in itself criminally irresponsible.

I have by the way mimeographed some more copies of my unpublishable book on peace [*Peace in a Post-Christian Era*] . . . I can send more now if you need them. Do you think it advisable to send any copies to any bishops? I do not think my own thoughts are of any special value, or that they contribute much. But they might be of slight use in some exceptional cases. Please let me know . . .

December 17, 1962

Under separate cover I am sending you three envelopes full of materials more or less related to the question of nuclear war.

In one is the book *Breakthrough to Peace* in which I have an essay on "Peace: A Religious Responsibility," which is pretty much a summary of what I have had to say on the subject. The introduction to that book, which I also wrote, is useful perhaps as a summary of the status questionis.

The most complete text I have written is that of the book *Peace in a Post-Christian Era*, which is not published, but I am sending you a mimeographed copy. I believe I sent you a copy before this but I am not sure. In any case I shall send some more copies by sea mail, and you can share them with others who may be interested. Together with this book, I am sending one or two other essays, like that entitled "Target Equals City." The substance of this is in the book, but I believe that it might be useful to present the essay separately as it points up the problem that is most acute: namely that when moralists and politicians acting more or less on moral principles have once committed themselves to a war that seems to be limited to certain acceptable opinions, in reality the war "escalates" to immoral and inhuman proportions before anyone is aware of the fact, and the moralists tend to be dragged along with it, even to the point of changing their "morality" to justify an immoral and criminal policy, *post factum*. This is where we have now arrived with nuclear weapons, I believe.

As to the political implications of the problem, the essay "Red or Dead" may be of some use. It seems to me that too many accept without any question the premise that there is no alternative but nuclear war or communism. In reality this is a delusion and an obsession which inevitably fixes the whole argument in a context in which it is not possible to make sense, and in which one remains completely out of touch with the moral realities which confront the Church in this crisis.

The third envelope contains pieces of a more literary nature, such as the "Original Child Bomb" (which has disconcerted any number of people who were not able to grasp the fact that it was satirical) and the "Letter to Pablo Antonio Cuadra" which was published in *Sur* (Buenos Aires) and has been read rather widely among intellectuals in South and Central America. These pieces are not theological, but I think they have their purpose, and they are the kind of thing most germane to my own craft, since I am a poet rather than a theologian.

I know that Dom Gabriel is certainly a very conservative and extremely authoritarian Superior. I am repeatedly experiencing these unfortunate realities. He has a good heart, in his own way, and willingly relents when he sees that one is not a furious rebel and heretic. But unfortunately he is extremely suspicious of anything that savors of pacifism. He simply does not seem to understand it, and I suppose he is much concerned about France having a *force de frappe*, etc. But in any case, whatever his anxieties and convictions, he has no right whatever to prevent this dossier from being shown to the Council Committee, for this is purely and simply a recourse to a higher Superior. He cannot legitimately prevent this, and if he tries to, then I think one should proceed through some bishop or cardinal, for this is a most urgent matter for the whole Church . . .

I am very grateful that you went to see him, and I hope that what little I have written may be of some assistance. It really seems to me that we must first distinguish the steps to be taken in arriving at a desirable conclusion.

First of all, it is most important for the Church to recognize clearly that the presence of nuclear weapons in the world has *essentially* changed the whole problem of war. The whole question must now be rethought in the light of an essentially new situation, which has never existed before. This is more even than a new set of circumstances which alter the same sort of war we have always known. War itself has completely new implications and a totally new character. Hence it is of no use discussing traditional ideas of the just war in a situation where the whole concept of war has been fundamentally altered. To treat this *merely* as a new means of self-defense is tantamount to suicide on a global scale. Even the use of this weapon as a deterrent is a whole new problem.

In order to grasp these dimensions of the question, I think books like *Kill and Overkill*, which I mentioned in my last letter, should be briefly summarized and the points of chief importance should be brought out.

I am convinced that in this question of nuclear war the Church confronts an issue similar to that which arose in the case of Galileo, but one with much more momentous consequences for man. I feel that the Church is in serious danger of making the same kind of error that was made in the case of Galileo, through failure to understand the nature of the question, and judging it in an unrealistic way, having no real relation to the issue. It was possible to err in Galileo's case, and still avoid destruction. Error in this matter may involve the Church in the most ghastly tragedy of human history, indeed a tragedy of possibly eschatological proportions.

Once the seriousness and essential newness of the problem is made clear, then there should be no trouble at all in arriving at the conclusion that the Catholic must decide for himself, in the forum of conscience, how far he can participate in dubious policies proposed by military men to governments which are not in possession of all the relevant facts behind the proposals.

My dear friends, I will share this Christmas with you in a special and intimate way by offering my third Mass for the success of your, and our, work for peace, especially in the Council . . . When you come to this country is there any possibility of your visiting Gethsemani?

January 15, 1963

Thanks for your good letter of January 8th. I am glad you can make some use of the material. Unfortunately I have no knowledge of who the German censor might be. I wonder, in any case, if the Abbot General is not expecting you to contact him directly, in the event that you use any of my material on peace? It seems to me this is what he wants, though he may have explained it in some particular way to you. I know that at the end of this month he will be in the hospital. It might be a good idea to get on the telephone to Rome and see if he is still there and find out what he wants you to do . . .

I do hope that his participation in the Council has made our General realize at least dimly that the whole Church is not clinging in desperation to rigid and conservative positions, and that those who seek renewal and strive for a spiritual awakening are not necessarily all heretics and rebels. And an awakening must be something other than a dogged return to conventionally accepted and authoritative curial positions.

I have been thinking seriously of sending *Peace in a Post-Christian Era* to Msgr. Capovilla, as well as to Cardinal Montini. I will perhaps do so if I get time. On the other hand it is possible that the title may sound too provocative (it is intended to provoke). Perhaps *Breakthrough to Peace* would be a better book to send. You are certainly right that a theology of peace needs to be developed. In fact it is quite probable that this demonstration of the necessity of Christian non-violence in political action, especially in international affairs, is of even greater importance than the other issue. The two go together.

Here, on the other hand, is where real creativity and originality are demanded. For the moment, I do not see the issue clearly enough in its totality. I only see various separated aspects of it. Of these, the most urgent is the recognition of the right of the individual conscience to dissociate itself from irresponsible public action. But it seems to me that this ought first of all to be associated with some form of Christian action based on love. It seems to me that while it may be all right to gain some kind of recognition for conscientious objection, it should be clear that the Christian objector is also one who dedicates himself to positive action based on redemptive love, ordered toward world peace. This is the great weakness of the peace movement in the United States: it is purely a movement of protest, often without even a solidly rational basis, against the evil of war. Unfortunately some of the elements in the peace movement are so weak, morally (and notoriously), that the whole idea of pacifism is discredited by their presence. I certainly recognize the need for a clear statement of the positive theology of love in connection with the question of war and peace. Whether I will be allowed to publish anything on the subject is another matter . . .

Hildegard Goss-Mayr wrote that she and Jean planned to spend a year in Brazil helping to form groups in support of non-violence. They wanted to get others involved. Dorothy Day had agreed to come for at least part of the time. Would it be possible for Merton to join them?

March 21, 1963

Thank you for your good letter, which brings news of your proposed plan for Brazil. I am especially glad that you thought of me in connection with it. I think it is a very necessary and vitally important project, truly in accord with the mind of Christ and of the Church (though not perhaps with all of her members).

Unfortunately I do not think there is the slightest possibility of my ever getting permission to join in the project in the way suggested by you. Not only would it be completely useless for me to even discuss it with my Superiors, but even if a bishop or someone else in high position were to put the project of my participation before them in the strongest terms, they would still refuse. They would be able to allege that the contemplative nature of our Order makes it impossible to allow one of the members of the Order to participate in active works of this kind, and in this they would be supported in Rome . . .

Hence I do not think there is any point in my trying to plan anything. On the contrary, it seems to me personally that I do not really have a vocation to participate actively in apostolic works (except by writing) outside the monastery. The only possibility would be if a foundation of our monastery were made in Brazil, and then perhaps the Abbot might consent to send me there to give moral support and encouragement to your work insofar as it could be done from the monastery. This is the only possibility I can see, and I doubt if it is likely to be realized as soon as next year. The Bishop of São Paulo might of course inquire, but I do not think there is much point in it.

I very much regret my inability to respond to your offer. It would give me great joy to do so if I thought it were God's will. Probably I am not worthy of the favor. But I can at least associate myself very closely with you in prayers and I may also be able to help you through friends in Brazil. As for the volunteer you seek, Dorothy Day will probably know the best one for you. I think personally it would be less ambiguous if he were a European or Latin American. If you ever go to Central America I have a lot of friends in Nicaragua who might be interested in such a project.

Do please keep in touch and tell me how the project advances. There is so much to be done. The very urgent task of trying to keep a little light and perspective available to the mind of the American public is already enormous. I doubt if people will be able to take a really sane and Christian view of Cuba and the Latin American problem here. The prejudices and absurdities are too great, and they are perilous . . .

October 28, 1963

Thanks for your warm and kind letter of last August. Soon after getting it I went into the hospital and am only now catching up with correspondence. I have not been able to do anything on *Pacem in Terris,* though I share your view that it would be right for me to mimeograph something on it. However I am enclosing a mimeographed copy of a message of acceptance for a "peace medal" that was awarded me by a non-religious peace-movement group in Massachusetts [see *The Non-Violent Alternative*]. It is made up mostly of university people and I was very touched and happy that they saw fit to make this gesture, partly because of my few writings on the subject and partly also because they were aware of the fact that I had been silenced on this point. I have not yet heard how the affair went off, as of course I was not able to be present . . .

The great March on Washington was in many ways triumphant, and it was certainly a magnificent expression of restraint, dignity, good order. The nobility of the thousands of Negro participants was evident in the highest degree, and when they "thanked the white people" who were there, one of my friends broke down in tears. Really, for the whites who participated, it was a very great grace, and something they needed. Indeed they needed this chance to give some sign of repentance, much more than the Negro needed to have them there. In fact, politically, the presence of these white people was perhaps not entirely an advantage to the Negro because it tended to confuse the real situation just a little. Everything that tends to preserve the atmosphere of illusion, the false optimism which supposes that the Negro has a place all ready for him in white America, once more strengthens the inertia of those attached to a status quo in which, in fact, the Negro has no place whatever. He is an outcast. You would be horrified to know to what extent even in the Negro ghettoes the Negro is oppressed and exploited by white men, even to the extent that it is very difficult for a Negro to own a store or run a business of any consequence even in the Negro ghetto, and the white shopkeepers bleed him with usury. This situation is very grave indeed and it is slowly creeping toward revolution of the violent kind, I very much fear. Yet the greatness of people like Martin Luther King is something to hope in and trust in. God can certainly use such men to work miracles, and perhaps He will. Indeed He already has.

Fr. Haring was here and we had a wonderful talk, all too short. He said he would read my peace book and try to intervene with Dom Gabriel. Unfortunately, I am afraid Dom Gabriel is too obsessed with the foreign policies of de Gaulle, and can never admit the possibility of disagreement on this matter of the bomb. It must not be condemned, according to him, even though *Pacem in Terris* is so clear on the subject . . .

December 2, 1964

Dear friends, it was so good to hear from you. I pray much for your work in Brazil and am very interested in everything about it. The translator of the Gandhi selection is a nun in Petropolis. Sor Emmanuel da Virgem, at the Convento da Virgem. She is a very lively person, liberal to a point I think, by background something of an aristocrat but I think she is open, certainly interested in everything good. I have asked her to send you the ms. which she has. But this may prevent her getting down to work on the translation, though I think she is working on something else now. The book is not out in NY and will not be until late spring, or later than that. She has been waiting for the finished book, so I think she can lend you the ms. However, I would like to see the job get under way soon. There is no time to be lost in Brazil.

I was very disappointed in the discussion of nuclear weapons in the Council. There were some good interventions from the European side, but Bishop Hannan of Washington was scandalous, it seemed to me. He showed how far one can go when nationalism is identified and confused with the Christian faith. Thereafter "my country right or wrong" becomes equivalent to a profession of faith in God. There is a lot of this in the United States, I am afraid, and we certainly have no monopoly.

The FOR retreat [see Berrigan letters] was good, very moving, and I think we all came away convinced that there is no hope to be placed in human or technological or political expedients, but that our hope is first and last in God and in the mystery of His will to save man, and His promise of a reign of peace. It is heartrending to read Isaias in these days of Advent: promises to which so many Christians seem totally indifferent. And judgments also.

. . . The new book [*Seeds of Destruction*] is finally in print, will be officially published in January. I will send you a copy in São Paulo. It contains more about peace than the material that was forbidden, and I think it says much that I have wanted to say. The publisher is sending copies to a few bishops. Do you have names of bishops or theologians to whom you would like the book to be sent? Please let me know. A French edition is on the way, also Spanish and Italian . . .

In October 1965, Hildegard Goss-Mayr, accompanied by Jim Douglass, visited Merton at Gethsemani. In the following letter Merton replies to her letter of October 25, 1965 (written from Glendale, Ohio), in which among other things she asked him if he would be willing to be on the editorial board of Der Christ in der Welt.

November 10, 1965

For the last week I have been wanting to answer your letter so as to reach you before you leave this country. I hope I am still in time— which I will be if the letter is not held up here.

First of all it was a great joy to meet you and see you. It is always disappointing to know a person only through letters. It was good to have you there if only for a short time. I hope you will come again someday. Also of course it is always a source of strength and inspiration to me to meet someone who actually does something: I often feel that I am quite useless and inert here . . .

About the magazine: yes, of course I know it well. Since my German is slow, I do not try to read it through when it comes, but of course I know what you stand for and am with you. But on the other hand I think it would be better if I did not attempt to join the editorial board. I was told by Dom Gabriel not to do this, for any magazine, and really I think it is more honest. The one exception was the magazine of our Order, I am on the editorial board of that, but it is very ambiguous since in reality I cannot do anything anyway, and the whole thing in the end gets to be a pure exercise of imagination. What I will certainly do is try to help you out with actual contributions if and when I can. That is less of a problem, and it is also more of a reality.

As usual I do not have too much information about what goes on but I hear that the atmosphere in this country is getting to be quite tense. One can see so clearly that the real trouble here is the lack of spiritual roots. This country would not be so unreasonable and so prone to violence if it were more firmly based in a spiritual tradition and had a few more solid principles to go by. That is easy enough to say, but what one can do about it is another matter. I think that actually the peace-movement people are not helping much, except that they are making a strong protest, which is all right. But what we need is a peace movement that will help the country to actually understand and want peace, and that is quite another matter. Burning draft cards will not bring this about, it only upsets a lot of poor confused people who are not capable of seeing what it means: except to interpret it as another threat in a time when they feel themselves already gravely threatened by millions of communists behind every tree.

. . . What is your feeling about the country, and the chances of the peace movement? . . . May God bless your trip home. Give my regards to Jean. I will certainly do all that I can to help you, insofar as it may be within my power to do so. I am sorry about not joining your editorial board, but I think it does not make sense and that my Superiors would not permit it.

December 8, 1965

Your letter arrived yesterday, and I want to say I will gladly try an article on "Demut" [humility] for you. I do not yet know quite what approach it will take but it will be in the context of non-violence. Some printed matter from Vienna arrived here for you yesterday: I am sending it along to you with a piece I wrote on "protest," which is naïve and unsatisfactory but it may have a few points in it.

It is true that I have had a little difficulty about adjusting my position as a solitary with the publicity that is connected with the peace movement. My name is still used and newspaper articles give the impression that I am somehow actively involved in actions about which I know nothing whatever. Hence I finally decided to ask Jim Forest to make it clear that I am *not* involved in any of the political activities of the CPF but that I still morally support their spiritual and pastoral aims. I thought that was fair enough. After all I have no way whatever of keeping up with events or with decisions, and I do not want to be saddled with responsibility for acts which I do not agree with or do not even, in some cases, understand.

. . . My very best wishes to you and Jean. I am most eager to hear about the Constitution on the Church in the World which has probably been promulgated by now. I have to write something on this for the English edition of the bit on peace that was in *Seeds of Destruction*. I think that from what I hear all the hopes of the peace people are justified . . .

January 14, 1966

It is the feast of St. Hilary, Doctor of the Church, who said: "The best way to solve the problem of rendering to Caesar what is Caesar's is to have nothing that is Caesar's." This is a good day then to send you the essay on "Demut," which turned out to be really an essay on the beatitude of the Meek, as applied to Christian non-violence. Since I really do not know what I am talking about, it is rather presumptuous to write on such subjects, but anyway I have done so. I hope what I have said makes sense. You and Jean can judge that.

The practice we are following here with censorship is that the American censors do not even require to read any article except that which is submitted, on some obviously theological topic, to a big important magazine. This would not apply to any magazine of moderate circulation, and certainly not to one like *Der Christ in der Welt* which has a fairly limited circulation. Unless you are explicitly told otherwise by the Order, on its own initiative, you can I think simply publish anything of mine without further formalities, unless I myself say otherwise . . .

There are hopes now that the Vietnam war may reach the conference table, thanks largely to the efforts of Paul VI. Something to be very thankful for. I have not any recent news, but I hope all will be going well and that the Pope's wishes for peace in the New Year (which we all share) may be granted. You will know better than I what chance there is of all this working out.

My best and warmest wishes to you and Jean. When do you come to this hemisphere again?

Hildegard in a letter of March 29, 1967, had asked Merton to write a preface for a book she planned to write on Latin America.

April 22, 1967

Thanks for your nice letter of March 29th. I had been wondering what happened to you. It is good to have some news. I will certainly be praying for the success of your efforts to teach non-violence in South America next July. Will you be returning through the U.S.?

As to the preface: your book sounds both interesting and important, and I wish I could do a preface for it. Unfortunately as you may imagine I have finally reached a saturation point with prefaces. Much as I hate to do so, I have to refuse to do any more at least for a while. I have had so many requests that if I continued to accept, I would do absolutely nothing but write prefaces . . .

The spring is really lovely here, but how can one enjoy it when things get worse and worse in Vietnam? There is a certain feeling of desperation among some in the peace movement when they see that they get nowhere with their efforts: but perhaps they ought to realize that efforts against war are not always popular in a nation which is at war, and it is a good thing that there is as much conscientious opposition as there really is here. But I wish the end were in sight . . .

To Philip Griggs

Philip L. Griggs wrote to Merton on June 17, 1965, identifying himself as a member of a Rama Krishna mission in California. He wanted to discuss Merton's review of the book In Search of a Yogi *by Dom Denys Rutledge, O.S.B. Though Griggs found much that was good in the book, he questioned some of its presuppositions, among them the assumption of the superiority of Christian faith to other religions. His Hindu name in the Rama Krishna order is Yogeshananda.*

June 22, 1965

Your long and interesting letter puts me, I am afraid, in a rather delicate position. Having written a preface to Dom Denys Rutledge's book, I suppose I ought to consider myself obliged to defend it. I am afraid I do not intend to do this . . .

. . . I wrote the preface at the request of the editor, who is also my own editor and publisher . . . Reading the book I was myself quite aware of the author's limitations as an Englishman, as a perhaps conservative Catholic type, etc. I could see that though he was earnestly trying to be open-minded, he was hemmed in by some characteristic prejudices and limitations of perspective. On the other hand . . . I was willing to accept it for the good it contained. In fact, it seemed to me that for all the shortsightedness and lack of perspective, the author was sincere in his "search for a yogi," and what got through to me (I think I say this in the preface) was that he did find some really authentic people, even though he may not have looked in the best places for them. My feeling, on putting down the book, was that it did bear witness to the fact of the presence of real contemplatives in India, and for that reason I felt I could write a favorable preface. I should have perhaps been more sensitive to the reactions of persons like yourself and other friends I have since made in India . . .

You ask about the relative nearness to God of a fervent Sadhu and a superficial Christian. The Church's teaching on nearness to God is that he who loves God better, knows Him better, and is more perfectly obedient to His will, is closer to Him than others who may love, know and obey Him less well. Since it is to me perfectly obvious that a Sadhu might well know God better and love Him better than a lukewarm Christian, I see no problem whatever about declaring that such a one is closer to Him and is even, by that fact, closer to Christ. The distinction lies in the fact that Catholics believe that the Church does possess a clearer and more perfect exoteric doctrine and sacramental system which "objectively" ought to be more secure and reliable a means for men to come to God and save their souls. Obviously this cannot be argued and scientifically proved, I simply state it as part of our belief in the Church. But the fact remains that God is not bound to confine His gifts to the framework of these external means, and in the end we are sanctified not merely by the instrumentality of doctrines and sacraments but by the Holy Spirit. And I repeat my conviction as a Catholic that the Holy Spirit may perfectly well be more active in the heart of a Hindu monk than in my own. I am prepared to recognize this in anyone I meet who seems to be genuinely holy and I am quite often struck by what seem to me to be signs of such holiness in people who have nothing to do with the Catholic Church. On the other hand, I would not be so naïve as to go around measuring the holiness of Hindu monks by this subjective standard in order to write a book about my conclusions.

. . . There is only one point in your letter with which I take issue. I would not agree that Pseudo-Denys teaches the "divine nature of all things," or that man is essentially divine by nature. This of course is the point where a genuine understanding between Christianity and Vedanta must seek to begin, and we must begin by making clear the distinction. It cannot be said that a Christian (or at least a Catholic) believes that man is by nature divine. If he did, the whole point of Christian teaching would be lost. The Christian belief is, let me state it clearly and without ambiguity, that man is divine *not by nature but by grace,* that is to say that his union with God is not an ontological union in one nature but a personal union in love and in the Holy Spirit, that is to say by God's gift of Himself to man, in Christ. Man is divine then not insofar as he has Being, but insofar as he is personally redeemed by and united with God in Christ. For a Catholic, this applies to Hindu saints as well as to any other. I am not questioning the fact of their sanctity at all. I am merely saying that for a Catholic the exoteric explanation of it is that these holy men have received the gift of God, the Holy Spirit, and have become "divine" not by nature but "by adoption," not by creation but in the Spirit and in love. I state this, you understand, merely as an exposition of what all Catholics must hold, not as an attempted "refutation" of Advaita. What is important at this point is to do the groundwork of clarification on the concepts of *nature* and *person* and the corresponding concepts in Vedanta. I for one might question whether the Vedantic position is really conveyed in its fullness by treating *Atman* as a concept of *Nature*. And as corollary to that I would like for my own part to strongly repudiate confusion between the idea of person with the idea of *individual nature*. In Christian metaphysics I think it will be seen eventually that the idea of person far transcends that of nature, and this applies also to Christian theology. But I readily admit that most philosophy and theology has not yet made this clear . . .

To Etta Gullick

Etta Montgomery grew up and received her early schooling at St. Andrews, Scotland. In 1935 she entered Oxford, where she studied theology, and in 1938 received a B.A. (Hons.). That year she married Rowley Gullick, a lecturer in geography who in 1950 became a fellow at St. Edmund's Hall, Oxford. Etta showed great interest in the college sports (St. Edmund's proved highly successful in rugby, soccer, and rowing). Contacts with the Orthodox Church through involvement in the founding and running of the House of St. Gregory and St. Macrina—an Anglican-Orthodox center and hostel—led in 1962 to a visit with the Ecumenical Patriarch, Athenagoras, in Istanbul.

In 1965 Etta began teaching on prayer at St. Stephen's House, an Anglican theological college at Oxford, and later lectured on the great spiritual writers. Some years earlier Dom Christopher Butler, Abbot of Downside, had become her spiritual guide. He suggested that she read the Rule of Perfection *by the Capuchin Benet of Canfield (1562–1610). She began to prepare an edition of the third part of the Rule, unavailable in English. This venture brought her in contact with Thomas Merton. She wrote asking him to read her edition and possibly prepare a preface for it. References to Benet of Canfield thread through the Merton–Gullick correspondence, even though Merton never got to write the preface and Etta never got the edition to a publisher. But their interests branch off from Benet to other spiritual writers, problems of prayer, the pains and joys of a dedicated spiritual life, the issues of war and peace.*

In April 1967 Etta and her husband visited Merton at Gethsemani and enjoyed a picnic with him at Monks Pond. Merton and Etta corresponded regularly and consistently over a period of eight years. In one of the letters, he writes of his joy in hearing from her: "It is . . . almost as if I had a sister . . . (in England). I never had a sister." Etta Gullick continues to lecture on prayer and resides on the Isle of Man.

March 5, 1961

I am reading Part III of Benet with the very greatest interest. It is true that he has a welter of divisions and subdivisions which I rather regret, but in between there are some marvelous passages. I find him very like Eckhart. We do have to open our hearts and "flow with God" with self-forgetfulness and the renunciation of mental objects, even the highest forms. In this of course we must always be called and led. He makes it clear. We are too rational. We do not permit anything to remain unconscious. Yet all that is best is unconscious or superconscious. Yes, the first and second mean are superb.

I am not a professional San Juanist and have no more labels by which to be known. I think *The Ascent [to Truth]* is my worst book, except for two early ones . . .

April 22, 1961

I now have the first two parts of Canfield's *Rule*, though I have not had a chance to read them. The notes arrived safely some time ago in case I did not thank you already.

Now: would you consent to my getting one of my friends to handprint, in a limited edition of not more than 100 copies, some selected passages from Part III, with perhaps a little note of introduction which I would write, *Deo volente*? This would not, of course, interfere with what they refer to as a "trade edition" of the complete *Rule*. And I would expand my introduction for that edition. I have at least three friends in mind, all of them great printers and two having a fine reputation among collectors. One of them will surely want to do this. What do you say? All we will "get out of it" (!) will be a few copies of the book, but I feel amply rewarded just in seeing something fine finely printed. For God's glory and for the honor of His saints!

. . . Do you know where I might get hold of the Vansteenberghe life of Canfield? If necessary you could order it from Blackwell's for me and the bill could be sent to my London publisher. Please let me know.

May 15, 1961

Thanks for your good letter. I will write to Eugene Exman as you suggest. I think that the selections will make a nice little book. I am sorry I got mixed up in the reference to what I thought was a biography of Benet. I do not have my notes here and so probably Vansteenberghe is the biographer of Nicholas of Cusa, not of Benet. I was quoting from memory. I would be grateful to borrow whatever is the standard book on Benet sometime, but I don't think I will need it now, as we have a mediocre French life that recently appeared, and this will do for the material I need.

I have heard of *The Mirror of Simple Souls*. It is attributed to Marguerite Porete, an unfortunate Beguine who was burned for some very innocent statements. I would like to get to know this book.

Which is the new Penguin version of the *Cloud*? I have read one that was printed in America by a man called Progoff. If this is not the one that has been put out by Penguin, I should be delighted to see it.

Can I send you my little collection of sayings of the Desert Fathers? You might perhaps like it.

This is a very hasty note.

June 10, 1961

Thank you very much for your typescript of the *Life of Benet*. I have been a bit rushed lately and have not had the leisure I would like in order to sit down and read it quietly. It is kind of you to send the book, and I will look forward to seeing it. I will have more to say when I have read these both.

I hope you are not too sanguine about my proposal of a little privately printed selection. One of the printers feels that he does not have room for this, and another to whom I sent it has been holding on to it for weeks without a word of acknowledgment. So I am not too sure what may come of it: perhaps nothing . . .

. . . I have found someone who is very interested in publishing Benet's *Rule of Perfection*. This is a Carmelite friar who is editing a series here corresponding to La Vigne du Carmel, in Paris. They have done several very good things, and Benet would fit in well with the rest of the series, but it is not nearly such a good publishing house as Harper's. I have at any rate mentioned Benet to this Father Kieran and he is very interested.

I will send you my selections, but once again I must wait a bit because I have not identified them by chapter and you might have to go through your whole text to find them. I will have to do this, and again this requires a bit of free time. We are in the midst of strawberry picking and I have had extra classes as well as some proofs to read and the usual chores of a novice master besides.

The Mirror of Simple Souls still interests me and I want to look into it more. I forget where I ran across the suggestion that it could be attributed to Marguerite Porete, but perhaps in the new *Histoire de Spiritualité*, in which case the suggestion would be due to Dom F. Vandenbroucke. Do let me know if you find anything interesting.

We did not begin taking the *Downside Review* until just recently, and so I have not read the articles on Eckhart. I like him, but now and again he leaves one with a sense of being let down, when he goes beyond all bounds. He is more brilliant than all the other Rhenish mystics and really more interesting. Yet I like Tauler for a more steady diet. Him too I read in French, I must get the German.

The Penguin *Cloud* did not come, but the *Orthodox Prayers* did and I am very happy with them . . .

July 1, 1961

I still have no word whatever from the man to whom I sent my selections from Benet a couple of months ago. I will have to get after him, but this is probably an indication that his answer is no. One of my regular publishers would probably be interested in a small edition of these selections however. I don't know if that would raise any kind of an issue with Harper's or Oxford. I have a feeling Harper's may make some difficulty about the version in seventeenth-century English. If the Oxford Press did it in New York that would be excellent.

. . . I do know C. F. Kelley's edition of the *Book of the Poor in Spirit,* as we have it on the shelves in the novitiate here. I will look through his preface. It would be nice if the *Mirror* were by Marguerite Porete, I feel sorry for her, and would be pleased if it turned out she had after all written a very orthodox spiritual "classic." Is C. F. Kelley the same as Dom Placid Kelley (or whatever the name was) who writes on Eckhart? I will certainly return copies of the *Downside Review* if you want to risk sending them. I will make sure they are not lost or put aside in the Fr. Abbot's office which is always the great danger with us. As for the Lossky [i.e., his book on Eckhart], I have seen it mentioned but do not have it. I hate to put you to the trouble of getting it for me. Why not just let us scrounge around and get a copy for ourselves? You are too kind.

I like the Penguin edition of the *Cloud.* It is clear and easy for the contemporary reader. Yet it does lose some of the richness of the older more concrete English. I like the fourteenth-century English mystics more and more. I am reading [Walter Hilton's] *The Scale* [*of Perfection*], which has such a great deal in it. And you are of course right about Eckhart. He is more and more wonderful, and when properly interpreted, becomes less "way out" as our beats say. There is more in one sermon of Eckhart than in volumes of other people. There is so much packed in between the lines.

I presume you are now liberated from the social occasions for a bit, until they all come back. I can think of nothing more dull than the College Ball, and indeed there is nothing more dull, except perhaps some of the other functions. Which college? It would be funny if it were Oriel, which nearly got me, but I escaped to Cambridge in time. (I probably would have done even worse at Oxford than at Cambridge.) Yet seriously there is an advantage in all those teas and whatnot, from the point of view of the undergraduate. Sometimes one learns more there than anywhere else: I mean by way of leads about books, and things to look into. One misses it a little on the American "campus." Or if they have teas here, they are awfully self-conscious and pretty much a waste of time.

But this is getting garrulous. All the best to you. Where do you go for the summer? Is there still room for anyone to be alone in England, anywhere?

July 25, 1961

Your copy of the Benet selections has arrived with your suggestions and I shall take them all into account, for I agree with them. At the same time my printer in Vermont has finally returned this text. He has taken to teaching, to keep body and soul together, and consequently he cannot print this now, but says he likes it very much and I believe him . . .

Your emendation of the biographical note is excellent too. Do you want me to keep this together with the text of the *Rule*, or is there anything you want returned? I have not read the early sections as yet. Perhaps I had better keep all together for the time being. Things have been very busy.

Now, above all. Today came the Lossky book on Eckhart. It is fabulously good, and not only that but it is for me personally a book of enormous and providential importance, because I can see right away in the first chapter that I am right in the middle of the most fundamental intuition of unknowing which was the first source of my faith and has ever since been my whole life . . . I cannot thank you enough.

Your last letter was very interesting and good to have. I am so happy now to "see" you, in the England that has always meant so much to me. There is a whole rugger-playing side of my own nature which in a way has been suppressed, for so many years. (I was bullied into the Clare Boat Club which was very bad, and I was very bad in the third boat, whereas I was good at rugger.) . . .

. . . I was up at Clare in 1933–34. Your years at Oxford coincided with mine at Columbia.

If you find out where C. F. Kelley is, I would be glad to know. He is always welcome here. The story of E. I. Watkin touched me deeply. I think he has a great and admirable courage that gives glory to God and I am sure in some obscure strange way he is loving God very much. I cannot doubt this. C. F. Kelley too. I have seen too many leave here for very good reasons that nevertheless could not be clearly formulated. Their reasons for staying could always be lucid and "right" and yet ultimately terribly wrong. You see, as a moral theologian I am closer to Zen than to St. Alphonsus . . .

September 9, 1961

Your last long letter, I mean the long one of August 1, was so good that I wanted to take a lot of time to think about it before answering and as usual that meant it went too long without an answer and I am really not going to answer it properly even now. To begin with, I envy you seeing all those wonderful places [in France] that I have not seen for so long. And you really seem to have living connections with them, in all sorts of various ways. I shall never forget the lycée: its grimness is in my bones. As for the mysterious redness and dustiness of Montauban, that too is an indescribable part of me. I remember all the walks we used to take on Thursdays, two by two. The *faubourgs* with the little one-story houses and the little colorless villas, the plane trees, and eventually some dusty field or other, some dried-up brook, some knoll with an umbrella pine on it. Caussade evidently was from Caussade. I remember going through it in winter. The usual red church and the frozen gray houses. But I loved St. Antonin. I don't think I ever liked a place so much, until the hermitage which has been built and to which I have access in the woods here. Did you see the house we built there? Banyuls is a place where my father painted a lot, but I was not with him that year.

No I did not read the *Rule* for Harper's, and I don't think I commented on it at all. But I am certain that they will not take the old text. It will have to be modernized a bit for them. Personally I see no harm in this at all. I am callous about too much emphasis on scholarship in things like this. In this case I think it is much more important that the book be *read* rather than put on a shelf and referred to in footnotes . . . And of course I am not trying to influence you unduly: it is your book and you know what you want to do with it. For my own part (witness *The Wisdom of the Desert*) I purposely edit the material in a way that seems to me to be attractive and interesting. I make it my own and do what I like with it. This is extreme left-wing activity, and one can do it with something that has been done over and over like the Apothegmata. I am fortunately in a position to do this if I want to, and the scholars can, as we say in this country, go and cry in their beer for all I care. This is shockingly independent and un-humble, I am afraid. Perhaps I will feel remorse when I examine my conscience at noon today, but I doubt this very much. Perhaps you had better send an urgent call to the Carmelites to pray for me.

And as you see, I took selections out of Benet in my own way. This by the way is still waiting for the preface. I have not been able to get at it at all, as I have too many other things to do. I had a mystical theology course which is getting prolonged by a "popular demand" which I suspect to be ninety percent nonsense and ten percent pure illusion. And it requires a lot of preparation. In the course of which, yes, I did see the *DS* [*Dictionnaire Spirituelle*] article on divinization which is splendid (as is practically everything in the *DS*).

I do not think strictly that contemplation should be the goal of "all devout souls," though I may have said this earlier on. In reality I think a lot of them should be very good and forget themselves in virtuous action and love and let the contemplation come in the window unheeded, so to speak. They will be contemplatives without ever really knowing it. I feel that in the monastery here those who are too keen on being contemplatives with a capital C make of contemplation an "object" from which they are eternally separated, because they are always holding it at arms' length in order to see if it is there. As for the call to solitude it is in some respects unavoidable, and imperative, and even if you are prevented by circumstances (e.g., marriage!) from doing anything about it, solitude will come and find you anyway, and this is not always the easiest thing in life either. It may take the form of estrangement, and really it shouldn't. But it does. However, that should not be sought or even too eagerly consented to. On the contrary. In any case the right result should be a great purity of heart and selflessness and detachment.

I know what you are trying to say about loving God more than anything that exists but at the same time this is a measure of self-preservation. Beyond all is a love of God in and through all that exists. We must not hold them apart one from the other. But He must be One in all and Is. There comes a time when one loses everything, even love. Apparently. Even oneself, above all oneself. And this will take care of the rapture and all the rest because who will there be to be rapt?

. . . And now I shall be envying you even more with the thought that you are rolling along the Adriatic and the Greek Islands. Do collect me up in the nothingness as I do also for you. All blessings. This is still only half the letter I wanted to write but things are impossible.

Fr. Illtud Evans [O.P.] was here. It was nice to see someone from England.

[*Cold War Letter 1*]

October 1961

I know you have been patient with me as a bad correspondent. I owe you replies for two or three wonderful letters and several cards. I was very interested in your marvelous trip through the Balkans, your visit to the Patriarch at Istanbul. It must have been most impressive. I hear he is wonderful. A friend of mine in New York has written back and forth and published magazine articles on him. He is very cordial. I hope the [ecumenical] chapel in Oxford will be a success. God bless you for it.

Thanks especially for the *Downside Reviews* with C. F. Kelley's excellent articles. These are very fine and I like them a lot. But do you realize that in sending me his address you did not give the name of any town? California is a big place, you know! Could you look again, please? I am not in a great rush to write to him as I have an awful stack of letters to answer.

One thing that has kept me very busy in the last few weeks is the international crisis. It is not really my business to speak out about it, but since there is such frightful apathy and passivity everywhere, with people simply unable to face the issue squarely, and with only a stray voice raised tentatively here and there, it has become an urgent obligation. This has kept me occupied and will keep me even more occupied, because I am now perfectly convinced that there is one task for me that takes precedence over everything else: working with such means as I have at my disposal for the abolition of war. This is like going into the prize ring blindfolded and with hands tied, since I am cloistered and subject to the most discouragingly long and frustrating kinds of censorship on top of it. I must do what I can. Prayer of course remains my chief means, but it is also an obligation on my part to speak out insofar as I am able, and to speak as clearly, as forthrightly and as uncompromisingly as I can. A lot of people are not going to like this and it may mean my head, so do please pray for me in a very special way, because I cannot in conscience willingly betray the truth or let it be betrayed. The issue is too serious. This is purely and simply the crucifixion over again. Those who think there can be a just cause for measures that gravely risk leading to the destruction of the entire human race are in the most dangerous illusion, and if they are Christian they are purely and simply arming themselves with hammer and nails, without realizing it, to crucify and deny Christ. The extent of our spiritual obtuseness is reaching a frightful scale. Of course there is in it all a great mercy of God Whose Word descends like the rain and snow from heaven and cannot return to Him empty: but the demonic power at work in history is appalling, especially in these last months. We are reaching a moment of greatest crisis, through the blindness and stupidity of our leaders and all who believe in them and in the society we have set up for ourselves, and which is falling apart.

Thanks especially for the Watkin book. I read first the chapter on Julian, whom I love dearly. Then Baker . . .

November 21, 1961

Well I have managed to find a moment clear on this feast of Our Lady and am trying as best I can to answer your questions about the introductions to Parts I and II of Benet. I cannot find the bit you refer to about Dionysus.

But first I hope that by now you have received the letter I wrote several weeks ago speaking of the *Downside Reviews* which I received and which I have enjoyed. Do tell me if you did not get the letter, for then something must have happened to it. I was answering your several letters from Greece, etc., which I enjoyed immensely. As for these air-letter forms, I not only read them but I also write them.

Now for your two introductions. I think they are unfortunately not really adequate. They do not read very well, because of all the mystifying complexity of the degrees one upon the other. And further I think you ought to go a lot deeper into the various questions raised, in relation to the whole history of spirituality. I think the present treatment is a little superficial, at least as far as situating Benet in the historical context is concerned. This needs badly to be done, and of course it is not going to be very easy . . . But all this should be considerably developed. I don't mean that you have to lengthen it, but really bring in the meaning of the questions you raise. For instance, the reference to Gregory of Nyssa and *epectasis*: it would do no harm to use the Greek word, and bring in briefly the material condensed in the *DS* article on *epectasis* and the chapter on this in Danielou's *Platonisme et Théologie Mystique*. The reference to Bonaventure could be filled out with more rich allusions to the spirituality of St. Bonaventure and his relation to Benet situating B. in the Franciscan–Dionysian tradition of Hugh of Balma and those people. (Not Hugh of Balma, but there is some Franciscan I am trying to think of: Harphius, Herp, is the man I mean. Perhaps also Gerson?) Finally the reference to Athanasius should go frankly, though briefly, into the question of divinization. I don't mean that you have to develop all these things in detail, but mention them in such a way that they are briefly described and identified and placed in the history of spirituality, and in their relevance to Benet. In this way your introductions would gain immensely.

Your manuscripts came at different times and I have still not read Parts I and II, so that these are a bit mixed up in the envelope where I have put them together. You do not identify the parts, only the chapters, and this makes it rather hard to find one's way without reading everything. And those degrees. Alas, I am afraid I am not a man of degrees and levels and I quickly lose patience with those complex systems. I have a horrible tendency to skip, I am afraid, when they start enumerating them. But of course you have to clarify . . .

In that other letter I also asked again for C. F. Kelley's address as through an oversight you had not given me the town where he is in California, or perhaps the *Downside* people forgot the town . . . Very busy trying to write about peace and sanity if such things are still possible in this world of ours.

[*Cold War Letter 14*]

December 22, 1961

The new book on Gregory of Nyssa by Danielou and Musurillo has been sent me for review by Scribner's. I wonder if it is published in England. It is excellent as far as I have gone with it. A good clear introduction by Danielou and plenty of the best texts, though unfortunately they are all from the old Migne edition and not from the new critical edition of Werner Jaeger . . . As for the man who said my essay on the Desert Fathers was not "sufficiently Eastern," well, is there any reason why it should be "Eastern"? Is it not enough that I am a Westerner who has some appreciation of the East? Since when does a person have to climb out of his own skin and put on that of somebody else? This is the kind of nonsense that is prevalent everywhere in the Church, I regret to say: people conforming to their little party lines and to the slogans of their movements for this and that. Let us not lose our perspective. It will not help the reunion of East and West if everybody in the West becomes Eastern and everybody in the East then, logically, becomes Western. All that is needed is for us to really reach a deep understanding of one another.

The question of peace is important, it seems to me, and so important that I do not believe anyone who takes his Christian faith seriously can afford to neglect it. I do not mean to say that you have to swim out to Polaris submarines carrying a banner between your teeth, but it is absolutely necessary to take a serious and articulate stand on the question of nuclear war. And I mean against nuclear war. The passivity, the apparent indifference, the incoherence of so many Christians on this issue, and worse still the active belligerency of some religious spokesmen, especially in this country, is rapidly becoming one of the most frightful scandals in the history of Christendom. I do not mean these words to be in any sense a hyperbole. The issue is very grave.

It is also, of course, very complex. Certainly I do not say that to be a Christian one must be a pacifist. And indeed there is the awful obstacle that in some schools of thought a Catholic "cannot be a conscientious objector." This is still open to debate even on the theoretical plane. In practice, since there is every reason to doubt the justice of nuclear war and since a Christian is not only allowed but obliged to refuse participation in an unjust war, there is certainly every reason why a person may on the grounds of conscience refuse to support any measure that leads to nuclear war, or even to a policy of deterrence.

I do think you ought to read something about it. A book put out by the Merlin Press in London, and edited by Walter Stein, a professor at Leeds, is very solid. There is a really good essay by a professor or whatever you call a lady don at Somerville, G.E.M. Anscombe. Do you know her? I think her contribution to this book makes a world of sense. The book is *Nuclear Weapons and Christian Conscience*. I hope to use all the material in a collection I am editing here. There will be a lot of other things too, by people like Lewis Mumford whom you must have read at one time or other.

What is worst about the Catholic silence on this subject (the Popes have certainly spoken out) is the idea that moral theology *obligates* one, almost, to take the lowest and most secularized position. We have actually got to the point where moralists are almost saying in so many words that the Sermon on the Mount is un-Christian and that the Christian way of "sacrifice" is to bow one's neck under the sweet yoke of Pharaoh . . .

One could certainly wish that the Catholic position on nuclear war was half as strict as the Catholic position on birth control. It seems a little strange that we are so wildly exercised about the "murder" (and the word is of course correct) of an unborn infant by abortion, or even the prevention of conception which is hardly murder, and yet accept without a qualm the extermination of millions of helpless and innocent adults, some of whom may be Christians and even our friends rather than our enemies. I submit that we ought to fulfill the one without omitting the other.

Enough of this unpleasant topic, but I feel it is quite necessary to speak plainly. It is impossible not to be in some way involved in the evil, but we must be very careful that we are not passively involved, or willingly involved: but that we are doing what we can to disengage ourselves from cooperation in mass murder and to remain Christian insofar as this is possible when so many issues are muddled and obscure . . .

January 29, 1962

Eric Colledge in an introduction to an English translation of some sermons of Tauler says that a Dr. Romana Guarnieri has advanced the thesis that *The Mirror of Simple Souls* was definitely by Marguerite Porete and that the Latin, Italian and French texts are being edited. If you see anything of this, or any articles about it, will you please let me know?

Certainly I feel there is a probability that the last chapters of the *Rule*, about the Passion, do not fit in naturally with the rest of it. They may have been a little forced. But in general I am more and more suspicious of hard-and-fast systems explaining the growth of the spiritual life. That it *must* do so-and-so at a certain point.

Your intuition that Christ suffers in us in the Dark Night of the Soul seems to me to be especially apt and true. In the Night of Sense it is we who suffer in our own emptiness; in the Night of the Spirit he is emptiness in us, *exinanivit semetipsum*. The special awfulness of that seeming void can certainly be taken as a personal presence, but without duality, without too much of the subject-object relationship. But above that.

Everybody is suffering emptiness. All that is familiar to us is being threatened and taken away . . . there may be little or nothing left and we may all have evaporated. Surely one cannot feel comfortable or at ease in such a world. We are under sentence of death, an extinction without remembrance or memorial, and we cling to life and to the present. This causes bitterness and anguish. Christ will cure us of this clinging and then we will be free and joyful, even in the night.

[*Cold War Letter 63*]

March 30, 1962

Another idea about the selections from Benet came to me: perhaps I can interest some Quaker friends of mine in printing it. It would of course be a very small and insignificant kind of publication, but anyway it would reach quite a few people who would profit by it. I am still convinced that the best thing to do with Benet is to get pertinent passages to the attention of people who can use them who might otherwise bog down in the rather elaborate structure of the whole *Rule*.

Did you ever get anywhere with Julian of Norwich? Though it might not seem so at first sight, I think there is much in her that is relevant to the Dark Night. At least theologically, if not exactly in the order of the classic experience. But certainly the great thing is passing with Christ through death out of this world to the Father, and one does not reduce this to a "classic experience." It must remain incomprehensible to a great extent.

. . . Where did I see, the other day, something about a new edition of *The Mirror of Simple Souls*, and definitely ascribed to Marguerite Porete? Perhaps it was somewhere in the new Molinari book on Julian of Norwich, which I have only begun and then had to set aside for more urgent matters. If there is a new one out, I will wait to get that instead of borrowing the Orchard edition. But I could also probably get an old copy of that from Tom Burns at Burns Oates.

Thanks very much indeed for the splendid Florovsky article in *Sobornost*. This is a treasure. I have the greatest respect for him. It seems to me that he of all men today has the sense of what theology really is supposed to be.

Am I unpopular because of the writing on peace? You ask this. The answer is yes and no. Unpopular with some bishops, yes. Probably get hit over the head. Yes. Certainly criticized vigorously and unfairly. I get the impression that people have not the time to really think about this issue. They have the wind up and are moved to vehement malevolence whenever someone suggests that the bomb might not be the solution to all their problems, and might not be a fully ethical solution to any problem. I cannot see problems of spiritual night otherwise than in the context of collective stupidity and crime in which we are all involved. I think a lot of the suffering and meaninglessness of the night comes from unconscious involvement in the general evil. I think your answers are in fact no answers, though they are correct. I would hesitate to be content to direct anyone now purely along the lines of John of the Cross. I cannot perhaps explain this adequately now, but may try later. The nothingness and emptiness are more important than their explanations, and I think you will find eventually that explanations are not needed. Yet of course you do need to communicate with someone and feel yourself understood. You are, I hope. But above all you are understood by Christ, and that is the great thing. And at the other end of it all, the least thing is to understand oneself, at least to feel that one understands himself well.

To return to the question of peace, I am interested in E. I. Watkin's book against nuclear war and am doing one myself. I like everyone that is mixed up with Pax in England. I think they make sense. We are starting a Pax over here, but of course too late to mean anything . . .

June 16, 1962

Many thanks for the good news about *The Mirror of Simple Souls*. It was very good of you to get in contact with M. Orcibal and I am delighted to hear the printing exists: perhaps if it is only a loan to you, I might find out some way of obtaining a copy myself. This is really interesting.

For the rest I have not done much about the later mystics, except that I have rewritten that study of the English mystics in greater detail and have inserted a page about Benet, including some quotes from your text which I hope you will permit me to use. I have still done nothing about finding another printer for the few selections I made, but that will come eventually. There has to be an element of slow motion in this life, and it is good, for otherwise one would just get involved in projects. This I cannot do, and will not. But it has its disadvantages, because it means that I can do only one thing at a time instead of twenty, which keeps me from being entirely modern. But really, I will eventually get a little edition of this done and I think it will be worthwhile. Did you ever get any kind of answer from Harper's, or have I forgotten . . .

Instead of the fourteenth- and fifteenth-century mystics, I have been back with the early Fathers. Tertullian, whom I have read for the first time. He is a great writer, but in many ways an awful person. His Latin is fascinating. Also Cassiodorus, who may seem very humdrum, but I have a great admiration for him. No mystic, of course. But a person of wonderful qualities and spirit. His place at Vivarium must have been quite something. This is what I am doing with the novices at the moment and I haven't time for much else in the way of study except the Prophets which I am also taking with them.

You can guess that what occupied me most for the first four or five months of this year was the war business. A lot of people have wondered why I got involved in this, and have complained about it, to such good effect that my Superiors have now asked me to stop publishing on that altogether. Which I expected. But no matter what people may think about it, this was absolutely necessary. There was not a single Catholic voice raised in this country, except for Dorothy Day at the *Catholic Worker*, and who listens to her? The moral climate was absolutely oppressive and vile. Total unquestioning acceptance of the bomb without distinctions made, without serious thought of the meaning of annihilation bombing. I would not have considered myself a monk, a contemplative or a Christian at all if in the face of that I did not say something. There are certain things which are fundamental, and the Ten Commandments among them. The monastic "revival" (if any), the liturgical movement, the biblical movement and all the rest, ecumenism, etc., what does it all amount to if we sit back and passively accept our state of affairs where we purely and simply rely on the H-bomb, and make our living by producing it, with no further questions asked. This is *impossible* . . . I do feel that it has been important to drop a few remarks on the situation. And so I have. But thank heaven I have said enough and can turn to something else. I think it has had rather a good effect, at least a lot of things have livened up and there is quite a bit of discussion now, in Catholic magazines, etc. I know of course that in England everyone was much more articulate. But they were not being heard here.

I even finished a book on the subject which is not even going to be submitted to the censors, but if you would like to see a mimeographed copy, I would be glad to send it [*Peace in a Post-Christian Era*] . . .

I do hope your operation will not be too serious or painful and that it will help you. I am sorry to hear you are ill, on top of everything else. The diet will probably be a good thing. I find that I eat more than I need and fast days are welcome. There is no harm in feeling hungry, and it helps with work, even. But do take care of yourself. Perhaps you are doing too much.

I can imagine how nice Oxford was this spring. Sorry to hear that St. Edmund's Hall was, as the sports writers here would say, "toppled." But they didn't topple very far, after all . . .

July 14, 1962

I remembered you especially at Mass this morning, and I want to get this letter off before you leave for France (and again I envy you). I wonder where you will go this time? Why don't you go to St. Antonin where they have a mineral water, which is claimed to be good for everything under the sun: there you could perhaps forget your diet for a few days. Or am I subverting your whole regime?

Your letters are always most welcome, and as a matter of fact I can hardly think of letters I enjoy more. You are, for one thing, my most real contact with England. I have lots of friends in England, but they never write much about England, just about this or that ax we happen to be grinding. But you write about the university and about people, and one gets echoes of Downside (which of course I never knew anyway), but it is really almost as if I had a sister still living there (in England). I never had a sister, and really I have felt this as a kind of lack. So really you must never feel diffident about your letters being "chatty." I am so glad that they are. Not that I could take all kinds of chat from everyone. I do get lots of letters that are an awful penance and it is real work to plow through them out of sheer charity. Not so yours at all . . .

. . . I wonder if the best thing in the world to read in a period of night is Ruysbroeck? Personally I rather doubt it. I think that he will only make you feel worse. Have you ever tried reading Sophocles or Aeschylus at such a time? In the first place they have the immense advantage of being people you at no time have to agree with. The whole notion of one's "spiritual state" is not called into question, and therefore they can get in under your guard, so to speak, and I find that the *Antigone* or *Oedipus at Colonus* is most helpful in a shattering sort of way. We simply have to get away from this business of weighing spiritual values in the balance against one another especially in the night when in any case it is almost impossible anyway. In the night it is intolerable to raise the question of right and wrong because we are in a sense simply wrong and in another sense out of the whole area of argument altogether. That is precisely the atmosphere of Greek religious tragedy. It is much healthier than our obsession with the fear that if we are not somehow optimistic we are lost. In the night optimism and pessimism are both meaningless.

Does this sound absurd?

In any case I am angry at Tertullian but admire his prose. I am definitely going to work on Cassiodorus and have already translated a prayer of his. I send you a copy. You can send me any criticisms of the translation, I will appreciate them. Am also getting involved in the monastic tradition of Lérins, together with Caesarius of Arles, and the whole question of the Regula Magistri. This of course for my classes for the novices and students, but also for my own interest. My private theory, without any support as far as I know, is that the Regula Magistri was really the Rule of Lérins. What do you think? Or what do your Benedictine friends think?

. . . Thank you for the wisdom and frankness with which you immediately took me up on my silly and priggish statement that I "only do one thing at a time." Of course I don't. But still, it does not seem to be the time to get after the selections from Benet. Later perhaps.

August 31, 1962

. . . Your letters from Somerset were totally charming and I envied you. I meant to ask you to send me a few postcards of Glastonbury for my novices.

I got a good letter from E. I. Watkin but very difficult to read! I think I am very much in agreement with him all along the line . . .

As to *epectasis*: I do not consider it a "state" at all but so to speak a basic law of the spirit, a kind of expression of the very nature of the spiritual life. I think this is most important for you in this "night," much of which comes from unconsciously hanging on to something steady and definite. We have got to travel in the void and be perfectly happy about it. This is what actually brings to the fore the idea of *epectasis*, but it underlies everything. All that we know clearly is insufficient. We must pass on to the unknown. The hunger for God cannot be satisfied except in the sense that an entirely new dimension makes the void itself our satiation, and this is nonsense as expressed here. *Who is there left to satisfy?*

Why not cry out to God in any way you like, as long as you don't expect it to console you.

Do send me a card from Arles, I have been studying Evagrius and all the people from Lérins (Honoratus, etc.). Much joy and blessing on your trip to France.

[*Cold War Letter 108*]

October 29, 1962

I really appreciated the letters and cards from France. Thank you so much. I did not envy you so much this year. The Dordogne is much more haunting, and I can imagine the coast crowded with Germans. The card of Arles was good, and I liked the one of St. Michel de Cuza, of course. It was pinned up with due pomp on the novitiate notice board with an awestruck sign, "Our Father Master was born at the foot of this mountain." Now I have gone and said the wrong name; I meant of course St. Martin du Canigou.

Banyuls I don't remember, Collioure I do. And I was always fascinated a bit by Narbonne, for no reason. It must be a dull place, nearly as dull as Perpignan. I am sorry I never got over the border into Spain. You ought to see Monserrate and Poblet. I think you would be impressed with the former and everyone says it has a lot of good scholars in it, besides clinging to the side of a cliff. An unusual combination.

Thanks so much for *The Mirror of Simple Souls*. I am really enjoying it, though I find that I have a hard time getting anywhere for great lengths in such books. A little goes a long way. It is an admirable book, but one which one does not really "read." I hold it in my hand walking about in the woods, as if I were reading. But it is charming and bold and right. I am more and more convinced that if you are in dryness and such, these books only increase the problem (if it is a problem).

At the same time I think we make problems for ourselves where there really are none. There is too much conscious "spiritual life" floating around us, and we are too aware that we are supposed to get somewhere. Well, where? If you reflect, the answer turns out to be a word that is never very close to any kind of manageable reality. If that is the case, perhaps we are already in that where. In which case why do we torment ourselves looking around to verify a fact which we cannot see in any case? We should let go our hold upon our self and our will, and be in the Will in which we are. Contentment is very important, of course I mean what seems to be contentment with despair. And the worst thing of all is false optimism.

I thought the opening of the Council was tremendous. You know the Roman joke that is going around now? Question: Where are Cardinals Ottaviani and Ruffini these days? Answer: Oh, hadn't you heard? They are on their way to the Council of Trent.

Apparently they are on the liturgy now. I don't know what will come, but the whole thing seems to be making sense. Probably it is bound to bog down a bit somewhere, but it is going better than expected.

I haven't heard much about the touchy situation in Cuba so I won't talk about it. Of course things being what they were, Kennedy hardly had any alternative. My objection is to things being as they are, through the stupidity and shortsightedness of politicians who have no politics . . .

January 18, 1963

I am really sorry for not having written for so long. Correspondence gets to be more and more of a problem, but that does not mean I do not greatly enjoy your letters, or that I do not mean to answer them eventually.

First, a whole lot of random things you brought up: Fr. Borelli, yes, I know him, through Fr. Bruno James who worked with him for a time and now is running some sort of a college in Naples. B. James is a mystic and is the object of a lot of potshots and criticism, but I think he is a genuinely holy man and really has something to do in this world. He has a lot of influence on people who come his way and helps them. But he does shock the conventional . . .

You keep talking of Harphius and I keep wondering if he is really worthwhile. I have been reading bits and pieces out of some of the Russian Startzi of Optina. Remarkable, really fine. I get them here and there, mostly in French. I think I may do an article on the Russian mystics. They have the Dionysian tradition but they have more. I think Western mysticism, and particularly the Dionysians in the West, tend to get departmentalized. Except the really great ones like Eckhart. I think more and more of him. He towers over all his century. I think we do ourselves a disservice if we let ourselves be narrowed down to the perspectives of the lesser Dionysians. I do not say Harphius, though I suspect he might be one of the ones I mean. But I haven't read him.

I have been working a bit on the School of Chartres—not mystics but very refreshing indeed and very original, more than people have realized. Especially William of Conches. Not much work has been done on them, texts are coming out, I might translate something.

. . . I was amused at your Jesuit who liked risqué stories if clever. The pure Jesuit line: just right. Just worldly enough, just sophisticated enough. I love Rabelais, he is one of my favorite authors. I go beyond the Jesuit line because I am a monk (and so incidentally was Rabelais: he left the Franciscans to become a Benedictine and was happy with "us"). I don't care whether it is clever, if it is sane and healthy and perhaps even a bit uncouth. Rabelais, though, had a fine active irrepressible imagination and mind. For that reason I *detest* pornography. I utterly loathe writing that seeks to work on the passions and to exploit them, instead of releasing them in a healthy form: laughter. I think that the periodical literature that exploits the weaknesses of men is a true disease and has much to do with the whole complex of all our troubles and problems: the utterly sick and subhuman reduction of "thought" to nothingness: to something that appears to be sensual but is not even that.

I don't get *The Month* but I would like very much to see the article on Wm. of St.-Thierry as I have to give lectures on the Cist. Fathers this year.

As for spiritual life: what I object to about "the Spiritual Life" is the fact that it is a part, a section, set off as if it were a whole. It is an aberration to set off our "prayer" etc. from the rest of our existence, as if we were sometimes spiritual, sometimes not. As if we had to resign ourselves to feeling that the unspiritual moments were a dead loss. That is not right at all, and because it is an aberration, it causes an enormous amount of useless suffering.

Our "life in the Spirit" is all-embracing, or should be. First it is the response of faith receiving the word of God, not only as a truth to be believed but as a gift of life to be lived in total submission and pure confidence. Then this implies fidelity and obedience, but a total fidelity and a total obedience. From the moment that I obey God in everything, where is my "spiritual life"? It is gone out the window, there is no spiritual life, only God and His word and my total response.

The problem comes when factors beyond our control make it impossible to respond in all our totality: I mean by that when a large part of our subconscious or routine or "obligatory" existence gets blocked off in such a way that it remains in opposition to, or not in union with, the will of God.

This is where you and I have to suffer much. In actual fact, if we could really let go of everything and follow the Spirit where He leads, who knows where we would be? But besides the interior exigencies of the Spirit there are also hard external facts, and they too are "God's will," but nevertheless they may mean that one is bound to a certain mediocrity and futility: that there is waste, and ineffective use of grace (bad way to talk, but you understand). The comfortable and respectable existence that you and I lead is in fact to a great degree *opposed* to the real demands of the Spirit in our lives. Yet paradoxically we are restricted and limited to this. Our acceptance of these restrictions cannot purely and simply be regarded as the ultimate obedience that is demanded of us. We cannot say that our bourgeois existence is purely and simply the "will of God." It both is and is not. Hence the burning and the darkness and the desperation we feel. The sense of untruth, of infidelity, even though we try as best we can to be faithful. I am not now talking of the illusory fidelity to some ideal of perfect purity of heart and apatheia, which is totally impossible and is a sinful angelism. But we are *held back* from the deep and total gift which is not altogether possible to make in a conventional and tame setting where we do not suffer the things that the poor and disinherited and the outcast must suffer. The crosses we may find or fabricate in this life of ours, may serve to salve our conscience a little, and legitimately so: but we are not in the fullest sense Christians because we have not fully and completely obeyed the Spirit of Christ. And in my case I am not permitted to do so. (That is a strange thing to say. Will explain someday.)

Result, an interior frustration and burning and desperation in which we are and must be aware of our lack of total honesty and self-renunciation. Yet I don't think there is much more we can do about it. Certainly the devices of "good religious" tightening up the nuts and bolts in their little observance here and there, this does not fill the bill. It only contributes to the illusion, and makes the pain worse.

Well, that is enough. I hope you will keep well, and that your work will go along peacefully and fruitfully, and that you will understand more and more the paradoxes in which you must live, and that you will obey God as best you can in your position. All that we have on earth is provisional in any case.

March 24, 1963

Thanks for your good long letter about the hard winter, the Abbot of Downside, the Council and the rest. We have had a hard winter too, but now it is nice spring weather.

What you say about the fact that you (and all of us) are unbelieving and that it is God in you who believes, is quite true. We do not realize how little faith we have, and the more people talk about "my" faith, the more I wonder if they have it. It can easily be simply a matter of subscribing to what other people, like oneself, think is proper to believe. But as to you being a heretic, I suppose in some theoretic sense you may be so to one on my side of the fence, but personally I have long since given up attaching importance to that sort of thing, because I have no idea what you may be in the eyes of God, and that is what counts. I do think, though, that you and I are one in Christ, and hence the presence of some material heresy (according to my side of the fence) does not make that much difference. Certainly truth is important but there are all sorts of circumstances one must consider, and as far as I am concerned you are what you should be, and what you can be, and thank God for it . . .

[Let me say] how much I love the *Mirror* and how much I thank you for letting me keep it. It is really one of my favorite books . . . The language is wonderful, the expressions are charming, and of course I like the doctrine. But I can see how it could have got poor Marguerite in trouble (you see, I am convinced that she is the author). As you say, one must fear delusion and heresy in such matters as this, but great simplicity, humility and purity of faith, and above all detachment from a self that experiences itself in prayer, or a self that desires anything for itself, is a sure safeguard. Along with a reasonably orthodox participation in the life of the Church: but I don't hold with these extreme liturgy people for whom all personal and contemplative prayer is suspect. If you make a meditation they think you are a Buddhist. I have been writing an article on Zen, and I think there is a lot to be learned from the Buddhists, as regards the natural and psychological side of contemplation, especially some of the most obvious psychological blocks, which we blithely ignore, and to our cost.

The nuns at Stanbrook are printing a little translation of a *Letter of Guigo* (enclosed) which I did. I think they would really be the ones to do the little book of small selections from Benet. I never went to that Quaker about it because I do not think he is the man. Do you agree to let me propose this to them? I might then write a little preface, and you might want to go over the texts, adding here and there or editing. What do you think? Hope you have a good trip to Rome.

April 29, 1963

Thanks for your letter from the Spanish steps, and the others. But especially from "the Spanish steps in the sun." I remember that well, especially the spring sun. I loved it. But I would not want to go there now. Friends who have been to Italy recently have terrible tales about the traffic, and in Rome we have our General's house, where there is a grueling and mad schedule going on all the time, and I would just as soon stay as far away from it as possible. No more Italy for me, anyway. Paestum, yes, I would love to see. I never did. I was also doing a bit of work on Cassiodorus last fall, as I probably mentioned, and I would like to see where his place was, even though nothing is left of it . . .

Yes, I knew of Christ's Hospital [English public school]. For a brief moment, long ago, there was a momentary thought of my going there, but I never saw it. I don't think I would have liked it. The school where I went was just right. I wonder if you ever get any boys from there? They used to all go to Cambridge, where we had closed scholarships. Oakham it was. Once in a while I hear from it. It has not changed much, if at all, except that some of the boys who were there with me are now Masters and so on.

How is your good Cowley Brother [Brother Raymond Molineaux, ordained when he was terminally ill]? I am awfully sorry to hear he is in bad shape and am praying for him. Of course there is every reason why you should want to carry part of his burden and should do so spiritually. And of course this is Christ in you and in him also. We cannot get too deep into the mystery of our oneness in Christ. It is so deep as to be unthinkable and yet a little thought about it doesn't hurt. But it doesn't help too much either. The thing is that we are not united in a *thought* of Christ or a desire of Christ, but in His Spirit. Anyway I will keep Brother in my Mass. I don't know if my letter about our oneness in Christ was clear. The other day a good distinction came to mind: but there is all the difference in the world between theology as *experienced* (which is basically identical in all who know and love Christ, at least in its root) and theology as *formulated* in which there can be great differences. In the former, it is the One Spirit who teaches and enlightens us. In the second it is the Church, and in this of course I believe that the Roman Church is the only one that can claim to say the last word. But I do not think it makes sense to be narrowly Roman in a sort of curial-party sense, and I am also very attracted to the orthodox *sobornost* idea. And of course I think in reality Pope John has been quietly moving in that direction, and he has been perfectly right in so doing, without affecting his own primacy and so on. As I look back on the sentences above, I can see that what I said is misleading too: I do not of course intend a hard-and-fast distinction between the Spirit on one hand teaching the individual and the Church teaching him: this would be erroneous. But I mean the Spirit teaching us all interiorly, and also exteriorly through the magisterium. In either case it is the Spirit of the Church, and the Church, living and speaking. But in exterior doctrinal formulations, where there are different groups, there are various confusions and differences. And so on. I am not a very sharp technical theologian, as you can see.

But I did like the Pope's encyclical on peace [*Pacem in Terris*] and it bore out a lot of the things I had been trying to say. But I still don't know if I will be allowed to say them . . . The stupidity of it is a little unnerving. The Pope can clearly say what he wants of the Church and of its members, particularly the clergy, and then people halfway down can contradict him: and of course preach obedience with supreme serenity themselves . . .

I haven't taken up the question of the Benet pieces with the Stanbrook nuns, but I really will. In fact I will try to get the selections off to them today or tomorrow. I think the idea of this little book is very attractive, and will keep at it. Have you any further suggestions?

. . . God bless you always. I do so enjoy your letters, especially when you travel. And I do think often of you and pray for you, and value your prayers for me. I keep all your friends and intentions in my own prayers, psalms and Mass. I think it would be wonderful if the Abbot of Downside became Archbishop of Westminster. However, I can see where he would rather stay where he is. But he seems to have made a great impression at the Council, in the best kind of way.

July 28, 1963

Thanks for the three letters I owe you. I cannot hope to answer them adequately now. But I envy you a little in Somerset: it is fiercely hot here. I suppose you are cool and everything is pleasant.

It would have been nice if the Abbot of Downside could have come here. Perhaps someday he will. I have been reading David Knowles's new book, with the long memoir on Abbot Cuthbert Butler, which is very well done and very interesting. He also has a very attractive chapter on Mabillon. I am afraid I am on the side of the Benedictines against de Rancé when it comes to study and so on, though perhaps some of the Benedictines do not think I would be that way. Perhaps they think I am a fierce ascetic, which I certainly am not, as anyone who knows me will gladly tell you.

I have been reading a very fine book of R. W. Southern on St. Anselm. I suppose you must know Southern. I think he did a very good job. I took this occasion to get into St. Anselm a little, too. I had always been put off him by the standard philosophy textbooks, but I find him fascinating. And am reading Erasmus too, since we have his collected works in one of those photo-offset editions of the old folios. This all doesn't sound much like Canfield, does it? Well, I do have a humanist and philosophical side. And Anselm was a mystic, certainly. I don't believe in being professionally anti-intellectual, as though the mind as such were an obstacle to contemplation. I think this is a big mistake, and the effects of it are unfortunate.

Certainly I agree that there can be no genuine contemplative life without suffering and without self-denial. Both are necessary. There is bound to be a great deal of unsought-for suffering merely because a contemplative is necessarily out of tune with most of what goes on around him. To be a contemplative is to be in some ways maladjusted and even though by forcing oneself, one can put up with the superficialities and pretenses of social life, one constantly sees through them and is very aware of their absurdity and meaninglessness. To live in state of more or less unrelieved absurdity is certainly not pleasant, and one suffers loneliness, frustration, confusion, and besides, one is always getting into somewhat humiliating situations because of it. However, that does not mean that we cannot function fairly smoothly and get along with people. Yet I for one (although I am thought to be very friendly and spontaneous) am always fairly well aware of the falsity of most "conventional" social relationships and the double talk that one has to indulge in, pretending that it all makes sense when it is really ludicrous.

A little self-chosen penance and suffering helps to make all this more intelligible because it is a kind of affirmation that the accepted standards all around one are not the real ones. However, this can become a temptation too. One can affirm himself in opposition to the world by penances.

This can get out of hand and turn into frank self-seeking. I think it is salutary to accept the absurdity and contradictions of life in good part, this is a very effective penance. Unfortunately I get angry and disgusted a lot of the time, and I suppose that spoils it to some extent.

How utterly *boring* people can make life, when they live together, and that includes monasteries. Though the monastic life itself is never boring.

Talking about Cowley, Fr. A. M. Allchin, of Pusey House (I suppose you must know him), is coming here next week. He has sent his book about the Anglican religious communities [*The Silent Rebellion: Anglican Religious Communities 1845–1900*] and I find it quite interesting. I am so happy that your friend [Brother Raymond] was ordained: yes, you did tell me that, I think. I shall remember him occasionally in my Mass, and may he rest in peace.

All your friends seem to be very noble and self-sacrificing and this is very fine. This gets back to something I said to you before, I believe: it is always helpful to be able to express our Christian charity in some way, and not just have to sit around with it all bottled up inside us. I think some active charitable work is good for the contemplative life, provided that we don't get into it purely out of restlessness and aimlessness. In everything, however, the great thing is God's will. A contemplative is one who has God's will bearing right down upon him, often in the most incomprehensible way. One feels that if one could only *see* clearly *how* it was God's will, the whole thing would be less painful. But it just is, and there is no explanation. This is painful. God is to us painful Himself, and we are to ourselves painful, during a great deal of our life. But we must not make too much of it, and I prefer not to think about it or talk about it.

. . . Hooray for [the] Henley [regatta] and for the beauties . . .

October 18, 1963

I have been a really abominable correspondent and now to add insult to injury I am writing without the typewriter. I have been a bit ill and cannot do a great deal of typing. Nothing serious, but my left arm won't take much work.

Have I written to you since the summer? I enjoyed Donald Allchin's visit and hoped to be in touch with the nuns at Fairacres Convent. I simply don't have time to write.

You are right about visits of course. They are exhausting (I don't mean Donald A. in particular). I feel that I have to see some people, that it is a real duty, but a series of visits is really wearing because actually there is so much interior resistance to the superficial side of it and so much attraction to the real center, in interior prayer.

Obviously, anyone living a life of prayer has to confront this kind of problem and each one has to solve it for himself in his own circumstances. You being married obviously cannot evade the duties of your state. I being a monk cannot nevertheless use "the duties of my state" as a blanket pretext for avoiding all contacts since some of them seem to be definitely willed by God. One can never work this out perfectly satisfactorily and therefore one always has to face the unpleasantness of a kind of insecurity, not knowing whether one has judged rightly. But it is a responsibility one must assume in one way or another. Once you form your conscience to abide by God's will, you will have all the fruits of prayer even though you may be deprived sometimes of the enjoyment.

Certainly the beauty and loveliness of Somerset must have had its compensation to offer for the other boring duties.

I have finished a long article on Anselm, occasioned by Southern's book. Thanks for telling me about him. He is as I imagined . . .

Have you read any of Zoë Oldenbourg's books about the Albigensians? Very moving and disturbing. She is right in many ways, yet you cannot call the Cathars "perfect Christians." I do not hesitate to add that the Inquisition is certainly no more perfectly Christian than the Cathars— probably a lot less!!

I have been reading George Herbert lately—again. He seems a bit thin and watery, but is so charming. And represents a world that has, alas, ceased to exist. I do so much want to read some of the seventeenth-century Anglican divines. Can you suggest some good ideas to investigate? I like William Law but have not read much . . .

A Martin Lings has done what I think is a very fine study of a Moslem called Ahmad Al-'Alawi. I have an extra copy and can send it if you like.

Thanks for your appraisal of the new Archbishop of W[estminster]. I rather fancied he was like that. He is the type we call in this country "an operator."

November 24, 1963

Just a word of thanks for the books, Wm. Law, and Lancelot Andrewes. I am so glad to have them both, particularly William Law. I like him very much. I will spend an afternoon in the woods with the *Preces Privatae* one of these days too.

Sooner or later I must do a study on Anglican spirituality. That is what Donald Allchin keeps suggesting and I think he is right, but I must move at it slowly, as I want to keep at several other things. I am still working on Anselm and still appreciating Southern. I would write to him if I had time. When something finally gets printed I will send it to him. I like the Canterbury School for some reason, though they are not my usual style. Perhaps because I know Canterbury so well. Perhaps their holiness affected me unconsciously, or their prayers, when I was in the place where they served God.

However, I have not abandoned my usual interests and I send you a bit I translated from Nicholas of Cusa. I hope the Stanbrook nuns will soon have printed the letter of Guigo so that I can send you one . . .

January 7, 1964

The "vast tome" on Anglicanism just arrived. I am sure it will be very helpful indeed and am really delighted to have it. I will also be looking forward to *English Spirituality*, which is still on the way. Vaughan I have, I think I told you. At least *Silex Scintillans*. I do not have his prose but I can easily get to it. I thought momentarily of editing his translation of St. Eucherius on "Contempt of the World." I like Eucherius, a former monk of Lérins and contemporary of Cassian. His little tract on the solitary life is beautiful. I wonder if it has ever been done in English. If not, I hope I will someday do it myself. But I am always promising myself irresponsibly to do translations which I cannot possibly get to at least in the present dispensation.

I am still novice master, and still have the usual other chores to do. One thing I seriously want to try to do this year is cut down on the contacts with people who come to visit. (But if you come to America I do not include you in those whose visits I will renounce. It is different for someone one may see only once in a lifetime.) There is really not a great deal of good I can do for all the people around here who want to be consulting with me about this and that, and I refuse to become a one-man ecumenical movement, which would be silly. It makes sense for me to see a few people, rarely, someone like Donald Allchin for example.

Then you have no idea how I am bothered by people who insist on sending me poems, manuscripts, privately printed books and the rest. I cannot even pretend to read this material, but just sending it back is a job in itself. Yet here again, I remember that you started by sending me Benet and I am grateful that you did. There are always exceptions and rightly. In other words one must be able to discriminate: but that too takes thought and time.

You ask about spiritual books. I have been reading all sorts of things, things which I find spiritual. Rudolf Bultmann's *Essays* is a challenging book, terribly interesting, and his anti-mysticism has a point. It is good to tussle a bit with something of this kind, in order to get down to the real foundation of everything, which is faith. I have also been reading [Karl] Jaspers. His *Way to Wisdom* has some good things in it. And a French phenomenologist, Merleau-Ponty, who seems to me at times to get close to Zen, though I am sure he has no intention of doing so. Zwi Werblowsky (I think I told you he was here, Professor of Comparative Religion at the Hebrew University in Jerusalem) has sent a very interesting Spanish Jew of the eleventh century who has Moslem elements. Bahya Ibn Paquda. Then there is Martin Lings's book on a wonderful Moslem mystic, which I may have mentioned when I was in the hospital: Shaikh Ahmad Al-'Alawi.

. . . About confession: it is not usually linked with direction, probably because of the shortage of time, with us. I mean with the RC's. Here in the monastery in practice we have confession and direction together. Mine is never more than ten or fifteen minutes, and actually I get very little direction. Not that I don't need it, but I just have nowhere to turn for it. In a way that is all right. It forces one to rely on the Holy Spirit, and to do so in stress and I hope with humility and the "dread" these existentialist lads are always talking about. Very salutary. It would be all too easy to get embedded in an institutional routine.

I enjoyed your account of your wedding anniversary (congratulations!). I will have my silver jubilee of entrance into the monastery in 1966 but nothing is ever made of that. Twenty-five years in a monastery is only a good beginning. But this year will be my fiftieth in existence, I will try to make a kind of quiet and determined jubilee, a year of prayer and self-dedication . . .

February 16, 1964

Just a brief letter to thank you for the big book *Crucible of Love*. I have not got into it because I am swamped with books on interlibrary loan that I have to return at definite times, and at the moment I am not too keen on reading Carmelites for some reason. I have had so much of them in the past, and I am discovering new things, for instance Abbot Ammonas, the successor of St. Anthony at Pispir. He is marvelous and so far completely neglected. The best texts have been edited in the *Patrologia Orientalis* since before the First World War, but no one has done anything with them except Hausherr (who has been doing good stuff on Oriental spirituality) . . . Also I am reading this great new Dutch Dominican, Schillebeeckx. (Isn't that a mouthful? But it is not as bad as it looks.)

. . . Your little bit of Latin [*Vita Jesu* by Ludolf the Carthusian] will get translated, but I will probably get a novice to do it. I am just too busy with too many things at the moment . . .

It is good for you to have someone to talk to there. You cannot really get direction by mail. As for your having defects and still knowing about the life of prayer, well, all I can say is that this is not unusual. I have never met anyone who did not have a lot of defects, and this seems to have relatively little to do with it, provided they are just things in their character which they can't really help. Such defects are very useful and do a lot for one, if one accepts them rightly. On the other hand there are a lot of defects which we could easily be without if we were not dominated by our environment, and caught as it were in a kind of trap by our own surroundings and our own history. I know that there are defects I have here which are precisely part of my situation in this monastery, blisters so to speak. I could be without them elsewhere, but then I might have much worse ones, and deeper ones too. Who can say? In any case we cannot expect to be without faults. As to your darkness, I really think it is also something of the blister type and that you could be without it if you really wanted to be, but I think it is just part of your life and you have incorporated it into your existence, it is almost something you unconsciously prefer. And of course it also has to do with grace, I don't say you are making it. But a thrust of higher liberty would get you out. How? Don't ask me.

God bless you always, anyway, and pray for me. Of course spiritual friendship is most important.

May 22, 1964

It is difficult for me to remember whether or not I answered your letters from Italy, but I think I haven't. I am sorry, because if I have not it must be a matter of months. But the letters were very lively and most interesting. Thank you for them. I really don't think I would like Italy today, except perhaps off the beaten track, and very far off. But I am more and more getting used to the idea that I shall probably never travel again. It is certainly an important aspect of monastic poverty, or so I think and one of the few real sacrifices. Still, I will always enjoy vicarious traveling with you, who are entitled to it.

Things have been inordinately busy here, and it is hard to know what to say first. But I did enjoy Fr. Hollings's thing on Chaplain craft [in *Black-friars*]. It was very well done . . . The book I have on my mind and like very much is Nora Chadwick's lectures on the Celtic Church. This is really first-rate, and especially interesting to me as I really intend now to do something on recluses and the Irish started all that, or so it seems, at least in Europe (though the ones Gregory of Tours talks of in Gaul seem to have had an independent origin??). Certainly the recluses of the English Middle Ages were very characteristic of the English Church, and I am getting back to the Ancren Riwle, Aelred's Rule for his sister, and so on.

My preface to the Fénelon letters is out, with the letters of course, and Harvill Press has done a rather attractive job. I don't think I have yet sent you the little book the Stanbrook nuns did for me, with Guigo on the solitary life. So I am sending it along together with some other recent things. I have been, I repeat, foolishly and perhaps scandalously busy with a lot of absurd things, not the least of which is a preface to Bolshakoff's book on the Russian mystics. The real job of that was that I had to go through his whole ms. written in longhand and in impossible English, trying to make it readable. The material is good, or at least quite interesting, but otherwise I am now I suppose an honorary Cowley Father by reason of my support of Bolshakoff.*

It is getting to be summer here, and already a bit hot. But after the

* *Sergius Bolshakoff, a Russian writer with friends in high places, often stayed with the Cowley Fathers (popular name for the Fathers of St. John the Evangelist) in Oxford. See letters to him.*

end of this month the heat is usually terrible. Yet I enjoy summer, especially the feast days when I try to get out into the woods as much as possible. I meditate best in the woods, no matter how hot it may be. And I hope to do more of it rather than less . . .

June 15, 1964

Yes, the *Clergy Review*: I am not sure if you wanted it returned. Somewhere along the line I got that impression, but not before I had first torn out the article to put on our novitiate board. The novices liked it very much. So I am returning the magazine, dismembered but whole.

I do not think contemplation can be taught, but certainly an aptitude for it can be awakened. It is an aptitude which quite a lot of people might have, in seminaries and monasteries at least, as well as in any walk of life. The important thing is that this be made real and credible by someone who knows by experience what it is, and who can make it real to those in whom it begins to awaken. In a word it is a question of showing them in a mysterious way by example how to proceed. Not by the example of doing, but the example of being, and by one's attitude toward life and things.

Certainly you have some sort of vocation in this regard, but you do not have to be too aware of it. Simply be content to let God use you in whatever way He wills, and be sure you do not get in his way with misplaced initiatives. The mere fact that you intuitively go straight for people like Benet of C. means that you will not be too tempted in this regard . . .

September 12, 1964

Thanks for the letters I owe you. This has been a very bad summer for letter writing here. Various things have kept me busy. There have been people dropping in, as usual in the summer, and this takes up time. Finally I have a nasty skin affliction, poison ivy, which takes the skin off my fingers and makes typing difficult. I have also been trying to get a little work done, and trying to pray. I do what I can to give prayer preference and so letters must necessarily suffer.

Your letters all sound good. I am glad you are in contact with so many people who are following a good and simple path. I have greater and greater confidence in the reality of the path that is no path at all, and to see people follow it in spite of everything is comforting. By rights they should all have forgotten and lost their way long ago. If they keep on it without really knowing what it is, this is because God keeps them there.

I am not surprised at the things you say. The climate of the Anglican Church seems to me to be quite favorable, especially with the background of the English school. I do honestly feel that the Anglicans have a special job to do, to keep alive this spiritual simplicity and honesty quite apart from all fuss and works. It seems to me that the atmosphere in our Church on the other hand is going to become more and more hostile to contemplative prayer. There will certainly be official pronouncements approving it and blessing it. But in fact the movement points in the direction of activism, and an activistic concept of liturgy. I think the root of the trouble is fear and truculence, unrealized, deep down. The realization that the Church of Rome is not going to be able to maintain a grandiose and preeminent sort of position, the old prestige she has always had and the decisive say in the things of the world, to some extent even in the last centuries. Contemplation will be regarded more and more as an official "dynamo" source of inspiration and power for the big guns out there: Carmelite nuns generating spiritual electricity for the Holy Office, not so much by contemplative prayer as by action and official public prayer within an enclosure.

In a word, the temper of the Roman Church is combative and "aroused" and the emphasis on contemplation is (if there is any at all) dominated by a specific end in view so that implicitly contemplation becomes ordered to action, which is so easy in a certain type of scholastic thought, misunderstood. When this happens, the real purity of the life of prayer is gone. I must say though that there is a good proportion of contemplative prayer in the novitiate. I don't use special methods. I try to make them love the freedom and peace of being with God alone in faith and simplicity, to abolish all divisiveness and diminish all useless strain and concentration on one's own efforts and all formalism: all the nonsense of taking seriously the apparatus of an official prayer life, in the wrong way (but to love liturgy in simple faith as the place of Christ's sanctifying presence in the community).

I have Oxford much in mind these days as we are reading an excellent new life of Newman (Merioll Trevor) in the refectory. I remember Oriel Hall and the exam I took there. They were going to give me a scholarship there the following year, probably, but I was put off by the noise of the High [Street] and went to Cambridge. I wonder what it would have been if I had gone to Oxford after all.

I am always glad to hear your news and the news of the people God brings close to you . . .

Pray for me: there is a meeting of abbots coming up here and it looks as though it were going to be quite difficult and unrewarding. I am supposed to give a talk and be present at the discussions, but do not relish the prospect at all. I think it is going to be terribly frustrating. They all have their minds made up firmly beforehand as to what they want and they are going to be playing politics to see that their own views are accepted. There will be small use in my being there, except perhaps that some will want to use me, for their own policies. I find this very distasteful.

January 25, 1965

You must be very tired of waiting for answers to your letters, and I hope you understand that I have been in an impossible position. I simply cannot keep up with correspondence adequately. And I am afraid I did not even have copies of the *Identity Crisis* to send. But the novice has finally got some run off again, and they will be on their way. I will enclose a couple of newer things. But for the last month or so I have hardly been able to get any writing of my own done either. Christmas always complicates everything here, and then there was the annual retreat (preached by Fr. Illtud Evans).

The book about Fr. William of Glasshampton [who left the ministry to become a solitary] interested me very much, especially as it has so much about the early days of Glasshampton. This interests me because I am at last, gradually, moving into a hermitage. Not that I can be completely solitary yet, since I am still novice master, but I do sleep there now and even spend a whole day and night there once in a while, and sometimes take supper up there too . . .

What you say about the Trinity in your life of prayer is of course the most traditional thing. It is good to understand the theology of it, because when it is put into words one gets the impression that the talk is about "three objects" which one is experiencing. The ancient way of looking at it, "to the Father in the Son by the Holy Spirit," reminds us of the *unity* and the un-objective character of it. And yet they are Three, or we are in their Three and One in the Three. The authenticity of the experience depends on the dissolution of the apparent "I" that can seem to stand outside all this as subject and observe it from somewhere else. Of course we fall back into this when commenting and explaining and that is the trouble with commenting and explaining. I still think that among moderns the most authentic expression of the experience is that of the Carmelite, Elizabeth of the Trinity, though I have not gone back to look at her writings for over fifteen years now. I might not like them so much now. I cannot say.

All the Benedictines and Cistercians and everyone will be totally swept along nowadays by the new liturgical changes, and since there has been an apparent opposition between "liturgy" and "contemplation," if you seem to confront them with a choice between them, they will panic and seize upon what seems to be secure because more popular. I think you may meet with little success in getting Benedictines interested in simple contemplative prayer at the moment. They have Baker and the Prophets, haven't they? If they do not listen to them, they will perhaps not listen too readily to you either. But I may be wrong. In any case, it is important precisely for monasticism and for the liturgy too that the whole thing does not become too much of a superficial movement, a matter of fashion. And if it is properly understood, the new liturgy ought to help people to be more deeply contemplative: unfortunately it may turn into a very busy-busy sort of thing with no time to breathe. I wonder how it is going in England, and in the monasteries. We are having our first concelebration here tomorrow, and I am not getting into it, as I want to leave a place for some of the younger ones who are more enthusiastic about it, whereas I am rather uninterested in it. I like the *idea* of concelebration, but I know how these things are, and being now among the seniors I can afford to sit back and let it become peacefully organized and settled before I become involved.

Regarding that Trinitarian formula: I should rather say: "In the Father, through the Son, by the Holy Spirit." This is much more "final" I think.

May 5, 1965

I was very sorry to get your letter announcing that you would not come. What a shame, to have to put off your whole plan. I do hope that perhaps in the future you may be able to come. Yet at the same time I do not know what my own position in the future will be. I have for a long time wanted to try the hermit life and it looks as if I can finally get permission for it, but naturally there will be conditions, and I probably will not be allowed to have visitors. We shall see. I do not mean of course that I would be leaving here, but living in a cottage in the woods, and as a matter of fact I am already spending a great deal of time there and sleeping there at night.

Things are rather gloomy here. The war in Vietnam is being pushed, against the protests and desires of most of the people. The country is not behind it, and yet Johnson insists on going on. I think he is very stupid and that he, and everyone else, will have cause to regret it. It may become quite serious, though it seems they are playing a daring political game rather than trying to start a nuclear war. But it might come to that, they are such fools.

Perhaps, too, you would have found the climate trying here. It is hot and damp at the moment, and we are having the unpleasant weather we often get later on in the summer. I think you would not have enjoyed that aspect of it much . . .

June 9, 1965

Several more copies of *Contemplation and Ecumenism* are on the way to you. I also put in some "versions" of Chuang Tzu I have dared to do, based simply on comparisons of various translations and on some guessing of my own. Chuang Tzu seems to have been on the right track in many respects, though without the theological depth that would come with true faith: still, he grasped the nature of things and of our orientation to God in silence. Tauler liked Proclus for the same reasons as I do CT.

I hope you will enjoy him. I am actually making a whole book out of bits like this, and it has been a lot of fun for me. Great occupation for the hermitage, in relaxation from the "work of the cell" which is the prime necessity.

The more I see of it, the more I realize the absolute primacy and necessity of silent, hidden, poor, apparently fruitless prayer. The whole monastic order is being swept with currents and backwashes of activism and anxiety over ways to make monasticism "count" in the modern world. The very fact that monks should be anxious about such things is already a strange symptom. However, it is balanced by the fact, as you say, that there are still very many who are drawn to the silent and solitary way which is really that of the monk. I think that this is one of the most encouraging things in Anglicanism, even though there is the honest-to-God set driving full speed away from center.

. . . Did I answer your question about September? I do not remember. The whole thing is very uncertain. At the moment the idea is to not undertake to have any more visits this year except for one or two that were arranged a long time ago, and would be once-in-a-lifetime affairs in any case probably. But yours might come under that heading. For the moment, I would say it is not certain that I could see you, but not totally impossible either. Do not plan on coming out here on the idea that it would be a sure thing, but then let me know if by any chance you could come, once you were in America. Then I might start asking and managing. Since you are coming from so far away, it makes a difference. Dom Leclercq might stop by in September. This has been planned for some time. A friend of mine went to see Padre Pio, has seen him before in any case, and is much impressed. So am I. I think Padre Pio is very authentic, from what I know about him. Certainly we all suffer together in and with Christ. And it is possible for this to be experienced in a way. On the other hand, experience of it may or may not add anything. It is the Holy Spirit who makes us one and our experience of Him may or may not make much difference. But faith in Him makes a very great deal of difference and this is the important thing. Deep faith and obedience. I see this more and more. So let us be united in prayer in Christ and in His Spirit.

July 16, 1965

I am glad to send you more of what I have. It is on the way by sea mail. If people like them, that is fine. I think it is natural that we reach people on the other side of fences these days. Your "Short Prayers" [in *Clergy Review*] is very good and I have posted it for the novices to read. There has been favorable comment.

Do you think the Abbot of Downside should see the enclosed? It is perhaps a bit cheeky of me to lecture the American bishops, but I heard they had expressed a quasi-approval of the bomb in the revised schema.

It won't hurt them to be reminded there is public opinion in the Church. I am sure non-Americans would be with me, and perhaps Dom Butler would like to see it.

August 26, 1965

I think I owe you a couple of letters. Your letters are always so good and full of interesting things, I am ashamed that I do not send something better in reply. Lately I have written almost no letters at all. Finally I got moved into the hermitage and out of the novitiate . . .

Life in a hermitage is really extraordinary. As you know I had been half in and half out for almost a year, but it is quite another matter to be here all the time, with no other responsibilities, and going down only once a day. I still have to say Mass at the monastery so I go down about mid-morning, say Mass, get one cooked meal, and pick up whatever I need, then come back to the hermitage. Even when I go down I seldom have any occasion to speak to anyone, just nod to a few people and come back. Really there is no question that this does something quite tremendous for the life of prayer. It enables things to open up, and also lets the trials get a good hold. I feel I am learning a whole new way of life, and it is really like being born again in a way. Certainly one of the things that strikes me most about it is that it is not at all what the opponents of eremitism always accuse it of being: a sort of vague life of abstraction and self-centeredness. Actually it is much less self-centered and abstract than the sort of drifting existence of irresponsibility one can get into in the community. I think that it is also far less petty. One has to be constantly concerned to do things well and do them in a manner that fits the life and the place. One certainly cannot trifle with a hermit vocation, I can see that.

Yesterday for example I got my baptism of fire when I was doing some work in the woods clearing brush and broke into a hornets' nest. Extremely unpleasant. They were all over me and bit ferociously, and even followed me into the house, some of them. I don't know if you have such things in England (wasps yes, I know) but I should think that a hermit's life in England or Wales would be much more tranquil from this point of view, I mean the insects, the snakes and the other natural things which are nevertheless quite proper to the life. One simply has to learn the rules, and this is a community life in which the rules are well kept, and broken only at a cost.

I am always very interested to hear all that you say about the interest in the real life of prayer in England. I have just reread the old article of C. F. Kelley in the *Downside Review*, on poverty and the Rhenish mystics, and thought it very good indeed again. Do you want that back, by the way? I can see that the real hermit life quickly brings one to precisely that kind of poverty and keeps one there. The business of being in direct dependence on God all the time is the key. Do keep me in your prayers, as the life is not easy. I remember you and all your problems and friends.

November 1, 1965

Thanks for your very interesting letters from Scotland. That is all ancient history by now, but I hope you had a good time. It is evident that I am not a better correspondent in the hermitage than I was in the monastery, and I suppose that is to be expected. Naturally I have to give most of my time to what I am here for, and even then I always seem to be short of time. There are things to be done, it is cold now, and wood has to be chopped and so on.

I am reading the life of an anchorite in Devon, or rather Somerset I think, St. Wulfric of Haselbury. It is written by John of Ford (Cistercian abbey). You must know that area rather well, though it is perhaps a bit far south for you. Could you possibly lend me an ordnance map of that bit of Devon and Somerset? Around Haselbury, Crewkerne, and wherever Ford Abbey is. It is all within fifty miles of Exeter. I just want to borrow the map and get my bearings. I may do a couple of articles on this.

Have you ever done anything more with Benet? Or did you tell me something recent about that? There is something hazy in my mind, but I cannot quite remember it.

Do please above all tell the Abbot of Downside how happy I was with his intervention in the Council on conscientious objection. I thought it was most important. From what I know of the discussion of peace and war there, it went well. There is a lot of fuss about that in this country now, since there is, quite rightly, a great deal of protest against this absurd business in Vietnam, which in the end cannot be anything but ruinous for the U.S. But also from the moral point of view it is a very dubious "just war." Feelings are running high, however. I don't know what will become of this country, but I still have hope in unsuspected moral resources somewhere.

There are a lot of people getting interested in prayer in this country, mostly in academic circles, and in a rather mixed-up context of psychoanalysis and Zen Buddhism. This is the area where people at the moment are most interested in our kind of contemplation. The Catholics are all hopped up about liturgy at the moment. If you would be interested to get in touch with people who are doing these things, though they may not quite be your line, I can establish such contact for you. There are people at McGill University in Montreal [the R. M. Bucke Memorial Society] who are studying from a "scientific" psychological viewpoint the phenomenon of this curious contemplation thing. I do think that with your Benet and Harphius and so on, you could contribute a lot, and they might even get you over to give a lecture or something. Let me know if you would be interested in hearing from them. Actually there is a variety of spirits among them, and they are not all as dull as this may sound.

November 11, 1965

. . . As to intercession: let each do what he likes. Sometimes I remember a lot of people by name, other times not. I always have a list that comes to mind at the diptychs at Mass, sometimes longer, sometimes shorter, and usually with a few people who are always there (v.g., novices when I was novice master) and a lot of others who pop in by inspiration. But obviously in one's meditation etc. one does not go dragging a lot of people in, unless it is an unusual situation. I think that in this whole question of prayer we make too many problems out of what one should do and what one should not do. These are entirely personal matters and in the same person they vary from moment to moment. The great thing is not to say that lists of names are bad or lists of names are good, but to let the person himself come to know by discernment of spirits when he should "intercede" for people by name and when not.

Archbishop Heenan (or is he a cardinal) made what I thought was an asinine intervention about priests in the Council. He attacked monasteries where there are a lot of "perfectly healthy monks who are priests and who never go out to work in a parish." He came along with the old stupid "lazy monk" argument. Incidentally when this was read in the refectory the approved schema on religious was read after it (probably by design) in which the Council explicitly approved contemplatives being exempted from active parish work. I wonder what Dom Butler thought of that one: that is to say I wonder not what he thought, because I can well imagine, but hope he had some fine blast that would give me consolation. However, it is wrong to seek consolation, even and perhaps especially in matters like these. I am only joking. Best of everything to you.

March 8, 1966

Thanks for the booklet on John of Ford [monastery]. The one or two pictures of twelfth-century buildings are quite charming. The rest is rather amusing in its own odd way. But I do like the gardens.

I am glad to hear you keep on doing so much good. Apparently at this moment you are intended to exercise a very real apostolate to bring people to prayer. I have a problem in that regard, not my own but someone else's, and material at that. It is a question of publishing Raïssa Maritain's *Journal* in English. It is very fine, a really important document on prayer. Naturally the state of RC publishing is now such that they will not touch it with a twenty-foot pole. Everything has to be super-active liturgical *épanouissement*, you know, and hence this book will not be published by RC's either in England or in America. I think the Anglicans would be a much better bet and have told Jacques M. so. Have you any ideas? We are at the moment trying a few non-religious publishers, or rather people who publish a few religious books but are not identified with any church group, in this country. If you have any good ideas for England, please let me know.

Did I ever tell you how much I liked your piece on intercession [in *Clergy Review*]? I thought you handled it very well.

Purgations all one's life? There are no rules for that. Each one gets what he needs, for himself or for others, and there is no use in trying to plan on having or not having any. My impression of you is that probably things will go on as they are for quite a long time, since you seem to be in a sort of a "bind." However, anything can happen, and really does it matter what happens? One's feelings can still make distinctions between consolation and desolation, but in the depths, do such distinctions really make much difference? Are they as real as they seem to be? As long as desolation is real, you have to have it, and so do I. You say you do not think you love God, and that is probably perfectly true. But what matters is that God loves you, isn't it? If we had to rely on *our* love where would we be?

I have sent more copies of monastic prayer [booklet entitled "The Climate of Monastic Prayer"], however some of these were offprints of the old, short version. I do not think we have any more of the longer one unless we run off some more. Glad people like it. Some monks do too.

If I don't have much to say for myself for another month or two, don't be surprised. I have to go to the hospital for a back operation. I hope it comes out all right, because my ability to chop wood next winter will very much depend on it. I like winter in the woods, spring even better. The life is fine but there is not much to be said about it. Writing letters is not easy. I have less and less inclination to or facility in talk.

April 6, 1966

I have very much enjoyed your letters from Rome and am interested in your meeting with Fr. Optat. I would like very much to read his book on Fr. Benet someday.

The operation went well—two very skillful surgeons. First week of recovery was a bit hard but I am all right now and they will let me get back to the monastery for Easter.

In the hospital I have read a lot of Eckhart and am more and more convinced of his greatness. Before coming I went back to Kelley's translation of *The Book of the Poor in Spirit*. This is the kind of thing I am going to stay with now that I am "free" and do not have to bother with nonsense that does not really interest me (politics).

More copies of "Climate of Prayer" will be run off.

August 1, 1966

Thanks for your letter from St. Andrews and for the others too. I thought I had answered one or other of them back in May, but perhaps not. In any case I have been writing fewer letters because I have a hard time typing. I have also done less writing work and naturally I am not able to do much manual work at all. I have tried some sawing, but even a little is apparently enough to start up trouble. I have to find very light things I can do. My whole back is bad because of injuries I got long ago playing rugger. They have finally caught up with me and I may have to have another operation, but I hope not. In any case I got back into the hermitage in the middle of May. It is the best place for me, though I may have it hard in winter. But now I sleep here better than anywhere else, and of course I am happy to have the early-morning hours up here where it is quiet, for meditation, reading and so on. I doubt if I could ever adjust happily to the monastery schedule now. I am so used to this one here. I never find it boring, and there is always plenty to do.

On personal and liturgical prayer, just by the way, I suppose you know Jacques and Raïssa Maritain's little book. Thanks for helping with her *Journal*. I believe that they still have not got a publisher but I am very grateful for the leads you gave us. I have just written an introduction to a selection of translations from Isaac of Stella by a nun at Wantage. She too is desperately looking for a publisher. Donald Allchin is helping her. Glad they have a good new warden now.

Progress in Prayer: all right, if you like, I will think about writing something on it, but it is a ticklish subject because the chief obstacle to progress is too much self-awareness and to talk about "how to make progress" is a good way to make people too aware of themselves. In the long run I think progress in prayer comes from the Cross and humiliation and whatever makes us really experience our total poverty and nothingness, and also gets our mind off ourselves. But I will think a little about it. I have a real repugnance for writing things that tell everyone specifically how to do something or other spiritual now. I suppose St. Ignatius was really much more flexible than we realize. As to Benet and your husband: I just finished a book by Warnock on *English Philosophy since 1900*, and in the chapter on metaphysics he manifested not a sign that such a subject could have any appeal to any philosopher: all right, in an atmosphere of logical positivism and all that, your husband (you give me the impression he is very commonsensical) has probably no inkling of what Benet could possibly be about. And no interest whatever in finding out. All the more reason why someone is needed to remind people that this exists. If you can't make it clear to everyone, so much the worse. Make it clear to some.

Incidentally, while I was writing this, a huge SAC plane flew directly over the hermitage: this letter has been under the H-bomb. The planes go over several times a day but not always right over me. They come over low too . . .

September 30, 1966

Sorry I have been so bad about answering, but I really thought that I had said, long ago, that I would be glad to read your introduction to Benet. Since I am no authority on him my reactions will probably be of very slight importance, but I would enjoy reading it for my own sake. Probably what Fr. Optatus says about you is quite correct [i.e., that she should persist in her efforts to bring out an edition of Benet], and I would not be bothered if others do not quite understand what you are trying to do. I am quite sure your work on Benet is important and I have long been anxious for you to get it done. I am only sorry that I never managed to get anyone interested in doing the little bits I once planned, as "selections."

. . . Jacques Maritain may be here next week. I am really grateful to you for all the efforts you made to help get Raïssa's *Journal* published. It seems to be something of a lost cause. I wonder why? Perhaps I can still try one publisher here. I am hoping Donald Allchin will be here early next year. I am sorry to hear he is overworking. That is a pity, and there is really no point in it. But it is easy to get carried away if one does not know how to say no to people. No is an important word, and so is yes. If we can use these two rightly . . .

November 24, 1966

This is not yet my complete letter on your ms. about Benet of Canfield. I think I have received all the bits and pieces. I have no hope of getting them all in the right order. I have a slight eye injury so I am not going through it fast but am saving my eye for work on my own. I will, however, give you just a few reactions—I am not reading very critically, since I am reading most for my own spiritual benefit.

I must say I think you have done a good job on Benet and I think it is very good to go into all his sources as thoroughly as you do. This will make a really valuable book on mysticism. On the whole I think your conclusions look right enough and I do not differ from you significantly anywhere. I made a few odd marks in the margins where I think you have something a little out of perspective, or some fact wrong, or simply where I think the writing breaks down. I think that is your main problem. The writing sometimes gets very involved and clumsy and falls over itself when the things you want to say could be said quite simply and directly. Doubtless in going over it yourself you will be able to straighten things out in a few places. Are you in a big hurry to get this back?

Sometime I will really try to write that little paper on progress in prayer but please do not expect anything right away or soon.

Of course I can understand your being a bit anguished about the obvious fact that there can be little hope of institutional or sacramental union as yet between Anglicans and Romans. Perhaps on the other hand I am too stoical about it all, but I frankly am not terribly anguished. I am not able to get too involved in the institutional side of any of the efforts now being made as I think, for very many reasons, they are bound to be illusory in large measure. And this kind of thing is for others who know more about it. To me it is enough to be united with people in love and in the Holy Spirit, as I am sure I am, and they are, in spite of the sometimes momentous institutional and doctrinal differences. But where there is a sincere desire for truth and real good will and genuine love, there God Himself will take care of the differences far better than any human or political ingenuity can. Prayer is the thing, and union with the suffering Lord on His Cross—and by the way I think you have got close to clearing up the difficulty about *that* on Benet's supereminent level . . .

On April 11 and 12 the Gullicks visited Thomas Merton at Gethsemani.

April 22, 1967

Thanks for your letters. I really enjoyed your visit and it was nice to meet you both. I enjoyed the picnic and hope we will have another someday. I also hope the rest of your journey was pleasant and that you are now back at home. This letter came the other day, several days after you had gone. I did not have any forwarding address in Canada. So now it comes all the way back to Oxford to you!

The weather is even more beautiful now than when you were here. The most perfect spring, with all the trees in full leaf. I am afraid that I have somewhat neglected work to get out in the woods, and having had a visit from my publisher into the bargain, am now behind with everything. So I am trying to catch up with my correspondence.

There is not a great deal of news. I am preparing some lectures on Sufism and doing some readings which interest me greatly. Probably I will try to get the notes mimeographed someday and will send them along, God willing. I hope your Benet book will meet with no more great obstacles.

August 31, 1967

I'm sorry to see your air letter is dated more than a month ago. This has been an unusually busy summer, and yet I do not seem to have got a lot of work done. So much of it a matter of being pulled this way and that with little things like articles, statements, even prefaces, though I am firmly resisting these. And of course piles of letters. One thing I have been doing: talks on tape for contemplative nuns. Not terribly good, but a start. I think something quite useful might be done in this way. Something for you to try perhaps.

Actually, this is because I am beginning to see that it is necessary to say some firm things about the contemplative life, and protect these people against the irresponsible gossip and nonsense of those who haven't the faintest idea what it is all about in the first place. I do hope that on your side the Anglicans will be very positive about contemplation—those who are interested. It is a matter for minorities and the majorities are all rushing off with banners waving to conquer something or other.

The other day I sent off two copies of *Conjectures*. Don't think of paying for them. If you want more, just let me know. For some reason English publishers are not interested in the book, which puts me in the category of other illustrious contemplatives such as Raïssa Maritain, you and Benet of Canfield. If you think someone would really be happy with the book, by all means give them a nudge (tell them to get in touch with Doubleday, New York, about it). I'm sure there must be someone who would be interested if you say your friends like reading it.

I was amused at your description of the Bluecoat boys [of Christ's Hospital school] in pink coats (the band at least).

As I say, this has been a busy summer. Have not read much that is exciting in a religious way. I like the Sufis and stick with them but most of the things I am reading are quite old . . .

April 26, 1968

I must owe you more than one letter, but it is just impossible for me to keep up with mail, and more and more I have to confine myself to what is absolutely necessary for business. But I do want to thank you for your letters and your piece on mortification which I thought was really very sensible and good. Like all your other things, it went on down to the library here. I am sure others will like it and benefit by it.

A Carmelite priest has sent me a long ms. on John of St. Samson, who is fairly interesting. Occasional references to Harphius and Benet make me think of you and your work. How is it coming along?

I will not go into a long discourse on the state of things here. The atmosphere is bad, in the country as a whole. There are a lot of sincere honest people who protest (like the American you mentioned in England, jailed etc.) but their protest seems to have little ultimate meaning. No one really trusts Johnson and it is evident that even the most seemingly honest gestures he makes, like his recent renunciation of candidacy and "the bombing pause," are ninety percent hoax.

Never was a deeply honest and simple life of prayer more necessary. It is about all there is left. But people don't trust God either.

As to your own desolation and loneliness: what can anyone say? It is the desolation of all of us in the presence of death and nothingness, but Christ in us bears it for us: without our being consoled. To accept non-consolation is to mysteriously help others who have more than they can bear.

To Shinzo Hamai

[*Cold War Letter 98*]

1962

The Hon. Shinzo Hamai
Mayor of Hiroshima, Japan

Most Honorable Mayor:

In a solemn and grave hour for humanity I address this letter to you and to your people. I thank you for the sincerity and courage with which you are, at this time, giving witness for peace and sanity. I wish to join my own thoughts, efforts and prayers to yours. There is no hope for mankind unless the truth prevails in us. We must purify our hearts and open them to the light of truth and mercy. You are giving us the example. May we follow.

I speak to you as a most humble and unworthy brother, as a monk of a contemplative Order of the Catholic Church. As such, I have learned to have a very great love for Japan and for its spiritual traditions. There are in Japan several convents and one monastery of my religious Order. The Japanese Trappistine nuns are the glory of our Order. The finest and most fervent of our convents are those in Japan. May their wholehearted prayers for peace and for the spiritual and temporal prosperity of your nation be heard.

Man should use political instruments in behalf of truth, sanity, and international Order. Unfortunately the blindness and madness of a society that is shaken to its very roots by the storms of passion and greed for power make the fully effective use of political negotiation impossible. Men want to negotiate for peace, and strive to do so, but their fear is greater than their good will. They do not dare to take serious and bold initiatives for peace. Fear of losing face, fear of the propaganda consequences of apparent "weakness," make it impossible for them to do what is really courageous: to take firm steps toward world peace. When they take one step forward they immediately tell the whole world about it and then take four steps backward. We are all walking backward toward a precipice. We know the precipice is there, but we assert that we are all the while going forward. This is because the world in its madness is guided by military men, who are the blindest of the blind.

It is my conviction that the people of Hiroshima stand today as a symbol of the hopes of humanity. It is good that such a symbol should exist. The events of August 6, 1945, give you the most solemn right to be heard and respected by the whole world. But the world only pretends to respect your witness. In reality it cannot face the truth which you represent. But I wish to say on my own behalf and on behalf of my fellow monks and those who are like-minded, that I never cease to face the truth which is symbolized in the names Hiroshima, Nagasaki. Each day I pray humbly and with love for the victims of the atomic bombardments which took place there. All the holy spirits of those who lost their lives then, I regard as my dear and real friends. I express my fraternal and humble love for all the citizens of Hiroshima and Nagasaki.

To Thich Nhat Hanh

In April 1983 it was my privilege to hear Thich Nhat Hanh speak in Rochester, New York, on "Non-Violence in a Violent World." The talk, sponsored by the Rochester Zen Center and the local Buddhist Peace Fellowship, drew a large and appreciative audience. The simple, soft-spoken manner and the poetic realism of this man who had seen his own country, Vietnam, practically destroyed by violence won the hearts and empathy of his listeners.

During the war in Vietnam, he had headed the Vietnamese Buddhist Peace Delegation in Paris. Presently he lives in France, though he travels frequently, speaking on behalf of non-violence and peace. A major poet of his country, he has written a number of books: The Cry of Vietnam, Zen Poems, The Miracle of Mindfulness *(a manual of meditation),* The Raft Is Not the Shore *(a collaborative work with Daniel Berrigan, while they were both in Paris).*

In company with John Heidbrink, Nhat Hanh visited Merton at Gethsemani at the end of May 1966. Merton wrote of the close ties he felt with this Vietnamese monk in an article called "Nhat Hanh Is My Brother," published in Jubilee, *August 1966.*

June 29, 1966

I suppose you are probably back in Vietnam by now. I thought of you today because I finished your excellent little book on Buddhism today. It is really a good book, and I especially liked the chapters about contact with reality and on the way to live the inner life. John Heidbrink speaks of translating it and I certainly think it ought to be translated. Meanwhile, as I said, I will try to write a review of it for some magazine or other.

You know that the FOR [Fellowship of Reconciliation] people have nominated you for the Nobel Peace Prize. I have written a letter in support of the nomination and hope you get it. It would certainly be very satisfying to us all if you did.

It was a great pleasure to have you here and I hope you will return sometime and stay longer. If you can send me any books on Vietnamese Buddhism in French (or English) I would be very glad to read them.

More of your own work ought to be translated into Western languages. I think you make very clear what Buddhism really is. And I certainly feel very strongly as you do that the essential thing is to escape ignorance and the inevitable suffering that follows from it by a real contact with things as they are, instead of an illusory relationship with the world. I think your problems with conservative and formalist religiosity are very much the same as ours in the Catholic Church. It is the same everywhere. A new mentality is needed, and this implies above all a recovery of ancient and original wisdom. And a real contact with what is right before our noses.

I certainly hope that everything goes well with you, and think of you often with much friendship. Come back and see us again, and meanwhile I hope that peace will come at last to your country. Please express my warm sentiments of brotherly solidarity to all with whom you work for the better understanding of the truth and for true peace.

September 12, 1966

Thanks for your letter from Paris. It is good to have news from you. I am sure that in Europe you will be able to do a great deal of good for the people of Vietnam. It would probably be very wise to stay out of Vietnam. Some people have been writing letters about you to the President and the Pentagon. The matter is now considered important enough for someone in the Pentagon to write long replies explaining that Ky is really very much in favor of Buddhists, would never hurt anyone, etc. etc. So at least there is some attention paid to the question, even if the answers are wrong.

I am sending the article on Buddhism and the notes on Dr. Suzuki. I read your book in French, as you see. But if you write another more detailed one in English that will be a very good thing. Naturally I want to read it, and I will give whatever help I can.

Good luck with your work. I have not had much news lately but I assume that things go on just the same. I certainly do pray for you and for all who are working to bring some measure of peace to Vietnam. Incidentally a book of mine [*No Man Is an Island*] has been translated in Saigon [also *Seeds of Contemplation*]. I am sending you a copy of it. I have no idea whether or not the translation is good or whether the book will help anyone there at the present moment.

To Bernard Haring

In 1953 Father Bernard Haring completed his three-volume work, The Law of Christ, *a work that established him as the instrument of a new approach to the teaching of moral theology. Haring was born in 1912, joined the Redemptorists in 1934, was ordained a priest in 1939. Ten years later, after serving as a medic in World War II, he came to Rome to begin what was to be his lifetime work— teaching moral theology at the Academia Alfonsiana of the Lateran University. A friend of Popes, a peritus at the Second Vatican Council, a popular lecturer, a man known for his deep sense of compassion, Fr. Haring is a highly respected leader in the efforts to renew the Church, especially in the area of her moral teaching. Of the several letters Merton wrote to Father Haring, only this one has survived.*

December 26, 1964

Thanks for your kind letter. It was good to know that the book [*Seeds of Destruction*] had reached you and that you found it interesting. I was not allowed to treat technically of the problem of nuclear weapons (I suppose I am not competent to do so in any case) but in the end I thought it was really better that I rewrote the essay, with quite a lot of new material, in such a way as to deal with the basic attitude toward peace, and stressing the importance of moral insight.

In effect, what is shocking about interventions like those of Bishop Hannon [auxiliary bishop of Washington] etc. is not that they are not in some sense "correct" within a certain limited framework, but the awful truth that one can remain in such a framework and be "right" technically, and yet totally lack all moral or practical insight whatever into the human realities involved.

Hence it seems to me that Schema 13 [preparatory draft of what was to become Vatican II's *Pastoral Constitution on the Church in the Modern World*] should above all reawaken the Christian moral sense in its depth and its catholicity and its humanity, its Christian concern for man and for God's creation and for human life. It would be a disaster if the Council Fathers could do no better than come up with a few sterile decisions of a more or less juridical character, deciding that "we can go this far" etc. without any real concern for the human needs and tragic plight of man today.

I also think that the Schema needs to rest on a deeper realization of the urgent problems posed by technology today. (The Constitution on Mass Media seems to have been totally innocent of any such awareness.) For one thing, the whole massive complex of technology, which reaches into every aspect of social life today, implies a huge organization of which no one is really in control, and which dictates its own solutions irrespective of human needs or even of reason. Technology now has reasons entirely its own which do not necessarily take into account the needs of man, and this huge inhuman mechanism, which the whole human race is now serving rather than commanding, seems quite probably geared for the systematic destruction of the natural world, quite apart from the question of the "bomb" which, in fact, is only one rather acute symptom of the whole disease. I am not of course saying that technology is "bad," and that progress is something to be feared. But I am saying that behind the cloak of specious myths about technology and progress, there seems to be at work a vast uncontrolled power which is leading man where he does not want to go in spite of himself and in which the Church, it seems to me, ought to be somewhat aware of the intervention of the "principalities and powers" of which St. Paul speaks. I know this kind of language is not very popular today, but I think it is so important that it cannot be left out of account. For instance I think that the monumental work of Jacques Ellul on *La Technique* is something that cannot be ignored by the Council Fathers if they wish to see all the aspects of the crucial question of the Church and the world.

In any case, dear Father, I am sharing these thoughts with you. I am sure you have already reflected on these problems much more deeply than I could. And of course I know that the prayers of the whole Church will bring the light and grace necessary to help us all find our way through this time of crisis. Yet at the same time it seems to me that the 1970s are likely to be one of the most difficult and perhaps even chaotic periods in the history of the world, though that does not mean that we should fear or lose hope. Quite the contrary. Yet we must be prepared to meet times that may be very confusing, and full of grave temptations.

I share your sentiments about the closing of the session, and I am sure it must have been quite a shattering experience for all the bishops as well as for the Holy Father, who, incidentally, said many very fine and inspired things at Bombay. Let us be grateful for all the good that has been done and for all God's gifts to us. I shall certainly keep you and all the Fathers in my prayers throughout the New Year, and I send you my cordial good wishes for 1965 . . .

To John Harris

John Harris, a schoolteacher in Devonshire (and later in Cornwall), England, obtained a copy of Doctor Zhivago *the very day it was published in England. Deeply moved by the book, he wrote to thank the author, addressing his letter simply to Boris Pasternak, Writer, Moscow. On November 7, 1958, he received a reply in the form of an unsigned postcard beautifully written in minuscule lettering with a mapping pen. Pasternak asked him to contact three persons— one of them Thomas Merton, "whose precious thoughts and dear bottomless letters enrich me and make me happy." Harris's letter to Thomas Merton initiated a correspondence that was to continue for nearly ten years.*

December 4, 1958

Your letter was a wonderful welcome surprise. The message from Pasternak was a joy and a relief. I shall treasure your letter as one of my most valued possessions.

Everything concerning Pasternak is extraordinary. The simplicity of this human voice speaking directly and reaching everyone, in spite of all the barriers erected around him, is a portent of immense significance in an age when men can communicate with the moon but not with one another. He is our greatest writer and poet, and more than that. He is a sign of hope and perhaps the first star of a new dawn for mankind. Such a thought might seem strange, yet I am convinced that there is much truth in it.

Every one of us who has been inspired to enter into some kind of a contact with him should be aware of the significance of that fact. It is bound to have great meaning in all our lives.

I am not writing to him, it would be too dangerous. If you think it prudent to write him yourself, please tell him I am overjoyed at his message and that my confidence in him is without measure. Tell him of my great sorrow at the stupid noise made about the Nobel Prize* and the pain that must have caused him. And ask if it would be dangerous for me to send books. You can word this prudently, as you see fit, but I don't believe they censor his incoming mail. They may be doing so now. I plan to send him a few books at the end of the year, and perhaps write later on when things get better. Meanwhile I have written an article about him, but am debating whether or not to publish it.

I am sending you a little privately printed work which Pasternak enjoyed last summer, a prose poem on Prometheus, which has a lot in common with Pasternak's own thought. It will serve to express my gratitude.

May God bless you, in your lovely corner of England. I have always loved Devonshire.

January 31, 1959

It is a long time since your letter of Dec. 11th. As a matter of fact it took a little time to get through to me, as sometimes happens. Then I have been waiting for time to write you a thoughtful reply, and something somewhere near adequate. This will not be that, but it will be as straight as I can make it.

And first of all it should be clear that I for one refuse to stick my head up from behind an impregnable barricade and declare, "Back here we are all safe, we have no problems, we know exactly what is what, we have all the answers and we can never be wrong." Reasons for not doing this, besides the fact that it is so obviously stupid and even dishonest— it is not even Christian. For Christ speaks in us only when we speak as men to one another and not as members of something, officials, or what

* *Pasternak was offered the Nobel Prize for Literature on October 23, 1958. At first he accepted, and then, realizing that accepting the prize would mean he would not be allowed to return to Russia, he declined.*

have you. Though of course there are official declarations and official answers: but they never come anywhere near the kind of thing you bring up, which is personal. No one is officially saved, salvation *cannot* be that kind of thing. The other reason for not claiming to answer all your questions and solve all your problems is that I really don't think your problems are as real as they seem to be: they are indeed, or they tend to be, created by the whole false position arising out of the fact that there are so many who insist on having, and giving, official solutions. As I say, declarations can and must be made but they never get into the depths where a person finds himself in God. You may think me flippant if I say you probably believe in God already, and your problem consists not in whether or not you doubt God, but in trying to account to yourself for a belief in God which does not sound like anything official you have ever heard about this matter. And in wondering whether, that being the case, it is "the same God" you believe in.

Whatever may be the intellectual aspects of the thing—I leave them to you, only suggesting that you do not have to apply yourself madly to "working" anything "out." If at the same time you can read and enjoy books by me and by Pasternak it is clear that you are a basically religious person. And in that case, explanations and manipulations of symbols are not the most important thing but the reality of your life in God. The symbols can later take care of themselves . . . But what you might do some time would be to go down (or over or up, whichever it is) to Buckfast Abbey and, if you feel like talking to anyone in particular, ask for a Father Hubert Van Zeller who is there, I think (he was at Downside). You can tell him you are a friend of mine and you don't have to commit yourself to anything special—just have a talk about anything of mutual interest and get to know a bit about monks and the Church.

If I may say so, I believe you are the kind of person who is basically Christian and realizes it and wants to be fully what he already is—and is disturbed by a lot of things that are superficial and accidental and really have nothing whatever to do with the real issue. But above all don't get the feeling that you can't get into the Church without being shoved: because then the logical and even honest thing to do would be to resist the shoving. No one is shoving, you are not even shoving yourself.

I wrote to Pasternak around Christmas time, and intend to write to him again for his birthday (February 10th). And I sent him a book—*The Sign of Jonas* . . . I know of someone in this country who has received a letter from Pasternak in the last few days and he seems well, says he is writing poetry. There are a lot of idle rumors going about, to the effect that things are likely to change greatly with him either for the better or for the worse . . .

. . . I am glad you read *Elected Silence*. The last part of *Bread in the Wilderness* says in a clumsy and involved way something that is brought out quite clearly in *Doctor Zhivago*—about our life in God, liberty, etc.

Do not hesitate to write if there is anything I can do for you, or send you . . . The important thing is who are you: you are not a "man with a problem," or a person trying to figure something out, you are Harris, in Devonshire, and that means you are not and cannot be another in a series of objects, you are you and that is the important thing. For, you see, when "I" enter into a dialogue with "you" and each of us knows who is speaking, it turns out that we are both Christ. This, being seen in a very simple and "natural" light, is the beginning and almost the fullness of everything. Everything is in it somewhere. But it makes most sense in the light of Mass and the Eucharist.

So God bless you, and let me know any news of Pasternak or of yourself . . .

March 14, 1959

I am sure that you are doing the right thing, and I say this not because by some kind of a reflex I automatically think everyone who enters the Church "is doing the right thing." One can do "the right thing" but without the right reasons and I can see that your reasons are quite right, and your understanding of the situation is correct. You are, in any case, seeking to become what you already are in so many ways. We have the good fortune to be born into a civilization that is still, insofar as it is still civilized, largely Christian. I am very glad that you were able to get in touch with someone at Buckfast and that there you can find the right approach.

There is and there can be nothing wrong with the Gospels and with Christianity. But often there are things and ideas that get mixed up with it, and seem even to be inseparable from it, or identified with it—and among these there are many errors, or wrong attitudes, or approaches to life that are not perfectly healthy. It is unfortunate that one has to run into these, and get mixed up in them to a certain extent. We cannot demand that our Christianity be absolutely pure . . . There is inevitably plenty of prejudice and cant wherever there is a religion. The point is that the wheat and the cockle are not the same thing, and that Christ Himself said, "Let both grow until the harvest." The temptation to demand that the wheatfield be absolutely pure of cockle is then a real and serious temptation. It is really an evasion. We have to take on the difficult job of constantly making distinctions and telling the difference and adjusting ourselves to the reality, in order to make sure that we ourselves are wheat and not cockle. And of course the thing is that one never can tell. Because we are not the ones appointed to do the judging. To look for an absolute assurance that one is pure wheat is to fall, after all, into the same old pharisaism. Dostoevsky saw it straight. We are sinners and we have to be very glad to take upon ourselves all the evil in the world as if we were responsible for it ourselves, and to love everyone else in their sins. In this way only is evil overcome and destroyed. But when it is always rejected and judged and pushed off onto others—it survives and flourishes mightily.

And poor Pasternak has had it all piled onto his back, the scapegoat of the whole world. How phenomenally terrible is the way the Mystery of Christ manifests itself in the lives of people like that. Thank you so much for giving me the contents of his Christmas postcard. I have heard since of his disappearance, I can only pray for him, and continue to do so, especially in every day's Mass . . .

Needless to say I keep you both (you and your wife) in my prayers and remember you often at Mass. Go ahead with peace and courage, you are on the right track and you will find far more than you are seeking. You are certainly on the only path that leads to anything really new: the newness of Easter. Please let me know how everything develops . . .

May 5, 1959

I should have sprung to arms immediately at your last letter, but as you said, the whole thing would probably have been settled before I came on the scene—and then, the truth is, I haven't the faintest understanding of the marriage red tape that the Church has brought into existence, and any advice I could give you would probably only make matters much worse. You will have learned all about the ins and outs of the case, and whether or not you are a candidate for what is (seriously too) called the "Pauline privilege." I always double up with laughter at the symbolic slips which the canonists can make with straight faces. After all the interminable talk about the sacredness of marriage, there is the equally straight-faced and "so-obvious" readiness to call it a *privilege* to get out of the sacred bond. "Well, why didn't you say that in the first place . . . etc. etc."

The best I can say is, be patient: God is not bound by the stupidity of theologians and canonists . . .

The great consolation that no one can take away from us is that we are Christians, that we have died with Christ and risen with Him and are free men, and that we not only have "privileges" which permit us to get away with little things here and there, through loopholes in the law—we are *obliged* by our Christian calling to be "no longer under the Law." This does not mean Antinomianism. The outlaw just runs away from the Law: he is temporarily out of reach of the Law. With us, not so. But there comes the equal obligation of being patient with the Law—and patience is possible insofar as we are above it, by Love. The trouble with those who have to struggle with the Law is that they want only something negative, to be without the Law. But what we want is a higher and perfect law, which is Love—the freedom of the sons of God. That is our highest obligation. Forgive the sermon . . . Do please remember that you *are* married, there is no question of it in the sight of God, in your hearts. This other business is part of the exterior routine that unfortunately goes with Church life. But the sacraments are so great and the Life that is in them so vast that a little patience with these externals is worth it in the long run.

And as for Dom Hubert Van Z.'s saying that he dropped *Zhivago* when adultery came into the picture: he is a good man and I respect him but I do not agree with everything he says. By this standard he would have to close Genesis as soon as bigamy rears its ugly head, or as soon as Abraham palms Sarah off on Pharaoh as his "sister." However, let's not bother with that. He wrote me a good letter saying he had seen you and agreed that you had a very real and serious vocation to the Catholic Church and that he thought your difficulties would iron themselves out without too much trouble.

The other thing that has kept me waiting is the need for time to digest the superb letter of Pasternak. Things have been in a rush here since Easter, and I have hardly had time to settle down to it until now. It is a tremendously important document, as I need not tell you. One of the things that please me most about it is that it confirms an intuition of my own. You compare him to Donne: I saw a very interesting analogy with an ancient Chinese book which P. probably does not know at all. It is the Book of Oracles called the *I Ching*. This consists of a series of symbolic configurations of events, or "changes" which one arrives at by drawing lots or tossing coins; but that is not the important thing. What is fascinating is the fact that each change is exactly that sort of fluid "style of movement" . . . "arrangement of groups" . . . which constitutes Pasternak's inclinations. Jung has written a fascinating preface to the *I Ching*, bringing in his archetypes. The *I Ching* had a tremendous influence on both Confucius and Lao Tzu, and what amazes me is that it is exactly the Pasternak approach. You really might be interested in it some time, though I would not recommend it now, it would be bad for you. It can be a very disturbing book, at the wrong moment. Because of its oracular character, one has to play the game it proposes, in order to see what it is really driving at. This should not be done by one who is not clear where fortune-telling ends and analysis begins. (I am sure you can be clear about that.) But there is always danger of setting off some kind of an interior explosion; the symbols are really powerful, and their strange conjunctions can turn out to be devastating if once we take them in some way seriously, which true understanding of the book requires. The whole subject is supremely interesting, and really beyond me, as I am not an analyst or that much of a scholar in these matters. But it is evident that Pasternak has, by his genius and simplicity, and by a kind of primitive quality, better *archaic* quality that is in him, reached down to those ancient springs. . .

. . . I am supposed to be writing an article on P.'s symbolism, and I do hope you will let me make use of the material in the letter. I mean, of course, very discreetly. Either quoting it only as "a letter," or "an unpublished letter"—or even not quoting it at all. Whatever you prefer. The article might appear in a volume that is being got up in honor of Pasternak, I don't know. Whatever you may decide, I am certainly glad to feel that his letter confirms the analysis I had made—as he also confirms yours. What was it you said to him about Donne? I have just been writing to the Japanese Zen man, D. T. Suzuki (a marvelous person), on very much the same sort of thing. I have done some translations from the Desert Fathers, who are so like Zen masters that I have got Suzuki interested in collaborating in a little study of them. I hope it will be very interesting.

You see that my concept of Christianity is far from being an old-maidish theology of hiding in a corner of the house and standing on chairs for fear of heretical mice. But the important thing for you at the moment is not Zen or *I Ching*, so please do not let me distract you from what really matters. All that these others have to teach is found in the Church also (and they too are of "the Church" in their own hidden way). There is such a sea of wonderful things for you both to fall into and swim in— where can you begin? What are you reading, or doing, or thinking? Perhaps I am wrong, but I keep thinking I ought to recommend to you a book by another English Dominican, Conrad Pepler, *The English Religious Heritage*. It is not perfect, but is full of many fine things and would give you many leads. And Bouyer's life of Newman . . . Best of all is to go to the sources, the Fathers, the Bible, and I am sure you do . . .

The great thing is not things but God Himself Who is not things but ourselves, and the world, and everything, lost in Him Who so fully IS that we come closer to Him by imagining He is not. The Being of all and my own Being is a vast emptiness containing nothing: I have but to swim in it and be carried away in it to see that this nothing is All. This too may be a distracting way of putting it: but everything is really very simple and do not let yourselves be disturbed by appearances of complication and multiplicity. *Omnia in omnibus Christus*. Let His Spirit carry you where He wills, and do not be disturbed if I sometimes talk like Eckhart . . .

June 22, 1959

There is a great long backlog of things to thank you for, and the greatest of them is the stupendous picture of Anne and Arthur [Harris's children], which I keep on the desk before me and which enlivens the grimmer moments of official life as novice master. (That, by the way, is my job.) And thank you for keeping me posted about the developments in your complicated journey. (Relax, you have arrived!) The business about your first "wife" being not baptized was what I was thinking about when I mumbled something about Pauline privilege in one of my letters. Or didn't I use the technical term? I must have, it is one of the only technical terms I know, and I use it whenever I can, as if to make people believe I know something about "marriage cases." If she is not baptized and does not insist on rushing back to hang on to you, everything will be relatively simple, as you must already know. I won't continue to say what must be obvious. For the rest, if they set their minds to it, the lawyers can do anything. After all they live in a purely fictitious universe, so since it is of their own making, they ought to be able to do what they like with it, with a little dogged patience and humorlessness.

I liked your article, or rather talk, on Pasternak's coincidences. But I think that to the people who demand an explanation for them, perhaps no explanation is necessary because none will suffice, and the rest understand it well enough: they would be comforted and enlightened by your use of the Donne tag . . . Incidentally I heard indirectly that he has emphatically dismissed Edmund Wilson's symbol-hunting as irrelevant, and has denied absolutely that he has a closed system of symbols that can be interpreted like *Finnegans Wake*. This refers to Wilson's second article, the one in *The Nation*, which you may not have seen. It is much more "thorough" and pedantic even—carries things altogether too far. I am relieved that P. dismissed it all. Of course not all: there is a lot that is good in the studies, when they do not get down to minute and silly details of etymology etc. . . .

Of course when you come into the Church you go through all the painful hesitations one must have about conforming, and wanting to learn, and wanting to do things the right way. Of course this is to be expected and I would not want to dismiss it lightly: you should want to learn and be "right"—the openness and "docility" of this period (which will never be recaptured!!!) is as a matter of fact tied up with a very special exposure to grace and the Love of God, and so the things you do are more than mere conforming. What goes on below the surface is so great that your care about genuflecting at the right times becomes something important and very sacred in the sight of God—but for deep and interior reasons which no one can see, least of all yourself. Just go ahead like that. But in the end, the right way about which you will naturally be concerned will often not exist at all—or be irrelevant. The Church has made such a fuss over her externals, or rather Catholics have, that one coming in from the outside tends to worry about what is and is not "done." But in fact almost anything is "done" in many cases, and it doesn't matter. Except that in England, of course, it may seem funny to be as free about things as Catholics in France or Italy. England is a very conformist nation (and yet independent too) and this will cause you trouble. But don't worry about it, do the best you can. Pray as you can, read as much as you can, find out what the monks are doing and then do what you like. The thing to avoid is getting stuck in any small limited area of Christian life: if you want to fall down on your face before God one day, that is all right, but it doesn't have to become a system to be followed thereafter until your dying day . . .

I heartily recommend, as a form of prayer, the Russian and Greek business where you get off somewhere quiet, remember what you may have known about hatha-yoga, breathe quietly and rhythmically with the diaphragm, holding your breath for a bit each time and letting it out easily: and while holding it, saying "in your heart" (aware of the place of your heart, as if the words were spoken in the very center of your being with all the sincerity you can muster): "Lord Jesus Christ Son of God have mercy on me a sinner." Just keep saying this for a while, of course with faith, and the awareness of the indwelling, etc. It is a simple form of prayer, and fundamental, and the breathing part makes it easier to keep your mind on what you are doing. That's about as far as I go with methods. After that, pray as the Spirit moves you, but of course I would say follow the Mass in a missal unless there is a good reason for doing something else, like floating suspended ten feet above the congregation.

I like the rosary, too. Because, though I am not very articulate about her, I am pretty much wound up in Our Lady, and have some Russian ideas about her too: that she is the most perfect expression of the mystery of the Wisdom of God. That in some way she is the Wisdom of God. (See the eighth chapter of Proverbs, for instance, the part about "playing before Him at all times, playing in the world.") I find a lot of this "Sophianism" in Pasternak, and hope he doesn't go and denounce *me* as he did Wilson. The article I wrote will be along soon now, it is in the July issue of a magazine you ought to know about, *Jubilee*: I'll send you a couple of copies of some back issues. It is edited by my godfather, Ed Rice, who lives in a slum with his wonderful wife and kids, in order to put everything he has in producing *one* decent Catholic magazine in this country. (*Commonweal* is fair, and so is *Cross Currents*.)

Anyway, pray and believe, and read the Scriptures, and love God very much. And pray for me. You put me in the Prophets—I have the feeling that it is not a very comfortable team to be playing on. But in the long run I don't play on any team, as far as I know. I am aware that I don't make for peace of mind in conventional groups, and I am wondering how long it is going to take for the average American Catholic to realize this, I mean realize it *keenly*. And for the American clergy to jump up madly and say, "You *see*, that is what we have been trying to tell you about him all along! The guy's a radical."

The most difficult kind of ethic is the kind which impels you to follow what seems to be your own inner truth. And of course, you always make plenty of mistakes that way. But that is the point. I cease to understand any reason for wanting to be always right. It is so hard to do the one thing that matters, which is to be not right, but sincere. And what a difference! The Grand Inquisitors are afraid of such an approach . . .

In any case I keep you all in my prayers. But be patient. You are *in*. You do not have the consolation of the sacraments, which of course is important, but you are "in" in the way God wants you to be at the moment, and you will see how much that means if you do not become confused or discouraged with the external complications of your position. God bless you.

September 12, 1959

I wonder how long it is since I last wrote you? I have been busy with some work, and have fallen behind with all correspondence. I remember your last two letters, however. By now I suppose you are back in Totnes [Devonshire] and getting ready to go at it again in school.

Recently I had some indirect news of Pasternak. Stephen Spender's wife stopped by here and showed me a letter Pasternak had written Spender about some pieces for *Encounter*. It was the same old Pasternak but at the end he said that his position was not too good. Or more precisely, "worse than ever." So at least we can pray for him. I have not been bothering him with letters, though actually I have been planning to send him my article. But I had entrusted that job to some people who are able to get through to him better than I. I haven't heard anything. A volume of his poetry has come out here but the translation is very unpoetic.

Be patient with your Pauline privilege. In due time it will all come through and I think perhaps the waiting is necessary in a way. Grace (we say glibly) works on nature, and can work suddenly if it pleases. But actually a deep interior revolution needs to go on and this takes time. A settling and a sort of aging of the strong new wine. We have no adequate idea of what takes place in our depths when we grow spiritually or change. Meanwhile you have had a chance to go through a lot of quick and volatile surface reactions, which are bare indications of the adjustment taking place deeper down. Let peace have time to settle and gain a firm grasp of those depths. And do not be troubled if you do not always feel settled. Time takes care of such things. And the Church with her sacraments, while doing infinitely much in your life, will not take away all anguish. On the contrary, the anguish must always be there. But it must deepen and change and become vastly more fruitful. That is the best we can hope for nowadays: a fruitful anguish instead of one that is utterly sterile and consuming.

How are the children? And your wife? How was Holland? I must say I envy them a little. When you wrote from Exeter I remembered a strange time in France, when I had a passionate desire to see Exeter and wrote a novel about it. Why, God only knows. I was fourteen and the novel was a kind of mixture of *Westward Ho* and *Lorna Doone*. I have only been once through Devon in a train, after landing at Plymouth, and that is all I saw of Exeter. It looked terribly small.

Ed Rice assures me he has sent you *Jubilee* . . .

February 18, 1960

First, thanks for the fabulous photograph of the great embracings which take place on top of Dartmoor. I am very happy that the austere landscape is made to glorify God by these unrestrained outbursts of affection. I posted the picture on the novices' board, not to remind them of what they are missing, but to get their prayers for you and Emy and the ecclesiastical courts. I feel silly saying periodically, "Well, well, be patient, everything will turn out all right," while year is added to year. I can at least guarantee that if it is not settled before, it will be taken care of at the Last Judgment. I don't mean this entirely facetiously: it is a way of saying what you and I know well enough, that in the eyes of God it doesn't matter. It would be a very fine thing if you could get to the sacraments, but if you are prevented by something that is beyond your control, then you have every right to count on the words "in spirit and in truth" as providing you with a shortcut. That will serve until finally the matter is settled, as they say in the external forum . . .

Yes, the jesuitical arguments: they present a serious problem. Especially when you apply them to something like an atomic bomb. I wonder when moral theologians are going to have to admit, finally, that things have gone so far and been blown up to such a magnitude that it is no longer humanly possible to hedge—because it too quickly becomes obvious, besides being useless. It is one thing to stick to traditional principles of morality, and quite another to imagine that one can easily reconcile them with some modern problems in what appears to be a "solution." I am in the fortunate position where I can say "I don't know" and stick to it. Who am I to say what is to be done about the population of China? And after all, what does the population of China care about it, anyway? My only contribution to the whole discussion is this: If I as a theologian insist that people in overpopulated countries must not practice birth control, then I am obligated in strict justice to take a practical and effective position to guarantee that they will be able to overflow into my own not overpopulated country. If I want the Japanese to go on having children at the normal rate, then I have got to, logically and ethically, invite them to take over the spare space we have here. And I have absolutely no right to resist them by force if they start to do it. The position is this: that pretty soon it is going to be clear that there cannot be a just war against a country like China if what that country wants is space and space is what we have. This is of course all too simple. No point in my going around insisting on it, because a theologian's job is to make the status quo inevitable. So some people seem to think.

. . . I am glad some copies of *Jubilee* have at least reached you in a roundabout way. They promised they would send some to you, but a lot of that sort of job is done there by volunteer workers on Wednesday evenings, and you can imagine what happens on Wednesday evenings. It is a very mad informal sort of a place, and the thing that everyone says about it is that the people who work there spend most of their time prostrate with laughter.

. . . Anne and Arthur have become two of my favorite people, and so of course have you and Emy. If I cannot write as promptly or as fully as I would always like to, you will understand. God bless all of you.

May 13, 1960

The French trip sounded very interesting and I was waiting to hear from you about it. I am glad it went off so well . . . Rocamadour is a wonderful place which I have never been able to forget, and I must admit that I envy you. There is just one river you missed: the Aveyron. It is like the Lot and the Dordogne, only better. At least I think it is better. A little wilder perhaps. You ought to see Najac. Someday I hope you will. I think that the things you saw this time are better than Albi. Cahors of course is wonderful. O that country! The only thing that tempts me more is Mount Athos—or Tibet. Except the Reds make the latter unappealing, and I hope they don't get to Athos someday.

You will miss Devon, won't you, when you go to the new job [in Cornwall]. As for your case, all I can say is that for some reason or other it has to be trying, but you really lack nothing except the consolation of the sacraments. That I admit is a great thing, but from the moment you are in the Church in your heart, you need not worry. But you are in a state of special destitution, I suppose, and that has its points. Though it may not seem especially consoling.

I have been reading a fabulous book, *The Human Condition* by Hannah Arendt, the one who wrote such a good one on [*The Origins of*] *Totalitarianism*. This is very fine, once one gets into it. And for once someone is saying something really new, though it is also really old. I recommend it.

Things are rather busy and I have a conference on Cassian to give in a few minutes, so this must end . . . Keep sending pictures of the children! Or just pictures, the human race, France.

On the 30th of May 1960 Boris Pasternak died.

June 17, 1960

Thank you for your letter about Pasternak and for the other ones too, and for all the postcards of the Lot and Dordogne. I heard also about the Pasternak funeral, at which evidently all his friends finally rallied round him. I cannot feel that we have lost him. I do not say this as a result of a kind of professional priestly pride which obliges me to be convinced that I am in a business which gets results (B.P. has been duly prayed for, ergo . . .) but because I believe that his whole life and his faith in life have been a sign of the divine mercy for all of us, in one way or another. Christ has manifested Himself in the life and work of Pasternak, and obviously because P. himself was one who had seen and recognized Him.

. . . The postcards and the map certainly gave me the *mal du pays*. When I was eleven I used to spend hours looking at the Michelin map, the red roads, the yellow roads, the roads without color, the pale green forests, and I not only looked at the map but went where my feet could carry me. Which of course was not by any means up and down the Lot Valley. But I saw something I had utterly forgotten, la grotte du Capucin, near St. Antonin. I remember it, a wild cave up on the side of a cliff in a corner of a glen where the river bends sharply and the train comes out of one tunnel only to plunge immediately into another. I climbed up there once. It was a big cave. I am secretly persuaded that it must be full of rock paintings far back inside and that no one has ever discovered them. Except I can't remember it going far back at all. I never understood the name. Now it occurs to me that a Capuchin must have lived there. Well, well. Who was this Capuchin? The word meant nothing to me in those days.

I don't think you are wrong in mumbling imprecations on America and Russia together for the U-2 and the other follies. As the twentieth century becomes more and more clear, I am beginning to have a wholesome respect for the nineteenth, which I used to despise. I admit England, France and Bismarck's Germany were pretty grim, but compared to Hitler, Stalin, Khrushchev and our huge, anonymous injured innocence over here, well, I'll take Queen Victoria any day. Of course there was that awful righteousness. But Russia is almost as bad as that today, and so was Dulles. Except that no one could take it too seriously. *Gott mit uns*. What makes me sick is the business in Latin America. And the absurd folly of our policy there. It must all serve to teach us to stop blaming "them" and stop hoping for impossible things to be done by "them," and start, each for his own part, to painfully find out where he stands and what he can do in the world, if only for the next man, then do it. But what?

One thing here is that I am having occasional meetings with good and earnest Protestant seminary professors, and we sit and talk and discover how much we really agree on many things and that if we cannot change the situation about our respective groups, we perhaps are not expected to change it. But that there are many other things we can change in ourselves. This I think can be fruitful.

You have never heard of Cassian? He is easily available in *Sources Chrétiennes* (Editions du Cerf) and makes very good reading, though perhaps he might appall you. He is the Boswell of the Desert Fathers, and wrote down everything they could be cajoled into saying. None of them were very talkative. Then Cassian went back to Marseilles and started a monastery and became a monastic best-seller. May the Lord rest his soul. (In the Oriental Church he is venerated as St. Cassian the Roman. In our Church he is suspect of heresy, but no one has ever stopped reading him on that account. And the heresy is just one little sentence he quoted from an old Desert Father one hundred years old who could no longer walk upright but crawled around on all fours. No wonder the poor old man could not be perfectly accurate on the fine shades of the doctrine of grace!)

If I tell you once again to be patient you will probably throw the letter on the floor and stamp on it. But your case will one day surely be settled and then you will have to find something else to worry about. Meanwhile you are in the grace of God and He is dwelling in your heart, though there is no need for you to see Him there. May He bless all of you.

September 7, 1960

Your letter came yesterday and I was glad to hear from you. In particular I had been looking for your new address . . .

I shall certainly pray that Rome gets galvanized into action and completes your case. It is said that the Church itself is a permanent miracle witnessing to her own divine origin by her manifestly divine qualities. However, I think the machinery of the Roman Curia does not always bear this out, unless the eternity of God is conceived as a vacuum without activity in it.

They (well, a publisher) sent me a book by Teilhard de Chardin to review: *The Divine Milieu*. It is fairly good. I have not yet read the other one. I think I sent you a French orthodox magazine with my article on Mt. Athos in it . . .

. . . God bless you all. I think of you and Emy and the children with affection, in prayer. I hope the new place will be better than the old and that whatever happens everything will go well with you . . .

I am very sorry about your father's death and will remember him in my prayers.

[*Cold War Letter 83*]

June 8, 1962

I suppose it was really rather foolish of me to send you the CW letters as a present on your entry into the Church instead of a letter which I ought to have written, and in which I could have said things a little more to the point. But I do now want to tell you how happy I am that it is finally settled. I was in fact mumbling to myself about getting some sort of action going, as if I could. But I thought it was about time someone built a fire under those people in Rome. I suppose I am the last man to do that. Rome does not want distant monks telling them what to do. Distant monks should neither be seen nor heard.

What can I tell you about the Church? You have been very patient with her human deficiencies, and that patience is also her gift. Your letter reflects the extraordinary serenity with which the new convert accepts *everything*. And one has to. In a sense it is true that one only comes in with blinders on, blinders one has put on and kept on. One has to refuse to be disturbed by so many things. And you are right in the refusal. These are temporal and absurd things which, in the eschatological perspectives, which are the true ones, must vanish forever along with many other things that are more precious and far from absurd in themselves.

The Church is not of this world, and she complacently reminds us of this when we try to budge her in any direction. But on the other hand we also are of the Church and we also have our duty to speak up and say the Church is not of this world when her refusal to budge turns out, in effect, to be a refusal to budge from a solidly and immovably temporal position. And that is the trouble with this war business. The Church's voice is clear enough, but the people who are responsible for applying Catholic principles to political action are acting in a way that is more secular than sacred. The current war ethic is pagan and less than pagan. There is very little of Christianity left in it anywhere. The truth and justice have been drained out of it. It is a lie and a blasphemy, and this has to be said. Not by you. But certainly if I have felt obliged to say it, I have been left without alternative. The urgency with which I have shouted what I wanted to say is due to the fact that I knew I would not go on shouting for very long and indeed the shouting is already over. You may perhaps see an issue of *Blackfriars* one of these days with the last echo of my outcry. I have written a whole book [*Peace in a Post-Christian Era*], but it has all been forbidden without even going to the censors. I have just been instructed to shut my trap and behave, which I do since these are orders that must be obeyed and I have said what I had to say. I will send you a mimeographed copy of the book if I can. Meanwhile with the letters of course you can use them discreetly, and I see no objection to their being quoted in class in a private school.

But to get back to you and Emy, I am so happy for you. You will have the grace to see through all that is inconsequential and unfortunate in the Church. She is still the Church, the Body of Christ, and nobody can change that, not even some of those who imagine themselves to represent her perfectly when they have simply twisted her teachings to suit their own secularism. Be true to the Spirit of God and to Christ.

Read your Prophets sometimes, and go through the Gospels and St. Paul and see what is said there: that is your life. You are called to a totally new, risen, transformed life in the Spirit of Christ. A life of simplicity and truth and joy that is not of this world. May you be blessed always in it, you and the children. I send you all my love and blessings.

May 15, 1963

I don't think the publication of the letters is a good idea. It would be difficult and complicated, and I would probably have to try to get them through the censors, who knows? Let us not attempt it.

If on the other hand you want to write an article and quote from them, there is much less of a problem, and I think that would be the better way to do it. If at all. And I do think there is a valid reason: for Pasternak. I believe that we owe it to him to recognize the real effect of his deeply and naturally religious outlook, and of his faith.

However, in quoting me, better omit my rather more lurid references to the Roman Curia and their hopeless delays, myopia, stupidity and so on. Remarks on art OK. Perhaps I had better refresh my memory a little on the bits you want to use, as I do not generally remember what I have said in letters, and perhaps that is a special mercy of God.

I will put another copy (I assume it is really another) of the *Peace* thing in the mail, with a bit on Fénelon I just wrote, and some stuff on Zen too. You had better brace yourself. Since a friend of mine took a picture of me, I might as well include that. How are the children? And all of you? As to the parish, ideally you are supposed to regard it as a community to which you belong and in which you worship God. But on the other hand if there are solid reasons for going elsewhere . . . viz., if the sermon drives you bats, then by all means do so. Especially for such a laudable motive as participation in sung liturgy.

June 29, 1963

I bless the day you got the cider.* That was a good letter. I forgot if it was in that one you sent the picture of the children. But I love those pictures. How the kids grow. I don't get the real point of looking into the pot on the stove during the hard winter: but I surmise it is something rugged, like "only soup of heather roots scuffed up by stags on Dartmoor" or something of the sort. It *must* have been a hard winter. Well, we had a hard one here too, and even a lot of evergreens were killed: types that flourish further south and don't expect hard winters.

Glad you like the picture I sent. That is of course exactly who I am: an

---

* Harris had written in a letter of June 13, 1963, that Merton's books had arrived at the same time as a barrel of cider, "the poor man's vin du pays."

Auvergnat curé with urbane connections, certainly not Savonarola* . . .

Under separate cover I will send a magazine with some things about the race problem here. It is getting to be extremely critical and it may blow the whole place wide open (or close it into a nice tight totalitarian state). The poem is about that. I suppose you read all about Birmingham, and now the other places.

In February 1965 John Harris sent Merton six letters of Pasternak's with comments on them. About a year later (May 24, 1966) he wrote: "Are you still there? We have grown used to your portrait on the wall and suddenly realized how long it is since we heard from or of you . . ." On January 20, 1967: "We hope that your hut in the woods is a real all-American hut with steam heat and running water and that the Abbot keeps your Huck Finn instincts civilized. Chuang Tzu is splendid. I'd never heard of him." Harris also mentions that his son Arthur (age twelve) has asked if Merton could send him some stamps for his collection.

April 10, 1967

Here are more stamps for our trusty secret agent in Cornwall. And, by the way, speaking of Cornwall: I am in a fury over that oil thing. How are you all now? How are the birds? Are there any fish left? I would be very interested to hear. I hope it will not be too bad. What I worry about most is the wildlife, because that is irreplaceable, but if you can't bathe this summer, that would not be too marvelous either. But I hope it will all be cleared up by now.

Did I thank you for your little Pasternak collection? You know I got it as I sent Arthur the stamps last time. But thanks very much. Have more fine picnics in Italy.

[My dear Arthur:

Since, as you realize, I conduct an immense and sinister traffic in hallucinogenic drugs and Argentinian soccer players and since this traffic has ramifications in five continents and many large and small islands, my secret agents everywhere keep me well provided with STAMPS.

Thus it is not difficult for me to send you from time to time a few of these, some of which are still impregnated with opiates, others scrawled with secret information concerning future interplanetary wars.

Please give my kind regards to your estimable father whom we in the transcontinental dope ring regard as a most deadly sleuth.

Sincerely yours

X 127†]

* *In the same letter Harris had also written: "We were delighted with your portrait. I had imagined you as Savonarolaesque . . . If this were one of those psychological tests, I would have put you down as an Auvergnat curé with urban connections."*
† *Merton's laundry number in the monastery.*

In a family Christmas card sent on December 19, 1967, Harris included a photograph of himself as well as his interpretation of the I Ching *on Merton and Christmas. Part of the interpretation was: "Departure toward the south brings good fortune."*

December 31, 1967

I am contemplating the great man and progeny: photo lies before me on work-and-dinner table of my hermitage. You enliven my frugal meals (soup, rice, ham sandwiches on occasion).

Now as to the offering from *I Ching*. I am suitably impressed. I am indeed quite awed. For there is much urging from a new monastery we have in Chile that I should come there ("south" if anything ever was!) and in lots of ways I would like to go, and have in fact tried to get there before. More than that, I have an even more attractive scheme for joining one of my former novices [Ernesto Cardenal], who now is running a very small out-of-the-way monastic encampment on an island [Solentiname] in a lake in Nicaragua ("south!!!") . . . We'll see in a little while. I'm not sure what is coming, but great changes are coming in two weeks (abbatial election, new man, Superiors coming from France—"great men"—). I will in any case do a great deal of conferring. But I have a feeling I am liable to get shipped north south east or west or maybe just stay here and get shot for my mad opinions. (The racial tension is going to be very bad indeed next year, it is going to be almost a revolution, certainly very violent and much chaos as a result.) (The KKK is getting strong in this area now.)

Sorry I haven't kept stamps for our secret agent this time. I am under an avalanche of mail and can hardly cope with one quarter of it . . . I am quixotically starting a small magazine to be done without cost on an offset press we have here. Any ideas for good material from England?? I would gladly print your bit about the correspondence with Pasternak (it would not have much circulation) or something else.

Best of all to you. My mind is fixed on the "south." Happy New Year.

To John C. Heidbrink

One of the things Jim Forest insisted on when I visited him in Holland was that I contact John Heidbrink, presently ministering to the Mill City Presbyterian Church in Oregon. I was unable to visit him but had several long telephone talks as well as some correspondence. His admiration for Thomas Merton seems to have grown with the years. From the first time he heard about him, from Dorothy Day and the Catholic Worker people, he was intrigued by this man totally com-

mitted to contemplation and the inner life. What did this mean for people like himself who were in the front lines of the work for peace and justice?

John Heidbrink has been in the forefront of the struggle for civil rights and for peace. He was born in Oklahoma City in 1926 and studied in Texas and Bern, Switzerland. After divinity studies at Harvard and Kenyon, he became Presbyterian chaplain at the University of Oklahoma, where in 1957 he participated in one of the earliest student sit-ins. At this time he became acquainted with Dr. Martin Luther King, Jr., then a young pastor in Birmingham, Alabama. He joined the Fellowship of Reconciliation (FOR) in 1960 as secretary for Church relations and worked at the FOR headquarters at Nyack, New York. Heidbrink's task was to get the churches committed to the civil rights movement. On the weekends he ran a coffeehouse to feed the hungry, the expenses were often paid out of the royalties Dan and Phil Berrigan received from their books.

Daniel Berrigan invited him to come to Le Moyne to speak to his classes on what Protestants expected from the Second Vatican Council; and in 1964 the two of them were in Prague for the International Peace Conference. It was during the time in Prague that Heidbrink assisted Berrigan and Jim Forest in making plans for setting up the Catholic Peace Fellowship (CPF). When Thich Nhat Hanh visited the U.S. in 1966, Heidbrink arranged his itinerary and made sure it included a visit to Gethsemani. His admiration for Thomas Merton remains strong. Speaking of Merton's last years, he commented: "His talents were in full bloom."

[*Cold War Letter 2*]

October 30, 1961

Thanks for your good letter of October 25. I am glad Dorothy Day and the *CW* got in touch with you. I am very anxious to be in touch with anyone who is working for peace at this hour. I do not think that Catholics realize the situation at all. They seem to be totally unaware of the gravity of the hour spiritually speaking, quite apart from the physical danger. It may very well be that we are faced with a temptation to a total interior apostasy from Christ, while perhaps maintaining an exterior rectitude of some sort. This is frightful. In this event, I feel that the supreme obligation of every Christian, taking precedence over absolutely everything else, is to devote himself by the best means at his disposal to a struggle to preserve the human race from annihilation and to abolish war as the essential means to accomplish this end. Everything else must be seen in this perspective, otherwise it loses its Christian significance at a time like this.

Since this is my attitude I am of course ready to help in any way that I can. Unfortunately I am in an extremely ambiguous and difficult position. Everything I write, unless it is to appear in "some small publication with limited appeal," is subject to a censorship which can drag out as long as two or three months, and then all sorts of trivial objections are raised to everything that is not purely a matter of pious homilies for the sisters on how to arrange the veil during meditation.

Fortunately you are a small and struggling organization [FOR] and I am willing to take it for granted that your publications are "small and of limited appeal" in the terms of our censorship statute. I shall check with Fr. Abbot to make sure. But this being the case, you can certainly quote what I say in letters, and even the mimeographed article I am sending under separate cover.

Yes, indeed I am anxious to have the *CW* article ["The Roots of War"] published as a pamphlet. There are technical points to be taken care of. It is from a book, *New Seeds of Contemplation,* to be published by New Directions in December. Please get permission from them, tell them I said OK . . .

There is no problem of censorship of course about the *CW* article. Go right ahead with it as soon as you please. Just make sure you refer to the book it comes from and to the publisher's permission. *CW* omitted this.

I cannot participate in your activities as a retreat leader, unless the retreatants come down here, which is pretty far. If a group wants to come down for an informal retreat and conferences with me, it can be arranged. I wish you would. But this is not strictly my line, and I couldn't give a whole series of them . . .

I am just about to get in touch with Archbishop Roberts [English, former Archbishop of Bombay who resigned in favor of a native bishop, one of the "liberal" bishops at the Council] . . . Sure I am Fr. Louis, but in the realm of writing and I might as well simply be TM.

November 13, 1961

. . . The enclosed article is for your publication ["Red or Dead"]. I have not sent it to the censor. Father Abbot has decided that you come under the article of the statute that does not require censorship since your publication has a "restricted influence," or words to that effect. Hence you can print and disseminate this in any way you like. Do you want to add it to the other one as part of the pamphlet?

The only trouble with censors will arise when others want to reprint this, but we will cross that bridge when we come to it.

I am very happy to hear that Pax is starting in this country (and it is about time). Jim Forest got in contact with me about that and asked me to be one of the sponsors. I am happy that I was able to obtain permission to be one.

. . . Time does not permit a longer letter at the moment so I must bring this to a close. I am grateful for your offer to read the life of Fr.

Metzger.* I think I can take responsibility for receiving and returning it if you tell me when you are mailing it and I can keep asking the secretaries in the front office whether it has arrived. I think I can get it back to you safely. With a little care these things can be managed, but on the other hand it is not totally without risk, as sometimes things fail to get through, or get lost, strayed, etc. I leave it to you to judge whether you should send it or not. I can say I am pretty certain it can be received and returned safely.

I would also like to know more about the FOR . . .

November 20, 1961

First, thank you for all the books and articles which have arrived. I am reading them with great interest, and I think some of the material may be useful for the paperback anthology I am preparing, though I think the English writers are a bit too chatty and informal. I want closely reasoned, tightly knit pieces, that are forceful and direct, but perhaps the E. I. Watkin piece in *Morals and Missiles* would be helpful. I have not begun the book on Father Metzger yet, but will in due course.

I have tightened up the "Red or Dead" piece by adding a page, numbered 1a, which clarifies matters a little and touches on the morality of the war situation without going into it. But it brings the question into the reader's consciousness, at any rate. Hence I am sending you the completed piece . . .

The numbers of *Fellowship* that have arrived are very interesting. I hope you will keep me on your list. I want to keep in touch. Jim Forest has written to me about the progress that is being made in Pax, and Archbishop Roberts has written, warning me to expect trouble from my co-religionists. I expect it. I hope I can handle it without being too hampered in my movements. That is the way it is with all efforts at truth. We all get too mixed up with what is less true, and then we get in one another's way. This whole present crisis is awfully symptomatic of the moral degeneracy of the world, including the Christian world, so-called. Well, let's hope that we can keep our sights on the target pointed out to us by the will of God, and work actively and positively for true Christian peace and justice, without compromising with error. For that we need much help from God.

December 2, 1961

I will be glad to get to know the FOR better. I had never heard of it, I must confess. But I have been here a long time and have been very much out of contact with everything. However, I now see that the FOR

---

* A Catholic leader in Una Sancta, an ecumenical movement in Germany. Metzger opposed Hitler's war and was executed for treason April 17, 1944.

is something very important for me. I must try to go along with you as much as I can, of this I am convinced. I think, however, that the most important thing is that we work along together quietly in a spirit of deep fraternal union and commitment to the cause of peace and unity, in other words stress the essentials as far as possible. I think it is important for me not to burst wildly onto the peace scene and create a stir, but simply to be there, because it is where I belong. The less I am involved in hot controversy, the less attention is drawn to my presence at the moment, the better it will be, and I will be able to go along quietly publishing here and there and above all establishing deep and firm contacts with the people involved, so that people will gradually get used to the fact that I am in the middle of all this as though in my natural habitat.

As for your proposal about condensing the first pages of "Red or Dead," by all means do so, I leave it to your editorial staff. I saw, on reading the issues of *Fellowship* you sent, that the article was overlong. I only wonder if there would be a possibility of running the entire "Red or Dead" piece in the pamphlet with "Roots of War"? . . .

Now that I know more about you, I can see that you must come down here, perhaps indeed certainly with one or two of your associates, so that we can have a good meeting and discussion of these big issues . . . Do please all of you at the FOR consider Gethsemani a place where you will always be welcome. If you want to be sure to see me, let me know a week or so in advance and I will get permission. I cannot always guarantee to see people at short notice.

The English book on *Nuclear Weapons* [Walter Stein, ed.] is without any doubt the best thing I have read for a long time. I am anxious to get the whole thing and use it in the paperback I told you about, if I possibly can. I may also write an article about it [Merton reviewed it in the *Catholic Worker*, November 1962], which you can use, but I am at present discussing the possibility with *The Nation*. It is really a splendid book, well thought out and well written . . .

The "Bridge of Faith," your article, represents exactly how I feel about Christian unity, especially about the need for a living dialogue with our brothers on the other side of the Iron Curtain who are being true to their faith under enormous difficulties. Who is to say they are not far better Christians than we are? I am deeply distressed and revolted by the idea that the West is somehow entitled to identify itself with Christendom and wipe out everyone else on that account. The Cross is the only way to establish peace. Until Christians come to know and understand something of the Cross, we cannot have anything but war. Unhappily the traditional Christian symbols and terminology have been exhausted by centuries of misuse and use without attention. We have lost the inner sensitivity to truth and to Christ, the fear of the Lord, without which we cannot see straight in the confusion of our world. Let us pray that Christians everywhere may recover this sensitivity . . .

[*Cold War Letter 38*]

February 15, 1962

Thank you for the tearsheets of "Red or Dead." I assume you don't want me to return them. I have just sent them off in a letter to Erich Fromm. In the note about the author, I presume there is no point in trying to make any changes and I do not wish to. I just observe that perhaps it would have been better with no mention of the Order. Not that it is important. It is only a very small point. But remember here we are in the realm of Byzantine and highly formal niceties, and in writing for *Fellowship* I am acting as a detached individual, while the Order, so to speak, looks the other way. And I am greatly relying on it looking the other way, for this will continue to be more and more important as we go on.

I think then in my relations with *Fellowship* it would be just best if I were (so to speak) taken for granted as part of the scenery, not requiring an introduction or an explanation, but I just happen to be on the scene somehow . . .

You speak about Una Sancta: definitely it ought to be started in America and I think it will. Things are moving along much more promisingly than one would have dreamed even five years ago. There is much to hope for . . .

I have had a lot of good reactions from the little piece on Fr. Metzger (which should not be published over my name, as it has not even been submitted to censorship; I regard it as his material rather than mine, since it consists mostly of excerpts). Do you know of Dr. Karl Stern, the psychiatrist and author? He speaks of having long "prayed to" Fr. Metzger every day. Evidently knew him in Germany . . .

As far as ecumenism and related "movements" go: I have no capacity to do anything that would even hint at organization. I am, once again, "not really there" or rather, if I happen to be on the scene, it is understood that nobody has adverted to the fact and this is the only way in which I can remain there. Even the small amount of work I am able to do here has been reduced and cut down to the minimum, and consists in nothing more than giving a few informal talks to groups who come, or chatting for a while with visitors. I had, by the way, a wonderful talk with Douglas and Mrs. Steere, the very day your last letter arrived.

The whole thing is this: I have in no sense whatever any mandate or approval or mission in the Church to work for ecumenism or for anything else. What I do I do purely as an isolated and articulate member of the clergy, whose actions are tolerated and within certain limits "approved" by Superiors so long as I do not involve them in embarrassing situations or long explanations. Hence the point is that you must always be very careful not to say anything that involves any institution to which I belong, except I assume it is legal to say I am a Catholic.

I agree with you that work must be done to clarify the practical meaninglessness of arguments based, in a purely theoretical and speculative way, on the just-war theory.

The great danger is that by isolating oneself from the unpleasant facts, one can spin out a theory that justifies almost any form of nuclear war. Within a very limited and even arbitrary set of suppositions and assumptions, one may end up by concluding "authoritatively" (with a theologian's authority, which cuts ice with bishops) that nuclear war "can be justified."

This theoretical statement having been generally accepted and blessed, the Christian is left at the mercy of *anything* that may be decided by the military according to an entirely different and more drastic set of assumptions.

The moralist may sweetly and benignly bless a nuclear war which he supposes involves a few five-megaton H-bombs directed at missile-launching sites, while the Pentagon is in reality contemplating massive high-megatonic terroristic attacks on bases and cities indiscriminately, plus a little chemical and bacteriological hors d'oeuvres to make it go down nice.

By the way, "Target Equals City" and "Christian Action" have been submitted to censors but not yet passed, so if you print them before I get the green light there may be trouble. However, I refer you to the recent *Commonweal*, with an article of mine which you can pick up if you want. There is a longer and more complete version which you may want to print as a pamphlet, perhaps. That will be in the collection I am editing, and maybe in the *Catholic Worker*.

No matter whether "Red or Dead" shows up with "Roots of War," I leave that to you. The Shelters for the Shelterless campaign seems to me to be very eloquent as well as fruitful.

Really Huxley is a great man. I would like to see his ms. about his wife very much. If you write to him, do please give him my regards and remind him of the great esteem and affection I have for him. I have a feeling he thinks that having become a hardened Roman and a monk into the bargain, I have drifted far from any common ground with him, but this is not so.

. . . Whether or not I can do anything about Una Sancta, I can always be a sounding board and a prompter, as well as an encourager. And we can always have our own Una Sancta underground. This is what I think my real mission is, an ecumenical underground that reaches out everywhere, to Buddhists and the Lord knows where.

God bless you always, and let me know when you would like to come

down. After Easter I have nothing special lined up yet, so any time after
then would be all right. I will wait until you set a definite time before I
ask Fr. Abbot about it, however . . .

May 11, 1962

I am just about a month behind with mail. It is not quite as hectic
here as there, but it can be hectic enough. At least I am out of the stained-
glass jungle, more or less. I am still going through all the material you
sent. One of the first things I did was answer the questionnaire, but I
got myself in a tangle with it because I began playing games and making
out like the novitiate was a parish. That got me in trouble later on, so if
all the answers don't come out perfectly straight in regard to what my
"parishioners" believe, discount it. I have a weakness for tests and seldom
take any, so I could not resist this one which is particularly good. I hope
I am not too late. Of course I want to know how it all comes out.

. . . How did your retreat with Dan [Berrigan] and the men from
Yale and Harvard go along? It sounds very good. Dan is certainly the
man to help you with Una Sancta. I am always being blocked in everything, and the fact that I am in an Order like this one means I am in a
systematic obstacle race as soon as I even think of trying to engage in
something active. I wanted to do some active and helpful things about
Pax, especially writing a lot of stuff for the bulletin, but I find I cannot.
The official frown has materialized all right; it is official and very much
of a frown. The best I can hope for is to get my new book on peace through
the censors. This is not the anthology, which seems to be going all right
at the moment, but the book I have written on the basis of various articles.
I hope it gets through the narrow gate.

. . . Jim Forest wrote me there was a meeting of Pax to discuss
whether they "should accept" the wonderful offer of FOR to help them
out with the printing, etc. Oh man, how silly can people get? I do hope
the meeting made sense and that they accepted.

Probably the Pax committee will be the hardest and slowest thing
in the world to get moving and when it comes it will move nowhere. I
know these movements. I wish I could do something. At least I can write
a few short things without signing them. Perhaps a statement of what it
is all about, that can go for everyone. I will see about it when I hear there
is going to be a bulletin at all. If and when . . .

May 30, 1962

Here is the little slip about using my name for the China project.
Notice that I am saying nothing about the Order. This may be something
that will get me in trouble but I think I ought to do it anyway. The Abbot
General has just vetoed a book of mine about nuclear war, just as the last
page was typed on stencils. I will run a few copies off anyway and my

friends can see it. But it must not be published. I have been told that I must cease writing and publishing on "controversial subjects" that have "nothing to do with the monastic life." There is no alternative but to accept the decision, which I do.

I don't suppose it affects the pamphlet *Roots of War*, which I assume is just about off the press by now, isn't it?

In any case this means I must keep my name out of print on the war question for the time being. I am glad I was at least able to say what I did, and that the anthology is coming out, regardless of anything else . . .

August 8, 1962

Fr. McDole is here. I am glad you wrote, as the letter reached me Monday. I had forgotten about him coming, and he was not going about asking, so that he would have been and gone without my doing anything about it. We had a good talk Monday and I will see him again today, and find him very alive and likable. I hope he will do a great deal of good, and hope I haven't made him twice as radical as he was already.

Every once in a while I come to myself and think that I have just been saying or writing something that would set half my fellow Catholics on their ear, and I begin to wonder why they aren't there on my account already. Perhaps they are. And yet when I ask myself if what I have said has something intrinsically wrong with it, I don't seem to find much, only the fact that it may have been too harsh, too blunt, too wounding. But heaven help us, one can't go about trying to avoid every statement that might wound the sensibilities of people who perhaps ought to be stirred up a little more than they are. The general attachment to the status quo is certainly not a sign of life, and the sensitivities that go with it ought perhaps to be stimulated a little, as they are perhaps an unconscious sign of conscience alive and working.

Well, that is neither here nor there. The book I wrote seemed to me to be most mild, and so full of qualifications as to border on compromise. I am glad you think it can be of some use. I am going to run off a few more copies and will send you half a dozen. But meanwhile, if you want to use quotes from the book, go ahead: but let us see what would be the best way to do this.

First would say, please make no reference to the book or its existence. Just quote me without giving any particular source.

The quotes should be short. I think in any case this will make them more effective. A box here and there, maybe.

Longer bits could be used on mimeograph, where there is less question of "publication." Or even in leaflets perhaps, though this may be getting beyond the limits that have been imposed on me. I am simply trying to practice obedience with the usual amount of "qualification" that is understood and tolerated and which you people have always found a little scandalous. It is, as far as I am concerned, a saving grace. Anyway, this is the way it has been understood in our long centuries of organization . . .

Fr. McDole confirms all the pessimistic impressions I had hitherto gathered about the deadness of American Pax. Steve Allen seems to have cooked up something more lively out on the Coast. On the whole they seem to be more awake in the Bay Area than anywhere else in this country.

I am glad to hear about the Metzger material. I don't know if I can do a whole book on it, but you might perhaps count on a preface or an article from me. The German will slow me down. I have his prison letters in German, but have not tackled them yet. Gordon Zahn sent me a card of the charming village church of Jaegerstaetter's little Austrian village . . . I look forward to Dan and Tony Walsh and I think Phil also being here next week.

P.S. I am going around telling people I am a member of FOR, by the way. I hope that is OK, though I am not an *absolute* pacifist.

September 25, 1962

Thanks for your good letter. I am glad to hear you are back from Europe and that you want to come down here in October. We will look forward to seeing you October 15th. The simplest way to get here is to hire a car at the airport and head for Bardstown. The map will show where we are, fifteen miles beyond Bardstown, you turn off about three miles before New Haven. There is a sign saying "Trappist" where you turn.

I am sending in the signed application for membership in the FOR. As I consider the principles set down, the aims of the Fellowship, it is difficult to see how I can do anything but join.* Hence I am glad to sign my name. In the present situation, I cannot align myself with those who sanction military preparations that must inevitably lead to violence on a world scale with colossal destruction of life and with the most flagrant violations of justice and morality.

It seems to me that every Christian has a moral obligation to do everything he can to help lead minds toward possibilities for peaceful and just settlement of international differences, even when there is great risk involved. We must take that risk. We have no right to eliminate what we consider political risks by military action on a totalist scale. This in any case, even the threat of this, is gravely harmful to the cause of the freedoms we are trying to defend. It calls into question the whole validity of our social ideals and the sincerity with which we proclaim them to other peoples who do not share our advantages.

Above all I feel myself most gravely obligated as a Christian and a

---

* *At this time (1962) FOR was considered a "Protestant" organization which Catholics simply did not join. Merton's action was unusual and ahead of his time.*

priest, as a monk above all, to a life devoted to charity and charitable efforts to solve social differences and problems. I mean here charity in the original Christian sense of the word, as a self-giving love: not a love that just gives money and never becomes personally involved. I am in the deepest sense personally involved in all that affects the good, the survival, the development and the salvation of my fellow man. It is with this in mind that I want to join the FOR.

On the other hand it would not be the desire of my Superiors to have this act of mine publicized, even for the benefit of a just cause like this. So long as I am just "there" and one of you, without any special attention being drawn to the fact, I think everything will be acceptable to them. Otherwise they might complain . . .

December 9, 1962

I was very sorry to hear, from Margaret Von Selle, that you were still in the hospital, or again in the hospital. I do hope you will get better soon, and that you will be all right, and well rested, by Christmas.

This is chiefly to thank you for the books. The Wright Millses were both terrific, as usual. The one on the Latin American problem was clear and persuasive, though he himself admits it is oversimplified. But one must see the other side of the case always. That is the trouble, people do not want to be objective. The Salisbury book on Russia is most valuable. Again, one has to be always adjusting one's views and taking into account the rapid movement of events and current developments. I was impressed to note the depth of the division between Russia and Red China at the present time. Of course it makes sense.

I have recently read the Lapp book, *Kill and Overkill*, and I think it is very important for this book to get to some of the people who will be discussing the question of nuclear weapons in the Council, when it resumes. Do you think you could possibly get copies to Jean and Hildegard Goss-Mayr, and also to Archbishop Roberts? I have mentioned it to the former and will tell the Archbishop about it soon. If they do not get the proper perspective, they will be talking about a problem that does not exist. Of course, I know the Goss-Mayrs know what the issue is, and so does Archbishop Roberts. But I think what is most important first of all is a clear recognition on the part of the Church that this is an *essentially* different kind of war and that therefore the question of defense in nuclear war takes on an entirely different character so that the categories of traditional warfare are irrelevant to the real moral issue in total nuclear war. In many cases these are stood completely on their heads. So much so that to proceed with the traditional moral approach to other war, and apply it as if there were no essential difference, would lead to solutions that would precisely favor the most immoral and most dangerous policies, rather than the ones which, if any, might promote less catastrophe. But at the same time once this issue has been made clear, then one can proceed to state the absolute seriousness with which the problem of abolishing large-scale wars must be approached. This has not as yet been regarded as even an interesting academic problem by most of the bishops. They must come to see it as a practical problem of utmost urgency not only for the Church but for everyone . . .

April 9, 1963

I just wrote to Glenn Smiley and gave him a message for you, but I might as well send along a copy of this letter I just wrote also to Paul Peachey about the retreat idea. You will see that within certain limitations it is entirely possible and I hope it will work out.

. . . Looking forward to the Pope's new encyclical on peace; I hope it will be a real awakening for the people that need to be awakened. If it is not too late.

Merton enclosed this letter to Paul Peachey.

[April 9, 1963]

. . . It would be better if a group of ten or so simply came down and spent a few days in the quiet of the monastery, in meditation, attending such offices as they would like, and devoting most of the afternoons to discussion and exchange of ideas. This last part would be under my aegis, I suppose. I have a suitable place for it, and can arrange the time fairly conveniently in the afternoon. My mornings are usually pretty well taken up with the novices. Naturally, three days is a rough idea of what might be feasible, and would fit my own plans for afternoons. But if anyone wanted to stay longer, that would be all right. It is just that three afternoons would be probably as much as I would be able to put into it.

I am sending a copy of this letter to John Heidbrink, and you can think it over with him, and let me know . . . I do hope it materializes, in the informal sort of way I have outlined above. Of course anyone is always welcome in the guesthouse, when there is room.

I agree with you that it should be a group of more or less "key" people. One other point that Fr. Abbot adds is that there should be no publicity, and in any case, I tell him, I did not think that any was likely.

May 20, 1963

. . . I look forward to hearing more about the program for the fall. It should be kept very small and informal. I am really not in a position to give a formal series of conferences in the sense of talks, lectures, exhortations, what have you. But informal conversations can be of great value. The chief thing would be the atmosphere of recollection and thought, and the exchange of ideas . . .

October 15, 1963

Thanks for your letter and for the prayers, which I appreciate. About the kind of group that is best: I think ten to fifteen are ideal. Beyond that it gets to be a bit confused, though in a pinch I suppose we could go up to twenty if it is not on a weekend. Indeed, ten or more would usually be preferable during the week. On a weekend we could not hope to fit in more than a few, three or four, unless it was in the dead of winter. I would suggest a small group to begin with, sometime during the week. Most of the rest of this year would be a little inconvenient for me, but next year is free. What about some time during the spring? Three days would be the kind of limit one would normally envisage, here.

Your mimeographed account of the trip was very lively and important. This is the kind of thing that is really significant. Such contacts mean infinitely more than a lot of theorizing at home. Thanks for writing it all down. I was especially interested in the East Germans since I have been getting to know Bonhoeffer and have read Pastor Hamel (which I think you sent).

. . . Do you know John Howard Griffin, who has been doing a lot of fine writing and speaking on the race thing? And P. D. East, editor of the so-called Petal Paper, who has defied the whole of Mississippi single-handed for a long time? He is now forced to get out before they do him in, I believe. He might come north and might possibly get interested in cooperation with FOR, though he has no special religion at all.

. . . I heard briefly from Douglas Steere at the Council. Pope Paul is most impressive and will probably go much further than Pope John . . .

February 23, 1964

Thanks for the material on Latin America. I am sorry to hear you are ill. Take care of yourself. Jim Forest has good news about the project. I hear from Dan Berrigan in Europe—his disappointments . . .

March 11, 1964

. . . The short visit of Jan Lochman was a great grace. We had a good talk in a deep agreement and sense of brotherhood in Christ. I am so glad you thought of having him come here. It was really something quite unique in the way of visits, a real encounter with a pilgrim, the sort of thing our Rule refers to. We are supposed to give preference, in the matter of hospitality, to "pilgrims" and I think that applies to my own contacts and visits. Certainly Jan Lochman filled the bill and I know that it was good for him to be here, as it was good for us to have him here. In these things, quiet and unassuming, the Kingdom of God consists.

The other day I also had a visitor from Argentina, a young poet called

Miguel Grinberg. I have told him to get in touch both with you and with Jim Forest when he is in NY a few weeks from now. He is a very lively and extraordinary person, a "pilgrim" too, but in another sense. He organized a fabulous meeting of poets from fifteen countries in Mexico last month and it was a great success. He is going about making contacts and opening up communication, and I think he will click with Fellowship of Reconciliation ideas and outlooks. He is not a Christian, but very open to Christian perspectives and to peace, etc.

Jim Douglass wrote recently and I was glad to hear from him. There again I would be keeping up a more lively correspondence if I had more time to think and compose intelligible letters.

By the way, I have been definitely sat on by the new Abbot General as regards writing about peace. It is a more or less final no.

Keep well and take care of your back. If you can bring yourself to rest more, you may be doing more for all of us than if you push yourself too hard . . .

May 9, 1964

I have your letter of April 29th here, and the memo about P. D. East, for which thanks. He was here, perhaps I did not tell you. I got some idea of his troubles and I can see they will continue. I hope he will find relative peace in his new place, and of course we here will do what we can to help.

The other day someone in Chicago contacted our Fr. Prior about Archbishop Roberts and I imagine he will be down here in a week or two. I look forward to seeing him very much.

Finally, about the session in the fall. October is out, so only November is available. As a matter of fact I had more or less counted on closing up shop after a rather busy summer, and was not going to take on anything more this year. Not only that, but I have more or less had to decide that I have too many irons in the fire and that a lot of them would have to come out. Chiefly this one of having groups down for discussion. Definitely I am going to have to cut this down if not eliminate it altogether.

What I would prefer to do would be simply to say: suppose two or three of those concerned drop down here for an informal visit sometime in November, preferably not on a weekend. Thanksgiving would be all right, though. I am afraid that a formal session with a planned topic and so on requires an organization which is just alien to this kind of life here and so I cannot undertake that. It would not work out, and we are not just geared for it. We could certainly discuss "spiritual roots of protest" in a very informal way, and if Dan is there the discussion would certainly be lively and fruitful. But let us not try to plan a formal session, and I will go along with the idea. I would tend to set the maximum at about six.

I hope this is not too disappointing, but I think I just have to face the realities of the life here. There is no use at all in our trying to get in with the rhythms of a more active and more organized existence and so I think that the only way to keep something like this fruitful and meaningful here is to keep it very small and informal and very spontaneous and relaxed.

Actually, though, as I mentioned, this kind of activity is going to have to be cut down somewhat here, and I am planning on much less of it in the future. Do you really think that just coming down for a visit would meet the expectations of the group? I know Ferry and Dan B., etc., would enjoy it.

How is your health? I am having my share of back trouble, trying to avoid an operation and so on, but the pain such as it is seems supportable most of the time; until I do something I shouldn't. I hope you will find some way of getting relief. Rest doesn't hurt, you know. It really sounds as if I am preaching quietism all down the line, but really I am convinced that we try to do too much and that our activity would be more fruitful if we kept it down a little . . .

September 14, 1964

How are you? And where are you? I thought I had better drop you a line and find out where things stand, about the possibility of you and some others coming down this fall. I would like to be able to plan more definitely one way or the other.

At the moment the first week of October is definitely taken up and will be so busy that I would rather have the second week free. At the end of the third I have someone coming through, so also the first week of November.

About the best times that leaves for me would be groups of days like Oct. 28, 29, 30 or November 11, 12, 13 or 18, 19, 20. Does that look any good to you at that end? Or do your plans call for something else? If we are to decide, I think now is the time, and of course I don't want to cling too rigidly to the dates mentioned if a change would really make a big difference in helping you to get down. But the previous commitments to other people must stand of course (above all, the very busy first week in October, when I expect to be running in circles and thinking exclusively with the top of my head).

Where is Dan B.? Is he back in the country yet? If so, where does one contact him? Do you know?

What Jim Forest writes these days is moving and alerting. I like the new peace move he is working on with you.

Old Archbishop Roberts really made a dent on his recent trip, and I am glad *Jubilee* picked up the ball and carried it down the field. I was very happy to meet him and will long remember it.

By the way, all the most important parts of my peace book finally got through the censorship of the General and they will be published this fall or next spring in the new book, *Seeds of Destruction* . . .

September 19, 1964

Thanks for the very good letter. Yes, I will be thinking about all those things. The great thing we can all try to do is get to those spiritual roots. My part is to offer whatever the silence here can give, and the slow tempo of the life, and you will probably enjoy coming to some of the Offices; that will be a rest and a change and probably a refreshment. Gregorian is good and it heals. The dopes here are thinking of getting rid of it and singing hymns. Yah.

The second and third weeks of November are, then, flexibly available, weekends being more or less out as being bad times for us here (crowded). We have the hermitage at our disposal, and I hope some decent weather. Anyway, we will camp around with the idea of roots, the need for them. I suspect that about all we all have is a great need for roots, but to know this is already something. I don't know what "way" there is to make contact with non-Christians on these things, except to get with them and stop emphasizing that we are different. We are all in the same boat, as far as our predicament goes. And we are all concerned with man living and surviving, which is pretty elemental, I think. The word of God reaches us somewhere in the middle of all that. But let us certainly arrange things so that those who most want to come can come, and seven is a good number. The optimum, I think. I will write to Dan . . .

I have been having some kind of skin trouble that I thought was poison ivy but perhaps is some other kind of affliction. I hope to have got rid of it by that time at least. It has been going on and off all summer.

What you write about marriage makes a great deal of sense. I should think that would be just the way it ought to be. Enough mystery and enough joy and the need to be patient and understand: much reward in all this. One of the things I miss most here is having children, but I suppose I would probably treat them miserably if I had them, or want to get away from them or something.

This is just a note then to say that I will be looking forward to November and will keep everything clear and open for you. I hope and pray that everyone will be able to get here and that it will be great for us all. Blessings always.

P.S. I agree about *Ecclesiam suam* [encyclical of Pope Paul VI]. I thought it was very cagy and political and not hopeful or especially enlightened, even the section on dialogue, though one felt he was "trying."

[Undated]

Thanks for your card. I think the best thing would be to plan on the group coming Nov. 18–20, it is much simpler like that, and then you can come later. Don't feel too limited about the time when you come. Christmas is not good but you will be busy then too. December tends to be dreary around here. But come when you can.

I will therefore plan definitely on the gang coming November 18 through 20. Which means I will be expecting them probably the night of the 17th for supper, which is what I will tell the guestmaster.

Fortunately the skin mends a bit. I think it will be OK. Am getting ready for the meeting of abbots next week, a great and perhaps useless chore. But there may be some point to it somewhere . . .

. . . Keep in touch and let me know when to expect you. I will look forward to seeing the others on the 17th or 18th of November. Who is coming?

The meeting on "The Spiritual Roots of Protest" was held November 18–20. John Heidbrink was in the hospital for surgery and therefore could not attend.

November 26, 1964

By now you may have heard reports from others of the retreat last week. I think we all felt it was a great experience. I will not use the word "meaningful," as I have heard this so much lately that the only bell it rings is the one for nausea. But certainly I think we were in contact with reality and truth in a way that is not met with every day. Thanks be to God for it. I would sum it up in two words: (a) a sense of the awful depth and seriousness of the situation; (b) a sense of deeper and purer hope, a hope purified of trust in the technological machinery and the "principalities and powers" at work therein. It was fine to meet John O. Nelson and John H. Yoder, and above all A.J. [Muste], who impressed me as much greater than anything that is said about him, and much simpler. I suppose this is true of all those who are really great in some way or other.

It was certainly a great shame that you could not be there, but it was a consolation to know from various quarters, especially from Dan, who had been with you, that your operation was a success. I hope that everything will go well and that you will be back in action without any troubles. My own back seems to have mended with a lot of traction and at the moment it is giving me little trouble. I am grateful for that too.

This is just a word to say God bless you. I am sure that we will always have light to follow the truth and the insights that are given us, if we seek that light. It is of course hard to go on when one's certainty in institutions is shaken, and it must be. Still, it all contributes to the purity of hope.

I suppose this retreat constitutes something of a "last fling" for me. My Superiors are really not too favorable to this sort of thing and developments seem to point to an end of retreats and a cutback in writing, contacts and so on. I understand what is up, and am able to accept it in a general way, so it does not call for commiseration, and if I wanted to force the issue I suppose I could. But there are reasons for going along with the policy, as I see it. We can be united in prayer and hope, and I hope we will keep in touch.

January 22, 1965

It was very good to have your special delivery letter, first because it gives me news that you are back on your feet, at least to some extent. I was worrying about you. Don't go and overdo things, you have to deny yourself the joy of daring too much. And I suppose that the business of feeling depressed when you have to leave work and get back into emptiness of mid-afternoon without a recognizable anchorage in custom, you think you are drifting and feeling guilty, because where after all do we drift except into extinction? That is the "condemnation of death" which Paul reminds us is so salutary because it makes us realize that we have nothing except the Lord's merciful love toward us. No amount of supposed achievement can alter this.

There is a demon of mid-afternoon for hermits also, but in my case I find that it also turns out to be a very good time for an hour's meditation, when I am not compelled to get wood chopped and do other such chores. I am not suggesting that you chop wood.

Now about the religious adjunct to the *Pacem in Terris* convocation.* I am glad there is one. The utter absence of any Catholic figure with any kind of recognizable status from the list of the ones in the main tent is something that strikes me hard. On the other hand, that fact is not going to guarantee that I participate. I just cannot. I have at least two deadlines to meet at that time, and other jobs that really have to be done. It is tempting to get at this, and I wish I could, but I have to be realistic about it. I know that if I undertook this I probably would not be able to do it and the other things would be left unfinished also. No one would gain by it. The best I can do would be to send a brief message which Dan could read perhaps, but I do not yet promise even that. I must think about it first.

However, there is no question in my mind that in the somewhat naïve approach to the "Church in the world" proposition there is all the danger imaginable that the Church will end up as a religious Madison Avenue for the computer boys. Yet to really say this with force one would have to have more technical competency than I have. I am not even good at high school math. Not that it takes math to see the danger, but one ought to be able to talk some science to prove that one has some title to make pronouncements on it.

* This convocation was the first of two conferences on Pope John's encyclical Pacem in Terris *organized by the Center for the Study of Democratic Institutions. (See letters to Wilbur H. Ferry.) It was held in New York City in 1965; a second was held in Geneva in 1967.*

The great thing is the true renewal, which is, as our hope tells us, certain: but it is not what the computers say, because this kind of thing cannot be programmed into a computer, and in the end, with all the "powers," the computers will be the object of that divine laughter that Bloy was always talking about: "*subsannatio*" or "laughter to scorn." There is then above all the question of raising our sights a bit and having a truer and more lasting hope. God will surely be manifest but not by the *hubris* and patronage of a society of con men. Although in that too he will be "glorified." Talking of *hubris*, it seems to me that our exploits in Vietnam are a superb example of it.

I am sorry not to come through with a share in the program, but you understand. God bless you and keep you. Be well and have joy.

April 30, 1965

I just got your note about Jean and Hildegard, and was planning in any case to answer your letter of the other day. I had just said Mass this morning for a broad sweep of peace-working people, including you, the Goss-Mayrs, Jim and the CPF, John Yoder (whose pamphlets I am reading with much profit) and so on . . . It is maddening at a time like this to have little or no exact news and not to find out clearly what has happened until two weeks after it is all over. In the age of nuclear war this does not help one to make very intelligent judgments, I am afraid, until long after they are worth making.

Still, this one I will make: I am very glad that the State Dept. and the White House took the FOR ad and protest seriously enough to write you about it. But at the same time I think they are just flattering you, and have no real intention of following a peaceful course if they can help it. They are of course concerned that there is very strong resistance to a war in Asia, and realize, they cannot help but realize, that most of the country for one reason or another is not interested in this kind of stupid adventure. In a sense I think it is unfortunate that the most articulate protests have taken a moral and pacifist stand. Unfortunate not because morality and pacifism are not relevant, they certainly are. But still, if the opposition is automatically defined as pacifist, it makes the war look ipso facto "practical" in a certain set of cliché terms, precisely because it wrongly divides the issue into pacifist idealism vs. hardheaded politics. This is the worst possible kind of illusion, because quite apart from the idealistic or even religious view of the question, aggression in Vietnam and escalation are lamentable politics, the fruit of stupidity, blindness and a messianic complex of some sort that makes the present policies of Washington the most absurd nonsense you might ever hope to encounter. Hence I would momentarily wish for a few of the old-style hardheaded power politicians of the eighteenth–nineteenth century who at least had the sense to avoid global crusades and to play their games in terms of a judicious balance. Maybe it turns out, after all, that this country is bent on ruin and can't help itself.

I would most certainly like if possible to see Jean and Hildegard in October. Since I am still novice master and still, for the rest of this year, in contact with occasional and exceptional visitors, there will be no objection from the Abbot (now away in Europe). It is probably my last chance, however, as next year he will probably want to stop all visits as his condition for letting me live as a hermit (which I am still doing only part-time). So let us provisionally arrange for a visit with Jean and Hildegard.

Thanks for the wonderful pictures of your family: they are all the most inspiring and happy faces: yours is a bit worn, but you seem to be holding up. Take care of yourself . . .

June 16, 1965

Many thanks for the card. You can certainly have the Simone Weil essay ["The Answer of Minerva"] to print, though I presume you know it was in *Peace News* some time ago, in the spring. The other little bit on ways to unity ["The Poorer Means"] is being printed in England [in *Sobornost*] and has also been accepted by a small Franciscan magazine, the *Cord*, published at St. Bonaventure, NY. If you want to pick it up after them, or before them for that matter, it is all right with me, but you should clear it with them . . .

I am looking forward to seeing Hildegard Goss-Mayr. It will be about my last visit of the year and for some time. By the way those Freedom Songs I wrote are being set to music by a young composer called Peloquin, in Boston, and they are to be sung at a concert premiere in Boston Nov. 22. Maybe a word on it would help. The composer Alexander Peloquin is at Boston College.

It was good to see Bob McDole, Dan Berrigan and Jim Douglass a few weeks ago. The big thing at the moment is not to let the Council get away with a very weakened and diluted chapter on war in Schema 13. It would certainly be tragic if the bishops came out with something completely inadequate on such an issue. The speech of [President] Johnson at Catholic University was read in the refectory here. It is really incredible that a man could stand up and claim to be guided by the highest moral motives while pouring troops into Vietnam, bypassing international discussion, claiming to keep the door open for discussion with the "enemy" when everyone knows that for both sides the only discussion they will contemplate is the capitulation of the other side, torture, napalm, etc., etc. But evidently he really believes that he and the nation are totally dedicated to the highest morality, and that our conviction that we are so is enough to make it so. He has apparently never stopped to consider the elementary fact that the other side also consider themselves dedicated to the highest principles, etc., etc., and that this is a universal trait, which calls for serious arbitration over objective rights, and not just the use of force justified by subjective righteousness. We live in an age of ethical moronism. And I suppose that there is not much that can be done about it, except to keep hoping that a vestige of common sense will still remain somewhere . . .

July 25, 1965

I have been waiting for a chance to make some thoughtful comment on your excellent notes on the just-war theory. I really think they constitute one of the best critiques of it that I have seen, and I am in fundamental agreement with you. After all, a Catholic is not bound to this theory as to an article of dogmatic faith and there is every evidence that the time has now come for a very serious revision of Catholic thought on the subject of war. Whether we can expect any such thing from the Council is another matter. (I will enclose my notes to the Bishop, on Schema 13.)

As you say so well, if the logic of the just war were followed, it would lead in practice to a "pacifist" position, and that is in fact what the Popes have actually done, especially Pope John in *Pacem in Terris*. His reasoning here is simply that new developments in war technology and the present political condition of the world have conspired to make the conditions of the just war practically unfulfillable. On the other hand, since the whole approach opened up by just-war thinking is one which permits unlimited casuistry, it is inevitable that casuistry should neutralize any logic of this kind, and in fact I hear that a revised version of Schema 13 does manage, by casuistically chosen terms, to neutralize whatever is said about the bomb, about total war, and about conscientious objection. Hence the just-war theory will really no longer serve even to check the unscrupulous use of violence or to give it a show of justification—except rather by the puerile eschatology of the right-wing Catholics with their holy-war mystique. I hear, by the way, that when Dan Berrigan gave a talk somewhere, some of these types were picketing the place with signs that read "Judas Berrigan."

Do I have any criticism of your notes? Not really, except perhaps to offer some ideas from a slightly different historical perspective, on the application of the just-war thinking in the so-called ages of faith. In the historical context, p. 4, you ask whether the "Christian" population ever protested against war on the just-war basis. Of course, until very recently, nineteenth century, the population as such was really not actively involved. In the heyday of just wars, the wars tended to be fought by professional armies only. Hence the conscience of the king was directly involved, along with the consciences of his advisors. The principles of the just-war theory were, like all Catholic moral thought at the time, useful chiefly for the confessor and director of conscience if any. If the king bothered to make a matter of conscience of it, his confessor should guide him by these principles. I have a strong text from Fénelon telling Louis XIV that his wars were absolutely unjust. F. was of course not L.'s confessor and the statement was made in an anonymous letter. It was in this kind of context, and not in that of public opinion, that appeal was made to the standards for a just war.

You are of course right in saying that, as a result of this kind of approach, there is really no practical way in which the ordinary Catholic can make use of the just-war theory to decide the question of war as a matter for his own conscience. This is the problem of the Catholic objectors today, and it makes the "pacifist" position much simpler.

I don't know what will come out of the Council on conscientious objection, but I think it may well be ambiguous enough to create a real problem in this area. The anxieties and conflict of conscience of objectors may well serve (at great cost to themselves) to finally force the issue back to an evangelical plane, even with Catholics.

I think then that the issue of war is one which constitutes one of the great challenges to the Catholic Church, and it is one where we are called upon to decide whether or not we are really Christians. God knows how we as a group are going to meet this. Cicero won't help us to make the grade any longer (if he ever did).

. . . At the end of August I will be officially permitted to live all the time in the hermitage and relieved of my responsibilities in the community (except of course the basic ones of the vows). Whatever else may come of it, I see clearly that it is for me the best and most providential way of finding myself in direct confrontation with and obedience to God's word. I will still receive some mail, and I don't consider personally that a complete rupture of communications with the rest of the human race would be an authentic confrontation with God. But He will determine to what extent my life is to remain directly relevant to other people. I suppose I will continue to write. But I will certainly feel very deeply united to all my friends and brothers in Christ and all those who in one way or another are striving for His Kingdom, and bearing witness to His mercy to us and to the living presence of the Spirit.

November 20, 1965

Yesterday I got very good letters from Dan and Jim and answered them immediately. Today I received yours, which set me back a bit, but it came clearer on a second reading. I will not go into long explanations of what I have already said to Dan and Jim. Your word "paranoia" is not so far wrong actually, because being in isolation and not knowing what is going on really puts one in a position where all of a sudden everything gets really kooky. I hope I have in part corrected the harm done by my telegram with them and I trust their charity to understand. I apologize to you for anything that may have splashed off on the whole peace movement.

At the same time, it is not all cowardice and betrayal. I think I do have something of a problem, but I am hoping to start over again and approach it more reasonably with them. As I did yesterday, I hope.

The problem is simply this: when people burn draft cards or themselves (and I appreciate your analysis of Roger La Porte's tragic act [self-immolation for peace] and its implications for society), I hear about it if at all from someone who is very upset by it, and who may or may not represent someone else who is even more upset and who in addition holds me in some way accountable if the people are Catholics. I am reputed to be "a pacifist," which in fact I am not, if you take the strict technical meaning of the term, and I am a Catholic, therefore it is automatic that I can know, explain, defend, etc., the burning of draft cards even before I know it has happened. Let alone before I know what it is about, whether I agree with it or not. Since I am not able to keep up with these things and since it is no longer possible for me to be making all kinds of pronouncements about them, I would appreciate not being expected to. For instance, at the moment, while a lot of people think I am solidly behind draft-card burning, others are urging me to come out against it, when I for my part, recognizing that I am really not in a position to make a really serious judgment, would prefer to say nothing. You may regard this as cowardice, I do not. I don't think that Christian courage demands that one speak his mind regardless of whether or not it makes real sense. For the same reason, I gave up signing manifestos for ads in the paper, on this or that issue. For me to do this would simply not be an authentic Christian and free act.

Now I suppose that in fact whether or not my name happens to be on the list of sponsors of CPF makes little difference in this regard. But in the light of the rather dramatic witness that is going on these days (not directly sponsored by CPF, but nevertheless members of the CPF are right in the middle of it), I realize that I am going to be constantly called to account in this way, and again, never knowing what next. Fear? I call that a reasonable fear, because after all one of the things it definitely includes is the possibility of another juicy "paranoid" judgment that would hurt my friends. Let's be a little realistic about this, John. What I am talking about is just the ordinary liberty of a human being who can make up his own mind without having it made up for him in advance on issues like these. And to some extent if I remain publicly committed to an organization that I can't keep up with, a lot of things are to some extent decided for me just by events. And even if Jim devotedly sent me packets of mail day after day, I would not want him to go to all that trouble, and I still would not have the kind of perspective one ought to have. And technically I have been more or less silenced anyway.

Jim understands now, I hope, that I do not mean to be dramatic or to torpedo the CPF. Also, let's face it, my name on their list is purely symbolic by now. I think that once the thing is seen in less dramatic and absurd terms than it appeared, last week, through my own fault, I have a perfect right to resign from the CPF without this being regarded as a betrayal or repudiation of those who are working in it and who are, as I gladly admit, much better men than I am.

I appreciate your frankness, John. And I see the ambiguities of my life well enough, I assure you. But this is the life I have to live whether people accept it or not. It is not that I disbelieve or distrust Jim and the others in their engagement in the CPF: it is myself that I disbelieve and distrust in that context . . .

December 4, 1965

First, thanks for your note and the enclosures. All were helpful. I owe you (and here you is almost plural, since I take you as FOR, CPF and all) a letter that speaks out frankly, not about the peace movement, not about the world, but simply about my own position, which you, in your Christlike charity, are willing to accept as is. This is not a matter simply of self-unburdening or solipsism or whatever you wish, it is perhaps relevant to you (plural) insofar as I am in a peculiar relation to you, a relationship made more peculiar by my solitude and positive withdrawal. Because I see that in no sense am I entitled to minimize or compromise this withdrawal, while at the same time retaining a genuine responsibility and service.

Obviously this peculiar relationship is not provided for in any of the current formulas. It is definitely not the kind of thing that is universally accepted and approved. It is in its own way a "no" even to much that is good and vital. And I will not attempt to prove in any way that my "no" and my "yes" are perfectly necessary and justified, because I have not reached statable conclusions and explanations. Thus in brotherly simplicity I simply offer you a provisional estimate, the way it looks to me now. If in stating this I say anything forceful, it is not at all an implicit criticism of you who have different ways. I accept your ways, as you have so rightly urged, and I needed no urging. I have always accepted your way as different from mine. I have always accepted Jim [Forest] as a person of unusual integrity and promise. I accept Tom [Cornell's] charismatic inspiration as necessary for him and right for him, but I question its rightness for the CPF, upon which it inevitably redounded, and upon which perhaps it was really intended to redound. But I am not talking about that.

No need to repeat that I recognize very clearly the wrong I did all of you with my telegram and first letter. I will add that certainly for me, as for all of you, Roger's immolation started off a deep process of examination and it will lead far. Wrong as I think his act objectively was, I believe it did not prejudice the purity of his own heart and I never condemned him. What I condemned and in some sense still very definitely question is a pervasive "spirit" or something, a spirit of irrationality, of power-seeking, of temptation to the wrong kind of refusal and impatience and to pseudo-charismatic witness which can be terribly, fatally destructive of all good. I do not, please understand me, accuse any individual, certainly no one among you, of incarnating that spirit. Quite the contrary. But the presence of such a spirit in the air, and it is in the air, a spirit of madness and fanaticism, summons me to deep distrust of all my own acts and involvements in this public realm.

In my peculiar position of solitude and lack of perspective on such matters, I would say that I was most vulnerable to this spirit of wrong, and that if I continued to try to be at the same time a solitary *and* actively involved and implicated in particular political decisions, at this present stage of my inner struggle, I would almost certainly turn out some kind of very dangerous false prophet. And the temptation might well be that this could cause such a commotion that it would recommend itself as "interesting" to this or that movement that could profit by it (I almost wrote prophet by it). Nor would the solution be for me to passively let you make my decision for me and funnel detailed commitments down here to me for me to sign. I believe in you, but this is not the form my belief takes and you would not want it to take such a form. You would not want me to be less than a person. Hence, for me now, to tag along with you in the day-to-day evolution of political witness would be a real betrayal of my own vocation. I feel this very strongly and very clearly. It is not by any means simply a matter of wanting to hold on to a wide public or anything like that, because in fact it may well be leading to a complete silence that would mean the end of all this "leadership" crap. Probably, the way I see it, the real road lies somewhere between, with a new development in thought and work that will, if it is what it should be, be much more true and more valid for peace than any series of ephemeral gestures I might attempt to make. But anyway, now is for me a time of searching, digging, and if I mention angst it is not to dramatize myself in any way but to assure you that I conceive my real and valid union with you all to take this form of silently getting ground up inside by the weights among which you are moving outside.

It is also understood of course that if I get any word, I hope reasonable word, to utter, I will not hesitate to utter it as I have always done before. But this word has to come from here, and from the center of this particular silence, not from there. That is why I have I think worked it out with Jim that I will remain a sponsor of CPF provided it is understood that in political matters and other questions of immediate practical decision I remain independent and autonomous and that your acts are not necessarily my acts in this realm. I think in all fairness that I need this clear autonomy for the sake of the free functioning my present life demands. I can be of use to you, I hope, if I don't have you hanging around my neck like what seems to me (rightly or wrongly) a millstone. I do not say this position is a wonderful one, or deny that it may be simply a reflection of a certain incapacity on my part, a definite limitation. All I ask is that if it is a limitation, you be willing to accept it patiently and not harass me for it, with enough confidence in me to hope that I will work my way through the woods in some good season.

Therefore, plainly what this means is that I consider myself not part of any peace movement in the active sense (the political sense). I am in the position I stated, I hope, clearly enough in the page I sent to Jim Forest. I am morally and spiritually with you, I back the stated aims of the CPF, especially the moral and pastoral ones, and of course this implies a general agreement with a liberal political implementation of the moral principles. An immoral war does demand *some* political protest. But I no longer consider myself able to underwrite a series of immediate practical decisions and I do not wish my name to be used in that connection. (This does not imply that I think the decisions will be right or wrong. Some will be of the kind I would heartily agree with, others less so. It is, however, the inactivity, the state of being a non-activist, a non-participant, that I think I am now bound to adopt, reserving the right to make my own protests in my own name when I see fit.) Obviously, if I do say anything political on my own, I do not claim a charismatic autonomy for myself after denying it to others, and if something I say turns out to be disastrous or idiotic I will certainly expect you to let me know about it. Also I will normally work through Jim, if it is a question of blasts that are to go out to the press . . .

Do you understand me, John? Or am I once again raving in my mad head? Above all, do you see that I can claim this for myself without in any way denying you others your own way and your own call?

About Dan and his exile: just as my own particular struggle and decision is something which I regard as a divine judgment visited upon me as the result of Roger's death, I think that Dan's exile is also in a way such a judgment, and his acceptance of it in faith will make his seemingly preposterous obedience very fruitful. Who knows what providential meetings will take place where he goes in the South? Which all gets back to my "Calvinism." One thing for which I respect Calvin is precisely his acute existential sense of evil as a positive cancer, an excrescence on being, not as a simple abstract lack of perfection. The man's sense of sin verged on the pathological, but we can at least learn from it about sin and judgment. And I feel called to meet up to such a judgment. (Obviously I don't accept his predestinationism.) With your charity I know that it will come through into healing for us all.

May 20, 1966

Your telegram arrived today and though I am not able to give an absolutely definite answer, the Abbot being away at the moment, I think it most important that Ven. Thich Nhat Hanh should visit here, and I shall do what I can to arrange it, even if it were only a visit to me, but I think he should also speak to the community and no doubt the Abbot will be interested. Much of course depends on when he comes. But we will be glad to see him whenever he gets here, and certainly I would like very much to chat with him a little and to see you again. I think it can be arranged but will have to see the Abbot about it next week. How long do I have to get you a final decision? Can do so by Wednesday or Thursday, I think; will wire if necessary.

It is good to hear from you. I have been meaning to write but I had a cervical-disc fusion a while ago and it is not easy to type as I also got bursitis in an elbow on top of it, so I have been resting the bones to some extent . . .

Let's hope something can be done to stop this miserable, futile, senseless mess in Vietnam. I am no better informed than ever but there does seem to be some rather more effective protest, and congressmen seem to be getting behind it. But whether that can stop the power people no one can say, as far as I can see. It seems to me the Vietnam Buddhists are about the only ones who are making much sense, though that is not an opinion shared by all in this monastery. (The Abbot reads *Time*.)

All the best always, hope to hear from you about when to expect you if you come.

John Heidbrink and Thich Nhat Hanh visited Merton at Gethsemani in late May.

May 30, 1966

. . . Will like plenty copies of the statement for Nhat. Wonderful weekend. May all your tour be blessed and may Nhat attain the best of ends.

June 1, 1966

My face is red like this pen. Proofs for "Blessed Are the Meek" just came in. I forgot entirely I had given it to the Cowley Fathers in Boston for their magazine. You can certainly use it, too, in any form you like (pamphlet?), but I forgot it was already being printed. Shows how addle-headed I am getting.

June 13, 1966

. . . If any copies have been made of Nhat Hanh statement ["Nhat Hanh Is My Brother"], I hope you will send me some, and I will be interested to hear how it did and so on. Glad of the good news of his visa extension and hope he will get to France. Incidentally, the French translation of "Blessed Are the Meek" is appearing in the same magazine (*Frères du Monde*) which printed Nhat Hanh's conference a couple of years ago.

Got a good letter from Dan the other day.

. . . Things are quiet here. Fr. Abbot is just returning from Chile, where we will be sending some monks shortly, I expect. Probably I will not be involved in it myself.

Your visit here is still remembered with joy, and I will be glad to see the pictures when they are ready . . .

June 26, 1966

Thanks for your letter: I think the idea of translating Nhat's little book on Buddhism is a good one. It ought to be done. But with translations I think it is always better that people who have other things to do should not do translations. There are always translators available. I am so far behind with my other work that I would not want to get into it now. You are much too busy and it would probably be slow work for you anyway, bad economy. Ping Ferry will be here tomorrow, I will ask him about it. I bet there is someone out at the Center who would be glad to do it, and in a better position to get it done without trouble.

. . . Glad to hear [Nhat] is or was getting a good reception in Sweden. I certainly hope that when he gets back to Vietnam—perhaps he is back already—they will realize that it is to their interest to respect his safety.

. . . Returning to Nhat's book: it is already a translation from Vietnamese into French. Ideally, it would be better if someone would translate it direct from Vietnamese. I realize it would not be easy to find anyone, however.

I liked the picture that Nhat signed. Don't forget to let me see the others on that roll, when convenient. This afternoon, too, I want to get busy on a letter to the Nobel people for Nhat. I think that whole Peace Prize idea is a good one. . .

August 1, 1966

. . . I am very happy to hear [Nhat] saw the Pope. That was very encouraging. Of all the people in the world, the Pope is still one of the few whose personal intervention really counts for a great deal. So that is wonderful news.

Have you got a European address where I could drop Nhat a line? . . .

March 5, 1967

Glad to have you come by yourself, or with just one or two others. I don't relish the large-group bit, and prefer just one or two, or just one.

It would be nice if you come at the same time as Dan Berrigan, who may show up sometime in late spring or early summer. But come when you can, and let me know in plenty of time. . .

About your book on mysticism. Candidly, I must tell you that I get swamped with manuscripts and you run the risk of having it put aside and never got to. But since the subject is an important one and since we will be able to talk about it, I will do my level best to read a good part of it. It is important anyway to defend mysticism, which is already under attack and, I believe, will be even more heavily attacked soon, particularly by the new Catholic theologians. We are facing a strong wave of anti-mystical, anti-monastic, anti-interiority theology. That of course is nothing new. My own feeling is that the main source of understanding and support in these fields will come from non-Catholics. Ironic, isn't it? All these are extra reasons why I will be anxious to read what you have to say, and therefore will take the presence of your ms. seriously, and not just forget it.

April 22, 1967

Thanks for your real good letter of the 1st. I was especially interested to hear something about your separation from the FOR, as I knew only the fact that you had left them, nothing more. That is the same thing that worries me in almost everything that gets organized these days. The speed with which everything gets sclerosis is amazing. Still, I think the FOR is probably better off than most outfits. Jim has been having a slightly rough time lately but I haven't heard much from him. Dan Berrigan should be down this way soon and things may get even rougher for him again, over Vietnam. I have not seen the papers lately but I understand that Haiphong has been bombed. I didn't even hear about the troubles in Louisville until they had been under way for several days.

I do think you are right to bide time and keep an eye open and see what comes up. If you are interested in dialogue with Marxists and so on, why not perhaps get in touch with a man in this country who is trying to get some things lined up for Cardinal Koenig of Vienna. He is the head of the Commission for Dialogue of Catholics and non-Christians, i.e., especially the East European Marxists. He is coming to this country . . . Why not write Carleton Smith [see letters to Carleton Smith]. Say I suggested that you write. The main opening would be to suggest someone the Cardinal could talk to when he comes here in the summer for conversations with atheists. God knows there is no official U.S. atheism, and there are no Marxists, but you might know what sort of people would fit in. It might be good, in any case, to talk with the Cardinal yourself about your own interest in this. Obviously, his urge to make you a Papal Legate or something would probably be minimal. And all in all, it might be some use.

Hildegard Goss-Mayr wrote, wanting me to do a preface for a book of hers [on Latin America], but I have finally had to drop prefaces for a while in order to get some work done. Lately, I have been getting very much behind because I have had an overload of visits. Hope I can get back to my stuff on Camus (I am going to do a book on him). I'll send you a new article on him. And when I get another chance, more of the old fruitcake and cheese routine.

My best love to all of you. I remember your wonderful visit last summer with Nhat. It is just as bright and warm here today.

To Abraham Heschel

Born in Warsaw, a descendant of Hasidic rabbis, Abraham Joshua Heschel (1907–72), emerged as a gifted writer who was able to combine intellectual insights with a profound poetic sensitivity. Studies at the University of Berlin produced as his doctoral thesis his classical study The Prophets, *published by the Polish Academy of Science in 1936 and subsequently published in English in 1962. He taught in Frankfurt for a time as Martin Buber's successor.*

In 1938 the Nazis forced him out of Germany. He returned to Warsaw as a teacher, but the Nazi invasion of his native country forced him to flee. He went to London briefly, then to Cincinnati, where he taught at Hebrew Union College from 1940 to 1945. In 1945 he went to the Jewish Theological Seminary in New York City, where, except for several visiting chairs that he accepted (University of Minnesota, 1960; Iowa State University; Union Theological Seminary, 1965), the remaining years of his distinguished career were spent.

In his writing he combines a sense of awe at the glory of God with a prophetic concern for the needs of God's people. His place was not just in the classroom and the synagogue but also at the side of Martin Luther King, Jr., in Selma, and with John Bennett and other clergy and laity concerned about Vietnam. Besides The Prophets, *his books include* Man Is Not Alone *(1951),* The Sabbath *(1952),* Man's Quest for God *(1954),* God in Search of Man *(1955),* Who Is Man? *(1965), and* The Insecurity of Freedom *(1966), among others.*

December 17, 1960

It was a real pleasure for me to get your good letter of October 23rd and the package of books, which are to me full of very satisfying intuitions and statements. It is an added satisfaction to have these books here at hand and to be able to meditate on them in a leisurely fashion, instead of rushing to get them back to the library.

I think the one that really appeals to me the most of all is *God in Search of Man.* I do not mean that I think it contains all your best and deepest thought, but it is what most appeals to me, at least now, because it has most to say about prayer. This is what I can agree with you on, in the deepest possible way. It is something beyond the intellect and beyond reflection. I am happy that someone is there, like yourself, to emphasize the mystery and the Holiness of God.

There are so many voices heard today asserting that one should "have religion" or "believe," but all they mean is that one should associate himself, "sign up" with some religious group. Stand up and be counted. As if religion were somehow primarily a matter of gregariousness. Alas, we have too much gregariousness of the wrong kind, and with results that do not need to be recalled. The gregariousness even of some believers is a huddling together *against* God rather than adoration of His true transcendent holiness.

Needless to say, I look forward eagerly to your book on the Prophets. This fall I went through Amos carefully with my novices. It is a frightening accusation of our own age, with its prosperity, its arrogance and its unbelief. And its poverty, its injustice and its oppression. And now we are in the season when, in our liturgy, Isaiah is read daily, a season of longing for the fulfillment of divine promises, those promises which are so infinitely *serious*, and which are taken so lightly. Nor are these expectations fulfilled, for Christians, at Christmas merely. That too is another expectation. I believe humbly that Christians and Jews ought to realize together something of the same urgency of expectation and desire, even though there is a radically different theological dimension to their hopes. They remain the same hopes with altered perspectives. It does not seem to me that this is ever emphasized.

. . . The monastery is near Louisville. We are about fifty miles south of it, fifteen miles beyond Bardstown. If you ever come down to Louisville, Cincinnati, or Lexington, you are close to the monastery. I do not know if you would be likely to come down to lecture at Hebrew Union Seminary in Cincinnati: if so, that would be a fine opportunity to get down here. But in any case I do hope you will take seriously the thought of coming to see me someday. You are always welcome at the monastery. Meanwhile, any letter from you is a joy to me. . .

January 26, 1963

It is a great pleasure to have received your fine book on *The Prophets*. I have been anticipating this for a long time, and my anticipation is not disappointed. It is a fine book, perhaps your very best. Or at least it is one that says a great deal to me. You take exactly the kind of reflective approach that seems to me most significant and spiritually fruitful, for after all it is not the Prophets we study but the word of God revealed in and through them. They offer us examples of fidelity to Him and patterns of suffering and faith which we must take into account if we are to live as religious men in any sense of the word. The book is in many ways just the kind of reflection germane to monks, and I hope to be able to use it in my conferences with the novices.

In any case, it is a privilege to be able to share your own meditations on the Prophets and indeed to find very little in those pages that I would not myself want to express in much the same way. Someday perhaps I will muster up courage to try the difficult task of saying what the Prophets must mean to a Christian: difficult because of the heritage of past interpretations and allegories. We have the bad habit of thinking that because we believe the prophecies are fulfilled, we can consider them to be fulfilled in any way we please, that is to say that we are too confident of understanding this "fulfillment." Consequently, the medieval facility with which the Kingdom of God was assumed to be the society inherited from Charlemagne. And consequently the even more portentous facility with which Christians did exactly what they accused the Jews of having done: finding an earthly fulfillment of prophecy in political institutions dressed up as theocracy.

The twentieth century makes it impossible seriously to do this any more, so perhaps we will be humble enough to dig down to a deeper and more burning truth. In so doing, we may perhaps get closer to you, whom the Lord has not allowed to find so many specious arguments in favor of complacent readings.

Abraham Heschel visited Merton on July 13, 1964.

July 27, 1964

Shortly after your visit, that warm and memorable occasion, which was a real and providential gift, I wrote this letter to Cardinal Bea. I have been meaning to send you a copy, and am only just getting around to it. Every time I approach any such statement, I am more deeply convinced of the futility of statements. But statements are easy. And the fact of not having made one when it was required can be a terrible and irreparable omission.

Your books and offprints arrived promptly. I am at the moment most involved in *The Earth Is the Lord's* and *The Sabbath*. I note that your preoccupation with the sanctification of time runs parallel to some ideas of my own in a recent ms. I have sent to the publisher on Liturgy [*Seasons of Celebration*]. But I am not at all satisfied with my book.

Fortunately I have received permission to publish the material on peace that was still swinging in the balance, I think, when you were here . . .

Please think of us when you are in this area again. The door is always open to you, if you let us know when you are coming. Also I would always be glad to hear any news, especially anything that may affect the Jewish Chapter in the Council, and other such things.

July 14, 1964

[His Eminence, Augustine Cardinal Bea
Secretariat for Christian Unity, Vatican City

Your Eminence:

Yesterday I had the very great pleasure of speaking at some length with Rabbi Abraham Heschel who visited us briefly here at the monastery. He spoke much of his hopes and fears for the Council and of course spoke very much of Your Eminence and of the Jewish Chapter, which we all have so closely at heart, and concerning which we share a certain sadness, not devoid of hope.

Naturally, one such as I, who am very far from the scene, can offer no constructive help save that of prayer. But this may turn out in the end to be more efficacious than other means. In any event, the purpose of this letter is to assure Your Eminence that I and my brothers here will certainly be praying that God may see fit to grant his Church the very great favor and grace of understanding the true meaning of this opportunity for repentance and truth which is being offered her and which so many are ready to reject and refuse. It is true that the Chapter can do much for the Jews, but there is no question that the Church herself stands to benefit by it spiritually in incalculable ways. I am personally convinced that the grace to truly see the Church as she is in her humility and in her splendor may perhaps not be granted to the Council Fathers if they fail to take account of her relation to the anguished Synagogue. This is not just a question of a gesture of magnanimity. The deepest truths are in question. The very words themselves should suggest that the *ekklesia* is not altogether alien from the *synagogue* and that she should be able to see herself to some extent, though darkly, in this antitypal mirror. But if she looks at the picture, what she sees is not consoling. Yet she has the power to bring mercy and consolation into this mirror image, and thus to experience in herself the beatitude promised to the merciful. If she forgoes this opportunity out of temporal and political motives (in exactly the same way that a recent Pontiff [Pius XII] is accused of having done) will she not by that very fact manifest that she has in some way forgotten her own true identity? Is not then the whole meaning and purpose of the Council at stake? These are some of the thoughts that run through my mind as I reflect on the present situation in the Church of God. I dare to confide them to Your Eminence as a son to a Father.

Would it not perhaps be possible, theologically as well as "diplomatically," to meet the objections raised by those who fear to alienate the Moslems? This too is a theological question, in view of the fact that Mohammed, before the decision which led to the beginning of Islam, stood face to face with the Christianity that existed in Arabia at that time, so that there was for a moment the question, in his mind, of Christianity. In any event Christians and Jews together in the Koran occupy a privileged position as "people of the book" and as spiritual descendants of Abraham. Perhaps this common theological root in the promises made to Abraham might bear fruit in a Chapter on anti-Semitism oriented to peace with *all* Semites and then with special emphasis on the relation of the Church and Synagogue and at least an implicit recognition of the long-standing sin of anti-Jewish hatred among Catholics.

In conclusion, turning to a more consoling topic, I can assure Your Eminence that the possibilities of ecumenical contact afforded by the monastic Orders are great and in some ways unique. Here at this Abbey, already for many years, we have been receiving frequent visits from groups of seminarians and ministers of various Protestant denominations, and of course, these visits are now more frequent and more significant. The fruits, to say the least, are most encouraging. I thought Your Eminence would be pleased to know this.]

On September 3, 1964, Abraham Heschel mailed a mimeographed statement about the declaration at the Council on Jewish–Christian relationship. The original statement, he said, had been in almost all respects a monumental declaration. Since the last session of the Council, reports had come to him that the statement had been rewritten in a way that made it ineffective and even offensive to Jews. It was said to state that "the Church expects in unshakable faith and with ardent desire the union of the Jewish people with the Church." Dr. Heschel pointed out that he had repeatedly said to leaders at the Vatican (and he had been received in audience by Paul VI): "I am ready to go to Auschwitz any time, if faced with the alternative of conversion or death." He also pointed out that no such expectations had been expressed by the Church regarding Islam. He hoped that the coming session of the Council would eradicate tensions between Catholics and Jews.

September 9, 1964

Your mimeographed bulletin referring to the revised Jewish Chapter has just reached me.

It is simply incredible. I don't know what to say about it.

This much I will say: my latent ambitions to be a true Jew under my Catholic skin will surely be realized if I continue to go through experiences like this, being spiritually slapped in the face by these blind and complacent people of whom I am nevertheless a "collaborator." If I were not "working with" the Catholic movement for ecumenical understanding, it would not be such a shock to take the three steps backward after each timid step forward.

I must, however, think more of people like Cardinal Bea, who must certainly be crushed by this development.

The Psalms have said all that need to be said about this sort of thing, and you and I both pray them. In them we are one, in their truth, in their silence. *Haec fecisti et tacui*, says the Lord, of such events.

[*Telegram*]

October 28, 1964

Gladly join you interfaith statement and protest against hypocritical distortion of morality in this campaign. It is nauseating.

December 6, 1965

This matter of business gives me opportunity to say "hello" and to hope you are well. Also to say how distressed I was about Dan Berrigan, and how thankful to you for your support of him . . .

As to the business: it is N.N. He wrote me telling me that he wanted to come down and converse with me about his dissertation and intimated that if I would not accede to this demand he would regard it as a personal betrayal, in other words he did not seem disposed to take no for an answer. Yet I have had to answer no because now I have been allowed to retire to a life of greater solitude and my Superiors have rightly required me to discontinue visits, at least of this kind, to give the experiment a good try . . .

The solitary life I find very fruitful and in some ways disconcerting. It has brought me face to face with things I had never had to consider before, and I find that some pretty drastic revaluations have to be made, in my own life. This keeps me busy. I would appreciate you remembering me in your prayer before Him whom we both seek and serve. I do not forget you in my own prayer. God be with you always.

December 12, 1966

Father Abbot spoke to me of your phone call, something about an article on the Bible for *Life*? Or is it for a book in a series to be put out by *Life*? The project is not totally clear. Though I am not too happy with big fancy projects organized by the mass media, I don't say no on principle: there is still room for yes if I can get a clearer idea of what is involved. Can you please tell me what it is? Fr. Abbot said you might drop by here and explain personally. That would be marvelous. But in any case, I need to know what the project is before I can commit myself finally. I sincerely doubt my capacity to write anything worthwhile on the Bible. I am not a pro. But if it is something within my powers I can at least think about attempting it.

I have still to thank you for a couple of books of yours which came in during the past months. I appreciate them very much, though I have not yet finished both of them. I have found much that is very stimulating indeed in *The Insecurity of Freedom* and I have been reserving *Who Is*

Man for a time of freedom and thoughtfulness. I should of course be always free and thoughtful but I get myself reading and thinking in terms of current work a lot of the time, and cannot always fit other things in.

In any case, it is good to hear from you again, however indirectly. I am, as you know, happily holed away in the woods where I belong and find the existence perfectly congenial. I could not ask for anything better, and in snow it is even quieter still . . .

To Aldous Huxley

Aldous Leonard Huxley (1894–1963), born in England and educated at Eton and Oxford, lived in Italy in the 1920s and came to the United States and settled down in California in the 1930s. Perhaps his best-known novel is Brave New World, *the narrative of a nightmarish utopian civilization in the twenty-fifth century. His writings expressed a growing disillusionment with the world. This may account for the fact that in his later years he developed a keen interest in mysticism, mystical phenomena, and Eastern thought. This interest bore fruit in a book called* Ends and Means *(a book that had a profound influence on Merton; see* The Seven Storey Mountain). *It was this same interest that occasioned his article "Drugs That Shape Men's Minds" (The Saturday Evening Post 231, October 18, 1958). It is to this article that Merton responds in his only letter to Huxley that has survived.*

November 27, 1958

Twenty years, or nearly that many, have gone by since a very pleasant exchange of letters took place between us. The other day, in correcting the proofs of a journal I kept then, and which is being published now, I was reminded of the fact. I shall send you the book when it appears. The final entries, in which you are mentioned, will testify to the gratitude and friendship with which I have continued to remember you since then.

Meanwhile, I am happy to open another discussion with you, and I intend to do so in a spirit which will, I hope, lead to something quite constructive. For I assure you that I have no wish whatever to enter into a silly argument, and that I approach you with none of the crudities or prejudices which I am sure annoy you in other clerics. I do not of course claim to be above the ordinary human failings of religious people, but I think I am at least relatively free of partisanship and fanaticism.

Your article in *The Saturday Evening Post* on drugs that help man to achieve an experience of self-transcendence has, you know, created quite a stir. We do not read *The Saturday Evening Post* here in the monastery, but a good lady sent me a copy of your article, together with a copy of a letter she sent to you advising you to read Fr. Garrigou

Lagrange on contemplation. May God preserve you from such a fate.

I am in no position to dispute what you say about the effect of drugs. Though occasionally fortified by aspirin, and exhilarated by coffee, and even sometimes using a barbiturate to get to sleep (alas), I have no experience of the things you speak of. Perhaps I shall make a trial of them one of these days, so that I will know what I am talking about. But since I feel, as you do, that this is a matter which merits discussion and study, I would like to put forward the things that occur to me after my first encounter with the subject. I hope by this to *learn* rather than to teach and I can see that this is your attitude also. Therefore, if you will permit me, I would like to take up the implicit invitation you expressed in the article, and invite you still further, if you are interested, to go into this with us. If you are ever in this neighborhood perhaps you could come here and we could talk at leisure. Our mutual friends, Victor Hammer and his wife at Lexington, would gladly bring you over.

After this preamble, here are the questions I would like to raise:

1. Are you not endangering the whole concept of genuine mystical experience in saying that it is something that can be "produced" by a drug? I know, you qualify the statement, you say that a drug can induce a state in which mystical experience can be occasioned: a drug can remove obstacles in our ordinary everyday state of mind, and make a kind of latent mysticism come to the surface. But I wonder if this accords with the real nature of mystical experience?

I think this point must be studied carefully, and I suggest the following:

2. Ought we not to distinguish between an experience which is essentially *aesthetic and natural* from an experience which is *mystical and supernatural*. I would call aesthetic and natural an experience which would be an intuitive "tasting" of the inner spirituality of our own being— or an intuition of being as such, arrived at through an intuitive awareness of our own inmost reality. This would be an experience of "oneness" within oneself and with all beings, a flash of awareness of the transcendent Reality that is within all that is real. This sort of thing "happens" to one in all sorts of ways and I see no reason why it should not be occasioned by the use of a drug. This intuition is very like the aesthetic intuition that precedes the creation of a work of art. It is like the intuition of a philosopher who rises above his concepts and their synthesis to see everything in one glance, in all its length, height, breadth and depth. It is like the intuition of a person who has participated deeply in a liturgical act. (I think you take too cavalier an attitude toward liturgy, although I confess that I am irked by liturgical enthusiasts when they want to regiment others into their way of thinking.)

By the way, though I call this experience "natural," that does not preclude its being produced by the action of God's grace (a term that must be used with care). But I mean that it is not in its mode or in its content beyond the capacities of human nature itself. Please forgive me for glibly using this distinction between natural and supernatural as if I were quite sure where the dividing line came. Of course I am not.

What would I call a *supernatural and mystical* experience, then? I speak very hesitantly, and do not claim to be an authority. What I say may be very misleading. It may be the product of subjective and sentimental illusion or it may be the product of a rationalization superimposed on the experience described above. Anyway, here goes.

It seems to me that a fully mystical experience has in its very essence some note of a direct spiritual *contact of two liberties*, a kind of a flash or spark which ignites an intuition of all that has been said above, *plus* something much more which I can only describe as "personal," in which God is known not as an "object" or as "Him up there" or "Him in everything" nor as "the All" but as—the biblical expression—I AM, or simply AM. But what I mean is that this is not the kind of intuition that smacks of anything procurable because it is a presence of a Person and *depends on the liberty of that Person*. And lacking the element of a free gift, a free act of love on the part of Him Who comes, the experience would lose its specifically mystical quality.

3. But now, from the moment that such an experience can be conceived of as *dependent on* and *inevitably following from* the casual use of a material instrument, it loses the quality of spontaneity and freedom and transcendence which makes it truly mystical.

This then is my main question. It seems to me that for this reason, expressed lamely perhaps and without full understanding, real mystical experience would be more or less incompatible with the *consistent* use of a drug.

Here are some further thoughts: Supposing a person with a genuine vocation to mystical union. And supposing that person starts to use a drug. And supposing further that I am correct in the above estimate of what real mystical experience consists in: then the one using the drug can produce what I have called a "natural and aesthetic" experience. But at the same time his higher "conscience" (here I mean not merely a moral censor but his inmost spirit in its function of "judge" between what is real and what isn't) will inevitably reproach him for self-delusion. He will enjoy the experience for a moment, but it will be followed, not by the inner permanent strengthening of a real spiritual experience, but by lassitude, discouragement, confusion, and *an increased need for the drug*. This will produce a vicious circle of repeated use of the drug, renewed lassitude and guilt, greater need for the drug, and final complete addiction with the complete ruin of a mystical vocation, if not worse.

What I say here is based on suppositions, of course. I do not attempt to impose the analysis on you, but I would be very interested in your judgment of what I have said and your opinion in the matter.

I will not weary you by prolonging this letter, but will close here in the hope that we can go further into the matter later on.

May I add that I am interested in yoga and above all in Zen, which I find to be the finest example of a technique leading to the highest *natural* perfection of man's contemplative liberty. You may argue that the use of a koan to dispose one for satori is not different from the use of a drug. I would like to submit that there is all the difference in the world, and perhaps we can speak more of this later. My dear Mr. Huxley, it is a joy to write to you of these things. I hope you can reply. God bless you.

To Lyndon Baines Johnson

Lyndon Baines Johnson (1908–73) was the thirty-sixth President of the United States.

May 31, 1964

As a priest and monk of the Catholic Church I would like to add my voice to the voices of all those who have pleaded for a peaceful settlement in Vietnam. A neutralized and united Vietnam protected by secure guarantees would certainly do more for the interests of freedom and of the people of Southeast Asia, as well as for our own interests, than a useless and stupid war. Quite apart from humanitarian and ethical considerations which, to me, are primary, it would seem that experience and realistic awareness of the situation ought to warn us that a prolonged war in Asia is not something that is going to benefit a non-Asian power, still less the interests of democracy. On the contrary, the only long-run effect will be a strengthening of communism—or else a desperate resort to nuclear weapons, in a possible extremity, which would be disastrous for everyone.

I therefore respectfully recommend a prudent and rational course, along the lines (which are universally acceptable, I believe) laid down in *Pacem in Terris.*

With cordial good wishes and the assurance of my prayers for the success of your policies in the area of civil rights and the war on poverty, I sign myself as a supporter of your campaign in this election year.

To William Johnston

William Johnston, an Irish Jesuit priest, has lived in Japan since 1951. He received a doctorate in Mystical Theology in 1968 from Sophia University in Tokyo and has served on their faculty as professor of literature and religion. He is the author of numerous articles and works on mysticism and on East–West religious dialogue, and his books include The Mysticism of the Cloud of Unknowing *(1967),* The Still Point *(1970),* Christian Zen *(1971),* Silent Music *(1974),* The Inner Eye of Love *(1978). It was his first book that occasioned his contact with Thomas Merton, when he wrote asking Merton to do a preface to it. Fr. Johnston visited Merton at Gethsemani in the summer of 1965 and Merton completed the preface for* The Mysticism of the Cloud of Unknowing *by Christmas 1966. In 1968 Fr. Johnston and the faculty of Sophia University were preparing for Merton's visit there, when they learned of his sudden and tragic death in Bangkok.*

May 29, 1964

Thanks for your letter of the 13th. Your project on *The Cloud* and Zen sounds interesting, and so, though I have made all kinds of resolutions to refuse this kind of thing, I want to make an exception and at least glance at your ms. The rest is up to the Holy Ghost: and time. I will send whatever comment is possible in the circumstances, long or short, and you will have to take your chance on it being either intelligent or idiotic.

At present I am reading Fr. Enomiye Lasalle's book in German with very great interest. Naturally I enjoyed Fr. Dumoulin's book as you and he know. I wrote a rather longer and more detailed article published in a more or less unknown new magazine, and I will send it along. I felt that Fr. Dumoulin had been a little unreceptive to Hui Neng, but I think that goes naturally with his instinctive preference for Soto Zen (*The Cloud*, too, is more like Soto).

It seems I am going to be writing reports on Buddhist literature for the magazine of our Order, so it is good to be in contact with you Fathers at Sophia. Though Zen seems to me to be something that will appeal to an elite only, and a very small one, yet it has great importance because it is so closely related to such movements as phenomenology and existentialism, besides responding to certain inarticulate spiritual needs of man today. It is important that we know about it, and also I add that I think a little Zen discipline is a very healthy thing. However, there will also be a lot of irresponsible talk floating around, and this too must be taken into account. But it will pass. Let us hope the true substance remains, even though from the Zen point of view there isn't any substance anyway.

January 25, 1965

A long time has elapsed since I received your ms. on *The Cloud*. I should have sent you some comments on it before this. But I need not give you much of an explanation, as you can understand how busy I am and how much correspondence I attempt to deal with.

I enjoyed the book very much. It is excellent. A good theological commentary on *The Cloud* is something very welcome indeed. You provide one which does not do violence to the essential simplicity and directness of the book. In other words, you do not bury the plain intuition of the contemplative author under conceptual and verbal exegesis. Perhaps there are places where you do not develop the resemblances with Zen. For instance on p. 166 that thing "which is hid betwixt" two opposites would give a very suggestive point of entry into the Zen experience and point up the similarity, on a certain level, between it and the experience of *The Cloud*. It is quite true that in Zen there is little or nothing said about love (but then there are also the Nembutsu people and perhaps they deserve mention—I forget what that is called—is it Shinn Buddhism?). Still, apart from the completely a-personal theodicy, if you can call it that, I wonder if there is not all the same some love buried deep in Zen. Perhaps I am only projecting my own Christian experience into the Zen framework. It is sadly true that I have no real knowledge of Zen as it actually is in Japan.

Fr. Dumoulin was very kind to try to arrange a trip to Japan for me. I am sorry it did not work out. It is unfortunate that our Order is not yet ready to understand this kind of thing, which of course would certainly fit into the pattern of a deeply Christian and ecumenical contemplation . . .

November 10, 1965

I don't know if *Monumenta Nipponica* came from you or Fr. Dumoulin. Thanks very much indeed for it and for the charming picture. I am sending you my book on Chuang Tzu. I have not touched the preface yet. I wish not to do so for a while as I am finishing other work and also my publisher is vexed with me for writing too many prefaces . . .

January 10, 1966

I was surprised and delighted to get the Shinzinger book on Nishida the other day, and am already well into it. It is really excellent. I am more convinced than ever that Nishida makes an excellent bridge builder between East and West. Thank you so much for taking so much trouble, and I am most grateful to Prof. Shinzinger. Is there something I can send him? Did you get my Chuang Tzu book? I might send him a copy of that. I hope you got one. And I hope you were not offended by a facetious remark I made about such and such a thing being "jesuitical" in the introduction. I did not of course mean it seriously at all, I was just fooling, and using the popular idea ironically.

. . . It was good to have the *Monumenta Nipponica*, and I am glad you are now concerned officially with its destinies. Do keep me in mind if anything on Zen comes along. I am finding the hermit life very profitable indeed. The mere fact of silence and solitude is most beneficial, added to the other factor of time. It gets better as it goes on and one begins to get rid of some of the outer coverings.

I have had some correspondence with university people in this country who have been attending sessions with Yasutani. He seems to be having quite an influence. The interest of these people in Zen is partly scientific, psychological, etc., though one, a Catholic woman, has apparently quite got into it and is doing well. She has had kensho, or at least I gather Yasutani has admitted this.

I never heard from Fr. Dumoulin but I gather in roundabout ways that he must have written and my Abbot must have said no. I would certainly have liked to see him. Please give him my best regards. I think of you all and keep you in my prayers. When your publisher has galleys of your book, be sure he sends me a set and then I will write the preface.

December 1, 1966

Just a word to say that Desclee have sent the proofs of your book and I am well into them. I think the new material in the beginning is excellent. I will get down to the preface in a day or two and hope to have it in your publishers' hands soon. Thanks for the letters and cards I have received from you in the past few months. With a back operation in the spring I got behind with everything and never caught up with letters. I will get a copy of the preface to you also . . .

December 20, 1966

Thanks for your fine article on Zen and Christian mysticism. If you will give me the exact references (in *Monumenta*?). I wish to do a brief summary for the magazine of our Order. I'd like to see that Hisamatsu article on "Oriental Nothingness," if there's some way of borrowing it.

July 5, 1967

Thanks for your good letter of June 14. Interested to hear about the Zen retreat. Honestly I do not think it matters a bit whether one can sit cross-legged or not. But perhaps in the peculiar situation where Fr. Lasalle wants (himself and you, too, implicitly) to be as much as possible the real article in the eyes of the Japanese, it may have accidental import. Much more deep and difficult is the question of satori.

Though I am far from the scene and do not have any experience of the real practical problems involved, I will give an opinion that may have some general bearing on the question: I hope it may. I suppose first of all that the Japanese Zen people have their own rather schematic idea of what it means to "believe in God." Obviously, if it implies essentially a sort of subject-object relationship, then it means a "dualism" which categorically excludes satori. They probably have never investigated the witness of mystics like Eckhart for whom it is possible to be "so poor" that one does not even "have a God." This does not mean "Christian atheism" or "God-is-dead theology." It is simply a fact of a certain area of apophatic experience. Also the Japanese Zen people probably think of

Christian mysticism in terms of "bridal mysticism," the gift of mystical rings, embraces, ecstasies and all that. Well, OK, no satori along those lines.

On the other hand, to look at it more subtly: I wonder if someone in Fr. Lasalle's position, wanting as a Christian to attain satori, does not inevitably get into a psychological position which makes satori difficult if not impossible. Because for there to be a real satori the idea of "a Christian who can attain satori" has to go out the window as utterly irrelevant. Hence, perhaps that is what the Zen people intuitively feel about your group as such.

Personally I do not think satori is impossible for a Christian any more than it is for a Buddhist. In either case, one goes in a certain sense beyond all categories, religious or otherwise. But perhaps our very attitude toward Christianity makes this harder for us. I do think it is probably best to simply take what Zen can offer us in the way of inner purification and freedom from systems and concepts, and not worry too much about precisely where we get. But I am all for Fr. Lasalle getting there if that is what he should do. I'm rooting for him! I'd be very interested to hear more about all this. By the way: do you know if the latest books of Fr. Lasalle and Fr. Dumoulin respectively (which I have received in German) will soon be in French or English? I am to review them, but my German is real slow.

To Ethel Kennedy

Ethel Skakel married Robert F. Kennedy on June 17, 1950. Senator Kennedy was murdered in Los Angeles on June 5, 1968, seven years after this letter was written. The Skakel family were longtime benefactors of the Trappists.

September 4, 1961

It was a very pleasant surprise to get your kind note and I am indeed grateful for it. I hope you will not take it amiss that I reply so soon with tiresome talk about a subject that is not personal at all but urgent and concerning everyone.

It seems to me that since I have the privilege of being able to communicate with you, who are so close to the President, and since he is certainly interested in what people think about important issues, I have a kind of obligation to put down in black and white my very strong objection to the resumption of testing nuclear weapons.

Without knowing anything about the immediate motives of political expediency, I base this objection on moral and humanitarian grounds. These grounds are, it seems to me, so important that there can be no longer any moral justification for all-out nuclear war. Consequently, no matter how good the motives for promoting nuclear armament may look on a certain superficial level, these motives mask a horrible, indeed diabolical, danger to mankind. I am not a man who has investments in anything. I have no cares about money and by the grace of God I live liberated from a lot of concerns which I have come to think of as entirely futile, though that is no reason why others should be blamed for engaging in them. But the point is this: there is no getting around the fact that the making and testing of nuclear weapons is profitable and indeed in some sense vital to many people in this country. Hence these people, however sincere may be their motives, tend to be prejudiced in favor of everything that endangers the peace of the world. They may not want war but they live by defense industries and they want weapons. And to want weapons as badly as they do is, I am afraid, tantamount to wanting war. That is how wars are made.

I therefore hope and trust that every precaution will be taken to prolong the ban on nuclear testing as long as possible. I believe we can only gain by a policy of this kind. If we can lead the world toward peace even with risk and sacrifice for ourselves, we will regain the prestige we have begun to lose. I think the other course would be disastrous and will cause us to be hated.

Naturally it is not for me to say how you are to evaluate these ideas of mine, and I leave it entirely to you to decide whether you want to bother the President with them. Or whether there would be any point at all in doing so. But I would not be faithful to the love I hope I have in my heart for all the peoples of the world, if I did not put this down in black and white and send it to you. Forgive me, and I know you will understand.

Sometime soon I will make amends for this by writing a more cheerful and personal letter. Dan [Walsh] talks so much of you and Bobby. It is wonderful, of course, to have him here . . .

God bless you all, and all your family, and the President . . .

[*Cold War Letter 10*]

December 1961

I liked very much the President's speech at Seattle which encouraged me a bit as I had just written something along those same lines. The interview granted to *Izvestia* was great also. We need more and more of that. Every form of healthy human contact with Russia, and above all China, is to be encouraged. We have got to see each other as people and not as demons . . .

It seems to me that the great problem we face is not Russia but war itself. War is the main enemy and we are not going to fully make sense unless we see that. Unless we fight war, both in ourselves and in the Russians, and wherever else it may be, we are purely and simply going to be wrecked by the forces that are in us. The great illusion is to assume that we are perfectly innocent, peace-loving and right while the communists are devils incarnate. I admit they are no angels and they have been guilty of some frightful crimes against humanity. They are without doubt a terrible menace, and a permanent one, to the safety and sanity of the human race. I admit also that we must not go to the extreme of condemning ourselves without reason. We have made mistakes and will make more of them, but I hope we can learn to be a bit more realistic about all that, as long as we avoid the biggest mistake of all: plunging the world into nuclear war by any deliberate decision of our own. I think also it is tremendously important for us to work out a collaborative control scheme with the U.S.S.R. to check on various possible accidents that might trigger a nuclear war.

Why is war such a problem to us? I do not pretend to be able to give a reason for everything under the sun, but if I am to be consistent with my own experience and my religious beliefs, as well as with the crying evidence that is all around us, one main reason is our moral decline. As a nation we have begun to float off into a moral void and all the sermons of all the priests in the country (if they preach at all) are not going to help much . . .

[The ones I am concerned about are] the "good" people, the right-thinking people, who stick to principle all right except where it conflicts with the chance to make a fast buck. It seems to me that there are dangerous ambiguities about our democracy in its actual present condition. I wonder to what extent our ideals are now a front for organized selfishness and systematic irresponsibility. The shelter business certainly brought out the fact that some Americans are not too far from the law of the jungle. If our affluent society ever breaks down and the façade is taken away, what are we going to have left? Suppose we *do* have a war, and fifty million people are left to tell the tale: What kind of people are they going to be? What kind of life will they live? By what standards? We cannot go on living every man for himself. The most actual danger of all is that we may someday float without realizing it into a nice tight fascist society in which all the resentments and all the guilt in all the messed-up teenagers (and older ones) will be channeled in a destructive groove.

This may sound pretty awful. You know of course that I am not trying to sit back and judge the whole country. These things are in every human being, and they have always been, and will be. But I feel strongly that in the condition in which we now live there is no adequate control for these unpleasant and dangerous forces, and that people are much too ready to give up trying to control them rationally . . .

The President can certainly do more than any one man to counteract this by word and example, by doing everything that can help salvage the life of reason, by maintaining respect for intelligence and humanist principles without which freedom is only a word . . .

There are plenty of wise and sane people in the country, and they are able to articulate. They can do a tremendous amount. I think, for example, of the group at Santa Barbara, the Center for the Study of Democratic Institutions. They have done a lot of serious and enlightened work. They can do much more.

There are people around like Senator Fulbright, who, it seems to me, has the right kind of ideas and works courageously in the right direction. But you can't do that without being regarded as a Red. The people who fail to see the value of our best liberal traditions, and who attack every moderate as a Fifth Columnist, are the ones who are really undermining the country and preparing it for ruin, if anyone is.

Anyway, these are not easy times to live in, and there are no easy answers. I think that the fact that the President works overtime at trying to get people to face the situation as it really is may be the greatest thing he is doing. Certainly our basic need is for truth, and not for "images" and slogans that "engineer consent." We are living in a dream world. We do not know ourselves or our adversaries. We are myths to ourselves and they are myths to us. And we are secretly persuaded that we can shoot it out like the sheriffs on TV. This is not reality and the President can do a tremendous amount to get people to see the facts, more than any single person . . .

I personally wish the Church in America and everywhere was more articulate and definite about nuclear war. Statements of Pius XII have left us some terribly clear principles about this. We cannot go on indefinitely relying on the kind of provisional framework of a balance of terror. If as Christians we were more certain of our duty, it might put us in a very tight spot politically but it would also merit for us special graces from God, and these we need badly.

May 14, 1963

Harper & Bros., the publishers, are going to send you at my request the autobiography of an interesting friend of mine, Fr. Bruno James. I think you will really enjoy it. I do not have to describe him, the book will. He is a most unusual, offbeat English priest who works like mad in the slums of Naples, running a sort of home-made university which is quite a thing.

He is going to be in this country in April, and if you are interested in the kind of person he is, you might enjoy meeting him. Because you could also help him quite a bit, I think. He comes to the country once in a while to try to get some support for his project. The people at Harper's are very much behind him. I cannot, however, claim that the whole American hierarchy is walking behind him with banners and bass drums.

(They are not against him, they don't know him.) Still, he is an amazing person.

I wrote a book on peace which the Superiors decided I ought to bury about ten feet deep behind the monastery someplace, but I still don't think it is that bad. I mimeographed it and am sending you a copy, just for the files or, who knows, maybe the President might have five minutes to spare looking at it. If you think he would, I will even send him a copy, but I know how that is. The Cuba business was a close call, but in the circumstances I think JFK handled it very well. I say in the circumstances, because only a short-term look at it makes one very happy. It was a crisis and something had to be done and there was only a choice of various evils. He chose the best evil, and it worked. The whole thing continues to be nasty. I am right behind Bobby in the Mississippi thing. This race question is one of the meanest and worst messes we have got, and the attitude of the South is just one of the best things we ever gave to communism, for the advantage of the world revolution. I hope the people of the U.S. can someday stop handing the Russians just what they want on a silver platter. I certainly don't envy any of the Kennedys in Washington, thank God you have high spirits and plenty of bounce . . . Dan got me to sign a *Reader* for you, which I did with great pleasure. I hope you enjoy it.

November 23, 1963

I have just come from offering Mass for the repose of the President's soul, and I want you to know how shocked we all are here by the tragic news that reached us yesterday afternoon. We are all offering many prayers for him and for all the family. A Solemn High Mass will be sung today, and I will offer my Masses for him tomorrow and Monday also.

Please offer my very special message of sympathy to Jackie. I feel for her most deeply. In a way she is perhaps the one who has had most to suffer from this cruel and senseless thing. I keep her most especially in my prayers along with all of you.

He was certainly one of the best and most promising Presidents we have had for a long time. He would have been a great support to the nation in years to come, and it is most tragic to think that his work was abruptly ended in the full vigor of his manhood, in his best years. This is a terrible loss for the whole country, and I am sure it is something that everyone finds it very hard to accept or understand.

It is easy enough to say that this is the will of God. The question arises, precisely what is the will of God in this mysterious situation. It would be tautology to say that it was the will of God just because it happened. But to me the whole thing is so uncanny and so strange that I think we must see it as a warning once again to the whole country: it is in some sense a reminder that our moral condition is very hazardous, when the rights of a whole race are flagrantly violated, when those who attempt to do right and uphold justice are menaced and even killed. It means we must certainly pray and work hard for this country, to try and bring it through the critical times that do not seem to become any less tense as time goes on. I suppose we must resign ourselves to the task of living under special difficulties. May we be generous in doing so . . .

With my deep sympathy and very best wishes to you, and Bobby and all of you. Dan is not here now but I will see him when he gets back after the weekend. I am sure he must have written to you . . .

February 26, 1965

Dan Walsh has no spirit of obedience whatever, especially when it comes to giving away books signed for him personally, but since he gave it to you I am glad. It has been getting an ambiguous press, but that is to be expected. And talking about the press, one of the few encouraging things I see in it, when I see it, which is rare, is an occasional picture of you and Bobby and six or seven dozen direct descendants. When this gets into the news I feel I can react as if the news were good. You have the distinction of appearing alive in a world of partial zombies. I congratulate you both on the latest addition to the family and may you all burst with happiness all the time.

Now to the question of the works of "art?" Here is the scoop on that. I have forty-three extremely way-out and abstract drawings going around the country causing senators to believe that there is yet another Red plot afoot to addle the American mind. They are at the moment, I hope, at Marquette in Milwaukee and from there they go to St. Louis, and then in Atlanta in June. Now they are to be at St. Louis in April and Atlanta in June. There is a hole between April and June, and I have always been told that this is called May. So I am looking for a place to subvert the nation with these drawings in the month of May. At first thought, what better place than Washington. Or does that make no sense at all? So far, they have been exhibited at colleges. But they don't have to be exhibited only in educational institutions. However, as you can now see, I am trying to enlist you in this: do you think maybe Trinity would want them? (Let's just forget Catholic U.) Or do you know of some group, club, clique, cell or cultural enclave that would dare to associate its name with these drawings? If you do and if you could get on the phone to them, then they could contact me and all the rest would be simple (in theory). (I know what it is in practice.)

What I am getting at is this: With the drawings in Washington you can go and see them and thus you can pick one, and then you will have the non-distinction of owning "a Merton." And if you have a good attic, you will not have too much trouble storing it.

. . . I enclose some notes on the drawings, you will see what I mean.

And I will try to induce someone around here to Xerox an article about them if I can find the article, which has a picture with it.

I know you are very busy, but perhaps this could easily be fixed with a phone call and hence I do not fear getting you involved in a lot of trouble. But I am grateful in advance for anything you can do to help out. If the pictures are sold, the money goes to a scholarship for a Negro girl in Louisville.

June 22, 1968

After sending my telegram I also planned to write you at least a brief letter. But I know you must have been simply swamped with mail and telegrams, so I have hesitated. However, I do want to send you the enclosed rather touching letter from a total stranger in Brazil. If you don't read Portuguese it would be worth having someone translate it for you.

Really it is hard to say anything that is capable of measuring the shock and sorrow of Bobby's tragic immolation. Nowadays we tend to expect almost anything. But there was something particularly awful and traumatic about this, just because Bobby represented a very real hope for the whole country and for the world. He was the only one with a real chance who might also have done something very definite for peace. And now it looks as if we will be faced with a completely illusory choice at the polls—so much so that I wonder if I'll vote at all. At least for the Presidency.

It has been a shock for everyone and I think you must have felt that the dimensions of your personal sorrow were multiplied in all directions. But that does not make it any easier to have to go through all that you and the family have suffered. I am glad Dom James was able to represent our community at the funeral. He brought me messages from you and Rose Kennedy. I do hope that things are getting settled down and that God is bringing peace in the middle of all the wretched agony of this.

Naturally I have said Masses for Bobby and I remember all of you at the altar. More and more we are forced to realize that God is our only real hope in the stark mystery of what we are all up against. Certainly we know that all will be well, but the ways in which He makes it well are apt to be difficult for us. Courage and peace be with you. My love to all the family, and God bless you . . .

To Jacqueline Kennedy

Jacqueline Lee Bouvier married John F. Kennedy in 1953. She was at his side in Dallas when, as thirty-fifth President of the United States, he was assassinated on November 22, 1963.

November 27, 1963

Thinking that one more letter might be a burden to you, I refrained from writing, though instinct and charity prompted me to do so. By now you must surely have heard everything. However, Dan Walsh has urged me very strongly to write and I am doing so at his suggestion.

The awful events of the past week have certainly been a kind of spiritual crisis for the whole nation, and a tragic, momentous, utterly mysterious expression of something hidden in the whole world, that had to express itself as it has done, in evil and in good. I think it is beginning to be clear that God allowed this that He might bring great good out of it. You know what help He has given you, and given us all. You can surely hope that from this tragic and cruel explosion of irrationality and violence, clarity and reason can emerge.

There can be no doubt now that the greatness of President Kennedy has been made dazzlingly clear to everyone, and that the scope and integrity of his work have established themselves beyond all question. It is now that people will perhaps be able to understand the necessity of the reforms he proposed and lend their willing cooperation which, if he still lived, they might have continued to refuse.

There can be no doubt too that your contribution to this has been enormous. Merely by being there, and by being you, you have impressed upon the entire world the meaning and validity of all those things President Kennedy stood for. I would like therefore to thank you simply for existing and for being you, and say how much your bravery has meant to us all here, as a manifestation of Christian strength, not the strength of natural heroism but the strength that comes from accepting the love of God in its most inscrutable form. Such praise as has been given you, you must accept humbly, because it is not for you alone. It is for Him who lives in you. It is for your husband, who obeyed God and served his country most loyally. And it is for your children. May they grow in Christ.

I know how sick you must feel of noise, and confusion, and all the rest. Perhaps, too, when this passes, you will be left slack and empty, and depressed. That too is part of the bitter gift that has been given you, and God will grant you to see the meaning of it, I am sure. Our faith demands of us that we find meaning in meaninglessness these days. It is not a source of unending comfort all the time. Those who claim that it is only tempt us against it.

If there is ever anything at all I can do for you, please be sure to let me know. Certainly I do not need to tell you that you have my prayers and have had them all along . . .

To Coretta Scott King

Coretta Scott (b. 1927) and Martin Luther King, Jr. (b. 1929), met in Boston in 1951. Martin came from Atlanta and was doing graduate studies at Boston University after having received his B.D. degree at Crozer Theological Seminary (Chester, Pennsylvania). Coretta, whose home was in Marion, Alabama, was a voice student at the New England Conservatory of Music, after graduating from Antioch College (Yellow Springs, Ohio). They were married in 1953. Coretta shared Martin's passion for racial justice and his commitment to non-violence. Coretta and their four children were at their home in Atlanta when the fateful news came of his assassination on April 4, 1968, in Memphis.

April 5, 1968

Some events are too big and terrible to talk about. I think we all anticipated this one: I am sure he did. Somehow when John Yungblut spoke of Martin coming here for a brief retreat before the big march, I had the awful feeling that it might be a preparation for something like this. It was to be Memphis instead of Washington—or somewhere else on the way.

Let me only say how deeply I share your personal grief as well as the shock which pervades the whole nation. He has done the greatest thing anyone can do. In imitation of his Master he has laid down his life for his friends and enemies. He knew the nation was under judgment and he tried everything to stay the hand of God and man. He will go down in history as one of our greatest citizens.

My prayers are with you and with him. May he find the rest and reward which God has promised to all who trust in His mercy. This morning my Eucharistic offering will be for him and for you.

To Ripu Daman Lama

Ripu Daman Lama was an Indian student who came to Cracow, Poland, to work for a Doctor of Science degree in mining engineering at the Mining Academy in that city. During his stay he came in contact with the Catholic Intellectual Club and through the influence of some of its members became interested in Christian philosophy. In a letter written on June 13, 1964, he says that Merton's name was frequently on the lips of the students with whom he discussed problems of philosophy and especially the problem of the growing atheism in the world.

August 16, 1964

Your letter of June 13th took some time to reach me, and then I have had to wait a little before having a chance to answer it. I will be very glad to send you some books that may be of interest to you and I beg you to keep them as my gift. The book *Elected Silence* was published in this country under another title [*The Seven Storey Mountain*]. I am sending you the American edition. Also a book, *New Seeds of Contemplation*, which I think generally interests Asian readers, and finally an anthology which has selections from various sources of mine. I will hope that these books reach you safely. If they do not, please let me know and I will try again somehow. One or two of my books have been translated into Polish, I believe, but I am not sure where, or which ones.

The phenomenon of atheism today is quite ambiguous. In one sense, it remains the naïve atheism of nineteenth-century scientism. The scientists of today have themselves traveled far beyond this point and it must be realized that nineteenth-century materialism created a scientific myth which endeavored to replace the religious myth. In effect, the communist countries are dealing in pseudo-scientific mythology today, when it comes to religion and to the basic philosophic truths. At the same time they take the true and deep concept of God and regard it in a light in which it is false and debased. They think that religious people believe in a God who is simply "a being" among other beings, part of a series of beings, an "object" which can be discovered and demonstrated. This of course is a false notion of God, the Absolute, the source and origin of all Being, beyond all beings and transcending them all and hence not to be sought as one among them. It is not hard to disprove that God "exists" as a being among beings, and this is no menace to religion. On the contrary. However, religious people make the mistake of replying to this argument as if it had some relevance, instead of trying to clarify the real meaning of God. In any case, the level on which atheist argumentation is carried out has not the remotest relation to true religion or metaphysics.

I should be interested to hear further of your experiences and thoughts. I am personally interested in Hinduism and Buddhism, and believe that it is very important for all the great religious philosophies to meet on a common ground to clarify the basic truths which they all hold together. This could be of great service to a world in confusion. Let us also hope and work together for peace and understanding among all peoples. May God bless your search and your love of truth.

November 13, 1964

Your letter of October 30th has reached me and it is very interesting. I think you are confronting rightly some of the big religious problems of the Western world. It is quite true that Christianity has been slow to abandon philosophical structures which do not have meaning for the man of today. It is even more true that among many Christians there is a lack of a *living* presence and witness to God, but rather an abundance of words and formulas, together with rites that many no longer understand. It is the old problem of institutional religion and of traditions that remain fixed in the past.

On the other hand, there is also a scientific dogmatism which belongs more to the nineteenth century than to the twentieth. Where the "dogma" of atheism has replaced the dogmas of official religion, there is I think nothing new and nothing that really appeals to modern youth either, though they may rest in a kind of vague skepticism. It seems that the most advanced scientific approaches to reality (for instance in physics) seem to exclude the rigid and dogmatic approach to the world and here eventually there may be a meeting with the highest spiritual notions. This remains perhaps for the future. But in the meantime, the struggle to establish a fixed concept of the divine essence that will state clearly "what he is" seems to me to be misleading. It is true that such statements can be made in their place, but they do not really solve anything because our experience of God tells us *that* he is but not *what* he is. We tend to experience him as one whom we do not know. I think you will find this in the Indian traditions also.

However, the great venture of our time is that which will help us make this encounter with God not only in the most advanced scientific thought but also in *man* and in our concern for our fellow man, for peace, for justice, and for truth. I wish you all success in your search.

To Martin Lings

Martin Lings, born in Lancaster, England, in 1909, was educated at Oxford (Magdalen) and at the School of Oriental and African Studies of the University of London. I was able in the fall of 1983 to contact him at his home in Kent, where he lives since his retirement. During the time he corresponded with Merton, he was Keeper of Oriental Printed Books and Manuscripts at the British Museum. His books include A Sufi Saint of the Twentieth Century: Shaikh Ahmad Al-'Alawi *(originally entitled* A Moslem Saint of the Twentieth Century), *and* What Is Sufism? *At the suggestion of Marco Pallis, Martin Lings wrote to Merton asking him if he would review Lings's recent book,* Ancient Beliefs and Modern Superstitions.

April 24, 1965

Your new book reached me this morning, and I must say it looks extremely interesting. I am not perfectly sure the review of our Order will want me to review it, this will depend on how germane it is to monasticism. But I think they probably will. On the other hand I have not yet done my review of [Frithjof] Schuon's book on Islam. I have a small pile of books on Sufism etc. building up and will probably do them all at once later on.

I must admit that in the review of our Order, still very conservative in a stuffy sense, and slowly evolving to a more open position, it is still quite difficult to know how to handle a review of a book like Schuon's, with which one is in the greatest sympathy. Yet I would still be expected by the censorious to point out small matters that would perhaps call for "criticism" from a strictly Catholic point of view, and to my mind this is not at all worth doing. Quite the contrary. Thus I, who am in any case no professional in dogmatic theology, find myself hesitant. I think that in a little while this will have cleared up sufficiently for me to go ahead without scruple. But not yet.

On the other hand I was able to give what I felt was a very enthusiastic review to your admirable book on Ahmad Al-'Alawi [*A Moslem Saint of the Twentieth Century*, 1961]. I am glad of this opportunity to express my thanks. The book was an inspiration to me and I often think of this great man with veneration. He was so perfectly right in his spirituality. Certainly a great saint and a man full of the Holy Spirit. May God be praised for having given us one such, in a time when we need many saints. I hope that in a few days I will have some offprints and will send you a couple.

Meanwhile I am very happy to be in contact with you, as I am with Marco Pallis, whose books have also been a great inspiration to me. I am most indebted to him for sending good books my way, and am in the middle of his translation of [René] Guénon's *Crisis*, which is first-rate. Contact with your "school of thought," shall I say, is of great help to me in rectifying my own perspectives in this time when among Catholics one is faced with a choice between an absurdly rigid and baroque conservatism and a rather irresponsible and fantastic progressivism à la Teilhard. The choice is of course not so restricted, and I am glad of influences that help me to cling, as my heart tells me to, to a sane and living traditionalism in full contact with the living contemplative experience of the past—and with the presence of the Spirit here and now.

June 20, 1965

Thanks for your kind letter. I should be interested to see your review of the Nasr book. I am very grateful for your comments on mine. Actually I need badly such advice as yours. I am really quite lost in the field of Islamic studies, since obviously I have only the most superficial acquaintance with the field, and it is really rather presumptuous of me to undertake to review books in it for the magazine of the Order . . .

To Martin E. Marty

Well-known author in the field of religious literature and longtime associate editor of Christian Century, *Martin E. Marty was born in 1928 in West Point, Nebraska. He was educated for the Lutheran ministry, studying at Concordia Seminary, Chicago Lutheran Theological Seminary, and the University of Chicago. His brief*

but important letter-dialogue with Merton came at the end of the "hot summer"
of 1967, occasioned by a book review that Marty had written much earlier of
Merton's Seeds of Destruction *in the New York* Herald Tribune. *The review was*
strongly critical, taking issue with one long section called "Letters to a White
Liberal," in which Merton questioned the sincerity of the white liberal's com-
mitment to reforms that would actually benefit black people. When the real crisis
came, Merton maintained, the self-interest of the white man would take over.
Marty pictured Merton safe behind his monastery walls, attempting to pose as a
white James Baldwin.

Two and a half years later, in the August 30, 1967, issue of The National
Catholic Reporter, *Marty wrote an open letter to Merton in which he apologized*
for having put down Seeds of Destruction. *With most of the summer of 1967*
past, he said, we can now "see that you were correct." He wrote: "Recently I
have had occasion to reread the book. What bothers me now is the degree of
accuracy in your predictions and prophecies in general. At the time you seemed
to be trying to be a white James Baldwin. Now it seems to me that you were
'telling it as it is' and maybe 'as it will be.'" Signing his letter "your regained
admirer and friend," Marty suggests that Merton might try his hand at what
could be called Seeds of Hope.

September 6, 1967

I long ago learned to live with the idea that I was half crazy. Lately,
seeing the reaction of some people to my more recent books, I have
become resigned to the possibility that I am completely crazy. Your open
letter awakens in me the hope that I am only half crazy after all. Restored
to where I thought I was, I am reassured. Thank you for your generosity . . .

This is not the reply you suggested in your closing lines, only a
spontaneous reaction of friendship and common concern: not a scenario,
but perhaps a few hopeful questions, based on a warm agreement with
your own tentative approach—I like the whole picture of tolerance, "play"
not being too deadly serious, keeping creative possibilities open even
when events are most destructive. I agree with you, it does no good to
be too raffishly apocalyptic at this point. It only adds to the violence where
there is already more than enough. I still think, though, that what I said
four years ago needed to be said, and said perhaps in that provocative
way. Today there is plenty of provocation everywhere, and I aim at
provoking no one if I can help it.

When I say we are in for a hell of a time in this country I am not
being apocalyptic: just saying what everyone now realizes. If my doubts
about the viability of optimistic liberalism are greater now than they were
before, it is because such liberalism presupposes a situation that can be
controlled by reasonable policies. There has been a shaking of foundations:
just a beginning. Reasonable control is not something we can rely on.

Nor even reasonable dialogue. We are not even going to find things fitting the names we have been accustomed to give them. We are in a great crisis of meaning. The fact that the racial identity of the Negro is now a central question is only a small part of it. Now more than ever generalizations, particularly old and familiar generalizations, are going to be dangerous. Perhaps we must now all be very careful to explain ourselves when we say "the Negro" or "the liberal." What Negro, and what liberal? And what radical?

I should imagine this summer's crisis has done a lot of winnowing among liberals, driving a great many to the right and a few to a hesitant left that is not quite there. I don't know, I am just guessing. I imagine, though, that there must be a few liberals around who are now fully convinced of the need for a new politics in this country. The old two-party system was finished decades ago. Perhaps there is some hope that out of this hot summer we may at last get the serious beginnings of a really effective radical coalition where, in spite of all the black separatism that is announced by "the Negro," there may in fact be collaboration between white and black on the left toward peace, new horizons, constructive change—not without a little more shaking of the foundation. This is perhaps the only hope of a third way, something other than complete anarchy on the one hand or a police state on the other.

I happened to be in Louisville right after the Detroit riots—and right after there was supposed to be a riot in Louisville itself. (The riot did not take place.) All the Negroes I met were being not only friendly but vociferously friendly. I did not feel that they were tense and mad, but relaxed and confident. It was the kind of feeling you used to get on the campus at Columbia the morning after we had burned down the Barnard fence. Not a sense of animosity and racial war. Obviously, I must follow my own rule and not generalize from this very limited experience, but I am quite sure that it is very important, at the moment, not to lump "the Negro" into one mad red-eyed monster with a Molotov cocktail in his hand. Nor to panic at the thought that the Negro's hate of the white man has now reached the point where it is completely irreversible and can be assuaged only by everybody's blood. This is just not true of "the Negro" in general, only a small minority. And in that small minority, the hate of the white man tends to be first of all a hate of white society, its institutions, its self-image, its property, its pretensions. I don't condone the senseless murder of firemen who are trying to put out blazes started by rioters: but still, it is the fireman as symbolic of white institutions and not the fireman purely and simply as white man that is being shot at.

In my opinion, the intransigence of the Black Power people is first of all aimed at one point: getting white liberals and radicals too off the back of the Negro activist so that the Negro can function freely by himself. Once this is quite clear, and I think it is now abundantly clear to everybody, if the white liberal or radical is willing to cooperate with the Negro *independently*, and *completely out of his way*, without trying to dominate the Negro and make up his mind for him about *anything*, the chances are that his support will be accepted. But it will be accepted grudgingly, without thanks, without demonstrations of wonderment and pleasure: it will be accepted merely as what is due. If this could have begun four years ago on these clear grounds of understanding, we would be better off today. I do not say we would not have had the Newark and Detroit riots. These were inevitable, and more like them are inevitable. The injustice and cruelty which are by now endemic beneath the surface of our bland and seemingly benign society are too deep and too serious to be cured by legislation, even if by some miracle the legislation were to mean anything in practice. This is all going to have to come out the hard way, and in my opinion (forgive the slight twanging of those apocalyptic wires) the un-Christianity of American Christianity is going to be inexorably exposed and judged: mine, perhaps, included. The form this Judgment will take will, first of all, be the panic, the hate, the violence, and the fanaticism of people who, calling themselves Christians, will resort to killing in "self-defense" because they are so obsessed with the fear that what they believe in—the affluent society—is being menaced by revolution. It is significant that the TV set, fancy clothes, furniture, liquor and of course weapons are so central in the rioting and looting of the ghetto. This is a religious war over what we all, white and black, really believe in!

It is here that I return to one of my more obvious suggestions. We Christians, some of us at least, were and are anxious to support the Negro non-violent movement for civil rights which is now, if not completely a thing of the past, at least seriously diminished in significance. But what about a white non-violent response to Negro violence? Strangely enough that has not been much preached, though in fact it has been practiced. I think for instance of Msgr. Robert Fox and his people in the Puerto Rican riots in East Harlem. Processions with flowers and lights, songs, in the streets on the nights of rioting certainly did a great deal to keep things calm. But of course the great thing is for this witness to be unambiguous, and it is hard for the clergy to be unambiguous insofar as the priest, like it or not, is aligned with the cop and the National Guardsman as a defender of the establishment. Christian non-violence in the presence of Negro violence must first of all mean a complete dissociation from and repudiation of an "order" which defends the money of the slum landlord and the white businessman against the people who are exploited by them in the ghetto. We have to clearly recognize that this order is disorder, and join the Negro in protesting against it. Such sentiments are by no means popular among Catholics today, but I submit they must be made and aired, and I think you will agree they are not apocalyptic. I am certainly all for your idea that in our search for ways of keeping elements of reason and humanity alive in an ugly and destructive situation, we can best study the ways of flower power. You do not use that expression which is already perhaps a bit outworn (it takes anything about six weeks to become phony in America today). But in conclusion, I take this opportunity to say precisely where I myself stand.

I am not convinced that Stokely Carmichael is the incarnation of Satan. I do not go along with violence, but I do not recognize in myself the slightest right to impose non-violence on the Negro. It is up to him to choose his own policies. I do not personally believe that there is much chance of the United States handing over Alabama to the Negro, though I wish it were possible. If non-violence is, as I think it is, a Christian duty in a time like this (because it is the only way to keep open really reasonable and creative possibilities in the mess that is to come), I think that we white Christians should get busy and find out about using it. But we must not use it for the interests of the white against the Negro. We must use it, as it is meant to be used, for truth, and for the good of everybody. To begin with, it must be used to keep open possibilities of authentic human communication when the bullets are flying.

My position is on the Christian non-violent left, particularly that segment of it which is occupied by Dorothy Day, the Catholic Peace Fellowship and people like Joan Baez. We are not liberals. We are still, I suppose, Christian anarchists, except that the term has no political relevance whatever. But the Christian anarchist remains—unlike the liberal—clearly non-identified with established disorder. Or at least he tries to. In so doing, he may exasperate everyone, but perhaps sometimes he may see an opening toward peace and love even when the sulphur and brimstone are at their worst, and others have given up trusting in anything except weapons.

Thanks for your fine letter, a most rewarding one for me. I am glad we understand each other after these four years.

To Hiromu Morishita

In 1964 a group of Hibakusha—people from Hiroshima who had survived the August 6, 1945, bombing of their city—toured various parts of the world (a number of cities in the United States, also Paris, East and West Berlin, Moscow) as ambassadors of peace. During their stay in the United States they came to Gethsemani to visit Thomas Merton. He read for them his poem "Paper Cranes." (The paper crane is the Japanese symbol for peace.) After their visit, Merton kept contact with them through the letters he exchanged with their leader, Hiromu Morishita.

Hiromu Morishita was the president of the Senior High School Teachers'

Society and a member of the Hiroshima Peace Education Institute. At Christmas 1965 he wrote to Merton of the birth of his second child, a girl, and two years later of a third child, a boy. The 1967 Christmas letter said: "We hope peace for all children." Morishita initiated the correspondence with a letter to Merton on July 10, 1964, thanking Merton for the "sympathetic kindness" with which they had been received at the monastery.

August 23, 1964

It was a pleasure to receive some news from you, and I am grateful for the photographs . . .

I am sure that the whole pilgrimage, which took you to so many different places, was deeply fruitful. Certainly your presence will have made a deep impression, and will have made many people think. How important the message of peace remains in our world: this is evident from the events in Vietnam and Cyprus. It seems that those who have the greatest power have not learned the lesson that destructive power cannot build a world of peace. Hence we must all continue our efforts to make the way of reason, negotiation, and peaceful settlement the one which men will seek to pursue, rather than the way of violence. International trust and confidence is most essential. Anyone who works for this mutual understanding of nations is doing a work that will be surely blessed, even though it may not seem in the eyes of men to attain immediate success.

A book of mine on the question of peace [*Seeds of Destruction*] is being published next year. If you would like a copy, please let me know. Also let me know if there are any others in Hiroshima, especially among those I had the privilege of meeting last summer, who would like copies of the book.

May your work and writing be blessed. I would be interested to hear more from you, and I am sorry I was not able to talk with you about calligraphy, which is a subject in which I am interested.

March 8, 1965

The books went off some time ago and you ought to receive them soon, if you have not received them already. They are in many respects unsatisfactory, but I hope the section on peace is, within its limitations, a contribution to valid thought on the subject. I am very much afraid that the American policy in Vietnam today is hardly calculated to promote true peace, and I observe with sorrow that the same rationalizations of force are offered. The great defect of American thought is lack of balance: too much science and not enough wisdom. This is a very serious defect. But there are many protests against the adventures of the military in Vietnam. Let us hope that somehow a calmer and more objective view may prevail.

I want to thank you for the calligraphies which you sent, and which

I treasure. They are very fine and full of delicate life, and the poems are indeed charming and inspired. I am very grateful to you. I am enclosing some poems which I recently translated from Portuguese [of Fernando Pessõa]. They lack the delicacy and suggestiveness of Japanese poetry, but contain something of the Japanese view of things, I believe. I have been reading the philosopher Nishida Kitaro, a great man, and these poems have something of his outlook.

Let me conclude by sending my cordial good wishes and warm friendship to you and all your associates there in Hiroshima, especially those whom I was privileged to meet here last summer. God bless you, and write when you can.

August 3, 1965

As August 6 approaches I want to write to you and all your friends and co-workers and join with you in concern and protest at this time when once again violence seems to be usurping the place of reason and humane understanding.

You know that there has been much protest and dissatisfaction here over the war policies of President Johnson in Vietnam. These policies are ridiculous and irrational and to the student of recent history they display the same "logic" of unconditional surrender that led to the bombing of Hiroshima and Nagasaki.

The great problem, it seems to me, is that those in power do not think in terms of human beings and living persons, but in terms of political abstractions which tend to become more and more unrelated to human reality.

Human protest must keep these realities very evident and obvious, lest they be completely forgotten. I am united with you in your efforts and aspirations.

[*This message was added to a form letter*]

Christmas Morning, 1965

I was very glad to get your card and hear from you again. Let us hope the shameful and disastrous war in Asia will finally end.

August 6, 1967

Today is Hiroshima Day and I think very much about you and all my friends there. It is a solemn and serious day, the lessons of which must not be forgotten: and yet so many appear to have forgotten them, and at times the rest of us wonder what to do next. Every form of protest has been tried and none of it seems to change the course of events in Vietnam. Yet we can keep trying, and still keep faith in man. But man can easily be blinded and deceived by his own passions. That is true of all of us.

Thank you so much for the special issue of *Prelude* which you sent last year. It tantalizes me, as I have as yet found no one who can translate any of its contents for me, but it is good to have your poems with me, even though I do not know what they say. I still have the little card and other calligraphies you sent, and I keep the card especially present with me in my book of prayers (the breviary).

I have a new book of poems [*Cables to the Ace*] coming out next spring—or rather a series of poems, which are largely experimental and may be hard to understand, full of ironies and ambiguities appropriate to the moment when we are saturated with the wrong kind of communication. It is perhaps a time of "anti-poems," and I have lately translated some such "anti-poems" by a friend of mine in Chile, Nicanor Parra. I hope to send you the book of his poems sometime, when it appears. Meanwhile I will send some other things that may interest you, by surface mail. The enclosed will perhaps remind you of the cottage where I had the pleasure of chatting with your group three years ago.

[*This message was added to a form letter*]

New Year's Day, 1968

Blessings for your family [Hiromu had enclosed family pictures with his Christmas letter]. Indeed we must hope and work for peace for all children and not permit them to be victims of criminal war!

To Christopher Mwoleka

Born in Bukoba, Kagondo, Africa, in 1926, Christopher Mwoleka was ordained a priest in 1962. Ten years earlier, while working as an office clerk, he purchased a copy of Merton's Seeds of Contemplation; *he attributed the growth of his spirituality in no small measure to the writings of Thomas Merton. On August 31, 1967, in his first letter to Merton, he said he wrote not to bother Merton but simply to communicate the joy he received from his books. Soon after, Father Mwoleka was assigned to teach at the Seminary of St. Charles Lwangas in Katoke, Biharamulo. In 1969 he was ordained a bishop. He is presently the Bishop of Rulenge, Tanzania, Africa.*

September 13, 1967

I was so happy and touched by your warm and kind letter. In this world where there is so much struggle and confusion, in which people seem to despair of peace, it is so good to receive a frank and understanding letter from a brother in a distant country—and in Africa. Surely the grace and love of Christ are evident in the way we are able to understand one another and to seek God in the same way, one prayer, one faith and one aspiration to life with God alone. I will thank Him also in my Mass for all the joy and light His Holy Spirit has given and will give you. I am glad that you are there to praise Him and pray for me.

Today I sent off a package of a few books which were not on your list [the list of Merton books he possessed]. I am also sending some mimeographed material which is not published or perhaps a few articles in magazines that would not normally reach you. Included will be some pages on the solitary life which I am now able to live in the woods about ten minutes' walk from the monastery. It is quite a solitary place and no one comes here. The arrangement is good, as I can get the food I need from the monastery, and go there for one meal a day. The rest of the time I am here. I continue of course to work, writing and so on.

You ask about the poem on "Melancholy." It is not a question of praise or of blame, but of stating the fact: there is bitterness in all of us, and sometimes we feel it. This must be understood, and we must deal with it humbly and realistically. We cannot be without feelings of various kinds, and we can simply use them as occasions for self-knowledge and trust in God's mercy.

You must above all be hopeful for Africa and for your people. The black people of the world have been treated unjustly, and they still suffer from the wounds of that treatment. But the future of Africa is in the hands of God, and I believe that African Christians will bring new life to the Church of the future. Perhaps God wants you to experience contemplation in a deeply African way, which I would surmise to be a way of wholeness, a way of unity with all life, a sense of the deep rhythm of natural and cosmic life as the manifestation of God's creative power: and also a great warmth of love and praise. If you realize that God has indeed given you His Spirit as the source of all joy and strength, and trust Him to purify your heart with His presence and love, in great simplicity, He will teach you the joy of being a child of God, an African child of God with your own special unique gifts.

I cannot promise to write many letters. I have so much correspondence that I really cannot do justice to all of it, and many letters go unanswered. But I do feel closely united to you in prayer and in the Spirit.

February 24, 1968

Thanks for your two very good letters. I am most happy and interested to hear about your reaction to Chuang Tzu.* That is indeed a hopeful sign: I had not realized that the thought of Asia would be welcomed so readily in Africa. On the other hand, just as Asian thought has been

---

* Fr. Mwoleka had written in a letter of February 10, 1968, of the great joy he had experienced in reading The Way of Chuang Tzu. He remarks: "This comes from the East and the East is not far from us; yet prejudices have barricaded the East from us."

unknown and misunderstood in the West, so too African thought, even more so, because there is much less written down, and more oral tradition. The thing they have in common is a very positive and affirmative view of nature: I mean Chinese thought (this is not so true of India). Chuang Tzu is very *open* to living things and relatively closed to artificial and social standards. I believe that one of the most beautiful things about African traditions would possibly be the sense of fellowship and brotherhood with other living beings, the animals etc., and with nature in general. I would be most interested to hear about this.

On the other hand, I am not surprised that *Raids* did not come through. To begin with, a lot of it is very obscure and involved, full of allusions which depend on a firsthand knowledge of Western urban culture. I believe you have some of this, but still you have not been immersed in our problems. Much of what I am trying to say in that book is negative and anti-Western, but in terms that Westerners would understand.

Fr. Haring is a really prophetic theologian for our day [Fr. Mwoleka had recently listened to a talk by him]. I have had the joy of meeting him here, and we talked much about peace and the struggle against violence. That reminds me that I must send you my little book on Gandhi if I did not do so already . . .

To Marco Pallis

After some months of search for Marco Pallis, I finally located him, through his publisher, at his second-floor flat on Chesham Street near Sloane Square in London, and visited him on September 28, 1983. He received me most graciously and over afternoon tea we talked about his life and work and his contact with Thomas Merton. His hearty appearance belied his eighty-eight years. (He was born in Liverpool, England, in 1895, of a Greek father and of a mother who, though born in England, was also of Greek parentage.) Marco Pallis has been a mountain climber and a student of Tibetan art, religion, and culture. His most famous book, Peaks and Lamas, *first published in 1939 and then in 1974 in a third, revised and enlarged edition, reveals both these interests.*

Marco Pallis's first contact with Merton came through a friend, George Zournas, who was editor of Theatre Art Books in New York. He had become patron of a group of young Tibetan monks who had fled their country after the uprising against the Chinese communists in 1959. When these young monks first arrived in the United States, it was suggested that they be placed temporarily in American homes in order to learn the language. George Zournas wrote to Thomas Merton, whose reply was that priority of concern should be given to their monastic vocation; hence they ought not to be dispersed among American families. Zournas wrote to Marco Pallis, telling him of this; Pallis heartily agreed and wrote Merton. This was the beginning of their exchange; in his first letter Marco Pallis asked

Merton's advice on the publication in America of an article he had written on the problem of evil. Merton was eager to learn what he could about Tibetan monasticism, and his contact with Marco Pallis helped prepare him for his visits to Tibetan monks on his Asian journey.

1963 [probably July]

First of all, I hope you will forgive the typewriter. I do not type well, but my writing is worse, and I am used to the machine, much as I regret to confess it to the author of *Peaks and Lamas*. I read your book several years ago and found it very congenial indeed. I certainly envy you your experience with Tibetan monasticism, and I hope at least the young lamas in New Jersey will eventually come down here, as I am not able to go to them, due to our strict interpretation of the laws of enclosure here. I have been very interested in the experiment there, and was worried about it at one point. Though there is now such a thing as an "American" monasticism, which is in its way fairly genuine, we must remember that this country lives by everything that is hostile to a truly monastic life, and even its most cordial embraces tend to prove deadly in the long run.

It is a pity that when you were in Louisville you were not able to come out here, but if you come this way again I hope you will visit us. If you let me know beforehand I will try to get permission to speak with you. I am very happy that you are sending me a new book of yours, which I shall enjoy reading if it is anything like *Peaks and Lamas*, or like your essay on the "problem" of sin.

This essay is really excellent, but I tell you at once that there is no point in trying it on any of the Catholic magazines in this country. First it is too long, even without the appendix. Then, though some of the editors would certainly be interested, it is very hard to fit it into any familiar context. The approach is not at all known to Catholics. Though of course there is no reason why it should be alien to anyone with a real knowledge of the Church's tradition. Yet for most readers and students there would be a gap to jump, and they would not be able to jump it.

My suggestion is that you let me send it to New Directions . . . and perhaps they will print it in one of their annuals in which they also printed, some time ago, a dialogue between myself and D. T. Suzuki. I am sending you an offprint of this, which is very close to the area which you are treating in your conference.

I have several works of [Frithjof] Schuon in French, also some of René Guénon [Pallis had translated both writers into English]. I like them both very much, though I have not really got into them thoroughly yet . . .

To my mind the meeting of Eastern and Western philosophy and mysticism is a crucially important matter. My general feeling is that the work that has been done so far, and the kind of thing I myself might be able to participate in, is not thorough enough and too intuitive. Of course a sapiential approach must be intuitive. But a great deepening is necessary. The task of getting to know the Eastern literature thoroughly is immense, and I do not have any Oriental languages. I might say, however, that I have a deep affinity and respect for Buddhism, and I think that I am as much a Chinese Buddhist in temperament and spirit as I am a Christian. I don't find any contradiction in matters of "faith" as I see it. But of course I say this without having an expert knowledge of the literature, and perhaps it is only irresponsibility and impressionism. I think one can certainly believe in the revealed truths of Christianity and follow Christ, while at the same time having a Buddhist outlook on life and nature. Or in other words, a certain element of Buddhism in culture and spirituality is by no means incompatible with Christian belief . . .

October 4, 1963

. . . I want to thank you especially for the books you so kindly sent. First of all, your own *The Way and the Mountain* is a very solid and valuable collection. Your essay on the "Active Life" belongs precisely to a tradition that I recognize and live in, and it is very well done. The one on Sikkim Buddhism is perhaps the one that moved me most. Can we hope for a revival of these values? As you say, it is really the cross of our time to see so much that is really valuable being destroyed or discarded in the most irresponsible sort of way. Even efforts to preserve the best things seem at times fated to be foolish and destructive. I wish the Church were more sensitive on this point. There is a glimmering beginning now, but perhaps too late, with the formation of a secretariat for relations with non-Christian religions, and with some beginning of understanding of primitive cultures on the part of people in the missions. Too few of them, I am afraid. It is a very sad thing that more Catholics were not the type of de Nobili, Xavier and Matthew Ricci . . . The essay "The Way and the Mountain" is the one I liked best. It is very fine indeed, and as a matter of fact the night after I read it, I dreamed about a "way," high on a cliff yet somehow secure. The Chinese painting of the "way" reproduced in the book is magnificent. I will send you my little book on Direction [*Spiritual Direction and Meditation*], which has many points in common with your essay . . .

And now above all, thank you for the superb book on Ahmad Al-'Alawi [by Martin Lings], superb because of its subject and because of the excerpts from his writings. I am immensely impressed by him, and by the purity of the Sufi tradition as represented in him. I am surprised Louis Massignon did not know him better or appreciate him more. I intend to reread the book meditatively; it is one of the richest things of its kind I have found lately. Surely the deepest expression of this kind of mysticism in our time. I have not yet got into Schuon's book on Islam, but will do so immediately. I do as a matter of fact know him and Guénon, though not well enough yet . . .

. . . Perhaps you would like a large omnibus book of my things. It is a bit pretentious but I think it says most of the things I am trying to say, or perhaps not quite. It does not say enough about my growing interest in Islam and Buddhism. I know I am going to profit very much by Schuon, and will perhaps have more to say when I have read a great deal more on these things.

Light little bits of news from time to time about the monks in New Jersey. I hope eventually some of them can come here, and I shall keep this in mind. I would write to Geshe Wengyal [a Mongolian monk in charge of the lamas] but I am already overloaded with correspondence. One would like to write a few really thoughtful letters and take one's time doing it, but "the reign of quantity" takes over, and one must move mountains of mail for little real purpose.

The race troubles in this country are very symptomatic of the ills of this quantitative society, its love for false and synthetic traditions. The spurious tradition of "the Old South," which seems by comparison with the total lack of tradition elsewhere to have some reality, is now coming out for what it really is: a mere illusion. It is rather pathetic, really, but the effects are terrible.

We have a vocation *not* to be disturbed by the turmoil and wreckage of the great fabric of illusions. Naturally we must suffer and feel to some extent lost in the tempest, for we cannot be complacently "out" of it. And yet we are, because of Him who dwells in us. But precisely in Him and by Him we are deeply involved by compassion: yet compassion is useless without freedom. I am sure our desire to understand this paradox and live in fidelity to it is the best indication that we can have the grace to do so. But none of it will come from our (outward) selves . . .

In an undated letter (probably summer 1964) Pallis writes that the musical group with which he played, the Early Music Consort of Viols, was making a second tour of the United States and would be traveling from Louisville to Berea, Kentucky, in October.

September 23, 1964

I see that I have let this reply go too long, but I hope it will reach you before you leave England.

It is very easy for you to stop at Gethsemani on your way from Louisville to Berea. It is only a little out of the way. We are fifteen miles southeast of Bardstown, or perhaps better south, but there are several roads from here to Berea. I think that the best idea would be to come here on your way to Berea. We will keep that day free for you. Would you and your group like to have lunch at the Abbey? There is no problem, just let us know.

One thing has been on my mind: would it be possible in any way for you to play some of the monks something? We never hear anything like this and would much appreciate some of the ancient pieces, in the spirit of the Middle Ages or early Renaissance. The latter part of the morning in the novitiate, this could substitute admirably for my class! . . .

October 17, 1964

Probably the best thing would be to come out somewhat early on the morning of next Saturday, the 24th. Those who would like to hear the sung High Mass (Gregorian of course) at eight o'clock would have to get started about 6:45 at the latest from Louisville.

I would be out to see you after the Mass. The best time for some music would be about 10:15, for forty-five minutes or an hour. But a problem has occurred to me; is the group all men, or are there some women? This would raise a problem as women are not allowed inside the enclosure, and I don't know if you would want to play without them. Please let me know if there are women in any case, because I can arrange for them to have lunch at the ladies' guesthouse, and of course would gladly meet them along with the rest.

The drive to Berea takes two or three hours, so I suppose you will be leaving in the early afternoon. In any case, I look forward very much to seeing you. If the program of music is not possible, no matter. It will be a great pleasure to talk with you and Mr. Nicholson . . .

There were, indeed, two women in the group. So the concert did not take place. Instead, Merton spent some time conversing with Marco Pallis and his friend Richard Nicholson.

December 10, 1964

Thank you for your very welcome letter. I had hesitated to write before I knew that you were back in England. But I have been wanting to write and return M. Schuon's really remarkable essay on monasticism. I like it very much, and like the whole tone of it from beginning to end. It is a much saner and more realistic approach to the question of "the monk and the world" than is being taken at times by some of the monks. The same problem we spoke of in connection with Tibetans. They do not want to be left out of the world!!

It is really remarkable that with all the unrest and perplexity about getting in touch with the world and engaging in "meaningful activity" (that word "meaningful" has come to take on an aura of magic in American religious circles), monks do not realize that they are manifesting a kind of despair, a kind of blind grasping and clinging to the evanescent aspects of life. The old structures, manifestly inadequate in some ways, are being taken away, and instead of being spiritually liberated, Christians are rushing to submit to much more tyrannical structures: the *absolute* dominion of technology-politics-business (or state capital). I think M. Schuon has exactly the right view, and I am pleased that he remarks in passing on the naïve infatuation with Teilhard de Chardin (though I think there is much that is good in Chardin, along with some grave illusions).

Have you by any chance read the book of Jacques Ellul on the *Technological Society* (perhaps *La Technique* in French)? It is monumental, and one of the most important treatments of the subject . . .

. . . I am always interested in news of the Tibetan monks in NJ. What you say about the successful formation of their American novices is very gratifying.

M. Schuon's essay is on its way back to you under separate cover together with a couple more pieces of my own, rather various. It is good to hear from you and I remember your visit with great pleasure . . .

The following reply to Pallis's twenty-four-page handwritten letter of January 23, 1965, is unfortunately incomplete, the last part having been lost or misplaced. In his letter Marco Pallis is particularly critical of the distinction which he believed Merton was making between "natural" religion and "supernatural" religion. Merton returns to the subject in his letter of Easter 1965.

March 10, 1965

Your splendid letter of January 23rd is much appreciated, except that in beginning to reply I am daunted by the consciousness that I will not be able to do it justice. The sheer quantity of mail these days . . . makes a qualitative reply something rare . . . But I must be concise, to at least touch on the main points.

1. Of course I agree completely that mere singling out "the bomb" for reproof and implying that everything else is tolerable is a gross error of perspective. I have recently written on Dresden, for example (just a note), where "conventional weapons" did twice as much harm as the bomb of Hiroshima.

2. Yes, it all hangs together. We cannot imagine that the human race somehow stands back and outside all that is going on, as a kind of absolute, deciding what must and what must not happen, while in reality being carried along by forces which no one understands. So the growth of population, the incidence of cancer, the splitting of the atom and chain reactions, the infinite noise of meaningless communication, so-called affluence in the big countries, and a thousand other symptoms all express the same thing, what it is we do not know because we are it. But we are

swelling up in a strange spiritual and a-spiritual ferment and God alone knows what will come of it.

3. *Pacem in Terris*: like all such documents, it is severely limited and somewhat abstract. Yet when one reads such things, this one proves itself to be, compared with the others, so full of deep human compassion that it is encouraging. But it is the compassion of a formal document, not of a sermon by St. Francis.

4. In the race question, I certainly do not advocate what the people in the South crudely call "mixing"—miscegenation. But I do not think there is any point in outlawing it either, because it is a fact, and one for which the whites are responsible above all. There is every reason to try to respect the proper characteristics of each race but—if there is a culture a hundred years from now it will probably be a sort of mestizo culture. With the limitations that this implies. And perhaps some accidental advantages, but I do not speculate on that.

5. Without touching on all the details of various observations you make (I agree heartily with all you say about wisdom and method, and regret that I have so little to offer in the way of method . . . which perhaps also shows a lack of wisdom), I would say that a point like the Ferrapont–Zosima contrast will obviously be seen from various viewpoints. The two actually represent aspects of the same thing, monasticism, and to prefer the one is . . . [The letter breaks off here.]

Easter 1965

Yesterday two more books arrived, Schuon on *The Self* and Guénon on *The Crisis of the Modern World*. I want to thank you for them . . . I am coming to the conclusion that I find Schuon hard going a great deal of the time, as his perspective is somewhat unfamiliar to me. In reading Schuon I have the impression that I am perhaps going along parallel to him, and once in a while I will get a glimpse of what he means in terms of my own tradition and experience. I liked very much his essay on prayer, for instance. But on gnosis I find it harder to follow him, I am not in tune with his conceptions, and it is hard to say whether I agree or not. I simply don't know.

. . . I agree entirely that one must cling to one tradition and to its orthodoxy, at the risk of not understanding any tradition. One cannot supplement his own tradition with little borrowings here and there from other traditions. On the other hand, if one is genuinely living his own tradition, he is capable of seeing where other traditions say and attain the same thing, and where they are different. The differences must be respected, not brushed aside, even and especially where they are irreconcilable with one's own view.

Of all the questions that I treated in my last letter to you (not nearly all those which you yourself raised), the one that still bothers me is that division "natural-supernatural" in religion and mysticism. I see more and more that it is misleading and unsatisfactory, and I also think that there is every solid reason even within the framework of Catholic orthodoxy to say that all the genuine living religious traditions can and must be said to originate in God and to be revelations of Him, some more, some less. And that it makes no sense to classify some of them as "natural." There is no merely natural "revelation" of God, and there is no merely natural mysticism (a contradiction in terms). However, this whole business of natural and supernatural requires a great deal of study. The terms are not clear or unambiguous even within the Catholic tradition, always. And outside it there is a great deal of confusion as far as I can see. It is something that requires a lot of study.

I hope you are well and that you have recovered from your sickness and can stay out of the hands of doctors . . .

June 17, 1965

This more or less immediate reply to your excellent letter, not a complete reply yet, is due to the fact that I had been thinking of writing to you for the last few days in any case. I have been wanting to tell you how much I have benefited by your translations of Guénon and Schuon. Not only the material, but also your own translations, which, I think, contribute much clarity to the originals. I meant to write you after Easter when I had finished the Guénon book on *Crisis*. Now I do so when I am in the middle of Schuon on the *Language of the Self*. The Guénon book is certainly a classic, and I appreciate Schuon more and more. The essay on Buddhism, for example, is most excellent. I am at one with him in his deep reverence for the spirituality of the North American Indian. Of that, more at some other time. The Indians of this country are a sign of the age, silent and frequently mistreated, at least in their legal rights. One feels that there is still, among some of them, a deep consciousness of their real calling, and a hidden hope. Yet there must also be much real despair among them. I have always had a secret desire to be among them in some way, and of course there is no fulfilling this, and it would tend to be highly ambiguous in any event.

About the question of prayer of petition: let me think about it. It is certainly no problem to me whatever, and never has been. I think that dealing with it might just make it more of a problem without helping those for whom it is a problem. But doubtless there would be no harm in setting down a few thoughts on the subject. I mentioned it in passing in the autobiography, but have never really dealt with the "question."

Since you are convinced of the undesirability of that last section on Jihad in the "Black Revolution," I will see that it is eliminated from future editions. I certainly respect your judgment and thank you for it.

. . . I do think that you representatives of the ancient traditions, and

I consider myself one of you, have a most important vocation in the world today. But we will not really be attended to. It does not much matter. I think that, for ourselves, we must consider at once a deeper penetration into and fidelity to the great wisdom of our fathers, *all* our fathers, with a deeper and deeper awareness of our unique responsibility to the wisdom of all the ancients, including the hidden and prehistoric ones. And at the same time be aware of our limitations, and the unlimited capacity of the power of the Spirit in us nevertheless, in the darkness and diaspora in which we live. I doubt if we are called upon to accomplish anything, but we will be what *we cannot help being*. This is the great truth that at once humbles and encourages us. On the basis of this awareness, I think there is every reason for a great boldness and freedom, but in a kind of Taoist dimension of not-striving. I am struck above all by the limitless depths of despair that are really implicit in the pitiful "hopes" of so many moderns, Christians, who are trying to come out with justifications for a completely secularized and optimistic eschatology of pseudo-science, in which the eventual triumph of religion is to discover that God is "dead" and that there is no religion anyway. The thing that we have seen is that this discovery is so old and so childish that it has been absorbed and explained millennia ago in the apophatic tradition, which results in the most positive of all the answers and affirmations, in apparent negation . . .

In one word, be assured of my deep sympathy and friendship, and my close solidarity, without any hint of institutional or "political" reservations and hesitations. I think we can accept ourselves as we are, and differences in terminology and exoteric formulation are of course neither underestimated nor overestimated. All this is perfectly taken for granted, and poses not the slightest problem . . .

November 14, 1965

I have owed you two letters for some time, and recently papers came about the painting that is being sent (it has not yet arrived) and which I eagerly expect. Your very good letter of last August, about your walking trip to Switzerland and the visit of Aelred Graham, was much appreciated and I have just reread it. It came, as a matter of fact, just when I was preparing to move out from the monastery to a hermitage to begin my vanaprastha, which is, I hope, definitive. I have been at it three months, and it is a splendid form of life. But three months have taught me many things and show me that I have more to learn, in order to get on the way without ambiguities. Well, that is what solitude is for and I am learning to be patient with the long task of gradually peeling off non-essential things. One would like to do it all at once but it is not possible, for various reasons.

Yes, I am learning now how true it is that one must take a passionless view of the great crises and perils of our time. There is no earthly use to getting tense about them as if something could be done immediately. This is the result of innumerable acts and sins, a huge accumulation of evil to which we have all more or less contributed, and "Christendom" has contributed enormously, I am afraid (I mean the half-Christianized culture that one can call by that name). However, I am not passionless about these things. I was shocked the other day when a young Catholic [Roger La Porte], not knowing what he was doing, tried to imitate the Buddhist monks of Vietnam who immolated themselves by fire. They had reasons which he could not possibly have and the whole thing was grotesque and tragic, precisely because springing from passion and confusion. But it was in its own way a sign too, since everything is a sign of some sort. But it makes one rethink some of the modern clichés about "commitment." I see that I have to slough all that off, in my own way, and take responsibilities on a deeper and simpler level. I have been deluded by a desire to "do good" when wu wei would have done more good. In my terms I would have let God work instead of trying to do it myself. Yet one must also act, and the business of feeling around for the balanced position is what requires time and patience.

. . . Life at the hermitage is peaceful and assumes a clear direction. One sees the way more clearly, and as you say, it is a great help to know that there are companions here and there. There is nothing whatever of any importance except this quest for inner truth, the truth that one "is" without being able to see it because we have all covered it over with the results of our selfish and deluded acts. The enormity of the task is great, yet simple, and one may have great desire and great hope of going on with the help of the Holy Spirit, in finding the path by His light in darkness. The path that leads home to Him in ourself, and the path which is also Himself. ("I am the way, the truth and the life.")

I envy Dom Aelred Graham if he will get a chance to visit the Orient. I was invited to Japan [by Father Dumoulin] but could not get permission to go, and I must follow my way by staying in one solitary place: which is just as good, really. About this I am unconcerned. If you do come to America let me know about it, but I think that Fr. Abbot is going to insist on one of the conditions he made when allowing me to be a hermit: restriction of visits. I do not personally feel that I need to be isolated from absolutely everybody but there remains always the crucially important exercise in selflessness which obedience offers. This is to say that if you write, I will ask permission to see you if you can come, but that I do not guarantee in advance that I will get this permission.

. . . One of the best things that came up in connection with the Council was, by the way, a fast organized by Protestant and Catholic women, in Rome, very quietly, for ten days during the discussion of armaments [see Dorothy Day letters and the Goss-Mayr letters]. Lanza del Vaste's people were much involved in it.

In a letter of October 14, 1965, Marco Pallis wrote to Merton: "Here is a small token of my love: this ikon, Greek, probably Macedonian, of the date probably 1700. It came to me in an unexpected way . . . and I thought of you. Your karma evidently wished you to receive it. Of the four saints in attendance on the Mother of God, one is St. Charalambos (only known to me by name); St. Nicholas, St. George and St. Demetrius . . . evidently call for no comment. Byzantine painting, which avoided luxurious additions and never sacrificed its essentially contemplative viewpoint to the love of anecdote, seems well-fitted to make its home in a Cistercian setting."

December 5, 1965

Where shall I begin? I have never received such a precious and magnificent gift from anyone in my life. I have no words to express how deeply moved I was to come face to face with this sacred and beautiful presence granted to me in the coming of the ikon to my most unworthy person. At first I could hardly believe it. And yet perhaps your intuition about my karma is right, since in a strange way the ikon of the Holy Mother came as a messenger at a precise moment when a message was needed, and her presence before me has been an incalculable aid in resolving a difficult problem.

I do not know if I told you I had received permission to move out to a hermitage in the woods. I have been here going on four months, about three and a half to be exact, and the adaptation is proceeding well, but there have been things to be peeled off, contacts and implications in the world, especially a difficult one I was caught in with the peace movement. As I told you in my last note, the Catholic peace movement in this country has been strangely agitated, and people have used my name in connection with events of which I had no knowledge and over which I had no control. It has been necessary to make quite clear that I am no longer in any way involved in a political movement for peace, be it Catholic or any other. Those who do not understand the contemplative life have no patience with such an attitude.

It all comes back to the question of the Church and the World, in which there lie grave temptations and struggles ahead for many. The myth of political efficacy will in many minds come to be a touchstone even of religious values. It already is. That has grave implications indeed. The abomination of desolation.

I am glad of your message about M. Schuon. I must send him my book on Chuang Tzu. Did you receive a copy? I asked the publishers to send you one. Please let me know about this. I have an article in that Indian magazine, *The Mountain Path*. Do you see that? They only sent me one copy, but I must try to get others.

But that is all business. Let me return to the holy ikon. Certainly it is a perfect act of timeless worship, a great help. I never tire of gazing at it. There is a spiritual presence and reality about it, a true spiritual "Thaboric" light, which seems unaccountably to proceed from the Heart of the Virgin and Child as if they had One heart, and which goes out to the whole universe. It is unutterably splendid. And silent. It imposes a silence on the whole hermitage . . .

Thank you, dear friend, for such a generous and noble gift. It will surely remind me often to pray for you and Richard to go deeper into your own truth as, I hope, I will go deeper into that which is granted to me to live. I see how important it is to live in silence, in isolation, in unknowing. There is an enormous battle with illusion going on everywhere, and how should we not be in it ourselves? . . .

This ikon now hangs in the hermitage that Merton had begun to live in at this time.

March 11, 1966

Since receiving your letter of February 20th I have given it much thought. It was very good of you to give me the information it contained [concerning the Tarikah*], and I assure you that I will not betray your confidence. Now that I know more about your group I will feel closer to you and will, of course, keep you in my prayers, relying also on your intercession in my behalf. I am glad you consider me a fellow traveler on the way, and I am happy that the mysterious ways of Providence have brought us together in this capacity. Nor do I doubt that we can all help one another in many simple and effective ways. I am especially grateful for M. Schuon's kind message. I hope you will thank him for me and assure him of my deep respect and friendship, indeed of my reverence now that I know him in a new capacity. I did of course know of his visits to the Indians and his deep interest in them. This is one side of his work that has most impressed me. I regret very much that I cannot have any contact with the Indians myself, here, but it is one of the drawbacks of my particular situation. I realize that there are many things I would like to do which, though very good in themselves, are unfortunately prohibited me here, and I must make the best of that, recognizing and accepting the fact that one cannot try to do everything and that I must work within the sphere in which God has placed me.

In solitude I have seen more and more that everything depends on obedience to God's will and the submission of a total and uncompromising faith. This for me at the moment comes down to the full acceptance of and adjustment to the particular situation He has willed for me here. I think that I am learning not to chafe at limitations that could objectively

---

* *A Sufi confraternity of which F. Schuon became the spiritual leader after the death of Shaikh Ahmad Al-'Alawi.*

seem quite unreasonable, but which certainly have a purpose in my life. Spiritually I am much more free in the solitary life, but materially the limitations remain and from certain points of view they are perhaps a little cramping. Correspondence is inspected, contacts which seem valuable are liable to be abruptly cut off without my knowledge, etc. I mention this to let you know that any relationship of mine with the Tarikah would be not only highly informal in itself but subject to this kind of control—which could even be arbitrary. On the other hand, as I said before, I do not chafe at such things and I find in them a certain freedom of indifference, realizing that such material limitations are really unimportant and that they never prevent anything that is really willed by God. I hope that it is in the area of this higher freedom we will always be at one.

However, there is no question that here everyone agrees on the meaning of my solitary life and on its necessity, in the same terms as those you yourself used. I am no longer concerned with writing about events or discussing them, or passing certain judgments (except where they may be evidently necessary). In fact I will probably do less writing in any case.

It has been a rigorous winter here, but I have profited by it in many ways. However, one result of a great deal of wood chopping is that my bad back gave out and I have to go to the hospital for an operation on it. I know that this is something that would be better avoided if possible, but I see no possibility, things have gone too far. I hope it will at least not do any harm. I am most suspicious of surgery, but as I say, doubtless it may even do some good. In any case it is one more thing to accept as part of God's plan for me—or part of my karma if you prefer. I am fully resolved, as far as my own part in it is concerned, that even were I to be partly crippled I would still want to continue in solitude and I think I would be able to work out some way of managing it.

Returning to the original point, of the need for an earnest life of solitude in the Catholic Church: popularly the trend seems to be in the other direction: all is action, liturgy and a thousand new projects and ideas. I think there is a great deal of good in a lot of it, and that some of it is very superficial and quite deceptive. This is another reason for a real contemplative life, not one that is half stifled by organization but one that is really lived in contact with reality and with life, in solitude. I can see that this is my real work and I certainly need to go about it in the right way. I am quite conscious of my own fallibility. One thing I can certainly profit by in my contacts with you and with M. Schuon will be an occasional reminder of the real nature of the work that is expected of me. Needless to say I will always be glad of general hints as to how to go about it better. I realize of course that an authentic spiritual guidance is not a matter of letters. Hence I would stress the informality of the situation, believing that precisely this would leave a certain openness for the Holy Spirit to bridge the gap between two distinct traditions. On the other hand it is a wonderful thing to be immediately in contact with Shaikh Ahmad Al-'Alawi and I deeply appreciate this.

I will write more perhaps when I am back from the hospital . . .

May 28, 1966 (Vigil of Pentecost)

I forget when it was that I last wrote you about the very important matter you set before me at the beginning of the year. Since that time I have been in the hospital and have come back to the hermitage. And of course I have not ceased to think from time to time of your proposal. I remember that my letter was inconclusive but remained open. The chief obstacle to a more or less full participation seemed to me then to be the fact that letters here are subject to complete control. However, as you see by this one, there is a way in which one is permitted to consult other masters without the censorship of the local Superior. You note that I simply put the letter in a sealed envelope which is within another envelope handed open to the Superior. The sealed envelope is marked "Conscience matter." A letter coming in would be the same: the outer envelope would be opened by the Superior but the inner one, properly marked, would be respected. In this form one might carry on a free correspondence with M. Schuon.

As things are now going, it seems to me that without disrespect to my own community, being now more or less detached from it, I no longer profit much by its teachings and its programs, which in any case are taking a quite different direction from that which I myself am following. On the other hand there is a considerable problem of my simply dispersing and squandering my energies in useless or fanciful pursuits which have little or nothing to do with any way at all. I am very conscious of this at the moment, feeling as I do that sporadically I get a certain amount of "illumination" which then goes off into nothing, produces perhaps a poem or an insight of some sort, but is it really fruitful in my life? Or is it simply a diversion?

In this situation I do think it is important to enter into contact with a source of guidance like that of Shaikh Ahmad Al-'Alawi and this is possible through M. Schuon. I believe this can be done without irresponsible confusions of one tradition with another, and without creating other worse diversions by involvement in a complex new set of practices, observances, techniques and whatnot. I do not know if this represents the right sort of attitude, but I mention it as it is my attitude now. It seems to me that my task is one of a positive and constructive spiritual freedom, as a "son of God" in the Holy Spirit and in Christ, to live the Christian life of grace in a creative, constructive and in some sense original way of my own, incorporating into it valuable insights and helps from other traditions insofar as these fit in with the Christian view of life. Does this make sense?

If you think it does, then perhaps you would simply forward this letter to M. Schuon and let him decide what he wishes to do about it. I do not by the way have his address, since I have lost the letter in which you gave it to me.

I have not heard from you in some time. I hope you are well, and I send you my best regards, as also to Richard . . .

December 24, 1966

This is Christmas Eve, and with the festivities I will probably not write letters for a few days, and I want to get this off to you. Of course you will be remembered in the liturgy and in meditation (at least in intention, as I do not actively remember people in meditation). May God grant you light and blessing.

Many thanks for the book *Born in Tibet*. I have already read your excellent preface, which faces the problems candidly without undue lamentation and yet without underestimating the seriousness of the situation. I see the book will be very important for me and will read it attentively.

I was most interested in all you had to say about Dom Aelred Graham's projected voyage. I envy him, I must say. I would love to visit monasteries. But obviously he has deserved this by his hard work and his devotion to activity. I on the other hand must pay for my hermitage with the sacrifice of not being a pilgrim too, except spiritually. One cannot have everything or rightly demand it. Still, it is a lack. I feel the loss, for I know I would gain spiritually. No matter.

This brings me to the fact that I have not yet written to M. Schuon as I intended. There again, I feel things would be so different if I had only met him personally and spoken to him. As it is, I do not feel it would be anything but artificial for me to write to him about prayer etc. at the moment. Something inside tells one when and when not to move in such instances, and so far I do not have the right impulsion. So it must wait. In any case, do be assured that I feel closely united to all of you in silent charity and in a common aspiration for deeper union with God in the Spirit.

. . . I will not write more at the moment. There is snow falling and it is getting heavier, so I must start down to the monastery and get this mailed . . .

To Sister Penelope Lawson

Ruth Penelope Lawson (1890–1977) was born at Clent in Worcestershire, England, where her father was vicar. She studied at Oxford, though an eye operation prevented her from taking a degree. In 1939 she did earn the highly respected Archbishop's Lambeth Diploma for a thesis on the Psalms. Soon after leaving Oxford, she joined the Anglican Community of St. Mary the Virgin (CSMV), where she was professed in 1915. She spent some time teaching in the schools that were staffed by the community, but her main work was as librarian at St. Mary's Convent, Wantage. From 1935 to 1972 she wrote a number of books, including The Wood: An Outline of Christianity, They Shall Be My People, *and two volumes of* Old Testament plays.

She was a great friend of C. S. Lewis; they corresponded from about 1939 till the time of his death. Many people think her translations are her best work. These include St. Athanasius and Origen; also some of the Cistercian Fathers— St. Bernard and William of St.-Thierry. It was her interest in translating the sermons of another Cistercian, Isaac of Stella, that brought her in contact with Thomas Merton. (See letters to Donald Allchin.)

October 17, 1965

Well, I have brought Migne up to the hermitage and am looking over the original text. I do find that sometimes you have condensed rather a lot and that perhaps you might go back over it and include a little more of the original. I think this would be important in Sermons IV and V, since they are important for the contemplative life. I think so also in VI, which I am reading now.

An example of what I mean comes in 1709 c. I have been reading people like Heidegger lately, and I find that Isaac here has resonances which will alert the ear of those who have been in contact with existentialism. I think that you probably skipped this bit with the idea that the modern mind would not accept it. But I believe that it is just the contrary. I think that in 1790 b-c you should take it word for word. For instance I think there are real reasons why *mors* and *vita* should be treated as "substantives" in all the force of the words (you tend to make them adjectival). I mean that when you say that "the mortal life of man is vital death" you are reducing two realities to one, making one a qualifier of the other. I think Isaac means two, hard, concrete facts and the "life-giving death" has all the concreteness of the Bible and the liturgy, apart from the *vita mortalis*, another distinct reality. I think also the *sentiendo* in 1709 c, line 3, is to be taken seriously. *Sentiendo discutimus:* it is a matter of conveying the idea of an experience that enters into the depths of our knowledge of life, whereas you treat it as a rather matter-of-course kind of experience. I am being very fussy about details, but here I think we have a powerful bit of Isaac and we must not miss our chance, though perhaps I admit I may seem to be rather demanding . . .

. . . I think too that though at first sight it might seem distasteful, there is rather a lot of power in the passage about the vices being nests of snakes and cradles of death etc. (1709 c). But I leave you to judge of that. One must certainly make concessions to modern taste and I know that kind of thing is not too welcome in England. (Or in America for that matter—it is more Luther's kind of thing. I have his version of the Scriptures here in one volume with the Vulgate, the Septuagint, and the Hebrew, which I cannot read.)

Tristitia in 1709 d. I think "gloom" is a good word. Depression might be another but gloom is better. The idea of sulking and brooding could get into it also. Maybe "sulking" is the best single word. What do you think? . . . Again in 1710 d, I think the *opus diaboli nihil nostrum*, the *nihil* should stand out as substantive. This is the work of the devil, our nothingness. Here again there are interesting resonances from existentialism, the void and so on. (I will send you a copy of an article I just did on the subject of existentialism and you will see what I mean, I think.) . . .

The bit in 1711 b-c on the structure of man is very important and here too I think we need to stick close to the original, since the terms are technical and go back to Platonism. But they also are very interesting since they have resonances in Jungian psychoanalysis today. Here again, let us take "these three" as substantives. The *caro*, body, flesh, and *anima*, might almost be left as *anima* since Jung uses that very word and *mens* means spirit, the higher self. The *anima* is the emotional and aesthetic self. The line on paradise is immensely important in this context. And quite original too, it will delight the Jungians no end (as it does me). That the structure of man is a paradise in which you have man (the *mens*), woman (the *anima*) and the serpent (concupiscence of the body in its fallen state). Hence the bit you ask about could be "Bodily desire incites, tempts, itches" (that is too strong), the emotional *anima* "takes delight in it, and the higher self, the spirit, consents." You see he is describing a dynamic process, man is for him this dynamic movement of the three selves . . . The bit you ask about is straightforward if we simply accept the old technical meaning of the terms: "Consider three things in yourselves: concupiscence of the flesh, the sensual (in the sense of aesthetic) response of the *anima*, and the rational mind or understanding spirit." I paraphrase so you will see what the whole thing is about. The *anima* is that in us which responds to beauty, to warm human affection, to pleasure (good or otherwise), to instinct on a higher level. The *mens* is that which is contemplative, intellectual, which enjoys the higher intuitions of the incorporeal, which makes the ultimate decision on which our whole destiny depends, and which, commanding the *anima* and the *caro*, is in immediate dependence on the will and word of God. It is the *mens* which contemplates Him and submits entirely to Him, bringing with it the *anima* and the *caro*. These others cannot go to God except when brought to Him by the *mens*. This is the old Cistercian picture of man. I really think you have got it very well, but I thought I would expatiate on it since you asked . . .

November 2, 1965

Many thanks for your letter of the 23rd of October. I must tell you that when I get enthusiastic about something I am liable to come out with too many ideas, and when I drink black coffee I get enthusiastic about what I am reading. My last letter was the result of an early, very early bout with black coffee about five in the morning and a long quiet period of reading. I am sure that you bravely stood up to the tidal wave, and your letter shows no bad results. Still, of course, all I said is to be taken with reservations . . .

July 4, 1966

I have safely received the manuscript of your translation of Isaac and have finished reading it. I think you have done an excellent job, very readable, very lively. I think it will really make a charming book. My only reservation—and I hope it does not make you despair because I know you cannot do anything about it—is that there really should by rights be something of Isaac's obscure philosophy. But I do not suggest that you try to tackle a Sexagesima sermon at this late date. The only thing is that any critic who knows Isaac will mention this fact. But let him mention it, say I. The book is good as it stands, and furnishes a nice, accessible introduction to Isaac. I hope the publisher likes it.

At the moment, I am about ready to do the introduction. Perhaps I may look up some articles on Isaac that I have not read yet, but I think I have enough material, and I don't want to make it too long . . .

July 27, 1966

Some time ago I finished the introduction to Isaac and I have been patiently (more or less) waiting for it to be typed and mimeographed. I have to have things mimeographed because I need more than a couple of copies and copies easily get lost anyway. This does not add greatly to the time required and is very convenient. But the typists available are not always free to work for me. My own typing is abominable and worse than ever now as I have a bad arm.

In any case, I write this with the intention of enclosing it with the introduction when I finally do get copies to send . . .

February 7, 1967

Please forgive me for waiting so long to reply to your inquiry. I had to get in touch with Herder, and then I discovered that they had written to me some time ago and I never received the letter. They are not able to use your book on Isaac, unfortunately. Of course we both anticipated this.

. . . It is a great shame that at present everyone is so obsessed with anything that can claim to be modern that they have no time for the old any more. It is almost impossible to get anything published on the Middle Ages, especially in theology, in this country. Herder put out a book on St. Thomas lately, but only with profuse apologies and all kinds of prefaces and introductions from people who are guaranteed up to date.

Any further news about your efforts in England? How about the magazine at Caldy? . . .

May 23, 1967

. . . The chances of publication of such a book in this country, without support from a special foundation, seem to be very poor indeed. No one here is interested in the Middle Ages, so it seems . . . Probably the best thing to do would be to get back to the idea of running bits of it in *Cistercian Studies*.

I have been terribly taken up with all kinds of extra work, and so I have been remiss in writing letters. Do you happen to know where Donald Allchin is now? In Oxford, perhaps? I had a lovely visit of two or three days with him here in Easter Week, and now I owe him a letter and thanks for a book. Doubtless I should write to Oxford . . .

To Pope John XXIII

Angelo Giuseppe Roncalli (1881–1963) was born near Bergamo, Italy, of peasant stock. He was educated at the Bergamo Minor Seminary and then at the Roman Seminary (Apollinare). Ordained a priest in 1904, he served as chaplain in the First World War. In 1925 he was ordained an archbishop and appointed Apostolic Visitator to Bulgaria. Later he became Apostolic Delegate to Turkey and then to Greece and in 1944 Papal Nuncio to France. In 1953 he was made cardinal and that same year became Patriarch of Venice. Five years later, on October 28, 1958, he was elected Pope.

Chosen for a transitional role, he inaugurated a new era in the life of the Church. In a consistory on January 25, 1959, he announced to an astonished College of Cardinals that he was calling an ecumenical council of the Church. A joyous moment in his life was October 11, 1962, when he convened the first session of the Second Vatican Council. His obvious love for people made him perhaps the most loved Pope of modern times. He realized that reforms were needed in the Church, and saw the need of demythologizing the Papacy and diminishing the cult of the pontifical personality. He wanted the Church to reach out to the world rather than isolate herself from it. He wrote seven encyclicals; the one most hailed by Merton and his friends in the peace movement was Pacem in Terris. The English translations of Merton's letters in French are by the editor.

November 10, 1958

My dear Holy Father:

This is one of your children who comes to kneel at your feet, to greet you and to congratulate you with my whole heart, and to tell you how happy we are to have you as our Father and the Vicar of Christ Our Lord. I am a Cistercian monk, born in France, educated in England and in America, master of novices and author of a few paltry books. On behalf of my novices and myself, I want to express our true, spontaneous and filial affection and to offer our prayers and our sacrifices so that God may deign to shower you, Most Holy Father, with all the graces that your formidable task requires.

I want to tell Your Holiness, as simply as I can, what came to my mind while I was saying Holy Mass yesterday. I hope that I can bring joy to the paternal heart of Your Holiness by sharing with you the aspirations of a contemplative monk who has always loved his vocation, especially the opportunity it offers for solitude and contemplation. Perhaps I have exaggerated this love in some of my books; but since my ordination nine years ago and through my experience as master of scholastics and then of novices, I have come to see more and more what abundant apostolic opportunities the contemplative life offers, without even going outside the monastic cloister.

It seems to me that, as a contemplative, I do not need to lock myself into solitude and lose all contact with the rest of the world; rather this poor world has a right to a place in my solitude. It is not enough for me to think of the apostolic value of prayer and penance; I also have to think in terms of a contemplative grasp of the political, intellectual, artistic and social movements in this world—by which I mean a sympathy for the honest aspirations of so many intellectuals everywhere in the world and the terrible problems they have to face. I have had the experience of seeing that this kind of understanding and friendly sympathy, on the part of a monk who really understands them, has produced striking effects among artists, writers, publishers, poets, etc., who have become my friends without my having to leave the cloister. I have even been in correspondence with the Russian writer who won the Nobel Prize in Literature, Boris Pasternak. This was before the tragic change in his situation. We got to understand one another very well. In short, with the approval of my Superiors, I have exercised an apostolate—small and limited though it be—within a circle of intellectuals from other parts of the world; and it has been quite simply an apostolate of friendship.

With the blessing of my Reverend Father Abbot, I am interested above all in Russia (I am going to learn Russian) and Latin America (I speak Spanish and Portuguese and we receive quite a number of vocations from down there).

Most Holy Father, with the encouragement of friends and a number of priests and bishops, I am beginning to think seriously of the possibility of a monastic foundation, whose purpose would be to exercise a contemplative apostolate of this kind. This is to say, a foundation in which the members would be monks and contemplatives, but at the same time would receive special groups, such as writers, intellectuals, etc., into their house for retreats and discussions. I especially think of South America as a place for such a house. Apparently the time for this has not yet come, still I wanted at least to share my hopes with Your Holiness.

Having presented this idea to you—an idea which also interests some of my priest novices who have come from other religious congregations— I want to ask, on my behalf and theirs, *if Your Holiness believes that there is a place for a limited apostolate of this kind*—publications, exchanges of letters (limited of course!), and gatherings of intellectuals in a monastery for conferences, etc.—in an Order that is strictly contemplative. And *if Your Holiness believes that special houses of this kind should exist*, with a staff that is more or less trained for this kind of apostolate. It goes without saying that such monasteries would be greatly needed especially in Latin America; in fact I would not even put the question.

Dear Holy Father, here are the very simple ideas of one of your children, who loves people and the Church and also his contemplative vocation. This son wants to show you his total and complete commitment to the salvation of souls and to the growth of the monastic and contemplative life in their world.

Humbly prostrating ourselves before Your Holiness, my novices and I beg you to grant us the favor of your Apostolic Blessing, so that we may be holy monks and deeply fervent priests, that we may unite in our hearts perfect contemplation and apostolic zeal and that Our Lord Jesus Christ, Who is the way, the truth and the life, may be known and loved by all.

Receive, dear Holy Father, this expression of the total devotion and the filial love of your sons in the monastery of Gethsemani.

M. LOUIS MERTON
NOVICE MASTER

February 11, 1960

With what joy we, your devoted sons, received the beautiful picture of Our Holy Father, and signed by Your Holiness's own hand, together with the warm and paternal letter granting us the Apostolic Benediction upon our choir novitiate! How deeply significant is the fact that these precious documents have reached us on the 11th of February when the whole Church joins in praising and thanking the Immaculate Virgin of Lourdes, our most loving Mother and powerful intercessor. We received all these graces as though directly from the hands of Our Blessed Mother and we join in thanking her for this signal favor and joy which will make us redouble our prayers for Our Holy Father, and renew our generosity in corresponding with our vocation!

The beautiful picture in full color will be given a place of honor and prominence in the sacristy, which is simply a corner of the novitiate chapel. There the Father Master and the novice priests (who form a large proportion of the novitiate) will be reminded, every morning, while vesting and unvesting before and after the Holy Sacrifice, to keep Your Holiness in their prayers at this most sacred and fruitful of all moments of the monastic day.

During the next eight days, the octave of this happy occasion, the collect *Pro Papa* will be said for Our Most Holy Father each day on which it is permitted, by the Father Master, assistant master, and the novice priests. The other novices will join them with a *Magnificat* each day for the same intention.

With the warmest expressions of deep filial devotion we prostrate ourselves at the feet of Your Holiness, with heartfelt gratitude for such unforgettable and paternal kindness. We will feel that our whole vocation and religious life have been powerfully affected by Our Holy Father's Apostolic Benediction.

We remain Your Holiness's most grateful and devoted sons in Christ Jesus Our Lord.

February 11, 1960

The joy that my novices and I experience exceeds all limits: how can I express it? Is it not really a little ray of that infinite light which comes from the love of the Heavenly Father for His children whom He has united in the Mystical Body of His Only Son? The kindness of Our Holy Father helps us to understand a little more the mystery of the infinite kindness of the Father *ex quo omnis paternitas in coelis et in terra nominatur.*

The attached letter in English attempts to express the sentiments of gratitude of your sons in the choir novitiate of the Abbey of Gethsemani. I would add a few words about a subject that may be of interest to Your Holiness. I have just received permission to start, very discreetly, a small retreat project here. This would be apart from the regular retreats which each year attract thousands of the faithful as well as Protestants and even people without faith. I have received approval for five or six retreats for what may be called specialized groups and even in some sense elite groups. For example, there will be a meeting of several theologians and heads of *Protestant* seminaries, another meeting of professors of a Catholic university (priests and lay people together), another of psychiatrists and writers, and possibly another of artists, poets, etc.

Our goal is to bring together in these various groups people highly qualified in their own field who are interested in the spiritual life, no matter what aspect, and who will be able to profit from an informal contact, from a spiritual and cultural dialogue, with Catholic contemplatives such as we are, or should be. It seems to me that this could create a marvelous atmosphere that would be most favorable for the action of the Holy Spirit and for the development of Christian faith and civilization. I wanted above all to share this good news with Your Holiness. I take much joy and courage from the hope that this venture will receive your paternal interest and even your blessing. I hope to send good news about this project by the end of the year, God willing. I am certain that the prayers of Your Holiness will obtain for us much light and strength for this so very delicate task; pray also that I may be a docile instrument of divine grace and nothing else.

Once again assuring Your Holiness of my filial and fervent devotion, I remain your unworthy son in Our Lord.

April 11, 1960

How can I express to you my gratitude and the emotion with which I received the honor bestowed on me by Your Holiness in sending me this beautiful stole,* worn and blessed by Your Holiness. It is truly the greatest honor of my life—aside from the honors of the supernatural order, such as holy baptism and the holy priesthood. This magnificent gift brings all of us many graces; and the whole community, especially Reverend Father Abbot and my novices, want to thank Your Holiness for the honor which you conferred upon us all and for your paternal kindness which is indeed the expression of a pastoral love that is universal.

The happy presence of our dear Dr. Barbato among us—he graciously agreed to speak to the novices—made so much more present and real the concern Your Holiness has for all his children, even those far away. We have the impression of a momentary glance through the door into the interior of the Apostolic Palace. What a joy to receive the personal blessing of Your Holiness.

As a token of my filial love and devotedness, I am sending a little book to Your Holiness through Dr. Barbato. It is a very simple book, much in the spirit of the *Speculum Asceticum*, which I received together with the stole and which is so fine a book for a priest and a monk. This little book contains a selection I did of some of the sayings of the Fathers of the Desert. It is a special edition, hand-printed by a friend of mine, Victor Hammer, an Austrian artist who found refuge here at the time of Hitler. If Your Holiness likes this book, I beg you to bless it and also myself, the unworthy translator. There are very simple and very profound stories in this collection, and some unforgettable sayings, including the words of St. Arsenius: *"fuge, tace, quiesce,"* which can be found in the *Speculum Asceticum* of Your Holiness.

I also thank Your Holiness for the interest you have so kindly shown in our little project of spiritual meetings with special and elite groups. A few days ago I had the pleasure of addressing more than fifty Protestant seminarians and pastors here in our monastery. They showed remarkable

---

* *This stole is in a display case at the Thomas Merton Studies Center at Bellarmine College, Louisville.*

good will. I always try to be for them first of all a sincere, open and humble friend. I speak to them not as a critic who blames them for errors, but as a brother who understands their desire to seek out God sincerely. They seem to appreciate this attitude and they ask: "Is the Catholic Church really interested in us?" I tell them "yes," that we want to understand each other better.

Another joy which the Lord granted me recently was receiving a very friendly letter from an orthodox priest in Paris who is interested in the articles I wrote about Mt. Athos and St. John Climacus and . . . [The rest of this letter is, unfortunately, missing.]

Monsignor Capovilla, private secretary to Pope John, wrote that the Holy Father was "impressed" by the following letter, only a part of which has survived. It possibly may have had an influence on the writing of Pacem in Terris.

November 11, 1961

. . . The most agonizing problem here is the very grave threat of a nuclear war. No one of course wants this kind of war. But lack of understanding, ignorance, and violent and subtle propaganda—all conspire together to create a very unsettling mood in the United States. There are many who hate communist Russia with a hatred that implies the desire to destroy this nation (a nation that admittedly poses a threat). But what is worse, the American economy depends more and more on these horrible preparatory measures that move us inevitably toward the greatest disaster. For this reason it is practically impossible to reverse the war machine and to disarm. Disarmament could actually ruin many people here. That is why the situation is so grave. Sad to say, American Catholics are among the most war-like, intransigent and violent; indeed, they believe that in acting this way they are being loyal to the Church. Just recently a very small peace movement, bringing Protestants and Catholics together, has come into being in the United States. I try to be a part of this movement as much as I can, here in the cloister, through my prayers and writings and also through the conversations I have with those who come here.

To Pope Paul VI

Giovanni Battista Montini (1897–1978) was elected Pope on June 21, 1963, and took the name Paul VI. He had worked in the Vatican Secretariat of State from 1924 till 1955, when he assumed his pastoral responsibilities for the archdiocese of Milan. Made a cardinal in 1958, he took an active part in the first session of the Second Vatican Council. Chosen as successor to John XXIII, he convoked the remaining sessions and brought the Council to a conclusion in 1965.

His historic visit to the Near East took place January 4–6, 1964. King Hussein greeted him in Jordan; Zalman Shazar in Israel. And it was in the Holy City of Jerusalem that he met and embraced Athenagoras, the Ecumenical Patriarch of Constantinople. On October 4, 1965, he journeyed to New York to make a fervent plea for peace before the United Nations.

July 26, 1963

To His Holiness Pope Paul VI
Vatican City

Most Holy Father:

Humbly prostrate at the feet of Your Holiness, I wish to express my most devoted and filial gratitude for the signal honor of the Pontifical Letter signed by Your Holiness, conveying to the novices and to myself the Apostolic Blessing. We all thank Your Holiness for this act of fatherly kindness to us and promise our fervent prayers at all times for all the intentions of Your Holiness.

It will be my own devoted effort to help the novices to become true contemplative monks, men of God, totally devoted to the love and contemplation of Jesus Christ, and deeply concerned, at the same time, with all the interests of His Church in the troubled times in which we live. Two intentions above all will concern us: world peace and justice and charity, and the plight of the American Negro struggling for his just civic rights, against the injustice of a treatment which is often most inhuman. We have only one Negro in our community at present. What a blessing it would be to have several more. We feel that the prayers and blessing of Your Holiness will bring down most abundant grace from on High, that we may serve Our Lord and Saviour with all the love and zeal of our hearts.

With renewed expression of my profound gratitude and loyal, filial devotion to Your Holiness, I remain as always Your Holiness's most humble son in Christ.

February 6, 1964

It was to me a deeply moving surprise and a great joy to receive from our Father Abbot the little souvenir which Your Holiness had the paternal kindness and bounty to send me by his hand. It was above all to me profoundly meaningful and consoling that Your Holiness should remember me and think of me, the least of your sons, and I express my warmest and most filial gratitude. I shall treasure this gift especially because it reminds me of the historic visit which Your Holiness recently made to the Holy Land [January 4–6, 1964]. The account of Your Holiness's first day in Jerusalem was to me almost shattering, in its expression of a reality and mystery which one does not ordinarily meet with in the news: the encounter of Christ in His Vicar on earth with the suffering and confused crowds—with all the echoes of Palm Sunday and some of its ambiguities also. I wonder if any of us can understand what this experience must have meant to Your Holiness? Like *Pacem in Terris*, this is certainly an extraordinary manifestation of Christ in His Church seeking the salvation of the multitudes and the preservation of mankind.

I know that Your Holiness is deeply interested in the problems of monasticism and of the contemplative life, which are numerous. We have great difficulties and greater hopes for monastic reform and renewal. We dare to believe that the monastic life may have a very special role in the renewal of the Church. There is much that is paradoxical in monasticism, and this paradox tends to be lost sight of when the monastic Orders are treated just like other religious Orders. In effect, the monk can do most for the world when he is most truly solitary. Yet even in his solitariness he must retain some physical contact with "the world." Does it seem that the somewhat charismatic character of this monastic apostolate might be more appreciated? Then the effect of the monk's life of prayer and his ability to share with others the fruits of contemplation would not be obscured or submerged in the routines and pressures of a more organized apostolate. In a word, we monks wish to assure Your Holiness of our deep sense of our need for a monastic renewal in deeper poverty, simplicity, solitude and prayer, which will at the same time give meaning to those contacts which we do and should have with intellectuals (Christian and otherwise) and with those interested in ecumenism, as well as with the ordinary faithful. If Your Holiness is interested I could perhaps at some time speak of the little we attempt to do here in this regard. It may be effective, though always remaining restricted.

I wish to take this opportunity once again to assure Your Holiness of my filial devotion and most profound respect, along with my earnest desire to be always more and more what I am called to be, a monk, seeking God in solitude, yet at the same time not unmindful of the needs and sorrow of the world I have left behind. I know Your Holiness in the past showed a deep interest in this desire for solitude which I have always had and which seems to be finding at least a relative fulfillment in a way that is not fully satisfactory but which nevertheless is a gift I receive with gratitude from the merciful hand of God.

I wish also to say that I sought in this relative solitude to devote myself, in prayer and concern, to the great problem of world peace in this atomic age: a problem which many in the Church, including some of the hierarchy, do not seem to be able to estimate in its full seriousness, and in its objective reality. There surely should be no doubt in the mind of anyone that now war is no longer a reasonable, indeed moral, solution to international problems, when it threatens at any moment to explode into a general catastrophe. How well this has been said both by Pope John and Your Holiness.

Your Holiness will pardon the length of this letter. I close in asking Your Holiness to bless me and my novices, who think of you each morning with deep affection, since Your Holiness's signed photograph is over the vesting table in our novitiate sacristy.

May 16, 1965

The main purpose of this letter is, in a spirit of filial obedience and devotion, to thank Your Holiness for the beautiful words on peace, so warm and so urgent, spoken to us in the recent encyclical *Mense Maio*. We in the monastery were deeply moved at the reading of these plain and simple words of the Vicar of Christ, and we have redoubled our prayers for peace. At the same time some of us are tempted to wonder if the appeal of Our Holy Father has been fully understood in all its gravity by the leaders of our nation, at present so implacably intent on the use of force to settle the grave problems that have arisen in Southeast Asia, and in Santo Domingo.

May I confess in simplicity that I sometimes wonder if the leaders of the United States and framers of its foreign policies are not perhaps afflicted with a certain moral blindness, due to the conviction that they are themselves perfectly sincere and disinterested, and to the belief that they have a certain "mission" to destroy communism. Secure in these beliefs, which are perhaps too simple and too sweeping, they seem to think that a use of power that would be wicked and unscrupulous when wielded by others is, in our case, perfectly just and reasonable. Thus arises a double standard in judging situations, and a consequent unwillingness to negotiate with an adversary who is considered, beforehand, as completely unreasonable and treacherous.

When Your Holiness appeals for peace, it seems to me that priests and faithful everywhere ought to be able to support this appeal with words and acts. Yet one of the few priests [Daniel Berrigan] in this country who has spoken out forcefully for a cessation of violence, torture and unjust methods in Vietnam has been silenced by his religious Superiors because of the opposition of certain newspapers and certain sectors of public opinion.

There is also a serious problem for lay Catholics who are disturbed by the fact that the conduct of the war in Vietnam or the arbitrary intervention in Santo Domingo seem to them to be in many respects unjust and not to be reconciled with the demands of a Christian conscience. They are therefore faced with the alternative of going to war in circumstances which seem to them unjust and immoral, or going to prison. Yet many of their fellow Catholics revile them as traitors and communists.

In all humility and submission I felt that I, the least and most unworthy of all Your Holiness's sons, ought to bring these thoughts to the attention of our Common Father.

It is my earnest desire that this letter be understood as an expression of sincere and humble concern in a most grave matter. For it seems to us here that we may in all truth now be on the verge of entering a third world war, for which it might turn out that the policies of our own nation would be in large measure responsible. In such a grievous predicament we can only turn to Our Holy Father with the assurance of perfect obedience to your directives and total support for your desires that peace with justice may be preserved on earth.

Therefore I humbly beg Your Holiness to grant to me and to my novices, as well as to all in the United States who sincerely seek a just peace and a cessation of violence, your Apostolic Blessing, and in return I assure Your Holiness of our poor prayers.

October 15, 1965

Permit me to thank you from the bottom of my heart, in my own name and in the name of those American Catholics who are working for peace, for your visit to the United Nations and your magnificent appeal to the world for peace. I shall continue to pray that God may bless the great effort made by Your Holiness, for it is daily evident that only from God can such fruit come. There are still so many Catholics in America who imagine themselves somehow deputed by the Lord to exterminate His enemies in a nuclear crusade. They do not know "of what spirit they are" (Luke 9:55).

As I do not read the newspapers, I do not know exactly what the reaction to the United Nations visit has been, but it will certainly be varied, and if there is a Babel of tongues, nevertheless the debate may prove fruitful. In any case I wish to thank Your Holiness for this great act which has been so significant and has done so much to remove the scandal of a certain silence and hesitation on the part of the Church in America with regard to the crime of total war.

As a gesture of filial devotion, I presume to enclose a copy of an open letter concerning Schema 13 and its statements about war.* I beg Your Holiness to accept this as a homage of obedient and affectionate loyalty. I beg Your Holiness's blessing upon my poor efforts to serve God in a more and more contemplative and silent life, while not neglecting to write what seems to be required or useful for the Church.

---

* "Schema XIII: An Open Letter to the American Hierarchy," published in Worldview, September 1965.

October 11, 1967

Since at the request of friends I am sending you herewith some pictures of the Crucifix done by the late Victor Hammer, as seen in the chapel of M. de Grunelius, at Kolbsheim, Alsace, I also take this opportunity to add a personal message of my own.

It was my privilege recently to contribute some very inadequate notes that were used, in part, in the composition of the "Message of Contemplatives" which Your Holiness had requested. [See letters to Dom Francis Decroix, abbot of the Cistercian monastery of Frattocchie.] This has caused me to think more deeply of some of the grave problems of the contemplative Orders today. I thought perhaps Your Holiness would be interested if I submitted these views on the subject from within a contemplative monastery where, as a matter of fact, I am now happy as a hermit. (I am in the forest near the Abbey of Gethsemani and remain of course a member of the community participating in some of the exercises.)

It would seem that the main question of renewal in the monastic Orders centers around the truly contemplative and interior life. I think most of us realize this, but there is a division of opinions between those who think that the interior life will be renewed if *external* protection is guaranteed (strict enclosure, etc.). Others see the importance of a deep *interior* renewal to be attained by a return to the ancient sources in spirit, while keeping in mind the mentality and special needs of modern man. It appears to me that both views have to be considered: silence and enclosure should be indeed maintained, but at the same time there must be new elements of openness and dialogue, better instruction and greater freedom for monks to participate in conferences and other useful meetings. In my own experience I realize the fruitfulness and importance of dialogue with visitors who come to the monastery and who belong to non-Catholic or even non-Christian traditions of spirituality.

In the light of this I ask myself if there might not be special possibilities of a monastic apostolate which would be primarily contemplative and which would consist not only in providing a place of prayer and retreat, with a certain amount of instruction and direction, but also Christian contemplatives could engage in well-informed and prudent dialogue with specialists in the field of non-Christian religions, particularly contemplative forms of non-Christian monasticism.

As to the problem of contemplatives engaging in the ordinary apostolate—a problem which excites fear in some members of our Order—a possible solution might be this: that the Order as such would maintain its strict contemplative character, but that individual members of it who might feel called to offer themselves for active work, for instance in a mission field, for several years, should not be prohibited or discouraged, but should be encouraged to do so, with the possibility of returning to their monasteries after a few years of active work. It is possible that their own religious vocations might benefit from this experience.

I sincerely hope that Your Holiness's health is now improved and I assure you of prayers, asking Your Holiness's blessing.

June 4, 1968

I write to you at the request of a small group of contemplative nun Superiors who recently met with me and an American bishop to discuss their very serious problems.

We all felt that the authentic renewal of the contemplative life among nuns in this country is seriously endangered by the fact that many communities, isolated and out of contact with each other, are full of fear and confusion. They do not dare make significant changes that would promote contemplative renewal because they are afraid that any change in the direction of openness would simply involve them in the active life and in the consequent loss of their contemplative character. On the other hand, unless real changes are made, to bring the contemplative life into harmony with the needs and aspirations of modern American youth, the contemplative communities, especially of nuns, will be almost extinct within one generation. This would really be a tragic loss to the Church.

These Superiors and this bishop therefore requested me to contact Your Holiness with a serious and urgent petition. We beg Your Holiness to appoint a commission of American bishops to study the special problems of the contemplative communities of nuns in this country, to facilitate the interchange of ideas and the study of their needs and to encourage ways of change and modernization that will not endanger the essence of the contemplative life but will promote its growth and development in accord with the situation of our times.

I take this opportunity to once again assure Your Holiness of my deep personal devotion and filial loyalty in Christ Our Lord, and to beg your Apostolic Blessing.

To Raymond H. Prince

Raymond H. Prince, professor of psychiatry at McGill University in Montreal, was born in Barrie, Ontario, in 1925. He received an M.D. degree from the University of Western Ontario in 1950 and an M.Sc. in anatomy at the same university in 1952. From 1952 to 1955, he trained in clinical psychiatry at various hospitals in Ontario, being awarded the Psychiatry Certification for Canada in 1955 and for Quebec in 1969. Dr. Prince is the author of some one hundred articles in scholarly journals. Since 1964 he has held the position of Research Director at the Mental Hygiene Institute of McGill University.

In 1964 he organized, with the assistance of Linda Parsons (now Linda Sabbath) and Martha Crampton, the R. M. Bucke Memorial Society. It was a time of widespread experimentation with mind-expanding drugs and various practices (meditation, etc.) of different world religions, as well as particular exotic sects or cults. The purpose of the R. M. Bucke Memorial Society was to study such phenomena from a scientific and cross-cultural perspective. It was named after Richard Maurice Bucke, a Canadian psychiatrist, whose book Cosmic Consciousness *(1901) was one of the first attempts to describe the common characteristics of mystical experiences and to point out their profound effects on personality and belief.*

On March 29, 1965, Linda Parsons wrote to Thomas Merton, not knowing he was a monk, and asked him for the names of individuals or groups that might be involved in research into religious experience. Merton's reply (see the letters to Linda Sabbath) was shown to Dr. Prince, who wrote Merton, enclosing an article on Sufism as well as the proceedings of a recent conference of the R. M. Bucke Memorial Society in which the topic of "Personality Change and Religious Experience" had been discussed. Merton's first letter to Dr. Prince was a comment on the conference paper.

May 22, 1965

I am grateful for the mimeographed conference proceedings on *Personality Change and Religious Experience,* and will read the essay on Sufism with interest. However, because the connection had occurred to me, I took up at once your own treatment of regression and mysticism. I think you have raised a good question and made something of a start. The material suggested many further questions to me, and I could perhaps write several pages of notes if I had time. I will try to suggest briefly some of the points that have occurred to me.

1. There is certainly a great deal of mystical material which consciously and explicitly makes use of terms suggesting regression. This is especially true in Taoist mysticism, for instance. And it is true wherever mysticism is couched in terms of passivity and abandonment, which are sometimes called "quietistic," even though they might not technically earn that designation. But I think that a great deal of discrimination is needed in evaluating different accounts of mystical experience. I think in your own approach there has been a tendency to treat experiences on quite different levels more or less as if they were all on the same level.

2. It seems to me that when ecstatic experiences take on a manic character (which they sometimes do), this should be regarded as calling their authenticity into question. I do not say that this would ipso facto invalidate any such experience, but it would be an indication that caution was required, because ideally the ecstatic experience should be beyond manic excitement. There are of course diversities of temperament and personal weaknesses that have to be taken into account in each case. Very

delicate problems of evaluation are involved here. In my opinion, experiences deep enough to be ecstatic or to be qualified as "unitive" should properly speaking be *beyond* all regressive symptoms. I would say a unitive experience that was merely regressive and narcissistic would be invalid religiously and mystically. There would be no self-transcendence, but only immersion in the self, in self-awareness as absorbed in an all which is undifferentiated. But this is not mystical union. Mystic union is not just an "oceanic feeling."

3. I think that regressive features are normal in a *transitional and early* phase of mystical development, in the so-called prayer of quiet, the night of the senses, and perhaps in some way in the Night of the Spirit (but I question this; here at least regression must be something other than what you are talking about). I believe that regression marks these early stages because it is necessary for one to *reculer pour mieux sauter* ["to move back in order to take a better leap"]. Regression, of sorts, enables the whole self to "rest" and "return to the root" establishing a deep continuity with the past so as to enter a future that is going to demand an experience of profound rupture. (Yet there must still be spiritual continuity in spite of the rupture and rift.) The paradox is that the "old" will be left behind, and yet the "new" will be the old transformed and renewed. Death and resurrection.

4. In my opinion, attachment to the "regressive" and narcissistic peace which is proper to early and transitional stages of development is *quite usually* the reason why so few people really become mature in the mystical life. Many reach the early stage, but become bogged down in this "peace" and "sweetness" and refuse to make the break with the past which is demanded of them in order to take the leap into a "new being." I think if one simply equates mysticism with regression, a fatal error will result, and people will be encouraged not to undergo the "death" that is required in order to "live again." Of course you may say, rightly, that this "death" is a climax of regression. But it is certainly something more than narcissistic and pietistic sucking at the breast of consolation (which many mystical writers describe, you have quoted Francis de Sales. St. Theresa and St. John of the Cross also use it).

5. In my opinion, regression, the "ego" and other terms current in psychoanalysis are not strong enough to bear the weight of description required to make clear what really happens in mystical experience. A considerable deepening is going to be needed, in order to discuss these questions adequately. At least this is the opinion of one who is by no means an expert and who has barely a layman's knowledge of psychoanalysis. For one thing, the assumption that rational and discursive knowledge is the normal peak of human intellectual and spiritual development is, to my mind, a real mistake. If we start to discuss mysticism from the viewpoint of the Cartesian *cogito* and the pragmatic scientific mind, we start with assumptions that make false perspectives inevitable. I think we

have to restore intuitive and "direct" apprehension of reality to its proper place as a *normal* perfection of the human mind, before we can begin to understand mysticism as something that is anything but pathological. The point is that primitive people excelled, so it seems, in this intuitive and direct grasp of reality, and our development as abstract thinkers is not necessarily in all respects a genuine progress. Here again, the idea of regression takes on another (cultural) aspect.

I will not make this letter longer, but I thought I would at least set down these few random thoughts . . .

December 18, 1965

I still have your long interesting letter of last summer, which I have been wanting to answer, and I still feel that perhaps I am not saying what I want to say because my knowledge of psychological terms is limited. But I have a couple of thoughts that might be useful to you, and might also help to clarify what I mean.

First of all, returning to the question of regression in mystical experience. As I understand it, regression is a retreat from reality and is essentially narcissistic. In deeper forms of spiritual experience there is often much that resembles regression, in that one seems to "withdraw" from external reality, though I think that this is a very misleading way to conceive it, and I think that in genuine religious experience, especially mystical, one's awareness of reality is immensely heightened, the external and the interior being transcended and recaptured in a unity which is neither and both and beyond the dichotomy of subject object, inside outside and so on.

Now the problem arises: in half-baked spirituality and partial religious experience there is a tendency to substitute precisely a narcissistic unity for this transcendence. That is to say the "oceanic feeling" which is, I think, certainly regressive, and which takes the self, the superficial empirical ego self, as a kind of paradise of all being and seems to experience everything in a heightened awareness of the self (in this ego sense, not the Self of higher religions). One of the great problems of spiritual training is then to help people *not* to confuse this narcissistic self-awareness with true mystical contemplation. And of course people have infinite ways of getting around this. By cleverly rationalizing the narcissistic awareness in certain kinds of philosophical, psychological, theological language, for instance. Or by the language of mystical and affective love-union. I notice, living as a hermit, that monastic community life permits a kind of communal narcissism which siphons it all off into community projects and a sort of communal awareness which is nevertheless centered in the self multiplied (rather than in real interpersonal love). In solitude one confronts narcissism in its brute form, and either resists or succumbs completely.

What I really wanted to tell you is this: in working on this idea I have been studying Rilke, who is very interesting from this point of view. He is a great poet, and had tremendous insights into the reality of spiritual experience, and yet I think he rarely if ever got beyond his narcissism. I can think of only one or two places where he might have done so. Otherwise, there is in him a magnificent regressive narcissism in full bloom, beautifully expressed, and wrong. Or, rather, misleading if you regard it as mysticism, which only few do. As an example I think you would be interested in a short prose piece in his *Selected Works* . . . called "An Experience." Here I think you have a classic example of narcissism as distinct from mysticism. It could hardly be clearer. I think that a discussion of "regression" and "mysticism" will be very much clarified by some consideration of this example. Then one might go on to numberless other examples in his poetry, which of course I think is magnificent, but short of genuine mystical transcendence and therefore very misleading. He is interesting because of his insight into Buddhism, too. Yet it is not the real thing.

I thought you might be able to use this idea to some advantage. I forget when your discussion of the point was scheduled. Was it in early December? I should be interested to hear what you said. It is an important point.

To Karl Rahner

Karl Rahner (1904–84), a highly respected Roman Catholic theologian, was born in Freiburg, Germany. He entered the Society of Jesus in 1922, and following his ordination to the priesthood in 1932, he returned to Freiburg for graduate work in philosophy at that city's university. Here he came under the influence of Martin Heidegger, whose style of thinking and investigating was to influence him in his theological writings. Rahner taught at the University of Innsbruck both before and after the Second World War; later he became professor of dogmatic theology at the University of Münster.

Much of his writing is in the form of long essays, which have been gathered together in a series of volumes called Theological Investigations. *He also wrote an encyclopedia of theology, entitled* Sacramentum Mundi. *He was a peritus at Vatican II and a member of the theological commission set up by Pope Paul VI to investigate theological trends since the Council; his theological thrust has been the development of a theological anthropology that would see the human person as the subject of the transcendent experience.*

March 16, 1964

I do not know whether you read English but I thought you might be interested in an article which took, as its starting point, your diaspora idea in the new book *The Christian Commitment*. I have also done a

review of the book, which I will send you if and when it gets published. But meanwhile I wanted to let you have a copy of this article. Reading your book from the monastic point of view, I was especially happy with your discerning insistence on the *person* as opposed to the rather naïve and sweeping collectivism that sometimes passes for pastoral theology today. Needless to say, I am in hearty agreement with your book and share with you the deep concern for a new and less rigidly institutional view of the Church, the concern that has been raised by the situation of the Church in her true "diaspora," the countries where unpleasant realities must be faced (and are not always faced).

Recently it was my great pleasure to have a conversation with Dr. Jan Milic Lochman of Prague, who visited our monastery and spoke of you, as well as of Barth, for whom I have a particular fondness.

Need I add that we are grateful to you for mediating to us some of the profound insights of modern thought, sc. Heidegger? I am quite interested in some of the French existentialists, notably Merleau-Ponty.

I will not lengthen this letter without need, but I thought, Father, that a word from a fellow disciple in a distant country would be of some cheer and encouragement to you. I too am often discouraged in encounters with the obtuseness of certain critics and censors, and find myself in a position where I am forbidden to speak on one of the most urgent issues of the time: nuclear war. In this country where so many theologians are proposing complacent and totally un-Christian arguments in favor of the bomb, I am not permitted to speak out against it. I do ask you to pray for me, and for us all. I will of course remember you in return. With most cordial and fraternal good wishes for Easter.

To Rosemary Radford Ruether

Rosemary Radford Ruether, born in St. Paul, Minnesota, in 1936, did her undergraduate studies at Scripps College and her graduate work at Claremont Graduate School. She received a Ph.D. in religion in 1965 and the following year joined the faculty of Howard University in Washington, where she continued to teach until 1976. Since 1976 she has been on the faculty of Garrett Evangelical Theological Seminary at Evanston, Illinois. In a letter to Merton in February 1967, Dr. Ruether wrote: "I distrust all academic theology. Only theology bred in the crucible of experience is any good." In her teaching and writing, she has drawn on the experience of women as a source and criterion of theological truth. Her books include New Woman/New Earth *(1976),* Mary, the Feminine Face of the Church *(1977),* Disputed Questions: On Being a Christian *(1982),* Sexism and God-Talk: Toward a Feminist Theology *(1983).*

Dr. Ruether wrote on August 12, 1966, that she had heard of Merton's

interest in her article on Vahanian. She offered to send him the manuscript of her book The Church Against Herself, *which included the Vahanian article.*

August 18, 1966

I do very much want to read your book, but there are several reasons why it would probably not be too good an idea to send your only carbon. First of all, things tend to get lost around here. Second, I am going to be hung up in various ways for the next few weeks and probably would not be able to get to it easily. Probably it would be better if I could get a set of proofs . . . On the other hand, this does not mean that I would necessarily be able to promise a preface. (I have to ration the prefaces almost out of existence these days.) But if the Vahanian piece is any indication, I think you have an extraordinary book going. Glad the Dutch Father [Robert Adolfs, author of *The Grave of God*] is so enthusiastic. It is absolutely necessary to do something about the pseudo-optimism that is floating around and is only the old static triumphalism in a new costume.

Vahanian is one man I must read. I have been reading a bit of [Thomas J.] Altizer, whom I respect, and [William] Hamilton, who is touchingly naïve and sometimes just plain stupid—but I felt very sympathetic to him in an essay called "Thursday's Child" . . .

. . . I would be happy if you would send along anything that you think would be good for me to read, I depend to a great extent on the light and love of my friends who keep me informed, notified, alerted, etc.

September 21, 1966

Thanks for your letter and for the essay on the Augustinian theology of sexuality which I liked very much. I don't know Bonhoeffer's *Act and Being*. I have read his *Ethics* and *Prison Letters* and have quoted the former here and there in my new book of which I will send you a copy . . . Did your essay make *Commonweal*? . . . The point you make about accepting the man-woman relation as a true acceptance of createdness is very necessary. That this is a relation of limit and not of fusion. I think, though, there is also the ecstatic element in the Augustinian tradition on love that can be emphasized too. Ecstasy is not fusion but the perfection of giving, *caritas*. Fusion, narcissism, are on the level of *cupiditas*. You bring this out well. There is a lot there, and I am all for you. I think as you do that this naïve optimistic naturalism only trivializes sex and adds to the speed with which it becomes impossible for people to cope with (some sentence, that). I haven't really read much Teilhard since an article of mine on *The Divine Milieu* was not allowed to be published by the censors of the Order (Teilhard too wicked). I was not sufficiently concerned to read him when I couldn't do anything with it—and not sold

enough on him to read it for pure illumination and uplift. So I didn't read him.

Bill Du Bay answered a sort of concerned letter I had sent him. He is very sure of himself. Knows his cause is right and therefore . . . But it is not enough just to be "in the right." That does not authorize one to forget all other considerations. My impression is that he is not going to listen to advice that does not go along the lines he has decided to take, and these are leading to a collision course that at best will result in his being a victim for everyone. Will it do any good? The point I was trying to make was that he was not really communicating anything clear either to the hierarchy or to the rest of us. He was just being dramatic. I don't think he accepted any of that at all. He exhorted me to embrace "radical honesty" and that settled it as far as he was concerned. Evidently to suggest going slow is conservative dishonesty . . .

January 29, 1967

I have been thinking of this letter for a while, and so I am writing it. The immediate occasion: the discussion on woman in *Commonweal*. Not that I want to add anything to that . . . I don't know where to begin on that, so I'll keep quiet. Yet in a way the letter has oblique reference to the question because it happens that you, a woman, are for some reason a theologian I trust. Almost the only one. And I do think I need the help of a theologian. Do you think you could help me once in a while? I do not intend to be very demanding on your time, but I would like to feel that I can resort to you for suggestions and advice. Not so much for my work, as just to help me think. I have no great project in mind. I just need help in two areas where I have serious trouble and where I have simply been avoiding a confrontation. The Bible and the Church.

To begin with the Church: I have no problem about "leaving" or anything. My problem with "authority" is just the usual one and I can survive it. But the real Church. I am simply browned off with and afraid of Catholics. All Catholics, from Ottaviani to Du Bay, all down the damn line. There are a few Catholics I can stand with equanimity when I forget they are Catholics, and remember they are just my friends, like Dan Berrigan and Ed Rice and Sister Mary Luke and a lot of people like that. I love the monks but they might as well be in China. I love all the nice well-meaning people who go to Mass and want things to get better and so on, but I understand Zen Buddhists better than I do them and the Zens understand me better. But this is awful because where is the Church and where am I in the Church? You are a person who might have an idea of the Church that might help me and that I might trust. An idea of the Church in which projects and crusades (ancient or modern) or ideas (new or old) or policies or orthodoxies (old or new) don't stand in the way between people. Is the Church a community of people who love each other or a big dogfight where you do your religious business, seeking meanwhile your friends somewhere else?

Could you suggest something good on this? I haven't been reading Catholic stuff, books or magazines, for a long time (except recently Guardini on Pascal). I'd be perfectly content to forget I am a Catholic. I suppose that is bad faith, because meanwhile I continue in a monastery and a hermitage where I am content with life and the institution is supporting me in this . . .

As to the Bible, I read it in peace and fruitlessly, I suppose. I don't try to follow the new stuff about it because there is just too much. But I ought to. And since you have mentioned that a couple of times, I wish you would recommend something.

I know this is a pretty bad letter (guilt about saying all this). But I do wonder at times if the Church is real at all. I believe it, you know. But I wonder if I am nuts to do so. Am I part of a great big hoax? I don't explain myself as well as I would like to: there is a real sense of and confidence in an underlying reality, the presence of Christ in the world which I don't doubt for an instant. But is that presence where we are all saying it is? We are all pointing (in various directions) and my dreadful feeling is that we are all pointing wrong. Could you point someplace for me, maybe?

. . . I have to write a book on monasticism and I wonder if I can make it relevant—or make any sense with it at all. (I have no problem with my vocation.)

February 14, 1967

Many thanks for your very good letter. It was what I needed, a sign that someone was there and that my own struggle with the institution was not madness, *hubris* or something. I do see, as you do, how demonic it can be. Your ms. is fine on that. I agree with you all along about the hardening of the Church as institution and idol and its becoming against what it ought to be a sign of. If we and others see this problem—and it is pretty terrible—then there *is* something going on, anyway, and if there is smoke going up here and there that is something. I also think we will be a very scattered Church for a while. But as long as I know what direction seems to be the one to go in, I will gladly go in it.

So, in your book first of all: what you say about the Church as happening clicks perfectly. I really think what I really wanted to know most of all was that my own personal "sense" of when Church happens was not just self-deception—at least not purely so. Because if that is where God speaks and the Spirit acts, then I can be confident that God has not abandoned us. Not left us at the mercy of the princes of the Church.

What I don't know about is the Christology. I am not arguing about it. It is just that my coming into the Church was marked by a pretty strong and dazzled belief in the Christ of the Nicene Creed. One reason for this was a strong reaction against the fogginess and subjectivity and messed-upness of the ideas about Christ that I had met with up and down in various kinds of Protestantism. I was tired of a Christ who had evaporated. But that is not what is bugging me and I will see about it all if I get to reading Loisy. What does bother me theologically (I am not enough of a theologian to be really bothered by theological problems) is the sense that, when you go back into the history of the Church, you run into a bigger and bigger hole of unconscious bad faith, and at that point I get rather uneasy about our dictating to all the "other religions" that we are the one authentic outfit that has the real goods. I am not saying that I want to be able to mix Christianity and Buddhism in quantities to suit myself, however. Far from it. I think you got me wrong on that.

About monasticism, my vocation and all that. I made too much of a shorthand statement there. I always tend to assume that everyone knows I have had a monumental struggle with monasticism as it now is and still disagree violently with most of the party-line policies. I am a notorious maverick in the Order and my Abbot considers me a dangerous subject, always ready to run off with a woman or something, so I am under constant surveillance. If I am allowed to live in a hermitage it is theoretically because this will keep me more under wraps than otherwise. So when I say I "have no problem with my vocation," I just mean that I am not for the moment standing over the Abbot with a smoking gun in my hand. In other words I have the usual *agonia* with my vocation but now, after twenty-five years, I am in a position where I am practically laicized and de-institutionalized, and living like all the other old bats who live alone in the hills in this part of the country and I feel like a human being again. My hermit life is expressly a *lay* life. I never wear the habit except when at the monastery and I try to be as much on my own as I can and like the people around the country. Also I try as best I can to keep up valid and living contacts with my friends who are in the thick of things, and everyone knows where my real "community" is. I honestly believe that is the right place for me (woods, not Gethsemani) insofar as it is the right battleground. It is a sort of guerrilla-outpost type of thing if you like. But from my experience I would myself be leading a less honest and more faked life if I were back in the cities. This is no reflection on anyone else. In staying here I am not just being here for myself but for my friends, my Church, and all those I am one with. Also, if there is one thing I am sure of too, it is my need to fight out in my own heart whatever sort of fight for honesty I have to wage and for fidelity to God. I am not by any means turning my back on other people, I am as open as the situation (of overcontrol) permits and want to make this more open as time goes on. Lots of people would like me to get out and join them in this or that, but I just don't see that I could do it without getting into some absurd role and having to act a dumb part or justify some nonsense or other that I don't really believe in. I know I firmly disbelieve all the favorite clichés about monasticism, and the community knows it too. I can't say where and how my life is eschatological, because as far as I can see I am a tramp and not much else. But this kind of tramp is what I am supposed to be. This kind of place is where I am finally reduced to my nothingness and have to depend on God. Outside I would be much more able to depend on talk. Maybe I am just protesting too much, but that is the way I feel about it. I assure you that whatever else it is it is not complacency, because there is ample material for not being complacent, I assure you . . .

Dr. Ruether had written that she believed that monasticism from the very beginning had involved a misunderstanding of the Gospel. Because it confuses the world (the spirit of the principalities and powers) with God's good creation. It has meant withdrawal from the latter rather than a willingness to do battle with the former. Monasticism should see itself as a ministry, offering a temporary *opportunity for contemplation that will give people the strength to return to the real arena of salvation, which is the sphere of historical action.*

March 9, 1967

Thanks for the new letter, received this morning . . .

Shock? No, not that. But just a sort of dismay because I felt that your last letter—perhaps written hastily—was not in tune with what you had been saying, and after reading the article on "Community and Ministry" (which I liked very much), I felt that the letter was not in tune with this either . . .

Honestly, your view of monasticism is to me so abstract and so in a way arbitrary (though plenty of basis in texts can be found) that it is simply poles apart from the existential, concrete, human dimension which the problem has for us here. The thing that dismays me is the problem of groping around for a place to start talking about it all. Perhaps the best thing would be to start from my own personal motives. Let me put it this way: I am so far from being "an ascetic" that I am in many ways an anti-ascetic humanist, and one of the things in monasticism that has always meant most to me is that monastic life is in closer contact with God's good creation and is in many ways simpler, saner and more human than life in the supposedly comfortable, pleasurable world. One of the things I love about my life, and therefore one of the reasons why I would not change it for anything, is the fact that I live in the woods and according to a tempo of sun and moon and season in which it is naturally easy and possible to walk in God's light, so to speak, in and through his creation. That is why the narcissist bit in prayer and contemplation is no problem out here, because in fact I seldom have to fuss with any such thing as "recollecting myself" and all that rot. All you do is breathe, and look around. And wash dishes, type, etc. Or just listen to the birds. I say this in all frankness, realizing that I can be condemned for having it so much better than almost anybody. *That* is what I feel guilty about, I suppose, but certainly not that I have repudiated God's good creation. Sure, it is there in the cities too, but in such a strained, unnatural, tense shape . . . Absolutely the last thing in my own mind is the idea that the monk de-creates all that God has made. On the contrary, monks are, and I am, in my own mind, the remnant of desperate conservationists. You ought to know what hundreds of pine saplings I have planted, myself and with the novices, only to see them bulldozed by some ass a year later. In a word, to my mind the monk is one of those who not only saves the world in the theological sense but saves it literally, protecting it against the destructiveness of the rampaging city of greed, war, etc. And this loving care for natural creatures becomes, in some sense, a warrant of his theological mission and ministry as a man of contemplation. I refuse in practice to accept any theory or method of contemplation that simply divides soul against body, interior against exterior, and then tries to transcend itself by pushing creatures out into the dark. What dark? As soon as the split is made, the dark is abysmal in everything, and the only way to get back into the light is to be once again a normal human being who likes to smell the flowers and look at girls if they are around, and who likes the clouds, etc. On the other hand, the real purpose of asceticism is not cutting off one's relation to created things and other people, but normalizing and healing it. The contemplative life, in my way of thinking (with Greek Fathers, etc.), is simply the restoration of man, in Christ, to the state in which he was originally intended to live. Of course this presents problems, but I am in the line of the paradise tradition in monastic thought which is also part and parcel of the desert tradition, and is also eschatological because the monk here and now is supposed to be living the life of the new creation in which the right relation to all the rest of God's creatures is fully restored. Hence, Desert Father stories about tame lions and all that jazz.

You will say this is not theology. Well, let's look a little at the literature. Though it is easier to find statements that seem to be and in fact are radically negative about material creation, I would say one must not oversimplify. This business of saying, as you do, that the monk is in the same boat with the Manichaean but just refuses, out of a Christian instinct and good sense, to be logical about it, is I think wrong. About early monastic literature, two things have to be observed first of all:

1. There are several different traditional blocks of texts. The Syrian tend to be very negative, gnostic, Manichaean (exception made for Ephrem, who is utterly different). But note for instance the development in the ideas of Chrysostom, for example. Then there is the reaction of Basil and the Cappadocians (blending Syrian with Egyptian–Greek lines).

The Greek–Egyptian hermit school, Origenist and Evagrian, less negative than the Syrians, more balanced. Here in the *Life of Anthony*, a classic source if ever there was one, Athanasius goes to great pains to have Anthony say that all creation is very good and nothing is to be rejected, even the devils are good insofar as they are creatures, etc. etc.

The Coptic school, especially in the Pachomian texts, the most biblical of the bunch, quite Old Testament, in fact, and with an Old Testament respect for creation and God's blessing upon the creatures.

2. In the literature itself there are questions of literary form and other such matters that are very important. Stories are told and statements are made that push one idea to an extreme. The balance is restored in other stories that push the opposite idea to its extreme. Thus there are stories which prove that no one can possibly be saved unless he is a monk, and other stories in which the greatest monastic saints are told in vision to go downtown and visit some unlikely-looking lay person (married and all), who turns out to be a greater saint than he by just living an ordinary life. A restudy and rethinking of these sources will, I am sure, show that you are much too sweeping when you say that monasticism is simply a repudiation of the world in the sense of God's good creation. On the contrary, it is a repudiation—more often—of the world in the sense of a decadent imperial society in which the Church has become acclimatized to an atmosphere which is basically idolatrous. Now, all right, the history of monasticism does show that the monks themselves got "demonized" by being incorporated into the power structure and all that. This I have said myself and I agree with you. But also the reactions are much more important than you seem to realize. For instance, the very significant lay-hermit movement in the eleventh century—lay solitaries who were also itinerant preachers to the poor and to the outcasts who had no one to preach to them (since there was no preaching in the parishes or even in many cathedrals). These were forerunners not only of Franciscanism but also of Protestantism and pre-Protestant sects like the Waldensians, etc. You have probably run into some of this, but not connected it with the hermits.

Once this more existential view of the whole monastic situation becomes possible, then I think it is possible to agree with you that monasticism has "lost its soul" insofar as it has become committed to an ironbound institutionalism built on a perverse doctrine of authority-humility-obedience. The bind here is worse than anywhere else in the Church, insofar as the emphasis on perfect obedience as "the" monastic virtue (which of course it is not) puts the monk bound hand and foot in the power of his "prelate" (now no longer charismatic and chosen spiritual Father but his boss and feudal lord and maybe general in chief). Then when renunciation of the world is fitted into this context by being a prohibition of any sight or sound of anything outside the walls, and so on, plus a Jansenistic repudiation of all pleasure, then you do get a real monastic hell: I don't deny that at all, I have lived in one. But again, the answer is to start with saving the poor blighters that are caught in such a mess, and to save the beautiful life that has been turned into a hell for them, when it should be what it was first intended to be.

Terms in which I have been stating this have been deliberately "humanistic" in order to emphasize the fact that we are NOT simply refusing to have anything to do with God's good creation, and that the idea of "salvation from the world instead of salvation of the world" makes a nice slogan but it does not really apply at all to our case properly understood, only to the distortion. I agree of course that the distortion has been terribly widespread, and is.

. . . More in tune with this letter: an example of what I myself am doing in my "secularized" existence as hermit. I am not only leading a more "worldly" life (me and the rabbits), but am subtly infecting the monastery with worldly ideas. I still am requested to give one talk a week in community, and have covered things like Marxism and the idea of dialogue à la Garaudy, Hromadka and so on, and especially all kinds of literary material, Rilke for some time, and now for a long time a series of lectures on Faulkner and his theological import. This is precisely what I think a hermit ought to do for the community which has seen fit deliberately and consciously to afford him liberty. I have a liberty which can fruitfully serve my brothers, and by extension I think it indicates what might be the monk's role for the rest of the Church . . .

Sorry this was so long, but I hope I have been able to make clear that the only world I am trying to get saved from is that of the principalities and powers, who may or may not have computers and jet planes at their disposal, that too is another question . . .

In her letter of March 1967 Dr. Ruether wrote that a paradise tradition that gets confused with agrarian romanticism does not take seriously enough the principalities and the powers. Paradise is brought out of the wilderness, not by planting trees, but by struggling against the "dehumanizing forces in the city of man."

March 19, 1967

Thanks for your letter which came the other day during the visit of an old friend of mine, a tough-minded, irreligious, Karnap-trained journalist. He and I went into the monastic question very thoroughly, including the *politike arete* bit and all the rest. Because he knows me, and knew me when I was a communist (of sorts) and all that, he knows very well that I am not "hostile to *politike arete*." But he saw, as I do, the real trouble: my lack of ability to communicate what I mean and to say what really needs to be said, because I am out of touch—in other words, it is not at all a question of repudiating political life but of participating in a way that makes sense here. And I would add, what is coming through to me now in your letters is that we both seem to be accepting a naïve and unreal separation between "city" and "country" that no longer means anything in the modern world. It seems to me in your last letter you were just using the old dualism, turned inside out. As if I were living in a sixth-century virgin forest with wolves. This is not "sub-human nature" out here, it is farm country and farmers are people with the same crucial twentieth-century problems as everybody else. Also tree planting and reforestation are not simply sentimental gestures in a region that has been ravaged by the coal and lumber companies. If reforestation were merely symbolic, I doubt if it would have the importance it seems to have, for instance, in Mao's China.

And while we are on that, another thing. I wonder if you realize that you (at least from your letters) are a very academic, cerebral, abstract type. You talk about God's good creation, the goodness of the body, and all that, but I wonder if you have any realization at all of the fact that by working on the land a person is deeply and sensually involved with matter. I return to the point I made in my last letter and which you dismissed as romanticism. It is not romanticism at all, my friend. It is something you city people need, and need very badly indeed. And for all their gnosticism, monks (at least in the West, where manual work has been held in honor) have had this sensual contact with matter and have not in fact despised matter at all, except in theory (and except where they have been warped by their own theory). Hence I would say that in my life the cultivation and expansion of the senses, and sensual awareness of things and people, and sensual response, are probably a whole lot more important than they are in yours . . .

To return to the city-country dichotomy. In actual fact, is there anything you can do in the city more effectively than I can do in the country, to stop the war in Vietnam? Except perhaps march with a sign in front of the White House (which is something I too ought to be allowed to do). But in reality are we not reduced to pretty much the same gestures, with pretty much the same hope of achieving anything? My negative ideas about political life today are trying precisely to say that political action is too often rendered futile by the massive corruption and dishonesty and fakery which neutralize it everywhere. But I do not mean by that to say that political action is ineffective and hopeless: just that something else is needed. Same with technology: it is not evil, but it is not beyond all criticism either. If used cynically and opportunistically for power and wealth, it becomes a disastrous weapon *against* humanity, and is the instrument by which the demons crush and humiliate and destroy humanity. Witness the Vietnam war. Obviously it has to be made clear that the old negative Jansenistic pietism that just turns away from the machine and murmurs prayers to the Blessed Mother, or St. Joseph the Worker, or something, has to be shown up for what it is. But the problem of getting technology back into the power of man so that it may be used for man's own good is by all odds the great problem of the day . . . I think it should be the job of the monk to do this kind of iconoclastic criticism, and I sense that you do not want such a thing to be done because maybe you are not willing to see that aspect of technology . . .

You will be interested to hear that Vahanian stopped here the other day. He was on his way to the airport and we did not have much time, a couple of hours, early in the morning when he was still half asleep. I enjoyed meeting him and we talked mostly about Faulkner, on whom I am working now.

Going back to your letter, let me repeat once again:

1. It is not a matter of rejecting historical responsibility and of equating the activity of the principalities and powers with history itself. But it is in history precisely that we confront their actions because history is the struggle of the old and the new, the fallen and the redeemed, the principalities and powers against man snatched out of their hands by Christ and in Him. Hence the problem is not just one of false spirituality versus incarnation, but much more dangerously, of a false and demonic parody of creation and incarnation and redemption, a demonic parody of the Kingdom: and this is where a naïve optimism about technology is a source of great problems. True historical responsibility cannot coexist with a blindness on this crucial point.

2. Certainly the demons down here are small-time. But it is by confronting them that a monk has to open the way to his own kind of involvement in the big-time struggle, or, as Vahanian said the other day, to be effectively iconoclastic in the modern world. I am personally keenly aware that if I threw up the sponge down here and went out to engage in something ostensibly more effective, it would be a real betrayal not of abstract obligations but of the Kingdom, in which the monastic life, however marginal, retains its importance. In many ways I would prefer to simplify the question, take matters into my own hands, and get going. On the other hand I observe so many people in the monastic Order doing this and ending up in the most ridiculous futilities—far worse than the ones against which they are protesting. Maybe there is a kairos coming, but I have no notion where or when: I am in the most uncomfortable and unenviable position of waiting without any justification, without a convincing explanation, and without any assurance except that it seems to be what God wants of me and that this kind of desperation is what it means for me to be without idols—I hope. I don't expect anyone on earth to congratulate me for this, and as far as I am concerned, it is just damned stupid, but it seems to be what I have to do. But I do think, given a more favorable situation, the monastic life can play a very helpful part in the worldly struggle precisely because of the different perspective which it

has and should preserve. What is needed is for the doors to open and for people to get around more and learn a little.

P.S. I am sorry to add more, but I am doing it in the fear that you may have thought the earlier pages a little insolent. They were not intended to be so. I do dimly realize—if only from scattered reading—that the situation now must be one in which my own small concerns with monasticism may seem completely irrelevant. And I am not defending them. Because they are not just monastic concerns, they are human and universal. What makes it difficult to express this is the fact that, for instance, "being a hermit" seems to mean trying to be a very peculiar and special kind of artificial man, whereas for me what it means is being nothing but man, or nothing but a mere man reduced to his simple condition as man, that is to say as a non-monk even, a non-layman a non-categorized man a plain simple man: not as an ideal status or a condition of "striving for spiritual perfection," but a reduction to the bare condition of man as a starting point where everything has to begin: incomplete and insufficient in the sense of being outside social cadres. But then, entering into these in a free and tentative way, in an exploratory way, to establish new and simple relationships. As of one who is not a doctor, a banker, a politician or this or that but a "mere man." And this condition of mere humanity does not require solitude in the country, it can be and should be realized anywhere. This is just my way of doing it. What would seem to others to be the final step into total alienation seems to me to be the beginning of the resolution of all alienation and the preparation for a real return without masks and without defenses into the world, as mere man. Pardon the mystique, but I got this idea and thought I would share it. Your critical mind will chop it down to size, but I think there is something valid there.

March 24, 1967

I am really grateful for your last letter, the one that came in with the litanies today. And I am sorry for being such a creep, but it is true that you did make me feel very defensive. First of all, I guess I have not caught on to your approach "the traditional dichotomies . . . dynamic and existential." Don't give up: I'll try again and promise not to prove any more that living in the woods is not really abandoning the Church (which is probably what I really want to do, I guess). Maybe that is why I make such a fuss about justifying my position. I think you've helped me to cool off on that one.

Of course I agree with you perfectly: obviously the city is the place where things are really happening, and obviously, too, a certain distance and marginality is good for monasticism because the country is *not* city and the perspective is slightly different. I agree with you too about nostalgia, pastoral simplicity and all that. So don't give up on me, I will be objective.

What helped most somehow was the tone of the letter. Before, you were simply professional or something, and I am not a pro at anything except writing: I am no theologian, and lately I haven't even been reading about monasticism, or monastic literature at all. I suppose I will get around to that again one of these days, with new perspectives. Right now I am working on Faulkner, and also writing on Camus, and am, I suppose, again sneaking out the back door of the Church without telling myself that this is what I am doing. I don't feel guilty about this, though, and am conscious of it. Anyway, in this last letter you were talking more my own language (about being so bloody defensive, etc.) and I feel perfectly at home with it. Thanks also for the last sentence of the P.S. "I am as fleshy as you, baby . . ."* OK, I recognize an idiom I am accustomed to and am not scared any more. I promise I won't get up in the air again. I don't know why you frightened me so. ("Cerebral" probably because I resented my mother's intellectuality) (or what I later interpreted as that).

You are perhaps more right than I think about the "crisis," though I have the impression I am not in much more of a crisis than I have been for the last ten years or more. It is perfectly true that I need to get out of here and get around a bit, and I know it only too well. This is one of the most frustrating things about the complete irrationality of my Abbot, who will not and cannot even discuss such a thing with equanimity. Since I can't even communicate with him on the point and discuss it reasonably, and can't get anything out of higher Superiors either, it is a bit frustrating . . .

March 25, 1967

Yes, I realize that you are right about the crisis bit, because I am in one of those situations when so much is surfacing that I can't even read and I have to talk to someone. Since you have been the catalyst, I trust your patience. You will have to be my confessor for a while: will you please? I think you have already implicitly taken on the job anyway.

Back to your letters and my insults. My misinterpretation worked like this. First I recognized in you someone I could really, I thought, talk to at last. Second: I felt that you were putting me, as monk, in a category of people to whom you refused to talk. Image: she is saying she won't recognize me as a human being until I leave the monastery. Problem: unrecognized assumption of my own that I have to get out of here. Below that: recognition that life here is to some extent (not entirely) a lie and that I can no longer just say the community lies and I don't. With that: sense of being totally unable to do anything about it that is not a feeble gesture. But also a genuine realization that this *is* my vocation, but that I have not yet found the way of being really true to it. Rock bottom: I don't know what is down there. I just don't know.

Her comment on Merton's charge that she was too "cerebral."

Yes, the monastic life here is an idol.

Provisional solution: the people are not idols, they are real, they are my brothers though they are also for the most part idiots (my Karnap friend told me last week, without any opposition from me, "you live among idiots"). Solidarity for me begins here. Author's vanity: would like to be part of a really groovy worldly in-group and can't. Being out here is really in some way exile, humiliation, desperation. Yet also I love the place on another level, which I defended vociferously before. I do need contact with you all outside. All I have is a kind of blind faith that this will work out somehow. Political machinations and pressures are not something I am good at, so I don't see a way to break out and don't know how. Incidentally, one reason why the Abbot so easily consented in letting me be a hermit is that this gives him extra leverage: "Hermits *never* travel." (Which is pure crap: hermits are the most traveling of all Christians.)

All this outcry about freedom.

Refusal to grapple with the idea of monastic renewal because I see that too much is really involved, and that what is going on here now is superficial: what is really in question is the survival of the kind of thing we have here. They are trying to save it, or at least the general structure. I realize obscurely that it can't be saved, has to be entirely rebuilt from the bottom up . . .

. . . I think this should clear things up a bit. I am not mad at you for being an "intellectual woman" but only for seeming to reject me. I don't take to rejection, I tell you. I need and value your friendship and I will also on my part be more or less grown up about it and try to give you what I can in my turn, once I know what you want. And now I think I do. (Before, I got the impression you didn't want anything from me except that I shut up and admit you were right about something or other.) . . .

April 9, 1967

It is a Sunday evening and, because the community has its day of recollection, I have had the day off (no conference to give). Have thought a lot, and straight I think, and got in the sun, and am in my right mind, and have now reread your letter again: it is very dense and tight and solid. It is very good to have you coming right through and no need to be defensive and perplexed about it. Helps me to be straight too . . .

You are right about the alienation bit. I think that is my own problem. To be a hermit without insisting on being "alienated." As if I needed alienation as an excuse. It is a way of chickening out on the charism, that. I really think my problem is simply that of being a hermit and not making a fuss about it. Of being without support and not complaining. Whether or not it means leaving this particular institution is not the issue at the moment. I have left it, as far as the practical conduct of my life is concerned (apart from things like laundry and food: like being on relief, though). I think the thing is really that I must stand on my own feet for real, and work out the relation of my life with, for instance, yours on a much deeper and more mature level. Without institutional justification. Without being in the groovy group and so on (not calling your group groovy). And maintaining the friendships and contacts I have. Poets and so on. If later it turns out that it is still a sham, my being a hermit and staying here, then the solution will also show. Right now I just don't see that part of it. What has come clear is that for the last year I have been shilly-shallying around with the solitude part of it, without realizing that that was what I was up to . . .

I am at the moment terribly suspicious of all monastic "solutions." They all seem to me to be as phony or more phony than the status quo. If I seek another Church it must be another honest monastic group: and there is one, started by a former novice of mine, in Latin America. He wants me there, but it is impossible to do it legally and not the kairos for a revolutionary break. At least that is how it looks today.

. . . I don't think I am rationalizing or evading when I say I think I owe it to you to pursue my own way and stand on my own in this sort of marginal and lost position I have. I am sometimes terribly hit by its meaning which is something I just cannot explain, because it is something you are not supposed to explain and must get along without explaining.

May 5, 1967

Sorry for the long delay in answering this time. I have had publishers here and lawyers here and visiting firemen—if you think I live in utter isolation you are quite wrong. I wish I had a little more of it sometimes. But the letters have been held up. Someday I ought to try to see what it is like to be really out of communication and isolated. Just to see what it is like. Not as a permanent thing, because I don't think that is important. But in other words, a hermit today is not all that isolated, with letters, planes coming down this way, and so on. I think I am probably much more in communication with people all over the place, all over the world, than most active lifers are. So much for the treetop: but I don't deny the water sounds fine where you are . . .

. . . What I do absolutely agree with is the need to be free from a sort of denominational tag. Though I have one in theory (people still have me categorized in terms of *The Seven Storey Mtn*) I am really not any of the things they think, and I don't comfortably wear the label of monk either, because I am now convinced that the first way to be a decent monk is to be a non-monk and an anti-monk, as far as the "image" goes: but I am certainly quite definite about wanting to stay in the bushes (provided I can make some sort of noises that will reach my offbeat friends) . . .

May 30, 1967

. . . Yes, this is about two hundred miles from Cincinnati. If you are down there, it would not be hard to get here as there are good new roads (via Lexington). Would enjoy seeing you . . .

. . . I liked your Pentecost thing* and hope it went off well. Your David had a good idea in his balloon message. On Pentecost I went to Dan Walsh's ordination and concelebrated in my own stumbling way. After which I got stoned on champagne.

There is supposed to be an exhibition of some far-out drawings of mine in Washington and I told the man that if anyone was mad enough to buy one the money should go to your church. But I haven't heard a thing from him and don't know what is happening . . .

One really lovely thing you should see if you are down this way is the old Shaker place near Lexington. I think they have a guesthouse now and one can even stay there. One thing eschatology seems to have done for them: it was connected with marvelous work with their hands. That strikes me as something very real!

July 7, 1967

Thanks for your letter—and the more recent mimeographed letter too. I showed this to Fr. Abbot and asked if we could not contribute something, so here is a small check [for a needy family for whom Ruether had made an appeal]. It is not much but it is something. That kind of situation is just horrible, and people forget that there are millions of others that have had to cope with it. I don't know if any drawings have been sold. I am not sure whether the exhibit is still on. I haven't heard anything. It was supposed to be at 3723 S St, NW, a place called, of all things, the Fun House, which sounds strange. But it is run by a poet called Jahn Pauker and his wife, and the fun as far as I can understand is a matter only of the arts.

Let's keep thinking of the possibility of your stopping by here late in August, and maybe talking a bit. You ask about the hippies and from what I know of them the idea sounds good, attractive, and also pathetic. I can't judge because I haven't seen them and this is something one needs to *see* all right, and I guess touch, etc. One can't judge without being all wound up in that for a while. Thirty years ago my friends and I were to some extent doing that, though not so colorfully, and I guess we were as much beat as hip, but there was a sort of millennial feeling about it too: but we were not that much of a group, just four or five of us really, living in the woods upstate NY. Some kids in California, though, have written

---

* *Liturgy at St. Stephen's Church with balloons. Her son David wanted to see the release of the balloons as a kind of attack on the city.*

asking me to write for "an underground paper" they are starting. It sounds most innocent and as you say full of grace, but yet one does not get the feeling that they are very happy . . .

I will pass your letter on, the one about the Parks family, and I do hope you succeed in getting them out of the crisis and at least relatively comfortable. And fed, and clothed, and all that they need. I finally got a sink in my place so I don't have to wash dishes in a bucket on the floor—or in the rain bucket outside, but I still can't drink the water here, have to carry it up from the monastery.

July 17, 1967

. . . About your remarks on the poverty hang-up. Good intuitions and you raise some of the more urgent problems, the right Problematik. It is thorny. Yet I think all such problems are harder to grasp now because everything has become slippery. We no longer have one unified set of ideas we start from: everything that we hold on the basis of one set of assumptions is questionable in terms of various other sets which remain open possibilities. For instance: there is a Christian vocation to voluntary poverty—because the poor are the eschatological people. So you do what you can to choose this eschatological lot, and try to be real about it, knowing you won't entirely succeed. This presupposes a world in which "the poor are always with you." Suddenly a new eschatology shows up: it is possible to abolish poverty altogether. So then what do you do! Abolish it. But when we set about doing that we find that we make poverty worse for the really poor, more inexorable, more hopeless, more grinding, more desperate. So then we see that there is yet another eschatological perspective: destroy the wicked society that is so full of contradictions.

. . . So for my part, even though it is only a gesture and largely unreal (obviously I am not one of the hillbillies), I hang on in desperation to what I think I have been called to, trusting not in it but in the mercy of Christ, who knows better than I that it isn't real, but that it is at least a choice. And there don't seem to be more meaningful ones around, for me, all things considered. So when I cite pragmatic reasons I am really being prudent, and setting up what is a non-rationale, in order to avoid the institutional clichés, the monastery propaganda. I know, maybe I don't succeed.

In the monastery now there is a whole new dialogue game going on and they are trying to grapple with the poverty thing among other things. I don't see any way out for them, in this context. No matter which way they turn, they end up in nothing but games and gestures. I do agree with you that we have to start out with the very sobering realization that voluntary poverty in the context of our society cannot be anything but phony insofar as we are identified with the top layer of people anyway, like it or not . . .

August 4, 1967

. . . For my part I have suddenly got engrossed in a whole new line of study, a new approach (for me)—the anthropological one, the question of the clash between cultures (white and advanced with non-white and more or less primitive) which has produced all sorts of strange things by which people have tried to cope with the trauma. So I am involved in looking up eschatological cults in Africa, Melanesia, among American Indians and so on. Very revealing, I think . . .

I guess all anyone can do is try to make sense out of his life. As to the Gospel side of it: I have always told Protestants coming around here that in my opinion a monk did not become a monk until he had gone through Luther's experience, and knew that the monastic life was futile. To abandon the monastic life because it is futile is to seek justification by works . . . no? Luther continued as a monk, as you say, and I have just reviewed a book by F. Parpert in German on this idea and on evangelical monasticism. He says (and I agree) that perhaps the most contemplative monastic people in the world today are the nuclear physicists (to me that means Bohr and the Copenhagen group, who are my culture heroes).

One real problem for me keeps coming up. I get invited out of here to get in conferences of this or that for two or three days: something perfectly legitimate even in the books of some of the more conservative types in the Order. But my Abbot will not allow it under any circumstance even when it comes through channels. Like the Archbishop tried to get me out to meet with Card. Koenig in the East this summer (Card. K. can't come down here) but the Abbot blocks it anyway. He does not realize, I think, that his unconscious objective is to keep me out of sight and under wraps and in a way to shut me up. It is a form of silencing which he can resort to with what he thinks is a good conscience, and "for my own good," when in fact it does deprive me of contacts and information and perspective. I try to tell him how wrong he is but it does not get through. Ambivalent about it: on one hand it makes me mad, for after all who wants to be castrated? But on the other hand these meetings and conferences do not amount to much and one could get involved in an endless series of really stupid functions. In the end I don't know. I know how the SNCC people feel.

In her letter of August 9, 1967, Dr. Ruether wrote, among other things, that she was puzzled by Merton's relationship with his abbot. It sounded, she said, very destructive. Perhaps he should consider becoming a "free hermit," not attached to a monastery.

September 11, 1967

Long time since your last letter. I am very interested in the new books, especially the Gregory one and most of all in your course on the theology of social change. Keep me posted on that one! I have been having trouble, just mechanical trouble, with the works and system in getting the books I need for my own work. Library red tape, etc. But I am coming along. The picture is slowly filling in. The Cargo syndrome which people regard as confined to a few "savages" seems to be pretty universal. Throw out everything, all the "old" and all property, shell money, native clothes, etc. etc. Then wait for Cargo to come from land of dead (U.S.A.). Shake, quake, have visions, etc., while waiting. Cargo will come in form of complete magic technology that does everything for you and fills the huts with so many goodies you can no longer move. Whiteman's Jesus religion was bum steer because there was no Cargo. This one is the real stuff. In the end it tapers off into a kind of Melanesian secular city pitch, we have to work for it after all, let's try liberal politics. Meanwhile the guerrillas are getting wised up. And so on.

Very good bit in your letter about my situation here. It is very unhealthy. I have thought about the various angles and still am. My present move is to try to get transferred to Chile. There the situation would be much better, at least. For the rest I still agree with you, but I'd need to talk about it more and see it clearer in this concrete case.

It is a pity you were not able to get down, but as it happened, that weekend I got a virus infection and was in no state to converse intelligently with anyone about anything . . .

December 31, 1967

Ah, yes, I have become very wicked. This is due in great part to my hanging around with these women theologians. What a downfall. Let others be warned in time. Young priests can never be too careful. Tsk tsk.

About the drawings: what you say about our friend fully confirms the impressions that have been growing on me from one direction or other. I don't want to get in a sordid little struggle over it. But I do want the drawings to be in the hands of someone who is not looking at them through that particular color spectacles.

Why don't I do it this way: I make a gift of all the drawings of mine that are in the "Fun House" (inauspicious name from the start) to your parish. They now (if the parish accepts) belong to the parish and you all can do what you want with them: sell them any way convenient or hang them up: or give them away and what you absolutely don't want or can't be bothered with just send on to the Bellarmine College collection. (To the Dean, Fr. John Loftus.) As to the wording of the above, frame it any way you want, so that you can get the pictures loose from the man . . . The drawings are yours. Unfortunately I don't have an inventory of them, but there must be about twenty available still. But get whatever you can. As to the rest, I really don't care . . .

February 18, 1968

. . . I agree with you about the theologians and think you were smart not to accept [the presidency of the Catholic Theology Society]. You are now an image, and if you don't look out they'll use you to comfort them in all kinds of irrationalities. Every once in a while we have to do a little iconoclasm in our own back yard.

Well, not even the new Abbot [Dom Flavian Burns] is going to send me to Chile, but he will at least let me go to things that are normal for a monk to go to. I may have a chance to get to some fairly interesting meetings abroad. Or if the meetings are not interesting, maybe I can see some worthwhile people on the side. But I don't anticipate getting around much, and don't really care—at least not for the nonsense and ritual of conferences.

To Linda (Parsons) Sabbath

Linda Parsons Sabbath was born Miroslav Projak in Saskatchewan, Canada. She remembers her Ukrainian-born parents as communist atheists and anarchists who punished her if she associated with Christian children. In May 1963, in her thirties, she became a Roman Catholic. Her conversion followed upon a series of vivid and even violent ecstasies, experiences of joy and elation which she first interpreted as part of a manic-depressive psychosis, but which her colleague, Dr. Raymond Prince, insisted were religious experiences. Indeed, it was their desire to know more about the reality of the religious experience that prompted Dr. Prince, Linda, and another colleague at McGill University, Martha Crampton, to organize the R.M. Bucke Memorial Society. (See the letters to Raymond Prince.)

From her brother, who was a Trappist monk at Oka, Martha Crampton received a book called The Ascent to Truth. *Linda considered it the best book she had ever read about Buddhism by a Western writer. Had she known Merton was a monk and a priest, she would probably not have written, but she interpreted the letters O.C.S.O. (Order of Cistercians of the Strict Observance) after his name as some special American degree. She and Merton became correspondents and friends. Moved by his call to solitude, she purchased land near Lake Magog (in the vicinity of the Benedictine abbey St. Benoît du Lac) as a place where people of various religious traditions could go for quiet, prayer, and contemplation.*

Soon after Merton's death, she set up the Thomas Merton Retreat Center at Lake Magog. One of the visitors to the center was Peter Sabbath, who was led to Christian faith by Linda. They married, and Peter became, by Linda's wish, the director of the Merton Center. Several years ago, at the request of the Bishop of Montreal, the center was moved into the city of Montreal, though the Lake

Magog property is still available for private retreats. Peter and Linda Sabbath continue to direct the Merton Center in Montreal. Retreatants come from all over Canada and the United States.

April 25, 1965

It took your good letter quite some time to reach me, and in any case my replies are always somewhat delayed. So you will understand that this letter has not been very prompt.

Thanks for the information about the R. M. Bucke Memorial Society. I am afraid that I am not too much in contact with the people who study religious experience from the aspect you mention, though I recognize the necessity and interest of such a study. I am myself of course living the monastic life, and also very much interested in contemplative disciplines of other than Christian traditions, especially Zen and Sufism. I am in fact charged with keeping in touch with new developments in these fields for the magazine of our Order [*Collectanea Cisterciensia*].

In answering your request for information, I would have to distinguish those who do "research in mysticism" (studying it objectively) and those who seek to deepen their own contemplative experience or that of others (subjectively and intersubjectively). I am much more acquainted with the second field. However, as regards those who would be more on the borderline of research, besides obvious names like those of Erich Fromm, Karl Stern, Abraham Heschel, I might mention the following:

Rabbi Zalman Schachter, Dept. of Judaism, University of Manitoba

Don Gregorio Lemercier, Monasterio de la Resurrección, Cuernavaca, Mexico

Dom Godfrey Diekmann, St. John's Abbey, Collegeville, Minn.

Dom Aelred Graham, Portsmouth Priory, Rhode Island

Prof. Serge Bolshakoff, 16 Marston Street, Oxford, England

The Mountain Path (magazine), Sri Ramanasram PO., Tiruvannamalai, So. India

The Yoga Vedanta Forest Academy, Rishikesh, India (North India, address not really complete)

Bro. Antoninus, 217 Laurel Grove, Kentfield, Cal.

Don Divo Barsotti, Casa San Sergio, Firenze, Italy

Frithjof Schuon, Chemin de Rochette, 40, 1009 Pully, Switzerland

These are a few that I can think of at the moment. As to bibliographies, I will have to put that off for a while . . . For my own part I would be interested to hear further about your work. I can, if you like, mail you much of the material that I have mimeographed for use here in the novitiate. It may have some bearing on your research. I will always be glad to offer whatever small amount of help I can, but I am no scientist, I am afraid.

August 8, 1965

By now you are probably at Pendle Hill, or maybe you are on your way home again. In any case, I hope the experience was fruitful. I will send a piece I wrote recently on Zen, and would be interested in your comments.

. . . Under separate cover I send you the Zen piece and a couple of others that might be of interest.

Naturally your letter clarified the situation, and I will not hesitate to send you anything I can that will be of use to you. The only way to make any sense about the inner dimensions of religious experience is to discuss it in a framework of practice and experience. The language of science may make statements about all this, from the outside, but are such statements really relevant? Or do they simply provide certain guidelines that are useful in attempts to communicate with those who are not really interested in the real dimension?

But I am not questioning the need for an academic and technically approved approach. It has its place.

Linda wrote on August 11 that she had canceled her plans for the Pendle Hill retreat. Though she reported on the experiences of some of the McGill people who had gone, she also mentioned that acting on a suggestion of his in Seeds of Contemplation, *she had purchased land near the monastery of St. Benoît du Lac with the hope of bringing together for quiet and solitude people of various religious traditions.*

October 3, 1965

Now that I go to answer your letter I find that I have misplaced it, but I think most of the points are in my mind. But first of all thanks very much indeed for the two books. Of course I like [Thomas] Traherne very much; I have the *Centuries.* I will try to find a copy of an essay I did on the English mystics and send it along. I have asked someone to send more copies of the ones you asked for, and you ought to have them by now. The book by Fingarette looks particularly interesting. I am just getting into it and I can see that it will be stimulating and probably very helpful to me.

Hermes looks like a worthwhile magazine. I know the work of most of the people involved and they are mostly very fine scholars with a good grasp of mysticism. Corbin is especially good at a kind of gnostic awareness of the meaning of Sufism, I suppose you know his work on the creative imagination in Ibn al-Arabi. It is first-rate. I wrote directly to *Hermes,* asking about a subscription, but have not heard from them . . .

. . . I was especially interested in your account of [your friends' involvement in] the session at Pendle Hill. Who was the Roshi? Yasutani?

There is a good new book out with a lot of material by and on him. (*Three Pillars of Zen*, by P. Kapleau . . . Best recent book on Zen I have seen.) But from the way you speak of it, this session sounds a little irresponsible, if people are thinking of suicide. What occurs to me is that most Americans and especially intellectuals are hardly prepared to meet Zen head-on, and I think every American who wants to know something of Zen had better begin with a long study and meditation on the basic principles of Buddhism, the four "Noble" Truths and the skandhas. Otherwise Zen will be dangerous. This concerted rush for "attainment" under pressure will, I am convinced of it, give most Americans a completely pathological grasp of Zen, something quite the opposite of what it really is . . .

Anyway, I was very glad indeed to get your letter, and I am sure we can begin to have some very interesting and fruitful exchanges, now that I see what you are driving at. I am glad Dr. Prince is going to take up the regression idea again, but thinking back on my letter [to him], I realize that I was perhaps taking the concept of regression too crudely as a mere return to infantilism in a negative and unproductive way, an evasion. If it means simply backing away from reality, then I think that one can hardly call mystical experience simply a regression, except in some of its transitory and anguished phases. But doubtless regression here means something more complex than that. I have a letter from Dr. Prince about that which I must answer.

Meanwhile, you may be interested to hear about developments in my own life here. Since I last wrote to you I have obtained permission to live as a hermit in more or less complete solitude. I go to the monastery once a day for Mass and a meal, and I give one conference a week to the novices, otherwise I see no one. I am in the woods, on a hill, in a nice location with a good view, have a lot of time for meditation and prayer, but I also have manual work to do, keeping the place up, chopping wood, etc., and then I do some writing each day . . . I like the life enormously and I am convinced that this is one kind of answer to the question of how to approach the real fundamentals of the inner life. To begin with, though this is customarily regarded as a withdrawal, it is not that at all. I find the life much more real, much more in contact with actual concrete realities and facts, than life in the community, which is full of ideological baggage and all kinds of stylized and formalized activity. I also quite frankly think that life here in the woods is much more "normal" than the life most people live in the cities, all city propaganda to the contrary. Of course it is true that it can be lonely and that if one does not have the right disposition and vocation the life could be completely sterile. Actually I have found it so far immensely fruitful in every way.

The monastic Orders in the Catholic Church are in fact discovering that without this opening toward a more solitary life their own communal monasticism will remain to a great extent sterile, or just "busy." Did I send you an essay I did on the eremitical renewal? . . .

October 4, 1965

. . . [Concerning] the question you ask about Zen experience and grace. Here are a few thoughts.

First of all, I think that any attempt whatever to sincerely discover a genuine center of meaning for one's life, a center that in some way or other is seen as "superior" to one's empirical, everyday, inauthentic existence, must have something to do with grace. Any attempt that sincerely seeks the ground of our being and the ultimate purpose of existence in a "disinterested" manner (i.e., not as a form of self-affirmation that simply reinforces one's superficial egoism) seems to me to very probably have some relation to grace. Of course in this matter it is not possible to do anything but make conjectures in the concrete case . . .

In the case of Zen, though, it seems to me that the genuine Zen experience implies so much of humility, of selflessness, of self-emptying and renunciation, and the "void" seems to me to be so capable of being a masked fullness which might well be that of the Spirit . . . All these things make me think that some of the great Zen masters were certainly very holy men and perhaps mystics in a certain sense. (The Zen people often reject the term "mystic," because to them it still implies a subject-object relationship with God. I think that is not so.) . . .

October 31, 1965

. . . I like very much the article of Arasteh.* I have written a note on it for Collectanea, and would like to have his book on Rumi [Rumi, the Persian and the Sufi, 1965] for review. Where can I contact him? I think that as a matter of fact he is much more on target than Fingarette.

. . . Freud has a place in monastic life, why not? But not "orthodox Freudianism" of the static variety. We need to make our own adaptation of Freud to our own needs and see it in terms of the rich psychological insights of generations of monks. The literature of the Middle Ages and of the Patristic period has really been hardly touched. It is a mine of material, but of course it has to be made accessible, it is not our kind of thinking.

. . . I am delighted that you keep sending things. I have looked at the yoga book and like the part that is direct commentary on Patanjali: the only clear one I have ever read . . .

On Hilda Graef. She is like that, a very testy and fussy critic, the fault-finding sort. Consequently one can be critical of her, and there is

* "A Unitary Theory of Natural Experiences," R. M. Bucke Newsletter, second issue, September 1966.

no obligation whatever to agree with Hilda Graef, imprimatur or not. I usually do not. I think she lacks perspective, though she seems to be a good enough scholar . . .

December 1, 1965

. . . I know my friend Zalman Schachter is quite enthusiastic about [psychedelics]. I of course cannot judge, never having had anything to do with them. However, my impression is that they are probably not all they are cracked up to be. For one thing, most of the accounts I have read or otherwise heard about seem to add up to what the Zen people call *makyo*, or the illusions that one has to put up with patiently until he gets rid of them, and things not to be taken seriously. I think that systematically induced *makyo* is hardly a good substitute for a genuine interior life, even though the latter may require one to do a little work. Theologically I suspect that the trouble with psychedelics is that we want to have interior experiences entirely on our own terms. This introduces an element of constraint and makes the freedom of pure grace impossible. Hence, religiously, I would say their value was pretty low. However, regarded merely psychologically, I am sure they have considerable interest.

Reza Arasteh sent me his book and I have begun it. It is very good to have something on Rumi in English, especially from this particular approach. I will write to him and will send him a copy of my own book on Chuang Tzu. I told the publisher to send you a copy of this. Did you ever get it? . . .

On December 6, Linda commented enthusiastically about The Way of Chuang Tzu: *"A sort of synthesis of everything you have thought, felt, experienced. I wonder how this Chuang Tzu fellow ever got in there."*

December 17, 1965

I have about fifteen things of yours to report on, and probably will not manage to say anything about half of them yet, but I will begin with the best. Your report on the Zen retreat is simply classic.* I enjoyed it immensely. It is very well done and also gives a clearer idea of the work than any book I have read about it. Of course, it is a little closer to home. But really it was very funny and extremely accurate, as far as I can judge.

About *makyo*. I think frankly that your approach is almost purely psychological. At least that is the impression you give me. If all you are looking for is psychological integration, then *makyo*, OK, then maybe mescaline, God knows, I don't. There is certainly a stage of the game at

---

* Her report on a retreat at Bishop Donegan Retreat House, Tuxedo Park, New York, November 24–28, 1965.

which it is important to bring all these images out. Your dreams in the retreat report were interesting, by the way. But what I am trying to say is that when the development of the religious (and mystical) consciousness really gets going, all this *makyo*, visions, oceanic feelings, lights and music, rapture, etc. etc, is really irrelevant and can become an obstacle. Haven't you read St. John of the Cross?

As to my participating in conferences by proxy, sending papers to be read: I think there is no use in my even considering it. Hence I will say no now, with many thanks, and just put the whole thing away. After four months in the hermitage, I realize that it is necessary for me to really reorganize my whole life . . . I simply cannot carry on the nonsense of having a rather elaborate social self, professorial, guru-like, poetic, political, whatever you wish. Nuts to all of it. It simply does not fit. Reza Arasteh has some good points about this in his book on Rumi. So, if you don't mind, I must simply decline all such offers, which I would gladly accept if I were in other circumstances. When I was down in the monastery I had, and rightly, a quite different view of this. In my opinion, as long as I was in the monastery it would have been right and good for me not only to participate in these things by sending papers, but I should have gone myself. I think it was foolish that I was not able to do so. But up here in the woods matters are entirely different, and there is no reason whatever for me to be anything but what I am here. This unfortunately even makes it impossible for me to travel to a Zen retreat, though that is a different thing again. I would like to very much. But since it is impossible (could not get permission) there is no need to think about it.

I hope you have got my book on Chuang Tzu by now. That book is what *I mean*, these days. So too is this little bit on the koans, by the way. I wrote it for a magazine in Europe. It does not indicate that I sit here musing on koans day and night. I have another approach of my own, but it comes to somewhat the same in the end.

Psychosynthesis I have not yet touched. I will work through a bit of it quietly and see how I like it, and then let you know. I don't like just skipping over things and giving a rapid impression . . .

I wish you could polish up your piece on the Zen retreat and publish it somewhere, like *Harper's* . . . It would be tremendous. But of course there are so many people involved. I won't tempt you. A very unhermit-like idea, wasn't it? Best wishes for Christmas. Of course, you did get Chuang Tzu, now I remember. Stupid of me.

January 13, 1966

. . . When I say you are interested in psychology rather than religion I do not mean it in the way you took it. Certainly I don't mean that you are preferring the world view of Freud to the Catholic faith. But I do mean that, Catholic and all, you are apparently focused more on the subject experiencing this and that rather than on God—whether as the transobjective content of the faith (*fides quae creditur*) or as the invisible source of faith by which we believe (*fides qua creditur*). There is nothing wrong with being subjective, and there is a time for it. The point is, however, not to get bogged down in it and examine too minutely what "I feel" and why "I" feel it. Because, after all, it is all pretty accidental.

Hence about your experiences over Christmas: they are nothing to be afraid of and nothing to desire. I would simply live through them patiently and not make too much out of them . . . You say you fear becoming, so to speak, amoral. I wonder why? I mean that "why" in several ways, of course: not merely that one should shrug off the prospect of being amoral. Why do you think you might become so? . . .

I don't know how much guru I am going to be. I keep telling people that I resign from being guru and never was one in the first place. I don't make disciples. As to the writing, I will probably continue to do some, as it is not a bother in itself. Publishing and dealing with people about it may be a distraction, but the writing itself is rather a help. It keeps the head clear. One has to have something concrete and definite to do. I like chopping wood also.

The great basic thing is remaining united by love with God's will considered as the pure ground and root of everything (not objectified necessarily in some anthropomorphic way). Here faith is the one point of contact. It brings one into immediate contact. What could be more real than that, even though one "feels" nothing. The great thing is the purity and simplicity of our consent . . .

January 29, 1966

If this letter turns out to be hard to follow, I tell you in advance that I am having a bad fight with this typewriter and the typewriter seems to be winning. I am sorry about that because I could use a nice cooperative typewriter at this point, so that I can think what I am saying instead of how to get the keys from sticking and the ribbon from tying itself in knots.

First of all, your letter of the 24th actually made a lot of sense all of a sudden. Not that I agree with your diagnosis of yourself as psychotic. But I can see where you could easily have one fantastic time. Nevertheless I don't see that you have anything to be really upset about or to be scared of. I just think you will have to suffer and put up with some funny things that most people don't run into, and that it is a good thing you are a Catholic, because that ought to help you quite a bit in getting rid of self-hate and some of that other jazz, if you go about it right. I will certainly help you if I can with a letter now and again, but you can't expect much that way, I warn you. Probably you know it already.

First of all, the question of diagnosis is none of my business. But I just don't think that you can sweep it all away with the word "psychotic," and I think you are just kicking yourself in the pants when you say it, which would be a good thing not to do. I think that there might be some point in getting treatment but the thing looks to me to be pretty mixed up: like you could be a mystic and you could also be getting a lot of static and side effects that are partly mental (which is quite usual).

However, my job is that of a priest, and the help I can give you if any is spiritual. And simple.

First of all, in the eyes of God and the Church all that business about your past and your background is zero. It makes no difference whatever. I mean you have to stop thinking of yourself as somehow less good than other people. Who knows anything about who is good and who isn't? I do want you to tell me about the "amoral" feeling because that is a point where something can perhaps be done, and I don't mean making you "moral," I mean getting the thing straight.

Each paragraph seems to begin with "first of all." I should have counted up to two. So, in the "second" place, I would say you are perhaps unwise to be reading a lot of stuff about religious delusions, especially clinical literature. Don't you think you ought to lay off that at this point? You will just fabricate symptoms if you don't, I think. Let me talk more about that some other time: but the point is you have got yourself standing before seven or eight imaginary law courts, each one judging you for something different, and you are trying to figure out ways to get off seven hooks you aren't on. I admit it feels as if you were on them for keeps. You are not, I am sure. Your judgment of yourself as psychotic is another way of the various ways in which you are calling yourself an outcast. But you are not an outcast and you don't have to be one unless you want it yourself. OK, probably back in the dark somewhere there is a you that wants to be an outcast.

I hope you will tell me more about the whole story so I get it clearer. You became a Catholic when: last August just before going to the Zen retreat? I would say be careful of what you mix with what at this point. The Zen I think is quite OK if you have good men like Yasutani on the job. But for pity's sake be careful of quacks, now above all.

From the priestly viewpoint, I think you need to get solid in your faith and in your understanding of the ways in which Catholicism copes with this sort of thing. Obviously you can't depend on the average confessor and I would just be as brief and objective as possible, i.e., follow the book, in confession. Confess only what is absolutely and certainly a sin, and don't fuss around with conjectures. Also don't examine your conscience too much. You know what is really a sin, fully deliberate, that's all that you confess. And of course serious matter. And when one has had a lot of trouble in the past, serious matter is sometimes easy to get, but full consent is not what you assume, if you have been trying to get out of the ditch. If you do something you don't really want to do and really want not to do, it is not a sin, or not fully so. But that is just the moral theology, and that is not what you need unless you are having trouble with confessors, getting them up in the air with things that are only vague possibilities.

Therapy and religion: if you are seriously going into therapy and they say you should not go to church, then I would say follow instructions and don't go to church. But you have to be sure your therapist knows what he is doing, and I would honestly recommend a Catholic. I think Karl Stern would be sympathetic with anyone having something like an ecstasy. I think he would be very fair about it. I know him.

Finally, what I mean about consent: You are obviously not in a condition of constant will-lessness (abulia). You have a concrete situation to face and accept as positively and constructively as possible. That is just about all you have to do, but it may be hard work to do it consistently. The basic principle is that you must stop wasting time blaming yourself for things which can no longer be helped and probably could not be helped at the time either. And you must accept the results of the past: your karma, let's call it. And you must go on from where you are, and try to go only where you can realistically go. And if on top of it your machinery stops functioning properly, well, that is just part of the situation you have to accept and work with. Eventually you will come through and figure out why, etc. Or you will see in some way what it is about. If you can't see now, don't panic, you will later.

The concrete existential situation you are in here and now, whatever it is, contains for you God's will, reality. Your only job is to accept it as it is, because it is His will, and seek to fulfill it because it is the truth, not because it pleases you, gets you off a hook, or on a hook, or makes you feel safe, or whatever. But in order to do this you have to really believe deeply in God's love for you, and see that even the "evil" in your life can serve the purposes of His love, now that it is over and the effects have to be suffered. Honestly, I assure you that from what I know of you, you seem to be a privileged person to whom God will refuse nothing that you need. I repeat, you may have a great deal to suffer, but if you accept it realistically and without too much fear, with real trust in Him, it will do great things for you. But it may be quite painful and confusing . . .

This business of believing in God's love for you not as an abstraction but as a reality, as *the* reality, is very important. It does not conflict with Zen, as a matter of fact. Though of course the way it is formulated is in subject-object terms. Never mind, it is real. Use your Christian faith a bit. I am not explaining it, as I assume you know what I am talking about. If not, I can suggest books.

This is a dry and hurried sort of a letter, because I want to get as much work done in it as I can without fooling around. Please tell me some more, especially about moral and amoral, and then again why you think you are a "fraud." I know it is painful to talk about this, but tell me, and I assure you that you are not all these bad things. It is mostly in your head, and in the society we live in. And tell me more about the ecstasies. If we can smooth out some of the ambivalence about all this, it will help . . . Dear Linda, stop hurting yourself. Be at peace. Realize God's love and mercy and your own freedom . . .

February 2, 1966

I have only glanced at *Battle for the Mind* but will read it carefully later, as I think it may have impressed you—too much? Catholic conversions are generally not emotional, or not *that* emotional (as in the book!) . . .

February 12, 1966

I don't see any problem about "amoral." To begin with, you mean it more speculatively than practically. I see exactly what you mean about the business of taking a "strong stand" on injustices. From a certain point of view one must certainly not do as Eichmann did, for example. But on the other hand this business of lining up the good guys and the bad guys and deciding for the good . . . deciding that one is oneself "just" and making sure of it by openly condemning the unjust. This is in fact condemned everywhere in the Gospel, isn't it? What about St. Paul's doctrine about those who felt they were just because they kept the law and others didn't. It seems to me you are only living up to the New Testament. There is certainly evil in the world, but we know nothing about who is morally responsible for it except when we ourselves act against love and life, and against everything that promotes life and meaning. In point of fact, the attitude of the professionally "just" does in fact become quite unjust in practice.

Furthermore, the conventional *feelings* about what is good and what is bad are usually very misleading, and often morally inane. Respect life, truth, growth, meaning, in yourself and in others, and you are not amoral. I think you are just saying that you have ceased to be a legalist. For this there is nothing due but congratulations.

. . . Finally, about being united with God's will: I don't mean that you should specially formulate this in words frequently but rather just develop a habitual awareness and conviction that you are completely in His hands and His love is taking care of you in everything, that you need have no special worries about anything, past present or future, as long as you are sincerely trying to do what He seems to ask of you. And of course by that I mean simply what is called for by the obvious needs of the moment, duties of state, people you meet, events to cope with, sicknesses, mistakes, and so on. "When hungry eat, when tired sleep." It is basically the same attitude as the Zenists', and presupposes that one has been able to let go of useless preoccupations with oneself. And with too clear a concept of God, too, for that matter. We don't always have to cultivate the "I–Thou" stance that people make such a fuss about. When it comes in handy or is appropriate, OK.

Have you ever read Caussades's *Abandonment to Divine Providence?* At times it is a bit overlogical, but still it is a good book.

I would not be *thinking about* God's love, but just have a habitual awareness of this fact, that whether you think about it or not, everything will be taken care of, and hence what I really mean by it is not thinking about yourself and not trying to figure everything out. As to trying to think of something horrible so as not to be carried away with "low-grade ecstasy," why do *that?* Why not just take things as they come and don't try to change everything. Sooner or later your system will get tired of experiencing everything intensely and you will go into something else, perhaps much more negative, or just neutral. In any case, there is no point anticipating it, for that will only give you more temptations to figure everything out.

As I said before, direction by letter does not make much sense, and anyway, I don't have a stock of wise fatherly answers, besides which I don't really know you. But if these suggestions come anywhere near being useful, OK. If not, ignore them . . .

March 19, 1966

Sorry, it is just not possible for me to keep up, but if I thought there was something very important I had to tell you I would have written. On the contrary, the notes you wrote on the past experiences you had and the more recent ones all are very satisfactory. You have nothing to worry about, you are certainly not pathological . . . Your nature is getting a bit rocked, and there is not much you can do about it. Do not attach too much importance to any individual happening or reaction, and do not look for very special significances: all is part of a purification process, with which you must be patient. You have an ego which you obviously cannot get rid of by ego-willing, and the more you try the more you will be in a bind. You cannot scheme, you cannot figure, you cannot worm your way out of it. Only God can unlock the whole business from the inside, and when He does, then everything will be simple and plain. Obviously the human element complicates everything but what else are we? Human, that's all. Dying is no answer either, but of course it is attractive since it promises liberation from all the ego jazz, emotions, etc. But what are you now, except what you are then? Identify with the Ground and you won't worry too much about the weeds. The Ground doesn't. And the Ground can't be anything but Good. In Himself He plants His own seeds without you knowing or being able to do much about it. Just don't go cultivating weeds on purpose, with the idea that they are something very special, either specially good or specially bad.

About *Seasons of Celebration,* don't waste your time reading anything but the "Easter Essay," or perhaps "Good Samaritan." Most of it is not worth the bother.

. . . I am going to the hospital this week for a back operation . . . When I get back, if I get back in one piece, I will want to do a lot of sitting around and just "being." If I never write another line I couldn't care less. And if the guy's knife slips and takes my head off, I couldn't care less either. This is no virtue, just a weed. Actually, life and death do not matter much and they are not our business to determine. The only thing we have to do is to seek in every way not to place any obstacle in the way of God's will that comes up inscrutably out of the Ground of our lives (this does not mean being totally weedless either).

Thanks for praying for me, however, in December. At that time I was arguing with the peace-movement people because this kid [Roger La Porte] burned himself to death and I was saying that if things like that happened they were slightly off the beam. They were saying he was another Joan of Arc, etc., so what finally happened was that it was made clear, supposedly, that I had nothing official or active to do with the peace movement but that I offered benign and moral support from afar. It worked out peacefully, which is unusual sometimes among peace-movement people. Perhaps that was what you were praying about. Anyway I am never sore to have one say a Mass for me, I assure you of that. I have a deeper and deeper sense of the great importance of the Mass, as you too intimate in your letter. There is no question of it . . .

Always very glad to hear from you. Thanks for all the things you have sent. If you want more copies of anything of mine, just say the word. I think I'll send you this preface to the Japanese *Thoughts in Solitude*. This is an uncorrected and bad typescript, and I'd ask you to send it back please as I don't have others. I am going to work it over a bit later, I think. It needs to be simplified a bit . . .

April 7, 1966

Thanks for the three letters and the enclosures. I am still in the hospital, but getting out Saturday. I will be back in the monastery for Easter. Can go to hermitage in daytime anyway. I am sick of the noise in here. The operation was a great success, they say. And I have made a super-fast recovery, was back saying Mass on Palm Sunday. So I guess you are right: the scenario calls for a quiet death among concerned chipmunks, and I'd like it that way.

Here I get a great deal of tender love and care from student nurses, and the rest of the time lay around reading Meister Eckhart. The first week was a little rougher, though, because I could not read without pain.

You are right about the Japanese preface* and I see more and more

---

* Writing about the preface to the Japanese edition of Thoughts in Solitude, *Linda suggests that his writing is more real when he speaks to the Japanese.*

that I should only work with what comes from Mother Tao and forget the dragons. What do I care about dragons, anyway? . . .

April 26, 1966

Thank you for everything: peanuts, graphology, everything. You are a woman of infinite variety. I am getting along. Going today for X-rays. Will see how the back is. I need to get down to some work.

Here is a poem I wrote in the hospital. You will get the other recent things as a matter of course, but I rewrote the preface to *Thoughts in Solitude* on a deeper level.

When will you be down in this area? Tell me and I will see what can be done.

May 14, 1966

Not much point in longing for solitude, it is not something you get but something you have. It is you. What are you looking for? To see yourself as a happy object? It is a waste of time. Being solitary, I no longer give it a thought, because solitude is an illusion like everything else. The only ground is emptiness, which is love. And this is not something we generate under nice and favorable conditions. The conditions are unimportant. You know all this but I might as well say it.

I don't know if I can swing a permission for June 29 or not. Maybe I can figure out something. Let us say provisionally that I hope to see you Wed., June 29, and if on that day you have the brother at the gate call the Prior, and ask him to contact me, that might do it, but I can't promise success. If you are coming *anyway*, then do that . . . I'll write more later.

May 26, 1966

How are you? I hope you were not distressed at my kidding you about solitude. I am back in the hermitage completely now, sleeping and all. It is a big relief to get back, it is my natural habitat and that is what counts. All is not simple and easy in the solitary life, but the thing about it is that the trials make sense and one sees that one has to go through them and put up with them, and one tries to meet it all in a constructive sort of a way. So it is work to do.

. . . Anything I can send you? I have a Buddhist [Nhat Hanh] from Vietnam coming here Saturday, perhaps I can report on him a bit. He sounds more like a political type, however. Peace pitch, I guess . . .

June 18, 1966

. . . I am not going to try and be guru to you about solitary life. I understand your yearning for it, obviously. With a great deal of prayer, humility, willingness to be changed and transformed interiorly, to be quieted down, etc. etc., and to do all the rest that God asks of you as time goes on, you will doubtless prepare to meet His grace. What are you looking for me to do? Tell you you are not an eccentric? If you need someone to tell you that, you are not by any means ready for solitude. But if you get up in the air about my saying so, it will confirm my saying it. In other words, take it easy. Take what God gives and trust Him. He will do the rest.

"All is not easy and simple in the solitary life." This is no mysterious statement. It simply means what it says, and is quite clear to anyone who has ever read anything about it, or been involved in it. It is an unusual life in which one has to find out a great deal by trial and error and in which there are few really valid road maps because each vocation is different, each situation is different, each one has in himself his own devils to fight with. This is ABC. It is not meant to be a disquieting statement. It is like saying "It is likely to rain hard today, better take a raincoat."

Actually, I don't say my life is crawling with problems. I have far fewer real problems in the hermitage that are specifically hermitage problems than I had in the community. I would not change the life for anything. I am not going around singing alleluias about how beautiful it is, because by now I am used to it and don't especially want to talk about it. I am not going to write much at all about solitude because when I am living it that is enough, there is no point in watching myself live it. I turn my mind to something else when it comes to speaking out. It is simply the only life I am at all ready to live seriously and for keeps. The rest does not interest me for five seconds. I lay no claims at all to being a first-class hermit or a first-class anything else. But I know this silence and this aloneness in the woods is for me: that's the best I can say about it. As to being the one who is going to make the road maps: sorry. I guess if that is needed someone will come along and do it. In any case my own solitude is quite peculiar because I am a writer and hence there are modalities in it which are not those of an "ordinary" hermit vocation, if such a thing exists. No hermit is ordinary. We are all cracked in slightly different ways, that's all. The first thing is to accept ourselves as we are and God's grace as it is given (to learn to recognize this, one may need help, I guess), and then learn to live without too many exorbitant plans and projects for the future. To do this now is already a good preparation for the solitary life, I think. It constitutes a kind of desert existence that has a validity of its own . . .

Linda visited Merton at the monastery on June 29 and 30, 1966.

July 9, 1966

Thanks very much for your letter of the 4th, the *New Yorker* piece on Nhat Hanh . . . At the moment I have a sprained ankle. Stepped in a hole outside the hermitage . . .

All you say about sattvic food makes sense as it stands, but if I go into that I don't just want to dabble around. I would say that food has always been one of my big problems around here, because after a few years I became allergic to milk products. For a long time I did quite well on rice and eggs (and of course other vegetables). Now I am supposed to eat in the infirmary refectory, where they give me meat. But in fact none of the food they give there interests me at all. It is nothing but industrialized canned stuff, tasteless and even repugnant, and as a result I have been eating little, which is perhaps a good thing. In the hermitage my eating habits are terrible: I will eat cans of sardines and potato chips. I am convinced that food is very important in the life of meditation. On the other hand, unless someone is going to make a big project out of sending a lot of stuff down, or unless I can get in direct contact with some source of supply near here, there is no point in just adding a little yogurt to the sardines and potato chips. On the other hand, it would really be quite a major operation to get around to the point of being completely on these unusual foods. It would involve a great deal of work and even some politics with the authorities around here, and getting (more than ever) the reputation of being a crank and so on. I don't mind this of course, if it really leads somewhere, but if it is just a matter of filling the place up with satchels of herbs I can't cook, then I don't want to get involved . . .

. . . Enclosed article on Buddhists self-explanatory. I am writing up a little piece for the RMB *Newsletter* ["Who Is It That Has a Transcendent Experience?" later published in *Zen and the Birds of Appetite*] and will send it along when typed. I am glad you got something out of your visit here, and I enjoyed meeting you and having you here for a couple of days. Come back when you can and when it is easy and possible.

July 19, 1966

The way this letter is typed may not indicate that I am thriving on sattvic foods. I want to thank you for the two cartons of various good things, and report on my use of them so far. We divided them up, and the things that required cooking were turned over to the brother who cooks in the diet refectory where I am: the hope is that he will give us all these things and I will be able to say what I like and what I don't. I just don't want to get involved in a lot of cooking in the hermitage, it takes up valuable time that could be used sitting around looking at the birds.

In the hermitage I have the things that can be of most immediate use to me here, things like the various spreads for sandwiches, etc., the rose tea or whatever it is, and the dried bananas, the medicines and that . . .

I would say that at this point the things I can use best are the things that don't need to be cooked. Nut butters, easily made drinks, herb teas and so on. But don't go overboard on any of it, please, because I eat little in the hermitage and a very little bit goes a long way. What I mostly need is something simple for breakfast and I can't digest milk products (though goat's milk seems less of a bother) . . .

Many thanks for your kindness in sending all these things: I am really grateful and I think that I can work out some way of making very good use of these foods. There is no question that I need to be more rational about what I eat. We all do here. But it is very hard to convince anyone of the value of the kind of things you sent, they are all sold on the ordinary commercial products and don't care about anything else. I speak now of providing for the community . . .

July 28, 1966

The tea has arrived and is most welcome. To me, that is the best of gifts. I can't think of anything better than really good tea. It is just what I need. It is my supreme luxury and most prized material good. So thanks very much indeed. This batch ought to keep me going for several months. I have also tried some of the rosebud etc. tisane from the sattvic-food place. This tisane seems quite good and I think it helps me relax and sleep. Tried it for that last night and it seemed to work. Reason I had trouble sleeping was that the bursitis is quite bad and also the new bad disc is troublesome. Have to see the doctor in a day or so . . .

July 5, 1967

Thanks for your good letter. I am glad you appreciate *Mystics and Zen Masters,* and share your hope that it will help people really understand Zen. I find that the misunderstanding of Zen by thinkers like De Lubac and Teilhard de Chardin is more fateful than the wrong ideas of a few enthusiasts. I am glad too that the notes on consciousness have reached appreciative readers. I hope to continue, although perhaps not too regularly, but as best I can. It gets better all the time, the [R. M. Bucke Society] *Newsletter.* That is encouraging. The Twining [teas] arrived and I am most grateful. I enclose a couple of items that might be useful.

August 7, 1967

Have I yet thanked you for the *Surangama Sutra?* If not, I do now. It is a book of essential importance. Of course a great deal of it is the product of a certain cultural milieu, but the main idea is of crucial significance: namely, liberation of/from consciousness . . . Of all religions, Christianity is the one that least needs techniques, or least needs to depend on them. Nor is the overemphasis on sacraments necessary either: the great thing is faith. With a pure faith, our use of techniques, our understanding of the psyche and our use of the sacraments all become really meaningful. Without it, they are just routines.

Sorry that I don't have a chance to write much. It is impossible for me to keep up adequately with correspondence, but in any case I wanted to reciprocate your kindness with these few lines . . .

To Zalman Schachter

Rabbi Zalman Schachter, born in Poland in 1924, was raised in Vienna. In 1940–41 he was interned in a prison camp by the Vichy French government. In 1941 he came to the United States, entered the Lubavitch Yeshiva in Brooklyn, and was ordained a rabbi in 1947. At Boston University he received a Master of Arts in psychology in 1953. From 1956 to 1957 he taught in the Department of Religion at the University of Manitoba, Winnipeg, Canada. Eventually he was promoted to the Chair of the Department of Near Eastern and Judaic Studies. He did his doctoral studies at Hebrew Union College in Cincinnati, earning in 1968 a Doctorate of Letters. His interest in the mystical aspects of Judaism created an obvious affinity with Thomas Merton. Zalman visited Merton several times during his stay in Cincinnati. Merton's first letter was prompted by Zalman's book The First Step, *sent to Merton by way of Jerry Steinberg, a student at Hebrew Union who came to visit Gethsemani.*

January 18, 1961

It was a real pleasure to get your kind greetings for Christmas and the New Year and I was very happy, sometime later, to receive the books you sent. *The First Step* seems to me to be very practical and well done, and I especially like the work of Rabbi Nachman and his message of fervor and hope. Too often today the idea of "hope" is presented in a totally untheological and secular form, as a kind of pious optimism that "everything will be all right," presumably because it is just somehow the nature of things to be all right. But as we know, it is not exactly the nature of things to be all right, since man has a way of following his sinful will in strange directions, and causes have effects. In the dark night through which we travel it is good to hear the voices of those who have not forgotten the Holy and Merciful God Who seeks to save us from ruin, Whose heart is set upon us as upon what is most precious to Him in His creation. Your gifts were therefore most welcome and I shall continue reading them with great attention and profit. I am very much interested in the Hasidim and respond to their fervor very readily.

It was a really good idea on your part to suggest that Jerry Steinberg come down here. I am sure he enjoyed his visit and we enjoyed having him and his friend from the seminary. I hope that perhaps some kind of annual event can be arranged when a group from there comes down. Of course anyone is welcome at any time, in the guesthouse, but my own contacts are restricted, naturally. I hope that if you come down this way you will let us know and we could arrange to meet and have a little talk.

If there is anything of mine you would like to read, just let me know the title and I will gladly have a copy sent to you . . .

Easter, 1961

. . . Dom Fulgence [of Our Lady of the Prairies Abbey in Manitoba] says he will lend you *Exile Ends in Glory,* which is out of print. It is a very poor book, I warn you. Though she was a good soul. The convents of our Order in Japan are the best and most fervent today.

I have a couple of volumes of Buber. I intend to read him, and am sending you *The Wisdom of the Desert* and a mimeographed thing on prayer.

December 15, 1961

I don't apologize for not having written, as you understand perfectly. And you know that whether I write or not, it makes no difference to the profound union between us in the glory of Him in Whose service we are hidden. And the lights are lit one by one outside the door of our Church, week by week. And we plunge more into the cold and the darkness. I wish I knew more about doing T'shuvah [metanoia or penance]. It is the only thing that seems to make much sense in these days. And in the political dark I light small, frail lights about peace and hold them up in the whirlwind. Do you get the *Catholic Worker?* I have had several things in that, among the poor, the outcast: I mean the ones that Catholics look upon as their own variety of beatnik. There is a wonderful complacency about the *Catholic Worker:* "We gotta have these jerks around and let them express themselves, because it shows the rest of us that we are completely right." You know what I mean.

Anyway, we need to make straight the paths for the coming of the Consoler. And I think the Christian needs to wait with the longing and anguish of the Jew for the Messiah, not with our foregone-conclusion, accomplished-fact-that-justifies-all-our-nonsense attitude . . .

. . . Too bad about Brother J. [one of the few black novices at Gethsemani]. I'll see what can be done, it will be a matter of notes back and forth. You have to understand he is a chewed-up and tormented person here, as many of us are, some being considerably more placid about it, which perhaps does not help much . . .

What is important is that the Lord comes to ask our life from us and when He asks that everything we are involved in now is completely finished, washed up, cleaned out, it is no longer seen or heard or thought of. This life of ours should then be right in His hands all the time, not as ours but as His, a match flame we have entrusted to Him after having received it from Him in the first place. What is important is that He regards the flame as precious. Nothing else is of any account.

Zalman, can you tell me about or send me any good magazine articles against nuclear war, especially something by one of your rabbis or by you, someone who knows and sees. I am doing a collection of such articles for a paperback anthology to be put out by New Directions and have already some very fine material . . .

[*Cold War Letter 37*]

February 15, 1962

Many things: first I sent the books to Joe [Manella] at the kibbutz. I want to know a lot more about this kibbutz.

Then too we will be looking for you August 8th. There may possibly be a Jesuit friend of mine, a poet, Dan Berrigan, here around then. If there is, you will like him. He has contacts with a boy in Chicago [Karl Meyer] who may come down at the same time, and who went on the San Francisco–Moscow peace walk. When he got to Russia, he offered to stay there as a hostage for peace but they didn't want any hostage for peace.

Rabbi Schwarzschild wrote two good letters and sent some offprints of excellent things of his. I especially liked one on silence and prayer, and will be writing to him soon.

Guess what, I just got through reading *The Last of the Just*. I think it is a really great book. It has helped crystallize out a whole lot of things I am thinking about.

Chief of these is of course no news to anyone: that the Jews have been the great eschatological sign of the twentieth century. That everything comes to depend on people understanding this fact, not just reacting to it with a little appropriate feeling, but seeing the whole thing as a sign from God, *telling* us. Telling us what? Among other things, telling Christians that if they don't look out they are going to miss the boat or fall out of it, because the antinomy they have unconsciously and complacently supposed between the Jews and Christ is not even a very good figment of the imagination. The suffering Servant is One: Christ, Israel. There is one wedding and one wedding feast, not two or five or six. There is one bride. There is one mystery, and the mystery of Israel and of the Church is ultimately to be revealed as One. As one great scandal maybe to a lot of people on both sides who have better things to do than come to the wedding.

And of course it is in no sense a matter of shuttling back and forth institutionally. Each on our side we must prepare for the great eschatological feast on the mountains of Israel. I have sat on the porch of the hermitage and sung chapters and chapters of the Prophets in Latin out over the valley, and it is a hair-raising experience is all I can say.

Therefore I am not at all surprised that you like *The New Man*, the best parts of which are Old Testament parts.

When the Christians began to look at Christ as Prometheus . . . You see what I mean? Then they justified war, then they justified crusades, then they justified pogroms, then they justified Auschwitz, then they justified the bomb, then they justified the Last Judgment: the Christ of Michelangelo is Prometheus, I mean the Christ in the Sistine Chapel. He is whipping sinners with his great Greek muscles. "All right, if we can't make it to the wedding feast (and we are the ones who refused), we can blow up the joint and say it is the Last Judgment." Well, that's the way it is the Judgment, and that's the way men judge themselves, and that's the way the poor and the helpless and the maimed and the blind enter into the Kingdom: when the Prometheus types blow the door wide open for them.

Enough. More some other time. May we enter into the Kingdom and sit down with Abraham and Isaac and Jacob and the Holy One, Blessed be His Name, to Whom Abraham gave hospitality in the Three Strangers.

February 24, 1962

Could you send more of your Hasidic mimeographed texts? I promised some dear friends I would ask you to send them some and am giving some you gave me. If possible send them to: Jim Forest, *Catholic Worker*, in NY.

I especially love the selections from Rav Kirk. Where can I get the book *The Banner of Jerusalem* by Agus? Is it in print? Have you another copy of your selections from Rav Kirk?

When you go to NY you must go to see them at the *Catholic Worker*.

May 21, 1962

Glad you got *The Banner* . . . I think it is a very interesting and illuminating book. So too is *The Garden of Hassidism*, which I love.

This is not an adequate reply to your letters. Hope to write a decent one before August.

September 11, 1962

. . . I am sending you a ms. of Rabbi Gendler, whom you know. It reached me from the fellows at Santa Barbara [through Ping Ferry], and with whom he is in contact. I think it is really powerful and clear. Reb Tamaret was a true man of God, and speaks clearly without hesitation, telling the truth about our time. It is powerfully moving and true. Maybe you know this already, doubtless you do . . .

October 15, 1962

Wonderful note. And above all I am moved by the quotation—*Liqutey Torah Ahre*. Especially the little phrase about creation, because I am absorbed in reading various twelfth-century masters of the School of Chartres, who under an impulse from Platonism and Arabic philosophy opened up a wonderful vision of the world. I am sure they must have been in contact with Jewish sources of the time, too. What would some of these likely be?

. . . I think the opening of the Council sounded most hopeful. The Pope, that wonderful little guy, got all the diplomats in the Sistine Chapel and pointed to the Last Judgment of Michelangelo and said, "Well, fellows, what's it going to be?" This struck me as what a Pope ought to be saying. Also he lined up an unofficial meeting of a lot of Protestants and Catholics in a hotel. Ha. I hope it will continue to develop like that.

Some friends of mine are over there trying to push for them to recognize officially the right to conscientious objection. It is a right which exists, and which they are not being asked to create out of nothing. But they ought to say it is there.

January 11, 1963

Thanks for your wonderful Christmas card . . .

I forget exactly what you were saying—something about the feminine: but it seems to me that the heart of the mystery of Israel is hidden motherhood, and that is the key to the dialogue between Israel and the Church—an impossible dialogue perhaps as long as we are all too far from our own inner reality (we = not you and me, but our groups). The Church should be the revelation and fulfillment of the Motherhood in Israel. No Father is involved but God and this is the great scandal to a community in which the Father is everything. But no matter, Father or Mother, what is important is the Child.

I have Heschel's *Prophets*—it is magnificent . . .

August 3, 1963

For the last couple of days we have been having a fine visit with Werblowsky. He had many interesting things to say, and I am glad you sent him down. I am sure we all profited by having him with us.

. . . As to T.G.: . . . For reasons which I cannot explain, I cannot easily get in touch with him myself, but if you write tell him I think of him a lot and am very interested in anything he may be doing. . .

I don't think that having him in the choir here would have fully solved the problem or even essentially changed it. On the contrary, I think it would have aggravated it, because the choir is very rough on anyone who likes music. (So much bad singing, so much pushing by cantors, so much tension, etc. etc. It would have driven J. nuts.) I think it was too complex a problem, one with which we should certainly have done better, but we didn't. I don't think it would have been possible to make it work definitely. I think that Negro vocations will not work out here until we get ten or so together (not instantaneously, but roughly in the same bracket). And of course get someone they can talk to, not just hand them the usual clichés.

. . . Was talking to Werblowsky about Bahya Ibn Paquda, who is, I think, my favorite Jewish mystic. I really like him tremendously . . .

Christmas, 1963

Many thanks for *Tract on Ecstasy*. I will read and pass on to Gerald Heard. It looks interesting, and I hope to get to it soon. Just heard recently from Werblowsky—nothing from T.G. He has probably gone sour on the white race completely. And I wouldn't blame him—except that it is what one must try not to do!

Thanks for the "ikon." You sent two, but both are welcome. It is very warm and good . . .

February 1, 1964

Thanks for your good note. I am sorry to learn that some of the inevitable grit and grime of my spirit is trickling into your prayer life. But thanks anyway for the support. I suppose I am a bit more gritty than usual, but nothing exceptional. Just a great deal of work and struggling with small and futile tasks and interferences. For one thing I have not even had a chance to get to your rebbe's *Treatise on Ecstasy*, because I have had a string of books on interlibrary loan (and still do) and have to get them back at certain times . . .

I have been quite tired, mostly of just beating the air and not getting down to work that is serious and waits to be done. The back is still bad once in a while and interferes with sleep . . .

That is certainly one reason why I am going to have to tell N.N. not to come down. I have already too many visits lined up, and I can see that he for one is going to be exceptionally demanding. What is more, I cannot see that there is much I can do for him, except stand by patiently and once in a while send a word of encouragement—by mail. He is a very mixed-up guy and sounds sick to me. That is not a reason for brushing him off, but it is a reason why I can't be of much help to him. He is always complaining of Heschel, and does so in a way that sounds a bit paranoid.

What is new with you? You have probably heard, at Prairies, that the Order is still struggling to change a lot of things and I am a little doubtful as to the value of what they are trying to do, where I can understand what they are trying to do. But something has to be done and will be.

. . . Zwi Werblowsky has sent Bahya Ibn Paquda and a couple of good books by Vajda on medieval Jewish mysticism. This is right up my alley and very helpful. I like this material very much.

I send you a little thing on monastic prayer, and so plunge into Lent . . .

April 7, 1964

Many thanks for your Easter note and I have not forgotten the long good letter dictated in the car about the prayer of dread, etc. Actually, according to Abbot Ammonas, my latest discovery, the prayer of dread is prelude to the gift of the Holy Spirit, after a "last purification" in which one seems to be in hell. I am not exactly looking forward to that kind of thing, as the minor purifications I am getting are hot enough for me right now. The usual weights and pressures, work, weariness, confusion, avalanche of meaningless yet necessary duties, and on top of that one of the brethren with misguided zeal denouncing me in a visitation, etc. Just the ordinary run of life, and I know you have much more of it than I have, except perhaps for the censors. That I gather is not the greatest of your worries. Needless to say, it is the great bane of a Catholic writer.

I am glad *Breakthrough* [*to Peace*] is going along in Hebrew. That is great, and a real consolation . . .

. . . I don't know if I ever sent you "The Message to Poets." It was read in Mexico City to a big group. It might be interesting.

. . . Let us keep one another in our prayers and may the Lord watch over us, for without Him we are nothing, not even dust and not even smoke. In the light of that, the mere fact that we are "here" ought to be an encouragement but sometimes it isn't. The capacity to be distracted turns out to be a blessing.

In a book which may or may not be permitted I have quoted from a letter I wrote you, about *The Last of the Just*. I hope that is OK, you are not identified and there is nothing personal about it.

April 25, 1964

About May 24th–25th and 26th. You will certainly be welcome if you and your group wish to come. I can also fling wide the doors of the hermitage for you at least for two of those days. The only slight problem about that is that there is a lot of construction going on right next to my novitiate office and I have no other place to work, but the construction may be finished and if it isn't, I can just take the day off. Sunday at the hermitage will be OK for you as I don't usually get there on Sunday myself, though some of the kids like to go and sit on the porch. They can go into the woods. Let me know what comes of it. I would be glad to meet the group on one of the days you are here, but doubt if I would have much illumination to offer. So anyway you can count on the hermitage for the 24th and 25th if you want it. I might be needing it the Monday afternoon of the 25th, though.

That was very touching about Dom Fulgence and the cowl.*

* *Dom Fulgence gave Zalman a monk's habit with a cowl. Zalman said that he would wear it for the Day of Atonement.*

May 6, 1964

Just got back from the hospital to this madhouse, and the machines are roaring outside the window. So I hope this letter is fairly coherent. Nothing serious in the hospital, just getting the back checked again.

About my last letter: I had to clear the business about the house with Fr. Abbot, who was away. I am afraid we will have to change the signals on that one. Fr. Abbot said that he did not envisage that kind of use of the cottage and did not want to make a precedent. I can see his point, because obviously the consequences might be more than we could cope with. So I am afraid that I will have to take back my consent on letting you and your group make use of the Shangri-la [the hermitage]. I . . . should have checked with Fr. Abbot first. Perhaps in any case there was some difficulty in getting all to agree at your end and so it may be less of a nuisance than I fear. I hope everything works out all right. We ought someday to have facilities for this kind of thing here and I will push this with Fr. Abbot . . .

November 28, 1964

Thanks for the wonderful long letter and the note with it. I will try to reply decently and in detail when I get a chance. I am afraid I am still going to be a frustrated correspondent to a great extent, and more than before, as the plan is to restrict visits and letters more. But we can still consider at least a brief visit in March. That will be Lent. I don't know when Easter comes. Beginning of March ought to be OK. We'll see, I think I will have still a certain latitude for short visits of an hour or so, but I think the long three-day ones or even one-day ones are going to get cut back. There are various reasons for it all. Perhaps I will talk about it in the next letter, but it is not just a question of my getting sat on . . .

Meanwhile I am sending the stuff available at the moment. I do not have any more *Identity Crisis* papers under the hand at the moment, but we will have to run some more of them off . . .

I am left in a state of doubt and confusion by the [Vatican Council's] Third Session. I do not know yet exactly how the Jewish Chapter came out, but I assume it was not as bad as it might have been. Some of the other developments were most disquieting. Still, since I have always had rather generous reservations about the institutional capacity for renewal, I cannot get too anxious about the behavior of the great corporation, as if everything depended on that. But I have had my usual share of skirmishes with the corporate machinery, and am bruised.

Really I think that a silence and a going underground are perhaps my best bet at the moment. I have been too much involved in bickering and fussing, though it was good to say the things that were said, and get called names in consequence.

More later. I must get ready for class. Blessings, joy, peace, the martial movements of big groups are always funny even when terrible. The laughter of the Lord in the Psalms is usually directed at this kind of comedy. But terrible comedy nevertheless, for us. I was deeply moved at your reaction to the Freedom Songs. I like very much writing that kind of thing and maybe will do much more. Who knows? Meanwhile, back in the hole, with our faces in the dust . . .

To Bruno Paul Schlesinger

Bruno P. Schlesinger, born in Neunkirchen, Austria, in 1911, was educated at the University of Vienna (B.A., 1938) and at the University of Notre Dame (Ph.D., 1949). He began teaching at St. Mary's College, Indiana, in 1945. In 1957 he was made chairman of the program of Christian Culture and in 1968 became chairman of the Department of Humanistic Studies. The Christian Culture Program, a search for unity in the study of the liberal arts, was based on insights put forth by Christopher Dawson, who served as a consultant. The program offered "a study of the culture process itself, from its spiritual and theological roots, through its organic historical growth, to its cultural fruits."

Dr. Schlesinger, in seeking comments and evaluations by various educators and scholars of the Christian Culture Program, wrote to Thomas Merton on November 10, 1961.

[*Cold War Letter 8*]

December 13, 1961

I have taken a little time to get around to your letter of November 10th about the program for Christian Culture at St. Mary's. This is a very important question and I am afraid I will not entirely do justice to it, but at least I can set down a few thoughts that occur to me, and hope for the best.

First of all, the urgent need for Christian humanism. I stress the word "humanism," perhaps running the risk of creating wrong impressions. What is important is the fully Christian notion of man: a notion radically modified by the mystery of the Incarnation. This I think is the very heart of the matter. And therefore it seems to me that a program of Christian culture needs to be rooted in the biblical notion of man as the object of the divine mercy, of a special concern on the part of God, as the spouse of God, as, in some mysterious sense, an epiphany of the divine wisdom. Man in Christ. The New Adam, presupposing the Old Adam, presupposing the old paradise and the new paradise, the creation and the new creation.

At the present time man has ceased entirely to be seen as any of these. The whole Christian notion of man has turned inside out, instead of paradise we have Auschwitz. But note that the men who went into the ovens at Auschwitz were still the same elect race, the object of the divine predilection . . . These perspectives are shattering, and they are vital for Christian culture. For then in the study of Europe and European Christianity, Latin Christianity, we come up against a dialectic of fidelity and betrayal, understanding and blindness. That we have come to a certain kind of "end" of the development of Western Christianity is no accident, nor yet is it entirely the responsibility of Christian culture, for Christian culture has precisely saved all that could be saved. Yet was this enough? These are terrible problems and I am sure no one can answer. In a word, perhaps we might profitably run the risk, at least those who are thinking about the course behind the scenes, not just of assuming that Christian culture is a body of perfections to be salvaged but of asking where there was infidelity and imperfection. And yet at the same time stressing above all the value and the supreme importance of our Western Christian cultural heritage. For it is the survival of religion as an abstract formality without a humanist matrix, religion apart from man and almost in some sense apart from God Himself (God figuring only as a Lawgiver not as a Saviour), religion without any human epiphany in art, in work, in social forms: this is what is killing religion in our midst today, not the atheists. So that one who seeks God without culture and without humanism tends inevitably to promote a religion that is irreligious and even unconsciously atheistic.

It would seem that the a-cultural philistinism of our society were the preferred instrument of demonic forces to finally eviscerate all that is left of Christian humanism. I am thinking of an appalling item read in our refectory yesterday in which we were informed that at last religion was going to be put on the map in America by the "advertising industry" (sic). Here with a sublimely cynical complacency we were informed that now everybody would be urged in the most shallow, importunate, tasteless and meaningless ways, that they had to go to some church or synagogue or conventicle of some sect. Just get into the nearest damned conventicle as fast as your legs can carry you, brother, and get on your knees and *worship*; we don't give a hoot how you do it or why you do it, but you got to get in there and worship, brother, because the advertising industry says so and it is written right here on the napkin in the place where you eat your fallout lettuce sandwich. Sorry if I sound like a beatnik, but this is what is driving intelligent people as far from Christianity as they can travel. Hence, in one word, a pretended Christianity, without the human and cultural dimensions which *nature* herself has provided, in history, in social tradition, etc., our religion becomes a lunar landscape of meaningless gestures and observances. A false supernaturalism which theoretically admits that grace builds on nature and then proceeds to eliminate everything natural, there you have the result of forgetting our cultural and humanistic tradition.

To my mind it is very important that this experiment is being conducted in a Catholic women's college. This is to me a hopeful sign. I think
women are perhaps capable of salvaging something of humanity in our
world today. Certainly they have a better chance of grasping and understanding and preserving a sense of Christian culture. And of course I
think the wisdom of Sister Madeleva has a lot to do with the effectiveness
of this experiment and its future possibilities. The word "wisdom" is
another key word, I suspect. We are concerned not just with culture but
also with wisdom, above all.

Here I might mention someone who I think ought to be known and
consulted as a choragos for our music, and that is Clement of Alexandria.
In fact I think one might profitably concentrate a great deal of attention
on the Alexandrian school, not only the Christians, but all that extraordinary complex of trends, the Jewish and gnostic and neo-Platonist, Philo
above all, and then the Desert Fathers too, just outside. And Origen.
And the Palestinians who reacted against Alexandria, and the Antiochians.
Here we have a crucially important seedbed of future developments . . .

But the whole question of Christian culture is a matter of wisdom
more than of culture. For wisdom is the full epiphany of God the Logos,
or Tao, in man and the world of which man is a little exemplar. Wisdom
does not reveal herself until man is seen as microcosm, and the whole
world is seen in relation to the measure of man. It is this measure which
is essential to Christian culture, and whatever we say or read, it must
always be remembered. I could develop this more, but have no time. I
could refer you to a booklet that is being printed in a limited edition by
Victor Hammer on this. I will ask him if perhaps he would consent to
send the college a copy . . . The booklet is my Hagia Sophia, which might
or might not have something to say that could be relevant. I hope I don't
sound commercial, but probably do, alas.

. . . Mark Van Doren was here talking about liberal education recently. He would be a good man to consult. He stresses the point that
liberal education is that which frees an (adult) mind from the automatisms
and compulsions of a sensual outlook. Here again we rejoin the Alexan-
drians and Greeks. The purpose of a Christian humanism should be to
liberate man from the mere status of *animalis homo* (sarkikos) to at least
the level of *rationalis* (psuchicos) and better still spiritual, gnostic or
pneumatic.

But I have gone far enough for this time. If you have any questions,
reflections or criticisms, they might stimulate another outburst one of
these days . . .

[*Cold War Letter 34*]

February 10, 1962

It was kind of you to send me the remarkably good essay by Fr.
[Georges] Tavard ["The Scope of Christian Culture"]. I have read it with

considerable interest and will discuss it with the novices here. He is clear and positive and I think he says very much that can be helpful.

Certainly it is first of all important to realize that Christian culture poses a question, and constitutes a problem. Too often we start out with the assumption that all the answers are quite clear, and that we of course are the ones who know them. That everybody else is ignorant or malicious, and that all that is required is for everyone to listen to us and agree with us in everything from faith to table manners and taste in art. Then the world will be all right.

This attitude, as I feel, together with Fr. Tavard, is precisely the most fatal and the most absurd we can possibly take. It assumes that "Christendom" is as much a reality today as it was in the thirteenth century, or at any rate after the Council of Trent, and that Catholic culture is the culture of those who are obviously and aggressively Catholic in the American sense of the word. We have failed to see that, in that sense of the word, we have come to be living contradictions. The "Catholic" who is the aggressive specimen of a ghetto Catholic culture, limited, rigid, prejudiced, negative, is precisely a non-Catholic, at least in the cultural sense. Worse still, he may be anti-Catholic in the cultural sense and perhaps even, in some ways, religiously, without realizing it. Do you think that is too bold and too sweeping a statement? I know it would shock and hurt many, but still I think there is a lot of truth in it. And I think we obscurely realize it and this contributes no little to our guilt and aggressivity.

. . . In any case I think Fr. Tavard's analysis is very acute, especially as regards the "cosmic" demands for Catholicity. I agree too, of course, as anyone with eyes and ears must inevitably agree, that "Christendom" has ceased to exist and that we are *bel et bien* in the post-Christian era. Unless we realize this fact, we cannot possibly make sense out of our situation and its claims upon us. Nor is it reasonable to expect the troubles of the world to be settled all of a sudden by miraculous mass conversions to what, for better or for worse, we actually have now in the way of Christian life, culture, etc., on top of our faith. We just simply do not deserve this, nor would it be merciful of God to bring such a thing about . . .

At one point I would amplify and clarify what Fr. Tavard has said: where he discussed Marx. He does not make clear the inner spiritual potentialities hidden under the surface of the Marxian dialectic and the genuine pretensions of humanism that Marx himself expressed. The subordination of man to the technological process is not something that Marx accepts with unqualified satisfaction. On the contrary, it is, for him, the danger and the challenge of a technology based on profit. He thought that the ultimate challenge was for man to free himself of his machines and gain control over them, thus breaking the bonds of alienation and making himself the master of his history. The early essays of Marx recently published by Erich Fromm (Praeger) have some interesting possibilities in the way of the kind of dialogue Fr. Tavard suggests. For in these early essays, in which he concentrates on the problem of alienation, there is a very clear demand for the kind of dimension that can only be supplied by wisdom. Marx himself was uncertain and ambiguous in his treatment of this, but in any case he finds himself compelled to toy with the idea of a human nature on which to base his humanism. Now of course to what extent his latent existentialism destroyed or fulfilled this is a question for experts. But in recent discussions among the "revisionists" in those Iron Curtain countries where the strict dogmatism of the Marxians is questioned, points like this are always agonizingly close to the surface.

Hence I would offer this as a further contribution to the question: if there is to be a collaboration between the Christian humanist and the technological humanist, based on the latter's eventual realization of the need for wisdom, this is going to require as of now a living and radical dialogue between Christian thinkers of the West and revisionist Marxists in the East. How this is to be brought about, the Lord alone knows. It is, however, vitally important . . .

January 16, 1966

. . . Are people giving you trouble with your Christianity and culture program? I imagine that with this rather empty-headed mood we are now in, with some rather naïve ideas of change, you will be coming in for some snide cracks . . . Obviously we must change, but just as obviously all meaningful change implies continuity. There is all the difference in the world between real development, growth, and mere change of fashion. A program like yours is a guarantee that minds will be to some extent protected against pure superficiality and mindlessness. All that is needed is a wide-openness to what is really new in the new and what really points to significant development (and not to plain immersion in totalism). In this connection I find a great deal of interest in Rilke, whom I am currently studying. With all his contradictions and inadequacies, and with his great intuitive sense, he really lived his way into the depth of our conflict. He lacked a scientific outlook, and so his resolution of the conflict is not all-embracing. But he has his points. I think he is a very interesting person to consider in connection with the whole idea of the cultural crisis of the present. He is far enough away from us for us to see him with detachment, yet he is close enough and prophetic enough to be really relevant in many ways, provided one does not make a cult of him and remains conscious of his shortcomings and eccentricities . . .

October 16, 1967

. . . With all the noise that is being made on all sides about where we are supposed to be going, one tends to forget that people are not always willing to let others decide who they are and what they want—

they tend in the end to decide for themselves. So though there may be lots of people around declaring that no one is interested in Christian humanism, or in contemplation, or in something else, there will still be enough others to give them the lie. To me one of the most amusing things that has happened lately is this: the progressive and activist Catholics began hailing the Beatles as very hip people (which of course they are). Then all of a sudden the Beatles start going to a yogi to learn contemplation—which is anathema to the progressive etc. Catholics. Hm. My feeling is that our progressives don't know what they are talking about, in their declarations about modern man, the modern world, etc. Perhaps they are dealing with some private myth or other. That is their affair . . .

To Lawrence Shehan

Lawrence Shehan, born in Baltimore, Maryland, in 1898, studied for the priesthood at St. Mary's Seminary and at the North American College in Rome. Ordained in 1922, he was made Bishop of Bridgeport, Connecticut, in 1953 and Archbishop of Baltimore in 1961. He was looked upon as one of the "liberal" American bishops, which probably explains why Merton wrote the following letter to him. Archbishop Shehan, elevated to the rank of cardinal in 1965, was the American member of the first Synod of Bishops held in 1967.

June 7, 1965

I write this letter to you directly after Mass and thanksgiving on Whitmonday with the sincere hope that all that I am about to say comes from the heart of a loyal and concerned priest who, in a spirit of filial trust, addresses himself to an admired and respected Shepherd, on a question of momentous importance for the whole Church.

The subject is the Chapter on modern war in Schema 13, to be discussed at the final Council session this fall. Reports have been circulating about this Chapter. It would appear that some very significant revisions have been made in it, revisions which, in effect, would seem to contradict the clear principles laid down by Pope John in *Pacem in Terris* and Pope Paul in *Mense Maio*, and indeed the consistent teaching of the modern Popes.

My purpose at this point is not to raise or to discuss an extremely complex theological question, the morality of this or that kind of modern weapon. It is my opinion that if theologians and the Council focus on this particular problem at the present moment, the possibilities of discussion will not be fully adequate and the solution arrived at (if any) might be premature. Above all, I do not speak from a partisan viewpoint. My plea is uttered, I hope, in the spirit of Pope John. It is an expression of *pastoral* concern (even though I may be a cloistered monk). It is dictated by deep concern for the reputation of the Church in the eyes of all those who do not believe in the Gospel.

Here is what I believe ought to be done. I think that at all costs the Church must make clear her true mind: that she "views with deep sorrow the enormous stocks of armaments that have been and are still being made in more economically developed countries . . . This production is allegedly justified on the grounds that in present-day conditions peace cannot be preserved without an equal balance of armaments . . . Justice, right reason and humanity demand that the arms race should cease." These quotations are from *Pacem in Terris*.

It is not a question of condemning nuclear weapons or other weapons. It *is* a question of condemning resort to total and unlimited war, which is plainly immoral and un-Christian. It is not a question of splitting hairs over what certain military technicians claim to be "controllable" and "limitable" use of modern weapons. A certain Herman Kahn has recently proposed forty-four steps of escalation in which he claims that every step up to the forty-fourth exclusive is "controllable." But this escalation ladder is a travesty of moral as well as tactical judgment. If there are American bishops who listen with confidence to the kind of arguments proposed by Herman Kahn, and I believe that there are, they will (if their opinions are allowed to prevail in the Council) bring irreparable harm upon the Church in a scandal as absurd as it would be avoidable. It is this scandal, above all, that I would avoid.

For this reason I think it is most important that a member of the American hierarchy, without necessarily committing himself to any technical moral position on nuclear or other weapons, should make a strong intervention in the Council to (a) prevent any wording of the Chapter on modern war that could be interpreted as a blessing pronounced by the Church on modern methods of warfare and an encouragement of their use by the Church, with the implication that they could be normally considered instruments of justice and reason (in contradiction to *Pacem in Terris*); (b) reaffirm strongly the Church's conviction that "the fundamental principle on which our present peace depends must be replaced by another, which declares that the true and solid peace of nations consists not in equality of arms but in mutual trust alone. We believe that this can be brought to pass, and we consider that it is something which reason requires . . ." *Pacem in Terris*.

The reason why I suggest this so strongly is that if in Schema 13 the Council appears to issue a formal blessing on the modern methods of technological warfare as adopted in a ruthless and unprincipled power struggle between nations that are, in principle, materialistic, it will give the impression that the Church has abandoned trust in God and confidence in man's power, aided by divine grace, to correspond to God's peaceful and merciful plan, and has instead aligned herself, for pragmatic reasons, with a political bloc which appears to be more favorable to her interests.

This letter is dictated not by certain theoretical convictions in regard to the morality of modern weaponry, but by an urgent practical awareness of the fact that those who are so eager to see the Church give some approval to nuclear war, or at least not disapprove it, show by implication that they are convinced that the methods of total and brutal violence are in fact effective and practical in preserving peace and that they are, indeed, the most effective means of doing so. This is not a theological question (except insofar as it seems to imply a peculiar modality of "faith" which I obviously cannot discuss here), it is a practical one. One has only to cast an eye on the scene in Vietnam to see to what extent this type of thinking leads to an increase of violence which, as far as I can see, is having the effect of confirming the "enemy" in its adherence to communism and in opposition to our own methods of "persuasion."

In conclusion, while, ideally speaking, it seems to me that the Chapter on war in Schema 13 should *go beyond* Pope John and Pope Paul's statements, at least it should not fall short of them. If it does so, and if the American bishops seem to bring this about by a concerted use of their influence in the Council, I can only say that the resulting scandal would be of such dimensions that it should almost nullify all the good work that has been done so far.

I therefore suggest that Your Eminence personally should intervene to prevent this kind of impression being created, and should urge other American bishops to do the same. I repeat that I in no sense advocate a precise theological solution to the complex question of the morality of modern weapons. It is rather a matter of deploring the implicit trust in force as the most reasonable and effective means of preserving peace, which seems to be the basis of so many difficulties and failures, as well as the source of great potential dangers.

What is needed from the Council is not a green light for war hawks but a voice of hope and encouragement to all those who still strive to settle international problems by reasonable communication and negotiation, by respect for the force of law, and by sincere concern for the common good as arbitrated in supra-national tribunals, rather than by resort to force backed by a philosophy of "my nation right or wrong" . . .

To Paul Sih

Paul K. T. Sih, born in the vicinity of Shanghai in 1909, had little religious upbringing in his family, though he was influenced by his Buddhist grandmother and her devotion to Kuan Yin, the goddess of mercy. He received a degree of

LL.B. at Soochow University (Shanghai) in 1933 and a Ph.D. at the University of Rome, Italy, in 1935. He served in government posts for the Republic of China. In Rome he became a good friend of John C. H. Wu, ambassador to the Vatican. Dr. Wu proved to be one of a number of important influences that finally led Dr. Sih to become a Catholic.

In 1959 Dr. Sih joined the faculty of St. John's University, New York, as professor of history and director of the Center for Asian Studies. This is the position he held when he was in correspondence with Thomas Merton. His books include From Confucius to Christ *(1952), his autobiography;* Decision for China *(1959), a brief history of China with emphasis on the period from the communist takeover of the mainland in 1949; and English translations of Chinese classics.*

May 23, 1961

It has been a little while since I received your kind letter and later on the copy of the *Hsiao Ching*, for which I am deeply grateful. I have also heard from *Jubilee* and they are willing to have me review the two books. So I intend in due time to do an article on them. I enjoy the *Hsiao Ching* very much indeed. In its simplicity it has roots in the highest wisdom and one is surprised at the "modern" sound of some of its basic intuitions. I hope to study these two books carefully and am trying to write of them worthily. I hope I will myself grow in wisdom.

I would be perfectly glad to give you permission to quote the lines* you desire in connection with Dr. Wu's translation of the *Tao Te Ching*. I would just ask you as a favor to suppress four words, "which I so love," as it seems to me better if I do not obtrude too much of my own personality into the picture . . .

August 16, 1961

It is already a long time since your letter of July 26th and the arrival of the two books, which I was so happy to receive. I began your auto-biography [*From Confucius to Christ*], and then one of the novices needed a book of this type as a change so I lent it to him (he enjoyed it very much), while I myself proceeded with your *Decision for China*. The latter is clear and illuminating. I have not yet quite finished it but it is a very meaningful book to me . . .

It is a pity that John [Wu] is not coming after all, as he is now on his way to Formosa. He urges me to try my own hand at Chuang Tzu, and although I was scared to even think of it, I did a couple of short passages the other day and found they came out all right. At least I thought they did, but probably I have no real way of knowing. Of course it is just

* *The lines he wished to quote from Merton's statement on John Wu's book read: "It seems to me that it is certainly the best English translation of this great classic which I so love. I can think of no other better qualified to communicate its spirit than John Wu."*

a matter of putting together three or four translations and then following hunches, which is what John advised me to do, saying he would go over the finished product and make all the corrections. But it is hardly a work of scholarship, and honestly if *this* is going to be the procedure, I wonder if there is any point in your publishing the book.

Can you recommend any collection of basic ideograms? I feel I ought to know about two or three hundred, in order to orient myself in the original text . . .

I am so glad you can plan to come down this fall. I don't know if John would be able to come with you, since he has not come this summer. By that time we might have some material to talk about, anyway, if I make any more headway with the versions. My aunt from New Zealand is probably coming through here in October, and I am not yet sure of the date. Hence November would be better . . . Of course Father Abbot would surely want you to talk here, and John also if he comes.

. . . Meanwhile, I am so happy with your books. I feel it is essential to know as much as possible about the situation in China today. The future of the world is being decided in Asia. Of this there can be no doubt whatever.

I am sending you a couple of my own books, which you probably have not read. One of them, *The Behavior of Titans*, is composed mostly of parables and myths which you might enjoy. In any case they come to you as a pledge of sincere friendship . . .

October 24, 1961

Very many thanks for your good letter of a week ago. I am glad to hear you have returned safely from Formosa, and are back at work at St. John's. As for the Chuang Tzu suggestion, since both you and John agree, I must say I resign myself to it, and will attempt to do the work, in fact will enjoy it shamelessly: but it will certainly take time. We have here Matthews' Chinese–English dictionary but I cannot make head or tail of it. However, I plan to go through it and learn a hundred or so ideograms that may prove essential for this kind of text. I wish there was some sensible way of learning the 214 radicals but perhaps that doesn't make sense either without help from a Chinese . . .

. . . I am especially happy to hear the *Platform Scripture* is coming along and I want very much to write a preface. I have not yet asked permission but I think there ought to be no special difficulty as this is a particular situation. I will let you know, but meanwhile do please send the text as soon as convenient as I am anxious to read it . . .

January 2, 1962

Please forgive me for my very long silence. I hope that the sending of *The Wisdom of the Desert* as soon as you referred to it was, temporarily, a sufficient sign of life and of friendship.

. . . John Wu says he wants to come down some time in the spring. As I say, you should feel free to arrange to come down with him, or come at some other time that would be more convenient for you . . . I don't remember if I suggested that as a feasible time when I last wrote to John . . .

Jubilee has said nothing whatever about publishing the article I sent them on the two Classics, the Lao Tzu and the *Filial Piety Classic*. I do not really know whether they have given up the idea or what . . .

I will look forward to receiving the Zen Sutra one of these days. I am in a mood for some Zen, with the complications of Christmas, cold war, and the Lord knows what behind me. There are times when one has to cut right through all the knots, and the Zen view of things is a good clean blade.

January 28, 1962

After much delay I have finally got the copy of the article on the two Chinese Classics back from *Jubilee*, and I am sending it right along to you. It is all ready for publication in the *New Scholasticism* or any other magazine you see fit. Of course you must feel free to make changes and corrections as I am no scholar in this field . . .

. . . With very best wishes to you and also to John Wu, whose Christmas letter I much enjoyed. I will reply to him when I get a chance.

Paul Sih visited Merton at Gethsemani on March 8, 1962.

May 9, 1962

Your letter of the 3rd reached me this morning. Thank you very much for it. The Wang Yang Ming has *not* reached me, however. I do not want to miss it. I hope it was not lost.

Above all I am happy about Zen scripture. I look forward to seeing it, and pray that I may be worthy to write a suitable introduction. I see more and more the awful complexity of the Western mind, which is my mind also, for better or for worse. I have been meditating here and there on Buddhist classics, in a small way, and find there an admirable therapy and simplification, wonderfully adapted to clear the way for grace, provided one does not become obsessed with a pride in one's own skill in meditating (not necessarily an urgent danger for me) or one's interior purity (still less, I am afraid). If Buddhism is humble, then it can be wonderfully, admirably humble and can offer for the humility of Christ a beautiful and appropriate dwelling.

In a word, I look forward to seeing the Zen Classic, and perhaps the Lord is just waiting for me to be simple enough to receive it.

Above all I appreciate your brotherly generosity in procuring for me the magnificent set of Legge [James Legge, *Chinese Classics*, 8 vols.] which is on its way from Taiwan. This I certainly look forward to with keen anticipation, and I will make room for plenty of time in which to study it. This is a wonderful gift, I can think of few that have been greater or more significant to me . . .

. . . I got a very entertaining letter from John Wu lately, which I will answer when I can. Meanwhile I want to get this off to you, with a copy of a prayer of mine which was read in Congress. By the way, I was glad to be able to write a different ending for the version of the article in the *Catholic World,* but sorry that in their introductory note they insisted on calling the *Tao Te Ching* a book of Confucian ethics.

With best wishes to you always and all blessings for your work at the institute.

June 28, 1962

John Wu left us the other day after a most pleasant visit. It was really good to see him face to face and talk with him at leisure, or more or less at leisure. He will have told you already of his visit, I suppose. It was a grace for me.

Yes, I have received Wang Yang Ming and I find him very interesting. The combination of Confucianism with, as John points out, a latent Buddhism has considerable possibilities, it would seem.

. . . As I told John I do not think I am ready to write a whole book on Zen. I do not yet have the capacity, and I must study much more. Also meditate much more. I do not know, either, whether a scholarly attempt is what is required of me now, or any other time, on this subject. It seems others might do a better job in that line . . .

Finally, the big volumes of the Classics have arrived and I am most pleased with them. They are a wonderful and treasured acquisition . . .

August 24, 1962

It is a long time since I received the remarkably interesting translation of the *Platform Scripture* and I ought to have acknowledged it long ago. The translation and the introduction by Wing Tsit Chan are both extremely interesting. It is an invaluable document, and will mean much to everyone who is interested in Zen Buddhism. I have not written about it, as I wanted time to comment fully. I have not had time for that yet, and also I would like to keep the manuscript a little longer and go over it again. I expect to be in the hospital for a checkup in a few days and I will meditate on the text there, I hope. In any case it will get a second and more serious reading.

. . . Keep me posted with regard to all your interesting projects at the Institute for Asian Studies. Fr. Dan Berrigan brought me messages from Fr. Beer and John Wu. I was glad to hear from them. The Chinese books are there but . . . I think that perhaps I will have to put off serious work in this field until I am replaced as novice master by somebody else and can devote more time to study . . .

October 16, 1962

The usual complaint of those who have too many occupations: I did not have time to get to your letter yet. But I am doing so finally. I am certainly very glad you liked the *Jubilee* article [September 1962]. I enjoyed writing it.

It is just not possible, though, for me to tackle the problem of sterilization and abortion for the *Redman* [St. John's University alumni magazine]. That takes professional handling, and I am completely incompetent. I have no real grasp of the complexities of the thing, and it would be disastrous simply to grind out a repetition of the hackneyed responses that are usually given. Respect for the depths of human tragedy compel me not to approach such a subject without being fully qualified to treat it.

I hope to send you a copy of the new *Reader*, a collection of my work that is just out. I think you will like it, and perhaps they would want to review it in *Redman* . . .

And so, I send you all my best wishes, hope you are well and flourishing, and wish I could get back to Chinese studies . . .

But the Lord holds all our affairs in the grasp of His loving peace, and we need not be too concerned.

June 26, 1963

I deeply appreciated your letter of April 9th, though I did not get around to answering it. The Temple Hill poem [by Chang Chien, a Chinese poet] was very attractive. I have written a brief review of the *Platform Scripture* for the Boston *Pilot*. I haven't heard anything from Ed Rice, and from the way he dallied with the review of the other two texts, finally not publishing them, I think there would be small hope of his taking a review article of this. Perhaps I am wrong.

In any case I think it is a most handsome book, and I compliment you on it. I wish I had been able to do at least enough work on Chinese to take advantage of the Chinese text with translation. Unfortunately it is just not possible for me, with my heavy schedule, to advance with Chinese. Perhaps if I get out of the job of novice master it may become possible . . .

August 18, 1963

I have been waiting to find out exactly what was going to be done with that review I wrote of the *Platform Scripture*. It still does not appear to have been printed in the *Pilot*. Maybe the editor thought it was too far-out for a Catholic diocesan paper. I have written to inquire and if they have not printed it, I want it back to send to *Jubilee*. I will let you know.

It would be great to do a small book for you on Zen, but whichever way I look at it now, the project is just impossible. The main reason for this is that I have been in a great tangle . . . which has resulted from my inadvertently violating a contract by offering a book to another publisher [Macmillan] without the proper clearance. This has caused untold trouble, and at the moment I do not think it would be wise in any way for me to propose doing a book for you or for any other publisher, at least until I have worked out my contract with them. Besides, I have really been spreading my work out all over the place too much, and it is necessary at the present moment to get back within certain limits. So therefore I simply must avoid branching out again . . .

This does not mean that you could not come down without this pretext. We do not need to be working on a book for you to visit here. September however is almost all taken up by the Louisville priests on retreat, but the rest of the fall, after the first week of October, is free as far as I know now. Do not hesitate to take a trip down if you feel like a couple days of peace in the monastery! You will always be most welcome.

October 2, 1963

Please forgive my failure to answer your letter sooner. I have been in the hospital, and am still not able to type effectively.

If you should be here over the Thanksgiving weekend, I would be happy to see you and perhaps you could participate in a discussion on mysticism with some Baptists.

I have not done much with Chuang Tzu but I might have a few pieces to discuss by then.

How is John Wu? I have not heard from him for a long time.

The review appeared in the *Pilot* after all. Did they send you a copy?

November 11, 1964

It was fine to hear from you again. I am glad that the [Asian] Center [at St. John's University] has developed and that so much good work is coming out of it. I am really delighted to have the essay of Dr. Chang and I will read it with great interest. The edition of the *Transmission of the Lamp* is important . . .

. . . You may certainly transmit the article on "Mystics and Zen Masters" to the *Chinese Culture Quarterly*, but first I must make a few slight changes. I will send you another copy when I have done this.

May I please have John Wu's address? I have not heard from him for a long time. Perhaps a letter went astray somewhere. Is he now in Taiwan? I suppose he must be very busy, but I hope he has not forgotten his old friends on this side of the world.

[Probably November 1964]

Here is the revised text of "Mystics and Zen Masters." As you see, it has been published in a little-known magazine. I don't suppose that will make any difference to *The Chinese Culture Quarterly*. So it is theirs if they will have it. Again many thanks in Christ.

April 23, 1965

It was a pleasure to get your letter. I had been thinking of you lately. Thanks also for the check [honorarium from *The Chinese Culture Quarterly* for publishing "Mystics and Zen Masters"], and I will anticipate reception of the *Quarterly* in due course.

The news of your book is interesting and auspicious. It is true that I am quite busy, but I would certainly be interested in what you have to say. So if you are not in too much of a hurry for a reaction on my part, do not hesitate to send the ms. As to an introduction, let me leave that open for the time being. Rather than bind myself by a promise, when I already have so many commitments, let me just say that I will keep the possibility in mind, and that it will depend on how I am able to negotiate the other jobs I have on hand at the moment. I am afraid I am quite crowded, but we shall see.

Spring seems to have come down here, and everything is opening up. The birds sing and the trees blossom. One would want to have the talent of a Tu Fu to praise it all. How are the publications of the Center of Asian Studies coming along? Anything new? I think John told me you might be doing his translations of Chinese poets . . .

May 27, 1967

It is so good to hear from you again. I often think about you and your work at the Center there. I haven't seen any books from there recently so I am happy to hear that Mencius is on the way. I want to get back into reading Chinese philosophy anyhow.

I am glad too that the *Legacy of Confucius* is on the horizon. The essay of mine on "Classic Chinese Thought" has now appeared in the book, however. I am perfectly willing for you to have it if you like, but it will be nothing more than a reprint. Evidently you have not seen the book *Mystics and Zen Masters*, though I thought a copy had been sent by the publisher. I will see that you get one. As I say, if you still want to use the essay, that is perfectly all right with me.

Recently I heard from John Wu, Jr., but not from John Sr. I must write to him. I wish he could get a publisher for his book on Zen [*The Golden Age of Zen*] . . .

July 18, 1967

Many thanks for the book on Mencius, in fact thanks for two copies. I was glad to get the extra one, and passed it on to our library. If I get a chance I may review it briefly for the magazine of our Order.

I was happy to hear of John Wu's engagement. I know he easily gets lonely and I hope the new marriage will bring him companionship and joy—I am also glad to learn he will be back in this country. Really, I agree that the new marriage is probably what he needs to get him working again with greater enthusiasm. Did his book on Zen ever get into print? I hope it will, because it is very worthwhile.

To Carleton Smith

Carleton Smith, art authority and foundation executive, was born in Bement, Illinois, in 1910. He studied at the Universities of Illinois (B.S.), Maryland (M.A.), and Chicago. His career has been most varied. He served as music editor for Esquire, *critic and columnist for* Coronet, *European correspondent for the New York* Herald Tribune, *and recorder of folk songs in many different countries. He is founder and chairman of two private corporations, the National Arts Foundation of New York and the International Awards Foundation. He has for many years been a close friend of Cardinal Koenig, Archbishop of Vienna, who often visits him and who has confirmed his three children. It was a visit of the Cardinal to the United States, as head of the Secretariat for Non-Believers, that occasioned two visits of Carleton Smith to Gethsemani as well as the correspondence with Merton.*

April 9, 1967

In regard to the visit of Cardinal Koenig to this country as head of the Secretariat for Non-Believers. I will resume the remarks I made the other day, as far as I remember them, and add a few new suggestions.

The dialogue with non-believers will be something quite different in this country from what it is in Eastern Europe. To begin with, this country still claims officially to be religious, and to be classified as a "believer" is at least respectable. Organized atheism is negligible here. What we do have in fact is a great deal of indifference to religion. The whole question of God is taken to be irrelevant. Behind the atheism of the Marxists one may perhaps say that there is still a nineteenth-century scientism. Behind the much more practical and more formless atheism of the U.S. is a more modern attitude and the roots are perhaps less easy to discover. Doubtless it would be worthwhile to bring these things out into the open. Americans themselves perhaps have not bothered to give the question much thought. What is studied is not the philosophical motivation of atheism but the sociological fact of indifference. This sociological fact, once established, is apparently regarded as its own justification. A typical American approach. I think it is very important for the Cardinal to understand the mental attitude of this country and of its scientists and intellectuals, and this is a more difficult and also more critical question than simply talking to them about God. Unless we see where this country really stands, there is no basis for dialogue in the first place.

This pragmatic "sociologism" (for want of a more accurate term) does in fact have a considerable effect on the American Church. For example, it seems to have a great deal of influence on the thinking of people like Cardinal Spellman on the Vietnam war: the pragmatic idea (which is also President Johnson's) that "now we are in it, we had better get it done with in the most efficient possible way and not monkey around in a lot of talk which will just give the communists a chance to put something over on us." The war is a fact. Communism is a fact. Our military technology is also a fact. Use the technology to crush communism in this war. The why of it, the philosophy behind it is not important. But a Catholic, as an afterthought, can always dig into his theological filing cabinet and find an appropriate justification for what is already accepted as a fact and as "unavoidable."

However, Cardinal Koenig must talk to someone, and about something. If the objective is to find out what really lies behind the indifference of American scientists and intellectuals to God, then he might talk to a wide variety of people, including believers, to find out what they all think. But of course he should find the intellectuals themselves: and who are these? Here I am not a trustworthy guide, as I never get around in academic circles and I have no idea who is who. Doubtless, philosophically speaking, he should meet the people who are influenced by the modern Anglo-Saxon trend in linguistic analysis, and also the phenomenologists and the people who follow Merleau-Ponty. But here he must ask a professional philosopher for advice. However, I do suggest that he contact people like Jacques Barzun and John Randall at Columbia, who will suggest names I am sure. The people at *Cross Currents* would probably have some ideas too: like Joseph Cunneen at Holt, Rinehart and Winston.

One of my own personal suggestions would be this. Instead of just confining his attention to the establishment academicians, I would love to see Cardinal Koenig meet informally with the really live element in the New Left, people like Stokely Carmichael of SNCC, some of the kids in the SDS. In fact I would dearly love to get in on such a meeting myself. I don't suppose it would be practical to hold it here at Gethsemani, so I would not be able to attend. I think it would have to be highly unofficial and informal and off the record. But I think we would really have a ball and I think the Cardinal would enjoy it and learn something of great value, for the future is popping in this area above all. The thing about these young radicals is that they are supremely indifferent to religion as their elders have proposed it to them, they want no part of any doctrine or any explanation, and yet they are in no sense aggressively anti-religious and are quite open to real Christian values when these are authentic. I have a hunch that the younger element in Russia and Eastern Europe is getting to be that way too. It is in these people that I see the only real constructive hope for the future—and in their counterparts in Latin America, where, however, atheism tends to be aggressive.

In conclusion, it would seem to me that a discussion of "God" as a theoretical problem, with no attention to the urgent existential problem of man and his survival and the humanization of his technical society, would be considered by all a waste of time. Where the practical atheism of the United States really bothers me is in its callousness toward human values, its obsession with technological efficacy at the expense of man. Now here is a point where I differ strongly from the supposedly liberal element in American Catholicism today. For this element, technology can do no wrong and to call American society godless is simply taboo. One is no longer permitted to criticize "materialism" and so on, and rightly so because the clichés and slogans against it are all worn thin by reactionary and hollow campaigns of the past. Nevertheless, the fact remains that this technological society *is* dangerously indifferent to authentic human values, and dangerously, indeed naïvely, obsessed with efficacy as an end in itself. On this point my friends at the Center in Santa Barbara [especially Wilbur H. Ferry] will certainly back me up a hundred percent. So will many other non-Catholic intellectuals.

Another suggestion: a meeting with a really intelligent dissenter like Lewis Mumford and the hearing of his views as to what the Church might do to preserve human values. [The Cardinal] should also perhaps meet Erich Fromm. In fact he should certainly meet Fromm.

Now I must close. I enjoyed your visit very much and hope that my few words have been of some use to you and to His Eminence . . .

April 28, 1967

Many thanks for your notes and clippings. I appreciate the latter and was especially interested in the coming of Alliluyeva [Stalin's daughter] to America, and the sincerity of her personal motives (or so it seemed to me). I hope she will find the peace she desires . . . I do see the *NY Times Book Review* here, as it is passed on to me by someone. I do not want to trouble you too much with cutting out clippings, but certainly anything of major importance about any critical event would be appreciated.

I am presuming to suggest to two people I know to get in touch with you on the chance that they might have some idea of interest to the Cardinal. One is a Presbyterian minister in Cornwall, NY [John Heidbrink], who has engaged in Marxist–Christian dialogue, and the other is a young Catholic professor [Dr. Denis Goulet] in the Department of Government in the University of Indiana who has some interesting ideas and is quite knowledgeable about developing countries.

. . . Thanks finally for the pictures. They are very good, some of them: and they give me a wide choice of apparent ages. My vanity prompts me to like the one where I seem to be thirty-five (scratching my head), but I also like the one where I might be sixty-five (looking across the front of the car). If I could have two each of these I would be most grateful . . .

August 20, 1967

I have your note from Paris. I suppose you know of the refusal of permission for me to come East and meet the Cardinal. It is unfortunate, but I must regretfully say that my Superior is so rigid in his conservatism on this point that I do not think an order from the Pope himself would move the man. To my mind it amounts almost to an obsession with him. The Bishop can do nothing, and apparently no one can do anything about it. It is unpleasant to be prevented from trying to do some small part of a good work for the Church, but evidently my Superior is dead set on preventing it, and there is nothing more I can do. Please convey my regrets to the Cardinal and explain the situation to him if you can . . .

To Archimandrite Sophrony

Archimandrite Sophrony, a priest of the Orthodox Church, lived in a monastic house in England: The Old Rectory, Tolleshunt Knights, By Maldon, Essex. There were six monks in their monastery, all of them from different places and speaking different languages. Merton's original French text has been translated by the editor.

January 26, 1961

The correspondence between monks cannot be as regular or as prompt as that of people in the world; and though my long silence bothers me, I do know that you will understand. I received with much joy your friendly letter of October and the shipment of books and articles, all of which I have read. I have also been moved by the simplicity of your gracious letter and by all you have told me about your monastic experience in England. There is so much truth and candor in your point of view that I know for sure that I can speak to you heart to heart. There are so many things to say that I know that I cannot even begin to express them all.

First of all, your book about the Staretz Silouane offers a striking example of a sanctity that is monastic, authentic and traditional, and also belongs to our time. I find there the mark of a contemporary holiness: this vision of the "dark side" of wisdom, this hope that struggles with despair, this feeling of being in hell. This is the "dark side" of the truth, the beauty of a wisdom which seems to be hidden in the chaotic disorder of sin. Oh, how discouraging it sometimes is to see what little good, true good, one is capable of. How false and disgusting so much conventional piety appears to be. Though the omnipresence of lies and of the Devil may frighten us, we must not surrender to tragedy. With the simplicity of the Staretz Silouane we must "keep our hearts in hell and not despair." It is not the lies we should see, but the truth with its darkened face, so like the Servant of the Lord who has no beauty, who is neither noble nor great, yet who comes forth like a shoot from the parched earth. And at the same time it is the Beauty of God who is always playing in the world before the Face of the Father.

Your essays on asceticism are excellent, solid and well-founded. I want to meditate on them again and try to learn how to be a better monk. As you know, I take great delight in the spirituality of [Mount] Athos, which seems to me to be authentic and integrated, while other monastic spiritualities are more or less static and watered down. I realize of course that all is not perfect on the Holy Mountain, but where can we expect to find perfection on this earth? If I seem to be able to understand this spirituality (and your remarks are a great comfort), it is simply because I like it. Nothing else.

But above all, I enjoyed your article on the Unity of the Church. I am under the impression that you did not quite succeed in saying all that you wanted to; but you have certainly sketched the beginnings of a doctrinal approach that I find very attractive. I confess quite simply that I very much admire the truth of this beautiful doctrine and that I have many times thought of it myself. Above all, I try to live out the consequences of that doctrine, namely, to unite in myself all Christian truth and all Christian love so that every Christian, and indeed everyone who is authentically in Christ, might take flesh in my life, or at least in my love. We must love the truth wherever it is found; we must go straight to the truth without wanting to glance backward and without caring about what school of theology it represents. The Church must truly be our Mother, which means that she must be the Church of the love of Christ; she must welcome us with a mother's love that shares her wisdom with us. You surely know the distress that one must experience in seeking to find the truth of love instead of the truth of formulas . . . and of laws, of programs, of projects . . .

I like everything you tell me about your small community. I pray for you at the Divine Liturgy. I am going to say the Jesus-Prayer for a while for you and in union with you with the hope that I may come to understand it more deeply . . .

To Daisetz T. Suzuki

Dr. Suzuki (1870–1966) had a world-wide reputation for his knowledge of Zen Buddhism. Born in Kanazawa, Japan, he taught at leading universities in Japan, Europe, and the United States. His writings have served as a bridge between East and West, and his mastery of English prose has meant that his works are widely read. His books include Essays on Zen Buddhism, 3 *vols.;* Introduction to Zen Buddhism; Mysticism: Christian and Buddhist; *and* Outlines of Mahayana Buddhism.

Merton paid a visit to Suzuki at Columbia University in June 1964, one of the rare occasions on which he was absent from the monastery. Merton was much impressed by this man, who was soon to be ninety-four years of age. In 1959 they had collaborated in a dialogue that appeared in New Directions 17 *and also in* Zen and the Birds of Appetite (1968). *This book includes a tribute to Suzuki that Merton wrote at the time of the great Japanese scholar's death in 1966. This eulogy was first published in* The Eastern Buddhist (*Otani University, Kyoto, Japan, August 1967*).

March 12, 1959

Perhaps you are accustomed to receiving letters from strangers. I hope so, because I do not wish to disturb you with a bad-mannered intrusion. I hope a word of explanation will reconcile you to the disturbance, if it is one. The one who writes to you is a monk, a Christian, and so-called contemplative of a rather strict Order. A monk, also, who has tried to write some books about the contemplative life and who, for better or worse, has a great love of and interest in Zen.

I will not be so foolish as to pretend to you that I understand Zen. To be frank, I hardly understand Christianity. And I often feel that those who think they know all about the teachings of Christ and of His church are not as close to the target as they think. And I think, too, that many of the Americans who are excited about Zen are perhaps dealing with something in their own imagination, and not with a reality . . .

All I know is that when I read your books—and I have read many of them—and above all when I read English versions of the little verses in which the Zen masters point their finger to something which flashed out at the time, I feel a profound and intimate agreement. Time after time, as I read your pages, something in me says, "That's it!" Don't ask me what. I have no desire to explain it to anybody, or to justify it to anybody, or to analyze it for myself. I have my own way to walk, and for some reason or other Zen is right in the middle of it wherever I go. So there it is, with all its beautiful purposelessness, and it has become very familiar to me though I do not know "what it is." Or even if it is an "it." Not to be foolish and multiply words, I'll say simply that it seems to me that Zen is the very atmosphere of the Gospels, and the Gospels are bursting with it. It is the proper climate for any monk, no matter what kind of monk he may be. If I could not breathe Zen I would probably die of spiritual asphyxiation. But I still don't know what it is. No matter. I don't know what the air is either.

. . . Enclosed with this letter are a couple of pages of quotations from a little book of translations I have made. These are translations from the hermits who lived in the Egyptian deserts in the fourth and fifth centuries A.D. I feel very strongly that you will like them for a kind of Zen quality they have about them. If you agree that they are interesting and that they show this particular quality, I wonder if you would let me send you the complete manuscript, which is quite short, and if you would do me the very, very great honor of writing a few words of introduction to it. The book will be published by one of two well-known New York houses, in this definitive edition. (Though at present a limited edition is being hand-printed by a friend of mine, without a preface.) I cannot assure you too strongly of my conviction that a preface from you would be a great and estimable favor. To be plain, I can think of no one more appropriate for the task, because in all simplicity I believe that you are the one man, of all modern writers, who bears some resemblance to the Desert Fathers who wrote these little lines, or rather spoke them. I feel therefore that the task belongs to you by right, and that the Desert Fathers themselves would want no one else to do it. I do hope you will be able to say yes to this clumsy request of mine.

. . . I have been rather fortunate in getting at some of the books available here and know the work of Alan Watts, including a recent book with a good bibliography. I have borrowed your books from libraries and have only two here, the American paperback collection and the *Studies in Zen* put out in London . . .

Are you coming back to America? Would there ever be a chance of your passing through Kentucky and visiting our monastery? Our Father Abbot has granted me permission to see you and speak with you, should you happen to come here, and it would be to me a most wonderful pleasure to do so. We are quite near Louisville. I am sure that a lecture by you could be arranged at one of the nearby universities to make it plausible for you to come to this out-of-the-way place.

April 11, 1959

What a pleasure to receive your kind reply to my letter. I was very happy to learn that my suppositions had been correct, and that you were indeed interested in the Zen-like sayings of the Desert Fathers. Thank you for quoting the two beautiful little poems about the monk and the burglar, so eloquent in their brevity. They show exactly the same spirit as that of the Desert Fathers. And one of the things the Zen masters and Desert Fathers share, among so many other qualities, is their quiet humor, blended with spiritual joy that transcends difficulties and sufferings.

Therefore I am sending on to you the manuscript which has received the provisional title of *The Wisdom of the Desert*. It is going by surface mail, and may take a little time to reach you. I hope you will feel free to say all that you like. I give you a free rein and hope that you will have many ideas. If you write a piece as long as my own introduction, or even longer (which would be very welcome), we could think about dividing the royalties in some way: some for our monks and some for you, or perhaps for some good monastic cause of your choosing. I leave that up to you. As for the Desert Fathers, they are not worried about their share of the material proceeds.

. . . We in the West are ready to talk about things like Zen and about a hundred and one other things besides, but we are not so eager to do the things that Zen implies: and that is what really counts. I only wish there were some way I could come in contact with some very elementary Zen discipline, even if it were only something like archery or flower arrangement. At the moment, I occasionally meet my own kind of Zen master, in passing, and for a brief moment. For example, the other day a bluebird sitting on a fence post suddenly took off after a wasp, dived for it, missed, and instantly returned to the same position on the fence post as if nothing had ever happened. A brief, split-second lesson in Zen. If I only knew some Japanese I would put it into a haiku, but in English the seventeen syllables somehow seem to have no justification except as translations from Japanese. But the gist of it would be that the birds never stop to say "I missed" because, in fact, whether they catch the wasp or not, they never miss, and neither does Zen. We in the West are the ones with the hit-or-miss outlook on life, and so we hit and we miss. And in both cases the results are likely to be tragic. I fear our successes more than our failures.

And now for your deeply moving and profoundly true intuitions on Christianity. I wish I could tell you with what joy and what understanding I respond to them. We have very much the same views, and take the same standpoint, which is, it seems to me, so truly that of the New Testament. I am sending you an article on Easter herewith which will show you how I approach it—in Pauline language on this occasion . . . Behind it is the same paradox you bring out in the words "we are innocent because of our sinfulness." That in fact is one of the great Christian paradoxes, one that has preoccupied thinkers like St. Augustine, Dostoevsky, St. Paul and a thousand others . . .

In your phrase "God wanted to know Himself, hence the creation," you touch upon a most interesting theological idea that has been developed by some Russian Orthodox thinkers and which has deep consequences and ramifications. Writers with this perspective are S. Bulgakov and N. Berdyaev. The Russian view pushes very far the idea of God "emptying Himself" (kenosis) to go over into His creation, while creation passes over into a divine world—precisely a new paradise. Your intuition about paradise is profoundly correct and patristic. In Christ the world and the whole cosmos has been created anew (which means to say restored to its original perfection and beyond that made divine, totally transfigured). The whole world has risen in Christ, say the Fathers. If God is "all in all," then everything is in fact paradise, because it is filled with the glory and presence of God, and nothing is any more separated from God. Then comes the question whether or not the Resurrection of Christ shows that we had never really been separated from Him in the first place. Was it only that we *thought* we were separated from Him? But that thought was a conviction so great and so strong that it amounted to separation. It was a thought that each one of us had to be god in his own right. Each one of us began to slave and struggle to make himself a god, which he imagined he was supposed to be. Each one slaved in the service of his own idol—his consciously fabricated social self. Each one then pushed all the others away from himself, and down, beneath himself: or tried to. This is Original Sin. In this sense, Original Sin and paradise are directly opposed. In this sense there is exclusion from paradise. But yet we are in paradise, and once we break free from the false image, we find ourselves what we are: and we are "in Christ."

The essentially Christian element in all this is the fact that it is centered in Christ. But what does that mean? Does it mean conformity to a social and conventional image of Christ? Then we become involved and alienated in another projection: a Christ who is not Christ but the symbol of a certain sector of society, a certain group, a certain class, a certain culture . . . Fatal. The Christ we seek is within us, in our inmost self, *is* our inmost self, and yet infinitely transcends ourselves. We have to be "found in Him" and yet be perfectly ourselves and free from the domination of any image of Him other than Himself. You see, that is the trouble with the Christian world. It is not dominated by Christ (which would be perfect freedom), it is enslaved by images and ideas of Christ that are creations and projections of men and stand in the way of God's freedom. But Christ Himself is in us as unknown and unseen. We follow Him, we find Him (it is like the cow-catching pictures) and then He must vanish and we must go along without Him at our side. Why? Because He is even closer than that. *He is ourself.* Oh my dear Dr. Suzuki, I know you will understand this so well, and so many people do not, even though they are "doctors in Israel."

I will have someone copy out the hymn called the *Exultet* which is sung on Easter Night in celebration and explanation of the mystery of the Resurrection. You will see in this what the Church really thinks about the "new creation" and new paradise in Christ. Right after the *Exultet*, the first chapter of Genesis is sung, with obvious implications.

As you know, the problem of writing down things about Christianity is fraught with ludicrous and overwhelming difficulties. No one cares for fresh, direct and sincere intuitions of the Living Truth. Everyone is preoccupied with formulas. Is this correct, is this absolutely in accordance with such and such a formula? Does this fit the official definitions? Etc. Hence, if you write anything about Christianity, I strongly suggest that you avoid any kind of commitment that would subject your statements to judgment according to this kind of standard. I hope you will present your ideas in such a way that you will not implicitly challenge the theological watchdogs. In other words, I would suggest that you do not preface your intuitions with even an implicit claim to state the nature of Christianity. If you say "This is Christianity," you will immediately hear a thousand voices shout "This is not Christianity." Which would be very sad, since in fact what you say *is* Christianity, and yet is probably hard to express in a way that would convince many Christians of its true nature. But you will certainly know how to proceed. If you say "This is what I think," well, nobody can deny it. It is certainly what you think.

Meanwhile you see that I enjoy talking with you of these things, and I assure you I will be very happy to hear how the ideas develop. And for the rest, we are in paradise, and what fools would we be to think thoughts that would put us out of it (as if we *could* be out of it!). One thing I would add. To my mind, the Christian doctrine of grace (however understood— I mean here the gift of God's Life to us) seems to me to fulfill a most important function in all this. The realization, the finding of ourselves in Christ and hence in paradise, has a special character from the fact that this is all a free gift from God. With us, this stress on freedom, God's freedom, the *indeterminateness* of salvation, is the thing that corresponds to Zen in Christianity. The breakthrough that comes with the realization of what the finger of a koan is pointing to is like the breakthrough of the realization that a sacrament, for instance, is a finger pointing to the completely spontaneous Gift of Himself to us on the part of God—beyond and above images, outside of every idea, every law, every right or wrong, everything high or low, everything spiritual or material. Whether we are good or bad, wise or foolish, there is always this sudden irruption, this breakthrough of God's freedom into our life, turning the whole thing upside down so that it comes out, contrary to all expectation, right side up. This is grace, this is salvation, this is Christianity. And, so far as I can see, it is also very much like Zen. And of course, personally, I like to see this freedom of God at work outside of all set forms, all rites, all theology, all contemplation—everything. But the rites and contemplation and discipline have their place. In fact they are most important.

And now one more thing. I feel obliged to say this because of the huge burden of the sins of the Western world, the burden of our sins toward the East: sins committed in the name of the Good and even in the name of Christ. I want to speak for this Western world which has been and is so utterly wrong. This world which has in past centuries broken in upon you and brought you our own confusion, our own alienation, our own decrepitude, our lack of culture, our lack of faith. And worst of all, that we have shamed the Truth of Christ by imposing upon you our own confusion as if it came from Christ. With us Christians tears of sorrow are supposed to be significant. If I wept until the end of the world, I could not signify enough of what this tragedy means. If only we had thought of coming to you to *learn* something. There are some who want to do this now, but perhaps it is too late. The victims of Hiroshima and Nagasaki are before me and beside me every day when I say Mass. I pray for them and I feel they intercede for me before God. If only we had thought of coming to you and loving you for what you are in yourselves, instead of trying to make you over into our own image and likeness. For to me it is clearly evident that you and I have in common and share most intimately precisely that which, in the eyes of conventional Westerners, would seem to separate us. The fact that you are a Zen Buddhist and I am a Christian monk, far from separating us, makes us most like one another. How many centuries is it going to take for people to discover this fact? . . .

October 24, 1959

Your article arrived very promptly—yesterday, when I returned to the monastery, it was already here. I have read it twice carefully and intend to study it much more, in fact I am having one of the novices copy it so that there will be no danger of losing the material. As you suggested I have modified a word here and there, and I will send you a copy of the slightly emended version. I will speak of the emendations in a moment.

But first of all I want to thank you for a really excellent and stimulating study. It is very fine indeed, and is to me one of the most significant short pieces of yours that I have read in very many ways. I am thoroughly pleased with it. But I feel in order to give it the full impact which it deserves, I will have to write a further text, to explain and integrate your own study in the whole plan.

Your commentary is excellent, but I am convinced that most readers will have no grasp of its real and intimate relation to the Desert Fathers, and will think it is a rather "unrelated" excursus on Zen, which of course is not the case at all. Hence, in order that they may grasp the import of your distinction between innocence and knowledge, which is so fundamental for the Desert Fathers and for ancient Christian tradition, I will absolutely have to bring to light some clear Christian texts which show conclusively that what you are saying really belongs to the authentic Christian tradition; it is not merely something that you, as a Buddhist, have read into it through Eckhart. Your use of Eckhart of course puts the whole study on a much more sophisticated level than the Desert Fathers' sayings originally suggest, since the Desert Fathers were really only simple Egyptian peasants—at least the ones quoted in these stories . . . Nevertheless they were all distinctly aware of this vocation to recover the paradisiacal innocence of Adam, and to do so by the kind of emptiness and poverty which you so perfectly describe, the only distinction being that they were less subtle about it than Eckhart or the Zen masters, and tended to see the thing more in objective, symbolic terms. Your point about the contrast of knowledge with innocence is deeply rooted in the tradition of the early Christian centuries and I shall adduce texts to show this. So my plan is to have your study and my comment *follow The Wisdom of the Fathers*, as a second section of the book, a kind of dialogue between East and West. Thus it is no longer a question of a simple preface.

I particularly value your astute remarks [see *Zen and the Birds of Appetite* pp. 107 ff.] about the necessity of combining spiritual ("recovered") innocence with a kind of practical, matter-of-fact acceptance of our necessity to deal with good and evil. This too is a deep point, much deeper than the average Western reader will realize, and your observations on the failure of some of the Desert Fathers to combine them is very illuminating. I am grateful for this insight, which is a considerable help to me personally (we are always tempted to be purists). However, I do think that you are unjust to the "great hermit" who had the monks let the robbers out of jail. Your point is interesting and true, but I think you are applying the story in a rather superficial way in that instance. You see, it is not at all just a question of whether or not robbers should be in jail. I do not have the text of the story by me, as I have no more copies here. But, as I remember it, the hermit reproached the monks because *through their fault*, that is through their spiritual sickness and attachment, robbers had come to be thrown into jail and delivered up to torture. What had happened was that the monks had failed to do what your Zen hermit did quite properly, when he helped the robber with the ladder. These monks, being "sick" with attachment to self and with fixation on their own proprietorship and security, had seized the robbers with anger and turned them over to the police—and thus put them in danger of torture. Surely they did not behave as monks, or as spiritual men: they were acting with violence, blindness and attachment. Now behind the action of the "great hermit" in liberating the robbers is the deep truth that the violence, attachment and sickness *of the righteous* is what causes, to a great extent, the delinquency of the unrighteous. He was in no sense saying that the guilty ought not to be punished, but that *the true guilty* were the ones who appeared to themselves to be innocent and righteous. They were the ones who were sick and in the wrong. These monks were in no way innocent, and their "knowledge" of good and evil had become the complete blindness of the man who thinks only that his own good is the good and his own evil is universal evil—surely this is the peak of attachment to an illusory "self." I think it is Lao Tzu who says somewhere that when a man praises virtue he turns other men into criminals. Certainly when a man praises "rightful" possession, he turns other men into criminals. This does not mean that laws ought not to be enforced, but it means that the obligations and responsibilities of the ones who make and enforce laws are beyond all comparison with what is actually thought—a very different kind of "morality" from that of the do-gooders, who are always complaining that Zen has no ethics.

I believe I understand why you insisted on this point—that robbers should go to jail—because America is now full of people who think that Zen is a mere yielding to irrational impulses, and who do not know the difference between satori and being dead drunk. For such people, naturally, the force of rule and law needs to be stressed.

One more small point—where I have presumed to change one word of your text. I think that on page one your use of the word "mythical" for the Christian concept of God will lead to serious misunderstanding and will make many readers miss the point of your study. I believe I know in what sense you use the term. It is quite true that the language which is used to describe God, and the very concept of God, is poetic, symbolic, imaginative, etc. But the connotations of the word "mythical" to the reader who is not "innocent"—is that a mythical term is one that is used for a kind of conscious and deliberate deception . . . I would suggest a use of the term "analogical." This means that we describe something that we do not and cannot know directly, by a reference to something that we do know. The terms "being," "power," "love," "wisdom," etc., applied to God are all *analogies*. We know what being, power, etc., are in the world of experience, but the things that we thus know are so infinitely far from the "being," etc., of God that it is just as true to say that God is "no-being" as to say that He is "being." This you will find in St. Thomas, the traditions of Pseudo-Denys etc.—in other words, in Eckhart's main sources. I would heartily recommend the use of the words "analogy" and "analogical," as thoroughly acceptable to Christian theologians, while "mythical" will give them all a fit of apoplexy . . .

November 30, 1959

I am so glad that you have added a few comments to your article. They are very wise, and I do hope that they can lead to further exchange of views, because really we have only *begun* to get into our subject. It would be a very great pity not to carry the conversation further. What a great shame it is that my way of life makes it practically impossible for me to get to Japan. But perhaps you will come to America again. I do hope you will take the occasion to arrange a meeting.

I recognize the validity of your criticism of my treatment of "emptiness." You are perfectly correct, and I felt quite uneasy about the point, especially as Cassian is clearly not deep enough in his idea of "purity of heart." This struck me as I was writing the article and unfortunately there was nothing much that could be done about it at the time. It must wait for further development. But again I think your insight is very acute and fundamentally Christian in its own way, though in the way you formulate it, the distinction between "God" and the "Godhead" runs into technical theological difficulties for us, that is, for the Christian writer. Do you know John Ruysbroeck? He develops your idea quite well. I shall try to send you a book of his . . .

. . . Speaking now as a monk rather than as a writer, I am much happier with "emptiness" when I don't have to talk about it. You have the knack of saying things about it that do not completely obscure it. But I do not. As soon as I say something, then, that is "not it" right away. Obviously the conclusion is to say nothing, and that for a great deal of the time is what I manage to do. Yet one must speak of it. Obviously, one must speak and not speak. I am glad you are far away or you would settle the question with thirty blows of the *hossu* [a stick carried by the Zen master to brush away flies and also to strike the pupil when this was deemed necessary]. But at any rate, I thought you would be happy to know that I struggle with the—not problem, but koan. It is not really for me a serious intellectual problem at all, but a problem of "realization"— something that has to break through. Every once in a while it breaks through a little. One of these days it will burst out . . .

June 11, 1964

I am really delighted to hear that you are in this country and that it is possible for me to meet you. I have received a special permission from my Father Abbot to travel to New York especially for this purpose, but I must ask you not to let this be too widely known. Obviously if your immediate companions know it, that is fine. But it should not become generally known around New York as this would cause difficulties.

It is my hope that I can arrive at New York Monday evening, June 15th, and I will stay somewhere in the Columbia neighborhood for two days, the 16th and 17th, leaving again on the 18th. Thus there should be ample time to see you. I will call you on my arrival, and find out when it would be convenient to see you. I hope to find you in the best of health and spirits.

Looking forward to a very pleasant visit with you.

P.S. I am enclosing a poem I wrote for some of the Hibakusha from Hiroshima, who passed through here recently.

October 14, 1964

Two packages of books have arrived and I am most grateful to you for them and for the kind inscriptions. I have begun immediately with *Zen and Japanese Buddhism*, which is very clear and has some fine things in it. I am especially struck with the idea of the purposeless life, "filling the well with snow." I suppose all life is just that anyway, but we are obsessed with purpose. I think of this because there was a very purposeful meeting of abbots and novice masters here last week, and we mightily filled all the wells in the country with snow, except that we thought we were doing something else. It is surprising how tired one can get of doing nothing, and how tireless the real "doing" always is.

The Jesuits in Japan have been writing to me (Fr. Dumoulin, etc.), and are very friendly. I wish I could someday see a Zen monastery, but I do not know if that would ever be possible. My Abbot is very opposed to travel.

. . . Meanwhile, here is a picture of me. There is no law against my visiting Japan in the form of a picture. It is taken in the monastery woodshed . . .

Don't forget that you were going to write out a few Japanese characters for me with a brush. I will put them up in the hermitage. And did any of the pictures taken by Mihokosan get developed? Are there copies? I would like very much to have one.

P.S. If you write out something in Japanese, please be sure to say what it is, and again I will be most grateful. The memory of our happy visit [at Columbia in June] remains as a joy and a wonder.

March 4, 1965

This year's Sengai Calendar reached me somewhat late with its intimations of the treasure ship heaped high with treasures from abroad. A few days later came a treasure indeed: your calligraphy, a presence of great beauty and strength which I have given a place of honor in the hermitage. It transforms all around it. Everything about the gift was admirable, and I am most honored and delighted to receive such a thing from Japan and from you. It is to me a deep bond with a world and tradition which I greatly love and admire. It is above all a special reminder of you whom I venerate.

. . . With my most cordial and respectful good wishes and the assurance that I remain united with you in the silence and peace of that Love which is the ground of all being.

May 3, 1965

I have been reading a remarkable passage in a Syrian Christian thinker of the fifth century, Philoxenus. In fact I think *Holiday* magazine sent you an issue in which I had an article which refers to him.* I think you will especially like this passage which discusses the *simplicity* which is a prime essential of spiritual life, and which was "normal" to Adam and Eve in paradise. Hence it is a description of the "paradise life" of prajna and emptiness.

Here is what he says. After saying that God was with them and "showed them everything": "They received no thought about Him into

---

* "*Rain and the Rhinoceros,*" *also in* Raids on the Unspeakable (*1966*).

their spirit. They never asked: Where does He live, who shows us these things? How long has He existed? If He created all, was He Himself created? By whom? And we, why has He created us? Why has He placed us in this paradise? Why has He given us this law? All these things were far from their minds, because simplicity does not think such thoughts. Simplicity is completely absorbed in listening to what it hears. All its thought is mingled with the word of him who speaks. It is like the little child, completely absorbed in the person speaking to it."

The mention of "law" here is actually no law other than that simplicity should be itself—namely, simplicity. That is to say, absorbed in what is said to it, and not aware of itself as existing outside of what is spoken to it. Is this not paradise?

I think that Buddhism is very aware of this, and it is therefore aware of that which is the intimate ground of all knowledge and all faith. And to the extent that Christian faith is unaware of this, it lacks some of the reality which it ought to have. However, I think it is there in the depths both of Christianity and Buddhism. Let us hope it is not being lost. In any event, there is only one meeting place for all religions, and it is paradise. How nice to be there and wander about looking at the flowers. Or being the flowers.

To Charles S. Thompson

Charles Stanley Thompson of the British National Health Service was received into the Roman Catholic Church in 1954. He became a member of an unofficial English Pax Society, serving as its bulletin editor from 1956 to 1963, and as its chairperson till 1971. The Pax Society is now a part of the British section of the international Pax Christi movement.

November 8, 1961

I am enclosing a check for five dollars, to cover the following: two years' subscription to Pax bulletin; *Morals and Missiles*; three copies of *From Arrows to Atoms*. What is left over is to be regarded as a contribution to your excellent work . . .

In addition . . . I would like to be of any help that I can. I understand that a Pax movement is starting in this country. It is about time, if it is not already too late. But in any case the world is in God's hands and if we seek His will we cannot fail to do good even in the midst of such great evils, for which we are all in some sense responsible.

Writing from Redhill, Surrey, Thompson asked Merton for permission to publish in the Pax bulletin his article from the October issue of the Catholic Worker. *He also invited Merton to let his name be added as a sponsor for Pax in England.*

November 27, 1961

Thanks for your good letter. I am glad you will reprint bits of the *CW* article . . . Also, since I have received permission from my Superiors for my name to be on the list of sponsors for Pax in America, I think there is no reason why I should not be on your list of sponsors if you think there is some point to it.

I look forward to receiving Pax and will mention it to people. The situation regarding war and the morality of war in this country is frankly most discouraging.

Here is a copy of an article that may appear here and there in the States ["Red or Dead"]. If you want to use bits of it, or use it as a pamphlet, or pass it on to someone who will print it in a magazine, go ahead.

March 17, 1962

. . . I wanted to assure you that I knew the book edited by Walter Stein. At first I planned to use all of it in the anthology of essays I have been editing [*Breakthrough to Peace*], then we had to cut down . . . so that in the end I have only one of Stein's essays left. But this book will contain much very interesting material, some of the best that has been done in this country . . .

If you have seen *Fellowship*, you will see that they did some rather intelligent cutting of "Red or Dead" and I will be happy if you do the same. I am glad you like it. Not everyone will. Yet it is only common sense.

An essay on "Christian Action and World Crisis" has been passed by the censors and will be shortly in *Blackfriars*. You may want to run a digest of it or parts of it. I mention that it got through the censors for this is always something of an achievement these days. In this country it is astounding to what an extent political thought, or rather preconceptions and unconscious obsessions, dominates religious thinking. I have been accused of almost condemning and rebelling against Papal authority on the subject of nuclear war: and why? Because I quote some of the very numerous statements the Popes have made against war and failed to mention the one or two in which they guardedly and with many reservations admit the possibility of a just war still. Hence your orthodoxy in this field consists in quoting *only* the statements in which the Popes say the nation may defend itself, and in applying these (not always with perfectly good reason) to *nuclear* war when they more probably refer to conventional warfare, in most cases. To round out the view, one must always say as a matter of form, "Of course the Popes desire peace." This is what is considered here to be the Church's teaching on nuclear war: practically a canonization of nuclear stockpiles as a Christian duty and an urgent necessity, without which the Kingdom of God cannot long survive . . .

In a letter of July 14, 1962, Thompson speaks of Eileen Eagan's visit to the Pax Center. They hoped to have her return to speak at a conference at Spode House to be held in November. One of the other speakers was to be the French Dominican, Fr. Régamey.

July 19, 1962

Unfortunately the Peace book [*Peace in a Post-Christian Era*, which Merton had sent to Thompson] has been forbidden by my higher Superiors. Hence none of it can or should be published as it stands. However, there is the peculiar circumstance that in fact some parts of it were published before, as articles, with permission of course. I would prefer, then, that if you want to use material that is in the book, you might go to the articles that were published with permission. I think, for instance, most of what you want from the first chapter will be found here and there in the material that was recently done in two installments in the *Catholic Worker*, under the heading "We have to make ourselves heard." I assume that in fact what you have set aside and want to use, from that chapter, roughly corresponds to the *Catholic Worker* stuff, which in any case was developed from an article in the *Commonweal*. I think there is really no objection to your using the material in this case. But for the rest of the book, I think we had better look elsewhere.

However, I might make one slight exception. Actually, we are permitted to print material in "very small publications" without further permission. I think that if you just lifted a paragraph here and there without further identification, once in a while and just use it, there would be no real objection. However, when it comes to actually publishing significant parts of the book, I am afraid we are forced to set that aside for good: or at least until there is some new decision from Rome.

The book was not condemned. It was simply forbidden because the topic was not considered to be proper for a "contemplative monk" and it was not even submitted to the censors: the Abbot General just asked me to stop putting out any new material on the question of war and peace.

Today one of the brethren showed me a shocking piece in which the Apostolic Delegate to the United States [Egidio Vagnozzi] with the most bland complacency displays the teaching that to prepare for war is the way of the Cross. "We must be willing to suffer, even to fight, to attain the peace of Christ. Not even the ominous shadow of the atomic cloud can bring about surrender to evil." This is a pretty forthright statement of what he considers "good" and what he considers "evil." Moral good is equated with the economic system of the West, moral evil with the economic system of the East. The moral problem of the unjust use of nuclear weapons, which is surely one of the great problems of the age, is simply ignored. How true it is that the Church needs renewal! This peculiar union of sophistry and the appeal to the Cross is shockingly eloquent of the complete confusion of secular and sacred values that has been going on quietly for so many centuries and has now reached its peak. I know that is a mixed metaphor but it will have to do.

Gordon Zahn will undoubtedly have seen you by now. You will thus have had the pleasure of meeting him, which I, as yet, have not.

The development of the American Pax affiliate seems to me to be marked with some confusion. I am of course not able to keep in touch with it, and only hear vague reports. I do hope Eileen Eagan will be able to get over there for your meeting at Spode House.

I liked Archbishop Roberts' contribution on the Problems of Authority, and am glad to hear of the favorable comments on my articles. I want especially to keep in touch with all of you in England who are, it seems to me, taking the honest and Christian position on this war thing.

I want to say this, too, that in the last few years, as I have had more and more to do with English Catholicism, as represented by its writers and by groups like Pax, I have been greatly inspired and "edified"—in the old traditional and good sense—by the quiet and solid reality of the faith and Christian sense which are there: and the basic spirit of liberty and devotion to truth which are blessed with modalities at once Christian and English. This is to me another sign of the eternal truth and validity of the Church's mission. And I might add that this forms part of the immensely important moral witness of England in the confusion of our world today. Obviously there is still, all around you, an enormous amount of the old fumbling and bumbling and the English evasions and blind spots which are unfortunately sometimes characteristic of official England: but how much better off you are, in the end, than we are here with our monumental edifice of absurdity built around business and public relations. It is much harder for truth to survive here, I think, than among you there. Or perhaps I just say this wishfully, remembering the love which I owe to and have for England.

In any case I am very sorry that I cannot just turn the book over to you to use as you like. Of course you may quote it out of print and lend it to people.

Thompson sent Merton the program for the November conference at Spode House. He asked Merton if he would be able to send a message to the conference.

[*Cold War Letter 106*]

September 27, 1962

. . . I may think up a more expanded message later for the Spode House meeting, but if I do not get a chance, here are a few words:

"I wish I could be with you to hear the talks and to share in the discussion, to carry away the light and encouragement they will certainly give. But in any case I will be there spiritually and will offer a Mass for the success of the meetings, if I can obtain permission to do so.

"The great issues that face us are the defense of man, the defense of truth, the defense of justice. But the problems in which we are immersed spring from the fact that the majority of men have a totally inadequate and rudimentary idea of what can constitute an effective 'defense of man.' Hence the transparent absurdity of a situation in which mass societies soberly and seriously prepare to defend man by wiping him out. Our first task is to liberate ourselves from the assumptions and prejudices which vitiate our thinking on these fundamental points, and we must help other men to do the same. This involves not only clear thinking, lucid speech, but very positive social action. And since we believe that the only really effective means are non-violent, we must learn non-violence and practice it. This involves in its turn a deep spiritual purification. May we all receive from God the grace and strength necessary to begin this task which He has willed for us. May we go forward in our poverty to accomplish this task insofar as may be given us by His Spirit."

Of course I see no difficulty in your quoting from things said in letters and from statements like this one, and even using bits from the Peace book, pieces of some three hundred words, without title, simply as quotations from somewhere.

I hope the American Pax will really develop more and more and become a force in the rather incoherent but active peace front in this country.

Peace News is coming and I am very grateful for it. It is perhaps better than the peace publications in this country.

I don't think the situation in the U.S. is any better. If anything, it gets worse, gradually. The war party is quite strong and gets stronger. It is not an organized group, but a very coherent stratum of rich people, backed by massive support from the middle classes in the less sophisticated and wilder areas, and above all California, which is getting richer and richer on the arms race. Catholics tend to be found in the belligerent pressure groups. There is a specious atmosphere of crusade in the popular Catholic press, with a lot of completely illogical and fanatical thinking that assumes any means is legitimate to wipe out the devil of communism. No apparent capacity to evaluate the disastrous consequences for "everybody."

To Paul Tillich

Paul Tillich (1886–1965) was born in the village of Starzeddel, Brandenburg, Germany. The son of an Evangelical Lutheran clergyman, he received an education in the humanities with special emphasis on Greek and Latin. He did his theological studies at several universities, receiving a Doctorate of Philosophy at the University of Breslau in 1910 and a licentiate in theology at Halle in 1912, when he was ordained a minister of the Evangelical Lutheran Church. During World War I, he served in the army as a chaplain. His war experiences helped him to perceive that the very foundations of Christian religion and culture were being shaken. He saw the need of correlating the questions of the day with the self-revelation of God. Much of his writing was directed toward the achieving of this correlation.

His academic career as a teacher included the universities of Berlin, Marburg, and Frankfurt; and, following the Nazi takeover of Germany in 1933, Union Theological Seminary in New York. Later he taught at Harvard and then at the University of Chicago. His books include The Courage to Be *(1952),* The New Being *(1955),* The Dynamics of Faith *(1957),* The Theology of Culture *(1959),* Love Power and Justice *(1960), and* Systematic Theology *(1951–63).*

September 4, 1959

For some time I have owed you this letter acknowledging your kind gift of *Love Power and Justice* with your own words and signature on the flyleaf. At the same time I want to thank you for the other books which Mrs. Leonard sent me. I will have more to say about them later on, when I have studied them more thoroughly. I have not yet finished *The Theology of Culture*, which in many respects is the most interesting—but I want at least to give you my impressions of the moment and convey to you something of the gratitude I owe you for the enjoyment derived from the books.

Love Power and Justice I found difficult at first. The book did not open up to me until your magnificent chapter on being and power with its, to me, central intuition that "the power of being is its possibility to affirm itself against the non-being in it and against it." From then on the book became an illuminating and exciting experience, and the concept you expressed has helped me to get much out of your other work too. Certainly your interpretation of the power of being is very important and of course very congenial to any religious thinker, because it leads directly into the most existential and most Christian reality of all—love. And your remarks on love reformulate the great Gospel truths with significant highlights afforded by depth psychology, and this is an approach which I really like. Love as the power of (personal) being to overcome what is against itself and achieve reunion or higher unity—that is everything. It seems to me that there is nothing here which should not be congenial to the best and most living Catholic thought these days.

I do not keep abreast of controversy, but I imagine your formula "ultimate concern"* has been hotly questioned. Before I go further with

---

* *"Ultimate concern": in his work* The Dynamics of Faith, *Tillich describes faith as the state of being ultimately concerned.*

it, I would like to say at once that I enjoy your forthright criticism of the overemphasis on the authoritarian aspect of faith, which tends to make Catholic theology on the point lopsided since the Reformation. If I tended to hesitate over your formula of ultimate concern, it was not from this authoritarian viewpoint at all, but rather because I thought it was not sufficient to embrace the Gospel idea of faith (rather grasping one facet of the "hope" side of Gospel faith) and then that it was not fully sufficient to express what you yourself want to say about faith. However, looking at it from the angle of "the power of being," your idea of faith becomes for me very noble, as well as attractive, when you point out that the power of faith is measured by its capacity to assume and rise above "existential doubt." This is of course the great point, and the Gospel point too. In the Catholic camp, this is every bit as actual as it is for you, but I would say that its actuality is not really discussed as a live issue until one gets into the field of mysticism. Have you read St. John of the Cross? In actuality his view of faith is a direct plunge into every possible form of doubt and contradiction and "night," the supreme intensification of "existential doubt," in which one's whole being becomes doubt and night, in order to burst out into that faith which is "pure night" to the soul. The dawn is in God. (I have not completed the book on faith, you may have said all this better.)

Finally I want to tell you how happy I am with the earlier chapters of *The Theology of Culture*, in which I find all my Augustinian and Franciscan instincts vindicated. True, I have been subjected to the Thomist formation, which is de rigueur for every priest, and it has made me a little suspicious of technical ontologism, but what you are after is the Franciscan instinct for immediacy which is to me the supremely important thing in religious thought—and experience. And the thing so easily frustrated, glossed over and rejected by the doctors of the law.

I close by warmly thanking you for these enlightening thoughts, and assuring you of my complete sympathy and communion in Christ Our Lord.

To E. I. Watkin

Author, philosopher, and linguist, E. I. Watkin (1888–1981) entered Oxford in 1907 after a diversified education at a private school with tutors, and at St. Paul's School, London. He completed his Oxford studies in Greek and Roman history, philosophy, language, and literature with one of the highest First Class Honours. His working knowledge of French, Italian, Spanish, and German enabled him to read and translate extensively in these languages.

Brought up Protestant, Watkin became an Anglo-Catholic in his teens. However, his love for the medieval past, together with his fear that the Church of

England lacked the authority to halt the strong tide of secularism, led him to the Roman Catholic Church. He was received at Downside Abbey in 1908. He felt keenly the need of showing Christianity as a credible alternative to prevailing philosophies. To do this, he stressed the importance of going beyond the letter of Catholic thought to its inner spiritual truths. This approach, ahead of its time, occasionally led to conflict with ecclesiastical authority.

He published many books, among which are Philosophy of Mysticism *(1920),* The Bow in the Clouds *(1931),* Theism, Agnosticism and Atheism *(1936),* Catholic Art and Culture *(1942),* Neglected Saints *(1955),* The Church in Council *(1960).*

Among his many friends were Frank and Maisie Ward, Evelyn Underhill, Martin D'Arcy, and Michael de la Bedoyere. His closest friend was Christopher Dawson, whom he had known since boyhood and who shared rooms with him at Oxford. A deeply humble man, he was eager to learn from others and equally ready to share generously with them.

August 1, 1962

Mrs. Gullick, in Oxford, led me to believe that you would not mind my sending you an unpublishable manuscript of mine on nuclear war [*Peace in a Post-Christian Era*]. We share very much the same views on this subject and I wanted you to see it, though it is very imperfect and in the end rather ambiguous.

So I sent you a mimeographed copy a week or so ago . . . Any suggestions you may have . . . will be gratefully appreciated.

I am also sending a mimeographed essay on the English mystics, in which you are referred to. When this comes to be published I shall need a reference to your Pax article on Knowles's book about the English mystics. Mrs. Gullick sent me the review but I cannot lay my hands on it now.

September 11, 1962

Your three good letters are awaiting an answer. I wish I could tell you how glad I was to get them. At a time like the present it is good to agree with someone for a change. I do not deny that I have more than a few people who agree with me, thank God, but they are widely scattered, and in not much communication with each other, generally speaking. I cannot say exactly that the Church has given me a bland security in which there is no further sense of isolation. I do not feel snug in her.

As you say, there are many disquieting things to face all around us. And humanly I sometimes wonder if there is any hope of it being otherwise in our lifetime. But it is a time of crisis, a long-overdue crisis, in which the anguish our fathers did not feel has come upon us, and compounded. I cannot smugly accept the mere fact of the Church as an *institution*, as if this alone were the answer to all problems. An institution that has held together since the year 33. I doubt if this is a fully comforting consideration. For me it is not enough, even when one adds the usual trimmings, "in spite of Pope Alexander VI" (wink and smile). "Surely this in itself is the greatest miracle!" And then we all go back to our stocks and bonds, and see how the missiles are helping the stock market. We too are perhaps not the least part of the miracle: the weapons have not yet gone off.

You are of course right about the *Peace* book. It is insufficient. I was naturally trying to write something "objective" that would pass as the common teaching of theologians or something of the sort. It did not even get to the censors, so I did not have a chance to find out if what I said accorded with the teaching of the Church. As if the quotations from the Popes were not enough . . .

Fortunately there are laymen speaking up, and I think you continue to be among them. In Canada, Leslie Dewart has been writing good things (a professor at St. Michael's in Toronto). Do you know Gordon Zahn's book [*German Catholics and Hitler's Wars*]? . . . Then there is also the anthology I put out, which got by (my articles got by, and I did not bother to explain that I had edited a whole anthology to go with them). I am waiting to get some more copies, and will send you one. It is called *Breakthrough to Peace*. Walter Stein is one of those represented, and also there is what I thought a very solid essay by Herbert Butterfield, at Cambridge. Others were Americans, and some of the best minds we have, I believe. You ought to be fairly pleased with the book.

. . . I am most impressed with the depth and subtlety of Oriental texts on mysticism, and I have no doubt that it is urgent for us to come to understand them and to see the correspondences between our thought and theirs. There can be no question in my mind that what is often passed off with a shrug as philosophical pantheism is in reality something quite different, an expression of a profound religious experience . . .

I think there is a great deal to be learned from Buddhist and Vedantist texts, especially, however, from the Buddhists. And lots of good material is coming out in English. You have Conze there in England. I also got into a dialogue with Suzuki, the Zen man, and I still have offprints so I will send you a copy . . .

In a word, my own feeling is that Christian thought is largely hampered by fear, and does not dare to do what we, in the Holy Spirit, ought to be most ready to do: to realize our *immediate* union with God in the order of grace. (We still talk most ambiguously about grace and nature: on the one hand we discard nature as if it were totally corrupt, and exalt grace, yet when we come to talk about grace in practice we treat it no better than if it were "nature," as if it did not make us sons of God and divinize us!) We have not known and tasted the things that have been given to us in Christ. Instead we have built around ourselves walls and offices and cells and chambers of all sorts, and filled them full of bureaucratic litter, and buried ourselves in dust and documents, and now we wonder why we cannot see God, or leap to do His will . . .

November 15, 1962

I owe you three letters: and I do at least want to say how much I appreciate your warm and generous lines. They convince me more and more that the true reality of the Church is precisely what the Gospel said it is: the communion of "saints" in the Holy Spirit. Let us dare to call ourselves saints because we know well enough that we are sinners and poor, and that we cannot possibly have any good that is not in and from Christ. But that in Him and from Him and with Him we have immense riches, which are, however, not our making but His gift.

That brings me to Buddhism. I am on and off thinking a great deal about it, when I can, because I think in many ways it is very germane and close to our own approaches to inner truth in Christ. Naturally, I am glad to find myself in the company of such a man as Don Chapman, in being called a Buddhist, because that is one of the standard jokes in the community here: that I am a hermit and a Buddhist and that in choir I am praying as a Buddhist (how do they know?), while others are all wrapped up in the liturgical movement and in getting the choir on pitch and in manifesting togetherness, whatever that is. Really I do not feel myself in opposition with anyone or with any form of spirituality, because I no longer think in such terms at all: this spirituality is *the* right kind, that is *the* wrong kind, etc. Right sort and wrong sort: these are sources of delusion in the spiritual life and there precisely is where the Buddhists score, for they bypass all that. Neither this side of the stream nor on the other side: yet one must cross the stream and throw away the boat, before seeing that the stream wasn't there.

I think that this is precisely where the Christian doctrine of grace gets you. If all is pure gift, then the idea of crossing a stream is of course a useful delusion. But there comes a time when one must see that one did nothing, one was and is a useless servant, and that this precisely is the heart of our joy in Christ Who does not estimate the value of our presumed service but only the gift of His love which makes us disappear in Him: not ontologically of course (the whole of Oriental "pantheism" is another Western myth, because their ontology is a mystery we have not yet penetrated), but in charity.

Even philosophically, however, I have a sneaking suspicion that what Buddhism is getting at is by no means a Platonic absolute, abstract, but right at the heart of the concrete *act of being* which is the great intuition of Thomism (not of "the Thomists," from whom may God deliver us). I should perhaps have said " of St. Thomas" . . .

January 11, 1963

Thanks for your last letter, dated in November. Christmas has intervened, and the New Year with changes in the work. I have been landed with a merged novitiate, that is to say the brother novices and the choir novices are one group with one Fr. Master, and I am giving them the same training. It is working better than I at first expected, thanks be to God. In the long run it should prove very good for the whole house. But it requires thought and preparation, especially as all the young professed brothers are in on my conferences too, as a kind of refresher course, though that is absolutely the wrong kind of term.

. . . I agree with your remarks about the Church. The problem is much deeper than many people seem to imagine, though the possibilities of renewal, with people like Pope John available, are great. Still, I think the approach is not radical enough. Or at least, we do not know as yet how radical it is, because for all the enthusiasm of some theologians, and I am enthusiastic with them, the first session did not really get down to the roots. Liturgy is all very well, but it is not the root problem. Nor is the schema on revelation. The great problem is the fact that the Church is utterly embedded in a social matrix that is radically unfriendly to genuine spiritual growth because it tends to stifle justice and charity as well as genuine inner life. It may well be the providential mission of communism to break this and set us free, but this is something that most Christians absolutely do not want to face. On the contrary, this risk appears to them to be the work of Antichrist and seems to them to justify the most extreme and un-Christian measures, and this alone is significant to such a point that I wonder we can continue to be so blind.

My *Peace* manuscript has gone to one of the bishops most concerned with lay affairs and he may be very sympathetic. But such an enormous work of clarification is necessary. The question is much greater than simply eliciting a declaration for or against nuclear war. We have to come to grips with the great facts of our time and see where we are in the midst of this colossal revolution. It is not primarily a political revolution, or even an economic one, that we are going through; it is the great technological revolution which began in the late Middle Ages and is turning man's whole life inside out, which is all very well, I am not opposed to genuine progress. But no one seems to recognize that the roots of all this are spiritual, or non-spiritual, depending on how you look at it. All this comes from inside man, and speaks eloquently in symbolic fashion; but we have become totally blind to symbols . . .

May 7, 1963

Thanks for your good letter. No one could agree more heartily than I. I have not seen the reactions in this country yet, but the description you give is entirely credible. One effect of the encyclical [*Pacem in Terris*] has, however, been that some of the lower clergy and the laity who had hitherto been silent are now beginning to speak up. But again, these few voices; what can they possibly mean against the din of the mass media? Still, I have heard favorable and respectful reactions in places where I would not have expected them. The fact remains, however, that even the undoubtedly awake bishops, of whom there are more than I expected in this country (the Council has had some effect in waking a few of them up), still only see nuclear war as a secondary and peripheral issue. This is a frightful expression of weakness and blindness. As you say, they are so committed to the categories of national sovereignty and so on that they do not know what is happening.

Hence they are putting an enormous amount of effort and palaver into the issues they think are crucial, and which in reality are more or less secondary, but which have the advantage of apparently knitting the organization of the faithful together: things like liturgy and so on. Quite all right, no doubt. But are they the most important issues today?

I know exactly how you feel about the Church, and I would say I felt the same way, except that I think I have got to the point where I have not much time to worry about it, and it does not constitute a personal problem. God's will for me is clear enough, and it certainly fits in with His will for the world, whatever that may be. The bishops can take care of themselves, that is their business. I am waiting to hear how the Abbot General will answer the letter in which I told him that I thought it was a good thing the Pope did not have to get his encyclical passed by the censors of our Order. And asking him if he would revise his judgment on my book. The trouble is that here, as everywhere, it is a secretary *under* the General who really dictates the policy about censorship, and he is one of these little French bureaucrats with a closed authoritarian mind with whom one cannot argue. The General himself is broader, and may override the secretary. But he is also a Gaullist, and so on this issue he probably will not.

. . . One thing is true, that in this country it is important for the people who are working for peace to keep together, and be alert, and to keep up an air of hope and positive activity. The mood of this country is much too close to suicide, and the noise of the salesmen and the advertising men keeps them from knowing it. Hence a really pessimistic view of the whole thing simply confirms them all in their conviction that the war *must* come, and this is precisely the worst attitude of all. Cuba was awfully close to beginning it, last October. I mean, of course, not the Cuban people, but the Cuban crisis. But I have no idea how this country can be brought to sanity. The huge machinery for lying and for self-deception is too complex and too far gone: as soon as anything gets into it, even if it be the truth, it takes on the same equivocal and half-meaningless appearance of everything else. The times are indeed Apocalyptic.

Yet I really do believe that the encyclical has done an immense amount of good, even in this country, and I still think it is possible that it may mark the turning of the tide. But obviously there is an enormous long way to go, and what the chances are of avoiding nuclear war in the next ten years, I do not know. All I can say is that I think they are better now than they were last year.

. . . I finished my essay on Fénelon and also got together a few excerpts from him on war and peace which are powerful, and which I can scatter around in mimeographed sheets. I will send you these.

Recently I have read *The Mirror of Simple Souls*, which Etta Gullick lent me. It is a marvelous book, and has some magnificent and original things in it. And is so splendidly written. I understand it is by Marguerite Porete, who was burned at the stake. Dom Porion, translator of Hadewijch of Antwerp, says this. There is no question that the mystics are the ones who have kept Christianity going, if anyone has. The Fénelon–Bossuet business, as an official and in some ways almost definitive victory for officialdom over mysticism, is a critical point in history. That is why it is interesting to see that Fénelon, before he got into mysticism, was already also criticizing the autocratic and unjust war politic of Louis XIV. It all hangs together.

Yet we have got to the point now where it does no good to swing from one side to the other, this reaction against that reaction. Unless the whole thing can be gathered up into a higher unity, it will all end by blowing up. Our task is to be something more than interior man against the bureaucrats. It is not enough to be against anything. We have got to save them all, along with ourselves. We have to somehow become capable of throwing all our limitations to the winds, so that the Holy Spirit can do through us works that are inconceivable. I do not know what all this might possibly be. But I think it is the only answer . . .

Holy Thursday, 1963

. . . I am supposed to be doing a preface of the new translation of selections from Fénelon's letters, and this means going into the background a bit. I have the greatest sympathy and liking for Fénelon as a man, and for his work when seen as a whole. His spirituality is so dried up and reduced to such rudiments by reason of the controversy with that ass Bossuet that it is no longer terribly interesting to me, though I respect its essence. I like him better when he is telling off Louis XIV for being an autocrat and waging unjust wars. This is an aspect of Fénelon that is too neglected. Everything has been squeezed down to textbook judgments on that damnably stupid controversy. Of course I like Michael de la Bedoyere's book about it.

It is not true that my book on peace is to be published. Yet I have thought of perhaps reopening the question now that the Pope has written his encyclical, which, at the time of writing, I had not yet seen. I have however been in contact with people in the peace movement here, and bits of things written before the ban are still being rehashed and printed. I send you one from *Fellowship*. It is possible that things are getting to be just a bit more hopeful, in some unaccountable way . . . But still I am deeply mistrustful, I regret to say, of superficial optimism. Is there not a real temptation to confuse a quasi-secularist wishful thinking about progress with true Christian hope? I think there is. There is so much madness and injustice and greed in the very essence of our society that a superficial interest in a few Christian slogans is certainly not enough to base one's hopes on. However, I do think Pope John has been entirely providential, a great and fine Pope, and so much better than the last one. He has shown that a little initiative at Rome can really work great changes in the general atmosphere, not only of the Church, but of the whole West. This may be something to reckon with, and I hope much good will come out of it . . . [But] as you say, there has been so much supine acceptance of injustice. Latin America is going to be the scene of terrible events . . .

December 12, 1963

I now have two letters for which to thank you, and as ever I appreciate hearing from you. Your remarks on the various things I sent you are very apt, and I am in fundamental agreement even where we seem to differ. The question of liturgy is of course a very complex one, and I think it is going to disturb very many people on both sides of the question. The adaptation is not going to be easy, nor is the sweeping optimism of liturgical reformers always a guarantee of the greatest intelligence. I am afraid that inevitably much that is good will be lost, and needlessly lost, and this will be very sad . . . However, it is certain that there must be a warmer and more intelligent relationship between what goes on at the altar and what is done by the people. It is easy enough for you and for me to appreciate the familiar forms which have remained to a great extent unchanged since Charlemagne. It is also easy for us to understand the Middle Ages and to feel our deep indebtedness to them, and to realize the continuity of our experience with that of the Middle Ages. A vast majority of Christians in our day cannot do this, unfortunately . . .

. . . I recognize the justice of your remarks on the liturgical paper and hasten to add that I am not much of a "liturgist" in the modern and fashionable sense, and really at heart I agree with you, for myself. I am very content with the simple Cistercian liturgy we have, and hate to think that it may be suddenly and violently wrenched out of shape for no particularly good reason, as the needs of a monastery are not those of a parish. But the obsession with the latest "thing" is so strong that even monks get swept away by it. And I am heartily in agreement with you in deploring this.

The race question is of course simmering, and ready to boil at any moment again. No one knows exactly what will come next, but without any doubt there must be a real, honest attempt to do justice. This is not a question of legislation, but also a matter of white people making up their minds to live in the same areas as Negroes and not move out immediately at the first sign of a Negro moving in . . .

I have been asked to write some notes on a notorious play [Hochhuth's *The Deputy*] which treats Pius XII as a renegade for not having openly protested against the mass murder of Jews by Hitler. The play is mediocre and heavy-handed, and there is obviously an air of resentment and prejudice everywhere in it, and yet after all one can see something of a justification for this viewpoint, in its essence. The idea that a Pope should put first of all the "duty" of retaining political advantage and power, and that the "good of souls" depends on this, is something that we cannot deny exists in Rome, and furthermore the play makes a great point of the fact that the whole Catholic notion of obedience and authority has come to be something dependent on this concept of power. In other words, obedience is something that ultimately has a political use: it makes the members of the Church pliant instruments of policy. This can be seen to have utterly shocking consequences. And amusing ones, for instance, in the curial indignation over the mere idea of reform. The shocked exasperation of the curial party when the bishops actually dared to question the value and honesty of certain curial procedures, and the flagrant opposition of the Curia to the Pope's own wishes, have been quite striking in the last Council session. Obviously for the Curia obedience means nothing outside the context of their *own* power. They obey a Pope as long as he plays their game. Only that. Apparently the definition of Papal infallibility in Vatican I was really understood as a definition of curial omnipotence.

The picture is usually grim, I fear.

. . . I will certainly keep in mind the difficulties you mention, and will pray for you. Often the best we can do is to want that which we cannot accomplish. And to trust in God, Who suffers in us in a way we do not understand. Since all that is ours is His, except sin, and even that becomes His affair when we surrender our will to Him in contrition, we can only rest in Him even when we suffer most.

To R. J. Zwi Werblowsky

Professor Werblowsky, a scholar in the field of comparative religion, was born in Frankfurt am Main in 1924. After teaching at Leeds and Manchester Universities in England, he went in 1962 to Jerusalem to teach at Hebrew University, where he became professor and later dean of the faculty of humanities. At present he is the Martin Buber Professor of Comparative Religion at Hebrew University. He has also served as Visiting Professor at a number of American universities (Harvard, Stanford, Notre Dame, Chicago Divinity, Brown). He was a friend and correspondent of Carl Jung.

In 1963, when he was Visiting Professor at Brown University, Zalman Schachter urged him to visit Thomas Merton. In an article in the Merton commemorative issue of Cistercian Studies *(Vol. 4, 1978), Professor Werblowsky writes of his visit to Merton, the talks he gave to the novices at Merton's request, his amazement at Merton's intuitive understanding of Zen, even though he had never experienced Zen life and discipline (as Werblowsky had). Only two letters have survived at the Merton Studies Center.*

July 16, 1963

It was a pleasure to get your letter, and to know that Zalman had acted as the Lord's instrument in bringing you this way. We will be very glad to have you here. I will be able to see you and talk with you on the Friday and Saturday of that weekend, the 2nd and 3rd of August. You may arrive whenever suits you best, on the 31st or the 1st. The best way is to come out by bus to New Haven (which is nearer than Bardstown and a little further on the same route).

If you let us know when you are coming, for sure, I will inform the Guest Master.

Thanks for the offprint of your article. I shall read it with interest, and look forward to discussing these things with you. Perhaps when you are here we could find a way to fit in a little talk on Hasidism, to my novices and students. They would appreciate it and so would I.

New Year's Day, 1964

I start the new year off with a letter to you. The Chinese call this the Year of the Dragon, so I suppose it will be an especially good one. First of all I want to thank you for the *Introduction aux devoirs des coeurs* [by Bahya] which has arrived. I really like it very much indeed. I thank you also for your offprint. I was especially interested in the one about Gilbert Crispin, about which you had told me. It fits with my own ideas about Anselm and his school. I have done two articles on Anselm, in which I agree with Barth that to call him an "apologist" is really absurd. I cannot imagine why Schmitt, the editor of Anselm's works, is so silly as to insist that Anselm is writing apologetics. Your thesis on Crispin seems to me exactly right.

Yes, the monks in Vermont were writing to ask about the mimeograph* and I sent them a copy. The whole thing is really a false problem, but it is one which exercises a lot of people. A pity. It all shows how reluctant monks are to let go of the external authoritative norm and launch out into the deep with the Holy Spirit, who knows how to resolve contradictions a lot better than the Holy Office, which seems to exist in order to maintain them.

By this time, when you get the letter, the Pope may be in your midst. I wonder what kind of eddies that will cause.

Thanks for the tip about the Buber article ["Interpreting Hassidism," *Commentary* 36, September 1963]. I asked some friends in New York to look up that copy of *Commentary*, but so far they have not. I will keep after them.

I send you a mimeo of a translation of a very short piece of Nicholas of Cusa. Here again the intention is in no sense apologetic, where he pits a "pagan" against a "Christian." In point of fact, one of the things that strikes the alert reason is that the "pagan" is really a "Christian" of the superficial type.

With this I will enclose a couple of other small things that might be of interest, and I will send my new book of poems too.

Let me hear from you sometime. It was good to see you here this summer, and I hope you will be back with us again one of these days.

Zalman has sent me a tract *On Ecstasy* by Dobh Baer of Lubavitch. I have not begun it yet. Have you read it? Any opinions on it?

To Robert Lawrence Williams

Robert Lawrence Williams, a young black tenor who had been born in Louisville, Kentucky, wrote to Thomas Merton in 1964 on behalf of the National Foundation for African Students, asking him to write a series of poems on faith and brotherhood. These poems were intended to be set to music and sung by Mr. Williams at a concert to be held in November 1964 as a tribute to President Kennedy and as a celebration of the commitment and contribution of black people to American culture. The proceeds were to go to the Foundation for the Education of Black Students.

Merton composed eight poems for Mr. Williams. Explaining them, Merton wrote: "These songs are all based on biblical themes . . . freely developed in the colloquial idiom of our time." The songs and their scripture sources are: I. "Sundown" (Michaeas 3); II. "Evening Prayer" (Ps. 140–41); III. "All the Way Down"

---

* *Dr. Werblowsky had talked to the monks at Weston Priory on St. John of the Cross. The monks found what he said difficult to square with their own idea about the Sacred Humanity as an object of meditation. He suggested they ask Merton for his article on "The Humanity of Christ in Monastic Prayer," which was to be published in* Monastic Studies *(1964) and in* The Monastic Journey *(1977).*

(Jonas 2); IV. "I Have Called You" (Isaiah 43:1); V. "Be My Defender" (Ps. 4); VI. "The Lord Is Good" (Ps. 7); VII. "There Is a Way" (Isaiah 35:8–10); VIII. "Earthquake" (Isaiah 52). The songs were first performed on August 20, 1968, at the National Liturgical Conference in Washington, D.C. Dr. Alexander Peloquin conducted the Ebenezer Baptist Choir (from Atlanta), together with some members of his own choir, in a memorial tribute to Dr. Martin Luther King, Jr.

March 21, 1964

Thanks for your letter and for your request, which I hope I will be able to fulfill. I have been giving it quite a bit of thought, and I really do want to do anything I can to help. But also I want to do only what is worthwhile . . .

It seems to me that anything I do must be an authentic expression of the Negro's struggle for his rights, and not just a friendly expression of concern by someone who lives comfortably looking on. A lot would then depend on who will be writing the music, who will be singing, and so on. I think that ideally speaking we should aim at a collaboration in which the music would be in the Negro tradition, and I would contribute words that would be (I hope) appropriate. When I say Negro tradition I mean, in this case, something between spirituals and the blues, and it seems to me that the jazz element is essential. Will this go over with the people who are supporting you there? Concretely, will it go over with the church authorities? . . . In any event, I hope you will come down and we can have a talk. Early in April would be a good time for me . . .

I look forward to seeing you and talking over the possibilities for this or some other project. Meanwhile, happy Easter to you and God bless you. I will keep your foundation in my thoughts and prayers.

Robert Williams wrote that his work in organizing the foundation prevented him from coming to Gethsemani in the immediate future. He suggested that the songs should present blacks as serious, determined individuals who were proud of their American heritage. One song he suggested was to present Harlem with its poor, lonely, frightened people as "the weeping city."

April 23, 1964

Don't let me keep you waiting too long for this letter. Thanks for your own letter and its suggestions. I have of course been giving them deep thought. It is not going to be too simple for me to carry them out just as you outline them, and here is why. I fully understand how important it is for you to stress the fact that the Negro is fully an American and that he has helped to build up this country. I could see my way to writing an article on this, for instance. But with a poem, a song, it is a little different, as I myself am not that much of an American. I am on the contrary more of a European. I was born [in France] and largely brought up abroad, though my mother was from Ohio. Still, I don't have that deep feeling for the land and the continent that you have, and consequently I find it hard to identify with you on this point, poetically . . .

On Harlem, on the other hand, I can certainly agree, since I used to know Harlem well. That goes back twenty-five years, and I did write a couple of poems at that time. Have you ever thought of "Aubade Harlem" as a possibility? You have probably not read it. I will send you a book containing this poem. I also wrote one about the Birmingham demonstrations, and that is on the way to you too as a possibility. It may seem a little ambiguous, as it is not about the little girls who died in the tragic September bombing, but about the children who demonstrated and faced the dogs and hoses. You might not be able to use it, as it is a bit cryptic and satirical.

The only thing I have written for you so far is this piece based on the Prophet Michaeas (Micah).

I will keep thinking about these various ideas and will get to town to hear a lot of spirituals in the library: that will be a help. I find myself here without material that suggests anything concrete.

All your ideas about the concert are very good ones and it would be great if you could get Aaron Copland in the project. On the other hand, I hope you are not banking on me to do all the songs for an entire concert program, as I cannot promise to have that many ideas that are worthwhile. How about some of the Negro poets? . . .

. . . As I reread this letter, I note that what I say about America above sounds a bit cold. I really love this country, but I love it as an immigrant and that is different. Your people have been here for generations, while I have my roots in France and England . . .

July 30, 1964

Don't apologize for the letter you wrote about Aaron Copland. Naturally you were disappointed. It was rather a lot to expect, and I hardly thought he would be able to do it. Certainly there are other composers . . .

Also I want you to be perfectly free about not using all the songs if you don't think they are all quite appropriate. I leave you to judge, according to the situation.

Even though the civil rights bill has passed, and that at least is something, there is going to be need of Freedom Songs for many a day yet, I fear. There is a deep, deep wound, and it is not healing. Let us hope that truth and song may begin to bring a little healing where it is needed. Those of us who recognize our duty and calling to work at this must remain very sober and realistic. A long and thankless task is ahead and we may not be able to do much. But the important thing is communication, openness, understanding, willingness to listen. On either side the majority are men of good will who want truth and justice to prevail. The problem is that the extremists are the ones who make all the headlines.

Williams wrote that they were putting their work for African students under the patronage of an African bishop in Kenya, Bishop Gatimu.

August 16, 1964

I am delighted to hear the good news of the possibility that your African work will be under the patronage of the Bishop in Kenya, and that the Mother Kevin Sisters are active in helping you out. Things will advance step by step . . .

. . . The big problem you run into in dealing with white people is that, in this matter, no doubt they are sympathetic, but they aren't black, and because they aren't, they don't know what it feels like and they are not able to enter into the experience except abstractly. Hence they may have good intentions, but these will lead nowhere or will easily peter out. There is nothing to back them. In the long run, if you could get a really concerned Negro composer it would be much more effective. Say, that reminds me, I know of a former jazz musician in Detroit. He does not compose, perhaps, but he might have an idea. I will write him. He is Tommy Glover, Jr. Why don't you write him too? He is Catholic and used to be here in fact . . .

October 28, 1964

I was glad to get your letter of the 11th, which was written evidently in good spirits, and I am happy too that you will be able to get down here sometime soon. The best time for me would be the first week in December. November 30th or December 3rd would be the best days . . . The Freedom Songs have been translated into French, for magazine publication there . . .

I am glad you liked the article that was in *Jet*, though I thought it was to have been in *Negro Digest*. I have not seen either one. We do not get all the magazines here and are supposed to be somewhat limited in that regard, but I would be very interested in seeing a good issue once in a while. I would like if possible to see the issue of *Jet* in which the article appeared, if that is still possible.

Can I send anything to your bishop friend in Kenya? I have mimeographed articles and essays that might be useful . . .

October 30, 1964

Your two letters have arrived. I am glad you reconsidered your decision to do the songs with the help of a tunesmith. I am sure your melodies would have been fine, but I wonder if the rest of the composition would have been up to it. Really I am sure that if we are patient something good will come up. You must realize that it is the ordinary way of God's dealings with us that our ideas do not work out speedily and efficiently as we would like them to. The reason for this is not only the loving wisdom of God, but also the fact that our acts have to fit into a great complex pattern that we cannot possibly understand. I have learned over the years that Providence is always a whole lot wiser than any of us, and that there are always not only good reasons but the very *best* reasons for the delays and blocks that often seem to us so frustrating and absurd. This applies certainly to anyone who has done what he can, though it obviously does not justify complete passivity in political affairs, such as the civil rights struggle. But even then, obstacles have a meaning.

I am greatly honored by your request, which I gladly accept: to be an honorary sponsor of your Foundation for African Students. This is a pleasure and I hope that my presence among the sponsors can be of use to you. Thanks also for writing to His Excellency. It will be a pleasure to send him some of the unpublished mimeograph material we put out here, it might be useful in seminaries or libraries . . .

Negro Digest has sent some copies: I do not know whether they are the ones you requested or others. I am glad to have them and will always be interested in other publications about the Negro. The lack of communication and understanding is appalling. There are some forms of curiosity which are not only legitimate but obligatory . . . I agree with your confessor in thinking that you will do a great work for the Church and for the Negro, but you will have to go through a lot of suffering and frustration if the work is to mature and be fruitful. So take a long steady look at the Cross and realize that it is only from Our Lord that strength can come. I will keep you in my prayers.

November 21, 1964

Many thanks for your letter of some weeks ago. I do not remember whether I actually answered it or only thought about the terms in which I wanted to do so. Lately I have been very taken up with retreats and so on and have not had time.

What I wanted to say was this: you must not feel that I was in any way surprised or put out by your change of plans. Doubtless you are sensitive and perhaps feel uncertain of yourself, which is to be expected since you have elected to go out and take risks in a new project for which there is not much precedent. However, let me reassure you: your feelings that you are perhaps offending others by little things will usually be without foundation, so you do not have to explain or apologize.

I will look forward to seeing you when convenient in the early part of January . . . After the retreat which begins the 18th I will, however, be on a different schedule and visits will be greatly reduced, so I hope you can arrange to come before that.

Many thanks for the copy of *Ebony*. I have been going through it and reading it with interest, especially the story of Sojourner Truth, which is very moving. The first thing that occurs to me on seeing this magazine is that a really integrated American culture would be much more lively and interesting than the present "lily-white" variety, which, I must confess, I find drab, dull and inadequate, at least as it is reflected in the mass media. I wish the American white people were capable of realizing how much the Negro can and does contribute to making American culture an authentic reality in its own right. Failure to realize this is not only an added injustice, but it deprives America of advantages it would otherwise enjoy.

I also want to say how happy I was that the Nobel Peace Prize was awarded to Dr. King. This is, or at least can be, something very significant for the whole civil rights movement. I am more and more hopeful that, in spite of all the frustrations and delays, truth and justice will come out on top, and that significant steps can continue to be made. But certainly much more depends on the courage and resourcefulness of the Negro than on the initiative of the white people, unfortunately. How sad it is to have to continue to admit this . . .

December 21, 1964

. . . You are right about the reactions of people, composers, who are on the lookout for money and prestige. It is true also that people are frightened of the civil rights cause. But that is no credit to them at all, and has nothing to do with the matter: except that of course anyone who is not committed would hardly be able to do a good job in writing the music. Never mind, though, I can tell you from long experience that when God wills to bring fruit from a work, He makes it wait and puts all sorts of obstructions in the way, or lets them be put there, in order to really bring the thing to maturity. I am sure it will work this way. Do not worry, Freedom Songs will be needed for a long time to come, I am afraid.

You are right about the Congo. This is another symptom of the same terrible blindness and confusion that is everywhere. People just do not seem to understand what is going on in Vietnam, Africa, etc, etc. They are so used to fiction and TV drama that they can't understand the complexities of the truth. They think that the world is divided up into good guys and bad guys, and they make up their own minds as to which is which, and once they have decided that they are the good guys, everything else automatically falls into place. This country needs lots of prayers. It is terribly misguided on a lot of crucial issues.

. . . God bless you, and may you have lots of grace, patience, and courage to go on with your work . . .

January 29, 1965

Your wonderful letter of January 15th has been waiting for an answer. The retreat was fine, and I remembered you in those hours of thought and prayer. After the retreat I was buried in an avalanche of mail that had been saved up, and I am only just getting around to your letter. But I am also returning the letter of Bishop Gatimu and the pictures, which I loved.

You are so right about the difficulty of communication. I suppose it is in large part a failure of the white imagination, first of all. Then when one is prosperous and comfortable, he becomes insensitive to the needs and sufferings of others; and then finally there is just the simple mendacity of the press seeing only one side of things and eventually distorting news to fit the one-sided view . . .

The tragedy is that when people have warm and generous hearts, and reach out impulsively to what ought normally to be a warm human response, and then meet with incomprehension, in the end the frustration gets to be just too much. The Negro is a warm and generous person, and he looks first of all for a human response. The white man is more calculating and he looks for a good deal, a return on his investment. This is nothing to be proud of. It is the source of the trouble. The refusal to be human with one's fellow man, and the insistence on treating him as an object to be used for profit and pleasure, covering this up with a superficial friendliness: that is the tragedy of the white man. But it is not his tragedy because he is white. It is his tragedy because he is rich. All rich people, irrespective of color, tend to get that way, and when the black man gets rich, as he one day will, and when he gets power, he will tend to be the same. But, I hope, in a warmer and more lavish kind of society . . .

March 10, 1965

Thanks for your letter of almost a month ago. I was delighted to hear that you and Tom McDonnell [book editor of the Boston *Pilot*, who introduced Robert Williams to Dr. Peloquin] had got together and that there were possibilities of a composer in the Boston area getting interested in the songs. I also know one in Detroit who might be interested. The only trouble is that I have only one copy left of the songs, and the stencils were thrown out. I thought I had many more. Do you have one extra copy left? I am going to have this one typed up with a few carbons, in case I need to send it to the man in Detroit . . .

However, in all such things as this we have to wait and be patient, because a human factor is involved, and there are always all kinds of things we cannot foresee or measure. In the end, God makes all come out for the best and we need never regret having been apparently blocked. You have undertaken something that will affect hundreds and thousands of people someday. You are right in feeling a little fear at the greatness of the task, and the possible difficulties. You will certainly meet great difficulties, and heartbreaking opposition and disappointment in many ways. You may in fact even be deprived of tasting the full fruit of success. But if you simply forget about the results and do the work with all your heart because it is pleasing to God and for the benefit of your brothers, and if you take that as reward enough in this life, you will achieve far more than you could ever hope . . .

May 27, 1965

It was great to get your letter from Paris, and to hear that you have a powerful sponsor. I hope that things will continue to go well, and I think often of your work. Your letter moved me deeply, because I am so much in accord with your ideas of Africa and African people, and so repeatedly shocked by the moral blindness of the white world. France can take a very critical attitude at times toward the United States, but I am afraid that France is as heartless and as hypocritical as the U.S., while having at the same time a little more finesse in her procedures. There is much good in France and also much pharisaism, and there is no white nation that can pride itself on having clean hands. The stupidity and grossness of the way things are done by Americans enables them to be condemned by everyone else, but in reality they are all in the same boat, and the boat is sinking.

There is a Vietnamese Buddhist who has been fasting, in Brooklyn, in protest against the violence exerted against his innocent fellow citizens and the North Vietnamese civilians. He has not had solid food since March. He will probably soon die, since he has vowed not to eat until there is a cease-fire and negotiation in Vietnam. Few people in this country even give the man a thought. His actions have nothing to do with business, so why notice them? But this is typical of the whole plight of all the colored races in the world. They try to enter some kind of human dialogue with the white races, and the answer is "You are just not *there*. We will only allow you to have existence on our terms, you have to conform to what our fantasy says about you, we will not admit that you are real."

. . . Alex Peloquin is coming down in June, and I hope by then there will be much to discuss. I want with all my heart to say something for the Negroes everywhere and to join my voice to theirs. It is one of the few honorable things I can think of at the present time. Every day I am ashamed of being a white man, and I suppose that is only just, since the white people have contrived for generations to make Negroes ashamed of their gift from God, their own skin. As if there were something wrong with it. How stupid people can be . . .

June 30, 1965

I hope you are enjoying Ireland and that your concerts are going well. This is just a note to say that Alexander Peloquin was here briefly last Saturday. He had not started anything with the songs yet, and we talked mostly about the right approach. He is definitely set on a folk-music approach and I do not feel that he is going to be "too classical" [Williams had expressed his fear of this to Merton], at least in this job. Naturally he is set on giving it the kind of seriousness that one expects of concert music, and I think that is only right. I think it is important that the voice of the civil rights movement be heard on this precise level, as well as on the others. This will be a most unique concert. He is at present studying your tapes to make sure that his settings are right for your voice . . . I keep you in my prayers and hope your trip is very profitable for you. I am sure it is. Now is the time to learn and grow. You will have experiences and see things you will never forget . . .

Williams wrote to Merton on December 12, 1965, that he had returned to America to find that Mr. Peloquin had turned the Freedom Songs into a symphony and had engaged a Metropolitan Opera soprano, Eileen Farrell, to introduce them. He said that he would forget about the songs, as it was obvious that his desires about them were not being respected: "I am used to stepping out of the white man's way when he decides he wants something."

December 17, 1965

Your card and note came as a considerable surprise to me, since I had heard absolutely nothing from Alexander Peloquin. He has not written a word since he was down here and I came to the conclusion that he had given up the songs as a bad job, and in fact that everybody had simply given them up. I was content with this solution, as I did not write them for my own interests, and I am not concerned with any interests of my own now.

It is hard to see what you yourself want, since you say you return the songs to me. But let us all think of the main issue: the question of raising funds for scholarships for African students, and let us see if we can't straighten things out.

First of all, there is the question of the ownership of the songs. I wrote them at your request, for you, and as far as I am concerned, they are yours, you have all rights to any income that may come from them, and as far as I am concerned it is for you to say whether or not you wish them to be performed, and under what conditions.

Therefore, if you object to the project Alexander Peloquin now has developed, it is for you to take that up with him. I will add my voice to yours if you request me to. But whether he performs the songs in his way or any other, if there is any money made on them it belongs to you. Hence I think the first thing you had better do is get busy with your lawyer and get yourself a contract with Alexander Peloquin. As I said, I will support you in this . . .

All I ask of you is that you let me know what you intend to do and also let me know what you want me to say if and when I write to Alexander Peloquin.

About the matter of the symphony and Eileen Farrell, about which I knew absolutely nothing at all: when Alexander Peloquin was down here I told him several times that I wanted your wishes respected in regard to the way the songs were composed. I felt that they could at the same time be simple and be of a high quality musically, and I thought both should be striven for. In any case, at that time I presumed that he was going to work that out with you, since he would compose his songs with a view to your voice and so on.

When you wrote in early fall that you were tied up in Dublin, and would not be able to come back, I wrote Peloquin and told him that he was free, if he wished, to consider composing the songs for another singer. I thought that was understood. I suppose he decided that he would then go about it in his own way. I regret if I failed in some way to be clear and to prevent this, if it was in my power to do so. As I say, I knew absolutely nothing of what he has since done.

Here are the practical possibilities open to you:

1. Make a contract with Peloquin so that any income from the songs will be available for scholarship funds. And let him do what he likes.

2. Demand that Peloquin drop the whole project. Then I think we had best forget all about it for good. This might be the best . . .

3. You can formally return the songs to me, in which case if there is any income I will see that it goes to CORE. Or, if you will accept it, I will gladly give it to the scholarship fund.

Will you please consider these three possibilities and any others that occur to you, and let me know what you intend to do? The songs are yours entirely, unless you decide to simply get rid of them, which is also your right. All I want is to help you make use of them in the best way possible, though the situation now may have become quite difficult. I have no idea how far advanced Peloquin is with his project. Can you tell me?

. . . As I said before, when he was here I repeated several times that I had written the songs for you and that I wanted all your wishes respected, and I said this with the idea that he would be *working with you*. But from the moment that you said you were staying in Ireland and I suggested that he go ahead with another singer in mind, he took the ball and started to run with it, and now we can't see him for dust. I certainly hope that I was not mistaken in thinking that this was what you yourself intended: I mean about giving the songs to someone else to sing (not as property). Did you mean that you wanted him to wait until you got back and still compose the songs for you? If you did, then the idea did not get across to me. But anyway, if there was an error on my part, it was here.

. . . I am very very sorry and grieved. Let me nevertheless send you my best Christmas wishes and prayers. Pray for me. I hope I will be a lot wiser the next time any project like this comes my way.

January 15, 1966

Thanks very much for your letter of the 6th. I was relieved to hear from you and to know that you were finally in touch with Peloquin. Since he did not get anywhere with the songs (which is understandable since he is so busy), it would surely be a good idea to give them to someone else if you can. Of course that might take some working out.

In my own personal opinion I think you ought to have a Negro composer, even though it might take a little time to find the right one. A white composer is hardly going to understand your viewpoint. For many white people, although they mean very well and have the best intentions, the race question is not something they deeply feel themselves. They realize that it is in the public eye and they want to be in the public eye too: so adding these elements together they don't mind writing an opera about it. But on the other hand, when it comes to saying what you want to say, I think you will find few white composers that are ready to say it effectively. I even thought it would be wonderful to get an African composer. Another possibility would be a South American, even though not a Negro, who might have a good understanding of the issue. But that might be hard too, the outlook would once again be different.

As for your own sensitivity on the question of what might happen to the songs: don't apologize. I would certainly feel the same way if I were in your position. I know how it is to be in the dark about what is going on and then suddenly discover that all one's plans have collapsed through the intervention of others. The monastic life is full of that kind of thing, unfortunately . . .

. . . [But] in the question of these songs, you are in a position to prevent them from being used in any way you don't want. Whoever does the composing needs to understand, I think, that he is composing them for *you* and not for anyone else unless you say so. I hope that is cleared up with Peloquin, anyway.

I shall keep thinking of the project and praying over it. I now live alone in the woods, by the way, though I may have told you. It means I have less correspondence and fewer visits, and I have to look after myself pretty much (especially as regards keeping warm), but I am writing along and studying, meditating, etc. It is a good life, and I think of you and keep you in my prayers . . .

Williams wrote on May 31, 1966, that he had just returned to Boston after touring the States on behalf of the foundation. He had met with Peloquin and received a promise, he said, that the songs would be ready by November.

June 19, 1966

It was very good to hear from you after all these months. I had been wondering what happened to the songs. Glad you are keeping on peaceful terms with the composer. I should imagine that with the complexity of artistic life and the innumerable projects someone like Peloquin must be involved in, it would be hard to keep things simple and clear. I shall keep praying that everything works out all right in the end.

I have been in the hospital for a back operation since I last wrote you but that is all over now, more or less, though I can't do any heavy work yet. I have been back in the hermitage for some time, and just living alone in the emptiness and silence of solitary life, waiting to see what develops in it, and trying simply to be with God—and to do a little writing work too . . .

The Freedom Songs appeared in an Italian book of mine, a collection of various items. I will ask the brother accountant to figure out how much of the royalties should go to you for the foundation, since the songs are yours. It won't be very much, just a sort of symbolic small sum, but anyway it will be something . . .

Best wishes always, and I wish you all success and joy in God's service, and working for the African students . . .

July 14, 1966

We are having really African heat here now. Unofficially, up to 104 around the monastery yesterday, but officially at least 101 in Louisville. Right now it is climbing back up though it is still early. I am trying to get my work done before the real heat. Then I will go out and meditate in the woods and forget the sweat.

Thanks for your last letter, July 8th, about printing the Freedom Songs in booklet form. That is a good idea and I am sending along a photo. It is the best one I have but it may not be totally appropriate, but I suppose it will do.

Two things I would mention: first, just a technical point and it does not really apply in this case as it is only a four-page booklet. If it were a *book* I would have to clear it with my regular publisher, so don't put a hard cover on it and I am OK.

The second thing is the number of copies you intend to print. You will never in a million years sell a million copies of that booklet at two dollars apiece. That is much too a high a figure. My own estimate would be much more conservative. To begin with, you will have a problem with the price. Obviously those who know that it is for a charitable cause and understand what the cause is will be willing to pay two dollars for a four-page booklet. But I assure you that most people will be antagonized by the price. I have seen this happen over and over when publishers have thought for some reason—often with very good reason, because of pro-duction costs—to make up a small book of mine into something that sells for three or four dollars when there are only a few pages, even though the design is special, there is artwork, etc. People do not think in those terms. My own suggestion would be to figure out some way of printing a fairly large edition (not over thirty thousand) and see if you could clear thirty or forty cents on each booklet, and that way you would really be doing very well—if you sold all the copies, but I doubt very much if you could distribute them all unless you got something like the Paulist Press to help distribute them. But honestly, when it comes to four-page book-lets, I wonder if it would not be better to keep the price far down or else count on a smaller edition. A million at any price is unrealistic. My guess is that you might be able to sell ten thousand if you are lucky, and if the price is low enough . . .

In a letter of September 29, 1966, Williams said he had received word from Peloquin that he was laid up because of an auto accident. He had written the music for some of the songs, but Williams did not know how many.

October 1, 1966

. . . May I please ask you a favor? I read with interest the leaflet you put out about my connection with this. You make statements such as "At the request of the author they will be sold at an estimated $30,000, etc." I have, as I say, no objection to your using the songs as you wish, but I do hope you will be careful in making statements in print about me, especially before I happen to know about them. This one is all right, I guess, but without realizing it you might make some such statement and get me in very great difficulties with a publisher. I am morally ob-ligated to send my poetry for book publication to one definite publisher, for instance. I know he is very broad-minded but the leaflet might give the impression that I was engaged in a thirty-thousand-dollar deal some-place and it would be very embarrassing for me. I know you have no experience of this kind of thing and that you mean very well by it, but I just want to tell you the situation . . .

It is perfectly OK to say that I am the author of the poems, that I gave them to you to sing (or put that in any form you like), and that the poems are your property. But please don't go any further than that, you would be perhaps acting against my interests—and even your own—without realizing it. I hope you don't mind me saying this simply, but that is the best way to avoid trouble in the future. I am sorry to hear there has been another slipup with Alex Peloquin but I hope things will work out. Your next year's tour sounds really grand . . .

October 13, 1966

Thanks very much for your kind letter of the 10th. I am glad you were not offended by my letter. It is a very good thing you have someone to advise you, because naturally public relations will be terribly important in advancing not only your own career but also the foundations you are devoting yourself to. And of course this is a field in which one must know all the little ins and outs, and realize the effect of shades of meaning, implications and so on . . .

My friend and editor, Naomi Burton (Mrs. Melville E. Stone), lives up in Maine and very much wants to hear the songs when you sing them. I asked her to get in touch with you. She would always be the one likely to give the best advice in anything that would concern me: I always rely on her in things involving the public, her advice is very reliable . . .

Meanwhile, Robert, I keep you in my prayers and hope that all will go well. Pray for me too, please. I am always having some kind of minor trouble with my health these days. I guess I am getting old and the machinery is wearing down.

On April 20, 1967, Williams wrote a letter expressing his bitterness over what was happening with the songs. Dr. Peloquin, he said, was insisting on payment for the writing of the songs. Williams finally decided the songs were not worth fighting for; after all, they were the white man's songs. He said he felt he should leave the Church, since to a black man it was just an organization to keep blacks in the place their white brothers had made for them.

May 1, 1967

I do not want to delay any longer in answering your deeply moving letter. First of all, I realize to some extent how much I am involved in the same problem you are. The behavior of so many white Catholics has effectively silenced me and deprived me of any possibility of giving you advice about the Church. All I can honestly say is that the decision is yours, and that the Church has to some extent forfeited the right to demand loyalty of her black children since she has not lived up to her role of mother in their regard. I speak now of the Church as institution. Invisibly, the union of believers who really obey God is another matter. The one thing that is essential is obedience to God in all sincerity, even when it may cut across the apparent obligation to obey men. At times

there are differences. On the other hand, while the white man has behaved in all truth like a devil, he is not the only one who has demons.
They are everywhere, so be on your guard. The demon of power and
hate corrupts everyone. The answer is true faith in God and a really
obedient heart that hears and follows His voice, careful not to be deceived.
Let us pray for each other that we may always follow that voice: we will
remain in a secret, underground way, united.

Robert, I have no illusions about the future. Many chickens are
coming home to roost in the white man's parlor. Some of them are going
to be pretty large chickens, and some of them are going to have the
manners of vultures. Too bad. The white man thinks himself sincere and
honest, but he will gradually begin to find out what a con man he has
been. It is a pity that you have run into such things: people who think
themselves disinterested and idealistic can be in reality the crassest kind
of operators, and never realize it. That is the pity of so many Catholics:
in the name of God and the Church they are ruthlessly ambitious, aggressive, arrogant, self-seeking characters. They cannot see it. But these
traits are universal, unfortunately, and if we imagine that they belong
only to this or that group, then we never get out of confusion. However,
I admit that for the time being the white man is the one who is getting
all the prizes in this contest.

My own part is to accept things as God gives them to me, and to
enter into the confusion without too many illusions and too many hopes
of making sense out of it all. I will try to diminish the evil and the hatred
where I can, and I will try to bring light into the confusion when I am
capable of doing so . . .

The only thing I regret is that you gave away the songs: but I hope
he won't use them. It would be ultimate foolishness if they came out with
melodies of his, and were sung by pious white Catholics. That is indeed
a rueful ending. But I preserve the ability to laugh even at that too—
with you. I don't care about any supposed achievement of my own. I
know too well that it is all wind. So good luck, man. Pray for me once in
a while, if you remember. And God bless you wherever you go and
whatever you do.

*On August 29, 1967, Williams wrote a moving letter to Merton in which he said
he could not leave the Church even though she had not been a mother to her
black children.*

September 5, 1967
I was happy to get your letter—a very moving and deep letter too.
It shows once again that the Spirit and the Church are far beyond any
lines of division that human beings can think up for themselves. And it
shows too that the Church can no longer continue to be a "white" Church.

And God will not let her do so. It is up to you not just to be part of a "white" Church but to help make the Church what she is really meant to be. Christ in the world today is not white, nor black either: but He is certainly present and suffering in the black people and colored people of the earth. The white world is purely and simply under judgment. And they don't know it.

What is going on today was something that inevitably had to come: the violence, the rejection, the separatism, etc. It cannot solve anything and it will increase the wounds and the suffering, but it is a stage that has to be gone through. For Christians and men of mature thought, the hard way is the only one left: the way that continues to understand, to make distinctions, to evade sweeping solutions that solve nothing, and to take each human being on his own merits and in his own situation as someone to help and heal. There will be a lot of us out in a kind of no-man's-land where we will be misunderstood and rejected by both sides. Well, that's all right. As you say very rightly, it constitutes a kind of monastic solitude . . .

On March 23, Williams replied to a letter of Merton's that is missing in which Merton apparently said what had happened was the will of God. Williams disagreed: "I no longer believe in you or your white Christianity. I believe in the sweet, kind, humble little Jesus who came to teach us how to live."

March 27, 1968

The note I sent you this morning was probably so illegible that you won't be able to read it, and I'd like this final message to be somewhat clear.

I agree, it is awfully easy to make vague statements about God's will. They might mean anything or nothing. The point is, however, what is *your* will? Do we have to be so vague about that? One time it is one thing, then it is another.

I am still not clear as to whether you own the songs or whether you transferred the rights to Peloquin. I don't much care, because either way it is quite clear that I am not the owner and have not been for a long time. Furthermore I have no desire to own the songs or to have anything whatever to do with them.

Two things I want to make clear:

1. I have done what I could to tell Peloquin that I don't want the songs produced. But if he controls the rights he is free to ignore my wishes. I am not responsible for something over which I have no legal control.

2. If you own the songs and don't want them produced, then take legal action to prevent them from being produced. He asked me if I had

any objections: I replied that I did not object if you did not. You seemed to say you had no objections . . . etc.

There is no point in my going on with this. My final word on these songs is that I do not want to have them produced by anybody, their production would be absurd in any circumstances, and I hope they are never heard of again. I'm entirely through with the whole business.

If it gives you personal satisfaction to kick me in the teeth about all this, then go ahead, it's been done before.

In a letter of March 28, 1968, Robert Williams apologizes to Merton for his recent letter. He suggests that Peloquin should go ahead with the songs: "Mr. Peloquin has probably worked hard on the songs and he deserves the fruit of his efforts. The poems are too beautiful to stick them away in a closet."

April 1, 1968

Your letter which I received Saturday meant more to me than I can ever say. It is one of the most noble I ever got from anyone. If it made me happy, it was above all because I was relieved to think that the bitterness had gone from your own heart and that I was not causing you pain. I am sorry if there was any harshness in my own letter. Actually— you have probably noticed it even more than I—this has been such a period of increased tensions that people have been much more touchy and have been exploding more easily. I have been in several painful situations on account of this. That was why it was all the more painful to think that you and I were at odds. I also feared that some dreadful mistake had somehow deprived you of any right to the songs or to the income from them . . .

Well, here is the situation. Peloquin has really put out an awful lot of work on the songs. I don't know yet how good it is, but I do realize that we cannot prevent him from producing them without a very serious reason to the contrary. All my own income from the songs will go to your African students. Peloquin also said that he would give half of his income. I don't think this is all going to amount to a very large sum, but I hope it will at least be useful. But in any case, you control the literary rights and anything that comes from the publication of the songs (my text, not the music) will be yours . . .

Yesterday I had the very great joy of offering Mass in the new home of a lovely black family I know and love in Bardstown. It was a great joy for me, and I thought of you too in the prayers of the Mass.

I will also think of you often in this season of the Cross and Resurrection. There is truly going to be a resurrection in the world, a new life for oppressed peoples. But the way to it will be marked with hard times and suffering. In all this, human values and personal bonds must always remain in high priority. My blessings and love to you.

April 2, 1968

I guess there was a mix-up and our letters crossed. But I hope by now you have my other letter (mailed yesterday) which shows you that as far as I am concerned this misunderstanding is as if it had never happened. I am sorry you were caused extra pain by this other accident.

Really it seems to me that things are unusually snarled up everywhere and in everything these days. There just seem to be mistakes, troubles, misunderstandings and mishaps without end. But let's not allow them to get us down. I assure you that I am completely out of all shadow of mistrust. I trust you completely and know that you have behaved very nobly under these difficulties. I shall always trust and value your friendship more than I can say. All will come out for the best, I'm sure.

As to the rights: be sure that you are the one who retains the property rights to those songs. You are granting Peloquin permission to use them, but the royalties due to me as author are all yours as proprietor of the literary rights. They belong by right to the African students for whom you intended them. I hope everything will work out well in that respect.

And let's hope this sad business will show us that we are both above the hazards and accidents that often try us all so sorely. We are bigger than the events that bug us! I know you are and I hope I am too . . . I'll always be your friend.

April 15, 1968

I know you said you didn't want to hear more about the songs, but there is one development I think you ought to know. I have sent my texts together with the music of two of them to Mrs. Martin Luther King, through a mutual friend [June Yungblut], who is very close to them. I thought there could be no more fitting use for the songs than to have them first presented as a memorial to the martyr for non-violence and civil rights. She is considering this, in the midst of all the other distractions and business by which she is assailed. If the songs can be presented as a small tribute to this greatest of Americans, in this tragic moment, I think you will feel as I do that something worthwhile has come out of our trouble and work after all . . .

May 5, 1968

I do not have too definite news about the songs except that Coretta King has approved the memorial-service idea. The rest is more or less in the hands of Peloquin still. And of course now the March is on: I haven't heard news of it yet, but keep it all in prayer and hope.

Few of us really realize what effect the brainwashing of the black people by the white has had in this country. Now at least it is surfacing, and the black people are fighting for their own *identity* first of all. I can only encourage everyone to resist the kind of mental domination exercised subtly by our affluent society: it means freedom for us as well as for you. Few white people know this. But the struggle will be immensely painful and confusing for everyone. Whitey isn't in a position to know how mixed up he is. But it is for you to get yourselves un-mixed-up, fighting the white man's values within your own soul . . .

July 16, 1968

It is a hot Kentucky night, the really stuffy kind that you know, and there is not much point in going to bed. So I'm going to try to write you a letter that maybe comes somewhere near saying what I want to say. I need to reply to your two letters which got in this morning—I read the second one first.

I am if possible as fed up as you are with the whole business of these songs. I see the falsity and hollowness of the whole thing. If I consent to go ahead with it, it is out of weariness more than anything else . . . Also, a really disinterested friend of mine, who is a friend of Coretta's too, has put out some effort in favor of the songs and I can't let that be wasted . . .

You are of course right to say that the failure of your plans, which were so beautiful and idealistic at the start, is partly because you are black. You are right also in saying that no white man can really understand all that a black man has to go through in a racist society. I don't deny that. On the other hand, you must not think that white people have it all the way they like just because they are white. I happen to be able to understand something of the rejection and frustration of black people because I am first of all an orphan and second a Trappist. As an orphan, I went through the business of being passed around from family to family, and being a "ward," and an "object of charitable concern," etc. etc. I know how inhuman and frustrating that can be—being treated as a thing and not as a person. And reacting against it with dreams that were sometimes shattered in a most inhuman way, through nobody's fault, just because they were dreams. As a Trappist, I can say I lived for twenty-five years in a situation in which I had NO human and civil rights whatever. Anything I got I had to beg for in an ignominious way. But I also had luck, as some do. I may be a success of sorts, but I can tell you what it amounts to: exactly zero. Sure, you run into a lot of praise, but you run into a lot of criticism, blame, jealousy, hatchet jobs and raw deals. In the end, a successful person is no better off than anybody else, as far as real gains are concerned. He may have a lot of apparent advantages, but they are canceled out by so many other things. Of course, I admit, some people are satisfied with success, a good image, and a fair amount of money. You would not be any more than I am. You are a different kind of person. For that very reason you cannot do the mean and ruthless things that have to be done in the jungle of contemporary life; you are not the kind of person that just ignores the rights of others. I hope I am not either. But that is the kind of person who is a success and goes places. So what I am trying to say is, if your dream of fame did not suddenly come true, you are perhaps a very lucky man. You will do it in some better way, and it will mean more.

In the end what really matters is not race, or good breaks, or bad breaks (though these are certainly important) but who you are as a person. And if you have real quality as a person (which you do, let me tell you), it does not matter whether the market is interested. The market does not know real quality, it just guesses sales value . . . It is when you are relatively indifferent to success that you will be able to make your way freely in the jungle . . .

As I said, I will go ahead more or less out of weariness, because someone has to take responsibility for the poems. I'll also keep my lawyer [John Ford] on the job to see that nothing goes wrong and that the money goes where I want it to go: to you and to the students. So I'll act, if you like, more or less as your agent. My lawyer will send you a release to sign, otherwise I wouldn't legally be able to make any agreement with the music publisher and the TV people.

. . . I wanted to try to say what was in my heart. I know it is not adequate and I have no illusions about glossing over the immense difficulties of the world we live in. But ultimately it all gets down to the individual, the person, and to each one's relation with his neighbor. Even if society itself is racist, in the end what is decisive is not that we are black and white but that we are people. And members of our own race can be to us as wolves or tigers—as well as saints and angels.

God bless you, Robert. Don't waste good feelings on these accidents of existence. There are much better things in store for you.

August 20, 1968

Great. Bravo. I am delighted that you have made up your mind to assert your ownership of the songs and not just let them drift into the public domain for no reason. I think it is the only clear and practical thing to do.

All the documents are in the hands of my lawyer at the moment and I'll contact him right away about returning the pertinent letters from the Gregorian Institute [which published the songs as arranged by Alexander Peloquin] and the TV people. I think the only thing to do is to let the lawyers handle it so as to be sure that it does not get fouled up in some way.

In any case, you are the owner of the songs and no one contests your ownership. I now hope that they will make a lot of money—though I can't guarantee it. But I got a telegram today saying they were sung last night in Washington [at the National Liturgical Conference memorial service in honor of Dr. Martin Luther King, Jr.] by the Ebenezer Baptist Choir and that the performance was great. I did not of course hear it and I was not even sure when it was going to be.

I certainly hope now that we are out of the valley of the shadow, at least as regards this project . . .

August 26, 1968

First, I want to congratulate you on the good news of your Carnegie Hall concert coming up. That is very fine, and it looks as though you are now going to have a chance to really do something with your talents. I shall pray that you do a great job. I am sure you will.

I liked your letter: and I think you have reasoned things out very well. I assure you that the best way to handle all business of contracts and so on is with the advice of a good lawyer who is interested in keeping things straight for you.

In the matter of these songs, I think that since John Ford is looking after my own affairs, and is very careful about forestalling useless problems and difficulties, he might want to contact you about it. I am bringing the matter to his attention, in any case.

Of course, you must realize that he is strictly business and will just want to handle the question objectively without emotional involvement. I hope you won't interpret this as coldness or lack of interest but it is just the way people are in business.

In any event, Peloquin seems satisfied that the songs are on the way up, and the next thing in line is the TV program, so I think you are wise to take advantage of your right of ownership . . .

That clipping about the new appointment in Harlem was certainly good news. That is another intention to pray for. It is a shame that there are not ten times more—a hundred times more—black priests in all these dioceses.

To John J. Wright

John J. Wright, born in Boston, was ordained to the priesthood in 1938. In 1947 he became Auxiliary Bishop of Boston; and when the diocese of Worcester was detached from the Springfield diocese, he was installed as its first bishop in 1950. Nine years later he was transferred to the see of Pittsburgh. Made cardinal by Paul VI, he went to Rome in 1970 to head the Roman Congregation of the Clergy. As Bishop of Pittsburgh he participated in the Second Vatican Council, during which he exchanged several letters with Thomas Merton, especially with regard to the pastoral constitution, Gaudium et Spes.

In a letter written in 1965 Bishop Wright, after expressing his view that the matters at the Council that Merton was most concerned about were going well, told him: "I sat in a Roman barber shop next to a man who was reading an Italian translation of one of your books while getting his hair cut. I said to him that I knew you, and he said, 'Dica lui per me, grazie.' So grazie!"

January 10, 1964

My friend Father Reinhold tells me that he has given you my mimeograph on peace, and that you are reading it. I am very grateful both to him and to you, and since this issue will probably come up in the Council, I am told, I thought I ought to share with you a thought that seems to me to be both central and urgent.

Of all the many aspects of the problem of nuclear war, one of the most challenging is also one which seems to offer chances of immediate practical solution. I refer to the matter of the individual conscience and so-called conscientious objection. It would seem that the Council both could and should clarify this issue and recognize the right of the individual Catholic to refuse participation in a war which he believes will violate the moral law.

In the first place, since historically "conscientious objection" developed in a Protestant context, it has always appeared to be somewhat equivocal to Catholic moralists, and as you know it has not always been easy for Catholics in this country to obtain support for claims to exemption from service on these grounds.

Whatever may have been the grounds for "conscientious objection" in the past, we are now in a new situation. In the past the assumption was that an individual could claim exemption even from a "just war," simply on the ground that he objected to all forms of war. Even though arguments could be put forward even in favor of this view, such arguments have become irrelevant. The question today is this: when total war (nuclear or otherwise) has repeatedly been denounced by the Popes as criminal, and when *any* war can at any moment escalate into a total war, it follows that the Catholic who claims exemption from service on the grounds of conscience is not simply claiming recognition for a subjective and arbitrary repugnance to something he does not like. He is on the contrary asking for recognition of a fundamental right, indeed obligation, to refuse to cooperate in something which he has good reason to believe may be, in God's eyes, a terrible crime.

In this case of course it is no longer a problem of law but a problem of *fact*. And the trouble is that the facts themselves are often ambiguous or secret. Hence if the Church insists that a Catholic base his decision, in conscience, upon the meager and slanted information that may be given him by a prejudiced press and a committed, non-Christian, military-industrial state, the Church is then in fact turning the Christian conscience over to forces that are not only secular but may perhaps even turn out to have been in some way demonic. This may sound like an exaggerated statement, but when we reflect on the bombings of the last war and the statements made by Pius XII even before the A-bomb, we may find some truth in it.

It seems to me that the Church today faces a great "temptation" which arises out of the last thousand years or so of her history: that of too closely identifying her policy in affairs of diplomacy etc. with her mission to save souls, and of tending to seek obedience in these matters of policy just as if they did in fact involve the salvation of souls. I call this a temptation, but others like the German playwright Hochhuth (most unjustly, I think) have accused the Church of yielding to it. So it is a problem.

There is at present a vacancy in the Generalship of our Order, but a new Abbot General will be elected next week. If Your Excellency should chance to meet him in Rome, and if you think there is some slight point to the things I have wanted to say in print about peace, it might be very helpful indeed to say a word in my behalf to the General, wherever he may be . . . The former General had forbidden me to submit any further manuscripts on this subject for censorship, on the ground that this subject was not one which a contemplative monk should treat . . .

February 20, 1964

Thank you for your kind letter telling me you had given the *Peace* mimeograph to some of the periti at Rome. Even though the book is not published, I am happy to think that the work was not wasted. Happily I am going ahead with publication in book form of some articles which were permitted (though they are now a bit out of date) and with these are two articles on the race question. All these things go together. Perhaps in the fall when the book appears I will have the pleasure of sending you a copy.

I am sending you another copy of *Peace in a Post-Christian Era*, and also a collection of essays by various hands which I edited, and in which I managed to publish some of the material which I later enlarged into the mimeographed book. This book, *Breakthrough to Peace*, is available, though the mimeograph is about running out. I can always send more. Since the problem of nuclear war is so largely one of the facts involved, some of the other essays may be enlightening.

At times, when we look at the enormity of the task before us, our mind is simply staggered by it. The Lord has willed us to live in perhaps the most difficult of all periods in man's history, and it is painful to us above all because the Catholic conscience has apparently been so slow to wake up to its responsibilities. Or rather, aware of the urgency of the problems, it has awakened itself to answers that are well meant but not yet concerned with the most crucial problems. Yet I feel, and I am sure you do, that we are really completely in God's hands and that, with all our incapacity, we can serve Him very well by staying there and responding to what our times ask of us, insofar as we can. If only He will give us the grace of lucidity and strength in all the diabolical confusion of the world—a confusion in which we share. How deeply we are involved in what we condemn.

In the race question, I wonder if things have not gone so far now that anything we may eventually do, in an explicit religious way, may be taken as totally irrelevant. On the other hand, the Church in Africa fills one with hope.

It is a great comfort to find a few here and there who are really able to be concerned about these things in all their depth. Do please believe in my total support, especially in my prayers such as they are . . .

July 17, 1965

I realize that it was perhaps presumptuous of me to draft the enclosed notes [on Schema 13], which I have sent to *Commonweal*. I am not yet certain they will be published, and I have no doubt some of the bishops will not like them. But on the other hand there is such a thing as public opinion in the Church, and now, if ever, is the time for it to be articulate.

As you know, I feel very strongly (and I believe you do too) that the question of war, of modern war technology, and of the right to refuse participation in massive or unjust use of force, all amounts to a kind of exposed nerve in the operation of Christian renewal. I frankly think that the ability of the Council to handle this situation with tact and understanding (if not with prophetic charismata) will determine the reality of the renewal that has been so convincingly proposed so far.

If the Council Fathers in this Schema in effect *determine beforehand* what is to be thought and done about such a problem as nuclear war, they will stifle genuine renewal and development in this and many other areas. Modern technology and politics are in a critical state of unusual development. Anything can happen in the next decades and we have no way of foreseeing what all the risks and opportunities may turn out to be. In meeting these risks and opportunities as they come, in making creative, perhaps heroic new decisions, Christians, especially laymen, will lay down the basis for a whole new theological interpretation of man's life in the world. If these decisions and new evaluations are blocked from the start by an arbitrary statement of the Council, renewal will hardly be possible. General guidelines are of course most desirable, and these have been repeatedly given by modern Popes. In this respect the Council should at least reinforce the teaching of *Pacem in Terris* on the irrationality of war as a means for solving international problems today.

On the other hand, an implicit approval and acceptance of modern war technology would have the most serious pastoral consequences. I am thinking particularly of some statements which might simply bind Catholics beforehand, without discussion, to participate in any and every war, to assent to and cooperate with the use of any and every means which a government may decide (for reasons not made public) to be expedient. I believe that if any statement is made at all on this, it should be one which liberates the Catholic from servitude to irresponsible strategists, propagandists and politicians in such matters as these. Rather than approving the use of force (even in the hypothetical case of self-defense), I think the Council should make clear the right to protest against the bomb in any situation where it is not clearly and obviously reasonable, just, right, and Christian. And when will this be found to be so except in a disinterested and manifestly necessary police action, directed by international authority? If enlightened and responsible protests are not allowed and encouraged, people will become more and more passive instruments of huge power structures. It would be a disaster if the Council simply made a statement that left Christians at the mercy of such power structures, under the pretext that this is sufficient obedience to God . . .

To John C . H . Wu

Dr. John C . H . Wu, author of many books on jurisprudence, philosophy, and literature, was born in Ningpo, China, in 1899. He distinguished himself as both a scholar and a diplomat in China, the United States, and Europe. For thirteen years he was a member of the National Legislature of the Republic of China. For three years he was Chinese ambassador to the Vatican. He has served as dean of the College of Chinese Culture in Taiwan, and as research professor of Asian studies at Seton Hall University in South Orange, New Jersey. Among his works are Beyond East and West *(his autobiography) and* The Golden Age of Zen *with an introduction by Thomas Merton.*

John Wu assisted Merton in producing his "version" of the Taoist philosopher Chuang Tzu by sending him four translations of the Chinese philosopher and also by making his own literal translations of the passages Merton selected. His high esteem for Merton is well expressed in a letter of September 6, 1966: "The beautiful thing about you is that your heart is as great as your mind. Thus in you love and knowledge are united organically. Herein lies your profound significance for this great age of synthesis of East and West."

March 14, 1961

Father Paul Chan wrote to me some time ago saying that he had kindly spoken to you about a project of mine which came to his attention, through a letter I had written to Archbishop Yu Pin. So you are already acquainted with the fact that I have been for some time persuaded of the immense importance of a prudent study of Oriental philosophy by some of us in the West, particularly in the kind of perspective that guided some of the early Church Fathers in their use of Platonism, and St. Thomas in his use of Aristotle.

Naturally, there is a great deal of irresponsible and rather absurd dabbling in things Oriental among certain Western types, and I don't want to make myself sillier than I already am by joining their number. Besides, I am very much lacking in background, and do not even have the most elementary knowledge of the languages that might be involved.

It is very important that one in such a position should have guidance and advice from someone who is an expert in the field. I am very glad Father Chan suggested you, as I am familiar with your books and realize that you are exactly the kind of person who would be of immense help. Since Father Chan says that you have expressed a willingness to do something of the kind, I therefore write to you without too many apologies, and indeed with deep gratitude for your kindness.

Where shall I begin? The one concrete thing that Father Chan seized upon in my letter to Archbishop Yu Pin was the tentative project of a selection from Chuang Tzu which New Directions would like to publish. But this is perhaps premature. I don't know if you saw a raw attempt of mine to say something about Chinese thought in *Jubilee*. It may have seemed articulate but I am sure you would have realized that I have only the most superficial grasp of the Confucian Classics, which is what I was mainly talking about. I do think it would be important perhaps for me to read some more and if possible discuss the Four Classics with you, on the most elementary level, like any Chinese schoolboy of the old days. I would like to really get impregnated with the spirit of the Four Classics, which to my mind is perfectly compatible with Christian ethics, and then go on to what really attracts me even more, the mysticism of the early Taoists. Then after that I might be able to talk sense about Chuang Tzu, and if you are still interested, we could perhaps work together on a selection, and you could do an original translation of the things we selected. I have the Legge translation here which looks suspiciously doctored to me.

I would be interested in your reaction, and would welcome any suggestions as to how to proceed and what to read now. And then, when you are free, I would like to invite you down to Gethsemani for a few days or a week . . .

Replying on March 20 to the above letter, John Wu praises Merton's grasp of the Chinese way of thinking and indicates that he would be delighted to cooperate with Merton in a translation of Chuang Tzu. He writes: "I have come to see that Chuang Tzu is neither a pantheist pure and simple nor a theist pure and true, but a mixture of the two—a prototype of what von Hügel calls panentheism . . . Only a man like yourself steeped in the works of the great Christian mystics can know what Lao Tzu and Chuang Tzu were pointing at, and how utterly honest and correct they were."

April 1, 1961

Your wonderful letter was a joy and an encouragement. I have no more doubts about the project being willed by God. It has the marks of the Holy Spirit's action upon it everywhere, doesn't it? The way you received the suggestion and your wonderful response is all the evidence one needs. I am sure we will go on to work together very happily and fruitfully . . .

So let us then proceed with love for the God Who manifested His wisdom so simply and so strikingly in the early Chinese sages, and let us give Him glory by bringing out the inner heart of that wisdom once again. One of the defects of a wrong kind of supernaturalism is that by rejecting those wonderful natural wisdoms that came before Christ and cried out for fulfillment in the Gospel, they set aside the challenging demands which would make us Christians strive for the highest purity of our own spiritual wisdom. And then, while claiming to be supernatural, we live on a level that is in some way *below* nature; the supernatural becomes the unnatural "sanctified" by legalistic formulas and appeals to gestures and rites whose inner meaning is not understood. And the whole thing is kept going by the magic formula *ex opere operato* . . .

I would not be able to explain this to many of my fellow priests, but I can say it to you with all confidence: it seems to me that this act of humility is demanded of us by God, that we condescend to *learn* and learn much, perhaps to acquire a whole new orientation of thought (which is simply the recovery of our own Christian orientation) from the ancient wisdoms which were fulfilled in Christ, so that we ourselves may reach a higher and deeper fulfillment which He demands of us . . .

What you say of the later Taoists taken up by Jung is very interesting and fits very well into some thinking I myself have been doing about personalism. One of the defects of popular personalism among us, including Christian personalism in some thinkers, is that the person is equated with the *anima* (P'o) and this is thought to be what survives, what is to be "cultivated" and "developed" so that actually a kind of practical anti-personalism is the result.

I am so happy you are doing a study of Chuang Tzu, and I look forward to reading it, avidly. I am more and more struck by the profundity of his thought. He is one of the *great* wise men: I will not say "philosophers" in the speculative sense, for his wisdom has a marvelous wholeness, and that is what makes it seem "simple." Indeed it is simple, but at the same time utterly profound. I think he has in him an element which is essential to all true contemplation, and which is often lacking in Western "contemplatives." His grasp of the fact that most of what is done in the name of "perfection" is actually perversion. His respect for the wholeness of reality which cannot be seized in a definition. The real meaning of *nature*. One must respect nature before one can rise out of it to be a person. Certainly he is well prepared for the "true light" which shines out in the Resurrection of Christ. The wisdom of Chuang Tzu demands the Resurrection, for the Resurrection goes beyond all moralities and moral theories, it is a totally new life in the Spirit.

Now as to the practical details. I have not seen the Giles translation and would be very glad to have it at hand while going through Legge. We do not have anything but Legge here. My edition of Legge may well be a reprint of the one you have. It too is very big, called the *Texts of Taoism*, but it was printed quite recently by the Julian Press with a preface by Dr. Suzuki. Hence the pagination may be different, that is the only problem . . . What I can do is tentatively send you a list of passages that interest me in the first four books, and see if you can locate them without difficulty . . . If I have the Giles book here I can give further references which will help you to locate the texts, but anyway with the subdivisions in Legge it should not be at all hard to give precise indications.

. . . God bless you, belatedly, on your birthday this Holy Week. I will be keeping you in my Easter Masses and ask the Lord to give you every blessing and joy and to keep ever fresh and young your "child's mind" which is the only one worth having. May He grant us (as you so well say) to be both inebriated and sober in Christ, Confucians and Taoists. It is all-important for us to *be* in Christ what the great sages cried out to God for. May our studies help us to live what they hoped for, and may we be able to bring to the Orient hope and light, which by right is theirs: for Christ rose up in the East, and we sing to Him *"O Oriens"* in Advent. His is what William of St.-Thierry called the *orientale lumen*. To that great light let us be humbly devoted and let us seek its tranquil purity in which all lights are fulfilled.

I look forward then to your coming later in the summer . . . Do let me know the date of Peter [Wu's] ordination and we will all be praying for him. I am so happy for you and for him and share with you the joy that is to be yours. God bless all of you. I will send you in a few days a list of selections from Chuang. Do please indicate to me any more books that would help me in my understanding and will broaden my background . . .

Your thesis on the natural law [as something that changes by addition] is vitally important . . .

April 4, 1961

I am having a really wonderful time with Chuang Tzu, and today I am sending you a first tentative list of selections from the first three books of the Legge translation in the edition that I have. I am only sending the selections from these first books so that you can see if my indications fit your edition. I am giving the number of the book and the numbers of these sections as given by Legge and the page number according to the edition I have here.

Please let me know if these indications are sufficient for you. If they are not, then I will make a complete list and send you the book I have here along with it. That ought to settle the difficulty.

The wisdom of Chuang Tzu delights and shames me. There is so much in him that we ought to be knowing and practicing at the monastery. Alas, we are all trying to be "Superior Men" and we are "standing on tiptoe" and "limping about" with our virtuousness.

. . . This is just a hasty note, but it brings you my best wishes, blessings and prayers. Yesterday I said Mass for you and for our project.

April 11, 1961

Thank you for your very good letter, for the Giles translation which I have now received and which is clear, idiomatic English, throwing light on Legge's more cautious and careful translation. Thanks above all for the first sample of your own translation. I like the almost poetic form and think we ought to use that often. I will discuss the details later—whether for instance it is better to use "benevolence" or "humanity," etc. . . .

Here is another list. I have given the sections according to Legge, and where it might be useful to do so, I have also added the page numbers in Giles. I think it will be all clear. More will follow soon.

Do you know what? We are reading *Beyond East and West* in the refectory now. It was Father Abbot's idea, highly encouraged by me, and everyone is enjoying it. You are so right in your great love for China and in your realization that Christianity transcends all racial and national limitations—a fact that has been too often forgotten.

I enjoy Chuang Tzu more and more. The liberty of spirit he seeks is found truly in St. Paul's Epistles and in St. John. We underestimate St. Paul. We do not realize what a liberation he went through and how carefree and undetermined a Christian really should be, with no care save to listen to the Holy Spirit and follow wherever He beckons! Let us seek more and more to do this in the gaiety and childlike joy of Chuang Tzu. I think spiritual childhood must be characteristically Chinese grace, I mean one which the Chinese temperament was prepared for . . .

April 21, 1961

Many thanks for your good letter. I am very glad the Mencius finally arrived and I knew you would like it. I am glad you approved of the "night spirit." It seems to me that Chinese is full of wonderful things that the West does not suspect—like your observation on the lunar month which deeply touched me in *Beyond East and West*. There are so many fine things in your book. I especially enjoy the notations from your diary that are being read now. The community was in a state of near riot when you described your marriage. I am in love with your parents. The book is most enjoyable and moving.

I have just finished reading the first paragraph (section) of Book XXIV of Chuang Tzu and really I believe it is one of the most superb passages in all literature. He is not only a wonderful thinker (he would repudiate the term, but in our poor English we have no alternative), but a fine poet. How modern he is! It has taken centuries to rediscover a little of what has been forgotten since Chuang Tzu. Legge's translation of this section seems quite good.

What are the ideograms for *True Man, Heaven-like-man*, etc.? What is their root meaning? What is their relationship to the ideogram for "Superior Man" in Confucius? I'd like to *see* these pictures if I can.

The Mencius will be in *Commonweal* [May 16, 1961] one of these days. Of course I did not translate it, just took the literal translation from the back of J. A. Richards's book and gave it form.

I was glad you liked *Seeds of Contemplation*. I have just completely rewritten it, leaving all that was there essentially, and adding more with a new perspective. It is the only book of mine that has been translated into Chinese. Would you like a copy?

Your ms. on St. Thérèse will be read with interest when it arrives. I am sure I can help you with other publishers. Frank Sheed is not endowed with infallibility. I am sure you will have a very special insight into the Little Way.

P.S. About the preface [to John's book on St. Thérèse], I will tell you if I think your book needs it and we can discuss the matter when you come down . . .

May 19, 1961

Forgive me for the delay in writing to you. I have been busy finishing up my course in mystical theology and various other tasks and now I have a little time to "return to the roots" and let the things that are more important come to the surface. Your manuscript on St. Thérèse I consider one of these "more important" things. I think the three items you sent me will go together to form a very fine little book and I do not understand Frank Sheed's criticism of it, unless he is allergic to some aspects of St. Thérèse, as most people are.

Actually I think your essay on St. Thérèse and Lao Tzu is very profound and interesting, and the one on Céline, which is Confucian, admirably balances it. I think the earlier pamphlet is less profound, more popular, and perhaps it ought to be redone to fit the tone and manner of the other two—that is to say, there ought to be more explicit references to Chinese Classical texts. Then all three would be on the same level. If you can think of a fourth essay, it would nicely round out the book, which is still a little short. I will gladly write a preface, if Fr. Abbot permits. We can see about that.

. . . I have finished making the selections from Chuang, but will type out the whole list in a few days to make sure you can read it.

Paul Sih sent me your translation of Lao Tzu, and this I like very much. I am hoping to write an article on this and the *Hsien Ching*, which is a beautiful little book. Your translation of the *Tao Te Ching* seems to me to be the best I know. I have two questions about it. In #23 the word "loss"—is it loss in a good sense, or in a bad sense? Would you enlighten me? And in #12, "The sage takes care of the belly not the eye." What is meant by "belly"? Does it by any chance correspond to the "bowels" in Scripture, i.e., the inmost heart?

I enjoyed very much your last etymologies. It is very important to me to get the wonderful differences of nuance and meaning, which have tremendous importance. It is so easy for the English reader to slur over "Superior Man" and "Heavenly Man" as if they were synonymous—especially in Taoism!!

Now I enjoy the quiet of the woods and the song of birds and the presence of the Lord in silence. Here is Nameless Tao, revealed as Jesus, the brightness of the hidden Father, our joy and our life . . .

May 27, 1961

. . . Here is my list. I hope it is comprehensible to you. I will try to clarify if you do not understand, but if you are in doubt I leave it to your discretion to edit the section suitably. I know these general indications are sufficient, you will be able to add what is better in Chinese and subtract what is useless. Please do not feel confined by my suggestions. Anything I have missed that is really good should not be omitted.

I look forward to seeing you and the translation and hope we will have weather as perfect as we have here now. It is delightful . . .

May 29, 1961

I had written out my list Saturday and I received your fine letter this morning. There is certainly no hurry, and if a trip to Formosa holds up your work a little, it is no matter. I do not know if I grasped your suggestion about how you believed I ought to proceed. If I work on some of the selections, it will really only be a manipulation of what has already been said in English by Giles and Legge, so of course it will be really nothing . . . I think that your insights into the meaning would be so much more real and profound that it is a question of you getting the real substance, and my merely polishing up the English expression. However, I might take a fling at a few passages I like just for the joy of doing it.

I am so happy that you want to complete the little book on St. Thérèse and Chinese philosophy, and that this will be an offering of piety in memory of your dear wife. We all love her here, since the book was read in the refectory . . .

I have carefully gone through your fine translation of the *Tao Te Ching*, and it is all superb. I really mean to get down to the article. I loved the *Hsiao Ching* too. It is so completely in tune with reality. The Zen books you speak of interest me, but my German is slow. I shall be eager to see if they appear in English translation. If I once reached Buddhahood and redescended to my present state, all I can say is that I made a really heroic sacrifice. But I don't regret it, as the other Buddhas seem to have done the same. Yourself for instance. Thus we go along gaily with littleness for our Mother and our Nurse, and we return to the root by having no answers to questions. Whatever I may have been in previous lives, I think more than half of them were Chinese and eremitical.

I hope soon to send you my dialogue with Dr. Suzuki, about which I think I told you. It is being printed. I like Zen, and from what I know of it, which is not much, I think the Rinzai school is probably more my line at the present stage, but I must say I don't like the looks of some of their masters and I would take good care to keep out of the way of their *hossu*.

All blessings for the forthcoming ordination, I will be there in spirit . . .

July 31, 1961

All this time I have refrained from writing to you because I supposed that you were in Formosa and I did not know when you would return. Now I am putting in the mail your manuscripts, which I had been holding here for the same reason. By the way, during this time I gave it (them) to a couple of novices to read and they enjoyed your work and were enlightened by it . . .

. . . Have you been doing anything with Chuang Tzu? I have been rereading some of the wonderful chapters and coming to the conclusion that I do not know anything about him yet, but want to more and more. Really one would like to put everything else aside and simply spend a good part of the day on this, but of course there are many other things to be done, and I have a few other studies on hand also: which is perhaps itself not in accordance with Chuang Tzu and accounts for my obtuseness.

I think much of you and of China. Dr. Sih is sending me a couple of his books, and he too plans to come down later on in the fall. If you did not come in August and wanted to come with Dr. Sih in October, that would be all right too. I leave you to decide.

. . . The picture of the ordination [of John's son, Peter, at Maryknoll] was on our bulletin board and the *Interior Carmel* is being read in the evening chapter, to the satisfaction of all.

Now I must close, but I will say at least this: I am glad you are not in Formosa and that we can hope to see you here soon.

August 12, 1961

Many thanks for the letter. It is too bad we cannot look forward to receiving you at the end of the month, but it is good that your uncertainty is now over and that you know when the meeting is to be. My prayers certainly go with you on this important trip. You have all my sympathy and best wishes in this critical time. I hope that the Holy Spirit will guide you and all your associates.

I am reading Paul Sih's book about China at the moment. It is very clear and informative, and tells me a lot of things about which I knew nothing. When we are up against a monster propaganda machine, the task is discouraging, but we must nevertheless stick to the truth. The trouble is that there is also a monster ambiguity to deal with at the same time, as though the propaganda machine had not only changed the "truths" but even changed the "truth" itself. As if it had somehow created a new kind of truth, in the face of which all former truths, however true, become irrelevant. This is the problem.

. . . Before I can attempt to do anything myself with Chuang Tzu I am going to have to learn two hundred fundamental ideograms. I don't think I can honestly approach the task otherwise. I need to orient myself somewhat in the Chinese text, which I am so glad to have. I have to make at least some kind of gesture at thinking through the ideograms and not just through sentences in Western languages. Can you suggest the best collection of ideograms for a beginner? Or is there some other approach?

The [Léon] Wieger [French translation of Chuang Tzu] is good to have. He is breezy and to some extent helpful, but above all it is fine to have the Chinese text. [Richard] Wilhelm [German translator of Chuang Tzu] has also arrived and I agree with you, he strikes one as very very solid and trustworthy. I like his work, and am glad to have this. With these translations I ought to be able to do something eventually. It will necessarily be slow and awkward, however.

Can we count on you coming down this fall with Paul Sih?

I am delighted to hear about your coming course in Oriental philosophies [at Seton Hall University]. I wish I could take it.

Best wishes to you and all the family, including Father Peter. And again, may God bless your journey. Perhaps you could convey my humble respect to Archbishop Yu Pin and ask his blessing for me.

October 11, 1961

Are you back from Formosa? I presume you must be. And you are probably very busy at Seton Hall. As for me, I have tried my hand at one or two little sections of Chuang Tzu and have enjoyed working on them in the way suggested, using the various translations. The German version is particularly helpful. But I find it takes an enormous amount of time to do it this way. Anyone translating from the original would move much faster. Consequently very little has been done. I have hopes of getting back to it, after I have cleared the way. I still have a couple of small writing jobs that have been hanging fire for many months . . .

On November 28 Dr. Wu wrote that he had just received Merton's book The New Man. *It is, he says, "a living synthesis of East and West . . . It seems to me that you read contemplatively. You are so deeply Christian that you cannot help touching the vital springs of other religions."*

December 12, 1961

Today is the Feast of Our Lady of Guadalupe, significant to us all in a very special way I am sure. At any event, Our Lady has brought me a moment of time in which to reply to your two good letters. I have got myself involved in a lot of thinking about peace and war, since it seems to be necessary for someone to speak out forthrightly on this awful problem. But it has taken up a great deal of my time, and the question gets so terribly involved when one listens to the opinions of men about it. And one has to. It is a great mystery, most of which is pure delusion and self-deception. It gets to be more and more subtle and more and more self-important, this thinking of experts, and yet in the long run the answer should be quite simple and quite plain: we should be Christians, and we should be prepared to follow Christ even if the consequences do not seem to us to be immediately profitable or expedient. It is the fact that we have unfortunately become so involved in expediency and in commitment to temporal interest above all, that we have had to follow the complications of military minds and of statesmen . . .

I think my time would probably have been spent better with Chuang Tzu, except that I cannot see my way to doing this at the moment. Perhaps after a couple of months, when I have settled my mind as to exactly what line I ought to take and how to clarify that position.

As to your illness, I am sorry to hear of it, but I hope you are now perfectly rested and reestablished. These fast air trips halfway around the world are not exactly restful, as far as I can see . . . It is more profitable and more comfortable to rise on the wings of the wind with the old Taoists and sport about among the clouds, but this is not possible until one renounces the idea of getting anywhere.

. . . Someone has recently sent me a marvelous book, *Poems of Solitude*, a collection including Juan Chi, Pao Chao, Wang Wei, Li Ho and Li Yu. Maybe you are right about my being Chinese, because this kind of thing is just what makes me feel most happy and most at home. I do not know whether or not I am always happy with mystical writings that are completely out of touch with ordinary life. On the contrary, it seems to me that mysticism flourishes most purely right in the middle of the ordinary. And such mysticism, in order to flourish, must be quite prompt to renounce all apparent claim to be mystical at all: after all, what difference do labels make? I know you agree, for this is what St. Thérèse so well saw. And by the way, how are you coming along with that book?

Your remarks on *The New Man* obviously made me very happy. What nicer compliments could any man have than to be told he has approached something which is the object of his greatest admiration and respect? To have been told that the book has a really Oriental quality is all the reward I ask for having written it, because I know that there is in the fact of having written it a value that cannot be taken away. I hope you will like the *New Seeds of Contemplation*, which will reach you soon.

. . . And now: when would it be convenient for you to come down this next spring? Would you like to come at mid-year, for example, at the end of January, or whenever the break in your school year comes? Or would you prefer to come later? The weather here is sometimes mild in winter and sometimes just as cold as it is in the East, we never know quite what to expect. It would be wonderful if you could meet my old friend Victor Hammer, an Austrian artist and printer who lives in Lexington . . . He is printing a thing of mine on Wisdom at the moment. He does very limited and rare editions which are quite beautiful. I think you received the Meng Tzu parable, which he printed last year. In fact I know you did, for you mentioned the printing.

All best Christmas wishes and warm blessings for the new year. May Our Lord come to us in peace and in simplicity, and increase our faith and love for Him. And may this poor world have peace, somehow, in spite of the madness and absurdity of men and weapons. For now it is the weapons themselves that make all the decisions: men humbly obey the creations of their own technology. I wonder if a few of us may persuade our fellows to retain at least enough freedom to use machines instead of being used by them.

[*Cold War Letter 82*]

June 7, 1962

I had better get this letter written before any more time flows under the bridge (what bridge? what time? this is our illusion). But in any case time has something to do with the fact that I am going to say Mass for your intentions on June 15th, a week from tomorrow, which will be Friday in Whitsun week . . . This Mass is being said for you at the request of Mrs. O'Brian and I promised her a long time ago I would let you know . . .

But it will be a joy to stand in the presence of the Heavenly Father, in Christ, and speak of you and all whom you love and of China.

Paul Sih has obtained for me a wonderful reprint of the Legge translation of the Chinese Classics, and has also sent the Wang Yang Ming. I am awed and delighted with the great volumes of the Classics. I do not intend to read them lightly however, they are waiting until other things can be cleared away. But I must admit I have done absolutely no work at all on Chinese, because I find that I simply waste too much time fumbling around in the dictionary and so little is done that it does not make sense to continue until sometime in the future when I can get some instruction. So it will all have to wait a bit. I am working on the Latin Fathers, with whom I can make enough headway to know what is happening. Perhaps I shall do a translation of an excerpt from Cassiodorus. I think you would like him. He is very much the Confucian scholar, Latin style. A great librarian and student and copyist of books, but also a polished writer and an engaging thinker, besides a man of prayer. His monastery of Vivarium is most attractive: it was a monastery of scholars.

And now to turn suddenly from scholarship to less pleasant subjects. I hesitate to send you the enclosed angry and bitter poem ["A Picture of Lee Ying"]. It is savage, and its savagery hits everything in sight, so that it is not kind to anyone, even to the poor and desperate Chinese girl whose picture broke my heart and suggested the poem. I wish I could have said something full of mercy and love that would have been worthy of the situation, but I have only used her plight to attack the hypocrisy of those who find no room for the Chinese refugees, and who always have a very good reason. And the sad plight of a whole society which nods approval, while pronouncing a few formulas of regret. I suppose I should not get angry, and that it represents a weakness in myself to get excited about the awful tragedies that are everywhere in the world. They are too awful for human protest to be meaningful, so people seem to think. I protest anyway, I am still primitive enough, I have not caught up with this century . . .

John Wu visited Merton at Gethsemani in late June 1962.

July 10, 1962

Many thanks for your two letters, and above all, thanks for coming. It was certainly a grace to have you here, a grace for me and a grace for us all. Therefore we hope you will return soon. And I am sure you will do that, now that you know what to expect: our disappearances and appearances, the long silences, the informality, and everything else down to Father Abbot's coy jokes about picture cards in the envelopes. This is just the way we are.

. . . Then I am preoccupied because one of my novices tells me that I have a neighbor: a snake has taken up residence in the woodshed up the hill. I don't want to disturb him. I knew he was there, since he left his skin on the woodpile. I did not know he was a permanent resident. He appears to be harmless. Yet I don't like to be pulling apart the woodpile and suddenly have a family of snakes fall out all around me. So I will have to get together with Tao and wait for something to work itself out. Maybe I will just talk to him reasonably, or maybe we will just settle down and be neighbors. I hate to kill even a snake, and anyway there seems to be no real reason for killing this one.

I thought I would finally type out one of the "versions" I did after Chuang Tzu. Very much "after," I fear. But anyway, it no longer even pretends to be a serious rendering. I might insert it in a collection of poems I am getting together, as an experiment.

. . . I also enclose a poem, landscape, especially with a quail in it. The quail, as I seem to remember, is also a bird loved by Chuang Tzu. The quail is called, popularly, "bobwhite" around here. I thought you might like this . . .

John Wu takes issue with Merton for calling his translation "after Chuang Tzu." He writes on July 17: "You have taken him by the forelocks not by the tail. I swear that I am not flattering when I say that this is exactly what Chuang Tzu would write had he learned English."

December 20, 1962

I was so happy to get your letter this morning. I am putting aside all others to answer you immediately: such is the power of Chuang Tzu and Tao to get action out of one buried in the inertia of too much activity. The very name of Chuang Tzu restores me to sanity, at least momentarily . . .

. . . Anyway, I am sure I will get back to Chuang Tzu in the spring and if you send me your article (you say you have sent it, good), then that will get me back where I belong, even before spring. It will be my Christmas reading.

Insanity. Anything but his quiet debunking view is plain insanity. Even within the framework of the Gospel message there is too much temptation to forget what Jesus Himself warned at every step. One thing is necessary. Christianity as it has developed in the West, including monasteries of the West, has become a complex and multifarious thing. It takes Chuang Tzu to remind us of an essential element in the Gospel which we have simply "tuned out" with all our wretched concerns. The whole Sermon on the Mount, for instance. And the Discourse of the Last Supper. Even the central message of the Cross and the Resurrection. And the crib full of straw, in which the Lord of the world laughs and says, "You should worry!"

I am proud that you should want to use my "versions" [in your class]. By all means do so. You know, by the way, one of my distractions, and

I think it is legitimate, is that I have "discovered" a Nicaraguan poet who is something like Chuang Tzu, but with of course many great differences. First of all he is mad. He is locked up. But he writes some of the most amazingly sane poetry. I will send you a few. He is called Alfonso Cortes. Nobody in this country has ever heard of him. Of course, he *is* mad, but in his madness he accuses all the right things for the right reasons.

. . . I am glad you like "Philosophy of Solitude" [in *Disputed Questions*]. It is one of the things I have most wanted to say, perhaps the only thing I have said that needed to be said.

All best wishes always, and every blessing in this holy season when the animals and the shepherds show us the way back to our child mind and to Him in Whom is hidden our original face before we are born. Be of good cheer. They cannot silence either Chuang Tzu or this Child, in China or anywhere. They will be heard in the middle of the night saying nothing and everybody will come to their senses.

June 23, 1963

Your two fine letters have been waiting long for a reply . . .

. . . Your remarks on Zen in the first letter are very helpful. Yes, the real point is this fact that Zen is NOT zazen. And everybody wants to reduce it to that, even with their koans and all the rest. In both cases a set of stinking skeleton. Let's throw out the skeleton for good and all and take off for nowhere with that Vagabond (that notorious illuminist, the Holy Spirit).

I have had a very amusing Chuang Tzuean experience. With deliberate intention to wreak mischief and with tongue deeply in cheek, I wrote a long fiery article defending Fénelon against Bossuet. (Of course I like Fénelon, but the idea was to puncture the Bossuet image and the French national collective ego, which is anti-Fénelon.) Then I sent it to the censors of the Order in England, who obviously rushed to approve it, and sent their approval to the Abbot General, probably letting him know the contents of the article (he can't read English). Report came back from our patriotic French General, a staunch Gaullist and a most humorless chauvinist when it comes to things like this. He granted the *nihil obstat*, I can almost hear the muttered recriminations with which he did so, and then added in a special note that he did not want his name associated in any way with such a piece of effrontery. It was magnanimous of him not to put me on bread and water for a year and stop me writing altogether.

But talking of Chuang Tzu: I am really hoping to get down to some work on him, and in fact I am well on the way to finishing a small book of selections. I thought I would send one piece along to you now, to see how you like it. It contains a few minor liberties with what must be the original meaning. You will tell me if I am too wild and wide of the mark, and what to change. But anyway, Chuang Tzu is my delight.

Thank you for the note on No Mind. Yes, the term Unconscious is misleading, and very much so. The thing is to get a real equivalent to the direct awareness *in depth*, the pure and complete immediacy implied by it. The problem of English terms like "no reflection" is that they seem to imply a kind of sensible quietism, a *surface* intuitiveness, more or less a rest in the immediacy of *sense* experience. That is of course only the least part of it. On the other hand we are bedeviled with the Platonist prejudice against senses, so that when it becomes an interior quietism of the zazen type, then some are satisfied with that. The old forced duality. And how they like to force it.

Yes, I did receive your article on Chuang Tzu, a long time ago, and it is very fine. I will be able to guide myself by it in writing the preface to my little pieces . . .

I am sorry we are going to lose you to Formosa in 1964. That is a long way off. With the mail it doesn't make much difference, but still there will not be much hope of seeing you if you are that far off. Still, I am sure they need you there.

Meanwhile, keep in touch with us. I hope we will see you before you go, perhaps sometime next spring or summer . . .

Paul Sih has sent me the *Platform Scripture* and it is handsomely done. He wants me to write a review of it, and I will earnestly try, but it is hard to fit in right now. But with a book like this an immediate reaction is not essential. Eventually I hope to come through with something.

Best wishes to you, John. I will be remembering you tomorrow on the Feast of St. John the Baptist, though I seem to remember your patron is the Evangelist. No matter, any day is a good day for prayers and blessings.

December 23, 1964

It was a great joy to get your card and note. What happened to our correspondence? The last letter I wrote was sent when I thought you were soon to go to Taiwan, and when I did not get a reply I thought I had missed you. And I did not know where to write next. Now I find you are still in New Jersey, and maybe that is better in the long run. But now I hear you met Suzuki in Honolulu and the deep secret of my mysterious voyage* is out. It had to be a total secret, and I saw no one in NY except Suzuki, none of my other friends yet know that I was there, I was under strict orders to slink around with false mustaches and dark glasses and foreign names. But I am glad you met him. I think you are perfectly right about his having a child's mind and heart. It is perfectly true, and that is his greatness.

---

* *Merton's secret meeting with Dr. Suzuki at Columbia in New York City in the spring of 1964.*

I am very anxious to see your history of Zen, and anything else you have been working on. I still have not given up the idea of various versions of Chuang Tzu, but have not been able to do anything about it lately. As a matter of fact, in my last letter I sent a version which may have been so bad that I attributed to it, also, your silence!

. . . This fall, Fr. Dumoulin wrote from Japan and urged very strongly that I ask permission to make a trip there and meet some of the Zen monks in their monasteries. He wrote quite a strong letter to the Abbot General about this, which ought to have meant something, since he is a member of the Secretariat for Non-Christian Religions. However, all my Superiors managed to gather from this request was that I was half out of my mind. They are completely unprepared to understand any such thing. They told me my request was completely incredible and that was that. I think I might have learned very much from it, but there are other ways of learning the same things and I must admit that I am not keen on traveling.

There is much Christmas mail to be attended to, so I must stop now . . .

January 31, 1965

Look how much time has passed since I received your letter and the chapter on Hui Neng [in Dr. Wu's book *The Golden Age of Zen*]. Time does not obey me, it will not stop for my convenience. This is very strange, but I must put up with it, even though time obeys everybody else. I will have to picket time for this unfairness.

Really I enjoyed your chapter on Hui Neng very much, as it has much new material and I like your insight about the quiet revolution on p. 10. Your pages bring out more of the real importance of Hui Neng. I like the concept of playful samadhi, which comes very naturally from you.

As to suggestions and criticisms: . . . The big question is the use of the term "self-nature," which I think the Western reader simply cannot avoid taking as the opposite to what it really means. You are right that "mind" is a "weasel word." And when you say that self-nature is the "substance and essence of mind" you are ushering in two more weasels, so that at this point self-nature is attacked on three sides by dangerous weasels. And since essence is big enough and fat enough to be the equivalent of two or even three weasels, then I think that you have self-nature entirely surrounded and I fear that he will not escape. But on the other hand, since nature is the biggest weasel of all, it turns out in the end to be a civil war, and the weasels are all fighting each other. From this kind of thing there is no resource left but to withdraw into the void and scamper about in nothingness where there cannot be a shadow of civil war. But of course this does not solve the problem of making the Western reader aware of what self-nature is all about. The main thing is that it is not about (1) self, and (2) nature, as these terms are understood in the West. Is that right? I may simply be mumbling the inanities of a half-frozen monk, but it seems to me that the problem lies somewhere in this area. It is a problem of communication. And if the word "self-nature" translates the Chinese ideograms, then it is a matter of explaining that there is more in this than meets the eye, or perhaps less. Or at any rate something else.

At every turn, we get back to the big question, which is the question of the person as void and not as individual or empirical ego. I know of no one in the West who has treated of person in such a way as to make clear that what is most ourselves is what is least ourself, or better the other way round. It is the void that is our personality, and not our individuality that seems to be concrete and defined and present etc. It is what is seemingly not present, the void, that is really I. And the "I" that seems to be I is really a void. But the West is so used to identifying the person with the individual and the deeper self with the empirical self (confusing the issue by juggling around a divided "body and soul") that the basic truth is never seen. It is the Not-I that is most of all the I in each one of us. But we are completely enslaved by the illusory I that is not I, and never can be I, except in a purely fictional and social sense. And of course there is yet one more convolution in this strange dialectic: there remains to suppress the apparent division between empirical self and real or inner self. There is no such division. There is only the Void which is I, covered over by an apparent I. And when the apparent I is seen to be void it no longer needs to be rejected, *for it is I.* How wonderful it is to be alive in such a world of craziness and simplicity . . .

John Wu wrote on May 11, 1965: "I have just read your nosegay of poems called The Way of Chuang Tzu. *I am simply bewitched. If Chuang Tzu were writing in English, he would surely write like this."*

June 9, 1965

What a wonderful letter that was! It was a pure delight, and it made me so happy that I had been insane enough to go ahead with the work on Chuang Tzu. To have one such reader would be enough! And to encounter living in you the spirit of Chuang Tzu himself with such liveliness and force is, I must say, an experience. I am glad there is still such a dragon hiding around corners and behind clouds in our rather stuffy world. And glad that, through your encouragement, I have had a glimpse of him.

Well, naturally, I have now produced practically a whole book. A great many more texts and a longish introduction. The publisher is delighted (New Directions) . . .

We will need illustrations, as New Directions wants to make a rather lavish book out of it. My idea is that perhaps some very fine free ancient calligraphy, perhaps something with some of the more important ideograms like Tao, wu wei and so on. I do have a little book where some Chinese drawings of trees, people and so on are found. They are adequate but not exciting . . .

Naturally, I want to dedicate the Chuang Tzu book to you. So I hope you will accept, indeed I will not permit you to refuse: then your name will appear on a good blank page and we will all fly away on the back of the same dragon.

I do not know what you think about what is going on these days in Vietnam. No matter what one's view of it may be, one has to forget about Law and good sense, if one is to be comfortable with the policies of Washington, as far as I can see. In the long run I think that our new President is pursuing a course that will get all those he is trying to subdue both very angry and unsubdued, and also will line them up in firm solidarity with communist China. I don't see how his absurd policies can have any other effect than this. He is doing his level best to make Asia communist, and is also trying hard in Latin America. The fact that he and his helpers cannot see this is all the more unfortunate, since it means that they will not give up until it is too late. What do you think about it all? In any event, the general acceptance of brute and useless terrorism as both reasonable and necessary, by many of the public here, is the most disquieting thing of all. Naturally it is easy to find fault and a lot harder to see what positively ought to be done. Meanwhile the brutality goes on, on both sides.

That is a less pleasant subject than Chuang Tzu. I leave you with best wishes for a pleasant summer. Later on I hope to send you the whole manuscript, but first it must be typed, and then I suppose I will have to send my extra copies to the official censors of the Order and the Lord alone knows what they will make of it . . .

July 11, 1965

I don't want to delay any longer in writing to you at your new address [in South Orange, N.J.] and telling you that of course I do have the three Zen chapters. But I have not been able to work over them, as I think this will require a bit of time and I don't quite know how to go about it. It is a question of making them more directly readable: your meaning will not always get across clearly. On the other hand, there is no more difficult job in the world than to try to edit another man's writing, or at least there is nothing that I find more difficult, and I warn you in advance that I may very well probably not be able to do it at all. At best I can make some suggestions. The material is terrific, and there is much that is new in the way of perspective and intuitions . . .

Chuang Tzu is finished, but all the copies are in use, with censors and so on. I don't know what on earth the censors will make of him.

This is just a hasty note. I am trying to catch up with my mail, a frustrating task, at which I know there is no chance that I will ever win. But why should one need to win? Tao will have to answer the letters.

July 22, 1965

. . . You will be pleased to hear the news: the Chuang Tzu book was not only passed with honors by both censors, but one of them even asked to keep the ms. for a good long time so that he might study it and use it more. So you must have said a good strong prayer and the Holy Spirit must have breathed over the waters of argument. In fact, though, now that I know who did the censoring, I can see they would be open to something like this. There are others who would have had seven kinds of fits.

. . . Facing a barrage of deadlines, I have no chance to work on your Zen chapters now, and will have to wait a bit. But I will do what I can by means of a general suggestion here and there. I would certainly not take upon myself the job of ruining your work for you: or I would have read Chuang Tzu in vain. I will concentrate on enjoying and profiting by the material and the way it is presented, you cannot deny me this. Then, if I go at it this way, the corrections that are really needed, if any, will arise quietly out of the truth you yourself have seen and intended. May the Holy Spirit bring it all to fruitful completion.

Dr. Wu writes in his letter of August 3 that he had met Father William Johnston, who said in a lecture that Merton's writings were "full of Zen even when they were not about Zen."

August 6, 1965

Your letter reached me here in the hospital. Nothing serious. I am getting out today. But all my work has been held up. I hope to get your Zen chapters back to you soon, but I have not been making corrections or suggestions yet. The time to think it all over has not been there, and I do not intend to say anything thoughtless. If I can, I will say *something*.

Fr. Johnston wrote a card that he might drop by the Abbey and I hope to see him. Fr. Dumoulin is going to be in this country too, soon.

August 10, 1965

Here are two of your chapters, I do not want to make you wait any longer. This is simply magnificent material, and I revel in it. I am especially fond of Tung Shan, who is rapidly becoming one of my very favorites. I can't wait to have the finished book so that I will be able to refer to it. I am also delighted with Lin Chi and his shouters. This is a wonderful book . . .

My only problem with it is that the way it is written often deprives it of its full impact. The material is all there and your exposition of it is fine, well planned, most lively and interesting. But often the statements seem to glance off the target rather than sticking in the bull's-eye: this being due to the way the statements are formulated and particularly the choice of words at times. I have attempted a couple of suggestions here and there but realize that they are totally inadequate. I am at a loss how to help out with this, because I feel myself on slippery ground. I think I know just what you mean in each case but I cannot seem to find a way to say it, or if I do, then I fear that I may be changing your meaning. It is purely a question of framing the statements in such a way that they will click with the American reader. I am not speaking at all about their content, but about getting it across. That is my only worry about the book. A publisher's reader might pick it up and fail to connect, and the whole thing would be lost on him. I don't think there would be any problem for people who have read other Zen books—there is now almost a Zen language in the book field. But for the general reader and the first-time-at-Zen people I think your book would be hard to understand. I think too you probably need to give more explanations of things which are familiar to those who already know about Zen but not to others. These are only impressions I have formed, and as I say I don't know what to say that will be more constructive and helpful. It is a wonderful book, and certainly one of the best things on Zen that has come out. It provides a very welcome change of pace and perspective from Suzuki, and throws such abundant light on Chinese Zen, it is going to be invaluable. I am delighted to have had this chance to read it and look forward to the rest of it . . .

. . . New Directions is coming along with Chuang Tzu. He is already in proof. Wu wei really works.

September 12, 1965

I am really very sorry to have kept your chapters on Zen so long, and I don't want to hold them up any longer. It has been a delight to read them: your book is indispensable. There has never yet been such a good, clear outline of the whole subject, and it is essential for students and for anyone who wants to enjoy Zen. My only regret is that you imposed upon me the task of reading with a pen in my hand, to look for corrections to be made. This really spoiled the pleasure of just going along with your Zen masters, and I really have left nothing to show for it. I have only tried to help you, here and there, to put it more idiomatically and correctly from the point of view of English syntax and style. But I am afraid I have not been much help. I am sure, though, that if you go over it all very carefully and self-critically, perhaps discussing it with someone there, you will iron out the wrinkles. The chief problem is that you get a lively intuition of how to say something, and I know what you are driving at, but you say it in such a way that it does not come off successfully from the point of view of English . . .

That is all the severity I can muster up. For the rest, I don't know which house I enjoy more. In Zen there are many mansions and my own inclination is to live in them all.

. . . Returning to your own book, I am delighted that it is going to be really full-length and no nonsense about it. One wants more and more. I can see that the material must be rich and plenteous, and the writers on the subject in English have not even scratched the surface. So dig in and keep digging, we are all waiting for you to come up with mountains of gold, and you have begun to do so already. Give us more . . .

November 11, 1965

If there is one truth I have learned about the hermit life, it is certainly this: that hermits are terrible letter writers. I have been meaning to get this off to you for days. I am sending off a copy of Chuang Tzu signed for you. I hope the publisher will by now have sent you other copies. I owe you a great debt for this. It has been a wonderful experience and something I cannot repay with a few words. I will keep you always in my prayers. And may we always live more and more in that wonderful spirit of acceptance that was his. It is of course the real key to all this talk about "turning to the world."

Where are the other chapters of your Zen book? I hope you are not going to give me up because I take so long to answer. I do not promise to be more prompt but I would like to keep up with you, even though I may be incorrigible about responding, the wrong kind of wu wei . . .

In a letter of November 19, Dr. Wu says that he is going to Taiwan in the spring. Then, writing on November 24, he expresses his joy at receiving the completed text of The Way of Chuang Tzu. *"I have come to the conclusion that you and Chuang Tzu are one. It is Chuang Tzu himself who writes his thoughts in the English of Thomas Merton. You are a true man of Tao just as he is. You have met in that eternal place which is no place and you look at each other and laugh together . . . The spirit of joy is written over all the pages."*

December 3, 1965

. . . Now about the Zen book (yes, I have the nine chapters and then one more), the man you must see at New Directions is Robert MacGregor. And he is probably the best person to see in the whole publishing business because he knows China and likes Buddhism, and I am sure he will be very interested in the book. Then, about the introduction: if you are not afraid that I will ruin the book and take away the readers' appetite, and afflict them with permanent allergies to Zen and all things related to it, I will gladly try my hand, though I have been forbidden to write any more prefaces by my publisher, who says I write too many. Since this is, I hope, a New Directions book, I am hoping that the (other) publishers will understand, and anyway, I had promised you more or less some time ago that I would do something of the sort. So it is not so bad. But I cannot do anything now, it must wait a bit, I have been too tied up in a lot of small jobs and have other urgent things to get out of the way. So you see that though I may on occasion talk like Chuang Tzu I don't live like him. But I guess I am learning to take these things with indifference.

As to what you said about the book, well, all I can say is that if Tao did the job through me, it was done in the usual way: without my knowing a thing about it. All I know is that in the beginning especially I was doing a job for which I felt no capacity whatever, and in the end, while I still felt I had no capacity, it did not make any difference, I was having a lot of fun. As to attributing it to me, well, you can do so if you like, maybe Tao is playing games and acknowledging who did the work in this particular way. Who am I to interfere with Tao? . . .

. . . Back to the Zen book, I think this revision is much smoother and reads very well. I am very happy to browse through it again, and will continue to do so until the preface pops out sometime later . . .

John Wu wrote on December 17, 1965, that Merton's name in Chinese was Mei Teng, which means "silent lamp."

December 28, 1965

Your letter and poem reached me on the Feast of St. Thomas, just as I was about to go to say Mass for Asia and all my Asian friends and for my own vocation to see things Asian in their simplicity and truth, if possible. So it was moving to be "baptized" in Chinese with a name I must live up to. After all, a name indicates a divine demand. Hence I must be Mei Teng, a silent lamp, not a sputtering one. Over these quiet feast days . . . I have been in the woods just staying quiet. And since the earth is one, I think I have plenty of Asia under my feet. The thing is to recognize it. This is the only real contribution I have to make to a tormented political situation. Instead of fighting Asia, to be it. And stubbornly, too.

Your calligraphy fascinates me, and of course so does the poem, in the great tradition of Chinese occasional verse, so polished and so human. I wish I could reply in kind, calligraphy and all. In desperation, or rather no, in considerable joy, I resort again to the green tea, and in fact the kettle is whistling by the fire right at my elbow, and the sun is rising over the completely silver landscape. Instead of putting all this into a poem, I will let it be its own poem. The silent steam will rise from the teacup and make an ideogram for you. Maybe sometime I will add a poem to it as an exclamation point of my own. But are such exclamation points needed?

In any event I am delighted with all you send, and especially with the sparks of Zen. Reading that, I easily saw why I had questions about your style in the other part of the book: this is what you were really aiming at all the time. In the other chapters you spoke academically to some extent, yet the informality kept bursting through. Here there is no longer any sense of uneasiness about it in the reader, since you are completely spontaneous and informal and it works like a charm. It is the best part of the book. And yet the other chapters had to be as they are too. I will certainly do my best to write a good essay on Zen as an introduction . . .

John Wu's letter of January 10, 1966, included the following haiku poem: "Silent lamp! Silent lamp!/I only see its radiance/But hear not its voice!/Spring beyond the world!

January 27, 1966

. . . The latest haiku and calligraphies are most impressive. I look at the calligraphies in wonderment, wishing I could begin to read them. When you tell me where Mei Teng is, I generally manage to pick that out, but it is no great achievement. Here then I have the privilege of being reduced to a state of complete infancy.

We have just been on retreat and so I am as usual caught with a lot of letters to answer, some of which will never get answered. But I must try, so I hasten on, leaving you for the moment. When are you planning to come down? The weather is very cold now, and the ax has plenty to do, but it will have more when the logs are out from under the deep snow. The retreat, in any case, accounts for my silence.

God bless you always. Keep warm and don't read anything that robs you of sleep: sleep is better than reading.

February 7, 1966

. . . A Moslem friend of mine is getting interested in Chuang Tzu and asked me if I could get him an offprint of your article. Do you have one—or is the new book soon appearing (the one I read in French)? Could you please send him the offprint if you have one. He is: Ch. Abdul Aziz, in Karachi, Pakistan. He would greatly appreciate it.

FR. LOUIS
Old cracked Mei Teng

In May 1966 Dr. Wu stopped in Tokyo on his way to Taipei and visited Suzuki. Two months later, on July 12, Dr. Suzuki died.

July 11, 1966

For a long time I have been trying to get over my consternation at the fact that you were in Asia. And then to write to you. Back in May, about the same time, Catherine de Vinck told me you had gone and your

letter came from Tokyo. I was especially glad to hear of your visit with
Suzuki. I have not heard from him, but I have heard from Richard de
Martino and have promised to write something for the *Eastern Bud-
dhist* . . .

You are probably wondering about the preface. I am still in the long
stage of preparation. I simply cannot rush into a thing like this, but I
think that by next week I will be ready to try getting something on paper.
I want to treat the question of Christianity and Zen: in what are they
alike, in what they are not alike, and so on. A brief simple contribution
to East–West understanding. But that is exactly the hardest thing to do
well. It would be much easier to write about the length of Chuang Tzu's
ears or something useless like that . . .

I hope by now you must be settled in Taipei and I hope things are
all right. I cannot convince myself that they are wonderful, but I am afraid
we all live in strange situations these days, in which nothing quite makes
perfect sense. If it did we would all drop dead from shock.

It has been slow going since the hospital. For a long time I had
trouble typing and only got back to work gradually. In fact I am still not
wildly producing and I doubt there is any harm in that. At the moment
it is very hot, anyway. I will be glad to get down to the preface. I have
really given it a lot of thought, perhaps too much. When you get this
letter, that will be the time for the extra prayer to the Holy Spirit. I really
need some inspiration to fuse it all together and make sense out of it,
otherwise it may just be an indefinitely long series of mumblings.

As I have other letters to catch up with, I will close this one. I hope
to hear from you soon . . .

*Dr. Wu returned to the States from Taiwan. His book had been published in
Taiwan.*

September 24, 1967

Hurray! So glad to have you back. Permanently I hope! And delighted
to hear that the book is so well advanced. Many thanks for [your] preface
[Merton had written the introduction]. It is a joy and a privilege for me
to be so closely associated with you in this. I must send you my own new
book: you have read most of the parts that have to do with Zen or the
East, I believe. There may however be some little corners that are new
to you.

It was also a joy to give what support [on conscientious objection] I
could to John Jr. and his friend.

Do please let me know if you are back permanently or at least for a
long time. Will I be able to reach you at this address? Will you be able
to get down here sometime? There is much to talk about. Could we plan
something for next spring? . . .

January 24, 1968

How are you? Snowed in? I haven't heard from you in a long time. This letter is a quick one, to ask you a favor. I am starting a small mimeographed magazine [*Monks Pond*]—an enterprise of no account, with no money involved, to be given out free, publishing mainly poetry. But I also want to devote some of it to Zen and to religious texts from Asia, etc.

Therefore I would like to run a few pages of your *Golden Age of Zen* book, in the next issue, first issue: specifically the pages about Pai Chang, his philosophy of work and the bit about the old fox. Is that all right? If so, and I hope so, please give me enough essential facts for the notes on contributors. (Are you teaching at Seton Hall again, for instance? What exactly was it you were teaching there? Etc. What is the exact name of the university in Taiwan—you were teaching there? Etc.)

How is the *Golden Age* book coming along?

. . . And above all, can you please send me some new and interesting texts, Chinese poems or Zen or Confucian texts that have not been done in English before or not done well?

There is at Indiana University a Richard Chi who has translated Shen Hui, and I hope to meet him this week.

Remember you are always welcome here, and we want to see you. We have a new Abbot now. You are invited to come and visit and give a talk to the community (which will help cover expenses) anytime you are out in the Midwest.

To June J. Yungblut

Born in the South, with a distinguished Quaker background (her ancestor Thomas Fitzwater came to America aboard the Welcome *with William Penn), June J. Yungblut did graduate studies at Yale and at Emory University. In 1958 she earned a master's degree in English literature and theology at Emory; nine years later she received a doctorate from there. At the time that she and her husband, John, contacted Merton, they were directing the Quaker House at Atlanta, Georgia. June and John had served in South Africa for the Friends World Committee in 1966. In 1968 John was attempting to arrange a retreat at Gethsemani for Martin Luther King, when the civil-rights leader was assassinated. June was at Coretta King's side during the terrible days that followed. June arranged a tribute to Martin Luther King at the Liturgical Conference in Washington (August 20, 1968) and on television. Both these events featured the Freedom Songs which Thomas Merton had written for Robert Williams, and which had been set to music by Dr. Alexander Peloquin. Merton's letters are addressed at times to June and*

Jan (i.e., John) and at other times to June. It was generally June who wrote to him.

June 22, 1967

The trouble with letters like yours that say so much is that they don't get answered, at least not easily. I am sorry for not replying sooner, but you understand. I had to get down to the commentary on *The Plague* and get it finished without too much interruption. So now it is finished and being typed. I hope it is adequate . . .

I am glad to have run into someone who likes and knows Beckett. As I say, I very much like that little piece "Ping." It seemed to me to be quite perfect. And I am all for *Godot*. But the longer books seem to me to be a morass of narcissistic brooding with a sort of objective excuse: that he is really not describing anything but playing with language. I can see where that could be interesting, because I am attracted to digging in large stores of linguistic mud myself. But somehow his mud is dull. Until it livens up in "Ping," for example. Maybe it lacks visual quality or the kind of visual quality that is needed to keep me awake . . .

Commonweal has sent me the De Lubac book on Teilhard to review. I think it will move Teilhard a few blocks closer to the Chancery Office and get him more established than he already now is. It is good at showing that what the Chancery Office looks for is all right there and everything is cozy. Teilhard really loves the exercises of St. Ignatius, etc. And I can believe that he did. But this is not after all a very inspiring book and it makes Teilhard look quite unrevolutionary. I don't know if that is the best thing for Teilhard or for the Church.

I got a lovely mad letter from a sixteen-year-old girl in [Campbell] California [Susan Butorovitch], saying she and a friend were running an "underground paper" and wanted me to send them something. They sounded very Beatle-struck, and suggested as subjects for me, besides "fight the baddy baddies," that I might also "promote Lennonism." So I sent them a piece of a new poetry-prose mosaic that I think New Directions is doing next spring. I don't know if it promotes Lennonism, but perhaps it is tinged with Dylanism.

For me, the turning-on that fails abysmally with Beckett comes with Kafka. I discovered a lot of his little short pieces lately and they are fine. I hope to compare *The Stranger* and *The Trial*.

I haven't heard from either Berrigan since Dan was here in May. I went into the airport with Dan and he was checking his ticket and vanished into thin air, probably transported like Elias. The plane he hoped for was not there and they must have whisked him to another one just as it was leaving the ground.

Jan, about your chapter on Christ,* it has got away from me and I can't comment articulately. I am still hung up in a very traditional Christology myself, and the reason I have difficulty latching on to any other kind is that in the end you are always dealing with some kind of authority anyhow: whether the Councils of Nicaea and Chalcedon or the works of Renan, Loisy, and the rest. And I am not sure how comprehensible I find some of the authorities. I remember your chapter as sounding quite as plausible as any other modern thing I have read, except that for me Christ is not simply "a mystic" among others, but then perhaps I have not much of a historical Christ anyhow: it is the Christ of the Byzantine ikons or of Transfiguration mysticism on Mount Athos, "I am the Light." It is hard for me to adjust and consider him as just receiving a little flash of the light like the rest of them. So I am not a good judge of that chapter.

How did the conference come out?† It is a pity that one has to run after shy bishops with a butterfly net. Did you catch him? He's big enough. I met our new Archbishop and he seems well disposed, open and all. I know he fully approves my ecumenical mischief on all sides. So does my own Abbot. So do remember that you are always welcome. Maybe I'll read some Beckett before you come again and I can talk sense. Why not think of coming this way later in the year, when the weather is cooler?

September 8, 1967

I just got John's letter. I have looked back to June's, which has been waiting for an answer, and I find you say something about sending a copy of the dissertation, or part of it, back in July. Did you? I never got any of it . . . I will be glad to read the dissertation and make any remark that might be useful. I regret that I *still* haven't read any Beckett but I very much enjoyed the piece from *Evergreen Review* that you sent . . .

Thanks too for the little bit of Teilhard. I have an article on him coming out in *Commonweal*. Nothing new here with Kafka, for some reason I haven't gone further with him. I am all bogged down trying to get material about Cargo cults right at the moment. Not sure why I am drawn to this strange eschatology, except that I think it may prove to say a great deal about us all in some queer oblique way. My book on Camus is at a standstill, but may pick up later in the winter . . .

Glad to learn anyway that the dissertation is all shipshape and accepted. Thanks, John, for remarks on *Mystics and Zen Masters*. I very much enjoy seeing you both, and though I have not officially checked on

---

* In a book John was writing, which was published in 1974, entitled Rediscovering the Christ.

† June had written on May 7 that she was helping to organize a conference of religious groups concerned about Vietnam. With the help of her friend Bishop Bernardin, she had been able to get Archbishop Hallinan of Atlanta to represent the Catholic Church.

it, I am sure I can arrange accommodations for a couple of nights for both, June at the ladies' guesthouse . . .

November 19, 1967

The presence of Fr. Methodius from Conyers [Trappist monastery in Georgia] reminded me that I had been owing you a letter and that Thanksgiving is a few days off: I haven't settled the business about your coming. I am tied up this next week, but I certainly hope to see you and John before you leave for South Africa! You would be welcome after Christmas, though there is a large family that comes here every year during that week: I don't think they entirely fill the ladies' guesthouse, though. Let me know if you want to come then (after Dec. 27) and I will check it out. And this time I will do it promptly.

Yesterday I got a letter from the AFSC in Philadelphia, inviting me to be on an unofficial team that is to go and talk to representatives of the NFL either in Cambodia or Czechoslovakia. Of course I would jump at it if I were the only one to decide. I had to turn it over to the Abbot, however. He did not have time to talk about it yesterday but I know what the fate of the invite will be. He is just not likely to see that this is important. He will regard it purely as a distraction from prayer. Which puts me in an uncomfortable position: because when it gets that far, I begin wondering if this place makes any sense whatever. Well, I'll suspend judgment until I see what he says. The paradox is that it is to a great extent because I am here that I am invited to go, while it is because I am here I can't go . . .

December 3, 1967

This is to let you know that I have received the dissertation, which arrived safely, and I am about halfway through it. I like it very much. You make a lot of good points and remind me of things I liked in *Godot*. You have yet to convert me thoroughly to some of the longer novels.

The article on Beckett in the latest *New York Review* is revealing. It throws a real light on the man. He is in fact a literary stylite, and his writing is full of a kind of ascesis of silence and non-communication. Also an ascetic criticism and rejection of the fatuity of "the world." Beckett indeed is a kind of monk. I guess that accounts for your (very flattering) intuition that brackets me with him. I think it is true that we have in common this same ascetic withdrawal and denial of an absurd world, but he is far more austere and consistent than I am! And in the end more apophatic. His pillar is much more remote . . .

I won't write more at the moment. Let me know if you and John will be able to come after Christmas . . .

June wrote on December 6 that she had successfully defended her dissertation and that the doctoral degree was to be awarded.

December 12, 1967

You have seen the globes. You have swum the Atlantic. You have spoken the unknown word. You have foundered in the sacred beer. You have been revived by Batman and Charlie. You are in. Congratulations. I should speak. My Dr. was purely honorary and I didn't have to swim even a small creek. But a Kentucky initiate with Cleanth nonetheless.

I'm saving for you like days 29 and 30 (with a guess you arrive on the 28th evening). If on the other hand spring turns out better for you, then better for me too, because that Xmas week is a big rassle . . .

June and John visited Merton at Gethsemani December 28–30. June wrote on January 11 that John was seeing Martin Luther King about arranging for a retreat at Gethsemani before the Washington March.

January 16, 1968

Thanks, June, for yours of 11th. As a sunken continent overgrown with seaweed, I gladly consent to being the subject of lectures in Capetown together with my fellow sea-monster Beckett.* We will make a pretty pair. But I have a suspicion that Providence would probably prefer that Capetown be spared the bewilderment, and that will keep you here . . .

. . . Also I do think that my overall work is such a mess and contains so much that is trivial and inconsequential, and hopelessly useless, that it would make a rather deadly project if you had to go through even most of it, not to mention all of it. If you really want to take on the project, I can think more about what would be more relevant in what is in itself over and done with. In other words, a more selective list . . .

Our new Abbot [Dom Flavian Burns] has just been elected. Probably the best man we have, but still quite young (thirty-five or so) but with some ideas anyway. Wants me to concentrate more on "the mystical" (sic)—as might be expected.

Frankly the new Abbot poses a small problem in one respect. I think that if Dr. King etc. came in a retreat before a march, in March, and it were publicized, it might constitute some sort of an adjustment problem for this new man. Whereas if the retreat of Dr. K. et al. were simply a private affair unconnected with any special event, it would be a very good thing; the Abbot could himself participate, learn a thing or two, and it would be a preparation for wider understanding on his part. I would suggest this gradual approach myself: Dr. King and others could come on a quiet private retreat sometime later in the summer, and we could all do some developing here. I think that in the long run this would be a much more organic and fruitful step. If the new Abbot suddenly found

* *June had agreed to give two lectures at Capetown University in South Africa on the topic "Samuel Beckett and Thomas Merton: Mystics with Opposing Views of Man."*

himself in the news in a situation he cannot yet cope with, it would be bad for him and everyone. And anyway, I think it is best for us not to be in the news one way or the other. A retreat before a march would be bound (and logically perhaps intended) to have some symbolic public meaning. I don't think this is the time for that yet. The new man has just about heard of civil rights and knows there is a struggle on, but that is all . . .

January 20, 1968

Beckett arrived in the midst of a flu epidemic and so it happened that last night, being holed in up here in the woods and unable to sleep, I finally hoisted my ruined frame out of bed, opened up the Mass wine and the Beckett underground Xerox special. Great midnight illumination. The book is every bit as good as [Joyce's] *Dubliners* and perhaps better. Anyhow I like it better. The writing is superb. "Dante and the Lobster" is a perfect piece of work, and shattering. Much to be said about all the loneliness stuff, solitude and society and so forth throughout the book. And merciful Mother Church ("Ding Dong"). The whole question of mercy, suffering. I mean, is the man such a cur if he demands that, after all, those who talk about mercy finally mean something by it? And if he declines to be convinced by their protestations in a dead language? (By which I don't mean Latin, either) . . . Still flung face down with flu.

About the other letter: of course we are available any time to anyone wanting to make a retreat, and if Dr. King prefers to come before the March, well and good, fine with us. The only thing was that from the long-term viewpoint, since the new Abbot opened our first official conversation in his new capacity by saying he wanted me to stick to my bloody mysticism and not get involved in all them outward works, it might be well to go a little slow on anything that might signify a tie-in with some onslaught on the bastions of squaredom. He is essentially open, just inexperienced and still a little closed in on set positions, but I think he can learn, given time. To have Dr. King, Vincent Harding and others here later in the year for a quiet, informal, deeply reflective session would probably get the Abbot to see where I really do belong, halfway between in and out of the action. Not just all the way out.

No more. I go to fling this at the beadles and get supplies of orange juice and return . . .

February ?, 1968

Fine letter, quick answer to only part of it. First I heard Martin L. King went to jail sometime back with the Styron book under his arm: he (and you) might be interested in the enclosed, "Faith and Violence." I forget if I sent it before, only part of a forthcoming book.

I would indeed be happy to get two of the books you refer to: *Road*

Belong Cargo, Lawrence; *The Rev. in Anthropology*, Jarvis. The others I have worked through except Eliade, and I'll get that for this library. We need all Eliade here.

I have Tom Altizer's book but have not begun it. He's welcome here any time.

Look forward to hearing about when Dr. King and Vincent Harding may come. Any time fine, but I have people jostling for March dates at the moment. As long as there is no publicity to mention, there is no problem for the new Abbot, who is quiet and I think shaping up well . . .

If you like, I can give you a brief list of the things of mine that seem to me to be me, as opposed to mere pious journalism. Could you spell out what is most wanted?

In a letter of March 2, June wrote that Jim Forest and Thich Nhat Hanh were visiting at Quaker House in Atlanta. She said she had thought of herself as a Quaker–Catholic but now it seemed she was a Quaker–Catholic–Buddhist. She mentioned her plans for post-doctoral study of four men of faith: Thomas Merton, Alan Paton, Elie Wiesel, Thich Nhat Hanh.

March 6, 1968

. . . As a Catholic Buddhist of long standing and also in fact Quaker, I naturally feel happy about the new Church . . . I must get in touch with Nhat. Too bad he couldn't come here. I hope he can later. And also I'd like to see some of his poems for my magazine. Can you Xerox any? I'm sure he won't mind and I'll clear it with him when I write him next. By now you should have the first issue of *Monks Pond*. I feel it is promising!

About the post-doctoral four: well, I'm honored to be in such good company. Anything I have sent or will send will be yours to mark up and do as you like with. I'll try to keep sending things as a matter of course, and will look up other items you ought to have. It is hard to say what I think is important in my work and what isn't. There are books like *Life and Holiness*, which are more or less religious journalism—that's not the right word—but secondary books written with a general line in mind, and not deeply personal. Also perhaps more superficial. Yet they do contain elements of what for better or for worse one could call my "thought" (?), if not theology at least philosophy, and that goes for some of the social-oriented stuff too. However, when I look back on this sort of editorializing or preaching whether about Christianity or monasticism or social justice, peace, etc., I find it thin and often a bit alien. I say things I think I have to say, and later become more and more oppressed with a sense of their inadequacy, untrueness to my own deep (?) intentions, etc. The work I feel more happy about is at once more personal, more literary, more contemplative. Books like *Conjectures, New Seeds, Sign of Jonas, Raids,* or literary essays, or poetry, or things like introductions to Chuang Tzu, Gandhi, Desert Fathers, etc. In the essay collections like *Disputed Questions* or *Seeds of Destruction*, still more *Mystics and Zen Masters*, there is a great unevenness—some is close to center and some way off from what I really want to say. The "Notes on the Philosophy of Solitude" in *Disputed Questions* is very central (I haven't reread it lately, though), and the thing on St. Bernard isn't. In *Mystics and Zen Masters* the Zen pieces are central, so is "Pilgrimage to Crusade," but much of the other stuff is peripheral to my thought. The existentialism piece is central, I think.

I have always felt strongly that much of the writing I was doing was beside the point, because it was not in a creative manner that really suited me. Working on the long Cargo etc. poem I feel much more in my right element. Though *Cables to the Ace* is in ways deficient, I feel it is also another right approach, though dour and perhaps shallow . . .

March 23, 1968

This to acknowledge receipt of the mss. The Beckett article is fine, will fit it into *Monks Pond* III or IV or maybe V. Poems too, will use as many as I can, depending on space. Do you want a quick decision or can I mull over them for a while—months? . . . Huge blizzard here. Three of the tall pines out front came crashing down last evening. Last night I was waiting for one to fall on the house. Didn't.

. . . I guess all the Nhat Hanh poems are published already . . .

March 29, 1968

I'll send some more of *Monks Pond* when I get a chance to sort and staple some more. Right now I have not been able to, busted in on by lots of people, etc.

Christ of the ikons. Disjointed ideas about that. Now that you pin me down, of course, I have all kinds of serious reservations on that one. Obviously to limit myself to the Christ of Byzantine theology would be absurd, and anyway it wouldn't be true and it isn't what I meant. The idea came to me simply as a contrast to the Christ of historical criticism. But first, what does the Christ of the ikons mean, what is the ground on which the Christ of the ikons is "my" Christ and what not?

The Christ of the ikons represents a traditional *experience* formulated in a theology of light, the ikon being a kind of sacramental medium for the illumination and awareness of the glory of Christ within us (in faith). The hieratic rules for ikon painting are not just rigid and formal, they are the guarantee of an authentic transmission of the possibility of this experience, provided the ikon painter was also himself a man of prayer (like Roublev). Thus what one "sees" in prayer before an ikon is not an external representation of a historical person, but an interior presence in light, which is the glory of the transfigured Christ, the experience of which is transmitted in faith from generation to generation of those who have "seen," from the Apostles on down. I don't say this is a highly scientific theory or anything, but it is what the ikon tradition believes. So when I say that my Christ is the Christ of the ikons, I mean that he is reached not through any scientific study but through direct faith and the mediation of the liturgy, art, worship, prayer, theology of light, etc., that is all bound up with the Russian and Greek tradition. But this is just by way of example, because obviously I am not hung up on orthodoxy.

The negative side: obviously this has the shortcoming of being tied in with a specific kind of culture and a culture that has a lot wrong with it: Byzantine theocratic imperialism. Thus there is something in the ikons of Christ as imperial ruler, the Kyrios in glory being referred to the Emperor himself as a kind of locus of the divine manifestation, and this I certainly don't buy. So yes and no. The Christ of the ikons as an example of a contemplative theology of light, as opposed to historical criticism: yes. But the Christ as ruler of a history in which the Basileus has a central and decisive "Christian" role, no. (Or any other ruler either, for that matter.) So one would have to multiply other examples to say what I mean. Like the Christ born in us in poverty, as Eckhart; but also the Christ of Julian of Norwich; the Christ of immediate experience all down through the mystical tradition, but in each case detached from special historical and cultural residues. I don't know if you get what I mean. The point is that I don't think the historical Christ can be known in a way that is as relevant as this, and this is the kind of knowledge of Christ that St. John talks about in the Gospel and in his Epistles. In comparison with this "knowledge" of Christ, the knowledge of Jesus as a man who "was" a Jewish mystic is to me somewhat irrelevant. That is knowledge "about" Christ, not knowledge "of" Christ, and not (what interests me more) knowledge "in" Christ. Christ not as object of seeing or study, but Christ as center in whom and by whom one is illuminated. I will be the first to admit that all this may be extremely ambiguous. And I am questioning it much more now than I would have, say, ten years ago. The ambiguities are of course those of monasticism itself, and the Christ I am talking about is essentially the "monastic" Christ. The real problem comes in when early monasticism lost its truly kenotic and eschatological character, and became dogmatic imperial shock troops in the service of a Christian social order (so called). To what extent is the Christ of monastic worship, with all the purity and refinement of ikon painting, Greek liturgy, theology of light, Hesychasm, etc., the justification of a certain "order"? To what extent is the experience of that Christ the experience of an inner security that came from supporting a "divine" social order? Hm. That calls for some thinking.

Even in the most static and established kinds of Christendom, monks have tended to be mavericks, if only interiorly, and one gets the feeling that there was a constant simmering of mystical revolt going on underneath the surface: and the focus of that revolt was in the Hesychastic kind of tradition, the "theology of light" and direct-experience types who were always breaking away to be hermits, to get as far as possible off into the woods, give up property, etc. The great example in the East is the struggle of St. Nil Sorsky vs. St. Joseph of Volokolamsk. But the "Order" always got its revenge by incorporating the hermits back into itself, canonizing and institutionalizing them. It would be interesting to study and find out if this were really reflected in the art of Russian monasticism.

Another focus of ambiguity: monastic world denial is originally a denial of a world that has not been penetrated with the light of the Resurrection, in order to see the world that *has* been transfigured and illuminated. But it later becomes the denial of the world, period, and the affirmation of the Resurrection as a proof of pure transcendence. To me the "light" of Christ in the ikons is simply a special case of the light which has now penetrated *everything*. But there is in monastic tradition a strong tendency to say the "light" of theophany is something that appears over against the world to repudiate it, not to transfigure it.

Hence my Christ is the "apophatic" Christ—light that is not light, and not confinable within any known category of light, and not communicable in any light that is not not-light: yet in all things, in their ground, not by nature but by gift, grace, death and resurrection.

All this is very provisional. I have more thinking to do, and perhaps some revising. Certainly some revising. Really what I was proposing was just an example, a partial view, that needs to be completed all round.

I'll send another copy of *Nat Turner*. Thanks for passing the first one along to Martin King. I hope he can come, and will do what I can to make it worthwhile if he does: but also feel acutely that I have absolutely nothing to say and am probably not expected to say much of anything. Just be around . . .

Dr. Martin Luther King, Jr., was assassinated in Memphis on April 4, 1968.

April 5, 1968

By a strange coincidence, I happened to be out in Lexington [with Donald Allchin] when Martin was shot and I heard all the news at once, instead of remaining for a day or more without finding out. What a terrible thing: and yet I felt that he was expecting it. In fact, almost at the very time of the murder I saw the TV film of his speech the previous night and heard what he said, in the place where we were eating a sandwich before starting home. A few moments later, the news came through on the car radio.

This all means something more serious than we can imagine. But he, at any rate, has done all that any man can do. It will be to his glory.

Could you please pass on the enclosed note to Mrs. King? [See letter to Coretta King.] I don't have their address.

On April 6, June wrote that she and other friends of the Kings had been at Coretta's house since the assassination. The Ebenezer Baptist Choir was singing and praying. Coretta had gone to Memphis for Dr. King's body. When she returned, "she spoke for a moment to each of us. She put her arms around me and held me a long time. Neither of us said anything."

April 9, 1968

Today is the day of the funeral. The other day I offered Mass for Martin, and two Anglican friends [Donald Allchin and an Anglican seminarian] joined me there. Yesterday I got your most moving letter and the note too. I was just on my way to Louisville, where I met a musician from Boston who had planned some time ago to come down and go over some songs of mine he had set to music. The songs were biblical "Freedom Songs" [see letters to Robert Williams] and were to have been first presented at the Liturgical Conference this summer at which Martin was to have been present, I understand. The music for them is powerful and they are quite effective. As Dr. Peloquin and I (he is the musician, fairly prominent at least in Catholic circles) went over them, we both agreed that they should not wait until August, but should be presented as soon as possible on TV and as a memorial to Martin. What we really need is a good strong Negro voice—someone like Harry Belafonte . . . I thought maybe you down there might speak to Belafonte or someone similar about the possibility of doing these songs. I'm sending the music of a couple of them, and also the text of my own poems—of which four out of eight are being used. I'll mark which ones. You and Coretta and anyone else likely to be interested might look them over. The music is somewhat arty and difficult but also basically popular, though not too "churchy." I think the whole project has possibilities. My only difficulty was that even in the August presentation Peloquin was thinking of a white singer. To my mind, that's out. One young Negro tenor was originally very interested and in fact started the whole thing, but Peloquin feels that this man's voice is not strong enough. And Peloquin does not seem to have other contacts.

These have been terrible days for everyone, and God alone knows what is to come. I feel that we have really crossed a definitive line into a more apocalyptic kind of time—the recent years were bitter enough, but mostly as anticipations of what now seems to be realizing itself. We will need a lot of faith and a new vision and courage to move in these new and more bitter realities . . .

June wrote on April 11 about the funeral. She told how Ralph Abernathy's children asked if it was all right to hate the assassin. Dr. King's two children (Martin and Dexter) both answered: "No, Daddy said not to hate anyone."

April 15, 1968

Your long and moving letter came today, with the two postscripts (but not the telegrams [sent to Coretta], which I'd very much like to see). This is just a note to say that *anything* that makes sense in the use of the songs is all right with me, and I guess also the composer. If you and Coretta feel they would be likely to fit into something in connection with the March, that's fine, perhaps that would make them more of a "memorial." I leave you and her to decide whatever you think would be best and she is the one who will surely know what ought to be done with them—if she feels they are worth the trouble.

As I may have mentioned, the songs are (as far as my poems go) the property of a young Negro singer at whose request I wrote them [Robert Williams]. Peloquin did not think he had the voice for them. (Not baritone enough.) But any of my royalties etc. would go to him. I'm sure he'd have no objection to their use in the March or anywhere like that—quite the contrary.

No more now, I just wanted to say I go along with anything you and Coretta decide.

Whitehorn, California
May 9, 1968

Your fine letter reached me out here in the California Redwoods. I am giving a few conferences at this really exceptional convent—best thing in the Order by far. (Don't tell the Holy Spirit guys that I'm roaming or they'll say why not come there and I haven't time yet.)

Thanks for everything you've done about the songs. You have to contact Peloquin about arrangements. If he is not at Boston College, he may be contacted at the Cathedral Rectory, Providence, Rhode Island (Catholic Cathedral). I don't know address or number.

Hope everything works out. This is a place you must get to know when you are out this way. Superb for a retreat . . .

May 23, 1968

I am writing this in the awareness that you are in the middle of everything now in the Poor People's March, but the letter will reach you perhaps when things are over, or less active. Meanwhile my prayers are with you and all who have gone to Washington, and especially Coretta and all the others who are leading it. I came close to some of it when I was in New Mexico, and talked to people who had been at the big rally in Albuquerque the day before. I just missed it in Louisville on the way back.

The main thing: thank you for all the wonderful work you have done in getting the Freedom Songs to the attention of those who can do something with them. I am most grateful, because you have done much more than I could have done myself, no matter how hard I might have tried. You have taken advantage of providential connections. I do hope that the results will be very fruitful. Peloquin tried to call me several times when I was away and once after I got back, but we did not manage to get to a phone at the same times. No matter, I am fully in approval of everything: the only condition I have is that the songs must be done by *some* Negro singer(s), whether Harry Belafonte or anyone else, who meets with the approval of you and Coretta and of course the composer. It would not be right to have them done merely by white people—though obviously a choir of white and black is to be expected. (If choral.)

One other thing. Those most moving telegrams you sent (in response to the death of Dr. King). I would very much like to use one of them in *Monks Pond*—the anonymous one from "Humbleness Nobody US Latin," which is to me as moving as the speech of Sacco–Vanzetti. I think it would not be wrong, as the message was anonymous and its intention was to be a sort of public witness. If Coretta would permit it, I want to use this in the next issue of *Monks Pond*. Would you please ask her? I hope she will say yes. It could form a kind of tribute on the part of the magazine.

I am trying to catch up with the mail that has accumulated while I was away. California, by the way, was marvelous—we'll talk of that sometime. I'll be busy with a group of nuns next week, and Bob Lax is coming later. Was hoping Nhat might, and of course he might send a last-minute message . . .

July 13, 1968

. . . Peloquin tried to reach me a couple of times and I tried to reach him, but it is just utterly impractical to try to keep in contact with anyone by phone here. Things would seem to be moving along toward the TV production.

Yes, I am in a sort of retreat for July and part of August, at least relative. But it looks as if there is no such thing as a real retreat possible here. It is too close to Louisville; there is too much of everything. But at least I have been able to slow down to a sprint. Instead of attempting to fly. Relative calm, anyhow, and some silence. But that doesn't need to affect anything important. Do let me know if anything comes up in regard to the songs, or the movement, or anything.

. . . It is possible that I may go to the Orient on some monastic business, but I think in that event I'd better take care to keep it all entirely and totally unpolitical in every respect. This is a first trip, and a lot depends on how it goes, so I would NOT be wanting to tie in anything like conversations with the NLF—which in any case would, I think, be futile at this point. There have been conversations in plenty, and they have ended in obvious fiasco and betrayal. I would not want to just perpetuate an illusion—which is about all I could do at this point . . .

Monks Pond III is in the works—slow—with your Beckett article. I'm saving the poems for IV . . .

July 29, 1968

I much appreciate your letter of a week ago. I did not know Nhat was possibly in Thailand. Have you an address where he might be reached there? If I can't see him here, then why not there? Yes, I am more and more convinced myself of the great need for understanding and brotherhood with Eastern religions, especially Buddhists. This to me is becoming more and more of a top priority, and that is one reason why I don't want to risk fouling it up with politics when I am convinced that there is no issue in that direction anyhow. I want to try to get going on a real religious dialogue in depth if I can, and really things are shaping up well so far, at least on paper. The prospects of contacts are very good. I hope it goes on that way.

Your Xerox did not get here yet. *Monks Pond* III is slowly moving but we have trouble with the machinery. I hope it will be ready in a few weeks. Nice concrete poetry section shaping up . . .

Am giving talks on Joyce to the brethren now. I regret anything I may have said that suggested Beckett's stories were halfway as good as *Dubliners*. I was out of my mind. But *Ulysses* remains one of my top favorites of all time. Such a great job! Am reviewing some current Joyce lore for *Sewanee Review* and find it atrocious. Half-literate, idiotic garbage. At least some of it. How does such stuff get by?

Have had at least a semi-retreat, relatively quiet, broken by a few trips in town for necessary shots, passport photos and all. Best always to you and John . . .

On August 20, 1968, Merton received a telegram from June: "Concert powerful and moving. Congratulations from Alex and me." The "Freedom Songs" had been performed in honor of Martin Luther King at the National Liturgical Conference in Washington, D.C., on the previous evening.

To Gordon Zahn

Gordon Zahn, well-known sociologist and pacifist, was born in Milwaukee in 1918. He received a doctorate from the Catholic University of America in 1952, after which he continued his post-doctoral studies at Harvard. In 1956–57 he went to Germany under a Fulbright grant to study at Julius Maximilian University in Würzburg. His research into Roman Catholic relations with Hitler's Germany resulted in a book, German Catholics and Hitler's War *(Sheed and Ward, 1962).*

It was during this year in Germany that he first heard of Franz Jagerstaetter, an Austrian peasant who refused to fight in Hitler's war and who, after a military trial in 1943, was beheaded. Zahn, who was himself a conscientious objector, felt a strong affinity with this man who had made a lonely decision of conscience. In 1964 Zahn published the story of the life and death of Franz Jagerstaetter, entitled In Solitary Witness.

After some years of teaching at Loyola University in Chicago, Zahn moved East in 1967 to Boston, where he taught at the University of Massachusetts. At present he is Professor Emeritus there and national director of Pax Christi U.S.A. Center on Conscience and War.

[*Cold War Letter 21*]

January 1962

Your article ["The Case for Christian Dissent"] reached me the other day and I read it immediately. It is very fine indeed, and I think it will be one of the most powerful and telling contributions to the anthology . . . I think we have a lot of superb things. The greatest problem will be to get everything together and not have to make the book too big or exclude anything really worthwhile.

In any case I am deeply grateful, and I am glad to hear that the book itself (your book) [*German Catholics and Hitler's War*] is coming along well. Frank Sheed is a good and courageous publisher. I wish you success with it, and look forward to seeing a copy. It certainly will upset some people. We have to face the fact that we have traveled a long way from the real Christian center. Centuries of identification between Christian and civil life have done more to secularize Christianity than to sanctify civil life. This is not a popular idea. I wonder if anyone in our time has really faced it in a satisfactory way without either too much evasion, too total and too oversimplified a rejection of the secular and the temporal, or too complete a submission to it? The problem is enormous, and of course your article, and your book, go right to the heart of it . . .

Jagerstaetter is to me a moving symbol of a lonely isolated Christian who was faithful to his conscience, in the supremely difficult question of the most real and the highest kind of obedience. In the case of St. Thomas More, we have obscured the issue by talking as if he had been obedient to the Pope and not to the King. Safe and cozy. There was nothing safe or cozy about it, and the Pope was miles and miles away.

This is only a short note, but I hope a very appreciative one.

April 30, 1963

I was very happy to get your letter and to hear from [Wilbur H.] Ferry about your talk* out at the Center. Now today I received a copy of the talk and read it. I am very impressed by it, and happy that you were able to use some words of mine. It seems to me that you continue to make your point very clear, and here you were able to do so quite plainly.

Certainly the issue is very grave. The quotations from your reviewers on page 11 and ff. are to me simply incredible. Incredible! Do I belong to the same Church as these people? Fortunately the encyclical is there to remind me that *they* may be the ones who are deluded. Yet I see the encyclical is not everywhere accepted with enthusiasm . . .

The momentous part of the encyclical was not the sentence about nuclear weapons (this had been said before) but the part about the possible obligation to cooperate even with communists in working for peace. But the first article in the creed of the American Christian is that the communist is a devil and to trust him is nothing but a pact with the devil. Of course, I admit they are not all bothered with scruples. But then neither, I note, are we. In fact, it seems to be recommended that we cast them away in dealing with communists.

Another indication of the unreality of our moral thinking is the inconsistency between the tough policy on birth control and our all-out acceptance of nuclear weapons. The thing this shows is that our objection to birth control does not spring from a respect for life, or not as much as we seem to think it does. I think it more probably comes from a hatred of pleasure, and consequently of a fear of life. If people insist on indulging their filthy desires by having carnal intercourse, then they must undergo the punishment and have children. They can't just have fun and get away with it. I wonder if this is really so much of a caricature after all? I am sure that in fact that is probably the way the minds of a great many of the clergy are working.

I am accused of being very much of a pessimist. But still, those who do so are usually basing their argument on the fact that I don't find much to hope for in the present climate of American Catholicism. This is interpreted by them as a failure of supernatural, theological hope on my part . . . I think that you are right in your implications, at the beginning of the talk: the climate of ecumenism is all very nice, but does it have all the wonderful meaning we read into it? Christ said: If you salute your brethren, what are you doing that the pagans have not done? I don't think

---

* *The reference is to a talk Zahn gave at the Center for the Study of Democratic Institutions at Santa Barbara, California, on the weekend that John XXIII's encyclical* Pacem in Terris *was released (April 1, 1963).*

that the glad gatherings of people who are exactly alike in every respect except their commitment to slightly different religious forms are exactly a presage of world peace. If they gathered together for something significant, like peace and disarmament, or the race issue, it would make more sense and I might find encouragement in it.

I hope some good discussion was stimulated by it. As far as I know, most of the people at the Center, except Ferry, are a little slow on the peace issue. Anyway, I am very glad you got out there and had a good trip. I am sure that the encyclical will make a great deal of difference for some people who will have been jolted by it . . .

Congratulations on the award you received there. One thing is certain, the peace movement is growing in strength and coherence, and this fact will make people think twice before trying to fire you. And if they ever do, there are plenty of other places in the world besides Loyola.

[Hans] Küng never showed up here for Holy Week after all. I recently heard that the Apostolic Delegate was planning to come then, and did not. (Thank God.) I don't know if that had any influence on Küng.

This fall sometime there may be a retreat for peace-movement people. I'll let you know when, in case you would like to come . . .

December 13, 1963

It was certainly good to hear from you. It is true that I was laid up for a while with a bad disc, but with traction and so on, it is getting back in shape. I am practically back to normal, except there are some things that I cannot do.

I am very glad to hear that the Jagerstaetter book is "in." Probably rewriting it for the average reader will do a lot to get it around, and that is what it needs. I look forward to seeing it.

As to Hochhuth: yes, I have read the play [*The Deputy*] and have dashed off some notes on it which George Lawler says he wants to include with some other notebook excerpts in *Continuum*. I am sending you a Xeroxed copy of the notes . . .

As to the play, I think it is awful: at least to read. Hochhuth strikes me as somewhat sick, not that I blame him for that. However, the question he raises is an important one, and though he has been grossly unjust to Pius XII (after all, there is no hint whatever of the real greatness of the man in the play), yet I think that the Vatican is at fault, and the hierarchy too, for favoring that kind of abominable and moss-grown concept of authority and of obedience. Here Hochhuth has something to be said for him. When such a temptation is presented to him, how can one blame him for taking it? There has been so much sickening nonsense about Pius XII, and such obviously interested efforts to promote him as a saint, that no one can blame this man for saying he does not agree. And after all, it is his business as well as ours, because if we set someone up as a saint we have to justify our choice to an extremely demanding and critical world. Here is one case where the world has decided to speak up, and we must admit that there is a foundation to the protest, though it is a pity that Pius XII should be so blackened as a person. Frankly, though the play raises this issue, it does not seem to me to treat it in a satisfactory manner and I do believe that it will not do anyone any good. It will confirm those who hate the Church in their prejudices, and it will not help Catholics to think about this real problem, so in the end I would be sorry to see it played: yet, on the other hand, do we really have a full right to demand that it be kept off the stage, and is it wise to attempt this? . . .

July 2, 1964

Thanks for your letter of June 11th. I look forward to "your" *Continuum*. Thanks for all the things you have sent. Yes, you sent the CRTA pamphlet and I agree, I am glad to be with you, and misrepresented by La Herzfeld, who does not seem to be overbright, and seems to be in the Pentagon rut as fairly and squarely as most other Catholic "intellectuals" who are near to the Society in one way or another (Loyola faculty excepted) . . .

I am very much tempted to write a parallel between *The Deputy* and the new Serafian book, *The Pilgrim*. Starting with the titles, there is soon seen to be a deeper analogy. Only in one chapter does the Serafian come out as a real hatchet job on Paul VI, the rest balances it off and makes nicer noises and gestures, and it is not as blatantly prejudiced as the Hochhuth. Yet at the same time it reinforces the justice in Hochhuth's accusation, and does so by dimming the focus that is too crudely and too insistently fixed on Pius. Actually, the great question is the Papacy itself in its post-Tridentine and post-medieval, indeed post-Constantinian shape.

The thing that really hits me hardest of all is that at this very moment the same issue of the Jews is right in front of our noses, just as much as it ever was before any German under Hitler, perhaps more so. And of course the Jewish schema,* or part of that schema, is central in *The Pilgrim*. Once again, when John brought up the obligation to make some kind of amends, the same old machinery that Hochhuth tries to show at work in the one man and mind of Pius is in full operation in the whole "Papacy," i.e. Curia and all.

Pius was the curial Pope, the saint of the office types, the one whom the conservative cardinals overheard conversing with Christ in vision, the one whose cause was all lined up until Hochhuth as devil's advocate had his say, and very pertinently this had to be said for the good of the Church,

---

* *Preparatory document: part of what became Vatican II's* Declaration on Relationships with Non-Christian Religions.

to preserve us from the monstrous canonization of the Holy Office and of all the Curia with Pius. Now Paul's curial side has won over his Johannine heritage and the Jews are being forgotten for precisely the same reason, only on a much more trivial scale: political expediency, the "good of the Church" in Moslem territory where, no matter what happens, the Church is going to have a rough time and fight a perhaps losing battle even with Nasser supposedly "favorable" (temporarily). Can't they see what this is about? Have they all gone blind to the significance of events and their religious typology?

Here we have Nasser with plenty missiles (not yet nuclear warheads, but how long?) provided by ex-Nazis to a great extent. Everything is set for the destruction of Israel, burn them up in an afternoon if possible, everybody knows this, nobody does or says anything, not expedient, bad politics. Anyway, they are still Christ-killers. All tradition says it, Chrysostom, etc. Thus we fail to see the high-priestly role of curial Rome, Sanhedrin. Christ will be crucified again in the Jews, by Gentiles, with the nodding approval of the Church now in the role of the Sanhedrin . . . Bizarre, isn't it?"

Another bizarre aspect of this whole thing: the curial people, convinced that they are "the Papacy" and really in a way the Pope, have now seen that they have the duty to override the Pope and disobey him for the sake of the institution which he represents. When the Pope goes against the Curia, the Curia must disobey him for his own good and that of the Church. The charism of infallibility is transferred to the Curia. It thus becomes anonymous and institutional. It is no longer a charism, it is a bureaucratic procedure . . .

Obviously, though, the Curia thus finds itself in the position of actually practicing the new morality, situation ethics (though this is not admitted because the Curia is really the vicar of Christ and therefore Christ). But to the rest of us it looks like situation ethics. So then we all start applying the same principles in our own lives. For the good of the Church, the Curia must be disobeyed, etc. Interesting prospects are opening up.

. . . About the preface to Jagerstaetter. Nothing I would like better, but I think really I should not. I have had to refuse prefaces lately and get out from under, otherwise I will soon be writing nothing but prefaces . . .

The new book is *Seeds of Destruction*. That includes the race essays, some cold-war letters, a short piece on Gandhi, and I hope also a long rewritten piece on *Pacem in Terris*, basically the same as *Peace in a PCE* but without controversy on the bomb, just peace peace.

. . . Congratulations on your fellowship [John Simon Senior Fellowship at University of Manchester, England]. I am sure your trip will be most fruitful . . .

December 17, 1964

It was very good to get your letter and to know where you are. I am glad Manchester turns out to be interesting, at least as far as the people around you are concerned. I don't know the place, but if it is anything like Birmingham, and I suppose it is . . .

Peace News asked me to review your book on Jagerstaetter [*In Solitary Witness*], and I did. Here is a copy of the review. I thought the book was extremely well done. It made very good reading, and any reader with average sense can surely get to it. Yet it is also scientific. I think it is really a fine contribution to the cause of peace, and will certainly make it hard for the disgruntled and pious supporters of the bomb to accuse you of being nasty, because the book does not really imply any special attack on anyone. It just says what the man did.

Right after I got through reading the proofs, A. J. Muste and a lot of other peace people whom you may or may not know, including Jim Forest, who used to be editor of *Catholic Worker*, were here for a retreat-cum-discussion. It was very lively and Jagerstaetter came up constantly.

. . . The general impression I got from the Council discussion on Schema 13 was that the Fathers were not really aware of the real nature and magnitude of the problem. As for Beck and Hannon, they are fighting for peace like Mao Tse-tung with his new bomb. It is incredible how all these people can sit with straight faces and declare, each as solemnly as the other, that *his* bomb is the guarantee of peace. Have they totally lost all sense of humor?

It is very good to hear from you and know you are well and happy. And that the future seems to have some good, if hazy prospects. When you propose to my Trappist imagination a place called Saskatoon [where Gordon had been offered a teaching position] I am afraid you draw a blank. All I see is a waste of level snow, broken by igloos. The igloos are largely fallout anyway, so I don't think it sounds like the best place.

However, I am gradually backing into a Saskatoon and igloo of my own, meaning a cottage in the woods. I hope to keep up the more creative work, and drop the journalism type of stuff for a while anyway, and why not for good? But everything remains pretty flexible and uncertain. The place is alive with rumors of a foundation in Norway, etc. etc. None of which I take too seriously. Next month I am fifty and that makes me too old for rumors or for most of the other nonsense of communal life . . .

Next spring my selections from Gandhi and a long introduction should be coming out. It ought to be quite good. They are already working on a French edition . . . and one in Brazil where the Goss-Mayrs are really working to set up a non-violent movement.

October 31, 1966

. . . Let me answer your question about Montreal or Xavier—as I suppose you want me to—as a question of religious conscience. This means considering the matter on the level of your relationship with God above all. Or as a matter of religious principle rather than of efficacy in this or that kind of action to be carried on. On that level, I would say decide the matter of principle, leaving the question of efficacy in the hands of God. In other words, if the paying of taxes is that much on your conscience, then decide that question and let God take care of the consequences, the effect on other people, whether or not you will be less influential and so on. That is the simple answer. But then when we reflect on all the realities of the matter, and see how impossible it is to have really clean hands anyway, maybe it would be preferable to consider other angles. On that level I am really no judge, but I don't suppose it would make an awful lot of difference if you were in Montreal, would it?

I would qualify any remark of mine on this subject by saying that personally I wish it were possible for me to be out of this country and living in some country too poor ever to have the bomb. On the other hand I recognize this to be a little quixotic, and I accept the fact of being here and the unavoidable moral ignominy. Still, if I were in your shoes, I myself would probably prefer Canada. But as you say, you must decide on the basis of your own life . . .

Don't worry about me: I was only in the hospital for some tests last week. Am living happily in the woods. I am glad the foreign editions of *Solitary Witness* are appearing. Will be interested in the German reaction . . .

August 14, 1967

Thanks for your letter telling me of the move East [to the University of Massachusetts] from Loyola. As I remember, they gave you rather a rough time there, so I hope you will now be better off—in the Prudential Center [the name of the apartment and office building where he had taken up residence]. That is as good a bet as any in this day when no one knows where the light is likely to come from, anyway . . . One of the young monks here reminded me on the right day that it was Jagerstatter's anniversary, so there are people here keeping track of things too.

. . . Do you know of anyone in the "American Church" who would like to participate in a seven-day fast of Catholics, Protestants and others at Geneva, for peace, in December? They have asked me and of course I can't go. As they are working through the FOR, I suppose the news may have reached you long ago. Let me know if you have any ideas, I'd like to be able to write something encouraging to this good pastor in Lyons.

. . . You are right of course about *The Seven Storey Mountain:* obviously I have gone a long way since then, and I am certain that I would preach a good deal less and have more reservations about many things if I rewrote it today. My health is not bad, in fact good enough for an old guy of fifty-two. Just trouble in bones, joints, etc., mostly old football injuries coming out into the open with wear and tear. Occasionally I have to get slightly patched up here and there. I suppose if I were more sprightly—i.e., less inclined to desperation about things in general—I would have more spring and be able to overcome these things effectively without getting cut up. Oh, well . . .

Correspondents

(A check list by selected categories)

Anglicanism
A. M. Allchin
Etta Gullick

Buddhism
Richard Chi
Thich Nhat Hanh
Marco Pallis

Christian culture
Bruno Schlesinger
E. I. Watkin

Democratic institutions
Wilbur H. Ferry

Hinduism
Amiya Chakravarty
Dona Luisa Coomaraswamy
Philip Griggs
Ripu Daman Lama

Judaism
Erich Fromm
Abraham Joshua Heschel
Zalman Schachter
R. J. Zwi Werblowsky

Mysticism, scientific study of
Aldous Huxley

Raymond Prince
Linda Sabbath

Orthodox Christianity
Sergius Bolshakoff
Archimandrite Sophrony

Pacifism
(also *non-violence, nuclear war, Vietnam war, peace movement, etc.*)
Daniel J. Berrigan
Dom Helder Camara
Dorothy Day
Catherine Doherty
James Douglass
Wilbur H. Ferry
James H. Forest
J. and H. Goss-Mayr
Shinzo Hamai
Thich Nhat Hanh
John Heidbrink
Abraham Joshua Heschel
Hiromu Morishita
Charles S. Thompson
E. I. Watkin
Gordon Zahn

Protestantism
James Baker
Cameron Borton

List of Cold War Letters

Index